CRIMINOLOGY
Second Edition

LEONARD GLICK
Community College of Philadelphia

J. MITCHELL MILLER
University of Texas at San Antonio

PEARSON

Boston • New York • San Francisco
Mexico City • Montreal • Toronto • London • Madrid • Munich • Paris
Hong Kong • Singapore • Tokyo • Cape Town • Sydney

Acquisitions Editor: Dave Repetto
Editorial Assistant: Jack Cashman
Senior Marketing Manager: Kelly May
Production Editor: Pat Torelli
Editorial Production Service: Progressive Publishing Alternatives
Composition Buyer: Linda Cox
Manufacturing Buyer: Debbie Rossi
Electronic Composition: Progressive Information Technologies
Interior Design: Progressive Publishing Alternatives
Photo Researcher: Katharine S. Cebik
Cover Administrator: Linda Knowles
Cover Designer: Susan Paradise

For related titles and support materials, visit our online catalog at www.ablongman.com

Between the time website information is gathered and then published, it is not unusual for some sites to have closed. Also, the transcription of URLs can result in typographical errors. The publisher would appreciate notification where these errors occur so that they may be corrected in subsequent editions.

Library of Congress Cataloging-in-Publication Data
Glick, Leonard.
    Criminology / Leonard Glick, J. Mitchell Miller.--2nd ed.
        p.   cm.
    ISBN-13: 978-0-205-53693-1
    ISBN-10: 0-205-53693-X
  1. Criminology.   I. Miller, J. Mitchell. II. Title.
    HV6025.G55 2008
    364--dc22
                                                                    2007035132

Printed in Canada

12 11 10 9 8   VONF   16 15 14 13

Brief Contents

Contents

2 The Nature and Extent of Crime: Measuring Behavior 28

3 Explanations for Criminal Behavior 62

4 Biological Explanations for Criminal Behavior   100

5 Psychological Explanations for Criminal Behavior — 122

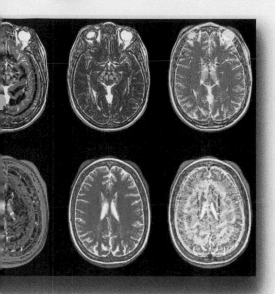

6 Sociological Theories I: Social-Structural Explanations of Criminal Behavior 142

7 Sociological Theories II: Social Control, Conflict, Feminist, and Labeling Theories 168

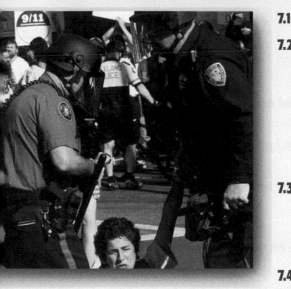

Violent Crime I: Assault and Rape

200

Violent Crime II: Robbery, Murder, Hate Crime, and Terrorism 240

10 Property Crimes 274

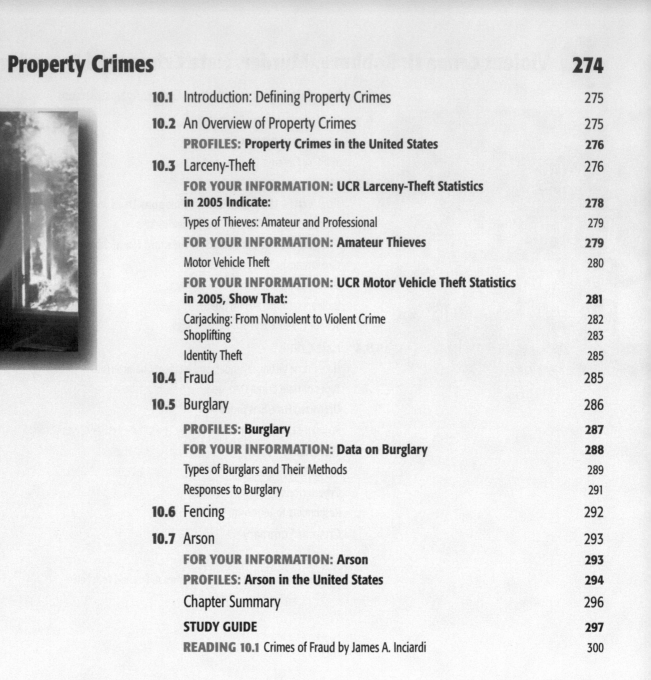

11 Organizational Criminality: White-Collar and Organized Crime 302

12 Morality Crimes: Drugs, Alcohol, and Sex 332

13 Responding to Crime: The Police and the Courts — 378

14 Responding to Crime: Corrections

Preface

WRITTEN WITH TODAY'S CRIMINOLOGY STUDENT IN MIND

Criminology has emerged as an independent field of study within the social sciences over the last decade and is now more diverse than ever before. The study of crime is more complex than one might first think; the discipline is an intriguing blend of complimentary academic fields that allow us to examine the diverse nature of crime from multiple scientific perspectives. Criminologists have historically focused on the causes of crime, including its distribution across social strata and demographics from a sociological tradition. In addition to sociological perspectives of crime, which feature cultural, social ecological, learning, routine activities, and critical explanations, biological and psychological influences have become increasingly prominent in both theoretical and applied criminology. In fact, attention to and interest in forensic criminology is at an all-time high both within academe and the popular culture, as evident by the popularity of "CSI" and the general attention to the use of science in crime-solving. Applied criminology, more broadly, entails the utilization of criminological work in the improvement of justice agency policies and practices. *Criminology*, Second Edition surveys these rich academic traditions and examines the multidisciplinary nature of criminology while emphasizing the natural relationship between scientifically understanding crime and effectively responding to it.

In addition to addressing traditional forms of property and violent crime, criminology today is confronted with new forms of crime such as terrorism, school shootings, and the persistent social problems of gangs, drugs, and illegal immigration. This new edition of *Criminology* features coverage of the breadth of the field while placing special focus on contemporary issues and events. Criminology, as a discipline, is quickly growing and continues to evolve. Heavily influenced by the theories and research methodologies from various academic fields, this text reemphasizes the themes of the original edition: eclectic, comprehensive, and objective (or at least evenly biased in advocating competing perspectives) in presenting, explaining, and evaluating the many philosophics, theories, and responses to crime. Instructors often emphasize specific schools of thought throughout courses, and this text enables the comparison and contrast of alternative theoretical and ideological perspectives. Classical and contemporary explications of the nature of crime and victimization and related applications of criminology are examined in conjunction with several useful pedagogical enhancements (described below) across the individual chapters toward four major objectives. This text will provide students with:

1. A thorough, definitive, and contemporary overview of the field of criminology.
2. An understanding of the major focus of criminal behavior and specific types of crime.

3. Familiarity with society's various responses to crime and the interrelated functions of the three main prongs of the criminal justice system, law enforcement, the courts, and corrections.
4. Critical and analytical thinking skills.

Criminology and criminal justice are thriving disciplines as the number of majors continues to steadily grow across the country. The success is no doubt driven in large part by the huge demand for graduates to fill diverse employment opportunities in the criminal justice system, related substance abuse, victimization, and youth service areas, as well as research and evaluation roles in both higher education and agency settings. The material in this book communicates the fundamental knowledge necessary for understanding the discipline and will serve as a foundation for more in-depth study of specific topics in later courses.

ORGANIZATION

The text has four major sections:

The first section (Chapters 1–2): Defines the field of criminology and the criminologist's role; examines the scientific approach and perspectives; evaluates the nature of deviant and criminal behavior; and examines patterns of crime and the measurement of crime.

The second section (Chapters 3–7): Focuses on criminological theories, ranging from the early explanations for criminal behavior to more recent biological, psychological, sociological, and other explanations.

The third section (Chapters 8–12): Covers the major forms of criminal behavior, including crimes of violence, property crimes, organizational crimes, and public-order crime.

The fourth section (Chapters 13–14): Focuses on society's response to crime and the U.S. criminal justice system, including the police, courts, and correctional system. These chapters are referred to by many as the "criminal justice system chapters" and are provided for those instructors who choose to cover this content in their criminology course.

INTEGRATED, FOCUSED READINGS

One of the ways in which *Criminology* is innovative and unique is that it exposes students to the works of classic thinkers and contemporary theorists and researchers through integrated readings in nearly every chapter. These readings present fresh insights into many of the latest developments in the field of criminology and include a variety of high-interest and contemporary articles by George B. Vold and Thomas J. Bernard, John P. Murray, Jeanne Flavin, Fran S. Davis, James A. Fox and Jack Levin, Judith A. Myers-Walls, Jan M. Chaiken and Marcia R. Chaiken, Clemens Bartollas and John P. Conrad, Anne Seymour and Trudy Gregorie, and others. Also included are classic works by Émile Durkheim, Edwin Sutherland, and Richard A. Cloward and Lloyd E. Ohlin.

READING 3.1

Contemporary Classicism: Deterrence and Econometrics, and Implications and Conclusions

Source: Theoretical Criminology, Fourth Edition by George B. Vold and Thomas J. Bernard and Jeffrey B. Snipes, copyright © 1997 by Oxford University Press, Inc. Used by permission of Oxford University Press, Inc.

BY GEORGE B. VOLD AND THOMAS J. BERNARD

DETERRENCE AND ECONOMETRICS

The classical school was the dominant perspective in criminology for approximately one hundred years, until it was replaced by the positivist search for the causes of crime. After another one hundred years substantial interest returned to the classical perspective in criminology, beginning in the late 1960s. This revival of interest was associated with a dramatic shift away from the positivist-oriented indeterminate sentencing structures and back to the determinate sentences similar to the French Code of 1791.[1]

Two principal branches of contemporary classicism can be identified. The whole question of deterrence has been the subject of voluminous literature in criminology in recent years.[2] Here an attempt has been made to develop the classical perspective in the light of modern knowledge of the human behavioral sciences, as well as through empirical studies of the effects of certainty and severity of punishment on crime rates. While deterrence theory and research has been dominated by criminologists and sociologists, the other branch of contemporary classicism has been dominated by economists. The field of economics holds a view of man that is quite similar to that of the classicists. For example, economic theory holds that a person analyzes the costs and benefits when he decides to buy a hamburger instead of a T-bone steak, or a Volkswagen instead of a Cadillac. The costs and benefits include not merely monetary factors, but factors such as taste, comfort, prestige, and convenience. Econometric techniques[3] have been developed to analyze these factors in terms of the resulting economic choice. Beginning with an article by Gary S. Becker in 1968,[4] many economists have approached crime as a similar economic choice. They have therefore applied their techniques to the analysis of criminal behavior, as well as to the choices of the criminal justice system.

The economic perspective views the decision to commit a crime as essentially similar to any other decision—that is, it is made on the basis of an analysis of the costs and benefits of the action. Because crime is seen as a free choice of the individual, the theories of crime which discuss cultural or biological "causes" are seen as unnecessary.[5] For example, [Richard E] Sullivan describes the choice of a career as a thief as follows:

The individual calculates (1) all his practical opportunities of earning legitimate income, (2) the amounts of income offered by these opportunities, (3) the amounts of income offered by various illegal methods, (4) the probability of being arrested if he acts illegally, and (5) the probable punishment should he be caught. After making these calculations, he chooses the act or occupation with the highest discounted return. To arrive at a discounted return he must include among his cost calculations the future costs of going to prison if he is apprehended. It is in this sense that the criminal is understood to be a normal, rational, calculating individual.[6]

The benefits of a criminal action may include not only increases in monetary wealth, but also increases in psychological satisfaction as well as the possibility of achieving these increases with very little effort. The expected cost of the crime is normally computed as the total cost associated with the punishment of the crime times the probability that the punishment will be imposed. For example, if the crime is usually punished with a fine of $1,000, and the probability of the punishment being imposed is 1/10, then the expected cost of the crime is $100. If the person can gain more than $100 in the crime, then it would be in his interest to commit it.[7] Often the costs and benefits cannot be computed in monetary terms, such as when the costs include time in prison or the social disapproval of arrest and conviction, or when benefits include the satisfaction of revenge or of outwitting the authorities. However, the individual must still compare these costs and benefits in order to decide whether the action is "worth it" to him or her.

This calculation does not presume that the criminal has a crystal ball to foresee future events. Many people make mistakes in calculating their future pay-offs, and when they do, they may end up in dead-end jobs or in bankruptcy. When criminals make similar mistakes, they may end up spending the better part of their lives in prison. As Sullivan says, "The basic economic assumption does not maintain that people do not make mistakes but rather that they do their best given their reading of present and future possibilities and given their resources."[8]

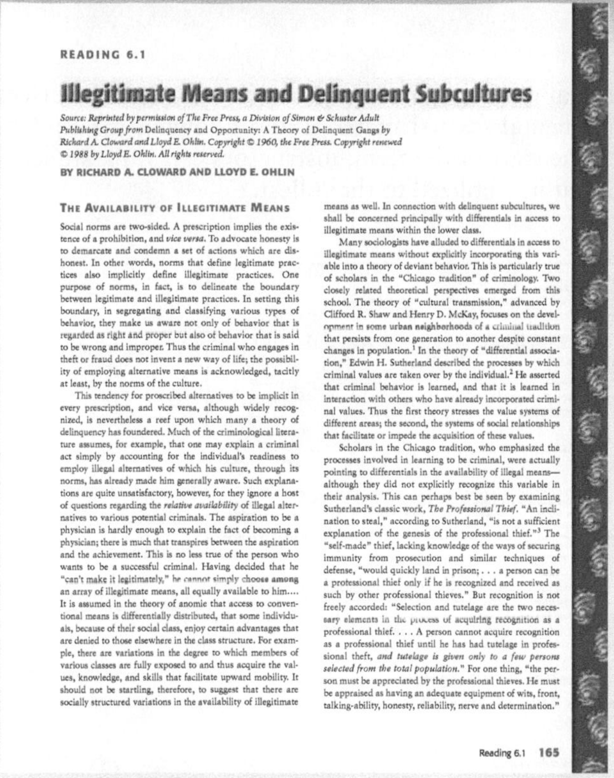

READING 6.1

Illegitimate Means and Delinquent Subcultures

Source: Reprinted by permission of The Free Press, a Division of Simon & Schuster Adult Publishing Group from Delinquency and Opportunity: A Theory of Delinquent Gangs *by Richard A. Cloward and Lloyd E. Ohlin. Copyright © 1960, the Free Press. Copyright renewed © 1988 by Lloyd E. Ohlin. All rights reserved.*

BY RICHARD A. CLOWARD AND LLOYD E. OHLIN

The Availability of Illegitimate Means

Social norms are two-sided. A prescription implies the existence of a prohibition, and *vice versa*. To advocate honesty is to demarcate and condemn a set of actions which are dishonest. In other words, norms that define legitimate practices also implicitly define illegitimate practices. One purpose of norms, in fact, is to delineate the boundary between legitimate and illegitimate practices. In setting this boundary, in segregating and classifying various types of behavior, they make us aware not only of behavior that is regarded as right and proper but also of behavior that is said to be wrong and improper. Thus the criminal who engages in theft or fraud does not invent a new way of life; the possibility of employing alternative means is acknowledged, tacitly at least, by the norms of the culture.

This tendency for proscribed alternatives to be implicit in every prescription, and vice versa, although widely recognized, is nevertheless a reef upon which many a theory of delinquency has foundered. Much of the criminological literature assumes, for example, that one may explain a criminal act simply by accounting for the individual's readiness to employ illegal alternatives of which his culture, through its norms, has already made him generally aware. Such explanations are quite unsatisfactory, however, for they ignore a host of questions regarding the *relative availability* of illegal alternatives to various potential criminals. The aspiration to be a physician is hardly enough to explain the fact of becoming a physician; there is much that transpires between the aspiration and the achievement. This is no less true of the person who wants to be a successful criminal. Having decided that he "can't make it legitimately," he cannot simply choose among an array of illegitimate means, all equally available to him.... It is assumed in the theory of anomie that access to conventional means is differentially distributed, that some individuals, because of their social class, enjoy certain advantages that are denied to those elsewhere in the class structure. For example, there are variations in the degree to which members of various classes are fully exposed to and thus acquire the values, knowledge, and skills that facilitate upward mobility. It should not be startling, therefore, to suggest that there are socially structured variations in the availability of illegitimate means as well. In connection with delinquent subcultures, we shall be concerned principally with differentials in access to illegitimate means within the lower class.

Many sociologists have alluded to differentials in access to illegitimate means without explicitly incorporating this variable into a theory of deviant behavior. This is particularly true of scholars in the "Chicago tradition" of criminology. Two closely related theoretical perspectives emerged from this school. The theory of "cultural transmission," advanced by Clifford R. Shaw and Henry D. McKay, focuses on the development in some urban neighborhoods of a criminal tradition that persists from one generation to another despite constant changes in population.[1] In the theory of "differential association," Edwin H. Sutherland described the processes by which criminal values are taken over by the individual.[2] He asserted that criminal behavior is learned, and that it is learned in interaction with others who have already incorporated criminal values. Thus the first theory stresses the value systems of different areas; the second, the systems of social relationships that facilitate or impede the acquisition of these values.

Scholars in the Chicago tradition, who emphasized the processes involved in learning to be criminal, were actually pointing to differentials in the availability of illegal means—although they did not explicitly recognize this variable in their analysis. This can perhaps best be seen by examining Sutherland's classic work, *The Professional Thief*. "An inclination to steal," according to Sutherland, "is not a sufficient explanation of the genesis of the professional thief."[3] The "self-made" thief, lacking knowledge of the ways of securing immunity from prosecution and similar techniques of defense, "would quickly land in prison; . . . a person can be a professional thief only if he is recognized and received as such by other professional thieves." But recognition is not freely accorded: "Selection and tutelage are the two necessary elements in the process of acquiring recognition as a professional thief. . . . A person cannot acquire recognition as a professional thief until he has had tutelage in professional theft, *and tutelage is given only to a few persons selected from the total population.*" For one thing, "the person must be appreciated by the professional thieves. He must be appraised as having an adequate equipment of wits, front, talking-ability, honesty, reliability, nerve and determination."

Reading 6.1 165

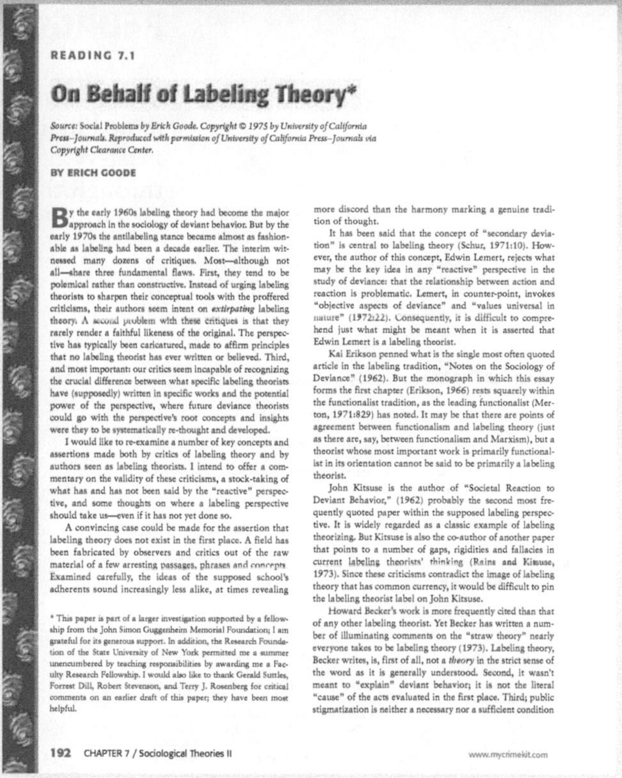

READING 7.1

On Behalf of Labeling Theory*

Source: Social Problems *by Erich Goode. Copyright © 1975 by University of California Press–Journals. Reproduced with permission of University of California Press–Journals via Copyright Clearance Center.*

BY ERICH GOODE

By the early 1960s labeling theory had become the major approach in the sociology of deviant behavior. But by the early 1970s the antilabeling stance became almost as fashionable as labeling had been a decade earlier. The interim witnessed many dozens of critiques. Most—although not all—share three fundamental flaws. First, they tend to be polemical rather than constructive. Instead of urging labeling theorists to sharpen their conceptual tools with the proffered criticisms, their authors seem intent on *extirpating* labeling theory. A second problem with these critiques is that they rarely render a faithful likeness of the original. The perspective has typically been caricatured, made to affirm principles that no labeling theorist has ever written or believed. Third, and most important: our critics seem incapable of recognizing the crucial difference between what specific labeling theorists have (supposedly) written in specific works and the potential power of the perspective, where future deviance theorists could go with the perspective's root concepts and insights were they to be systematically re-thought and developed.

I would like to re-examine a number of key concepts and assertions made both by critics of labeling theory and by authors seen as labeling theorists. I intend to offer a commentary on the validity of these criticisms, a stock-taking of what has and has not been said by the "reactive" perspective, and some thoughts on where a labeling perspective should take us—even if it has not yet done so.

A convincing case could be made for the assertion that labeling theory does not exist in the first place. A field has been fabricated by observers and critics out of the raw material of a few arresting passages, phrases and concepts. Examined carefully, the ideas of the supposed school's adherents sound increasingly less alike, at times revealing more discord than the harmony marking a genuine tradition of thought.

It has been said that the concept of "secondary deviation" is central to labeling theory (Schur, 1971:10). However, the author of this concept, Edwin Lemert, rejects what may be the key idea in any "reactive" perspective in the study of deviance: that the relationship between action and reaction is problematic. Lemert, in counter-point, invokes "objective aspects of deviance" and "values universal in nature" (1972:22). Consequently, it is difficult to comprehend just what might be meant when it is asserted that Edwin Lemert is a labeling theorist.

Kai Erikson penned what is the single most often quoted article in the labeling tradition, "Notes on the Sociology of Deviance" (1962). But the monograph in which this essay forms the first chapter (Erikson, 1966) rests squarely within the functionalist tradition, as the leading functionalist (Merton, 1971:829) has noted. It may be that there are points of agreement between functionalism and labeling theory (just as there are, say, between functionalism and Marxism), but a theorist whose most important work is primarily functionalist in its orientation cannot be said to be primarily a labeling theorist.

John Kitsuse is the author of "Societal Reaction to Deviant Behavior," (1962) probably the second most frequently quoted paper within the supposed labeling perspective. It is widely regarded as a classic example of labeling theorizing. But Kitsuse is also the co-author of another paper that points to a number of gaps, rigidities and fallacies in current labeling theorists' thinking (Rains and Kitsuse, 1973). Since these criticisms contradict the image of labeling theory that has common currency, it would be difficult to pin the labeling theorist label on John Kitsuse.

Howard Becker's work is more frequently cited than that of any other labeling theorist. Yet Becker has written a number of illuminating comments on the "straw theory" nearly everyone takes to be labeling theory (1973). Labeling theory, Becker writes, is, first of all, not a *theory* in the strict sense of the word as it is generally understood. Second, it wasn't meant to "explain" deviant behavior; it is not the literal "cause" of the acts evaluated in the first place. Third; public stigmatization is neither a necessary nor a sufficient condition

* This paper is part of a larger investigation supported by a fellowship from the John Simon Guggenheim Memorial Foundation; I am grateful for its generous support. In addition, the Research Foundation of the State University of New York permitted me a summer unencumbered by teaching responsibilities by awarding me a Faculty Research Fellowship. I would also like to thank Gerald Suttles, Forrest Dill, Robert Stevenson, and Terry J. Rosenberg for critical comments on an earlier draft of this paper; they have been most helpful.

192 CHAPTER 7 / Sociological Theories II

www.mycrimekit.com

The articles have been carefully selected and integrated into the text to support and illustrate the subject matter, and to add important dimensions and depth to the reader's knowledge and understanding. Each reading—whether it comes from *Fortune*, *The Economist*, *The Futurist*, a classic work, or a criminological journal—was selected for its presentation, scholarship, and ability to capture and hold interest. **Critical Thinking Questions** appear at the end of each reading.

- To avoid disrupting the flow of the text, the readings are located at the back of each chapter. Reading Abstracts are located in each chapter where the reading is most relevant. These Reading Abstracts provide a brief synopsis of each reading and prompt students to the exact location at the back of the chapter.

READING ABSTRACT

The Professional Thief

BY EDWIN SUTHERLAND

A classic example of the case study method is illustrated in Edwin Sutherland's *The Professional Thief* (1937), excerpted in Reading 2.1. Sutherland interviewed a professional thief and obtained in-depth information that would be difficult to get through other methods. He learned what it means to be a professional rather than an amateur thief, how professional thieves are organized, and how they communicate and network with one another.

See reading on page 56.

READING ABSTRACT

Crime as Normal Behavior

BY ÉMILE DURKHEIM

This reading is a classic in the field of criminology. Durkheim believed that

- the collective conscience of a people defines what is crime and that it (crime) is a normal phenomenon of societies;
- crime is the natural and inevitable product of collective life and social evolution;
- crime actually helps to ensure the stability of the society by identifying and clarifying social standards for acceptable and unacceptable behavior (i.e., it is functional);
- rather than disrupting society, crime actually serves to strengthen group solidarity by uniting people in disapproval against the deviant.

See page 24 for reading.

READING ABSTRACT

Contemporary Classicism: Deterrence and Econometrics, and Implications and Conclusions

BY GEORGE VOLD AND THOMAS BERNARD

This reading examines the economic model of crime and deterrence, and its implications for crime control.

See reading on page 84.

PEDAGOGY

Criminology also contains a wide range of important pedagogical devices aimed at reinforcing fundamental textual material and allowing for student mastery of the content. At the start of the term, instructors can walk students through this pedagogy so that it is utilized to the fullest.

exploded firecrackers in its mouth. In the United States, there appears to be a connection between family violence and animal cruelty and violence. It is not uncommon to find the assault and abuse of animals in the histories of people who have committed murder.

After reading this section, you should be able to

1. distinguish between conflict and violence;
2. discuss the incidence and prevalence of violence in American families;
3. analyze patterns of abuse between spouses and intimate partners;
4. identify risk factors in parental abuse of children and profile the typical abuser;
5. describe the dynamics of domestic violence between siblings, toward elders and parents, and toward animals.

8.4 EXPLAINING AND RESPONDING TO ASSAULTIVE AND ABUSIVE BEHAVIOR

Three main types of explanations exist for violent and assaultive behavior in American society:

1. ***Psychopathological theories*** explain assaultive and abusive behavior in terms of abnormal psychological characteristics among people.
2. ***Sociocultural theories*** focus on the approval of violence by a society's value system and norms.
3. ***Economic or exchange theories*** stress the idea that violence is a means that can be used to attain wanted ends. That is, when other resources, such as love, respect, money, or shared goals, are not available or insufficient to achieve desired ends, assaultive behavior—abuse and violence—tends to be employed.[34]

Psychopathological Explanations for Violence

Mental illness may contribute to family violence.

Psychopathological explanations for assaultive and violent behavior involve the idea of mental illness. There is, for example, an assumption that distinctive, psychopathic personality traits are present in an abuser. Psychopathy in child abusers is traced to their childhoods, when they themselves were abused. Ironically, the cause of psychopathy in abusive parents is the fact that they were reared in the same way they re-create with their own children. But are abusers simply insane?

One problem with the psychopathological explanation is the inability to specifically determine what personality traits and mental traits characterize the pathology. Attributing abusive behavior to mental illness also tends to ignore other variables, for example, the cultural, social, economic, and demographic factors that are involved.[35]

Explaining and Responding to Assaultive and Abusive Behavior 213

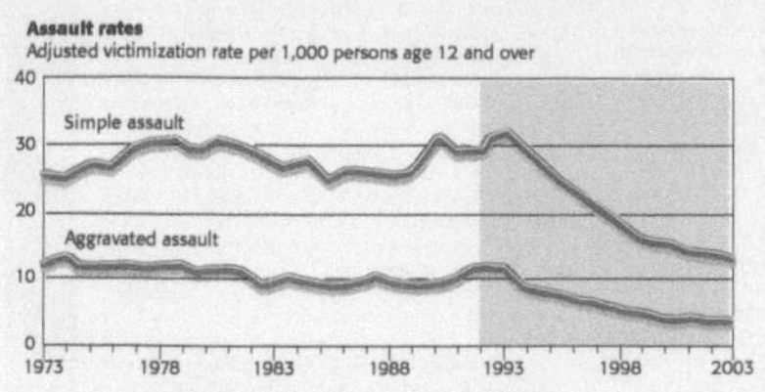

Note: The National Crime Victimization Survey redesign was implemented in 1993; the area with the lighter shading is before the redesign and the darker area after the redesign. The data before 1993 are adjusted to make them comparable with data collected since the redesign.

Source: U.S. Department of Justice, Office of Justice Programs, Bureau of Justice Statistics, *Bureau of Justice Statistics Assault Trends*, Washington, DC: Government Printing Office, September 10, 2006, p.1.

FIGURE 8.1

As shown in Figure 8.1, between 1994 and today, simple and aggravated assault rates have been declining in the United States. In 1994, there were about twelve aggravated assaults per 1,000 persons twelve years of age and older. Today, there are about five aggravated assaults per 1,000 persons.[6] What factors do you think might account for this decline?

Battery is an attack that results in striking or touching the victim.

Assaultive Behavior in the Workplace

Assault and violence have become a serious problem in the American workplace.

Workplace violence, or assaultive behavior in the American workplace, has increased over the past decade. One of the most serious problems in the workplace is the escalation of employer-employee conflict and violence. One reason is that many employers have used unpleasant psychological methods to force employees to resign.

- According to the Bureau of National Affairs, about one in four managers abuses employees to the extent that the workers slow productivity, call in sick, or change jobs, costing the economy billion of dollars annually.
- Downsizing in the work world and downturns in the economoy have cost hundreds of thousands of people their jobs and have caused a widespread malaise among workers.
- These events have engendered a "cycle of vengeful acts by angry and frustrated employees and punitive and abusive acts by management."[7]

Not only do workers steal, commit sabotage, and sell company secrets to their employers' competitors, they also become angry and assaultive. Many employees who have been overlooked for a promotion, restructured, downsized out, or fired from their jobs have responded with violent acts, even homicide. In the United States, homicides account for 17 percent of all occupational deaths. In fact, homicide ranks second only to vehicle accidents as a cause of death on the job.[8]

DID YOU KNOW
For the most recent statistics on assault, use the keywords "Bureau of Justice Statistics" in an Internet search, or go to the following BJS web site: http://www.ojp.usdoj.gov/bjs/.

Assault 203

BOXED FEATURES

- **FYI Boxes** in each chapter provide additional information for those readers who are interested in reading more about particular topics.

FOR YOUR INFORMATION

The Nation's Two Crime Measures

- In 1994, law enforcement agencies active in the UCRP, which began in 1929, represented approximately 249 million U.S. inhabitants—96 percent of the total population.
- The UCRP provides crime counts for the nation as a whole, as well as for regions, states, counties, cities, and towns. This permits studies among neighboring jurisdictions and among those with similar populations and other common characteristics.
- UCR findings for each calendar year are published in a preliminary release in the spring, followed by a detailed annual report, *Crime in the United States*, issued in the following calendar year.
- Following a five-year redesign effort, the UCRP is currently being converted to the more comprehensive and detailed National Incident-Based Reporting System (NIBRS), which will provide detailed information about each criminal incident in twenty-two broad categories of offenses.
- The NCVS, which began in 1973, provides a detailed picture of crime incidents, victims, and trends.
- Two times a year, U.S. Census Bureau personnel interview household members in a nationally representative sample of approximately 45,000 households (about 80,000 people). Approximately 160,000 interviews of persons age twelve or older are conducted annually.
- Publication of NCVS data includes *Criminal Victimization in the United States*, an annual report that covers the broad range of detailed information collected by the NCVS.

Contrasting the UCR and the NCVS

- The two programs were created to serve different purposes. The UCRP's primary objective is to provide a reliable set of criminal justice statistics for law enforcement administration, operation, and management. The NCVS was established to provide previously unavailable information about crime (including crime not reported to police), victims, and offenders.
- The two programs measure an overlapping but nonidentical set of crimes. The NCVS includes crimes both reported and not reported to law enforcement. The NCVS excludes, but the UCR includes, homicide, arson, commercial crimes, and crimes against children under age twelve. The UCR captures crimes reported to law enforcement, but it excludes sexual assaults and simple assaults from the Crime Index.
- Because of methodology, the NCVS and UCR definitions of some crimes differ. For example, the UCR defines burglary as the unlawful entry or attempted entry of a structure to commit a felony or theft. The NCVS, not wanting to ask victims to ascertain offenders' motives, defines burglary as the entry or attempted entry of a residence by a person who had no right to be there.
- For property crimes (burglary, theft, and motor vehicle theft), the two programs calculate crime rates using different bases. The UCR rates for these crimes are per capita (number of crimes per 100,000 persons), whereas the NCVS rates for these crimes are per household (number of crimes per 1,000 households). Because the number of households may not grow at the same rate each year as the total population, trend data for rates of property crimes measured by the two programs may not be comparable.
- Each program has unique strengths. The UCR provides a measure of the number of crimes reported to law enforcement agencies throughout the country, including the most reliable, timely data on the extent and nature of homicides in the nation. The NCVS is the primary source of information on the characteristics of criminal victimization and on the number and types of crimes not reported to law enforcement authorities.
- NCVS and UCR data can be used in concert to explore why trends in reported and police-recorded crime may differ.

FOR YOUR INFORMATION

Ferri and Social Reform

Ferri's contributions to the etiology of criminal conduct were "incidental means for achieving a greater understanding of the course which the reformation of criminal justice should take."[1] That is, Ferri was basically a social reformer. He desired to achieve a "demonstrably effective criminal justice, which would afford maximum protection or defence of society against the criminal."[2] In his writings, Ferri examined many crime-preventive measures, or, as he termed them, "substitutes for punishments," such as "free trade, abolition of monopolies, inexpensive workmen's dwellings, public savings banks, better street lighting, birth control, [and] freedom of marriage and divorce."[3] These preventive measures were very much in line with his political theory, which was that "the state is the principal instrument through which better conditions are to be attained."[4] Ferri was the chief architect of the positivist school, which stood in clear opposition to the classical school. Ferri felt that a positivist perspective was necessary to "put a stop to the exaggerated individualism in favour of the criminal in order to obtain a greater respect for the rights of honest people who constitute the great majority."[5]

[1]T. Sellin, "Enrico Ferri," in *Pioneers in Criminology*, H. Mannheim, ed., 2nd ed., Montclair, NJ: Patterson Smith, 1972, pp. 378–79.

[2]Ibid.

[3]G. B. Vold and T. J. Bernard, *Theoretical Criminology*, New York: Oxford University Press, 1986, p. 41.

[4]Ibid.

[5]Sellin, "Enrico Ferri," p. 378.

FOR YOUR INFORMATION

The Controlled Experiment: Drug Therapy Research for Children

Some criminological research has focused on the development of different forms of drug therapy to alleviate various types of aggressive, delinquent behavior in children. The application of such a controlled experiment involves the following steps:

1. Two groups, an experimental (or test) group and a control group, are organized. Each of these groups must be alike in age, IQ, sex, social class, and any other characteristics believed to be associated with aggressive, potentially delinquent behavior.
2. The experimental group receives the medication while the control group, without knowing it, receives a placebo, which is a harmless solution such as water.
3. Differences in the manifestation of aggressive behavior are compared between the two groups.
4. A series of measurements of aggressive behavior are taken in both groups sometime after the termination of the medication and compared with the children's behavior as observed and measured before the treatment.
5. A reduction in aggressive, potentially delinquent behavior on the part of the experimental group as compared with the control group would be viewed as resulting from the medication received by the experimental group.

- **Profile Boxes,** which occur primarily in Chapters 8–12, highlight many of the different crime types discussed in these chapters and provide a quick summary of the major points.

PROFILES

Crime Patterns: Time of Day and Place

- Personal crimes of theft are more likely to occur during the day, between 6 AM and 6 PM, than at night.
- Household crimes more frequently occur after dark than in daylight. Although violent incidents occurring at night are most frequently committed between 6 PM and midnight, household crimes are more likely to be committed sometime between midnight and 6 AM.
- Robberies and assaults in which the offenders are armed are more likely to occur at night than during the day.
- Violent crimes committed by strangers are more likely to occur at night than those committed by persons who are known to the victims.
- The crimes most likely to occur during evening or nighttime hours are motor vehicle theft (63 percent) and serious violent offenses, such as robbery with injury (60 percent) and aggravated assault (58 percent).
- Among the crimes least likely to occur at night are simple assault (45 percent), purse snatching, pocket picking (34 percent), and personal larceny without contact (35 percent).
- About half of all violent incidents occur five miles or fewer from the victim's home.
- The largest proportion of violent incidents occur on a street away from the victim's home.
- The victim's home is the next most common site for a violent crime: about 25 percent of violent crimes take place inside or near the victim's home or lodging; 27 percent of rapes occur in the home.
- Overall, almost 11 percent of violent crimes occur in a parking lot or a garage, and 11 percent inside a school building or on school property.
- Four out of ten robberies take place on the street.
- The most common place for a motor vehicle theft to occur is in a parking lot or garage (36 percent).

Sources: The Uniform Crime Report and the National Crime Victimization Survey.

PROFILES

Assault

- Overall, aggravated assault and simple assault are more likely to be reported to the police when the victim is female (61 percent for females, 52 percent for males).
- Aggravated assaults against black victims (61 percent) are reported to the police at a significantly higher percentage than aggravated assaults against white victims (54 percent).
- In terms of offender characteristics for assaultive behavior, gender makes little difference. That is, the percentage of aggravated assaults reported to the police differs very little when the offender is male (54 percent) or female (55 percent). For simple assaults, the percentage is the same—37 percent.
- In terms of race of the offender, only somewhat higher percentages of aggravated assaults are reported to the police when committed by black offenders (59 percent) than by white offenders (54 percent).
- Simple assault percentages are the same for both white and black offenders (38 percent).
- In terms of age, the younger the offender, the lower the percentage of assaultive behavior reported to the police.

Source: U.S. Department of Justice, Office of Justice Programs, Bureau of Justice Statistics, *Reporting Crime to the Police, 1992–2000,* Washington, DC: Government Printing Office, March 9, 2003, NCJ-195710, pp. 3, 5.

BUILT-IN STUDY GUIDE

A comprehensive Study Guide and workbook section has been incorporated at the end of each chapter and contains a wealth of review and quizzing opportunities for students. This Study Guide is designed to help students organize their study of the chapter content, evaluate their understanding, and help them prepare for exams. Before reading each chapter, students can review this Study Guide section, especially the Chapter Objectives and Key Terms, so that they can focus their reading. An Answer Key is provided at the end of the text.

The Study Guide includes:
- chapter objectives and key terms
- short answer questions
- multiple-choice questions
- true-false questions
- fill-in questions
- matching questions
- essay questions
- answer section

SUPPLEMENTS

We carefully designed a supplement package that supports the aims of *Criminology* in order to provide both students and instructors with a wealth of support materials to ensure success in teaching and in learning. Several of the student supplements are available for FREE when packaged with the textbook so that students can benefit from them without incurring additional cost.

Instructor's Manual and Test Bank:

This author-written supplement contains an Instructor's Manual section with instructive chapter outlines, objectives, and key terms. In addition, a Test Bank with approximately 75 questions per chapter in three question types—true–false, multiple choice, and fill-in-the-blank—includes questions on the chapter material as well as the readings.

Computerized Test Bank:

This computerized version of the test bank is available with Tamarack's easy-to-use TestGen software, which lets you prepare tests for printing as well as for network and online testing. Full editing capability for Windows and Macintosh.

PowerPoint Lecture Presentations:

Featuring the figures from the textbook, this complete set of chapter-by-chapter PowerPoint lecture presentations, containing approximately 20 slides per chapter and specific to *Criminology*, is also available to qualified adopters giving instructors countless presentation options for their introductory course.

The Blockbuster Approach:

Teaching Criminal Justice and Criminology with Video, Second Edition: This supplement effectively guides the instructor on how to successfully integrate feature films into the introductory course and offers hundreds of film suggestions for the general topics covered in the course.

CourseCompass:

Instructors can focus on teaching the course—not on the technology—and create an online presence with no headaches. CourseCompass combines the strength of Allyn and Bacon content with state-of-the-art technology that simplifies course management. This easy to use and customizable program enables instructors to tailor the content and functionality to meet their individual needs. Visit http://cms.abacon.com/coursecompass/ for more information.

ACKNOWLEDGMENTS

This new edition of *Criminology* was facilitated by several talented people whose contributions deserve mention. Holly Ventura Miller was instrumental in updating the examples of major concepts and theories across the chapter and ensuring that chapter material was based in contemporary criminological and criminal justice research. Natalie Dominguez performed the majority of research assistant tasks and we are grateful for her assistance. Alison Routh resolved many lingering issues near completion and we likewise appreciate her assistance. Wesley Jennings has developed new instructor supplements for this edition and we also appreciate his important contributions. We would also like to thank the reviewers of this project whose many helpful suggestions are reflected throughout the text. They include: Gina Respass, Old Dominion University and Kenneth E. O'Keefe, Prairie State University.

The people at Allyn and Bacon made this edition possible and are due much deserved thanks. Dave Repetto facilitated Mitch Miller joining the project as an author, was a source of encouragement and assurance, and kept the project on schedule. Jack Cashman expedited matters along the way, trouble-shot many issues, and eased communication.

ABOUT THE AUTHORS

Leonard Glick is a retired professor of sociology from the Community College of Philadelphia where he has taught criminology for over thirty-five years. He played an essential role in the development of the college's criminal justice program. Dr. Glick's students came from a variety or roles in the criminal justice field, including police, probation, parole, prison personnel, and administrators. He has conducted and directed research for the Law School of the University of Pennsylvania, the Ford Foundation, the American Association of Community Colleges, Children's Hospital of Philadelphia, The Philadelphia Child Guidance Clinic, and various federal programs.

Working as a therapist and psychologist for Cigna, Humana, The Metropolitan Clinic of Counseling, and various hospital systems, Dr. Glick has counseled local, state, and federal law enforcement personnel on both an inpatient and an outpatient basis. He has also provided psychiatric and psychological services for criminals, crime victims, and their families.

Dr. Glick's undergraduate and graduate degrees are from the University of Pennsylvania, the Graduate School of Bryn Mawr College, and California Coast University. He is the coauthor or author of several professional papers and textbooks in criminology, sociology, and social problems.

Occasionally writing and doing research, Dr. Glick has retired with his wife Mary, children, grandchildren, their standard poodles, and siamese cat on the beaches of Galveston, Texas and the Adirondack mountains of New York State.

J. Mitchell Miller is professor and chair of the Department of Criminal Justice at the University of Texas at San Antonio. Dr. Miller received his Ph.D. from the University of Tennessee, Department of Sociology, in 1996. During doctoral study, he served as research associate in the Executive Office of the Society for the Study of Social Problems and participated in the American Sociological Association's Honors Program. He served on the faculty of the College of Criminal Justice at the University of South Carolina from 1996–2006, holding joint appointments with the College of Social Work and

School of Environment. From 2003–2006, Dr. Miller served as Director of Graduate Studies in Drugs and Addictions at USC.

Dr. Miller has been heavily involved in criminal justice pedagogy and student development. He was selected Advisor of the Year in 2004 by *Alpha Phi Sigma*, the National Criminal Justice Honor Society and is developing a research-based learning pedagogy for the criminal justice sciences through a Hewlett Foundation grant. He is the former editor of the *Journal of Crime and Justice* and the *Encyclopedia of Criminology (Vols. I–III*, Taylor and Francis) and is the current editor of the *Journal of Criminal Justice Education*. Dr. Miller is active in several national and regional criminology and criminal justice professional organizations, most notably as president-elect of the Southern Criminal Justice Association. Author of five books and over fifty academic journal articles and book chapters, Dr. Miller pursues an active research agenda of employing theoretical criminology to better assess the effectiveness of practices and policies across the prongs of the criminal justice system. His applied criminological research agenda has been supported through grants from the National Institute of Justice, the Bureau of Justice Assistance, the U.S. Department of State, and the U.S. Department of Justice. He is currently conducting evaluations of the effectiveness of a statewide truancy reduction initiative in South Carolina for the South Carolina Department of Education and a jail inmate reentry initiative in Auglaize County, Ohio for the Ohio Department of Mental Health.

CRIMINOLOGY
Second Edition

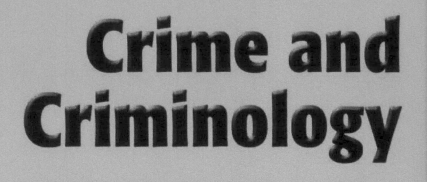

Crime and Criminology

1.1 INTRODUCTION: WHAT IS CRIMINOLOGY?

Crime is a pronounced reality of contemporary American life. Acts of violence and greed seem to dominate daily news across the nation in both traditional and new forms. It is the responsibility of criminologists to define, explain, and measure crime as well as provide recommendations for improving criminal and juvenile justice system policy and practice. Today's criminologists remain focused on the causes, nature, and distribution of violent, property, and morality crimes, but must also address a variety of less known criminal phenomenon. These include foreign and domestic acts of terrorism, child abductions, school safety, and billion dollar white collar crime scandals.

Americans fear crime yet, at the same time, are fascinated by it. For much of America, Sunday evenings since 2000 have centered on the hit television series, the "Sopranos," a mafia soap opera of violence and corruption. In that crime is commonly perceived as a social problem demanding a solution, many Americans are interested in the study and understanding of crime. Many people also want something to be done about our crime problem. This long-term concern has encouraged the continued scientific study of crime and criminal behavior, giving rise to the academic discipline of **criminology**, which represents a systematic effort to understand crime and criminal behavior.

In this text, you will learn about crime. You will also learn why people commit a wide range of criminal acts, from rape and murder to corporate and computer fraud. You will also learn how society responds to crime and America's crime problem.

This chapter

- discusses the criminological approach to studying and understanding crime (section 1.2);
- examines criminology and the criminologist's role in the study of criminal behavior (section 1.2);
- reviews how the criminologist attempts to be scientific in studying crime (section 1.3);
- explores the theoretical perspectives on the study of crime and the nature of deviant and criminal behavior (sections 1.4 and 1.5);
- concludes with an examination of the legal definition of crime and a classic reading on crime by Émile Durkheim (sections 1.6 and 1.7);
- includes a reading new to the second edition which defines the field of criminology.

Chapter Outline

Millions of Americans are fearful of crime in their communities. To what extent is this fear justified?

1.2 CRIMINOLOGY AND THE CRIMINOLOGIST'S ROLES

Criminologists scientifically study the nature and extent of crime, patterns of criminality, explanations for and causes of crime and criminal behavior, and the control of crime and criminal behavior. Criminologists

1. contribute to the study of crime mainly through scientific research that enables them to obtain facts and develop conclusions concerning crime;
2. help to identify the public's values and attitudes and major issues of public concern about crime and criminal behavior;
3. attempt to measure the actual extent of criminal behavior in society and its relationship to factors such as age, sex, race, religion, social class, location, and time of year.

Data on the type, extent, and variation of criminal behavior are obtained and presented from a variety of sources. For example, information concerning the extent of crime is available from official crime statistics published by the Federal Bureau of Investigation and the Bureau of Justice, and from independent criminological studies on the incidence of crime based on reports provided by crime victims.

Criminologists define and describe the many issues and problems raised by criminal activities and behavior in society. They also provide us with factual data on a variety of crimes and criminal behavior. However, the role of criminologists is not merely to identify a crime problem and list various facts and figures; they also analyze, interpret, and organize this information within a systematic framework. This process leads to a clearer understanding of the dimensions and scope of the crime problem. Prior to understanding how crime and criminal behavior develop or why they exist, we must have organized, valid data on various social, deviant, and criminal phenomena. An organized description of the important factors and dimensions of criminal behavior and crime is a necessary prerequisite to any analysis and understanding of crime.

DID YOU KNOW

The term *crime* is defined and examined later in this chapter. For now, a crime is an act that is in violation of the criminal law, and a criminal is a person who commits such an act.

DID YOU KNOW

Edwin Sutherland first defined criminology as " . . . the body of knowledge regarding delinquency and crime as a social phenomena. It includes within its scope the process of making laws, breaking laws, and of reacting toward the breaking of laws."

Criminology is the scientific study of crime, criminals, and criminal behavior.

The Criminologist Explains the Causes of Crime

Explanations that account for the causes, variations, and extent of crime are as complex as people and society, including, for example, people's social values and society's structure.

Criminologists identify crime problems, collect and analyze data, and communicate research findings to inform criminal justice and related public policy.

An additional major goal of criminology is to attempt to explain the existence and prevalence of crime and criminal behavior. Simply stated, criminologists attempt to answer the question, "What are the causes of crime?" To answer this question, criminologists draw from many fields, such as sociology, psychology, biology, criminal jurisprudence, political science, anthropology, public administration, and history. The explanation for crime and criminal behavior is not a simple task. Our society is complex. The explanations that account for the causes, variations, and extent of crime are as complex as our society. Criminologists and the discipline of criminology explore the many conditions and causes of crime and examine those factors in society that contribute to crime's continued existence. Criminological knowledge can help students develop an understanding of the connections between crime, criminal behavior, and current American values and social structures.

The Criminologist as Theoretician and Researcher

Criminologists relate scientific theory and research to the practical questions of how to predict and prevent crime and how to treat criminals.

To explain how and why criminal behavior or crime develops, the criminologist adopts the roles of both theoretician and researcher. For the criminologist, simply gathering the facts about a particular crime pattern (e.g., whether crime is increasing or which particular groups in society are most affected by a particular type of crime) is not enough; the causes of crime must be discovered as well. To do this, the criminologist must develop theories and then test the adequacy of those theories by means of scientific research.

In the role of theoretician, criminologists develop **theories**, or tentative explanations, concerning the causes of criminal behavior. Some theoretical

A **theory** is a means of explaining natural occurrences through statements about the relationships between observable phenomena.

As a social scientist, the criminologist is both a theoretician and a researcher. This criminologist is interviewing a juvenile offender as part of a research project on a criminological question, such as the causes of juvenile violent crime. In this process, the criminologist uses the scientific method and may link theory and research to policy and practice.

explanations for violent crimes—rape, homicide, and child abuse, for example—stress a number of causal factors, including physical characteristics and personality traits within the psychological makeup of the individual. Other, more sociological theories stress the importance of learning and the socialization process as causes of criminal behavior. Still other theories note the strong influence that social and economic inequality have on the development of personal stress, frustrations, and conflicts that may, in turn, induce people to engage in crime.

Criminologists provide a wide variety of theories regarding criminal behavior. These theories

1. contribute to the understanding of crime;
2. provide a framework within which people can examine current social policies and treatment proposals;
3. help us to understand the success or failure of treatments that have been established to prevent or alleviate crime.

Criminologists clearly recognize that theories are important for the development of political and social policies and treatment programs for criminals and their victims. The fact is, any proposed social or political policy or treatment program for dealing with crime is based on some type of theory, regardless of whether the authors of the proposal are aware of it. For example, many different proposals have been advanced to deal with the problem of the first-time minor offender. Some proposals have recommended treatment in a therapeutic community, others have recommended probation, and still others have recommended incarceration. Underlying each proposal, however, is a distinct theory on the causes of minor crimes and the possibilities, if any, for deterrence. Thus, the question is not whether we should have theory or whether we need theory; rather, the important question is how adequate are theories in helping us to understand the causes of crime and to know how best to deal with criminal activity and criminals. It is in this area that the criminologist can make important contributions in the dual role of theoretician and researcher.

The Criminologist as Critic and Evaluator

The criminologist sometimes plays the role of sociopolitical critic and policy advocate or evaluator of anticrime measures and criminal treatment programs.

Because of his or her unique understanding of criminal behavior and crime, the criminologist may be engaged in a number of additional roles related to the field of criminology. For example, some criminologists engage in the role of sociopolitical critic, presenting opinions and expertise for assessing the adequacy of current perspectives and policies on criminal activity and rehabilitation programs. While acting in the role of social critic, criminologists may

- take an active part in formulating and advocating the adoption of policy decisions aimed at alleviating society's crime problems;
- propose social, economic, and legal reform measures to reduce crime;
- use their knowledge and skills to evaluate and test the adequacy of specific programs for treating criminals.

The analysis and evaluation of treatment and rehabilitation programs are important areas of criminological inquiry. Criminologists, penologists, and other social and behavioral scientists have amassed much evidence on the effectiveness of treatment programs for delinquents and criminals, such as the influence of different therapeutic programs on delinquents or the effects of imprisonment on subsequent criminal behavior. In the role of evaluator, the criminologist analyzes many kinds of programs for dealing with criminal behavior, recommends changes, if any, and suggests the direction that new programs should take.

After reading this section, you should be able to

1. define criminology as the scientific study of crime, criminals, and criminal behavior;
2. explain the relationship between theory and research in criminology;
3. describe the roles of criminologists in terms of their basic goals:
   a. to identify, define, and describe crimes and criminal behavior in society;
   b. to collect, analyze, interpret, and organize reliable data about crime;
   c. to develop and test theories of the causes of crime and criminal behavior;
   d. to evaluate current and future responses to crime, including treatment and rehabilitation programs designed to help both criminals and victims;
   e. to propose or support research-based anticrime measures, programs, or reforms.

1.3 CRIMINOLOGY AND THE SCIENTIFIC APPROACH

Approaches that one can take to examine and understand criminal behavior include literary, journalistic, religious, and philosophical approaches. The criminological approach to understanding crime can be distinguished from these and many other approaches in that criminology attempts to use the scientific method in its investigations. In using the scientific approach to study crime, the criminologist follows certain guidelines in conducting research and developing conclusions. This section examines some of these guidelines as well as the characteristics of the scientific point of view: objectivity, factual data, precision, and appraisal and verification.

Objectivity

Criminologists attempt to conduct research and draw conclusions without personal bias or preconceptions.

The first major characteristic of the scientific method is objectivity. **Objectivity** refers to the ability and willingness to study the subject matter of a given field without prejudice or bias. A criminologist may personally believe, for example, that the death penalty represents a feasible, logical, and desirable way of dealing with someone who commits first-degree murder. However, in being objective, she or he would not allow such personal feelings to interfere with the research or the conclusions on capital punishment.

It is important to understand that objectivity can never be fully achieved in any scientific inquiry. Nevertheless, any biases or preconceptions on the part of the scientist must be reduced or held to a minimum and must be stated.

Objectivity refers to the ability and willingness to study the subject matter of a given field without prejudice or bias.

Criminologists constantly attempt to be objective when doing research. To maximize objectivity in scientific inquiry, criminologists must be aware of their own feelings and guard against imposing their values on their data or interpretations of data. They must also receive adequate training in the scientific approach. A researcher trained in the scientific method knows that data on a particular criminal activity or criminological question must be based on factual evidence from scientific research, not on speculation, commonsense notions, or personal preferences.

Factual Data and Precision

In criminological research, factual (empirical) data are important, and the collection and analysis of these data must be precise (accurate).

Criminologists insist that any research they do must be based on factual, or empirical, observations and not personal beliefs or idle speculation. For example, some people believe that crime generally is more prevalent among the lower social classes than in the higher classes. Some believe that if juvenile delinquents receive ongoing group therapy, their delinquent behavior will decrease. The criminologist would not accept these beliefs as constituting factual or observable evidence. Rather, the criminologist would insist that valid data on these subjects be obtained by means of scientific research.

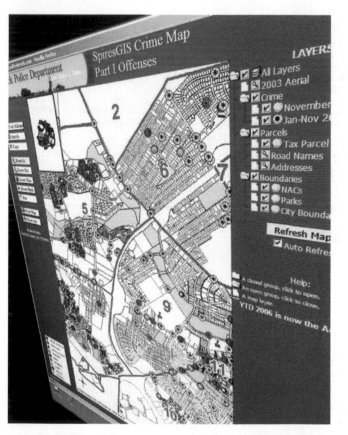

Criminologists use the scientific method in conducting their research, which may involve quantified (numerical) data or descriptive accounts of people's experiences (qualitative data). In both quantitative and qualitative research, the scientific method demands objectivity, accurate empirical data, and precision in the research design and in all other facets of operation.

Another characteristic of the scientific approach is the demand for **precision** in all facets of research. Thus, the criminologist must maintain accuracy in the collection and analysis of data from research on any criminological question or problem. To ensure precision, the criminologist develops a research design prior to investigating a particular problem or question. The **research design** precisely defines the specific kinds of data to be collected and the sources to be used in gathering these data. For example, data may include the age and sex of offenders, the types of offenses, the types of sentences, the lengths of incarceration, and so on, whereas the sources of data may be official crime reports, victimization reports, and court or prison records.

In addition, the research design specifies the time period during which the data will be gathered and gives a thorough description of the methods to be employed in the data gathering. Such methods may include using questionnaires or interview surveys, or developing and conducting a set of experiments. The research design also specifies the methods by which the data, once gathered, will be classified and the procedures that will be used to develop conclusions.

> **Precision** involves maintaining a high degree of accuracy in the collection and analysis of data.

> **Research design** precisely defines the types of data to be collected, the sources and the methods to be used in gathering data, and the time period for the study.

Verification and Appraisal

Vital elements in the scientific approach that criminologists use in conducting research are the critical verification and appraisal of research by competent peers.

In building a body of knowledge about crime and criminals, criminologists try to achieve critical consensus, based on their ongoing evaluations of the research conducted by their peers. For example, criminologists may replicate a colleague's study to see whether they obtain the same results. Studies may be challenged or supported by others' research.

Studies also are evaluated for their adherence to the scientific method. For example, data that are not collected properly or do not measure what was intended or claimed will be regarded as invalid. Data that do not consistently show the same relationships or correlations will be regarded as unreliable. And conclusions that do not accurately reflect the data will be regarded as biased. As you can see, appraisal and verification are vital steps in the scientific process that criminologists use.

After reading this section, you should be able to

1. explain how the scientific point of view relates to a criminological approach to understanding crime;
2. define and describe objectivity and precision as key elements in the scientific approach;
3. list the elements of a scientific research design that could be used in a criminological study;
4. give examples of kinds of data in criminological research;
5. explain the role of verification and appraisal in criminology.

1.4 CRIMINOLOGICAL PERSPECTIVES

Criminologists use theoretical perspectives as frameworks for the scientific study and analysis of crime and criminal behavior. A wide variety of criminological perspectives exist that provide both a foundation for criminal analysis and insight into the nature of crime. These perspectives are complex, and no one perspective is correct. Each helps us to focus on different aspects or dimensions of reality. This textbook uses elements of each perspective to attempt to analyze and explain crime, because no one perspective can adequately explain all the various types of crime and dynamics of criminal behavior. The three main theoretical perspectives in criminology are the functionalist, or consensus, perspective; the conflict perspective; and the interactionist perspective.

The Functionalist or Consensus Perspective

The functionalist perspective stresses cooperation and harmony in society and defines crime as a threat to the social order through the violation of society's laws.

Functionalism is a theoretical perspective which contends that social order is realized because people reach a normative consensus, that is, agreement over right and wrong.

The first theoretical perspective to be examined is the **functionalist**, or **consensus, perspective**. Functionalists view society as consisting of a set of interdependent and related units, called social groups and social institutions. Thus, society is viewed as a system of interrelationships between people and various groups and institutions. The most basic relationship between these parts is cooperation and harmony, as people are bound by consensus to society's common values. According to the functionalist perspective, so long as people are appropriately socialized—that is, they conform to society's common values—the social system functions smoothly as a whole.

Functionalists, or consensus theorists, believe that this highly coherent society is fundamentally stable, so that social change is only gradual and adjustive. Crimes are viewed as dysfunctional—consequences of a belief, behavior, or group activity that interferes with the functional requirements of the social system.

All social systems have the basic requirement that people conform to the rules and laws of society. Systematic, widespread violation of these laws and rules is dysfunctional as well as disruptive, in that it undermines the order and consensus that perpetuates the social system. In the functionalist perspective, then, society is viewed as a system of interdependent parts or units, each of which plays an important role by filling a particular need in maintaining the total system.

Criminal behavior is any behavior that is in violation of the criminal law.

Consensus theorists define **criminal behavior** as behavior that is in violation of the criminal law. Crimes are perceived as acts that violate the accepted legal code of the jurisdiction within which they occur. That is, behavior is "not a crime unless it is prohibited by the criminal law [that] is defined conventionally as a body of specific rules regarding human conduct which have been promulgated by political authority, which apply uniformly to all members of the classes to which the rules refer and which are enforced by punishment administered by the state."[1] Implied in this perspective is the idea that the definition of crime is a function of the values, beliefs, morality, and goals of the existing legal power structure or legitimate authority recognized in a society.

The Conflict Perspective

The conflict perspective stresses that value conflicts are the basis of crime and that definitions of crime reflect the vested interests of certain groups in society over others.

Conflict theory is another major perspective that criminologists employ in the study of crime. Unlike the consensus or functionalist perspective, which views

In general, according to the functionalist perspective, why has this youth engaged in the illegal behavior of shoplifting? According to the conflict perspective, what are the causes of this crime? How might the act of shoplifting be explained from an interactionist perspective?

society as having an overall unity that is impaired by conflict, the conflict approach has as its starting point the diversity, heterogeneity, and lack of uniformity in contemporary society. In other words, conflict, rather than consensus, is normative. The **conflict perspective** is based on the premise that many social values conflict with one another and that these value conflicts are the basis of much crime.

Conflict theorists believe that different segments of society compete for wealth, scarce resources, high social status, and power. This competition is seen as the basic form of social interaction. To understand crime, relationships between the competing interests and values of different social classes (or of labor, business, and government) must be examined, because this competitive interaction can and does lead to conflict. Conflict, in turn, leads to social problems, including deviant and criminal behavior.

Conflict theory focuses on issues such as who makes rules and laws, who decides who is criminal, and which groups benefit or suffer as a result of these decisions. As stated earlier, ideas of dominance and power are central to this perspective. Dominant groups have the power to decide which laws and **social norms**—patterns of expected behavior, or the "rules" of society—govern the society. The dominant groups also ensure that these laws and norms favor their own standards, values, and interests. Groups whose interests and norms conflict with those of the dominant groups, therefore, are judged deviant or criminal and are subject to punishment by authorities who represent and enforce the laws and norms of the dominant groups.

Conflict theory, then, challenges the functionalist view that a consensus regarding values, morality, and ideas exists in society and that the law is simply the embodiment of this consensus. The conflict perspective also rejects the notion that laws serve to benefit and protect everyone in society.

The Interactionist Perspective

The interactionist perspective is a microlevel approach that focuses on interacting individuals and defines crime as criminal behavior learned in social contexts.

The functionalist and conflict perspectives focus on society's organizations, institutions, and structure. They are macrolevel perspectives. The **interactionist perspective**, in contrast, focuses on human behavior and social life from the standpoint of the individuals involved in day-to-day interaction—a microlevel perspective.

The conflict perspective is based on the premise that wealth and power vary across groups. Inequality generates conflicting social values, the basis of much crime.

Social norms are patterns of expected behavior that govern society.

The interactionist perspective focuses on social behavior from the standpoint of the individuals involved in day-to-day interaction and defines criminal behavior as a product of social learning.

The interactionist perspective assumes that people bring to each social situation certain ideas about the nature of the situation, about the meaning of their behavior, and about others. These ideas, in turn, play an important role in determining how and why people act as they do. People may act in a socially acceptable manner, or they may act in a deviant or criminal manner. People learn noncriminal and criminal ideas and behaviors from others through the ongoing process of symbolic interaction—the use of words, gestures, and actions to communicate the meaning of events, situations, and behavior.

From the interactionist perspective, then, to fully explain people's criminal behavior, one must go beyond factors such as age, sex, marital status, social class, and so forth, and determine how they interpret the world. What do their social situations and behaviors symbolize to them? This perspective emphasizes how criminals are socialized into the criminal world—how they learn the attitudes, values, beliefs, and symbols conducive to committing crimes—through their interactions with other criminals.[2]

For symbolic interactionists, the definition of crime reflects the desires and preferences of people who maintain social power and use their power and influence to impose definitions of right and wrong on others. Symbolic interactionists view criminals as people whom the community chooses to label as deviants or outcasts because they have violated social rules.

In sum, the functionalist (or consensus), conflict, and interactionist perspectives are the most common schools of thought by which criminologists analyze crime and criminal behavior. Each perspective leads to a different set of theories about the causes and treatments of crime, and each perspective offers different solutions to crime and other social problems. All three perspectives have value in criminology.

After reading this section, you should be able to

1. compare and contrast three theoretical perspectives on the study of crime and criminal behavior;
2. explain the basic premises that underlie the functionalist perspective on crime;
3. describe the role of social norms in definitions of crime;
4. show how the conflict perspective is applied to the problem of crime;
5. contrast macrolevel and microlevel approaches in criminological theory;
6. explain the symbolic interactionist perspective on criminal behavior.

1.5 THE NATURE OF DEVIANT AND CRIMINAL BEHAVIOR

From a criminological perspective, crime represents a major form of deviant behavior. Criminologists, in discussing and analyzing concepts of deviant behavior and crime, point out that all human groups and societies establish systems of social norms or rules that specify how people are expected to act in their social relationships. In this sense, social or cultural norms bring about a degree of stability and order within society. This helps to ensure the fulfillment of many social values and basic needs.

For criminologists, **deviant behavior** is behavior that does not conform to the social or cultural norms of society. Deviant behavior is behavior that does

Deviant behavior is behavior that does not conform to the social norms of society.

not meet the expectations of a group, community, or society as a whole. Criminal behavior, in contrast, is behavior that violates the criminal laws of society.

Conformity and Mechanisms of Control: Norms and Laws

To understand deviance and criminal behavior, one must first understand conformity and why most people conform to most of the norms or rules of society.

Before we further analyze deviant and criminal behavior, we must first develop two general points about conformity and why people comply with the norms of their respective societies:

- **Conformity** refers to behavior that complies with the norms of a community or society. In all societies, groups of people develop a variety of procedures and techniques to help ensure that social control and conformity to social norms and laws are maintained. Chief among these mechanisms is the socialization process.
- **Socialization** is the process by which individuals internalize many of the socially approved values, attitudes, beliefs, and behavioral patterns of their society. Early socialization consists mainly of developing habits that conform to the customs, traditions, and laws of the groups and community into which a person is born. Children also learn a system of values that provides motivation and justification for deciding to do certain things that are approved by significant others, such as parents and peers, and not to do things that are disapproved by significant others.

For the great majority of people in society, socialization results in the development of an internal system of controls—a self-regulating conscience—that incorporates the internalized values and norms of parents and peers. To a great extent, then, conformity to the norms and laws of a community results from internal restraints developed within the person during the process of socialization.

Conformity to social norms and laws is also achieved through a variety of external mechanisms, either informal or formal. Many social groups, and, in particular, less complex and smaller societies, rely on systems of informal control. Violators of community norms are subject to the censure of others—perhaps even that of the community as a whole—in the form of ostracism or public ridicule. As societies grow and become more complex, informal mechanisms of social control become less effective and tend to be replaced by more formal controls. Formal control mechanisms include such things as

- a system of written law;
- legislative and judicial bodies;
- a variety of enforcement agencies;
- the state as the final authority in society.

The state possesses a monopoly over the use of coercion for the purpose of maintaining order and stability in society. In addition, it has legitimate authority to apply various penalties—fines, imprisonment, and death—for behavior that violates society's laws. Reliance on formal authority for maintaining law and order tends to increase as societies grow larger and more complex. A growing ineffectiveness of informal social control mechanisms invariably results in a greater development of formal law and an increased use of the state's law enforcement and judicial agencies.

Conformity refers to behavior that complies with the norms of a community or society.

Socialization is the process by which individuals internalize many of the socially approved values, attitudes, beliefs, and behavioral patterns of their society.

DID YOU KNOW
Conformity to norms and laws is the result of both internal and external mechanisms of social control.

DID YOU KNOW
Consensus theory: Norms become laws because they reflect society's social consciousness.

Deviant behavior is found in all groups and societies and throughout human history. What internal mechanisms of social control did not work to prevent these American youths from engaging in deviant behavior? What external mechanisms of social control are available to protect communities from this kind of deviance? What determines whether or not this deviant behavior is defined and treated as a crime?

Laws are **formal norms** that have been codified as punishable offenses against society or its citizens.

Felonies are the more serious of the two basic types of crime, usually resulting in a penalty of one year or more in prison.

Misdemeanors are the lesser of the two basic types of crime, usually punishable by no more than one year in prison.

How Do Social Norms Become Laws?

Consensus and conflict theorists disagree on how social norms become laws: through public mandate in the consensus view, and through economic power in the conflict view.

Functionalist or consensus criminologists believe that social norms become laws because they reflect the society's traditions, customs, and a general agreement about appropriate behavior or the social consciousness of the society. Laws are said to reflect public opinion. They are a measure of society's values. This perspective emphasizes social cohesion in society.

Rooting their theory in the writings of Karl Marx, conflict criminologists believe that those who control the means of production also control the power of the state and use this power to enact as well as to enforce laws that support their economic interests and control the lower classes. It is economic power that determines what becomes law. Conflict criminologists stress the idea that our legal system serves the interests of the upper classes and not society as a whole.

Internal and external mechanisms for maintaining conformity and social control are never totally effective. Deviant and criminal behavior, like conformity, can be found in all groups and societies and throughout human history.

Deviant behavior manifests itself in many ways. Some people violate codes of etiquette, such as being polite to other people and using good table manners. Others are negligent in fulfilling family or work obligations. Still others are deviant because they behave in ways defined as criminal, such as by gambling, selling drugs, or robbing a storekeeper at gunpoint.

When criminologists speak of crime, they are referring to behaviors that violate specific types of social norms we call laws. **Laws** are **formal norms**, in that they are formally written rules that govern behavior considered to be offensive against the state. The state has the authority to establish laws that define certain actions as illegal, because such acts are seen to threaten the interests and general welfare of the society. As pointed out earlier, the state also prescribes certain punishments for these violations in the form of fines, jail, or death. Violations of serious laws, such as those prohibiting homicide, rape, aggravated assault, and robbery, are legally termed **felonies** and involve substantial penalties, such as heavy fines and/or imprisonment. Other, less serious offenses, such as vagrancy and petty theft, are termed **misdemeanors** and carry penalties such as limited fines, short jail sentences, or community service.

After reading this section, you should be able to

1. define conformity and deviance and explain why most people conform to society's norms;
2. compare and contrast internal and external mechanisms of social control;
3. compare and contrast formal and informal mechanisms of social control;
4. compare and contrast the consensus and conflict explanations for how norms become laws;
5. define formal norms and give examples of violations of those norms;
6. define laws and distinguish between felonies and misdemeanors.

1.6 DEFINING CRIME

Most criminologists use a legal definition of crime. Others broaden the definition to include other antisocial or deviant behavior. Arguments in favor of a broader definition of crime include:

- Some antisocial behavior is more damaging to our social order than much of our traditional crime but is not made punishable by our criminal codes.
- Some social behavior patterns closely resembling violations of criminal law are not included in the criminal code.[3]

Arguments for accepting a legal definition of crime include:

- There is no general agreement on what constitutes antisocial behavior or on norms the violation of which would constitute nonnormative behavior of a criminal nature.
- Our Constitution and state laws provide safeguards to protect individuals from unjust stigmatization.

Many people would consider it an unfortunate mistake to give up these important safeguards to make the term *crime* more inclusive.[4] The reasons for accepting an exclusively legal definition of crime are compelling. As criminologists Martin R. Haskell and Lewis Yablonsky report: "Immoral or unethical behavior, no matter how socially damaging or reprehensible it may be, cannot be meaningfully equated with criminal behavior because the status of criminal is not conferred on the perpetrator. This status, in our society, is conferred only upon those found guilty of a violation of a provision of the criminal law."[5]

The Legal Definition of Crime

The legal definition of crime includes an act or omission that violates and is punishable by law and is committed with criminal intent.

This textbook exclusively uses the legal definition of crime. According to *Black's Law Dictionary*, a *crime*, or public offense, is defined as "an act committed or omitted in violation of a law forbidding or commanding it, and to which is annexed, upon conviction, either, or a combination of the following punishments: (1) death; (2) imprisonment; (3) fine; (4) removal from office; or (5) disqualification to hold and enjoy any office of honor, trust, or profit."[6] When using a legal definition of crime, there are several specific variables that must be present in order to establish an organized understanding of what a crime is. The following conditions must be met for an act to be a crime:

1. There must be an act or omission.
2. The act or omission must be in violation of a law forbidding or commanding it.
3. There must be **criminal intent** (*mens rea*) or criminal negligence.
4. There must be a union or joint operation of act and intent or criminal negligence.
5. Punishment must be provided by law.[7]

In other words, intending to commit a crime is not a crime. Just thinking about a crime is not enough. Some action must be involved for there to be a crime. In a crime by omission, there must be an obligation to act and a failure to do it. For example, a person may be required to make child-support payments each month but fails to do so. Failure to act is considered a crime in many states. In addition, for an act or omission to be a crime, it must be specifically defined as a crime in the laws of the state in which it is committed. If a law does not exist in the statutes or case law of the state, then the act or omission is not a crime.

Mens rea (literally, "guilty mind"), or criminal intent, must also be present for an act to be a crime. Without criminal intent (or criminal negligence), an act is not a crime. In addition, to constitute a crime, the act must also be the act that the accused intended. That is, if the accused did not intend to take the

Mens rea means "guilty mind."
Mens rea defines **criminal intent.**

This offender is under arrest for engaging in a criminal act. According to the legal definition of crime, what five conditions have to be met in order to determine that a crime was committed?

action, then the act is not a crime. Finally, unless the statute provides for punishment (a fine or jail term, for example) for the prohibited act, the statute "is not part of the criminal law and the act is not a crime."[8]

The criminal law recognizes a variety of situations in which criminal intent is absent. These are termed "defenses to crime." If one of these defenses—insanity, self-defense, duress, or age, for example—exists, the criminal defendant is not considered responsible for the criminal act and is absolved from criminal liability.

Crime Is Relative

What is considered criminal varies, depending on geographic location and time period.

As you have read, acts are not crimes unless and until laws exist that prohibit them. Implied in this statement is the idea that crime is relative, because the content of the criminal law varies with place and time. Behavior considered criminal in one place may not be considered criminal in another; that is, behaviors considered criminal vary according to geographic area. For example, gambling is legal in Atlantic City and Las Vegas, but it is illegal in most other U.S. cities. Drug users may be fined in some states and go to jail or prison in others.

Crime is also relative to time period. Behaviors considered criminal during one decade may not be considered criminal during another. For example, before the passage of the Pure Food and Drug Act of 1906, the sale of patent medicines containing opium was legal. After the passage of the act, it was considered illegal. At one time or another, the following acts were considered crimes, and the communities or states in which the behaviors occurred could impose punishments on the offenders: drinking tea, mistreating an oyster, printing certain books, a woman moving furniture in the house without her husband's permission, and a man kissing a woman in public. Most people today would find these examples humorous, given that laws such as these often prohibited essentially harmless behavior. A number of laws still exist in our society that define many essentially harmless acts as criminal. However, many acts that can injure others are not considered crimes, because they are not prohibited by criminal law.

Mala Prohibita and *Mala in Se*

There are crimes that are inherently wrong and crimes that are wrong only because the laws say so.

There is wide variation in the criminal law and in the behaviors that people define as either harmless or harmful. Many people would not consider the crimes mentioned previously, such as drinking tea or kissing a woman in public, as being inherently bad. Yet the acts could be viewed as wrong because the law says so. Such laws are referred to as *mala prohibita*. According to *Black's Law Dictionary*, "Crimes *mala prohibita* embrace things prohibited by statute as infringing on others' rights, though no moral turpitude may attach, and constituting crimes only because they are so prohibited."[9]

Other crimes, such as larceny, rape, murder, and cannibalism, are viewed by most people as being wrong, immoral, or evil in themselves. Laws that prohibit such behaviors are referred to as *mala in se*. According to *Black's Law Dictionary*, "Crimes *mala in se* embrace acts immoral or wrong in themselves, such as burglary, larceny, arson, rape, murder, and breaches of peace."[10]

Mala prohibita: acts that are viewed as criminal because the law says so.

Mala in se: acts that are viewed as criminal because they are wrong, immoral, or evil in themselves.

Civil Law and Criminal Law

Civil law concerns noncriminal offenses, but sometimes a violation of civil law is also a violation of criminal law.

Civil, or tort, law deals with non-criminal offenses that are handled by civil rather than criminal courts.

In addition to criminal law, there is a body of legal regulation termed **civil law**. Civil offenses are not considered to be offenses against the state or the general welfare of society at large, even though they may cause suffering, harm, or injury to a person or persons. Thus, the civil courts do not defend the interests of society but, rather, function as arbitrators between particular individuals. Civil law typically deals with matters such as car accidents or libel suits, in which one party brings a civil suit against another.

Some acts end up in both civil and criminal courts. Aggravated assault and rape, for example, are violations of the criminal law. However, they are also torts, or wrongs done to a person. The victim of a rape or an aggravated assault may sue in the civil court to recover damages for injury. Criminal courts cannot award damages to a victim. A criminal court can impose punishment only on behalf of the state. It can also levy fines, but solely for the benefit of the state.[11]

Juvenile Delinquency

Juvenile delinquency refers to illegal acts committed by young people, especially offenders under age sixteen.

Juvenile delinquency refers to illegal acts committed by young people, usually sixteen to eighteen years of age or younger.

As will be explored in the following chapters, another important area of law violation is juvenile delinquency. **Juvenile delinquency** refers to illegal acts committed by young people, usually sixteen to eighteen years of age or younger. From a legal perspective, delinquency pertains to all acts that, if committed by adults, would be considered crimes. Delinquency also includes a variety of additional offenses, known as *status offenses,* that apply specifically to youths, such as incorrigibility, truancy, and running away.

After reading this section, you should be able to

1. give the legal definition of crime and arguments for and against accepting it;
2. list the conditions that must be met in order for an act to be a crime;
3. give three examples of how definitions of crime are relative to place and time;
4. distinguish between *mala prohibita* and *mala in se* and between civil law and criminal law;
5. define juvenile delinquency.

1.7 DURKHEIM ON THE NORMALITY OF CRIME

The final section of this chapter examines some of Émile Durkheim's views on crime. Any introduction to the field of criminology and crime would be incomplete without a review of his classic ideas on the "normality" of crime. Émile Durkheim (1858–1917), one of the most distinguished European scholars of the nineteenth century, made an outstanding contribution to the field of criminology. His eminence in the field rests on his broad approach to antisocial

READING ABSTRACT

Crime as Normal Behavior

BY ÉMILE DURKHEIM

This reading is a classic in the field of criminology. Durkheim believed that

- the collective conscience of a people defines what is crime and that it (crime) is a normal phenomenon of societies;
- crime is the natural and inevitable product of collective life and social evolution;
- crime actually helps to ensure the stability of the society by identifying and clarifying social standards for acceptable and unacceptable behavior (i.e., it is functional);
- rather than disrupting society, crime actually serves to strengthen group solidarity by uniting people in disapproval against the deviant.

See page 24 for reading.

behavior. Criminologists before and after Durkheim have attempted to find the causes of crime in such external factors as population density, economic conditions, natural forces, and ecological areas. Durkheim, however, believed that if one is to find an explanation for crime, it is necessary to look at the nature of society itself. He suggests that the individual is a small image of the world within which he or she lives. Crime, for Durkheim, proceeds from the very nature of humanity, results from social interaction, and is normal. There can be no evolution in law without crimes occurring in society, according to Durkheim.

Émile Durkheim is considered a major figure in the fields of criminology and sociology. The functionalist perspective was first based on Durkheim's theories.

1. explain how Émile Durkheim contributed to the development of criminology;
2. argue for Durkheim's claim that crime is normal in society, and assess the implications of this view for criminology;
3. answer the critical thinking questions that follow Reading 1.1, "Crime as Normal Behavior," at the end of this chapter.

CHAPTER SUMMARY

This chapter focuses on a general discussion of the criminological approach to understanding crime and criminal behavior. Criminology, drawing from many fields, is the systematic, scientific study of crime, criminals, and criminal behavior. Criminologists study the nature and extent of crime, patterns of criminality, explanations for crime and criminal behavior, and the control of crime and criminal behavior (p. 5).

Criminologists perform a number of roles in their inquiries into criminal behavior. As scientific researchers, criminologists attempt to identify, define, and measure the extent of crime within society. To this end, they must identify people's values, determine issues of public concern, and attempt to measure the actual extent of criminal behavior. In addition, criminologists attempt to explain the origins of crime. To do this, they adopt the role of theoretician. In this role, criminologists must develop theories that tentatively explain the causes of crime. Criminologists also engage in the role of social critic, presenting opinions and knowledge that are useful in assessing the adequacy of current policies and programs dealing with crime and the criminal. As social critics, some criminologists have taken an active role in formulating and advocating the adoption of new policies to deal with crime and criminals. Criminologists also sometimes play the role of evaluator, analyzing the effectiveness of specific programs for treating offenders (pp. 5–7).

Distinct from other approaches to examining and understanding crime, criminology attempts to employ the scientific method in its investigations into criminal behavior. The scientific point of view that criminologists maintain stresses that (1) objectivity be maintained as fully as possible throughout all phases of the research; (2) research be based on factual data; (3) precision be maximized; and (4) the research be subject to evaluation and verification by professional peers (pp. 7–9).

Three major criminological perspectives on the study of crime are the functionalist (or consensus), conflict, and interactionist perspectives. The functionalist and conflict perspectives stress society's organizations, institutions, and structure. Interactionists emphasize how criminals are socialized into the criminal world (pp. 9–12).

From a criminological perspective, crime represents a major form of deviant behavior. Deviant behavior is behavior that does not conform to the expectations of a group, community, or society as a whole. Criminal behavior is behavior in violation of the criminal laws of society. Conformity to the norms and laws of society results from a variety of internal and external control mechanisms. The state represents the final authority or external mechanism of social control used to maintain conformity and order within society. Society's mechanisms of social control are never totally effective. Deviant and criminal behavior can be found in all societies (pp. 12–14).

There are arguments for rejecting or accepting a legal definition of crime. This text uses an exclusively legal definition of crime. The text discusses the specific variables that must be present in order for an act to be a crime and stresses the idea that crime is relative to the variables of place and time. *Mala prohibita* and *mala in se*, as well as criminal law and civil or tort law, are specific types of law. Juvenile delinquency is a specific area of law violation (pp. 15–18). The chapter ends with Émile Durkheim's classic reading, "Crime as Normal Behavior" (pp. 24–26) and J. Mitchell Miller's, "Criminology as Social Science" (pp. 26–27).

Study Guide

Chapter Objectives

- Write a clear and concise definition of criminology.
- List the things that criminologists study.
- Identify and briefly describe the major goals of criminology and criminologists.
- List and explain the guidelines and characteristics of the scientific point of view.
- Identify and briefly describe the three criminological perspectives on the study of crime and criminal behavior.
- Compare and contrast internal and external mechanisms of social control.
- Briefly explain how norms become laws from the perspectives of consensus and conflict criminologists.

- Define crime, felonies, and misdemeanors.
- Briefly list the arguments for and against accepting a legal definition of crime.
- Give the legal definition of crime.
- List the conditions that must be met in order for an act to be a crime.
- Briefly give three examples of how crime is relative to place and time.
- Define *mala prohibita, mala in se*, civil or tort law, and juvenile delinquency.
- Briefly describe what Durkheim means by "crime as normal behavior."

Key Terms

Civil law (18)
Conflict perspective (11)
Conformity (13)
Consensus perspective (10)
Criminal behavior (10)
Criminal intent (16)
Criminologists (5)
Criminology (4)
Deviant behavior (12)

Felonies (14)
Formal norms (14)
Functionalist perspective (10)
Interactionist perspective (11)
Juvenile delinquency (18)
Laws (14)
Mala in se (17)
Mala prohibita (17)
Mens rea (16)

Misdemeanors (14)
Objectivity (7)
Precision (9)
Research design (9)
Socialization (13)
Social norms (11)
Theory (5)
Tort law (18)

Self-Test
Short Answer

1. Briefly describe what criminologists study.
2. List the criminologist's goals in the study of crime.
3. List the four characteristics of the scientific approach.
4. List three characteristics of the functionalist perspective on crime.
5. List three characteristics of the conflict perspective on crime.
6. List three characteristics of the interactionist perspective on crime.

7. Define deviant behavior.
8. Briefly give the legal definition of crime.
9. List the conditions that must be met in order for an act to be a crime.
10. Briefly describe what Durkheim means by "crime as normal behavior."

Multiple Choice

1. Criminologists scientifically study
   a. the nature and extent of crime
   b. patterns of criminality and the explanations for and causes of crime
   c. the control of crime and criminal behavior
   d. all of the above
2. Criminologists attempt to
   a. identify crime
   b. define crime
   c. measure the extent of crime within society
   d. all of the above
3. Criminologists do not study
   a. criminal behavior
   b. explanations for criminal behavior
   c. the behavior of animals other than humans
   d. delinquent behavior
4. Functionalists
   a. view society as consisting of a set of interdependent and related units
   b. consider competition to be the basic form of social interaction
   c. focus on issues such as who makes rules and laws
   d. reject the notion that laws serve to benefit and protect everyone in society
5. For an act to be a crime, which of the following is not true?
   a. There must be an act or omission.
   b. *Mens rea* must be absent.
   c. There must be a union or joint operation of act and intent or criminal negligence.
   d. Punishment must be provided by law.
6. Which of the following is not true according to Durkheim?
   a. There can be no evolution in law without crimes occurring in society.
   b. Crime actually helps to ensure the instability of the society.
   c. Crime proceeds from the very nature of humanity and is normal.
   d. To explain crime, it is necessary to look at the nature of society itself.
7. According to the text, which of the following is not one of the guidelines and characteristics of the scientific point of view?
   a. factual data
   b. classification
   c. objectivity
   d. precision
8. Criminology does not have its roots in which of the following fields?
   a. anthropology
   b. physics
   c. psychology
   d. sociology
9. Criminologists
   a. define and describe the crime issues and problems, criminal activities, and behavior that exist in society
   b. provide factual data on a variety of crimes
   c. adopt the roles of theoretician and researcher
   d. all of the above
10. An act may be
    a. a criminal offense
    b. a civil offense
    c. a criminal and civil offense
    d. any of the above

True–False

T F 1. The chance of being a victim of a crime is greater than that of being hurt in a car accident.
T F 2. Any proposed social or political policy or treatment program for dealing with crime is based on some type of theory.
T F 3. A criminologist's research design precisely defines the kinds of data to be collected but not the sources to be used in gathering the data.
T F 4. Unlike the conflict perspective, which views society as having an overall unity that is impaired by conflict, the consensus approach has as its starting point the diversity, heterogeneity, and lack of uniformity in contemporary society.
T F 5. Criminal behavior is behavior in violation of the criminal laws of society.
T F 6. The state represents the final authority within society.
T F 7. Violation of laws termed misdemeanors involve substantial penalties, such as heavy fines and/or imprisonment.
T F 8. Laws that prohibit such behaviors as murder and rape are referred to as *mala prohibita*.
T F 9. Some acts end up in both civil and criminal courts.
T F 10. For Durkheim, there is no society that is not confronted with the problem of criminality.

Fill-In

1. _____ is a systematic effort to understand crime and criminal behavior.
2. In the role of _____, the criminologist analyzes many kinds of programs for dealing with criminal behavior and recommends changes and their direction.
3. The criminological approach to an understanding of crime can be distinguished from other approaches in that criminology attempts to use the _____ method in its investigations.
4. _____ refers to the ability and willingness to study the subject matter of a given field without prejudice or bias.
5. The _____ perspective focuses on human behavior and social life from the standpoint of the individuals involved in day-to-day interaction.
6. For criminologists, _____ behavior is behavior that does not conform to the social norms of society.
7. _____ to the norms and laws of a community results from a system of internal controls developed within a person during the process of socialization.
8. _____ are formal norms.
9. Crime is _____ to the factors of time and place.
10. _____ law deals with noncriminal offenses.

Matching

1. Crime
2. Deviant behavior
3. Criminal intent
4. Criminology
5. Felonies
6. Laws
7. Objectivity
8. Conflict perspective
9. Misdemeanors
10. Functionalist perspective

A. Society as a system of interrelated parts
B. Minor crimes
C. Theory rooted in the writings of Marx
D. Scientific study of crime
E. *Mens rea*
F. Behavior that does not conform to social norms
G. Serious crimes
H. Formal norms
I. Willingness to study the subject matter of a given field without prejudice or bias
J. Violation of criminal law

Essay Questions

1. Explain how crime can be viewed as a major social problem in the United States.
2. What are the criminologist's roles in the study of crime and criminal behavior?
3. Explain and examine the major guidelines and characteristics of the scientific point of view.
4. Compare and contrast the three major criminological perspectives on the study of crime.
5. Explain why people conform to the norms of their society.
6. How do norms become laws from the perspectives of consensus and conflict criminologists?
7. Compare and contrast the legal and extralegal definitions of crime.
8. Give examples of how crime is related to time and place.
9. Review the major points in Durkheim's classic reading, "Crime as Normal Behavior."

Crime as Normal Behavior

Source: Reprinted with permission of The Free Press, a Division of Simon & Schuster Adult Publishing Group, from The Rules of Sociological Method *by Émile Durkheim, translated by Sarah A. Solovay and John H. Mueller. Edited by George E. G. Catlin. Copyright © 1938 by George E. G. Catlin, Copyright © renewed 1966 by Sarah A. Solovay, John H. Mueller, and George E. G. Catlin. All rights reserved.*

BY ÉMILE DURKHEIM

There is no society that is not confronted with the problem of criminality. Its form changes; the acts thus characterized are not always the same everywhere; but everywhere and always, there have been men who have behaved in such a way as to draw upon themselves penal repression. If, in proportion as societies pass from the lower to the higher types, the rate of criminality, i.e., the relation between the yearly number of crimes and the population, tended to decline, it might be believed that crime, while still normal, is tending to lose this character of normality. But we have no reason to believe that such a regression is substantiated. Many facts would seem rather to indicate a movement in the opposite direction.... There is, then, no phenomenon that presents more indisputably all the symptoms of normality, since it appears closely connected with the conditions of all collective life.... No doubt it is possible that crime itself will have abnormal forms, as, for example, when its rate is unusually high. This excess is, indeed, undoubtedly morbid in nature. What is normal, simply, is the existence of criminality, provided that it attains and does not exceed, for each social type, a certain level, which it is perhaps not impossible to fix in conformity with the preceding rules.... To classify crime among the phenomena of normal sociology is not to say merely that it is an inevitable, although regrettable phenomenon, due to the incorrigible wickedness of men; it is to affirm that it is a factor in public health, an integral part of all healthy societies. This result is, at first glance, surprising enough to have puzzled even ourselves for a long time. Once this first surprise has been overcome, however, it is not difficult to find reasons explaining this normality and at the same time confirming it.

In the first place crime is normal because a society exempt from it is utterly impossible. Crime . . . consists of an act that offends certain very strong collective sentiments. In a society in which criminal acts are no longer committed, the sentiments they offend would have to be found without exception in all individual consciousnesses, and they must be found to exist with the same degree as sentiments contrary to them. Assuming that this condition could actually be realized, crime would not thereby disappear; it would only change its form, for the very cause which would thus dry up the sources of criminality would immediately open up new ones.

Indeed, for the collective sentiments which are protected by the penal law of a people at a specified moment of its history to take possession of the public conscience or for them to acquire a stronger hold where they have an insufficient grip, they must acquire an intensity greater than that which they had hitherto had. The community as a whole must experience them more vividly, for it can acquire from no other source the greater force necessary to control these individuals who formerly were the most refractory. For murderers to disappear, the horror of bloodshed must become greater in those social strata from which murderers are recruited; but, first it must become greater throughout the entire society. Moreover, the very absence of crime would directly contribute to produce this horror, because any sentiment seems much more respectable when it is always and uniformly respected.

One easily overlooks the consideration that these strong states of the common consciousness cannot be thus reinforced without reinforcing at the same time the more feeble states, whose violation previously gave birth to mere infraction of convention—since the weaker ones are only the prolongation, the attenuated form, of the stronger. Thus robbery and simple bad taste injure the same single altruistic sentiment, the respect for that which is another's. However, this same sentiment is less grievously offended by bad taste than by robbery; and since, in addition, the average consciousness has not sufficient intensity to react keenly to the bad taste, it is treated with greater tolerance. That is why the person guilty of bad taste is merely blamed, whereas the thief is punished. But, if this sentiment grows stronger, to the point of silencing in all consciousness the inclination which disposes man to steal, he will become more sensitive to the offenses which, until then, touched him but lightly. He will react against them, then, with more energy; they will be the object of greater opprobrium, which will transform certain of them from the simple moral faults that they were and give them the quality of crimes. For example, improper contracts, or contracts improperly executed, which only incur public blame or civil damages, will become offenses in law.

Imagine a society of saints, a perfect cloister of exemplary individuals. Crimes, properly so called, will there be unknown; but faults which appear venial to the layman will create there the same scandal that the ordinary offense does in ordinary consciousness. If, then, this society has the power to judge and punish, it will define these acts as criminal and will treat them as such. For the same reason, the perfect and upright man judges his smallest failings with a severity that the majority reserve for acts more truly in the nature of an offense. Formerly, acts of violence against persons were more frequent than they are today, because respect for individual dignity was less strong. As this has increased, these crimes have become more rare; and also, many acts violating this sentiment have been introduced into the penal law which were not included there in primitive times.

In order to exhaust all the hypotheses logically possible, it will perhaps be asked why this unanimity does not extend to all collective sentiments without exception. Why should not even the most feeble sentiment gather enough energy to prevent all dissent? The moral consciousness of the society would be present in its entirety in all the individuals, with a vitality sufficient to prevent all acts offending it—the purely conventional faults as well as the crimes. But a uniformity so universal and absolute is utterly impossible; for the immediate physical milieu in which each one of us is placed, the hereditary antecedents, and the social influences vary from one individual to the next, and consequently diversify consciousness. It is impossible for all to be alike, if only because each one has his own organism and that these organisms occupy different areas in space. That is why, even among the lower peoples, where individual originality is very little developed, it nevertheless does exist.

Thus, since there cannot be a society in which the individuals do not differ more or less from the collective type, it is also inevitable that, among these divergences, there are some with a criminal character. What confers this character upon them is not the intrinsic quality of a given act, but that definition which the collective conscience lends them. If the collective conscience is stronger, if it has enough authority practically to suppress these divergencies, it will also be more sensitive, more exacting; and, reacting against the slightest deviations with the energy it otherwise displays only against more considerable infractions, it will attribute to them the same gravity as formerly to crimes. In other words, it will designate them as criminal.

Crime is, then, necessary; it is bound up with the fundamental conditions of all social life, and by that very fact it is useful, because these conditions of which it is a part are themselves indispensable to the normal evolution of morality and law.

Indeed, it is no longer possible today to dispute the fact that law and morality vary from one social type to the next, nor that they change within the same type if the conditions of life are modified. But, in order that these transformations may be possible, the collective sentiments at the basis of morality must not be hostile to change, and consequently must have but moderate energy. If they were too strong, they would no longer be plastic. Every pattern is an obstacle to new patterns, to the extent that the first pattern is inflexible. The better a structure is articulated, the more it offers a healthy resistance to all modification; and this is equally true of functional, as of anatomical organization. If there were no crimes, this condition could not have been fulfilled; for such a hypothesis presupposes that collective sentiments have arrived at a degree of intensity unexampled in history. Nothing is good indefinitely and to an unlimited extent. The authority which the moral conscience enjoys must not be excessive; otherwise no one would dare criticize it, and it would too easily congeal into an immutable form. To make progress, individual originality must be able to express itself. In order that the originality of the idealist whose dreams transcend his century may find expression, it is necessary that the originality of the criminal, who is below the level of his time, shall also be possible. One does not occur without the other.

Nor is this all. Aside from this indirect utility, it happens that crime itself plays a useful role in this evolution. Crime implies not only that the way remains open to necessary changes but that in certain cases it directly prepares these changes. Where crime exists, collective sentiments are sufficiently flexible to take on a new form, and crime sometimes helps to determine the form they will take. How many times, indeed, it is only an anticipation of future morality—a step toward what will be! According to Athenian law, Socrates was a criminal, and his condemnation was no more than just. However, his crime, namely, the independence of his thought, rendered a service not only to humanity but to his country. It served to prepare a new morality and faith which the Athenians needed, since the traditions by which they had lived until then were no longer in harmony with the current conditions of life. . . . It would never have been possible to establish the freedom of thought we now enjoy if the regulations prohibiting it had not been violated before being solemnly abrogated. . . .

From this point of view the fundamental facts of criminality present themselves to us in an entirely new light. Contrary to current ideas, the criminal no longer seems a totally unsociable being, a sort of parasitic element, a strange and unassimilable body, introduced into the midst of society. On the contrary, he plays a definite role in social life. Crime, for its part, must no longer be conceived as an evil that cannot be too much suppressed. There is no occasion for self-congratulation when the crime rate drops noticeably below the average level, for we may be certain that this apparent progress is associated with some social disorder. Thus, the number of assault cases never falls so low as in times of want. With the drop in the crime rate, and as a reaction to it, comes a revision, or the need of a revision, in the theory of punishment. If, indeed, crime is a disease, its punishment is its remedy and cannot be otherwise conceived; thus, all the discussions it arouses bear on the point of determining what the punishment must be in order to fulfill this role of remedy. If crime is not pathological at all, the object of punishment cannot be to cure it, and its true function must be sought elsewhere.

CRITICAL THINKING

1. What reasons does Durkheim give for regarding crime as normal behavior in a healthy society?

2. What does Durkheim mean by "collective conscience," and what might be some examples?

3. According to Durkheim, in what way might crime contribute to social evolution?

READING 1.2

Criminology as Social Science

J. Mitchell Miller, "Criminology as Social Science," Copyright © 2004 From Encyclopedia of Criminology, *vol. 1 (pp. 337–39) by Richard A. Wright and J. Mitchell Miller (Eds.). Reproduced by permission of Taylor & Francis, a division of Informa plc.*

BY J. MITCHELL MILLER

Criminology consists of the study of the social problem of crime, including the processes of making and breaking laws as well as society's reaction to the phenomenon (Sutherland, 1939). As an academic field of study, criminology meets the standards of a social science, defined as:

The entirety of those disciplines, or any particular discipline, concerned with the systematic study of social phenomena. No single conception of science is implied by this usage, although there are sociologists who reject the notion that social studies should be seen as scientific is in any sense based on the physical sciences (Jary and Jary, 2001).

The social sciences (e.g., sociology, political science, anthropology, economics) differ from the natural or hard sciences (e.g., chemistry, physics, biology) in more ways than just addressing dissimilar subject matter. The natural sciences enjoy a much longer history, dating back to the European Enlightenment era, whereas most of the social sciences did not appear on the university setting prior to the 20th century. The utilization of society as laboratory yields implications for inquiry surrounding the inability of social scientists to adequately eliminate mitigating factors in hypothetic, deductive, and experimental research designs. As an alternative methodological approach, social science largely relies on quasi-experimental research design, which emulates hard science, generally.

The social sciences are heavily rooted in and subscribe to the major philosophies of science, most notably positivism and subjectivism. Positivism has been the dominant paradigm influencing research theory symmetry throughout the social sciences for several decades. According to the *Dictionary of the Social Sciences* (Gould and Kolb, 1964, 530), positivism is "a philosophical approach, theory or system based on the view that in the social as well as in the natural sciences sense experiences and their logical and mathematical treatment are the exclusive source of all worthwhile information." Derived from the social thought of Comte, Newton, and the Vienna Circle, the logic of positivism sets the standard for contemporary social science theory testing and both pure applied research, primarily through the logic and use of variable analysis. Variable analysis emphasizes reductionism, categorization, and measurement toward the goals of establishing correlation and casuality. This style of inquiry, called positivistic criminology, is rooted in empiricism, which is often erroneously thought to characterize quantitative research featuring statistical analyses.

Subjectivism or interpretivism, differs from positivism in its fundamental assumptions concerning the nature of inquiry. A dynamic and developmental perspective that fosters a qualitative naturalistic research style, subjectivism, also known as interpretivism, has become established as the foremost inquiry alternative to positivism in the social sciences, generally, and in criminology, specifically. Subjectivism is a methodological approach to inquiry positing that social phenomena cannot be objectively observed *per se*, rather each concept is constructed and understood by shared meanings. Whereas positivism seeks to eliminate any subjectivity or bias from both the researcher and the subject, interpretivism encourages consideration of participant perception of human actions. Qualitative research methods, both observational and interactional, facilitate this approach, which, despite the widespread equaling of empiricism and statistical analysis, is inherently sense oriented and thus empirical.

Another standard by which to define a filed of study as a science is theory, that is, a set of explanations specific to the field in question. The various social sciences are shaped by specific theories, typically derived from larger social perspectives, namely functionalism, power conflict, and symbolic interactionism. Criminology certainly draws on each of these larger perspectives in its leading theories. Functionalism and its emphasis on normative consensus clearly influences classical criminology and its more modern extensions of deterence and rational choice theories. Virtually all of critical criminology is either directly or indirectly derived from social conflict perspectives on society and symbolic interactionism affects a variety of crime causation and response theories, such as routine activities theory, reintegrative shaming theory, and labeling theory.

Whether attempting to validate a theory, exploring new phenomena, or evaluating the operational effectiveness of a juvenile or criminal program, criminologists employ a broad range of research methods, both quantitative and qualitative, but strive to do so from a theoretical orientation. Accordingly, a strong case can be made for criminology as a social science.

The issue of criminology as a social science stems from both its embeddedness in sociology and the erroneous assumption that criminology and the complimentary field of criminal justice are synonymous. Although it is clear that criminology is a social science, the boundaries between and hierarchal order of the other crime-focused academic fields relative to criminology are muddled. Criminology, historically, has been considered a major area of specialization within its mother discipline, sociology, the refinement and evolutionary outcome of the sociology of deviance. Criminology today remains both a primary research focus and formal track of undergraduate and graduate studies within sociology departments, but has also splintered from sociology at many colleges and universities to become an independent discipline (a trend in the social sciences since the 1970s responsible for several relatively "young" fields such as child and family studies, women's studies, and African American studies).

Criminology is often confused and contrasted with criminal justice, which emerged on the college setting during the 1970s—about the time criminology was becoming somewhat independent from sociology. Criminal justice was largely shaped by and reflected the spirit of the times, which included the civil rights movement, the Vietnam War, and a general liberalization of the popular culture.

These social movements, along with unprecedented levels of juvenile delinquency, presented widespread challenges for law enforcement management and social order maintenance. The nation's response was the Law Enforcement Administrative Act (LEAA) that sought to resource criminal justice and enhance the professionalism of police administrators. Accordingly, criminal justice (originally known as "police studies" or "police science") programs of study were established in institutions of higher education throughout the country. The LEAA served to define criminal justice as an applied and practitioner-oriented field of study, contrasting it with the more theoretical orientation of criminology.

Today, the paradigmatic conflict between criminal justice as applied science and criminology as social science lingers, but has been largely resolved. The two are naturally complementary and have become so interwined in coverage and research focus that differences are often a matter of semantics.

REFERENCES AND FURTHER READING

Gould, J. and Kolb, W.L., Eds. (1964). *A Dictionary of the Social Sciences*. New York, NY: The Free Press of Glencoe.

Jary, D. and Jary, J. (2001). *Sociology: The HarperCollins Dictionary*. New York, NY: HarperCollins.

Schuetz, A. (1943). The problem of rationality in the social world, *Economica*, 10, 130–149.

Schuetz, A. (1953). Common-sense and the scientific interpretation of human action, *Philosophy and Phenomenological Research*, 14, 1–38.

Schuetz, A. (1973). *Collected Papers*, Natanson, M. The Hague: Martinus Nijhoff.

Sutherland, E.H. (1939). *Principles of Criminology*, 3rd ed. Philadelphia, PA: J.B. Lippincott.

See also **Criminology and Criminal Justice: A Comparison; Criminology: Definition; Criminology: Historical Development**

The Nature and Extent of Crime

Measuring Behavior

2

ZIP code 60615 | chicagocrime.org - Mozilla Firefox

File   Edit   View   Go   Bookmarks   Tools   Help

http://www.chicagocrime.org/zipcodes/60615/

E CHICAGOCRIME.ORG AV
4200 N

A **freely browsable** database of crimes reported in Chicago.

Browse by: Crime type · Street · Date · Police district · ZIP code · Location · City map   Search: GO

Crimes by ZIP code / 60615

Latest reported crimes

MAY 19
9:20 p.m.   Criminal damage
4900 block S. St Lawrence Ave. Apartment

MAY 19
6 p.m.   Criminal damage
4900 block S. Champlain Ave. Residence-Garage

MAY 19
6 p.m.   Motor vehicle theft
5200 block S. Cornell Ave. Street

MAY 19
2:55 p.m.   False fire alarm
600 block E. 51st St. School building (public)

MAY 19
2:20 p.m.   Battery
5000 block S. Blackstone Ave. Sidewalk

MAY 19
11:05 a.m.   Battery
5400 block S. Dr Martin Luther King Jr Dr. School building (public)

MAY 19
7:55 a.m.   Burglary
100 block E. 50th St. Apartment

MAY 18
9:02 p.m.   Criminal damage
4900 block S. Forrestville Ave. Apartment

2.1 INTRODUCTION: RESEARCHING CRIME

This chapter examines the nature and extent of crime in the United States, presenting data on the amount, distribution, and growth of crime. Specific attention is given to the different ways criminologists collect and analyze data. This chapter also addresses the following questions:

- How do criminologists measure crime (sections 2.2 and 2.4)?
- How much crime is there and how is it dispersed across society? (section 2.3)?
- Who commits crimes (section 2.5)?
- What is the nature of criminal behavior (section 2.5)?
- What are some of the major crime trends and patterns (section 2.5)?

The chapter also explores information from official crime statistics published by the Federal Bureau of Investigation and the U.S. Bureau of Justice Statistics, and reviews victimization and self-report studies, which are important sources of information on crime. It also critiques the accuracy and adequacy of these resources. Before we begin this analysis, however, we must first look more closely at the variety of methods criminologists use in collecting data on crime and criminals.

2.2 CRIMINOLOGICAL RESEARCH AND DATA COLLECTION

Criminologists use a wide variety of methods and techniques to measure the nature and extent of crime. Criminological data are collected by conducting surveys and experiments, using observational techniques, and compiling case studies. Knowing how data are collected helps us to understand how criminologists develop, comprehend, and assess criminological theories and criminal behavior patterns. In the scientific approach, the step of collecting data follows that of establishing the research design.

Survey Research: Questionnaires

Survey research, consisting of questionnaires and/or interviews, is a major method of data collection for criminologists.

One of the most common methods of data collection that criminologists use is **survey research**. Survey data are obtained through the use of questionnaires and/or interviews. **Questionnaires** are forms filled out directly by study participants. They are frequently sent by mail to a specific sample of people thought to be representative of a larger population. A representative sample has certain qualities or

Survey research, involving the use of **questionnaires** and **interviews,** is the most common method of data collection for criminologists.

characteristics in similar proportions to those found in the larger population. Criminologists frequently use questionnaires because

- they are less expensive to administer than other forms of data collection;
- information can be obtained from large numbers of people (citizens, known criminals, victims of crime, etc.) over a short time period and with minimum effort on the part of both researcher and respondents.

The use of questionnaires poses several problems, however, for the criminologist:

1. Nonresponse on the part of the subjects is a problem. People who have committed criminal acts or who are crime victims may not want to provide personal information, for various reasons. Nonresponse has serious consequences, because the partial or selective return of data may later result in incomplete or distorted findings and conclusions on the researcher's part.

2. A significant number of respondents may misinterpret or misunderstand particular questions developed by the criminologist. Questions such as, "How many guns do you have in your house or apartment?" and, "How many times have you been a victim of crime during the past year?" usually pose little difficulty for respondents; but questions about people's beliefs and attitudes are often difficult for the criminologist to construct and difficult for the respondent to interpret.

3. Many other problems are inherent in the use of questionnaires. For example, many respondents prefer to give answers that please the researcher, or a respondent may not answer the same question in the same way if asked on two separate occasions.

4. The unconscious bias of the investigator may affect his or her questions. Data from biased questions will support predetermined conclusions; therefore, the survey is not scientific.

5. The quantitative data obtained through a questionnaire are only raw data and require interpretation. This interpretation can be quite difficult.

Some of the problems in using questionnaires can be overcome by techniques such as repeating the same question with paraphrased wording or giving the questionnaire a test run by administering it verbally to a small sample of respondents, which permits the researcher to revise and improve the questionnaire.

Survey Research: Interviews

Interviews, conducted face-to-face or over the telephone, are a major method of data collection for criminologists.

Survey data on crime, as well as descriptive data in qualitative studies, may be obtained by means of interviews. An **interview** is a meeting between a subject or respondent—such as a criminal, prisoner, or crime victim—and an interviewer. Interviews are conducted face-to-face or by telephone. An interview is different from a questionnaire in that a questionnaire is completed by the respondent independently, whereas an interview is carried out by a trained interviewer who asks the subject questions from an interview script (sometimes called an interview schedule or protocol) that has been specifically developed by the researcher. Interviews are almost always more time-consuming and expensive than questionnaires, but these drawbacks are often outweighed by the following advantages:

1. The problem of nonreturn is largely eliminated.
2. More intimate or personal questions can sometimes be asked.

3. The interviewer can sometimes reword or explain certain questions to lessen any misunderstanding on the part of the respondent.

Surveys (questionnaires and interviews) are used by criminologists to gather data and information regarding the attitudes, beliefs, characteristics, and behavior of a variety of people, including criminals and crime victims. Surveys measure the extent of crime; different types of crimes committed by different populations (the young, the aged, males, females, and so on); and attitudes toward criminals, victims, the police, and the courts. **Victimization surveys** seek information from victims of crime, and **self-report surveys** ask respondents to describe current and past criminal activities.

Criminologists use surveys to gather information about a large category of people termed a population. In research, a **population** is defined as a large category of people from which a sample is selected. A population, for example, might be all men under the age of eighteen, all crime victims, all police, or all prisoners. A population is usually too large to enable everyone to be surveyed; therefore, the criminologist must take a representative **sample** or a representative subset of the population. If samples are carefully drawn, the representative sample will have the same characteristics as the larger population being studied. For example, in a study of middle-class attitudes toward capital punishment, if 25 percent of all middle-class American people are over fifty-two years of age, then the sample of middle-class people used in the study should include 25 percent of subjects over fifty-two years of age. Any generalizations from the research findings can then be applied to the whole population.

> **Victimization surveys** seek information from victims of crime, whereas **self-report surveys** ask respondents to describe current and past criminal activities.

> A **population** is a large category of people from which a sample is selected.

> A **sample** is a set of subjects selected from a population.

Experimentation

To test specific hypotheses, criminologists may use controlled experiments as a method of data collection.

For many years, biology, physics, and chemistry have used **controlled experiments** for collecting data and conducting research. Criminologists also use this precise and rigorous method of data collection. In a controlled experiment, all factors or conditions that are believed may influence the outcome of the experiment are held constant or controlled, with the exception of the variable or factor hypothesized to account for some change in the subjects under study.

One might wonder why a control group is necessary in an experiment. Why can't a researcher, for example, simply prescribe the experimental medication to aggressive, potentially delinquent children and observe what happens to them? Let's consider the example of testing a new medical treatment for such children without the control group. If a group of aggressive children were given the medication, and if their behavior improved over several weeks of experimentation, researchers could not be sure that the improvement resulted from the medication itself. The improvement might be due to other factors totally unrelated to the experiment that simultaneously changed during the period of experimentation. For example, an improved diet low in sugar, salt, and food coloring also may have been implemented during the study and may have caused improvement in behavior. Therefore, a control group is necessary to determine the effects of the medication alone.

Although the experimental model might be viewed as the ideal, most rigorous method for scientific data collection, its use in criminology is limited in that it can be extremely time-consuming and costly, particularly when large numbers of subjects are involved.

> The **controlled experiment** is a scientific method for collecting information in which measurements of behavior in an experimental group and in a control group are compared.

The Controlled Experiment: Drug Therapy Research for Children

Some criminological research has focused on the development of different forms of drug therapy to alleviate various types of aggressive, delinquent behavior in children. The application of such a controlled experiment involves the following steps:

1. Two groups, an experimental (or test) group and a control group, are organized. Each of these groups must be alike in age, IQ, sex, social class, and any other characteristics believed to be associated with aggressive, potentially delinquent behavior.
2. The experimental group receives the medication while the control group, without knowing it, receives a placebo, which is a harmless solution such as water.

3. Differences in the manifestation of aggressive behavior are compared between the two groups.
4. A series of measurements of aggressive behavior are taken in both groups sometime after the termination of the medication and compared with the children's behavior as observed and measured before the treatment.
5. A reduction in aggressive, potentially delinquent behavior on the part of the experimental group as compared with the control group would be viewed as resulting from the medication received by the experimental group.

Observation: Detached and Participant

Criminologists use two basic types of observation: "detached," in which the observer remains in the background, and "participant," in which the observer joins the group under study.

Detached observation is a method of observation wherein the observer remains outside of the group under study.

In **detached observation**, the observer remains in the background, outside the group under study, using firsthand observation of criminals and delinquents to systematically gather data, develop knowledge, and perhaps gain insight into people's activities and motives. One-way mirrors, night-vision scopes, and camcorders have enhanced the criminologist's ability to study behavior that was previously difficult or impossible to observe.

Participant observation is a method of observation wherein the observer actually joins and participates in the group or community being studied.

Another form of observation criminologists use is called **participant observation**, wherein the observer actually joins and participates in the group or community being studied. This form of observation often allows the researcher more insight into the "way of life" of the group she or he is observing, because it provides a fuller opportunity to experience and understand the world from the point of view of the subjects. A classic example of participant observation is found in the research of William Foote Whyte as described in his book *Street Corner Society*.[1] For several years, Whyte lived and participated in a lower-class Italian immigrant neighborhood in Boston. During this time, he developed an in-depth analysis of neighborhood life in Cornerville (as he termed it), as well as analysis of the activities of various neighborhood gangs found in the community.

The Case Study

A case study involves the comprehensive study of a single person, group, community, or institution.

A **case study** is a scientific method of data collection used in the study of crime; it involves the comprehensive study of a single person, group, community, or institution.

The **case study** entails the intensive study of a single individual, group, community, or institution. The study can be conducted at one particular point in time or over a period of time (in a longitudinal study). A major advantage of

READING ABSTRACT

The Professional Thief

BY EDWIN SUTHERLAND

A classic example of the case study method is illustrated in Edwin Sutherland's *The Professional Thief* (1937), excerpted in Reading 2.1. Sutherland interviewed a professional thief and obtained in-depth information that would be difficult to get through other methods. He learned what it means to be a professional rather than an amateur thief, how professional thieves are organized, and how they communicate and network with one another.

See reading on page 56.

using an individual or group case study is that the criminologist is dealing with human beings in their natural environment and not with cold statistics.

Case studies are favorable when one wishes for a more in-depth examination of a particular individual or social phenomenon. The case study method produces more qualitative findings than statistical analyses, although this can result in generalizability issues. The following is an excerpt from a case study of a recovering heroin addict, Ron Santiago.

Ron Santiago had been out of the halfway house for only a couple of months when I first met him. A colleague of mine had invited Ron to talk to his counseling class about some of his experiences with drugs and suggested that, as a sociologist, I ought to get acquainted with this intriguing person. I arranged a meeting with Ron, a forty-two-year-old black man of Cuban ancestry who is a recovering heroin addict. He told me a little of himself, his recent experiences in drug treatment programs, and a bit about his criminal past.

At the time, Ron was barely surviving on welfare, trying to stay clean from drugs, and attempting to put his life together in a small town in

If a criminologist wanted to study patterns of interaction and affiliation among prison inmates, what research methods might the criminologist use? What would be the advantages and disadvantages of using participant observation as a method? What would be the advantages and disadvantages of conducting a survey using questionnaires?

northern New York, far from the streets of Harlem and the South Bronx. When I invited him to talk to my criminology class, he seemed eager and interested in sharing his experiences with a college audience. The students in my class were mesmerized as they listened to the accounts of this articulate man who had been deeply engulfed in the life of a dope addict; a man who had committed hundreds of robberies and burglaries to finance his drug habit; who had worked as a numbers runner and operated his own drug selling network; who had frequently manipulated and slipped through the flawed and sometimes corrupt criminal justice system; who knew personally of men thrown off third floor tiers of brutal jails, like New York City's Rikers Island; who had been deeply thrust into the violence, illicit contraband, and corruption of correctional officers; who understood the dynamics of inmate subcultures in several New York State prisons, and, yet, a man who was attempting to turn his life around.

When I suggested to Ron that his fascinating life might be worth sharing with other audiences in the form of a book, he embraced the idea with both enthusiasm and trepidation. From May 1990 through February 1991, we spent countless hours tape recording his story in a series of loosely structured sessions, each of which lasted from two to three hours, during which I asked him about different aspects of his life.

Ron's story is told in his own words and from his own perspective.[2]

Aggregate Data Research

Criminologists utilize databases to analyze secondary data on crime and criminal behavior.

In addition to collecting data by survey, experimentation, observation, and case study, criminologists use secondary data collected by private organizations, research foundations, public organizations, and agencies. Large databases, which can save the researcher much time and expense, are available from such organizations and agencies as the U.S. Census Bureau, the Department of Justice, and the Department of Labor. These and other agencies provide extensive data to help criminologists ascertain—without having to research and collect new data—the relationship between crime and such social variables as class, sex, age, and family structure. Problems may arise from using some secondary data that has been collected for administrative or political purposes rather than for a particular criminological study. However, large-scale databases are an invaluable asset criminologists widely use.

After reading this section, you should be able to

1. distinguish survey research, experimentation, and observation as three major methods of data collection in criminology;
2. argue the strengths and limitations of using questionnaires and interviews in survey research;
3. describe a controlled experiment and give an example of the use of experimentation in criminology;
4. argue the strengths and limitations of using detached observation and participant observation;
5. define the case study and aggregate data research as methods used in criminology;
6. summarize what Edwin Sutherland learned in his famous case study.

THE UNIFORM CRIME REPORTS

An important source of data and information about the amount, distribution, and growth of crime is survey research conducted through the Federal Bureau of Investigation's **Uniform Crime Reporting Program (UCRP)**, which focuses on crimes reported to the police. Each year, the **Federal Bureau of Investigation (FBI)** publishes a report containing the most extensive set of U.S. crime statistics available. This report is entitled *Crime in the United States*, also referred to as the **Uniform Crime Reports (UCR)**.[3] The UCR statistical data on crime are based on reports submitted monthly to the FBI by more than sixteen hundred police departments throughout the United States. Each police department submits data on the numbers and kinds of crime reported in its specific jurisdiction. The UCRP is thus the country's major source of crime data and information produced by city, county, and state law enforcement agencies.

> The **FBI** is the **Federal Bureau of Investigation**. The **UCR** is the annual **Uniform Crime Reports**. Each year, the **FBI** publishes a report containing the most extensive set of U.S. crime statistics available—the **UCR**. The FBI's **Uniform Crime Reporting Program (UCRP)** is the country's major source of crime data and information produced by city, county, and state law enforcement agencies.

Part I and Part II Crimes

The Uniform Crime Reports include data on two broad categories of crimes reported to the police: Part I (or index) crimes and Part II crimes.

The UCR is divided into two parts: **Part I crimes**, or **index crimes** (such as murder, nonnegligent manslaughter, forcible rape, robbery, aggravated assault, burglary, larceny-theft, motor vehicle theft, and arson); and **Part II crimes** (all other crimes except traffic violations, including fraud, embezzlement, vandalism, and gambling).

Part I offenses

> **Part I crimes,** or **index crimes,** include murder, nonnegligent manslaughter, forcible rape, robbery, aggravated assault, burglary, larceny-theft, motor vehicle theft, and arson.
>
> **Part II crimes** are all other crimes except traffic violations, including fraud, embezzlement, vandalism, and gambling.

- are more serious crimes (felonies);
- typically involve serious offenses against persons or property and therefore elicit much public interest and concern;
- are typically used to estimate the seriousness of the crime problem in the United States;
- include the offenses of criminal homicide, rape, robbery, and aggravated assault, collectively termed **crimes of violence**;
- include the offenses of burglary, larceny-theft, motor vehicle theft, and arson, termed **crimes against property**.

Table 2.1 lists and defines both Part I and Part II offenses.

> **Crimes of violence** include the offenses of criminal homicide, rape, robbery, and aggravated assault.
>
> **Crimes against property** include the offenses of burglary, larceny-theft, auto theft, and arson.

TABLE 2.1   OFFENSES IN UNIFORM CRIME REPORTING

Offenses in Uniform Crime Reporting are divided into two groupings, Part I and Part II. Information on the volume of Part I offenses known to law enforcement, those cleared by arrest or exceptional means, and the number of persons arrested is reported monthly. Only arrest data are reported for Part II offenses.

The Part I offenses are:
Criminal homicide   a. Murder and nonnegligent manslaughter: the willful (nonnegligent) killing of one human being by another. Deaths caused by negligence, attempts to kill, assaults to kill, suicides, accidental deaths, and justifiable homicides

are excluded. Justifiable homicides are limited to: (1) the killing of a felon by a law enforcement officer in the line of duty; and (2) the killing of a felon by a private citizen. b. Manslaughter by negligence: the killing of another person through gross negligence. Traffic fatalities are excluded. While manslaughter by negligence is a Part I crime, it is not included in the Crime Index.

Forcible rape   The carnal knowledge of a female forcibly and against her will. Included are rapes by force and attempts or assaults to rape. Statutory offenses (no force used—victim under age of consent) are excluded.

(Continued)

TABLE 2.1 OFFENSES IN UNIFORM CRIME REPORTING *(Continued)*

Robbery The taking or attempting to take anything of value from the care, custody, or control of a person or persons by force or threat of force or violence and/or by putting the victim in fear.

Aggravated assault An unlawful attack by one person upon another for the purpose of inflicting severe or aggravated bodily injury. This type of assault usually is accompanied by the use of a weapon or by means likely to produce death or great bodily harm. Simple assaults are excluded.

Burglary—breaking or entering The unlawful entry of a structure to commit a felony or a theft. Attempted forcible entry is included.

Larceny—theft (except motor vehicle theft) The unlawful taking, carrying, leading, or riding away of property from the possession or constructive possession of another. Examples are thefts of bicycles or automobile accessories, shoplifting, pocket-picking, or the stealing of any property or article which is not taken by force and violence or by fraud. Attempted larcenies are included. Embezzlement, "con" games, forgery, worthless checks, etc., are excluded.

Motor vehicle theft The theft or attempted theft of a motor vehicle. A motor vehicle is self-propelled and runs on the surface and not on rails. Specifically excluded from this category are motorboats, construction equipment, airplanes, and farming equipment.

Arson Any willful or malicious burning or attempt to burn, with or without intent to defraud, a dwelling house, public building, motor vehicle or aircraft, personal property of another, etc.

The Part II offenses are:

Other assaults (simple) Assaults and attempted assaults where no weapon is used and which do not result in serious or aggravated injury to the victim.

Forgery and counterfeiting Making, altering, uttering, or possessing, with intent to defraud, anything false in the semblance of that which is true. Attempts are included.

Fraud Fraudulent conversion and obtaining money or property by false pretenses. Included are confidence games and bad checks, except forgeries and counterfeiting.

Embezzlement Misappropriation or misapplication of money or property entrusted to one's care, custody, or control.

Stolen property; buying, receiving, possessing Buying, receiving, and possessing stolen property, including attempts.

Vandalism Willful or malicious destruction, injury, disfigurement, or defacement of any public or private property, real or personal, without consent of the owner or persons having custody or control.

Weapons; carrying, possessing, etc. All violations of regulations or statutes controlling the carrying, using, possessing, furnishing, and manufacturing of deadly weapons or silencers. Included are attempts.

Prostitution and commercialized vice Sex offenses of a commercialized nature, such as prostitution, keeping a bawdy house, procuring, or transporting women for immoral purposes. Attempts are included.

Sex offenses (except forcible rape, prostitution, and commercialized vice) Statutory rape and offenses against chastity, common decency, morals, and the like. Attempts are included.

Drug abuse violations State and local offenses relating to the unlawful possession, sale, use, growing, and manufacturing of narcotic drugs.

Gambling Promoting, permitting, or engaging in illegal gambling.

Offenses against the family and children Nonsupport, neglect, desertion, or abuse of family and children.

Driving under the influence Driving or operating any vehicle or common carrier while drunk or under the influence of liquor or narcotics.

Liquor laws State or local liquor law violations, except "drunkenness" and "driving under the influence." Federal violations are excluded.

Drunkenness Offenses relating to drunkenness or intoxication. Excluded is "driving under the influence."

Disorderly conduct Breach of the peace.

Vagrancy Vagabondage, begging, loitering, etc.

All other offenses All violations of state or local laws, except those listed above and traffic offenses.

Suspicion No specific offense; suspect released without formal charges being placed.

Curfew and loitering laws (persons under age 18) Offenses relating to violations of local curfew or loitering ordinances where such laws exist.

Runaways (persons under age 18) Limited to juveniles taken into protective custody under provisions of local statutes.

Source: Federal Bureau of Investigation, "Crime in the United States, 1992," *Uniform Crime Reports,* Washington, D.C.: U.S. Government Printing Office, October 3, 1993.

The UCR uses a variety of basic methods to present data on crime:

- the numbers of crimes reported to law enforcement, expressed in raw figures;
- the percentage changes in the incidence of crime occurring in a particular time frame;
- crime rates per 100,000 Americans.

The equation that the UCR uses to calculate the crime rate is as follows:

$$\frac{\text{Number of Reported Crimes}}{\text{Total U.S. Population}} \times 100{,}000 = \text{Rate per 100,000 Residents}$$

By expressing the incidence of crime in terms of rates, the UCR is able to indicate whether an increase or a decrease in crime resulted from a population change or a change in the numbers of crime committed. For example, an estimated 12 million index crimes are reported to the police annually in the United States. The annual rate of reported index offenses is about 4,000 per 100,000 U.S. residents. Over the past decade or so, there has been an overall decline in reported offenses of about 20 percent.

Violent crime is composed of four offenses, according to the UCR Part I:

- murder
- forcible rape
- robbery
- aggravated assault

Property crimes, according to the UCR Part I, include the following:

- burglary
- larceny-theft
- motor vehicle theft
- arson

The object of property offenses is the taking of money or property; there is no force or threat of force against the victims.[4]

Criminologists, sociologists, legislators, municipal planners, and students of criminal justice use the UCR crime statistics for varied research and planning purposes. The statistics' value for criminological research is questionable, however, because of reporting and methodological flaws.

The American public looks to the UCR for information on crime statistics and changes in crime levels. Criminologists, sociologists, legislators, municipal planners, and students of criminal justice use the statistics for varied research and planning purposes. Why is the value of the UCR questionable for application to criminological research?

Limitations and Criticisms of the Uniform Crime Report

The UCR is limited in that certain crimes are excluded from the index, not all crimes are reported to police, and police reporting of crimes varies.

1. *Many Crimes Are Excluded from the Index.* The accuracy and adequacy of the UCR as a data resource in the field of criminology is questionable. Even though it provides a widely used index of national crime statistics, one must recognize its limitations for criminological research. A broad range of crimes are excluded from the index, such as white-collar crimes and crimes against the public order and morals. For example, the index includes a $300 theft on the street, but not a computer hacker or savings-and-loan executive who steals $300,000, $3 million, or $3 billion.

2. *Many People Do Not Report Crime.* An additional problem in using the UCR as a source of aggregate criminal statistics is that many crime victims do not report crimes to the police. As a result, such crimes do not become a part of the UCR. This creates an inherent limitation in official crime statistics, in that the figures presented in the UCR do not include criminal acts that never come to official attention. These are crimes committed in society that remain undiscovered, unreported, and unrecorded. Criminologists term the missing official statistics the "**dark figure of crime.**"

The "**dark figure of crime**" is the range of crimes that are committed in society but are undiscovered, unreported, or unrecorded.

There are many reasons why persons who are victims of crimes don't report them. Many victims believe "it won't do any good" to take the time to get involved with the police and fill out forms and reports. Some victims also believe that "nothing will be done about the crime anyway," or the crime "wasn't important enough" to complain to the police.[5] In some cases, a victim will not report a crime for fear of reprisals by the offender or the offender's family or friends. Many victims believe that it is "too inconvenient" to report the crime. A person may not report a crime such as a theft or burglary because he or she does not have insurance, or because he or she does not want the insurance rate to increase. Also, many victims of crime view some criminal incidents as private matters—for example, those involving family or friends—and therefore do not report them to the police.

3. *Not All Crime Index Offenses Are Recorded.* An additional major problem with the UCR is that it fails to record all index offenses known to the police. Reporting procedures permit police departments to record only the most serious index crime when several index crimes occur during one event. For example, if a drug addict burglarizes a house, steals money and jewelry, rapes an occupant, and kills the owner (thus committing four index crimes), only the homicide is recorded as a crime by the police department because the UCR considers homicide to be the most serious of these index crimes.

4. *Crimes Are Recorded Inconsistently.* In a critical analysis of the UCR, Leonard Savitz reported that not all police departments submit crime reports.[6] Also, some types of crimes are listed and counted one way and other types of crimes are recorded another way. For example, if a person robs five people in a restaurant, the incident is reported as one robbery; however, if that same perpetrator assaults the same five people, the incident is recorded as five assaults.

5. *Other Criticisms of the UCR.* The UCR does not include federal crimes, and significant differences exist between local and state definitions of crimes and those used by the FBI. Further, because city, county, and state police departments lack uniformity in their arrest definitions, many crime-reporting inaccuracies regularly occur. The definition of arrest in the UCR guidelines is not routinely applied by all police department personnel. According to Lawrence W. Sherman, many department agents cannot even recall the UCR definition of arrest.

This victim of crime is giving information to a local law enforcement officer. What factors will determine whether or not this crime is reported in the FBI's UCR? What factors will determine whether or not this crime is reported in a victimization survey?

- 11 percent stated driving a suspect to the station;
- 16 percent stated any restraint imposed on a citizen;
- 29 percent stated more than four hours of detention;
- 58 percent stated telling a suspect, "You're under arrest";
- 100 percent stated charging and booking.[7]

Lawrence Sherman and Barry Glick reported that many police departments regularly make systematic errors in UCR reports. Of the 196 police departments they studied, all counted an arrest only when the suspect was formally charged. This occurred in spite of the fact that the UCR requires arrests to be counted if the suspect is released without being formally charged with a crime. The UCR also requires citations and summonses to be counted as arrests. However, almost one-third of the departments surveyed did not report citations, and more than half did not include summonses as arrests.[8]

UCR statistics, then, provide us with the numbers of crimes *known* to city, county, and state law enforcement agencies, but they do not tell us the number of crimes that have actually *occurred*. One can never determine the actual extent of crime in our society. However, one can attempt to fill the gap between recorded crime and unreported crime by examining victimization surveys and self-report studies. Figure 2.1 shows the total crime reported to police from 1992 to 2005.

After reading this section, you should be able to

1. describe and explain the UCR as a data resource in criminology;
2. explain the difference between the UCR's Part I and Part II crimes;
3. describe the basic methods the UCR uses to present crime data;
4. identify and describe five limitations or criticisms of the UCR.

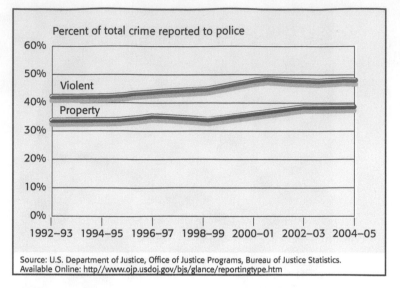

FIGURE 2.1 Total Crime Reported to Police, 1992–2005

Source: U.S. Department of Justice, Office of Justice Programs, Bureau of Justice Statistics.
Available Online: http//www.ojp.usdoj.gov/bjs/glance/reportingtype.htm

2.4 OTHER WAYS TO MEASURE CRIME

Criminologists clearly recognize the limitations of the UCR in providing data regarding the extent of crime in America. Other ways to measure crime include using victimization surveys that measure the extent of crime or criminal behavior based on researchers' interviews with individuals about their experiences as crime victims. Victimization surveys have helped criminologists overcome some of the limitations of the UCR. Basically, victimization surveys help to uncover the "dark figure of crime," that is, those crimes that are committed in society but are undiscovered, unreported, or unrecorded.

The National Crime Victimization Survey

The National Crime Victimization Survey is used extensively by criminologists and criminal justice researchers to measure the nature and extent of criminal victimization in the United States.

The **National Crime Victimization Survey (NCVS)** annually presents information on criminal victimization in the United States. The Census Bureau has administered the NCVS for the Bureau of Justice Statistics (BJS) since the program began in 1973.

The **National Crime Victimization Survey (NCVS)** annually presents information on criminal victimization in the United States. The Census Bureau has administered the NCVS for the **Bureau of Justice Statistics (BJS)** since the program began in 1973. NCVS researchers estimate the total number of crimes committed in the United States using data derived from a continuing survey of the occupants of a representative sample of housing units in the United States.[9]

As the NCVS reports, the success of a victimization survey depends on the victim's ability to identify specific crimes. This requires that the victim not only be willing to report a crime but also understand what happened and how it happened.

Recent studies by Alfred Blumstein; Joel Wallman, Gary Lafree, and M. Quimet; and others have pointed out that America is in the midst of the largest decline in violent crime rates in more than fifty years. Reasons for the decline in crime rates include

- an increase in the number of police officers;
- more aggressive policing;

The National Crime Victimization Survey (NCVS)

- The NCVS measures the crimes most likely to be identified by a general survey, namely, rape, robbery, assault, burglary, personal and household larceny, and motor vehicle theft. The UCR's Part I offenses of homicide and arson are omitted.
- Because crime victims are asked directly about crime, all crimes are measured, whether or not they are reported to the police.
- NCVS interviewers ask household occupants if anyone age twelve or older living in the house was a crime victim during the past six months.
- The interviews provide specific information, such as the victim's age, race, sex, income, and educational level.
- Data from the NCVS also provide specific information about the crimes, such as location, extent of personal injury, and economic loss.
- Sections of the NCVS examine the characteristics of offenders, circumstances surrounding the crimes, and patterns of reporting to the police.
- The NCVS also provides general information on the frequency and impact of crimes.
- According to the NCVS, about 24 million crimes are committed annually in the United States, and crime has decreased since 1981. This decrease includes a downward trend in levels of violent crime, theft, and household crime since the survey began.

- increased use of incarceration;
- demographic shifts;
- generally improved employment opportunities;
- changes in collective values.[10]

Limitations of the National Crime Victimization Survey

As with other methods of data collection, there are limitations to the NCVS, which include underreporting of crime by victims, fabrication of crimes by survery respondents, and reports of crimes that happened outside the time frame of the survey.

Victimization surveys such as the NCVS provide information on crimes not reported to the police. However, just as there are limitations in UCR data, there are limitations in NCVS data. For one thing, some victims fail to report many crimes to NCVS interviewers. Some fail to report because they are related to or are friends with the offender. Others simply forget the criminal incident, especially if it was a less serious crime. Still others are ashamed of being a victim and fail to inform the interviewer for fear of being embarrassed. At times, victims of crime believe they will get into trouble if they admit to being a victim. Some interviewees are apathetic and do not care to make a report. James Levine reports that crime victimization survey respondents at times fabricate criminal incidents because they want to please the interviewer. Also, some crime victims overreport crime because they misinterpret events and facts (perceiving, for example, a lost piece of jewelry at home as a burglary).[11] In crime victimization surveys, respondents may report criminal events that occurred many months or even years prior to the study's time frame. This is termed **telescoping**. Other problems are the NCVS's exclusion of many criminal offenses and the fact that, when several offenses are committed during an event, the NCVS, like the UCR, records only the most serious crime.

In spite of these problems, NCVS data, in addition to crime data provided in other victimization research, are invaluable to the criminologist. Because NCVS sampling is done carefully and the interview completion rate is very high (96 percent), the data and information obtained are believed to constitute a valid, unbiased estimate of all victimization for crimes that are surveyed.

The UCR and the NCVS are the nation's two major crime measures. Table 2.2 summarizes the differences between these two sources in offenses measured, scope, collection methods, kinds of information reported, and sponsor.

TABLE 2.2   How Do the Uniform Crime Reports and the National Crime Victimization Survey Compare?

	Uniform Crime Reports	National Crime Victimization Survey
Offenses measured	Homicide Rape Robbery (personal and commercial) Assault (aggravated) Burglary (commercial and household) Larceny (commercial and household) Motor vehicle theft Arson	Rape Robbery (personal) Assault (aggravated and simple) Household burglary Larceny (personal and household) Motor vehicle theft
Scope	Crimes reported to the police in most jurisdictions; considerable flexibility in developing small-area data	Crimes both reported and not reported to police; all data are available for a few large geographic areas
Collection method	Police department reports to FBI or to centralized State agencies that then report to FBI	Survey interviews; periodically measures the total number of crimes committed by asking a national sample of 49,000 households encompassing 101,000 persons age 12 and over about their experiences as victims of crime during a specified period
Kinds of information produced	In addition to offense counts, provides information on crime clearances, persons arrested, persons charged, law enforcement officers killed and assaulted, and characteristics of homicide victims	Provides details about victims (such as age, race, sex, education, income, and whether the victim and offender were related to each other) and about crimes (such as time and place of occurrence, whether or not reported to police, use of weapons, occurrence of injury, and economic consequences)
Sponsor	Department of Justice Federal Bureau of Investigation	Department of Justice Office of Justice Programs Bureau of Justice Statistics

Source: **http://www.ojp.usdoj.gov/bjs/**.

FOR YOUR INFORMATION

The Nation's Two Crime Measures

- In 1994, law enforcement agencies active in the UCRP, which began in 1929, represented approximately 249 million U.S. inhabitants—96 percent of the total population.
- The UCRP provides crime counts for the nation as a whole, as well as for regions, states, counties, cities, and towns. This permits studies among neighboring jurisdictions and among those with similar populations and other common characteristics.
- UCR findings for each calendar year are published in a preliminary release in the spring, followed by a detailed annual report, *Crime in the United States*, issued in the following calendar year.
- Following a five-year redesign effort, the UCRP is currently being converted to the more comprehensive and detailed National Incident-Based Reporting System (NIBRS), which will provide detailed information about each criminal incident in twenty-two broad categories of offenses.
- The NCVS, which began in 1973, provides a detailed picture of crime incidents, victims, and trends.
- Two times a year, U.S. Census Bureau personnel interview household members in a nationally representative sample of approximately 45,000 households (about 80,000 people). Approximately 160,000 interviews of persons age twelve or older are conducted annually.
- Publication of NCVS data includes *Criminal Victimization in the United States*, an annual report that covers the broad range of detailed information collected by the NCVS.

Contrasting the UCR and the NCVS

- The two programs were created to serve different purposes. The UCRP's primary objective is to provide a reliable set of criminal justice statistics for law enforcement administration, operation, and management. The NCVS was established to provide previously unavailable information about crime (including crime not reported to police), victims, and offenders.

- The two programs measure an overlapping but non-identical set of crimes. The NCVS includes crimes both reported and not reported to law enforcement. The NCVS excludes, but the UCR includes, homicide, arson, commercial crimes, and crimes against children under age twelve. The UCR captures crimes reported to law enforcement, but it excludes sexual assaults and simple assaults from the Crime Index.
- Because of methodology, the NCVS and UCR definitions of some crimes differ. For example, the UCR defines burglary as the unlawful entry or attempted entry of a structure to commit a felony or theft. The NCVS, not wanting to ask victims to ascertain offenders' motives, defines burglary as the entry or attempted entry of a residence by a person who had no right to be there.
- For property crimes (burglary, theft, and motor vehicle theft), the two programs calculate crime rates using different bases. The UCR rates for these crimes are per capita (number of crimes per 100,000 persons), whereas the NCVS rates for these crimes are per household (number of crimes per 1,000 households). Because the number of households may not grow at the same rate each year as the total population, trend data for rates of property crimes measured by the two programs may not be comparable.
- Each program has unique strengths. The UCR provides a measure of the number of crimes reported to law enforcement agencies throughout the country, including the most reliable, timely data on the extent and nature of homicides in the nation. The NCVS is the primary source of information on the characteristics of criminal victimization and on the number and types of crimes not reported to law enforcement authorities.
- NCVS and UCR data can be used in concert to explore why trends in reported and police-recorded crime may differ.

The National Incident-Based Reporting System

The National Incident-Based Reporting System is a system in which crime data are collected on each single crime occurrence.

The FBI's **National Incident-Based Reporting System (NIBRS)** attempts to overcome some of the problems of the UCR and the NCVS. NIBRS is a new system of crime reporting based on each single crime occurrence. As more U.S. states

The FBI's **National Incident-Based Reporting System (NIBRS)** is an incident-based reporting system through which crime data are collected on each single crime occurrence.

The National Incident-Based Reporting System

The U.S. Department of Justice is replacing its long-established Uniform Crime Reporting (UCR) system with the more comprehensive National Incident-Based Reporting System (NIBRS). While the UCR monitors only a limited number of index crimes and, with the exception of homicides, gathers few details on each crime event, NIBRS collects a wide range of information on victims, offenders, and circumstances for a greatly increased variety of offenses. Offenses tracked in NIBRS include violent crimes (e.g., homicide, assault, rape, robbery), property crimes (e.g., theft, arson, vandalism, fraud, embezzlement), and crimes against society (e.g., drug offenses, gambling, prostitution). Moreover, NIBRS collects information on multiple victims, multiple offenders, and multiple crimes that may be part of the same episode.

Under the new system, as with the old, local law enforcement personnel compile information on crimes coming to their attention, and this information is aggregated in turn at the state and national levels. For a crime to be counted in the system, it simply needs to be reported and investigated. It is not necessary that an incident be cleared or an arrest made, although unfounded reports are deleted from the record.

NIBRS holds great promise, but it is still far from a national system. Its implementation by the FBI began in 1988, and participation by states and local agencies is voluntary and incremental. By 1986, jurisdictions in nine states had agencies contributing data; by 1987, the number was twelve, and by the end of 1989, jurisdictions in seventeen states submitted reports, providing coverage for 11 percent of the nation's population and nine percent of its crime. Only three states (Idaho, Iowa, and South Carolina) have participation from all local jurisdictions, and only one city with a population greater than 500,000 (Austin, Texas) is reporting. The crime experiences of large urban areas are particularly underrepresented. The system, therefore, is not yet nationally representative nor do findings represent national trends or national statistics. Nevertheless, the system is assembling large amounts of crime information and providing a richness of detail about juvenile victimizations previously unavailable. The patterns and associations these data reveal are real and represent the experiences of a large number of youth. For 1997, the twelve participating states (Colorado, Idaho, Iowa, Massachusetts, Michigan, North Dakota, South Carolina, Tennessee, Texas, Utah, Vermont, and Virginia) reported a total of 1,043,719 crimes against individuals, with 119,852 occurring against juveniles (including more than 15,000 perpetrated by caretakers). Nevertheless, patterns may change as more jurisdictions join the system.

More information about NIBRS data collection can be found at these web sites (1) **http://www.jrsa.org/nibrs/**, (2) **http://www.fbi.gov/ucr/nibrs/manuals/vfall.pdf**, (3) **http://www.fbi.gov/ucr/nibrs.htm**, and (4) **http://www.search.org/**.

submit NIBRS data, they will become an increasingly important source of information for criminologists.[12]

Self-Report Surveys and Their Limitations

Self-report surveys attempt to measure crime by asking people to report on their own criminal activities.

Self-report surveys are another method of measuring and obtaining information regarding the types and extent of criminal behavior in the United States. They measure crime by asking people to report on their own criminal activities. Respondents report by completing an anonymous questionnaire or by partaking in a confidential interview.

A classic self-report survey was conducted in the 1950s by James F. Short and F. Ivan Nye, who asked juveniles to report on their delinquent behavior. They found that about one-third admitted to committing delinquent acts that were not officially reported.[13] A more recent major self-report study is the National Youth Survey, which has produced much information on delinquency. For example, the study reported that, although most delinquent behavior is minor and sporadic, a small group of "chronic" offenders is responsible for a disproportionate amount of all types of self-reported delinquency.[14]

Conversely, another major self-report study, conducted by the University of Michigan's Institute for Social Research, shows that criminal behavior among high school students is widespread and not at all restricted to a few hard-core delinquents. Surveying more than twenty-five hundred high school seniors nationally, the institute reported a stable pattern of youth crime from the late 1970s to the 1990s. The researchers found that one-third of the seniors surveyed reported stealing during the past year, more than one-fourth reported breaking and entering, one-fifth reported committing violent acts, and one-third reported shoplifting.[15]

In a classic 1940s study, James S. Wallerstein and Clement J. Wyle reported that more than three-quarters of the men they studied said they had committed such crimes as larceny, disorderly conduct, and malicious mischief.[16] In more recent research, Mark A. Peterson and Harriet B. Braiker sampled six hundred twenty-four incarcerated male felons in California prisons. The researchers asked the respondents to self-report on violent crimes, such as attempted murder, armed robbery, aggravated beating, and use of a weapon, that they had committed during a three-year period. The respondents reported committing many violent crimes for which they had not been convicted. Those felons who considered themselves criminals (75 percent) reported committing the highest number of crimes. In this same study, when asked what led them to crime, half of the men claimed economic hardship, one-third claimed a desire for high times and fast living, and about one-sixth of the incarcerated felons cited their temper. Respondents who cited economic need reported less violent crimes; respondents who said a need for high living led them to crime reported committing the most crimes.[17]

In later chapters dealing with violence, delinquency, and white-collar crime, you will see that self-report studies provide the criminologist with much information about criminality. However, just as there are limitations with other methods of collecting data, there are limitations with self-report studies. For example, with few exceptions, self-report studies do not represent national samples but focus only on a local population. Self-reports tend to survey particular groups of people, such as juveniles or felons, and any of these subjects may forget or be deceptive in their responses. Respondents who have committed crimes—especially serious crimes—are understandably reluctant to report these behaviors to anyone. Even though the criminologist assures confidentiality, the respondent is not naive and questions the security of the information.

In general, then, self-report studies are limited in estimating the amount and overall rate of crime in the United States. The two more commonly used sources of criminological data that help us to estimate the nature and extent of U.S. crime are the UCR and the NCVS. Each source of data adds different information and a different dimension to our knowledge base on crime. Each source, in its own way, provides information on the characteristics of crimes, criminals, and victims.

After reading this section, you should be able to

1. compare and contrast the three main sources of data on crime in the United States;
2. explain how the UCR measures crime and identify five limitations of the UCR;
3. describe the purpose and procedure of victimization surveys and some findings of the NCVS;
4. explain how the NIBRS attempts to overcome the problems of the UCR and NCVS;
5. analyze the strengths and weaknesses of self-report surveys as a measure of crime in the United States.

CRIME PATTERNS: CHARACTERISTICS OF CRIMINALS AND CRIME VICTIMS

This final section of the chapter reviews some of the general crime patterns in addition to many of the characteristics of criminals and crime victims in the United States. Examination of this information helps criminologists and others concerned about crime to better understand and develop insight into the nature of crimes and the reasons people commit them.

Data resources, such as the UCR and the NCVS, tell us much about crime in the United States. Recall that about 12 million index crimes are reported annually in the UCR[18] and the NCVS reports that 24 million crimes are committed annually in the United States.[19] According to Timothy C. Hart and Callie Rennison of the BJS

- in 2000, about half the violent crimes (rape, sexual assault, robbery, and simple and aggravated assault) committed against persons age twelve or older were reported to the police, according to the NCVS;
- about one-third of both property crimes (burglary, motor vehicle theft, and property theft) and pocket pickings or purse snatchings were reported;
- 39 percent of the 25.4 million crimes estimated from victims' survey responses were reported.[20]

Clearly, the number of crimes reported in the NCVS is much greater than the number reported in the UCR, even considering that the data presented in the two sources are not totally comparable because of crime category differences. This discrepancy reflects a tremendous amount of crime not being reported to the police. Self-report studies reflect similar findings.[21]

Because the UCR and the NCVS use very different methods of acquiring data, contradictory as well as confusing results are sometimes obtained. However, the UCR, NCVS, and self-report studies are in much greater agreement about the relationship between crime and variables such as population density, season, age, and gender.

Ecological and Time Factors

Ecological and time factors, such as geographical location, time of day, and time of year, reveal patterns that are important to understanding criminal behavior.

According to the UCR, patterns relating to geographic region include the following:

- the largest number of Crime Index offenses is reported in the southern states, accounting for 41 percent of the total;
- western and midwestern states follow the South, with about 23 percent of reported crimes each, and the northeastern states with 14 percent.[22]

Population, time of year, time of day, and specific place also are important factors. For example, differences in crime rates vary in relation to population density.

According to the UCR, the Crime Index rate is highest in metropolitan areas and lowest in rural counties. In general, Crime Index offenses reported in the UCR occur most frequently in August, whereas the lowest totals are recorded in February. Violent crimes occur more frequently in the summer; the lowest totals, in the winter. The UCR monthly figures also show that more

Crime Patterns: Time of Day and Place

- Personal crimes of theft are more likely to occur during the day, between 6 AM and 6 PM, than at night.
- Household crimes more frequently occur after dark than in daylight. Although violent incidents occurring at night are most frequently committed between 6 PM and midnight, household crimes are more likely to be committed sometime between midnight and 6 AM.
- Robberies and assaults in which the offenders are armed are more likely to occur at night than during the day.
- Violent crimes committed by strangers are more likely to occur at night than those committed by persons who are known to the victims.
- The crimes most likely to occur during evening or night-time hours are motor vehicle theft (63 percent) and serious violent offenses, such as robbery with injury (60 percent) and aggravated assault (58 percent).
- Among the crimes least likely to occur at night are simple assault (45 percent), purse snatching, pocket picking (34 percent), and personal larceny without contact (35 percent).
- About half of all violent incidents occur five miles or fewer from the victim's home.
- The largest proportion of violent incidents occur on a street away from the victim's home.
- The victim's home is the next most common site for a violent crime: about 25 percent of violent crimes take place inside or near the victim's home or lodging; 27 percent of rapes occur in the home.
- Overall, almost 11 percent of violent crimes occur in a parking lot or a garage, and 11 percent inside a school building or on school property.
- Four out of ten robberies take place on the street.
- The most common place for a motor vehicle theft to occur is in a parking lot or garage (36 percent).

Sources: The Uniform Crime Report and the National Crime Victimization Survey.

property crimes occur in August; the lowest number, in February.[23] The NCVS data also indicate that most personal and household crimes are more likely to occur during the warmer months of the year, but they point out that the impact of seasonality on crime rates varies from one type of crime to another. For example, robbery usually displays no regular pattern of high and low months from one year to the next.[24]

Crime and Age

Young people commit more crime than older people.

The relationship between crime and age is very clear. Regardless of social class, sex, race, or marital status, older people commit less crime than younger people. All three major sources of criminal statistics—official records, self-report surveys, and victim surveys—indicate an inverse relationship between crime and age; that is, as one variable—age or crime—increases, the other decreases.

Figures indicate that young people are arrested at a disproportionate rate to their numbers in the U.S. population. Consider the following:

- Age-distribution figures for persons arrested for Crime Index offenses showed that 26 percent are under the age of eighteen years, even though they are only about 6 percent of the population.
- Seventy-four percent of those arrested are over the age of eighteen.
- Well over one-half of the annual arrests for Crime Index offenses are of persons under the age of twenty-five years.

- The under-twenty-five age group also makes up almost one-half of murder offenders.
- People age forty and over make up only about 15 percent of all arrests in the United States.[25]
- Persons under twenty-five years of age comprised 44.3 percent of all those arrested.
- Arrests of juveniles (under eighteen years of age) for murder climbed 19.9 percent in 2005 compared with 2004 arrest data; for robbery, arrests of juveniles rose 11.4 percent over the same two-year period.
- In 2005, juveniles were arrested most often for larceny-theft offenses.
- Juveniles have a high involvement in arson offenses. In 2005, 48.6 percent of persons arrested for arson were juveniles, and of those juveniles, 59.4 percent were under the age of fifteen.[26]

According to the BJS's 1998 *Report to the Nation on Crime and Justice*, arrest data indicate that the intensity of criminal behavior slackens after the teenage years and continues to decline with age. Arrests, however, are only a general indicator of criminal activity. The greater likelihood of arrests for young people may result partly from their lack of experience in offending and also from their involvement in the types of crimes for which apprehension is more likely (e.g., purse snatching as opposed to fraud). Moreover, because youths often commit crime in groups, the resolution of a single crime may lead to several arrests.[27]

The *Report to the Nation on Crime and Justice* also indicates that the decline in crime participation with age may also result from the incapacitation of many offenders. When offenders are apprehended repeatedly, they serve increasingly longer sentences, thus removing them from society for long periods as they grow older. Moreover, a RAND Corporation study of habitual offenders showed that their success in avoiding apprehension declined as their criminal careers progressed.[28]

A study by John Laub and associates reported that

- the offending rate for eighteen- to twenty-year-olds was approximately three times greater than that of people twenty-one years and older;
- twelve- to seventeen-year-olds offended at a rate twice that of people eighteen years and older.[29]

Criminologists have termed the decline in criminal activities with age the *aging-out phenomenon*. Some criminologists consider the relationship between age and crime to be constant; other criminologists believe that the relationship between age and crime varies according to the type of offense and type of offender.

Michael Gottfredson and Travis Hirschi report that an inclination to commit crime peaks in the late teen years and then declines with age. Regardless of sex, race, country, time, or offense, they believe the relationship between crime and age never changes. In other words, because all people commit less crime as they age, it is not essential to consider the factor of age in explaining criminal behavior.[30]

Even for frequent offenders, crime decreases with age. According to this perspective, all offenders commit fewer crimes as they age, because they have less ambition, energy, strength, and mobility. Even so, differences in group offending rates for men and women, which exist at any point in their respective life cycles, are maintained throughout their lives. For example, if sixteen-year-old boys are four times more likely to be criminal than sixteen-year-old girls, then fifty-five-year-old men will be four times more likely to be criminal than fifty-five-year-old women, even though the number of committed crimes will decline with age.[31]

The view that the aging-out phenomenon is very much a part of the criminal life cycle is also supported by James Q. Wilson and Richard Herrnstein. They report that teenagers are involved in a process of becoming independent from their parents, but lack the resources needed to support themselves. Thus, they are frustrated in their search for legitimate ways to obtain status, money, and sex. They then get together with their peers and find illegitimate sources to meet their needs. As teenagers mature, legitimate means to status, money, and so on, become increasingly available, and criminal means become less attractive. More powerful adulthood ties to conventional society (e.g., a family and job) and adult peers further make crime an unattractive choice.[32]

Other criminologists report that social factors, such as one's economic situation, lifestyle, and peer pressure, affect frequency of criminal involvement and help to explain the aging-out phenomenon. For most offenders, frequency of offending may decline as they age; for other offenders, however, the rate may remain the same because of negative social factors, such as friends who are criminals or a continuing inability to find a job.[33] The point here is that the relationship between crime and age is not the same for all criminal offenders. Life-cycle situations and changes affect people and their behavior differently.

Still other criminologists report that there are many different types of criminal offenders. For some offenders, criminality declines with maturation. For others, it remains the same. Crimes that provide economic gain, such as fraud, embezzlement, and gambling, are less likely to decline with aging. Crimes that are high-risk or low-profit are more likely to decline with maturity.[34]

In any event, criminologists have varied and complex views with respect to the relationship between age and crime. These differing views have brought about much debate and research in this area.

Crime and Gender

The crime rates of males are much higher than those of females, and the types of crimes committed also vary by gender.

The crime rates of males are much higher than those of females:

- Men account for 73 percent of Crime Index arrests, 83 percent of arrests for violent crimes, and 71 percent of arrests for property crime.[35]
- Men are more likely to be offenders than women in violent victimizations involving a single offender. Eighty-four percent of crime victims report that the gender of the offender is male.[36]

The kinds of crimes committed in the United States also vary by gender:

- About 35 percent of the people arrested annually in the United States for larceny-theft are women.
- Only 7 percent of people arrested for robbery and 11 percent of those arrested for aggravated assault are women.[37]

However, the UCR indicates that, during the past decade, arrest rates for women increased at more than twice the rates of men. Since 1990, the annual number of female defendants convicted of felonies in state courts has grown at more than twice the rate of increase of male defendants.[38]

The increase in the arrest rate for women has caused some debate. Some criminologists believe that the women's movement in America has largely succeeded in achieving equality for women in a variety of legitimate ways, but that the women's movement has also been successful in providing women with opportunities for illegal activities previously reserved for men. Others believe that the

All measures of U.S. crime report a significant increase in crimes committed by women. Why might that be? According to crime profiles, what kinds of crime are women more likely to commit compared to men? What explanations might account for the great difference in crime rates that nevertheless persist between men and women?

impact of the women's movement has been less direct; they argue that law enforcement agencies have generally been paying more attention to women and their criminal activities since the movement's inception than they had before.[39]

Crime and Race and Class

Some researchers link crime to socioeconomic background, whereas others stress social maladjustment.

Race-distribution figures for annual arrests made in the United States indicate the following:

- 70 percent of arrestees are white, 27 percent black, and the remainder are of other races.
- In terms of rates per 100,000, the BJS reports that blacks are eight times more likely to commit homicide than are whites.
- Over one-third of female violent offenders are described by crime victims as black.
- Blacks make up only about 12 percent of the U.S. population; yet, according to the UCR, they account for over one-third of the Crime Index arrests, 45 percent of the arrests for violent crimes, and one-third of the arrests for property crimes.[40]

Even though blacks have proportionally more contact with the criminal justice system than whites, the preceding statistics do not indicate that race influences criminal behavior. As D. Stanley Eitzen and Maxine B. Zinn report in their analysis of U.S. social problems, "Many crimes on the street are committed by racial minorities because the social conditions of unemployment, poverty, and racism fall more heavily on them. . . . [O]fficial statistics reflect arrest rates and are not necessarily a true indication of actual rates. . . . [T]he bias of the system against . . . the poor minorities makes the likelihood of their arrest and conviction greater."[41]

According to the *Report to the Nation on Crime and Justice*, the relationship of an offender's social and economic background to crime has been hotly debated. The report states that there is no agreement on the relationship between crime and socioeconomic factors; some researchers believe that crime results from deprived backgrounds, whereas others see criminal behavior as a symptom of maladjustment.[42]

The majority of people who enter the criminal justice system for committing street crimes are those who constitute America's lower classes—the poor, the unemployed (or those in low-level jobs), and the undereducated. Some researchers explain this statistic by observing the following:

- The FBI lists "crimes of the lower classes" (i.e., white-collar, corporate, and political crimes are omitted).
- Many personnel in the criminal justice system assume that people in the lower strata are more likely to be criminal than those in the upper strata.
- More criminal justice personnel are assigned to lower-class than to upper-class neighborhoods, which ensures that more criminal activity will be uncovered there.
- Economic deprivation "may induce people to turn to crime to ease their situations."[43]

Some research by criminologists reports that a class-crime relationship does exist in the United States. Delbert Elliot, Suzanne Ageton, and David Huizinga's self-report study of more than seventeen hundred youths ages eleven to seventeen indicated that lower-class youths were much more likely than middle-class youths to engage in serious delinquent acts such as robbery, burglary, assault, sexual assault, and vandalism.[44] Nevertheless, other criminologists have arrived at different findings:

- James Short and F. Ivan Nye, in their classic 1958 study of class and crime, found no direct relationship between crime by youths and class.[45]
- Charles Tittle, Wayne Villemez, and Douglas Smith, in a 1978 review of thirty-five studies, also found that little evidence exists to support the claim that crime is primarily a lower-class phenomenon.[46]
- In a more recent review of existing data, Charles Tittle and Robert Meier again found little, if any, evidence that a consistent association could be made between the variables of crime and social class.[47]

Because criminologists use different research methods to examine the crime-class relationship, they often come up with conflicting findings. These problems indicate that additional research is needed in this area.

After reading this section, you should be able to

1. identify crime patterns in the United States that relate to geographic location, time of day, and time of year;
2. summarize U.S. crime patterns that relate to demographic factors such as age and gender;
3. explain what the aging-out phenomenon is and why it may occur;
4. compare and contrast research findings on the influence of socioeconomic factors such as race and class on criminal behavior.

CHAPTER SUMMARY

This chapter examines the nature and extent of crime in the United States. Criminologists use a wide variety of methods to measure crime, including surveys, experiments, observational techniques, case studies, and aggregate data research. Survey data are obtained through the use of questionnaires or interviews. Questionnaires can provide researchers with a reasonably inexpensive method of data collection from large samples of criminals or crime victims. Interviews can provide in-depth information on criminal behavior. Both, however, have their disadvantages (pp. 29–31).

Criminologists may conduct controlled experiments using control groups. They may also use direct and participant observation to collect information. In direct observation, the observing is systematic, with the observer remaining outside the group under study. In participant observation, the criminologist participates in the group or community being studied. The case study method entails the intensive study of a single individual, group, community, or institution. Criminologists also use large-scale databases to obtain extensive information on crime (pp. 32–34).

Major sources of data and information on the amount, distribution, and growth of crime are the UCR, the NCVS, the NIBRS, and self-report surveys. The UCR provides us with the most extensive set of U.S. crime statistics available. Part I crimes, or index crimes, are the more serious crimes, or felonies. Part II crimes encompass all other crimes. The UCR reflects changes in the number, distribution, and frequency of index offenses, as well as data on violent crimes and property crimes. The UCR has value for criminological research, but it also has limitations and criticisms (pp. 35–39).

Victimization surveys have helped criminologists to overcome some of the limitations of the UCR, measuring the extent of crime through criminologists' interviews with individuals about their experiences as crime victims. The NCVS presents information on the nature and extent of criminal victimization in the United States. The UCR and the NCVS are the nation's two major crime measures (pp. 40–42).

The NIBRS is a system in which data are collected on each single crime occurrence. The NIBRS holds great promise, but, at present, it is far from a national system of crime reporting (pp. 43–44).

Self-report surveys measure crime rates and provide criminologists with information regarding the types and extent of criminal behavior. These instruments ask people to report on their own criminal activities, but they too have limitations (pp. 44–45).

Ecological and time factors, including geographic region and population density, influence the general crime patterns in the United States. Examining the characteristics of criminals (comparing age, gender, race, and social class) provides information that helps criminologists and others concerned about crime to better understand and develop insight into the nature of crimes and the reasons people commit them (pp. 46–51).

Study Guide

Chapter Objectives

- Identify and briefly describe the major methods of data collection in criminology.
- List and explain the major advantages and disadvantages of each method of data collection.
- Describe the UCR as a data resource in criminology.
- Describe the basic methods the UCR uses to present data on crime in the United States.
- Identify and briefly describe five limitations or criticisms of the UCR.
- Define victimization survey and describe how the NCVS is administered.

- Describe some of the major findings and limitations of the NCVS.
- Compare and contrast the UCR and the NCVS.
- Describe the NIBRS.
- Examine how self-report surveys measure and provide information regarding the types and extent of criminal behavior in the United States.
- Describe three or four of the general crime patterns in the United States.
- Briefly examine four of the characteristics of criminals and crime victims in the United States.

Key Terms

Bureau of Justice Statistics (BJS) (40)
Case study (32)
Controlled experiment (31)
Crimes against property (35)
Crimes of violence (35)
Dark figure of crime (38)
Detached observation (32)
Federal Bureau of Investigation (FBI) (35)

Index crimes (35)
Interviews (30)
National Crime Victimization Survey (NCVS) (40)
National Incident-Based Reporting System (NIBRS) (43)
Part I crimes (35)
Part II crimes (35)
Participant observation (32)

Population (31)
Questionnaires (29)
Self-report surveys (31)
Survey research (29)
Telescoping (42)
Uniform Crime Reports (UCR) (35)
Uniform Crime Reporting Program (UCRP) (35)
Victimization surveys (31)

Self-Test
Short Answer

1. List and define the methods of data collection in criminology.
2. Briefly describe the UCR.
3. List four criticisms of the UCR.
4. Outline the NCVS.
5. Briefly compare the characteristics of the UCR and the NCVS.
6. Define the NIBRS.

7. Briefly describe a self-report survey.
8. Briefly describe the relationship between crime and region, population, time of year, time of day, and place.
9. Describe the relationship between crime and age as well as crime and gender.
10. Briefly indicate the relationship between crime and race, and crime and social class.

Multiple Choice

1. Criminologists use which of the following methods to measure the nature and extent of crime?
   a. surveys and experiments
   b. observational techniques
   c. case studies
   d. all of the above

2. The disadvantages of using interviews in criminological research are often outweighed by the fact that
   a. the problem of nonreturn is largely eliminated
   b. less intimate questions can sometimes be asked
   c. the interviewer can less adequately explain certain questions
   d. none of the above

3. Which of the following crimes is not one of the UCR's index crimes?
   a. nonnegligent manslaughter
   b. fraud
   c. aggravated assault
   d. larceny-theft

4. The UCR
   a. excludes a broad range of crimes from the index
   b. fails to record all index offenses known to the police
   c. does not include federal crimes
   d. all of the above

5. Victimization surveys help to overcome some of the limitations of the UCR by
   a. focusing on all crimes
   b. measuring the extent of crime based on interviews with crime victims
   c. including self-report studies
   d. all of the above

6. The NCVS estimates that there are about _____ million annual crimes committed in the United States.
   a. 14
   b. 24
   c. 34
   d. 55

7. Self-report studies
   a. primarily represent national samples
   b. tend to survey particular groups of people, such as juveniles or felons
   c. are considered to be the most accurate picture of criminal behavior in the United States
   d. are more widely used by criminologists than victimization studies

8. The largest number of UCR Crime Index offenses is reported in
   a. the northeastern states
   b. the southern states
   c. the western states
   d. the midwestern states

9. Crime rates are highest in
   a. metropolitan areas
   b. rural counties
   c. suburban communities
   d. none of the above

10. Crime rates are higher
    a. for women than for men
    b. for middle-aged men than for teens
    c. for teens than for men in their thirties
    d. for suburban dwellers than for city dwellers

True–False

T F   1. One of the most common methods of data collection that criminologists use is the experiment.

T F   2. Questionnaires are almost always more time-consuming and expensive than interviews.

T F   3. The UCR Part I offenses are the more serious crimes, or felonies.

T F   4. Today, very few crimes are excluded from the UCR index.

T F   5. Even though many crimes are not reported to the police, they still become a part of the UCR.

T F   6. Victimization surveys help us to uncover the "dark figure of crime."

T F   7. One limitation of victimization surveys is telescoping.

T F   8. The NIBRS is an outdated reporting system.

T F   9. The NIBRS collects more details on more categories of crime.

T F   10. Self-report surveys measure crime by asking people to report on their own criminal activities.

T F   11. The UCR and NCVS data indicate that most personal and household crimes are more likely to occur during the colder months of the year.

T F   12. Because of social and political advances in the United States, rates of crime for women are now almost as high as those for men.

Fill-In

1. In an experiment, one group is called the experimental group and the other group is called the _____ group.
2. A classic example of the case study method is Edwin Sutherland's *The Professional* _____.
3. The most extensive set of U.S. crime statistics can be found in the _____.
4. Criminologists term the unrecorded crime statistics the "_____ of crime."
5. The _____ annually presents information on criminal victimization in the United States.
6. With few exceptions, _____ studies do not represent national samples but focus only on a local population.
7. The NCVS and self-report studies indicate that the number of crimes committed is far _____ than official statistics indicate.
8. The _____ increases what we know about crime by providing detail on individual crime incidents.
9. The NIBRS is assembling large amounts of crime information and providing a richness of detail about _____ victimizations previously unavailable.
10. With respect to time of occurrence, personal crimes of theft are more likely to occur during the _____, whereas household crimes more frequently occur during the _____.
11. Criminologists have termed the decline in criminal activities with age the _____ phenomenon.
12. According to the *Report to the Nation on Crime and Justice*, the relationship between an offender's social and _____ background and crime has been hotly debated.

Matching

1. Aging out
2. UCR
3. Index crimes
4. Part II crimes
5. Dark figure of crime
6. Survey research
7. Experiment
8. Participant observation
9. Edwin Sutherland's "The Professional Thief"
10. Victim data

A. William Forte Whyte's Street Corner Society
B. Crimes unrecorded in official statistics
C. More serious UCR crimes
D. Source of aggregate criminal statistics
E. NCVS
F. Case study
G. Decline in criminal activities with age
H. Less serious UCR crimes
I. Use of a control group
J. Use of questionnaires and interviews

Essay Questions

1. Describe the survey as a method of collecting criminological data. What are some of its advantages and disadvantages?
2. Describe the controlled experiment as a method of data collection.
3. Describe the difference between detached and participant observation.
4. Briefly describe the Uniform Crime Reporting Program (UCRP).
5. List and explain three limitations or criticisms of the UCR as a source of crime data.
6. Briefly compare and contrast the UCR, the NCVS, and the NIBRS.
7. Briefly describe self-report surveys and their limitations.
8. Describe three of the general crime patterns that emerge from crime statistics.
9. Briefly describe the link between crime and age.
10. Examine the relationship between crime and gender, race, and social class.

The Professional Thief

Source: Excerpted from "The Professional Thief," in The Professional Thief; Annotated and Interpreted by Edwin H. Sutherland, Chicago: University of Chicago Press, 1937. Reprinted by permission of University of Chicago Press.

BY EDWIN H. SUTHERLAND

The following reading, "The Professional Thief," is adapted from Edwin H. Sutherland's book *The Professional Thief*. As you read this excerpt, keep in mind the following:

- This particular subject's information is not necessarily generalizable to other professional thieves.
- A criticism of the individual case study method is that the information provided may be incorrect, biased, and limited.
- In spite of these shortcomings, criminologists have continued to use this technique to obtain in-depth data content.

Contemporary methods have involved the examination of a single criminal's lifestyle, such as that of a "fence" (a receiver of stolen property who resells the stolen goods for profit). For example, Carl Klockars and Darrell Steffensmeir have used this observational method to gain insight about the fence's behavior, techniques, associations, and motives.

The professional thief is one who steals professionally. This means, first, that he makes a regular business of stealing. He devotes his entire working time and energy to larceny. . . . Second, every act is carefully planned. The selection of spots, securing of the property, making a getaway, disposing of the stolen property, and fixing cases in which he may be pinched [arrested] are all carefully planned. Third, the professional thief has technical skills and methods which are different from those of other professional criminals. Manual skill is important in some of the rackets, but the most important thing in all the rackets is the ability to manipulate people. The thief depends on his approach, front, wits, and in many instances his talking ability. The professional burglar or stickup man [robber with a gun], on the other hand, uses violence or threat of violence. . . . Fourth, the professional thief is generally migratory and may work in all the cities of the United States. He generally uses a particular city as headquarters, and when two professional thieves first meet, the question is always asked: "Where are you out of?" . . .

The professional thief has nothing in common with the amateur thief. . . . The professional thief will be in sympathy with the amateur's attempt to steal something but will not be interested in him, for they have no acquaintances or ideas of stealing in common. . . .

The professional thief has nothing in common with those who commit sex crimes or other emotional crimes and would not even be courteous to them if he should chance to meet them in the can. . . .

Sympathy and congeniality with professional burglars and stickups is nearly as close as between thieves in one racket. They are all thieves, and the fact that one has a different racket does not alter this feeling. To professional burglars whom he knows on the street he will tender ideas and spots. . . . He will render assistance to a professional burglar in fixing cases, securing bonds, or escaping from a jailhouse. . . .

There are few fixed rules of ethics, but there are some common understandings among thieves. . . .

It is understood that no thief must squawk (inform) on another. . . . If a thief should squawk, the other thieves would not descend to the same plane and squawk on him. They use better methods. The worst penalty is to keep him broke. This is done by spreading the news that he has squawked, which makes it impossible for him to get into any mob. That is the greatest disgrace and the greatest hardship that can befall a thief. . . .

A thief is not a professional until he is proficient. When a thief is taken on for unimportant tasks by some mob, he is not regarded as a professional. He may develop into a professional in the course of time if he does these unimportant jobs well enough to lead the mob to give him more important jobs. . . .

Members of the profession make their exit from the profession in various ways. Some die, some get too old to work and wind up in a home for old people, some develop a habit [drug] and become too inefficient to be professional thieves, some violate the ethics of the profession and are kicked out, some get in bad with the fix and can no longer get protection and are therefore useless as members of a mob, some become fixers in resort cities, some become big shots in gambling, vice, junk, or booze rackets, some get "the big one" [an extraordinarily large theft] . . . , and some settle down to legitimate occupations without getting "the big one." . . .

The essential characteristics of the profession of theft . . . are technical skill, status, consensus, differential association, and organization. Two significant conclusions may be derived from analysis of these characteristics. The first is that the characteristics of the profession of theft are similar to the characteristics of any other permanent group. The second is that certain elements run through these characteristics which differentiate the professional thieves sharply from other groups. . . .

The professional thief has a complex of abilities and skills, just as do physicians, lawyers, or bricklayers. . . .

The professional thief, like any other professional man, has status. The status is based upon his technical skill, financial standing, connections, power, dress, manners, and wide knowledge acquired in his migratory life. . . .

The profession of theft is a complex of common and shared feelings, sentiments, and overt acts. Pickpockets have similar reactions to prospective victims and to the particular situations in which victims are found. This similarity of reactions is due to the common background of experiences and the similarity of points of attention. These reactions are like the "clinical intuitions" which different physicians form of a patient or different lawyers form of a juryman on quick inspection. Thieves can work together without serious disagreements because they have these common and similar attitudes. . . .

Differential association is characteristic of the professional thieves, as of all other groups. The thief is a part of the underworld and in certain respects is segregated from the rest of society. . . .

The final definition of the professional thief is found within this differential association. The group defines its own membership. A person who is received in the group and recognized as a professional thief is a professional thief. One who is not so received and recognized is not a professional thief, regardless of his methods of making a living. . . .

Professional theft is organized crime. It is not organized in the journalistic sense, for no dictator or central office directs the work of the members of the profession. Rather it is organized in the sense that it is a system in which informal unity and reciprocity may be found. . . .

The complex of techniques, status, consensus, and differential association . . . may be regarded as organization. More specifically, the organization of professional thieves consists in part of the knowledge which becomes the common property of the profession. Every thief becomes an information bureau. For instance, each professional thief is known personally to a large proportion of the other thieves. . . .

Similarly, the knowledge regarding methods and situations becomes common property of the profession. "Toledo is a good town," "The lunch hour is the best time to work that spot," . . . and similar mandates and injunctions are transmitted from thief to thief until everyone in the profession knows them. . . .

Informal social services are similarly organized. Any thief will assist any other thief in a dangerous situation. . . . In these services reciprocity is assumed, but there is no insistence on immediate or specific return to the one who performs the service.

CRITICAL THINKING

1. According to Sutherland, what four types of behaviors define a professional thief?
2. What are the five essential characteristics that distinguish a professional of theft from an amateur?
3. What does Sutherland mean by "differential association"?

READING 2.2

Covert Participant Observation: Reconsidering the Least Used Method

Source: Miller, J.M. 1995. "Covert participant observation: Reconsidering the least used method." Journal of Contemporary Criminal Justice, 11(2), May 1995. Reprinted by permission of Sage Publications.

BY J. MITCHELL MILLER

"The goal of any science is not willful harm to subjects, but the advancement of knowledge and explanation. Any method that moves us toward that goal is justifiable." (Denzin, 1968)

Social scientists have virtually ignored the qualitative technique covert participant observation. This variation of participant observation is either not mentioned or described in less than a page's length in social science research methods texts. The majority of qualitative methods books provide a few illustrative examples, but scarcely more in terms of detailed instruction. Manifested in the selection of alternative field strategies, this disregard has made covert observation the truly least used of all the qualitative research methods.

It is unfortunate that covert research is so rarely conducted because a veiled identity can enable the examination of certain remote and closed spheres of social life, particularly criminal and deviant ones, that simply cannot be inspected in an overt fashion. Consequently, covert research is well-suited for much subject material of concern to criminology and the criminal justice sciences. Also applicable in some situations where overt designs appear the appropriate or only option, covert schemes are infrequently considered. Clearly, complicated ethical issues inherent to secret investigations have created a methodological training bias that has suppressed their application. New generations of researchers therefore remain unfamiliar with a potentially valuable research option.

This brief commentary reintroduces covert participant observation and presents the principal advantages of using the technique. Theoretical, methodological, and pragmatic grounds are offered for exercising covert research. Ethical matters long associated with the stifling of its use are also reconsidered in the context of criminal justice research. The ethicality of secret research, relative to other qualitative methods, is upheld for some research problems with certain stipulations.

DEFINING COVERT PARTICIPANT OBSERVATION

Covert participant observation is a term that has been used rather interchangeably with other labels: "secret observation" (Roth, 1962), "investigative social research" (Douglas, 1976), "sociological snooping" (Von Hoffman, 1970), and most frequently "disguised observation" (Erickson, 1967; 1968; Denzin, 1968). Disguised observation has recently been defined as "research in which the researcher hides his or her presence or purpose for interacting with a group" (Hagan, 1993, 234). The distinguishing feature is that the research occurrence is not made known to subjects within the field setting.

Disguised observation is too inclusive a term often used in reference to those who simply hide in disguise or secret to observe, such as Stein's (1974) observation via a hidden two-way mirror of prostitutes servicing customers. Covert participant observation likewise involves disguise, however, the researcher is always immersed in the field setting. Additional elements—intentional misrepresentation, interpersonal deception, and maintenance of a false identity over usually prolonged periods of time are entailed. "Covert participant observation" is therefore a more technically correct term than "disguised observation" because it better indicates the active nature of the fieldwork essential to the technique (Jorgensen, 1989).

Covert participant observation is essentially "opportunistic research" (Ronai and Ellis, 1989) conducted by "complete-member researchers" (Adler and Adler, 1987) who study phenomena in settings where they participate as full members. Admission to otherwise inaccessible settings is gained by undertaking a natural position and then secretly conducting observational research. Examples of the method include Steffensmeier and Terry's (1973) study of the relationship between personal appearance and suspicion of shoplifting involving students dressed either conventionally or as hippies, Stewart and Cannon's (1977) masquerade as thieves, Tewksbury's (1990) description of adult bookstore patrons, and most recently Miller and Selva's (1994) assumption of the police informant role to infiltrate drug enforcement operations.

The most pronounced example of covert research, however, is Laud Humphreys' infamous Tea Room Trade (1970). Shrouding his academic interest in sexual deviance, Humphreys pretended to be a "watchqueen" (i.e., a lookout) for others so that he might observe homosexual acts in public bathrooms. He also used this role to record his subjects' license plate numbers to obtain their names and addresses in order to interview them by means of another disguise—survey researcher interested in sexual behaviors and lifestyles.

There are other versions of disguised or covert participant observation wherein certain confederates are made aware of the researcher's true identity, purpose and objectives (Formby and Smykla, 1981; Asch, 1951). The reasons for working with cooperatives are plain: to facilitate entry and interaction in the research site, to become familiar with nomenclature and standards of conduct, to expedite the happening of that which the researcher hopes to observe, and to avoid or at least minimize potential danger. Such reliance may be counterproductive, though, in that observations and consequent analysis of the social setting may be tainted by confederates' values, perceptions, and positions within the research environment.

If only a few individuals within a research site are aware of the researcher's true identity, it is possible, indeed likely, that interaction will be affected and spread to others within the setting. Hence, data distortion can become a potential validity and reliability problem with the use of confederates. The researcher must be completely undercover to avoid this problem and utilize the covert role so as to optimally exploit a social setting.

The goals of covert participant observation are no different than the standard objectives of overt participant observation; exploration, description, and, occasionally, evaluation (Berg, 1989). Epistomological justification is similarly derived from an interpretive, naturalistic inquiry paradigm (Patton, 1990). Most aspects of the methodological process, such as defining a problem, observing and gathering information, analyzing notes and records, and communicating results, are nearly identical to conventional participant observation as well. The covert approach may thus be considered a type of participant observation rather than a distinctive method.

There are aspects of the covert participant observation research cycle, however, that are unconventional. One controversial point is gaining entry to a setting through misrepresentation. It is the closed nature of backstage settings and the politics of deviant groups that negates announcement of the researcher's objectives and requires deception via role assumption if certain topics are to be examined.

The character of the participation is also much different and more demanding on the researcher. Covert role assumption means full participation in various group and individual activities, many of which contain risks. The direct study of crime by means of an undercover role can be doubly enigmatic to both the researcher's well-being and the inquiry. Assuming a role either as a criminal or in close proximity to crime for the purpose of research does not absolve the researcher from real or perceived culpability; thus moral decisions and the possibility of arrest and legal sanction must be considered prior to the onset of fieldwork.

The recording of notes from a clandestine position would divulge the researcher's cover and is obviously inadvisable. Extended periods of time in the field often yield rich and rare insight, but, without a chance to withdraw and log events, recollection of temporal/causal sequence can become muddled due to information overload and understandable fatigue. Resolves to this concern have been the use of mnemonics—a process of memorizing through abbreviation and association (Hagan, 1993, 195), taking photographs when possible, and the use of hidden mini-tape recorders and even body wires (Miller and Selva, 1994).

THE ETHICS OF COVERT OBSERVATION

The ethicality of disguised or covert observational techniques has long been controversial, as evidenced by the "deception debate" (Bulmer, 1980; Humphreys, 1970; Roth, 1962; Galliher, 1973). Participants in this debate have tended to assume one of two polarized positions: moralistic condemnation or responsive justification. Deception is explicitly equated with immorality and is so unconscionable for some they would have covert observation banned from social science research altogether (Erikson, 1967). The major objection is that deceptive techniques often violate basic ethical principles including informed consent, invasion of privacy, and the obligation to avoid bringing harm to subjects.

Critics further contend that misrepresentation not only causes irreparable damage to subjects, but also to the researcher, and to science by evoking negative public scrutiny and making subject populations wary of future researchers (Polsky, 1967). Risk to the researcher, however, is a matter of individual decision. To set restrictions on academic investigations in an a priori fashion on the basis of potential harm is at odds with both the ideals of an open, democratic society (individual freedom and autonomy) and traditional social science precepts (free inquiry and, ironically, informed consent).

The argument of isolating future research populations is seemingly unsound as well. Many settings of interest to criminal justice researchers are essentially restricted and typically occupied with subjects already suspicious of strangers due to the threat of legal penalty associated with disclosure. Because researchers as outsiders will usually be distrusted and excluded from such settings, it is logical to assume that its occupants are already ostracized from researchers. The more substantial points that remain and must be confronted are interrelated: the use of deceit and the harm subjects may encounter as a result of the research process.

The topic of dishonesty in covert research is not as clear as opponents of the method suggest and nebulous in comparison to the frequent disregard for ethical standards demonstrated in other qualitative deviance research. Klockars' award winning *The Professional Fence*, for example, describes research conduct far more offensive than the duplicity intrinsic to covert participant observation. This case history of a thirty year career of dealing in stolen goods was enabled by an intentionally misrepresentative letter in which the researcher admittedly lied about: 1. his academic credentials, 2. his familiarity and experience with the subject of fencing, 3. the number of other thieves he had interviewed, and most seriously 4. the possible legal risks associated with participating in the project (Klockars, 1974, 215). Klockars' deception is reasoned in near blind pursuit of his research objective:

> "I thought the claim would strengthen the impression of my seriousness" and "the description of what I wanted to write about as well as the whole tone of the letter is slanted . . . and did not warn Vincet (the research subject) of his rights." (Ibid)

Surprisingly, Klockars' book and similar projects have not produced controversy on par with covert strategies. The terms "case history" and "personal interview" simply do not provoke the interest and suspicion generated by the labels "covert" and "disguise." Covert methods can be considered, relative to the exercise of some techniques, forthright in that the level of deception is predetermined and calculated into the research design (Stricker, 1967). The decision of whether or not to use deception to gain entry and thus enable a study can be made based on the ends versus the means formula described below.

A BASIS FOR COVERT RESEARCH?

Justifications for the use of covert techniques have been presented on various levels. The most common practical argument is that those engaged in illegal or unconventional behavior, such as drug dealers and users, simply will not submit to or participate in a study by overt methods. Likewise, those in powerful and authoritative positions have been considered secretive and difficult to openly observe (Shils, 1975). Police chiefs, white-collar criminals, prison wardens, and drug enforcement agents benefit from the existing power structure which inhibits study of their behavior in these official roles. A covert design is often the only way to conduct qualitative evaluation research of certain enforcement and intervention programs closed to principal participants.

Beyond a "last-resort" rationale, there are other reasons, methodological and theoretical, for employing the covert technique. An evident reason is that of qualitative methodology in general—the desirability of capturing social reality. By concealing identity and objective, researchers can avoid inducing a qualitative Hawthorne effect (i.e., a covert approach can minimize data distortion). Covert participant observation is justified theoretically by dramatulurgical and conflict perspectives. If Goffman (1959) is to be taken seriously, then all researchers should be viewed as wearing masks and the appropriateness of any inquiry viewed in its context. Following Goffman, Denzin has also argued that ethical propriety depends upon the situation:

"the sociologist has the right to make observations on anyone in any setting to the extent that he does so with scientific intents and purposes in mind." (1968, 50)

Dramaturgy also provides a theoretical framework from which to assess topics of concern to the covert observer. The duplicity of roles already present in criminal settings under analysis (e.g., undercover police, fence, snitch, racketeer) are only multiplied when such a role is assumed with the additional post of social scientist.

Consideration of the well known consensus-conflict dialectic also provides logic supportive of covert research. Conventional field methods, such as in-depth interviewing and overt observation, are based on a consensus view of society wherein most people are considered cooperative and willing to share their points of view and experiences with others (Patton, 1990). This assumption is highly suspect, however, in stratified and culturally diverse societies. To the extent that acute conflicts of interests, values, and actions saturate social life to the advantage of some and not others, covert methods should be regarded proper options in the pursuit of truth.

This rationale should resonate with critical criminologists as it is in sync with the accepted view of much crime and delinquency as definitions and labels unjustly assigned to persons and events by operatives of an oppressive criminal justice system. John Galliher, well-known for commentaries on research ethics, supported a critical approach to covert research at a recent meeting of the Society for the Study of Social Problems by qualifying "upward snooping that might expose institutionalized corruption."

Perhaps the most compelling basis for the use of disguise in some research, however, is "the end and the means" position first stated by Roth (1962), then Douglas (1972) and Homan (1980), and most recently Miller and Selva (1994). Employing this reasoning in defense of covert observation, Douglas (1972, 8–9) notes:

"Exceptions to important social rules, such as those concerning privacy and intimacy, must be made only when the research need is clear and the potential contributions of the findings to general human welfare are believed to be great enough to counterbalance the risks."

That the purpose may absolve the process has also been acknowledged by the British Sociological Association, which condones the covert approach "where it is not possible to use other methods to obtain essential data" (1973, 3); such is the case in many criminal justice research situations. The benefits of investigating and reporting on expensive, suspicious, and dysfunctional facets of the criminal justice system, then, may outweigh its potential costs. Failure to study how various initiatives and strategies are actually implemented on the street could condemn other citizens to misfortune and abuse should the behavior of the system be inconsistent with stated legitimate objectives.

To rule out study of covert behavior, whether engaged in by the powerful or the powerless, simply because it cannot be studied openly places artificial boundaries on science and prevents study of what potentially may be very important and consequential activities in society. The propriety and importance of research activities must always be judged on a case by case basis. Drug enforcement's use of asset forfeiture, for example, has been questioned by the press and media with such frequency and intensity that scholarly evaluation is warranted. The very nature of the allegations, however, have prompted the police fraternity to close ranks, thus compelling covert analysis. Abandoning such a study because it can not be carried out overtly would mean that potential misconduct and betrayal of public trust by government officials would remain unexposed.

The means and end rule, of course, requires the subjective interpretation of plausible harm to subjects, what exactly constitutes benefit, and who will be beneficiaries. To assess the balance between these elements it is necessary that they be highly specified, a requirement that is not easily met. The means and end formula is thus ambiguous and the choice to use a covert technique must be carefully deliberated. Certainly, deceptive observation carries ethical baggage less common to other qualitative methods, yet its ethicality is negotiable through detailed purpose and design.

CONCLUSION

The study of crime invites and sometimes requires the covert method as does examination of the clandestine nature of many facets of the formal social control apparatus. How other than through covert participant observation can topics such as undercover policing and inmate-correctional officer interaction be fully understood and evaluated? Those in the criminal justice system, as well as criminals, have vested interests in maintaining high levels of autonomy which require degrees of secrecy. This is evident in various labels such as "police fraternity," "gang," and "confidential informant."

The very things that make a criminal justice or criminological topic worthy of investigation and suitable for publication in a social science forum can preclude overtly exploring it. Methodologically sustained by the theoretical foundations of qualitative inquiry, covert designs tender opportunities to reach relatively unstudied topics.

The solidification of criminology and criminal justice as independent academic disciplines have resulted in a greater number, breadth, and specification level of refereed journals—all of which may indicate a general research surplus (Vaughn and del Carmen, 1992). This is a debatable point for new technologies and the ever evolving nature of the criminal law present still developing and unstudied forms of deviance; but it is also true that the last thirty years have witnessed the near-exhaustion of most obvious crime oriented research foci. It is not uncommon to hear the sagely professor remark how much more difficult it is to now market one's intellectual work in choice outlets (e.g., *Justice Quarterly, Criminology*) than in years past. Covert research is simply one particularly inviting means by which to meet the expectations and competitive realities of today's social science arena.

This comment has briefly surveyed the methodological, theoretical, and practical reasons to utilize covert participant observation in criminal justice research. The most difficult facet of using this method will undoubtedly remain ethical factors that must be dealt with on a case by case basis. But these too can be overcome with caution, conviction, and adherence to established scientific guidelines for qualitative research (Glaser and Strauss, 1967). The spirit of selecting methods on technical merit and relevance to research objectives rather than ethical pretense is an outlook consistent with the goals of social science. To the extent that this perspective thrives, covert participant observation may well become more commonplace; perhaps to the point of no longer being the least used method.

REFERENCES

Adler, P.A. and Adler, P. (1987). The past and future of ethnography, *Contemporary Ethnography*, 16, 4–24.

Asch, S.E. (1951). Effects of group pressure upon the modification and distortion of judgment, in H. Guetzkow (Ed.), *Groups, Leadership and Men*. Pittsburgh: Carnegie Press.

Berg, B.L. (1989). *Qualitative Research Methods for the Social Sciences*. Boston: Allyn and Bacon.

British Sociological Association. (1973). *Statement of Ethical Principles and Their Application to Sociological Practice*.

Bulmer, M. (1980). Comment on the ethics of covert methods, *British Journal of Sociology*, 31, 59–65.

Denzin, N. (1968). On the ethics of disguised observation, *Social Problems*, 115, 502–504.

Douglas, J.D. (1976). *Investigative and Social Research: Individual and Team Field Research*. Beverly Hills, CA: Sage.

Erikson, K.T. (1967). Disguised observation in sociology, *Social Problems*, 14, 366–372.

Formby, W.A. and Smykla, J. (1981). Citizen awareness in crime prevention: Do they really get involved? *Journal of Police Science and Administration*, 9, 398–403.

Galliher, J.F. (1973). The protection of human subjects: A reexamination of the professional code of ethics, *The American Sociologist*, 8, 93–100.

Glaser, B.G. and Strauss, A. (1967). *The Discovery of Grounded Theory*. Chicago: Aldine.

Goffman, E. (1959). *The Presentation of Self in Everyday Life*. New York: Doubleday.

Hagan, F.E. (1993). *Research Methods in Criminal Justice and Criminology*, 3rd ed. New York: Macmillian.

Homan, R. (1980). The ethics of covert methods, *British Journal of Sociology*, 31, 46–59.

Humphreys, L. (1970). *Tearoom Trade: Impersonal Sex in Public Places*. New York: Aldine Publishing.

Jorgensen, D.L. (1989). *Participant Observation: A Methodology for Human Studies*. Newbury Park, CA: Sage.

Klockars, C.B. (1974). *The Professional Fence*. New York: The Free Press.

Miller, J.M. and Selva, L. (1994). Drug enforcement's double-edged sword: An assessment of asset forfeiture programs, *Justice Quarterly*, 11, 313–335.

Patton, M.Q. (1990). *Qualitative Evaluation and Research Methods*, 2nd ed. Newbury Park, CA: Sage.

Polsky, N. (1967). *Hustlers, Beats, and Others*. New York: Anchor Books.

Ronai, C.R. and Ellis, C. (1989). Turn-ons for money: Interactional strategies of the table dancer, *Journal of Contemporary Ethnography*, 18, 271–298.

Roth, J.A. (1962). Comments on secret observation, *Social Problems*, 9, 283–284.

Shils, E.A. (1975). Privacy and power, in *Center and Periphery: Essays in Macrosociology*. Chicago: University of Chicago Press.

Stein, M.L. (1974). *Lovers, Friends, Slaves...: The Nine Male Sexual Types*. Berkeley: Berkeley Publishing.

Stewart, J.E. and Cannon, D. (1977). Effects of perpetrator status and bystander commitment on response to a simulated crime, *Journal of Police Science and Administration*, 5, 318–323.

Stricker, L.J. (1967). The true deceiver, *Psychological Bulletin*, 68, 13–20.

Tewksbury, R. (1990). Patrons of porn: Research notes on the clientele of adult bookstores, *Deviant Behavior*, 11, 259–271.

Vaughn, M. and del Carmen, R. (1992). An annotated list of journals in criminal justice and criminology: A guide for authors, *Journal of Criminal Justice Education*, 3, 93–142.

Von Hoffman, N. (1970). Sociological Snoopers, *Washington Post* (Jan. 30).

Explanations for Criminal Behavior

3.1 INTRODUCTION: THEORIES OF CRIME

Criminology is scientific because crime is studied *systematically*. A systematic or scientific approach is realized through a combination of theories and research methods. Theories suggest what causes crime in terms of what characteristics are common to criminals and high crime areas. The explanations for crime are not simple; we live in a complex society, and the causes of crime are as complex as the society itself. As discussed in Chapter 1, the criminologist attempts to explore the conditions leading to criminal behavior and the factors in society that contribute to its continued existence. This chapter and those that follow explore a wide variety of theories regarding crime. These theoretical explanations contribute to an understanding of criminal behavior and also provide an important framework for examining current policies and past as well as present treatment efforts established to deal with or alleviate the crime problem.

As shown in Chapter 1, theories are important for the development of political and social policies and treatment programs for dealing with criminals and their victims. Chapter 1 examined the three major criminological perspectives on the study of crime and criminal behavior: the functionalist or consensus perspective, the conflict perspective, and the interactionist perspective. Each perspective provides insight into the nature of crime and helps us to focus on different aspects or dimensions of reality. As this chapter extensively explains and analyzes crime and criminal behavior, you will see how elements of each of these perspectives are used to help us explain crime. This chapter focuses on what are considered to be the most important explanations for crime. In particular, this chapter

- contrasts early spiritual and natural explanations for crime (section 3.2);
- defines and analyzes the classical school of criminology (section 3.2);
- describes the contributions of Cesare Beccaria and Jeremy Bentham to the development of criminology and criminal justice (sections 3.3 and 3.4);
- defines and analyzes the positivist school of criminology (section 3.5);
- describes the contributions of four positivist thinkers to criminology and criminal justice (section 3.5);
- identifies four present-day forms of classical and positivist theories (section 3.6).
- adds two new readings on specific and general deterrence.

3.2 TRADITIONAL EXPLANATIONS FOR CRIME

Attempts to explain crime date back through many centuries of recorded history. During the sixteenth and seventeenth centuries, for example, people who engaged in crime and other forms of deviant behavior were thought to be possessed by demons or evil spirits. Exorcism and banishment were among the treatments against crime. At the same time, victims of crime might view their loss as divine retribution for some wrong that they or a family member had committed in the past.

Spiritual and Natural Explanations

Many traditional explanations for crime were based on beliefs in supernatural or spiritual powers or in laws of nature.

Spiritual explanations for crime were rooted in people's religious beliefs and superstitions. The guilt or innocence of a criminal, like victory or defeat in battles or disputes, was believed to be decided by divine intervention. Cures for criminal behavior ranged from religious conversion to torture and death.

Natural explanations for crime were rooted in people's ideas about the nature of reality in the physical world. Ideas about reality were based on observations of nature but were not scientific. For example, the natural world was thought to include inherent good and evil, and crimes often were regarded as crimes against nature or the natural order rather than crimes against victims or against God. Seeking explanations for crime in the natural world provided a basis for the development of legal definitions and treatments of crime.

During the Salem, Massachusetts witch trials of the late 1600s, women were condemned to death for "crime waves" caused by the devil. This "work of the devil" is an example of a spiritual explanation for the causes of crime. What are some other types of explanations in the history of criminological theory?

Spiritual Explanations for Crime

- Spiritual explanations of crime are part of a general view of life in which many events are believed to be the result of the influence of otherworldly powers.
- In the Middle Ages in Europe, feudal lords instituted methods by which they thought God could indicate who was innocent and who was guilty. The first such method was trial by battle, in which the victim or a member of his or her family would fight the offender or a member of his or her family. God was said to give victory to the innocent party.
- Somewhat later in history, trial by ordeal was instituted. In this method, the accused was subjected to difficult and painful tests from which an innocent person (thought to be protected by God) would emerge unharmed, whereas a guilty person would die a painful death. For example, a common method of determining whether a woman was a witch was to tie her up and throw her into the water. If she sank she was considered innocent, but if she floated she was guilty. Other forms of ordeal included running a gauntlet and walking on fire.
- Trial by ordeal was replaced by compurgation, in which the accused gathered together a group of twelve reputable people who would swear that he or she was innocent. Again, the idea was that no one would lie under oath for fear of being punished by God. Compurgation evolved into testimony under oath and trial by jury.
- Our modern prison system originated in association with a spiritual explanation of crime. Around 1790, a group of Quakers in Philadelphia conceived the idea of isolating criminals in cells and giving them only the Bible to read and some manual labor to perform. The Quakers thought criminals would then reflect on their past wrongdoing and repent. They used the term *penitentiary* to describe their invention, a place for penitents who were sorry for their sins.
- Today, some religious individuals and groups still attribute crime to the influence of the devil and to sinful human nature.
- The problem with these theories is that, because spiritual influences cannot be observed, they cannot be proved. Thus, these theories cannot be considered scientific.

Source: George B. Vold and Thomas J. Bernard, *Theoretical Criminology*, 3rd ed., New York: Oxford University Press, 1986, pp. 6–9.

Natural Explanations for Crime

- Natural explanations of crime make use of objects and events in the material world to account for what happens.
- Among the Greeks, Hippocrates (460 BC) provided a physiological explanation of thinking by arguing that the brain is the organ of the mind. Democritus (420 BC) proposed the idea of an indestructible unit of matter called the atom as central to his explanation of the world around him. With Socrates, Plato, and Aristotle, the ideas of unity and continuity came to the fore, but the essential factors in all explanations remained physical and material.
- In Roman law, the Hebrew doctrine of divine sanction for law and order merged with Greek naturalism to provide a justification based on the "nature of things."
- Thus, the rule of kings by divine right became a natural law looking to the nature of things for its principal justification.
- Modern social science continues this natural emphasis; social scientists seek their explanations within the physical and material world.

Source: George B. Vold and Thomas J. Bernard, *Theoretical Criminology*, 3rd ed., New York: Oxford University Press, 1986, pp. 6–9.

The Classical School of Criminology

The field of criminology began with the classical school of criminology. The classical school views human behavior as rational and assumes that people have the ability to choose right from wrong.

During the past three hundred years, a variety of scholars have developed important theories or explanations of crime. These writers have come from many fields. In the eighteenth and nineteenth centuries, they came from such fields as philosophy, theology, medicine, and psychiatry. In the twentieth and twenty-first centuries, many of these theorists have come from such fields as economics, psychology, political science, history, and sociology.

Writers from earlier schools of criminological thought were not primarily concerned with developing generalizations about crime, criminal behavior, and the relationship between varying crime rates and social conditions. Instead, most early scholars who developed theories about crime causation did so, as the criminologist Donald R. Cressey has stated, "in an attempt to find a panacea for criminality." He also indicated that early writers made few, if any, efforts to "verify the many theological or moralistic assertions by actually investigating relevant situations; writers usually selected a general 'cause' of all criminality and then sought to convince their readers that elimination of that cause would eradicate crime both by reforming criminals and by preventing future criminality."[1]

Even though writers and philosophers for many centuries have expressed interest in criminal behavior, criminologists have traditionally marked the beginning of the discipline of criminology with the establishment of the **classical school of criminology**, which purports that people rationally choose to commit criminal acts. The classical school of criminology was developed by Cesare Beccaria and Jeremy Bentham in response to the primitive and cruel European justice system that existed prior to the French Revolution of 1789. Basically, the eighteenth-century classical school

- viewed human behavior as essentially rational in nature;
- felt that people had the ability to choose right from wrong;
- believed that the major element governing a person's choice of action was the basic human desire to obtain pleasure and avoid pain.

Leaders of the classical school about two hundred years ago proposed a number of legal and judicial reforms premised along these lines to curb the problem of crime in their day. These reforms included the imposition of penalties and deterrents severe enough to outweigh any pleasure encountered through the commission of a criminal act. It was thought that people would willingly refrain from crime once they had calculated that the penalties attached to it would exceed the pleasure involved in the act itself. Because factors far beyond personal calculation and motivation are involved in the manifestation of crime, however, proposals such as these had little effect on the crime problem.[2]

Before examining Beccaria's ideas and contributions to criminology, you should understand that the classical school has its roots in the idea that people who commit crime choose to do so after weighing the consequences of their actions. Classical theory is based on the following three assumptions:

1. All of us have free will to make a choice between getting what we want legally or illegally.
2. The fear of punishment can deter a person from committing a criminal act.
3. The community or society can control criminal and noncriminal behavior by making the pain of punishment and penalties more severe than the pleasure from criminal activities and their gains.

According to the **classical school of criminology,** human behavior is rational, people have the ability to choose right from wrong, and people rationally choose to commit criminal acts.

After reading this section, you should be able to

1. explain the basis of spiritual explanations for crime and treatment of criminals;
2. explain the basis and effects of natural explanations for crime;
3. give historical examples of spiritual and natural explanations for crime;
4. describe the origins of the classical school of criminology;
5. list the basic assumptions on which classical theory is based.

3.3 CESARE BECCARIA

Cesare Beccaria, a major contributor to the classical school of criminology, was born in Milan, Italy, on March 15, 1738, and died in 1794. Born an aristocrat, he studied in Parma and graduated from the University of Pavia.[3] In 1763, the protector of prisons, Pietro Verri, gave his friend Beccaria an assignment that would eventually become the essay, "On Crimes and Punishments." It was completed in January, 1764, and first published anonymously in July of that year. The article caused a sensation, but not everybody liked it. The fact that it was first published anonymously suggested that "its contents were designed to undermine many if not all of the cherished beliefs of those in a position to determine the fate of those accused and convicted of crime. . . . [An] attack on the prevailing systems for the administration of criminal justice, . . . it aroused the hostility and resistance of those who stood to gain by the perpetuation of the barbaric and archaic penological institutions of the day."[4]

Eighteenth-Century Criminal Law

Cesare Beccaria, a major contributor to the classical school of criminology, responded to eighteenth-century criminal law, which was repressive, uncertain, and barbaric.

To understand why Beccaria's essay created such controversy, one need only consider the state of criminal law in Europe at the time. Eighteenth-century criminal law was repressive, uncertain, and barbaric. It also permitted, as well as encouraged, abusive and arbitrary practices. The law gave public officials unlimited power to deprive people of their freedom, property, and life with no regard to principles embodied in the concept "due process of law":

> Secret accusations were in vogue and persons were imprisoned on the flimsiest of evidence. Torture, ingenious and horrible, was employed to wrench confessions from the recalcitrant. Judges were permitted to exercise unlimited discretion in punishing those convicted of crime. The sentences imposed were arbitrary, inconsistent, and depended upon the status and power of the convicted. . . . A great array of crimes were punished by death not infrequently preceded by inhuman atrocities. . . . In practice no distinction was made between the accused and the convicted. Both were detained in the same institution and subjected to the same horrors of incarceration. This same practice prevailed in regard to the convicted young and old, the murderer and the bankrupt, first offenders and hardened criminals, men and women. All such categories of persons were promiscuously thrown together, free to intermingle and interact.[5]

Beccaria's Proposed Reforms

Beccaria's specific suggestions for a system of criminal justice based on the social contract covered the areas of guilt and punishment. Even though people had to surrender part of their liberty for protection, Beccaria believed they would want to give up "the least possible portion": "The aggregate of these least possible portions constitutes the right to punish; all that exceeds this is abuse and not justice; it is fact but by no means right." Given this view, Beccaria advocated that only legislators should be the creators of laws. He stated that the authority for "making penal laws can reside only with the legislator, who represents the whole society united by the social contract." In addition, unless it was ordained by the laws, judges were not permitted to inflict punishment on any member of society. Beccaria also made some important points about being termed "guilty": "No man can be called guilty before a judge has sentenced him, nor can society deprive him of public protection before it has been decided that he has in fact violated the conditions under which such protection was accorded him. What right is it, then, if not simply that of might, which empowers a judge to inflict punishment on a citizen while doubt still remains as to his guilt or innocence?" This new concept, "innocent until proven guilty," underlies our criminal justice system today.

Source: C. Beccaria, *On Crimes and Punishments,* translated by H. Paolucci, New York: Bobbs-Merrill, 1963, pp. 8–13, 30–33, 45–58, 62–64, 99.

The preceding description applies to the status of criminal law when Beccaria wrote his essay on crime. It helps us to understand why his essay was considered humane and revolutionary in character. For Beccaria, it was bad laws, not evil people, that were the root of the crime problem. A modern system of law that guaranteed people equal treatment was needed to replace the old, unenlightened criminal justice system of his time.

Social Contract Theory

Beccaria based his call for reform on the theory that citizens and the state have a "social contract" that entitles people to legal protections against crime.

Beccaria's blueprint for reform had its roots in social contract theory, which stresses the idea that people were originally without government. People then created the state through a "social contract," by which they surrendered many of their "natural liberties." In return, people received the security that government could provide "against antisocial acts."[6] Beccaria wrote, "Laws are the conditions under which independent and isolated men united to form a society. Weary of living in a continual state of war, and of enjoying a liberty rendered useless by the uncertainty of preserving it, they sacrificed a part so that they might enjoy the rest of it in peace and safety. The sum of all these portions of liberty sacrificed by each for his own good constitutes the sovereignty of a nation, and their legitimate depository and administrator is the sovereign."[7]

Pleasure, Pain, and Punishment

Pleasure and pain, according to Beccaria, are the only "springs of action," and the purpose of punishment is to prevent a criminal from doing any further injury to the community and to prevent others from committing similar crimes.

Beccaria believed that punishment should be based on the pleasure/pain principle. For him, pleasure and pain were the only "springs of action" in people who are in possession of their senses: "If an equal punishment be ordained for two crimes that injure society in different degrees, there is nothing to deter men from committing the greater [crime] as often as it is attended with greater advantage."[8] He also believed that punishment and penalties should be imposed on the guilty according to a scale determined by the degree of danger the given crime poses for the community: "If mathematical calculation could be applied to the obscure and infinite combinations of human actions, there might be a corresponding scale of punishments descending from the greatest to the least."[9] With such an exact scale of crimes and punishments, people would know which penalties were attached to which criminal acts.

What, then, was the purpose of punishment? For Beccaria, its purpose was to prevent a criminal from doing any further injury to the community or society. The purpose of punishment was also to prevent others from committing similar crimes. These purposes required setting penalties that would make strong and lasting impressions on others with the "least torment to the body of the criminal."[10] Punishment should be no more severe than deemed necessary to deter individuals from committing crimes against others or the state. Maximizing the preventive, or deterrent, effect would be achieved by prompt, effective, and certain punishment: "The more promptly and the more closely punishment follows upon the commission of a crime, the more just and useful will it be . . . . I have said that the promptness of punishments is more useful because when the length of time that passes between the punishment and misdeed is less, so much stronger and more lasting in the human mind is the association of these two ideas, crime and punishment; they then come insensibly to be considered, one as the cause, the other as the necessary inevitable effect."[11]

After proposing that the rich should be punished in the same way as the poor, and that both torture to obtain confessions and capital punishment should be abolished, Beccaria concluded: "So that any punishment be not an act of violence of one or of many against the other, it is essential that it be public, prompt, necessary, [as] minimal in severity as possible under given circumstances, proportional to the crime, and prescribed by the laws."[12]

After reading this section, you should be able to

1. explain what the classical school's perspective on crime was and how it contrasted with the state of criminal law in eighteenth-century Europe;
2. describe Cesare Beccaria's ideas of the social contract and the pleasure principle and their implications for criminal justice.

3.4 JEREMY BENTHAM

An influential early classical theorist was the British philosopher **Jeremy Bentham**, born in 1748. He believed that people have the ability to choose right from wrong, good from evil. His explanation for criminal behavior included the idea

Jeremy Bentham was an early classical theorist who based his ideas on utilitarianism, *felicitous calculus*, and "the greatest happiness."

How would Cesare Beccaria and Jeremy Bentham explain this person's criminal behavior? According to utilitarianism, how should this criminal and crime be treated by the criminal justice system?

that people are basically hedonistic, that is, they desire a high degree of pleasure and avoid pain. People who choose to commit criminal acts think they stand to gain more than they risk losing by committing the crime. Bentham believed that the criminal justice system should deter people from making this choice.

Utilitarianism

Jeremy Bentham, a major contributor to the classical school of criminology, based his theories on the principle of utilitarianism.

Bentham's perspective on human behavior had its roots in the concept of utilitarianism, which assumes that all of a person's actions are calculated. **Utilitarianism** is the doctrine that the purpose of all actions should be to bring about the greatest happiness for the greatest number of people. For Bentham, people calculate actions in accordance with their likelihood of obtaining pleasure or pain. Bentham stated that an act possesses utility if it "tends to produce benefit, advantage, pleasure, good or happiness (all this in the present case comes to the same thing) or (which again comes to the same thing) to prevent the happening of mischief, pain, evil or unhappiness to the party whose interest is considered."[13]

Bentham developed a **felicitous calculus**, or **moral calculus**, for estimating the probability that a person will engage in a particular kind of behavior. People, he believed, weigh the possibility that a particular behavior pattern or action will cause current or future pleasure against the possibility that it will cause current or future pain. In response to the question of why a person commits a crime, Bentham would probably reply that the pleasure that the person anticipated from the criminal act was much greater than the subsequent pain that might be expected from it.

The Greatest Happiness and Social Control

Bentham advocated the "greatest happiness" principle and the use of punishment to deter crime.

Bentham expounded a comprehensive code of ethics and placed much emphasis on the practical problem of decreasing the crime problem. He aimed at a system of social control—a method of checking the behavior of people according

Utilitarianism is the doctrine that the purpose of all actions should be to bring about the greatest happiness for the greatest number of people.

Felicitous calculus is a **moral calculus** developed by Jeremy Bentham for estimating the probability that a person will engage in a particular kind of behavior.

to the ethical principle of utilitarianism. He believed that an act should be judged not by an "irrational system of absolutes but by a supposedly verifiable principle. The principle was that of 'the greatest happiness for the greatest number' or simply 'the greatest happiness.'"[14]

For Bentham, checks or sanctions needed to be attached to criminal behavior and set up by legislation, which would then serve "to bring the individual's pursuit of his own happiness in line with the best interests of the society as a whole."[15] Punishment, Bentham believed, was a necessary evil— necessary to prevent greater evils from being inflicted on the society and thus diminishing happiness.[16] Social control based on degrees of punishment that both fit the crime and discourage offending is part of our system of criminal justice today. As you can see, Jeremy Bentham, Cesare Beccaria, and the classical school of criminology had many influences on the American system of criminal justice.

Influences of the Classical School

The U.S. Bill of Rights is rooted in Beccaria's writings. Beccaria and Bentham also influenced the development of the modern correctional system.

Beccaria's groundbreaking essay strongly influenced the first ten amendments (the Bill of Rights) to the U.S. Constitution and played a significant role in bringing about many of our present-day penal practices. It was also of primary importance in "paving the way for penal reform for approximately the last two centuries."[17] Reviewing European history, we see that the essay greatly influenced the French penal code adopted in 1791, Russian law at the time of Catherine the Great, Austrian law during the reign of Emperor Joseph II, and Prussian law during the reign of Frederick the Great. By stressing that the goal of punishment is to deter criminal behavior in people, Beccaria reflected Jeremy Bentham's utilitarian concepts of free will and hedonism.

Both Beccaria and Bentham advocated a new philosophy and a new system of legal and penal reform. These classical theorists argued that the proper objective of punishment should be to protect society and its laws. It was their view that punishment should not be inflicted for vengeance; rather, the primary purpose of punishment should be the reduction or deterrence of crime. They advocated that the excessively brutal punishments of mutilation and death be abolished and that penal reforms be introduced so that the punishment fit the crime. Thus, it was their belief that

- the punishments inflicted should be just severe enough to outweigh any pleasures, either contemplated or actually experienced, that could be derived from the commission of the criminal act;
- in this way, the threat of punishment would deter most people from committing crimes in the first place;
- the actual infliction of punishment would deter an offender from committing additional criminal acts.

Beccaria also presented convincing arguments for imprisonment as a form of punishment, saying it would be the most effective and efficient method for carrying out punishment. As it happened, a more than adequate number of jails and prisons were already conveniently in existence throughout Europe. Prior to this time, these buildings were used for the temporary confinement of minor offenders and those awaiting trial, and they were easily adapted for use in implementing Beccaria's and Bentham's programs.[18]

Thus, the classical theorists influenced the development of the modern correctional system.

After reading this section, you should be able to

1. describe Jeremy Bentham's ideas of utilitarianism and the "greatest happiness," and his moral calculus;
2. compare Beccaria's and Bentham's views on deterrence, guilt, and punishment;
3. identify some contributions of the classical school of criminology to American criminal justice.

3.5 THE POSITIVIST SCHOOL OF CRIMINOLOGY

The classical perspective on crime and criminal behavior dominated the thinking and understanding of crime, law, and justice for almost a century. However, many of the proposals that the classical theorists made had little effect on the crime problem. In the decades that followed, statistical improvements in crime measurement began to reflect the existence of certain patterns in the manifestation of crime. For example, scientific research revealed that crime varied by age, race, sex, and geographic area; that is, it became obvious that factors far beyond personal calculation and motivation were involved in the manifestation of crime and criminal behavior. With the development of various scientific disciplines during the nineteenth century, attention was drawn away from notions of rationalism and punishment, and toward an investigation of the causes of crime, stressing in particular the influence of hereditary, psychological, and social factors.[19]

In the decades that followed the classical theorists, the logic and basic methods of science evolved and took root in Europe. In the past, during the classical and medieval periods of history, interpretations of and explanations for human and societal existence had come mainly from a strong belief in an unchanging natural law and in the supremacy and sanctity of traditional as well as theological dogma. The philosophical systems of these periods were based on simple speculative analogies to so-called eternal truths coming from the revered sources of divine will and tradition.[20]

With the development of the Industrial Revolution, however, the world began to change radically. Old patterns of social relationships and daily routines changed. The revolution ultimately brought about an intellectual crisis in Europe. People questioned their old beliefs about the nature of human existence and society; no longer could they take society for granted. New answers were needed to the questions, "What is society? How does it change? How can it be reorganized to meet individual and social needs?"

People also began to question previously relied-on sources of knowledge that answered such questions. No longer could traditional authority and speculative philosophy explain people's present and future life circumstances. Speculative social philosophies gave way to the idea that society and social change could be studied factually, objectively, and scientifically. Answers to ancient questions about human nature and human behavior, including deviant and criminal behavior, began to be offered in terms of objective science and not in terms of religion or philosophy. One of the earliest positivist thinkers was the French sociologist **Auguste Comte.**

Auguste Comte, the founder of sociology and positivism, believed that both external and internal forces are important for understanding human behavior.

Auguste Comte

Auguste Comte was the founder of sociology and positivism.

Impressed and inspired by the revolutionary discoveries in biology, chemistry, astronomy, and physics, the founder of sociology, Auguste Comte (1798–1857), advocated that human behavior and society should be studied using methods similar to those used in the physical sciences. Comte encouraged social scientists to use the perspective of **positivism**, which emphasizes techniques of observation, the comparative method, and experimentation in the development of knowledge concerning human behavior and the nature of society. This approach was different from more traditional speculative systems of social philosophy.

The positivist perspective also stressed the idea that much of our behavior is a function of external social forces beyond individual control, as well as internal forces such as our mental capabilities and biological makeup. With the advent of positivism, people were beginning to be perceived and understood as organisms that are part of the animal kingdom whose behavior is very much influenced (if not determined) by social, cultural, and biological antecedents, rather than as self-determined beings who are free to do what they want.[21]

There is great diversity in positivist theories on the causes of crime: some stress external (or social) factors more, and others stress internal (or individual) factors more. Based on Comte's positivism, Cesare Lombroso (1835–1909) and his distinguished pupils Enrico Ferri (1856–1929) and Raffaele Garofalo (1852–1934) founded positivist criminology—the modern, positivist school of penal jurisprudence—and led what has been called the Italian school of criminology.

Positivism emphasizes the techniques of observation, the comparative method, and experimentation in the development of knowledge concerning human behavior and the nature of society.

Cesare Lombroso

In his view on crime, Lombroso called for scientific explanations, focused on internal biological factors, and believed that people who engage in crime are throwbacks.

Cesare Lombroso was born in Venice, Italy, in 1835. Educated in medicine and psychiatry, he became a professor of criminal anthropology at the University of Turin in 1906.[22] In his book, *The Criminal Man*, published in 1876, Lombroso explained criminal behavior on the basis of biological characteristics and heredity. Using various physiological and cranial measurements of known criminals, Lombroso developed the theory that certain persons who engage in criminal behavior are "born criminals."

Lombroso believed that criminals could be distinguished from noncriminals by a variety of what he termed **physical stigmata**, such as a long lower jaw, flattened nose, and long, apelike arms. The stigmata themselves did not cause criminal behavior; rather they were visible indicators of a personality type that was, in essence, a primitive **atavism**, a throwback on the Darwinian scale of human evolution.[23]

Lombroso's approach "suggested that criminals are distinguished from noncriminals by the manifestation of multiple physical anomalies, which are of atavistic or degenerative origin. The concept of atavism (from Latin *atavus*, ancestor) postulated a reversion to a primitive or subhuman type of man, characterized physically by a variety of inferior morphological features reminiscent of apes and lower primates, occurring in the more simian fossil men and, to some extent, preserved in modern 'savages.'"[24] In addition, Lombroso's theory

DID YOU KNOW
Lombroso was one of the first theorists who attempted to scientifically study criminal behavior.

Lombroso believed that **physical stigmata,** such as a long lower jaw, flattened nose, and long, apelike arms, identify a criminal. These biological characteristics were seen as **atavism,** or a throwback to earlier states in human evolution.

Lombroso's Study of a Criminal's Brain

Lombroso was unhappy with the abstract, judicial methods of studying crime in his day. He wanted to apply the experimental method in studying the differences between criminals and noncriminals. He did his research by studying criminals in Italian prisons, where he became acquainted with a famous bandit named Vilella. When Vilella died and Lombroso did a postmortem examination, he found a distinct depression at the base of the skull, a "characteristic found in inferior animals, and a depression correlated with an overdevelopment of the vermis, known in birds as the middle cerebellum."[1] In reviewing this moment in his life, Lombroso later stated: "This was not merely an idea, but a revelation. At the sight of that skull, I seemed to see all of a sudden, lighted up as a vast plain under a flaming sky, the problem of the nature of the criminal—an atavistic being who reproduces in his person the ferocious instincts of primitive humanity and the inferior animals. Thus were explained anatomically the enormous jaws, high cheekbones, prominent superciliary arches, solitary lines in the palms, extreme size of the orbits, handle-shaped or sessile ears found in criminals, savages, and apes, insensibility to pain, extremely acute sight, tattooing, excessive idleness, love of orgies, and the irresistible craving for evil for its own sake, the desire not only to extinguish life in the victim, but to mutilate the corpse, tear its flesh, and drink its blood."[2]

[1] M. E. Wolfgang, "Cesare Lombroso," in *Pioneers in Criminology,* H. Mannheim, ed., 2nd ed., Montclair, NJ: Patterson Smith, 1972, p. 248.

[2] C. Lombroso, from his opening speech at the Sixth Congress of Criminal Anthropology, Turin, Italy, April 1906; quoted in ibid.

implied that the "mentality of atavistic individuals is that of primitive man, that these are biological 'throwbacks' to an earlier stage of evolution, and that the behaviour of these 'throwbacks' will inevitably be contrary to the rules and expectations of modern civilized society."[25]

Although Lombroso is considered the father of criminology, there are many criticisms of and misconceptions about his ideas. Many scholars, including Lombroso's most ardent advocates, criticized his methods of research, such as his sources of information, his use of statistics, and the absence of adequate control groups in his experiments (although he did challenge his opponents to test his research and ideas by a controlled investigation of criminals and noncriminals).[26]

Lombroso not only focused on the "born criminal," atavism, and degeneracy; as a positivist, he also expressed concern for factors such as the social and physical environment of the offender. In *Crime, Its Causes and Remedies* (1899), he reported that economic and political developments give rise to the appearance of abnormalities that induce social reactions. In discussing socioeconomic factors, he emphasized a mutual interactive relationship between heredity and environment and, in other written works, stressed environmental conditions as causing or having an effect on criminality. For example, he discussed the influences of poverty on crime, the relationship between the cost of food and crimes against property and person, and the relationship between alcohol and crime.[27]

Lombroso also investigated the etiology (or origins) of crime. He used a wide variety of research techniques and procedures, ranging from historical and clinical methods to anthropometric and statistical techniques. These were important strides in the study of crime; nevertheless, Lombroso's research methods would not be accepted today as scientific.[28]

Enrico Ferri

Ferri coined the term "born criminal" and developed a five-fold scientific classification of criminals.

Enrico Ferri was born in Mantua, Italy, in 1856. His dissertation, published in 1878, was entitled *Criminal Sociology*. It was in its fifth edition when Ferri died in 1929. He was, for many decades, an acknowledged leader of the positivist school of criminology.[29] Ferri studied under Lombroso at the University of Turin because of his belief that, "in order to formulate principles concerning crimes, penalties and criminals, it is first necessary to study . . . criminals and prisons, since facts should precede theories."[30]

In 1880, Lombroso began to edit his periodical, the *Archive of Psychiatry*. In its first volume, Ferri contributed a paper on the relationship between criminal anthropology and criminal law. In this paper, Ferri first coined the term "born criminal," to designate Lombroso's atavistic type of criminal, and developed one of his basic ideas: a scientific classification of criminals.[31] Ferri's classification included the following:

1. The *born or instinctive criminal*, who carries from birth, through unfortunate heredity from his progenitors, . . . a reduced resistance to criminal stimuli and also an evident and precocious propensity to crime.
2. The *insane criminal*, affected by a clinically identified mental disease or by a neuropsychopathic condition which groups him with the mentally diseased.
3. The *passional criminal*, who, in two varieties, the criminal through passion (a prolonged and chronic mental state), or through emotion (explosive and unexpected mental state), represents a type at the opposite pole from the criminal due to congenital tendencies.
4. The *occasional criminal* who constitutes the majority of lawbreakers and is the product of family and social milieu more than of abnormal personal physiomental conditions.
5. The *habitual criminal*, or rather, the criminal by acquired habit, who is mostly a product of the social environment in which, due to abandonment by his family, lack of education, poverty, [and] bad companions . . . , already in his childhood begins as an occasional offender.[32]

Ferri carefully pointed out that not every criminal would fit into his classification system, nor would criminals in daily life appear so well-defined as the system suggested. Classes of criminals do not exist in nature, according to Ferri. However, they are a necessary "instrument by which the human mind can better understand the multiform reality of things."[33]

Ferri expressed interest in Lombroso's ideas of the basic biological causation of criminal behavior, but he stressed the importance and interrelatedness of social, economic, and political factors as well. In *Criminal Sociology*, Ferri presented his original thesis on the causes of crime, which centered on the following factors:

- physical (race, climate, geographic location, seasonal effects, temperature, etc.);

Enrico Ferri was a positivist who developed a scientific classification of criminals and focused on the causes of crime, criminal sociology, social reform, and effective criminal justice.

Ferri and Social Reform

Ferri's contributions to the etiology of criminal conduct were "incidental means for achieving a greater understanding of the course which the reformation of criminal justice should take."[1] That is, Ferri was basically a social reformer. He desired to achieve a "demonstrably effective criminal justice, which would afford maximum protection or defence of society against the criminal."[2] In his writings, Ferri examined many crime-preventive measures, or, as he termed them, "substitutes for punishments," such as "free trade, abolition of monopolies, inexpensive workmen's dwellings, public savings banks, better street lighting, birth control, [and] freedom of marriage and divorce."[3] These preventive measures were very much in line with his political theory, which was that "the state is the principal instrument through which better conditions are to be attained."[4] Ferri was the chief architect of the positivist school, which stood in clear opposition to the classical school. Ferri felt that a positivist perspective was necessary to "put a stop to the exaggerated individualism in favour of the criminal in order to obtain a greater respect for the rights of honest people who constitute the great majority."[5]

[1] T. Sellin, "Enrico Ferri," in *Pioneers in Criminology,* H. Mannheim, ed., 2nd ed., Montclair, NJ: Patterson Smith, 1972, pp. 378–79.

[2] Ibid.

[3] G. B. Vold and T. J. Bernard, *Theoretical Criminology,* New York: Oxford University Press, 1986, p. 41.

[4] Ibid.

[5] Sellin, "Enrico Ferri," p. 378.

- anthropological (age, sex, somatic [body] conditions, psychological conditions, etc.);
- social (density of populations, customs, religion, organization of government, economic and industrial conditions, etc.).[34]

For Ferri, the positivist school cultivated a "science of criminality and of a social defence against it." This science involved "an individual fact

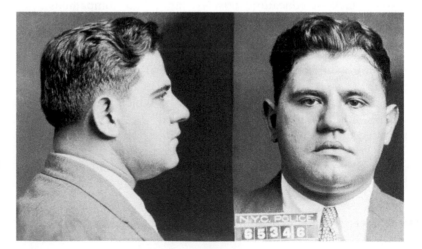

How might the early positivists regard this criminal and the causes of his crimes? How might Lombroso describe him? How might Ferri classify him as a criminal type? How would Garofalo's classification differ? What would the positivists say should be done to protect society from this criminal?

(somatopsychological condition of the offender) by anthropology, psychology, and criminal psychopathology; and a social fact (physical and social environmental conditions) by criminal statistics, monographic studies, and comparative ethnographic studies for the purpose of systematizing social defence measures (a) of a preventive nature, either indirect or remote (through 'penal substitutes') or direct or proximate (by the police); or (b) of a repressive nature through criminal law and procedure, techniques of prison treatment, and aftercare." Ferri called this science **criminal sociology**.[35]

Raffaele Garofalo

Raffaele Garofalo was a positivist who rejected the doctrine of free will, classified criminals into four types on the basis of moral deficits, and believed in incapacitation as the best social defense against crime.

Raffaele Garofalo (1852–1934) was the third of the leading exponents of positivism. Garofalo was born of Italian nobility in Naples in 1852. He was a professor of criminal law at the University of Naples and is known principally in the United States for his major work, *Criminology*.[36]

Garofalo also rejected the doctrine of free will. He believed that crime and criminal behavior can be understood only by using scientific methods, and that science deals with universals. He, therefore, developed a sociological definition of crime that was universal and would "designate those acts which no civilized society can refuse to recognize as criminal and repress by punishment."[37]

Because he believed it to be inadequate for scientific purposes, Garofalo rejected the definition of crime as "that conduct for which the law has provided penalties and has denominated criminal."[38] He found this "juridical" conception of crime inadequate because it included as well as excluded behaviors that he thought should be a part of a sociological notion of crime. His definition of **"natural crime"** was "that conduct which offends the basic moral sentiments of pity (revulsion against the voluntary infliction of suffering on others) and probity (respect for property rights of others)."[39] Garofalo's theoretical system holds that "the concept of natural crime serves the primary end of identifying the true criminal against whom measures of social defence must be taken. Natural crime is behavior which violates certain basic moral sentiments. The true criminal is he whose altruistic sensibilities are lacking or are in a deficient state of development. The concepts of crime and the criminal are thus integrally related."[40]

Garofalo advanced the concept of psychic or moral anomaly. That is, he believed that the true criminal is abnormal and "lacks a proper development of the altruistic sensibilities. This lack or deficiency is not simply the product of circumstance or environmental conditioning but has an organic basis."[41] For Garofalo, "[t]here is no such thing as a casual offender."[42] He believed that this moral anomaly was "hereditarily transmissible" and "established by unimpeachable evidence."[43] Thus, Garofalo believed that congenital and inherited factors are important, and he downplayed external factors. Making environmental and social factors less important affected his conclusions regarding crime-prevention measures. For example, Garofalo did not believe that education was an agent for eliminating crime; in fact, he viewed education as "chiefly determinative of the kinds of crime committed."[44] He was also skeptical of economic distress as a cause of crime, but he stressed the importance of a sound family environment and religious instruction for children as a crime-prevention measure. Garofalo stated that, without a doubt, "external causes such as tradition, prejudices, bad examples, climate, alcoholic liquors, and the like are not without important influence. But in our opinion, there is

Natural crime, for Garofalo, consisted of conduct that offends the basic moral sentiments of pity and probity.

always present in the instincts of the true criminal, a specific element which is congenital or inherited, or else acquired in early infancy and become inseparable from his psychic organism."[45]

Garofalo developed a classification of four criminal types or classes, based on the concept of moral anomaly. Even though they are distinct from one another, they are related in the sense that each type is characterized by "a deficiency in the basic altruistic sentiments of pity and probity."[46] Garofalo's four classes of criminals are

> The murderer is the man in whom altruism is wholly lacking. The sentiments of both pity and probity are absent, and such a criminal will steal or kill as the occasion arises. . . . Lesser offenders fall into two major groups: violent criminals, characterized by the lack of pity, and thieves, indicated by a lack of probity . . . such offenses are committed by a small minority of the population. . . . The violent criminal may also commit crimes of passion, sometimes under the influence of alcohol . . . such crimes . . . are indicative of inferior innate moral capacities. . . . Certain environments . . . contribute to crimes against property . . . [such as] two or three evil companions. . . . Nevertheless, many manifestations of such behavior can only be attributed to "a remote atavism" and in other cases to a general deficiency in "moral activity." . . . Lascivious criminals . . . [are] a group of sexual offenders . . . whose conduct is characterized less by the absence of the sentiment of pity than by a low level of moral energy and deficient moral perception.[47]

Garofalo's concepts of crime and criminals provide a base for his "social defense" against criminality. For Garofalo, because of the "absence or deficiency of the basic altruistic sentiments," the criminal demonstrates his "unfitness" or "lack of adaptation" to his social environment: "Elimination from the social circle is thus the penalty indicated."[48] This emphasis on elimination results in "a theory of penalties or treatment which makes incapacitation of the criminal the consideration of central importance."[49] Deterrence of potential offenders and reformation of offenders are of secondary importance.[50] Incapacitation through death or imprisonment or "transportation" (banishment to penal colonies) was the key to eliminating criminals from society.[51] Garofalo presents three means of elimination:

1. Death, for those whose acts grow out of a "permanent psychologic anomaly which renders the subject forever incapable of social life."
2. Partial elimination, including long-time or life imprisonment and transportation for those "fit only for the life of nomadic hordes or primitive tribes," as well as the relatively mild isolation of agricultural colonies for young and more hopeful offenders.
3. Enforced reparation for those lacking in altruistic sentiments who have committed their crimes under exceptional circumstances not likely to occur again.[52]

Garofalo believed that his theory of punishment met three conditions needed to make it "an effective instrument of public policy": it satisfied the deepseated public demand for punishment of the offender simply because he committed a crime; its general principle of elimination was sufficiently intimidating to contribute to deterrence; and the social selection resulting from its operation offered hope for the future by slow eradication of the criminals and their progeny.[53]

Comte, Lombroso, Ferri, and Garofalo reflect the diversity of positivist views in their various emphases on internal or external causes of criminal behavior. However diverse its elements, the perspective of positivism significantly contributed to the development of criminology and criminal justice in the United States, chiefly because the positivists embraced the scientific method and focused on society's need for protection against criminals.

After reading this section, you should be able to

1. list the characteristics of positivism and describe the circumstances in which it arose;
2. explain the concept of atavism as a feature of Lombroso's general theory of criminality;
3. list Ferri's five types of criminals and three causes of crime;
4. describe Garofalo's four criminal types, the sources of their criminality, and the three ways of eliminating them from society;
5. compare and contrast positivism and the "science of criminality" with the classical school of criminology.

3.6 CONTEMPORARY CLASSICISM AND POSITIVISM

The contributions of the early schools of criminological thought have been many and profound. Classicism and positivism have provided us with many theories of crime and criminal behavior, laying a foundation for the discipline of criminology and the related fields of criminal justice and penology. Most modern theories combine elements of both the classical and positivist perspectives. Four modern examples are described in this section: rational choice theory, deterrence theory, an economic model of crime, and routine activities theory.

Rational Choice Theory

For rational choice theorists, a criminal rationally chooses the crime to commit and the target of crime.

A recent reformulation and integration of earlier classical and positivist theories is found in rational choice theory. Developed by Derek Cornish and Ronald Clarke, **rational choice theory** focuses on the situational aspects of criminal behavior. Rational choice (or situational) theory stresses the point that society can achieve a high degree of crime prevention by focusing on the situational aspects that influence particular types of criminal behavior. According to rational choice theory, a criminal rationally chooses both the crime to commit and the target of the crime. The criminal, in other words, does not randomly select his or her target.[54]

Recently, some criminologists have categorized rational choice theory as a neoclassical theory, because of its focus on rationality and choice. Others, however, have argued that rational choice theory is a form of positivist theory, because it stresses empirical techniques to evaluate and reduce vulnerability to crime and does not focus on the dispensing of justice.[55]

Whatever position one maintains, rational choice theory is one of the integrated classical theories that have merged the classical and positivist

Rational choice theory focuses on the situational aspects of criminal behavior and stresses that a criminal rationally chooses both the crime to commit and the target of the crime.

This citizen may be about to get robbed. According to rational choice theory, what factors will determine whether and how a crime will occur? According to deterrence theory, what factors will influence the potential offender's decision?

An **integrated theory** is a theory in which two or more of the major criminological theories are used together in a new theoretical perspective.

perspectives to crime and crime prevention based on a person's rationality and freedom of choice. An **integrated theory** is one in which two or more of the major criminological theories are used together in a new theoretical perspective. Rational choice theory stresses the idea that an individual's ability to choose is merged with the empiricism of positivism, enabling criminologists to analyze and understand how one's choices are influenced by situational factors. As later chapters in this analysis of criminal behavior and crime control will demonstrate, many situational factors or opportunity factors (e.g., access control, entry and exit screening, surveillance, brighter streetlights, and home alarms) can be altered in order to deter criminal behavior.[56]

Deterrence Theory

Deterrence theory stresses that an individual's choice to commit or not commit a crime is influenced by the fear of punishment.

Deterrence theory stresses the idea that an individual's choice is influenced by the fear of punishment.

Deterrence is the act of preventing a criminal act before it occurs, through the threat of punishment and sanctions.

Rational choice theory says that criminals are rational beings who evaluate available information to decide whether a crime is attractive and worthwhile. **Deterrence theory**, on the other hand, stresses the idea that an individual's choice is influenced by the fear of punishment. **Deterrence** is the act of preventing a criminal act before it occurs, through the threat of punishment and sanctions. Rooted in the classical perspective, deterrence theory focuses on the following premises:

- For punishment to be a deterrent to criminal behavior, it must be certain, swift, and severe.
- The severity must be sufficient to outweigh any rewards that the criminal may obtain from a criminal act.
- Deterrence is both general and specific. (See Readings 3.2 and 3.3.)

Deterrence is at the center of neoclassical thinking.

Why are crime rates so high in the United States? Using the deterrence perspective, one could argue hypothetically that they are high because many criminals believe that many police officers will not make an arrest even if they are aware of a crime; therefore, there is only a small chance of being arrested for committing a particular crime. In addition, the perpetrator may believe that, even if arrested, there is a high probability of receiving a lenient punishment.

How, then, can we reduce high rates of criminal behavior? From a deterrence perspective, crime rates should decline if there is an increase in the rates of arrest, conviction, and severity of punishment. Studies have indicated three significant findings, however:

1. Where there have been increases in police activity, crime rates are not necessarily reduced; nor are crime rates reduced by increasing the number of police in a community.[57]
2. In a famous Kansas City, Missouri police study, the absence or presence of police patrols did not affect the crime rates.[58]
3. At times, high, intense, short-term levels of police presence and intervention in a community may initially and temporarily deter crime and lower crime rates. However, once the intervention ends, crime rates return to previous levels.[59]

Considering the relationship between deterrence and severity of punishment, can the threat or implementation of severe punishment reduce the crime rate? The research findings are mixed. Some studies report that increasingly tougher laws have a deterrent effect and lower crime rates; but other studies question this relationship.[60] A recent study by the National Center for Policy Analysis examined the relationship between the probability of going to prison and various crime rates. For example, the study reported that as the probability of going to prison increased for the crimes of robbery and murder, the rates for these crimes significantly declined. The study concluded that there is a relationship between the probability of incarceration for a particular crime and a subsequent decline in the rate of that crime.[61]

Deterrence theory also includes the idea that forced retribution for a crime should reduce crime rates. **Retribution** is the notion that a wrongdoer should be forced to "pay back" or compensate for his or her criminal acts. During the 1970s and into the 1980s, there was a return to retributivism and the justice model. The **justice model** stresses the idea that offenders are responsible people and therefore deserve to be punished if they violate the law. Do criminal offenders deserve the punishment they receive from the laws and the courts? Should punishments be appropriate to the type and severity of the crime committed? These are questions central to the concept of "just deserts," which is the pivotal basis of the justice model. **Just deserts** is a justice perspective according to which those who violate others' rights deserve to be punished. The severity of the punishment should also be commensurate with the seriousness of the crime.

In addition to returning to the justice model, the United States in the 1970s and 1980s reverted to a **utilitarian punishment philosophy** to deal with crime. Utilitarianism in punishment is based on the assumption that punishment is necessary to protect society from crime and also to deter offenders, a subject that will be addressed in a later chapter.

An Economic Model of Crime

An economic model of crime assumes that an individual will choose the same course of action when confronted with the same alternatives regarding costs, rewards, and risks.

Do criminals control their own actions and behavior? Do people commit crime when they believe the benefits of crime outweigh the risks? Like earlier classical theories and the modern rational choice theory, the **economic model of crime** is based on the assumption that a person chooses to commit crime. The economic model assumes that when confronted with the same alternatives, a person will choose the same course of action. In other words, criminal behavior follows a

Retribution is the notion that a wrongdoer should be forced to "pay back" or compensate for his or her criminal acts.

The **justice model** stresses the idea that offenders are responsible people and therefore deserve to be punished if they violate the law.

Just deserts is a justice perspective according to which those who violate others' rights deserve to be punished.

Utilitarian punishment philosophy is based on the assumption that punishment is necessary to protect society from crime and also to deter offenders.

The **economic model of crime** stresses that criminal behavior follows a calculation whereby the criminal explores the perceived costs, rewards, and risks of alternative actions.

READING ABSTRACT

Contemporary Classicism: Deterrence and Econometrics, and Implications and Conclusions

BY GEORGE VOLD AND THOMAS BERNARD

This reading examines the economic model of crime and deterrence, and its implications for crime control.
See reading on page 88.

calculation whereby criminals explore the perceived costs, rewards, and risks of alternative actions.

Routine Activities Theory

Routine activities theory stresses the idea that criminals balance the costs and benefits of committing crimes.

Classical theorists explain crime as a rational course of action by offenders who seek to minimize pain and maximize pleasure. Routine activities theory is a product of the classical approach. **Routine activities theory (RAT)** stresses the idea that criminals are not impulsive or unpredictable, because they balance the costs as well as benefits of committing crimes.

In an analysis of crime and routine activities, Lawrence E. Cohen and Marcus Felson consider the trends in crime rates in terms of the changing routine activities of everyday life. RAT explains why crime and delinquency occur in particular places under specific conditions. It does this by focusing on the convergence of motivated offenders, suitable targets, and the absence of capable guardians against a violation. RAT assumes that

Routine activities theory (RAT) stresses the idea that criminals are not impulsive or unpredictable, because they balance the costs as well as benefits of committing crimes.

1. self-interest motivates criminal offenders to commit criminal acts;
2. many individuals may be motivated to break laws.

Suitable targets may be things that are valued (e.g., jewelry, cars, or cash) or people who, when assaulted, provide positive rewards or pleasure to the perpetrator. Guardians are defined as objects (e.g., gates, surveillance cameras, or burglar or auto alarms) or individuals (e.g., guards or police) who are capable of protecting possible targets or victims. To the offender, the presence of protective guardians raises crime costs and lessens target attractiveness.[62]

Predatory violations are illegal acts in which someone definitely and intentionally takes or damages the person or property of another.

RAT studies focus on direct-contact **predatory violations**—illegal acts in which "someone definitely and intentionally takes or damages the person or property of another."[63] Focusing on crime events and not on criminal offenders themselves, RAT examines how structural changes in everyday activity patterns influence crime rates by affecting the convergence in time and space of three requisite conditions for a crime to occur. These three conditions include

1. a motivated offender
2. a suitable target
3. absence of guardianship

One way of examining routine activities theory is to focus on the locations where crimes are most likely to occur. Where, for example, would you expect the theft of textbooks to occur most often? The answer depends on the daily routine activities of typical victims and offenders, and their relationships. It stands to reason that textbook theft is most likely to occur on college campuses; the greater the availability of valuable texts to potential thieves, the greater the probability that such a crime will occur.

For Cohen and Felson, criminality is a given. The concept of routine is derived from the fact that the elements of a criminal act merge together in normal, regular activities. RAT stresses the idea that there are plenty of motivated offenders in society and that it is important to focus on the prevention or deterrence of crime and not worry about the "nature of criminality." If we are to reduce crime in America, the attractiveness of and/or accessibility to the target needs to be reduced.[64] Routine activities theory, then, focuses on criminal events, not on offenders. RAT makes no attempt to account for why some individuals do offend but others do not.

After reading this section, you should be able to

1. explain rational choice theory as an integrated theory in criminology;
2. evaluate deterrence theory and the justice model in relation to studies of crime rates and punishments;
3. describe how the economic model of crime works;
4. briefly describe the major points from Reading 3.1, on contemporary classicism and contemporary positivism;
5. compare and contrast contemporary classicism with ancient classicism in relation to the role of economic theories, based on Reading 3.1;
6. list the assumptions on which the routine activities theory is based.

CHAPTER SUMMARY

This chapter discusses many of the early theoretical explanations for criminal behavior (pp. 63–66). Early scholarly explanations for crime came from a wide variety of fields. Criminologists have traditionally marked the beginning of their discipline with the establishment of Cesare Beccaria's and Jeremy Bentham's classical school of criminology, which purports that people rationally choose to commit criminal acts (pp. 67–72). The positivist school of criminology, founded by Auguste Comte, purports that behavior is determined by measurable factors beyond human control, a principle developed further in the theoretical contributions of Cesare Lombroso, Enrico Ferri, and Raffaele Garofalo (pp. 72–79).

All of these theories from the past have formed a foundation for modern criminology and related fields. Rational choice theory is a reformulation and integration of earlier classical and positivist theories. Rational choice theory stresses the idea that a criminal rationally chooses the crime to commit as well as the target of the crime. It also stresses the idea that a high degree of crime prevention can be achieved by focusing on the situational aspects that influence particular types of criminal behavior (pp. 79–80).

According to deterrence theory, an individual's choice to commit or not commit a crime is influenced by the fear of punishment. According to the economic model of crime, criminal behavior follows a calculation whereby the criminal examines the perceived costs, rewards, and risks of alternative actions. The chapter concludes with an explanation of routine activities theory, which stresses the idea that criminals balance the costs and benefits of committing crimes (pp. 80–83).

Study Guide

Chapter Objectives

- Compare the spiritual and natural explanations for crime.
- Write a brief explanation of the classical school's perspective on crime.
- Briefly explain the state of criminal law in eighteenth-century Europe.
- Briefly list the dimensions of social contract theory.
- Briefly describe Beccaria's beliefs on punishment and its purpose.
- Identify and briefly describe the concept of utilitarianism and Bentham's moral calculus.
- Briefly explain "the greatest happiness."
- Describe Beccaria's and Bentham's views on deterrence and punishment.
- Briefly describe the development of positivism.

- Write a clear and concise statement on what Lombroso's general theory suggests about criminals.
- Briefly outline Ferri's scientific classification of criminals.
- List Ferri's causes of crime, and explain the "science of criminality."
- Briefly explain what Garofalo meant by the term *natural crime*.
- Briefly describe rational choice theory.
- Describe deterrence theory.
- Briefly describe the economic model of crime.
- Briefly describe the major points from Reading 3.1 on contemporary classicism and contemporary positivism.
- Identify the major points of routine activities theory.

Key Terms

Atavism (73)
Beccaria, Cesare (67)
Bentham, Jeremy (69)
Classical school of criminology (66)
Comte, Auguste (72)
Criminal sociology (77)
Deterrence (80)
Deterrence theory (80)
Economic model of crime (81)

Felicitous calculus (70)
Ferri, Enrico (75)
Garofalo, Raffaele (77)
Integrated theory (80)
Just deserts (81)
Justice model (81)
Lombroso, Cesare (73)
Moral calculus (70)
Natural crime (77)

Physical stigmata (73)
Positivism (73)
Predatory violations (82)
Rational choice theory (79)
Retribution (81)
Routine activities theory (RAT) (82)
Utilitarian punishment philosophy (81)
Utilitarianism (70)

Self-Test
Short Answer

1. List the six major theorists and their "schools" examined in this chapter.
2. List three characteristics of law in eighteenth-century Europe.
3. Define social contract theory.
4. Define utilitarianism and moral calculus.
5. Briefly state how Lombroso viewed the criminal.
6. List all of Ferri's causes of crime.

7. Define natural crime.
8. List Garofalo's classes of criminals.
9. List Garofalo's means of elimination.
10. Briefly define contemporary classicism.
11. Describe rational choice theory.
12. Describe routine activities theory.

Multiple Choice

1. Scholars in the field of criminology during the eighteenth and nineteenth centuries came from such fields as
   a. philosophy
   b. medicine
   c. psychiatry
   d. all of the above

2. Classical theorists believe that
   a. all of us have free will
   b. social factors are important in criminal behavior
   c. most crime is economically determined
   d. all of the above

3. Cesare Beccaria's *On Crimes and Punishments*
   a. undermined many cherished beliefs of those in power
   b. was an attack on the prevailing system of justice
   c. was written in response to the positivist school of criminology
   d. *a* and *b*

4. Eighteenth-century European law was characterized by
   a. secret accusations
   b. torture
   c. arbitrary sentences
   d. all of the above

5. Jeremy Bentham believed
   a. that criminals are a primitive throwback on the Darwinian scale of human evolution
   b. that an act should not be judged by an irrational system of absolutes
   c. in the power of the scientific method
   d. *a* and *b*

6. The positivist perspective stressed that much of our behavior is a function of
   a. external forces that are within individual control
   b. external forces that are beyond individual control
   c. internal forces, such as our mental capabilities and biological makeup
   d. *b* and *c*

7. Cesare Lombroso explained crime mainly on the basis of
   a. economic factors
   b. biological characteristics and heredity
   c. social factors
   d. all of the above

8. According to Enrico Ferri, crime is caused by such factors as
   a. race, climate, geographic location, seasonal effects, and temperature
   b. age, sex, and somatic and psychological conditions
   c. density of populations, customs, and religion
   d. all of the above

9. Raffaele Garofalo
   a. accepted the doctrine of free will
   b. believed that crime could not be understood only by using scientific methods

   c. believed in elimination
   d. all of the above

10. According to rational choice theory
    a. a criminal rationally chooses the crime to commit
    b. a criminal rationally chooses the target of the crime
    c. a criminal is irrational in the choice of crime and victim
    d. *a* and *b*

11. According to deterrence theory
    a. criminals are not rational beings who evaluate available information to decide whether a crime is attractive or worthwhile
    b. an individual's choice is influenced by the fear of punishment
    c. virtually all criminal behavior is biologically inherited
    d. virtually all criminal behavior can be explained psychologically

12. The economic model views the decision to commit a crime as
    a. essentially similar to any other decision—that is, it is made on the basis of an analysis of the costs and benefits of the action
    b. a function of one's socioeconomic position in the marketplace
    c. not a function of economic validity
    d. all of the above

13. According to routine activities theory,
    a. criminals are impulsive
    b. criminals are not impulsive or unpredictable
    c. criminals balance the costs as well as benefits of committing crimes
    d. *b* and *c*

14. Routine activities theory focuses on the convergence of
    a. a motivated offender, a suitable target, and a lack of guardians capable of defending the target
    b. unsuitable offenders, unsuitable targets, and capable guardians
    c. routine offenders, routine targets, and routine guardians
    d. none of the above

15. The early explanations for criminal behavior focused on
    a. the psychological reasons for committing crimes
    b. the biochemical causes of crime
    c. the genetic causes of crime
    d. none of the above

True–False

T F 1. Attempts to explain crime date back some three hundred years.

T F 2. The positivist school purports that people rationally choose to commit criminal acts.

T F 3. The classical school purports that behavior is determined by measurable factors beyond individual control.

T F 4. The classical school believes that the major element governing a person's choice of action is the basic human desire to obtain pleasure and avoid pain.

T F 5. Beccaria's blueprint for reform had its roots in social contract theory.

T F 6. Bentham's perspective on human behavior had its roots in the concept of utilitarianism.

T F 7. Beccaria's general theory suggested that criminals can be distinguished from noncriminals by the manifestation of multiple physical anomalies that are atavistic.

T F 8. Garofalo's ideas relegate environmental and social factors to secondary levels of importance.

T F 9. Rational choice theory focuses on the "born criminal."

T F 10. The economic model of crime challenges the assumption that a person chooses to commit crime.

T F 11. Routine activities theory focuses on the criminal offenders themselves, not on criminal events.

Fill-In

1. Criminologists have traditionally marked the beginning of the discipline of criminology with the establishment of Cesare Beccaria's and Jeremy Bentham's _____ school of criminology.

2. The classical school of criminology was founded by _____ and _____.

3. Beccaria believed bad _____, not evil people, were the basis of the crime problem.

4. Beccaria believed that punishment should be based on the pleasure/_____ principle.

5. Bentham developed a moral _____ for estimating the probability that a person will engage in a particular kind of behavior.

6. It was the founder of sociology, _____, who advocated that human behavior and society should be studied using methods similar to those used in the physical sciences.

7. _____ explained criminal behavior on the basis of biological characteristics and heredity.

8. Lombroso is considered to be the father of _____.

9. _____ thought that the positivist school cultivated a "science of criminology and of a social defence against it."

10. Garofalo presents three means of elimination: _____ , _____ , and _____ .

11. _____ theory stresses the idea that an individual's choice to commit or not commit a crime is influenced by the fear of punishment.

12. _____ theory explains why crime and delinquency occur in particular places under specific conditions.

Matching

1. Industrial Revolution
2. Spiritual explanations of crime
3. Beccaria
4. Lombroso
5. Ferri
6. Utilitarianism
7. Moral calculus
8. Comte
9. Natural crime
10. Primitive throwback
11. Routine activities theory
12. Rational choice theory

A. Founder of sociology
B. Bentham
C. Criminal sociology
D. Salem witch trials
E. Garofalo
F. Classical theorist
G. Radical, worldwide social change
H. Atavism
I. Father of criminology
J. The greatest happiness for the greatest number of people
K. Situational aspects of criminal behavior
L. Suitable targets and motivated offenders

Essay Questions

1. Do you believe that many Americans still explain crime using spiritual explanations? Elaborate on your answer.
2. Why, in your thinking, are many of the principles of the classical school of criminology experiencing a revival in criminology today?
3. Do you believe that people have free will and make a choice to commit or not commit a crime? Explain your answer.
4. Examine the growth of positivism and its impact on the field of criminology.
5. Compare and contrast the major principles of the classical and positivist schools of criminology.
6. Do you believe that social, political, and economic factors have anything to do with why a person becomes a criminal? Explain your answer.
7. Does the individual make the choice to commit a crime? Explain you answer.
8. How does routine activities theory explain criminal behavior? Do you agree with this theory? Why or why not?

Contemporary Classicism: Deterrence and Econometrics, and Implications and Conclusions

Source: Theoretical Criminology, Fourth Edition *by George B. Vold and Thomas J. Bernard and Jeffrey B. Snipes, copyright* © 1997 by Oxford University Press, Inc. Used by permission of Oxford University Press, Inc.

BY GEORGE B. VOLD AND THOMAS J. BERNARD

DETERRENCE AND ECONOMETRICS

The classical school was the dominant perspective in criminology for approximately one hundred years, until it was replaced by the positivist search for the causes of crime. After another one hundred years substantial interest returned to the classical perspective in criminology, beginning in the late 1960s. This revival of interest was associated with a dramatic shift away from the positivist-oriented indeterminate sentencing structures and back to the determinate sentences similar to the French Code of 1791.[1]

Two principal branches of contemporary classicism can be identified. The whole question of deterrence has been the subject of voluminous literature in criminology in recent years.[2] Here an attempt has been made to develop the classical perspective in the light of modern knowledge of the human behavioral sciences, as well as through empirical studies of the effects of certainty and severity of punishment on crime rates. While deterrence theory and research has been dominated by criminologists and sociologists, the other branch of contemporary classicism has been dominated by economists. The field of economics holds a view of man that is quite similar to that of the classicists. For example, economic theory holds that a person analyzes the costs and benefits when he decides to buy a hamburger instead of a T-bone steak, or a Volkswagen instead of a Cadillac. The costs and benefits include not merely monetary factors, but factors such as taste, comfort, prestige, and convenience. Econometric techniques[3] have been developed to analyze these factors in terms of the resulting economic choice. Beginning with an article by Gary S. Becker in 1968,[4] many economists have approached crime as a similar economic choice. They have therefore applied their techniques to the analysis of criminal behavior, as well as to the choices of the criminal justice system.

The economic perspective views the decision to commit a crime as essentially similar to any other decision—that is, it is made on the basis of an analysis of the costs and benefits of the action. Because crime is seen as a free choice of the individual, the theories of crime which discuss cultural or biological "causes" are seen as unnecessary.[5] For example, [Richard F.] Sullivan describes the choice of a career as a thief as follows:

The individual calculates (1) all his practical opportunities of earning legitimate income, (2) the amounts of income offered by these opportunities, (3) the amounts of income offered by various illegal methods, (4) the probability of being arrested if he acts illegally, and (5) the probable punishment should he be caught. After making these calculations, he chooses the act or occupation with the highest discounted return. To arrive at a discounted return he must include among his cost calculations the future costs of going to prison if he is apprehended. It is in this sense that the criminal is understood to be a normal, rational, calculating individual.[6]

The benefits of a criminal action may include not only increases in monetary wealth, but also increases in psychological satisfaction as well as the possibility of achieving these increases with very little effort. The expected cost of the crime is normally computed as the total cost associated with the punishment of the crime times the probability that the punishment will be imposed. For example, if the crime is usually punished with a fine of $1,000, and the probability of the punishment being imposed is 1/10, then the expected cost of the crime is $100. If the person can gain more than $100 in the crime, then it would be in his interest to commit it.[7] Often the costs and benefits cannot be computed in monetary terms, such as when the costs include time in prison or the social disapproval of arrest and conviction, or when benefits include the satisfaction of revenge or of outwitting the authorities. However, the individual must still compare these costs and benefits in order to decide whether the action is "worth it" to him or her.

This calculation does not presume that the criminal has a crystal ball to foresee future events. Many people make mistakes in calculating their future pay-offs, and when they do, they end up in dead-end jobs or in bankruptcy. When criminals make similar mistakes, they may end up spending the better part of their lives in prison. As Sullivan says, "The basic economic assumption does not maintain that people do not make mistakes but rather that they do their best given their reading of present and future possibilities and given their resources."[8]

Economic theories can also be used to explain the policies of various criminal justice agencies. The economic view maintains that if society were willing to pay the social costs, virtually all crime could be eliminated.[9] These social costs would include a tremendous increase in budgets of criminal justice agencies, as well as the willingness to convict large numbers of innocent people.[10] By maintaining the crime rate that we have, our society is saying in effect that the cost of reducing crime to a lower level is more than we are willing to pay. If crime were reduced to a lower level, it would result in a net social loss, since the costs would be greater than the benefits we would receive. Therefore, according to economic theory, the present level of crime represents an "optimality condition," the point at which the total social loss for the society is minimized.[11]

IMPLICATIONS AND CONCLUSIONS

The classical and neoclassical schools represent an abandoning of the supernatural as an explanation of criminal behavior. Instead of viewing humans as puppets of the supernatural, the early classical criminologists argued that humans act on the basis of reason and intelligence and therefore are responsible for their own actions. To that extent classical criminology marks the beginnings of the natural approach to criminal behavior.

The classical school also marks the beginnings of the rationalistic, bureaucratic approach to criminal procedure. As such, the classical school was responsible for a wide-ranging reformation and restructuring of the criminal justice system. But after one hundred years of such reforms there was considerable dissatisfaction with the ability of classical ideas to achieve reductions in criminal behavior. This ultimately resulted in a break with the classical system of thinking, beginning with the positive school of Lombroso and his pupils. That school extended to criminology some of the ideas about human behavior that were beginning to dominate biology, medicine, psychiatry, psychology, and sociology at that time. In part, this school proposed an explanation of the failure of classicism to reduce crime: if crime is caused by forces beyond the control of the individual, then punishing the criminal will not be effective. Instead of punishing criminals, positivist criminologists argued that it is necessary to address the causes of criminal behavior whether they be biological, psychological, or social.

The recent revival of interest in classical criminology seems to reflect, at least in part, dissatisfaction with the effectiveness of positivist-oriented policies for the control of criminal behavior, just as the original switch to positivism reflected a dissatisfaction with the effectiveness of classically oriented policies.[12] Whether punishing criminals will be more successful today than it was one hundred years ago remains to be seen. Several recent reviews of the empirical research on the question of deterrence have all concluded that at the present time it is not possible to say whether or to what extent punishments actually deter crime.[13]

The appeal of classicism rests on its promise of crime control through manipulations of the criminal justice enforcement and punishment systems. As such, it is more attractive than the later theories that argue that crime can be reduced only by changing more fundamental social arrangements, such as redistributing legitimate opportunities or changing the capitalist economic system. Ultimately classicism must be judged on the basis of its ability to produce the results it promises.

NOTES

1 See the entire issue of *Corrections Magazine* 3 (3) (Sept. 1977).
2 For a review of theoretical issues, see Franklin E. Zimring and Gordon J. Hawkins, *Deterrence*, University of Chicago Press, Chicago, 1973; Johannes Andenaes, *Punishment and Deterrence*, University of Michigan Press, Ann Arbor, Mich., 1974; and Jack P. Gibbs, *Crime, Punishment, and Deterrence*, Elsevier, New York, 1975. Gibbs's book reviews the empirical studies, as does Alfred Blumstein et al., *Deterrence and Incapacitation*, National Academy of Sciences, Washington, DC, 1978. For a briefer but very thorough presentation of both theory and empirical studies, see E. A. Fattah, "Deterrence: A Review of the Literature," *Canadian Journal of Criminology* 19 (2): 1–119 (Apr. 1977).
3 This term refers to the use of mathematical techniques to test and apply economic theories. See Richard F. Sullivan, "The Economics of Crime: An Introduction to the Literature," *Crime and Delinquency* 19 (1): 138–149 (Apr. 1973).
4 Gary S. Becker, "Crime and Punishment: An Economic Approach," *Journal of Political Economy* 76 (2): 169–217 (Mar.–Apr. 1968).
5 Becker, op. cit., p. 14; Sullivan, op. cit., p. 139.
6 Sullivan, op. cit., p. 141.
7 George J. Stigler, "The Optimum Enforcement of Laws," *Journal of Political Economy* 78: 526–536 (May–June 1970).
8 Sullivan, op. cit., p. 142.
9 Becker, op. cit., pp. 18–19.
10 John R. Harris, "On the Economics of Law and Order," *Journal of Political Economy* 78: 165–174 (Jan.–Feb. 1970). See also Stigler, op. cit., p. 80.
11 Becker, op. cit., pp. 18–24; Stigler, op. cit.; Sullivan, op. cit., p. 143.
12 For example, James Q. Wilson, *Thinking About Crime*, 2nd ed., Basic Books, New York, 1984; Ernest van den Haag, *Punishing Criminals*, Basic Books, New York, 1975.

13 See, for example, Gibbs, op. cit., p. 217; Daniel Nagin, "General Deterrence: A Review of the Empirical Evidence," in Alfred Blumstein, Jacqueline Cohen, and Daniel Nagin, eds., *Deterrence and Incapacitation: Estimating the Effects of Criminal Sanctions on Crime Rates*, National Academy of Sciences, Washington, DC, 1978, p. 136; Charles R. Tittle, *Sanctions and Social Deviance*, Praeger, New York, 1980, p. 24; and Linda S. Anderson, "The Deterrent Effect of Criminal Sanctions: Reviewing the Evidence," in Paul J. Brantingham and Jack M. Kress, eds., *Structure, Law, and Power*, Sage, Beverly Hills, CA, 1979, pp. 120–134.

CRITICAL THINKING

1. What do you think is meant by the term *econometrics*?
2. How can a cost-benefit analysis be applied to crime?
3. How is an economic model of crime rational? As a criminological theory, how is it classical?
4. What is the solution to the crime problem in the neoclassical view?

READING 3.2

Deterrence, General

Source: David L. Myers, "General Deterrence." Copyright © 2004 From Encyclopedia of Criminology, *vol. 1 (pp. 385–389) by Richard A. Wright and J. Mitchwell Miller (Eds.). Reproduced by permission of Taylor & Francis, a division of Informa plc.*

BY DAVID L. MYERS

General deterrence is a major justification for prescribing and imposing punishment in response to law-breaking behavior. When the criminal justice system threatens or inflicts punishment, it is expected that there will be less overall crime than would otherwise occur if no penalties existed. In other words, people in the general population will refrain from committing crime due to a fear of being punished. This belief that individuals will curb or avoid criminal behavior because of the potential adverse consequences is essential to virtually any system of criminal law (Zimring and Hawkins, 1973).

The concept of deterrence usually is traced to the development of the classical school of criminology during the latter half of the 18th century. According to classical criminology, humans are rational beings who are guided by their own free will, and both criminal and law-abiding behavior results from conscious choice. Behavioral decisions are made following a consideration of the costs and benefits associated with various actions, and crime generally is selected when it is deemed more beneficial or less costly than non-criminal behavior. Therefore, in order to deter crime, would-be offenders must be persuaded that likely punishments will outweigh the possible gains achieved through breaking the law.

Based on these underlying beliefs, in 1764 Cesare Beccaria proposed a rational system of punishment in his *Essay on Crimes and Punishment*. In reaction to the often arbitrary and cruel systems of justice that were in place at that time, Beccaria presented a series of criminal justice system reforms. His proposals covered such topics as making laws public and easy to understand, eliminating the torture of suspects, the presumption of innocence until proven guilty, equal treatment under the law, and abolishing the death penalty. Furthermore, he stressed that the central purpose of punishment should be deterrence, and to attain maximum deterrence, punishment should be based on the principles of certainty, severity, and swiftness.

Beccaria specifically argued that to deter crime, punishment must be perceived as a highly probable reaction to criminal behavior. He emphasized the certainty of punishment over its cautioning that overly harsh punishments could actually be counter-productive. In line with classical criminology, Beccaria proposed that deterrence would occur if the harm of a punishment simply exceeded the potential gain from a crime. Finally, he placed great emphasis on swiftness (or celerity), maintaining that punishing offenders as quickly as possible following the commission of a crime would leave a lasting impression. Overall, a strong association between crime and punishment is necessary to ensure that would-be offenders choose not to break the law when deciding on a course of action. Deterrence, then, should occur to the greatest extent when potential offenders believe a punishment will likely and swiftly follow a criminal act, and the sanction will be of adequate strength to outweigh any expected benefits from the crime.

In the later 18th and early 19th centuries, Jeremy Bentham extended the ideas of Beccaria and the classical school of criminology. While maintaining that individual behavior is governed by free will and rational choice, he asserted that humans engage in a process of "hedonistic calculus," whereby they spend much effort weighing the costs and benefits of their behavior and choosing the one that would be expected to maximize pleasure and minimize pain. This, according to Bentham, necessitates a carefully crafted approach to identifying various types of offenders and supplying an exact amount of punishment to be applied to a specific offense. Like Beccaria, he believed that crime could be deterred if punishment was properly provided, and that the criminal justice system should be responsible for ensuring a fair and effective system of punishment. Finally, Bentham was one of the first to suggest that informal sanctions (those coming from outside the criminal justice system) also may be an effective deterrent for criminal behavior.

It is important to note that two separate types of deterrence were inherent in the writings of Beccaria and Bentham. Specific deterrence pertains to the effect of a punishment on the future behavior of an individual who is sanctioned (Andenaes, 1974). This type of deterrence occurs when someone is punished for a crime and subsequently refrains from breaking the law due to a fear of further punishment (e.g., a speeder receives a ticket and drives more slowly in the future to avoid another citation). In contrast, general deterrence refers to the effect of threatened or imposed punishment on other potential offenders (Blumstein, Cohen, and Nagin, 1978). In other words, general deterrence takes place when sanctions are in place and inflicted on law-breakers, and others in the population are thereby discouraged from committing crime (e.g., a vehicle operator sees another driver receiving a ticket and slows down to avoid a similar penalty). Overall, specific deterrence has been thought to impact on offenders who have been caught and punished, whereas general deterrence most often has been applied to those in the general public who have not experienced sanctioning. The discussion that follows is centered on general deterrence.

Although the concept of deterrence is well over 200 years old, it has only been examined through research during the past few decades. Modern scholars have emphasized the certainty and, to a lesser extent, the severity of punishment, although the swiftness of punishment has received little consideration (Blumstein et al., 1978; Paternoster, 1987). Furthermore, deterrence research has progressed in a number of clearly defined states. The findings produced from these studies have not always been consistent, but overall, the best evidence available suggests that the sanctions provided by the criminal justice system do produce a significant general deterrent effect, at least for some people and under certain conditions.

In the later 1960s and early 1970s, deterrence research was conducted at the "objective level," whereby comparisons were made between jurisdictions in terms of their levels of punishment risk and corresponding levels of crime (Blumstein et al., 1978). For example, it was expected that states with higher levels of punishment certainty (i.e., greater rates of arrest or imprisonment for specific crimes) and severity (i.e., lengthier time served for the offense) would exhibit lower crime rates. These studies by and large found inconsistent support for this hypothesis, but it did appear that the certainty of punishment had a greater general deterrent effect than punishment severity (Zimring and Hawkins, 1973). However, it was hard to determine from this research whether levels of punishment impacted on crime, or whether crime rates actually impacted on punishment levels. It could be that jurisdictions with lower crime rates are better able to arrest and incarcerate those who break the law. It was also suggested that at lower levels, punishment certainty and severity might fail to deter, but at higher levels, a "tipping effect" may occur when punishment does become a credible threat. Finally, it was proposed that deterrence could depend more on individual perceptions of punishment certainty and severity, rather than objective risk levels, meaning that someone's personal beliefs about punishment risk might be much more important in guiding their behavior than the actual risks that exist at the objective level (Paternoster, 1987).

This recognition of the importance of individual perceptions in the process of deterrence guided much research from the mid-1970s through the mid-1980s. Numerous cross-sectional studies were conducted to examine whether those who perceived punishment to be a certain and severe response to crime were less likely to self-report criminal behavior than were those who believed there was little risk (Paternoster, 1987). By the early 1980s, many of these studies appeared to indicate a moderately strong inverse relationship between perceptions of certain punishment and various criminal behaviors, as those who perceived a higher likelihood of receiving some sort of punishment reported less prior criminal behavior than did those who perceived a lower likelihood of punishment. This same research generally failed to find a similar inverse relationship between the perceived severity of punishment and illegal acts, because a belief that harsh punishment would be imposed was not found to be associated with less criminal behavior.

The perceptual studies discussed above were also questioned concerning their methodology. In this research, individual perceptions were measured at a given point in time, and then people were asked about their past behavior. Other researchers began to demonstrate with longitudinal (or "panel") data that active participants in crime often do not get caught and that leads them to lower their estimates of punishment risk (Paternoster, 1987). Therefore, the earlier, cross-sectional studies were actually measuring an "experiential effect" of prior behavior on current perceptions of risk, rather than a true deterrent effect of perceived risk on behavior. When the experiential and deterrent effects were separated using a longitudinal design, a much weaker deterrent effect from the perceived certainty of punishment was found than had been suggested through the flawed cross-sectional research. Furthermore, better studies that considered a wider variety of factors that potentially impact on criminal behavior (e.g., rewards, informal sanctions, peer influences, moral beliefs, etc.) found the weakest evidence of a general deterrent effect from the perceived risk of formal sanctions.

By the mid-1980s, perceptual deterrence research seemed to indicate little reason to be optimistic about the general deterrent effect of formal punishments. However, the most methodologically rigorous, longitudinal studies also suggested that people's perceptions of punishment risk were unstable, meaning that these perceptions could change from time to time or situation to situation (Paternoster, 1987). This finding led to a major improvement in recent deterrence research, resulting in conclusions that are more in favor of the presence of general deterrence. In the late 1980s and early 1990s, researchers began to use scenarios or detailed descriptions of risk and if they would commit a crime in the presented setting (e.g., "given the situation described, how likely is it that the person in the scenario would be arrested, and would you commit the crime under the same circumstances?"). Using this technique, risk perceptions and behavioral intentions were measured at the same time, overcoming the problems of experiential effects and unstable risk perceptions that had plagued earlier research. These studies have found that, while controlling for a variety of other factors that may influence behavior, a more highly perceived sanction risk does have a significant deterrent effect on a variety of criminal behaviors (Nagin, 1998). Moreover, this research shows that perceptions of sanction risk depend greatly on the context of the situation that encompasses such things as relationship to the victim, presence of witnesses, security devices, and so on.

In addition to the recent scenario-based studies that suggest formal sanctions do produce a general deterrent effect (particularly when the perceived certainty of punishment is high), other types of research have also provided evidence that the presence of legal penalties deters crime. Several studies in a variety of countries have used a time-series design to examine the effect of targeted policy interventions, such as police drunk-driving checkpoints and crackdowns on drug markets (Nagin, 1998). The evidence suggests that these efforts are usually successful in producing an initial general deterrent effect, again based mainly on the increase in punishment certainty that occurs as a result of the intervention, rather than any increase in punishment severity (Sherman, 1990). For instance, Ross's (1982) international research on the impact of police crackdowns on drunk-driving consistently reveals significant decreases in automobile fatalities in the aftermath of highly publicized checkpoints. Unfortu-

nately, this deterrent effect typically begins to decay over time, thereby limiting effectiveness. However, the decrease is often slow and gradual, probably due to individual perceptions of elevated risk taking some time to change. Based on this research, it has been argued that general deterrence can be maximized by a regular rotation of police enforcement strategies that can both create initial deterrence and leave behind "residual" deterrence once police move to another location (Sherman, 1990).

In addition to the time-series research discussed above, the general deterrent effect of the police has been examined through other methods. First, a consideration has been made of what would happen if the police ceased to exist. Studies of police strikes have examined the extreme situation where punishment risk has been greatly reduced or eliminated, due to the police not being available to make arrests. The evidence from a variety of jurisdictions, including the U.S., Europe, and Canada, consistently suggests that in times of minimal or no threat of law enforcement, serious crime substantially and suddenly increases (Andenaes, 1974; Sherman 1995). For example, Makinen and Hannu's (1980) study of crime in Helsinki before and during a police strike uncovered large increases in violent crime and emergency room admissions for assault related injuries following the initiation of the strike. Furthermore, research also suggests that cities with greater numbers of police on duty have less crime, apparently due to the increase in punishment risk associated with more police (Nagin, 1998). It appears, then, that police are needed for general deterrence purposes, and again the importance of punishment certainty comes to the forefront.

Other police research has sought to clarify the impact of what police do and where and how they do it. In the mid-1970s, a highly publicized study conducted by the Kansas City, Missouri, police department appeared to indicate that varying amounts of police patrol presence had no effect on crime (Sherman, 1995). Many scholars concluded that although some police presence was obviously needed (in light of the evidence from police strikes), it was foolish to think that more specific police practices could substantially reduce crime. Since that time, however, other research has produced contrary findings. In general, this evidence suggests that a proactive approach, targeting specific places, people, and times, can produce a significant general deterrent effect.

To begin, it is known that crime does not occur in random locations, as certain "hot spot" sites (e.g., certain bars, intersections, parking lots, etc.) are much more crime prone than other places (Sherman, 1995). This piece of information conflicts with the traditional approach to law enforcement that seeks to provide even police visibility throughout a jurisdiction. With this in mind, research has demonstrated that when police patrol efforts are concentrated in high crime areas, crime can be reduced (Sherman, 1995). Other studies suggest that aggressive policing of minor crime and disorder (e.g., public drunkenness, prostitution, or disorderly conduct) can produce a more general deterrent effect on serious crime (Nagin, 1998). Finally, similar findings have also been produced when police focus their efforts on confiscating illegally carried weapons and monitoring known offenders (Sherman, 1995).

Research on the impact of the police supports the presence of a baseline general deterrent effect that appears to be enhanced punishment certainty. Other studies have considered whether increasing the severity of punishment generates any crime reduction effect. Over the past 25 years, prison populations have grown rapidly, and recent reforms (e.g., mandatory and determinant sentencing, parole abolition, transferring juveniles to adult court) are often supported on the grounds that they will deter crime. Unfortunately, there is no clear answer to the question of how much general deterrence has been produced from these efforts. Some research suggests that the impact has been negligible, whereas other evidence indicates a significant or dramatic effect (Myers, 2001; Nagin, 1998). These mixed findings are further complicated by the difficulty associated with separating deterrent effects from incapacitating and rehabilitative effects (i.e., crime could be reduced simply by incarcerating offenders, rehabilitating them, or both). Furthermore, there is little support for any general deterrent effect produced by modern and highly popular incarceration policies directed at drug offenders. In fact, these strategies may actually increase the attractiveness of other crimes to potential offenders. All in all, it seems that efforts to increase punishment severity are not nearly as successful in producing general deterrence as those directed at increasing punishment certainty.

In addition to the major areas of research discussed to this point, there have been other efforts to extend the study of general deterrence beyond the restraining effect of the threat or use of formal, legal punishments. Several scholars have suggested that formal sanctions may deter best when they lead to informal sanctions (Andenaes, 1974; Zimring and Hawkins, 1973; Nagin, 1998). Here, people are deterred from crime because they fear such negative consequences as losing a job, being dismissed from school, or receiving disapproval from significant others. Informal sanctions could also be internal or self-inflicted, as in the case of feelings of remorse and shame. When researchers have included these types of punishments in their studies, they have often been found to inhibit crime better than the threat of formal sanctions (Nagin, 1998). It should be noted, though, that for informal sanctions to deter, individuals must have a stake in conformity (i.e., they must have something to lose). Obviously, if someone has few valued social relationships, a lack of commitment to conventional activities, and poor moral values, it would be hard to expect that the threat of informal sanctions would inhibit their criminal behavior.

Another area of interest concerns the importance of formal sanction delivery. First, it is illogical to believe that general deterrence will occur if a sanction threat is not viewed as credible (Nagin, 1998). If policies are not administered as intended or if penalties are rarely imposed (owing to a lack of enforcement of the law, plea bargaining, or some other reason), perceptions of punishment risk are likely to be low. Therefore, general deterrence probably will be weak or nonexistent if the population has knowledge that punishment will not be imposed for certain behavior (e.g., in the case of drug laws not being enforced in certain locations or jurisdiction). Another important and related factor concerns perceptions of the fairness of the sanction. If police officers, prosecutors, judges, or juries believe that a punishment is being unfairly threatened or imposed, they may act to eliminate the sanction or reduce its magnitude. This process likely will impact on punishment credibility, resulting in diminished general deterrence.

Much has been learned about general deterrence over the past 30 years. However, as discussed by Nagin (1998), there is a strong need for further research and theoretical development. Although the weight of the evidence suggests that formal and informal sanctions do produce at least a marginal, short-term, general deterrent effect (i.e., people seem to at least curtail their criminal behavior under certain circumstances because of the fear of punishment), relatively little is known about any longer-term effects. Secondly, although the importance of individual perceptions of punishment risk has been established, it is not yet clear as to how these risk perceptions are formed (e.g., by some overall knowledge of criminal justice system effectiveness, information obtained from others, or by personal experience with sanctioning). Third, recent research suggests that some targeted policy interventions (e.g., drunk driving crackdowns, hot spot policing) can produce a general deterrent effect, but questions remain concerning the significance of how these efforts are implemented in different locations and under various circumstances. Finally, the discrepancy between policies in their intended form and the way they are actually administered should be a central issue in the continued study of general deterrence.

REFERENCES AND FURTHER READING

Andenaes, J. (1974). *Punishment and Deterrence*. Ann Arbor, MI: University of Michigan Press.

Beccaria, C. (1986). *Die delitti e delle pene*, 1764; as *On Crimes and Punishments*, translated by D. Young. Indianapolis, IN: Hackett Publishing.

Bentham, J. (1962). An introduction to the principles of morals and legislation, in J. Browning (Ed.), *The Works of Jeremy Bentham*. New York: Russell and Russell.

Blumstein, A., Cohen, J., and Nagin, D. (1978). *Deterrence and Incapacitation: Estimating the Effects of Criminal*

Sanctions on Crime Rates. Washington, DC: National Academy of Sciences.

Makinen, T. and Hannu, T. (1980). The 1976 police strike in Finland. *Scandinavian Studies in Criminology*, 7.

Myers, D.L. (2001). *Excluding violent youths from adult court: The effectiveness of legislative waiver*. New York: LFB Scholarly Publishing.

Nagin, D.S. (1998). Criminal deterrence research at the outset of the twenty-first century, in M. Tonry (Ed.), *Crime and Justice: A Review of Research*, Vol. 23, Chicago, IL: University of Chicago Press.

Paternoster, R. (1987). The deterrent effect of the perceived certainty and severity of punishment: A review of the evidence and issues, *Justice Quarterly*, 4 (1987).

Ross, L.H. (1982). *Deterring the Drinking Driver: Legal Policy and Social Control*. Lexington, MA: D.C. Heath.

Sherman, L.W. (1990). Police crackdowns: Initial and residual deterrence, in M. Tonry and N. Morris (Eds.). *Crime and Justice: A Review of Research*, Vol. 12, Chicago, IL: University of Chicago Press.

Sherman, L.W. (1995). The police, in J.Q. Wilson and J. Petersilia (Eds.), *Crime*, San Francisco: Institute for Contemporary Studies.

Zimring, F.E. and Hawkins, G.J. (1973). *Deterrence: The Legal Threat in Crime Control*. Chicago, IL: The University of Chicago Press.

READING 3.3

Deterrence, Specific

Source: David L. Myers, "Specific Deterrence." Copyright © 2004 from Encyclopedia of Criminology, *Vol. 1 (pp. 389–393) by Richard A. Wright and J. Mitchell Miller (Eds.). Reproduced by permission of Taylor & Francis, a division of Informa plc.*

BY DAVID L. MYERS

Along with general deterrence, specific or special deterrence is commonly offered as a major reason for punishing criminal offenders. When known lawbreakers are punished for their behavior, there is usually an expectation that they will refrain from committing further crime due to a fear of additional punishment. In other words, it is anticipated that the experience of some unpleasant punishment will inhibit offenders from breaking the law in the future. As first discussed by Gibbs (1975), it may be that for some offenders the experience of punishment will lead to a complete cessation of criminal behavior (i.e., absolute deterrence), whereas others subsequently may exhibit a reduction in the seriousness or frequency of their offense (i.e., restrictive deterrence). In general, the widespread belief in specific deterrence often leads to calls for stricter law enforcement and harsher sentencing, as applying more certain and severe sanctions would seem to enhance the specific deterrent effect.

Specific deterrence, like general deterrence, has its roots in the development of the classical school of criminology during the 1970s. Based on the classical school's notion that humans are rational beings, guided by free will and conscious choice, it seems logical that those who are punished for committing crime would choose not to do so again. Assuming that the administered sanction was of great enough magnitude to outweigh the gains achieved through breaking the law, punished offenders subsequently should decide on a course of action that would not trigger further adverse consequences. These beliefs were inherent in the writings of both Cesare Beccaria and Jeremy Bentham in the latter 18th and early 19th centuries, and the idea that criminals will alter their behavior in response to imposed punishment remains highly popular among politicians and the public alike.

Unfortunately, the question of how legal punishments actually affect future criminal behavior is not an easy one to answer. An enduring debate in the field of criminology concerns whether formal sanctions reduce or amplify future criminal offending. In other words, rather than producing a specific deterrent effect, the experience of legal punishments could increase the future offending of those who are sanctioned. This increase in criminal behavior may be due to diminished opportunities for success in legitimate activities (e.g., school or jobs), or it may arise through a process of self-identification and value development in which the individual who is "labeled" a criminal adopts the norms and behavior patterns that are characteristic of the label (Paternoster and Iovanni, 1989). In any case, in contrast to the notion of specific deterrence, being sanctioned or negatively labeled might actually increase someone's involvement in future criminal behavior that has been referred to as a "deviance amplification" (or "backfire") effect.

While studying the effects of legal sanctions requires recognition of the two contradicting behavioral predictions discussed above, the task of conducting research on this topic is made even more difficult by the potential obstacle of selection bias (Smith and Paternoster, 1990). For example, a simple test of whether formal punishments have any effect on subsequent criminal behavior could involve comparisons of future offending across two or more groups that naturally received different court dispositions (e.g., diversion, probation, boot camp, or incarceration). In this case, the findings could indicate that offenders receiving harsher punishments are more likely to recidivate in the future than are those receiving more lenient sanctions that would appear to suggest that harsher punishments fail to provide specific deterrence. However, the design of this hypothetical study is problematic, as assignment to the groups is the result of a nonrandom process where judges are more likely to sentence high-risk offenders (i.e., those committing more serious crimes and/or having more extensive offending histories) to harsher dispositions. These individuals therefore would be more likely to commit future crime regardless of the punishment imposed. Selection bias, then, is a major concern when groups under study differ in terms of more than just the "treatment" that was received. Therefore, research on the specific deterrent effect of formal sanctions needs to be interpreted with caution.

One area of relevant research involves examining the impact that arresting juveniles has on their future behavior. A few early studies suggested that arresting young offenders might escalate (rather than deter) their future offending, although this research tended to suffer from such methodological problems as small sample sizes and poorly matched treatment and control groups. A study by Smith and Gartin (1989) improved upon those earlier efforts. Using data on police contacts for all males born in Racine, Wisconsin, in 1949 and followed until age 25, the authors examined the influence of arrest on subsequent criminal behavior. Contrary to earlier research, Smith and Gartin uncovered evidence that supported the presence of specific deterrence. While controlling for the seriousness of the current offense and the extent of prior offense, being arrested was found to reduce future criminal behavior among those offenders who were arrested as compared to those who were contacted by police but not arrested. More specifically, being arrested was associated with an increased probability of desistance from crime for novice or new offenders, but as offenders acquired

more police contacts, the effect of arrest on future police contacts diminished. Still, for those offenders who persisted in their criminal behavior, being arrested increased the time until next police contact. Overall, arrest was found to have a consistently negative effect on the total number of future police contacts.

Whereas the research discussed above focused on the future offending of juveniles who were apprehended relative to those who were not, other studies have looked at the effects of varying degrees of punishment on known offenders. In the much debated and somewhat controversial "Prove Experiment," delinquent boys in Utah were randomly assigned to experimental and control groups (Empey and Erickson, 1972). The experimental intervention was community based and provided intensive treatment services. Comparisons were made with a randomly selected group that had been placed on regular probation, as well as a matched group that was institutionalized in a training school. The effectiveness of the treatment program was evaluated based on arrests both during program participation and after the treatment had ended.

Empey and Erickson (1972) reported that boys in the community-based program were significantly less delinquent while under supervision than those placed on regular probation, and they were no more delinquent than youths in the training school. Juveniles in the latter group committed as much delinquency while at home on short furloughs or following escape as did the experimental group that was free in the community. An analysis of postprogram recidivism revealed little difference between the experimental and control groups. However, when preprogram arrests were compared to postprogram arrests, the results supported both the community program and institutionalization as an effective deterrent to offending. Compared with probation, lower case arrests were reduced by 25% for those juveniles who were institutionalized and by 70% for those in community-based programs.

In a somewhat similar study, Murray and Cox (1979) examined chronic delinquents in Chicago who were either incarcerated in a state reformatory or were diverted to one of several less-custodial community-based programs. All of the youths had lengthy records of delinquency, although those who were chosen for the community programs were presumed to be somewhat less dangerous and perhaps more amenable to treatment as compared to the incarcerated offenders. However, the study did produce several striking outcomes that would appear to support a deterrent effect from increasingly severe formal sanctions. A comparison of preprogram and postprogram delinquent behavior revealed a larger reduction in offending among youths sent to reformatories relative to those who remained in the community. Additionally, for youths who remained in the community, the greatest reduction in arrests occurred among those who experienced the most restrictive forms of supervision. The authors suggested that the findings indicated evidence of a "suppression effect" of recidivism brought about by restrictive sanctions, and that court mandated intervention is the most effective deterrent to chronic juvenile offending. As with the Provo Experiment, these conclusions can be challenged on the grounds that they could be the product of subject maturation over time and on the issue of whether the decline in official arrests represented a decrease in criminal behavior or an increase in the ability to avoid apprehension.

Subsequent researchers studying the effects of varying levels of formal punishment sought to improve the methodology of earlier works. Klein (1986) randomly assigned 306 juvenile arrestees, all initially considered referable for further processing, to four different conditions: release, referral to a social service program, referral to a social service program with purchase of treatment, and formal petition for prosecution. By the end of a six month follow-up period, a trend had emerged that as the level of case processing increased, so did the chances of rearrest. This trend continued through a 27-month follow-up period, with released offenders rearrested less commonly than all others, and petitioned offenders rearrested most commonly. In the middle, there was a widening gap between the two social service conditions. The purchase of treatment, designed to ensure a greater level of rehabilitation, actually yielded an increasingly greater number of arrests.

In general, Klein's (1986) findings on future rearrests indicated that diversion to a community agency was less harmful than petitioning to juvenile court, but more harmful than outright release. In a more detailed study of the same issue, Wooldredge (1988) examined the relative effectiveness of 12 different juvenile court dispositions on eliminating recidivism among 2038 youthful offenders in Illinois. Court actions ranged from case dismissals to incarceration, with a variety of combinations employed. Recidivism was measured based on future juvenile and adult arrests during a follow-up period of three to seven years. While controlling for a wide range of individual and environmental characteristics (but not eliminating the possibility of selection bias), a combination of probation supervision and community treatment was found to be associated with the least recidivism. Contrary to the findings of Klein (1986), 8 of 11 dispositional options yielded lower recidivism rates than the case dismissal option. Shorter terms of supervision and longer terms of community treatment were found to be effective in eliminating and prolonging recidivism, whereas longer terms of incarceration were found to be counterproductive.

Research by Gottfredson and Barton (1993) would appear, at least at first glance, to contradict the findings of Klein (1986) and Wooldredge (1988). Their study investigated the effects of the 1988 closing of the Montrose Training School in Maryland. A group of 673 youths who had been incarcerated in the institution was compared to a group of 254 youths who had a high statistical probability of being institutionalized, but juveniles in the latter group did not go to Montrose because they were referred to the Department of Juvenile Services after admissions had ceased. These youths spent little or no time in any other institution and were instead placed in community-based programs. The authors found that during a 2.5-year follow-up period, the incarcerated juveniles had significantly fewer arrests than the noninstitutionalized youths, but the difference was less substantial when only serious offenses were considered. Nevertheless, the results indicated that recidivism was greater among youths in the community-based programs than among those who were incarcerated, which would imply a specific deterrent, rehabilitative, or combined effect from the more restrictive sanction. However, this study was conducted immediately after the closing of the institution, when the community programs were at the earliest stages of implementation. It may be that if the less restrictive programs had been operating for a longer period of time, the quality of services provided would have been greater, and different results would have occurred.

To continue with the theme of the effects of varying degrees of punishment, several studies have examined the juvenile court's response to offenders referred for the first time. Brown and his colleagues (Brown, Miller, Jenkins, and Rhodes, 1991) reported on a random sample of 500 juveniles who were adjudicated delinquent in Pennsylvania between 1960 and 1975. Their analyses indicated that whereas the type of disposition (i.e., probation vs. placement facility) was not related to future criminal behavior, adjudication at first court referral was associated with less recidivism than was postponed adjudication. Additionally, juveniles who were not adjudicated on their first referral had a rate of ending up in prison as an adult that was double that of youths who were adjudicated on their first referral. In a similar study, Jacobs (1990) reported slightly different findings. Among first-time juvenile court referrals, youths who were formally processed displayed less recidivism than those who were diverted. However, for those juveniles placed under formal court supervision, youths who received out-of-home placements exhibited greater recidivism than did those who received in-home supervision. Finally, in a recent study from the same mold, Minor, Hartmann, and Terry (1997) found that for first-time juvenile court referrals, there was minimal relationship between type of court action and recidivism. The one exception was that for persons entering adulthood during the follow-up period, those who had been formally petitioned for further processing during the first court action were significantly more likely to be charged in adult court than those who were diverted.

The findings of Brown et al. (1991), Jacobs (1990), and Minor et al. (1997), although varying somewhat appear consistent with those of Klein (1986) and Wooldredge (1988).

None of these studies found support for a specific deterrent effect from the harshest of formal sanctions. Some of the findings indicate better results from outright release relative to more intermediate community-based programs, although the weight of the evidence appears to support formal supervision in a structured community setting. The results of these studies contrast with those of Murray and Cox (1979) and Gottfredson and Barton (1993), who found support for institutionalization over other less restrictive programs. It is important to point out that the research by Murray and Cox (1979) and Gottfredson and Barton (1993) focused on more serious and frequent offenders. It is quite possible that the specific deterrent effect of legal punishments varies with the extent of past involvement in delinquent or criminal activity among those who are sanctioned. In other words, formal sanctions may have a different effect on beginning offenders than on experienced offenders.

As previously discussed, Smith and Gartin (1989) found arrest to be associated with an increased probability of desistance among less experienced offenders more so than among the more experienced. Along these same lines, the literature appears to indicate that youths referred to juvenile court for the first time and offenders referred for relatively minor delinquent behaviors exhibit less recidivism when they are not forced to undergo incarceration (Jacobs, 1990; Klein, 1986; Minor et al., 1997; Wooldredge, 1988). On the other hand, for the most serious and frequent offenders, institutional confinement may be an effective response that reduces the likelihood of recidivism (Gottfredson and Barton, 1993; Murray and Cox, 1979).

The answer to the question of whether imposing formal sanctions provides specific deterrence probably is not as clear-cut as the previous paragraph would indicate. The final conclusion may be closer to the argument of Sherman (1993), who claimed that legal punishments can either reduce, increase, or have no effect on future criminal activity, depending on a variety of factors related to the offender, offense, and social setting. In presenting a theory of "defiance," Sherman further suggested that the future criminal behavior of formally sanctioned individuals will be influenced by such things as the degree to which offenders perceive punishment as legitimate, the strength of the social bonds that offenders have with the sanctioning agent and the community, and the extent to which offenders accept the sanctioning without becoming angry and feeling rejected. According to this perspective, rather than asking if imposing punishment on those who break the law deters future offending, it may be much more useful to consider under what conditions various types of sanctions reduce, increase, or have no significant effect on future crimes.

As reviewed by Sherman (1993), research has shown that people tend to obey the law more when they believe a criminal sanction has been administered fairly. On the other hand, those who perceive that they have experienced unjust sanctioning (e.g., by courts or the police) are less likely to comply with the law in the future. Furthermore, a number of well-designed, randomized experiments that examined the impact of arrest on future domestic violence found that arrest reduced repeat domestic violence among employed men who were married, but increased it among those who were unemployed and unmarried. Finally, there is at least limited evidence that older people, who generally have more of a stake in conformity, are more effectively deterred by formal sanctions than are younger people. These findings also suggest that formal sanctions are more likely to provide specific deterrence for those from "in-groups," while punished individuals from "out-groups" are less likely to reduce (and may even increase) future offending. This might explain, for example, why juveniles who are transferred to adult court for prosecution and sentencing consistently exhibit greater, more serious, and faster recidivism as compared to similar youths who are retained in juvenile court (Myers, 2001). It is likely that on average, transferred offenders are more weakly tied to conventional society, and they reasonably could perceive a greater level of unfair treatment coming from the criminal justice system.

A final area of theory and research relevant to the topic of specific deterrence is that of situational crime prevention. A number of countries, such as England, France, Sweden, and the Netherlands, have devoted much attention and research toward preventing future crime through the use of techniques other than traditional law enforcement and criminal justice system efforts (Tonry and Farrington, 1995). Situational crime prevention is one such approach, which, like the notion of specific deterrence, assumes that offenders assess the risk, effort, and payoff in deciding whether to commit a crime. Along these lines, then, offenders could be deterred from committing future crime by increasing the perceived efforts and risks associated with certain criminal behaviors, reducing the anticipated rewards from these same acts, or inducing guilt or shame on the part of the offender (Clarke and Homel, 1997). The belief that offenders are capable of making choices, and that these choices are shaped by a variety a factors surrounding a specific criminal incident, links situational crime prevention with rational choice theory, a modern version of deterrence theory.

As reviewed by Clarke and Homel (1997) and others, situational techniques have been applied internationally in response to diverse criminal behaviors. Corresponding research suggests that these efforts have been successful in reducing drunk driving, income tax evasion, sexual harassment, and theft, in such places as Australia, Great Britain, and in the U.S. Although many of these efforts would appear to provide both a general and specific deterrent effect, some strategies focus on preventing repeat crime by known offenders. For example, along the lines of inducing guilt or shame on the part of an offender, the use of family or community accountability conferences has spread through many countries, including New Zealand, Australia, Singapore, Ireland, South Africa, Canada, the United Kingdom, and U.S. (Braithwaite, 1999). The goal of this "restorative justice" approach is for victims, offenders, and family and community members to participate in forming a collective response to a specific offense. A strong emphasis is placed on victim empowerment and offender reintegration into the community, with agreed-upon sanctions often being informal and less punitive in nature than traditional justice system punishments. As discussed by Braithwaite (1999), this approach has been found effective in preventing future crime and delinquency among a variety of juvenile and adult offenders, although further research is needed.

To sum up, research on the specific deterrent effect of formal sanctions has not established that punishing offenders will consistently reduce their future criminal behavior. This suggests that expectations for a uniform effect from various punishment efforts, common among politicians and the public, are unrealistic. It does appear that a more certain and moderate justice system response (e.g., arrest, adjudication, and supervision with treatment) provides more benefit than a more severe response (e.g., incarceration), but even this conclusion is based on mixed evidence. Furthermore, it maybe that for the most serious and frequent offenders, specific deterrence will only take place following harsher or lengthier punishment. To add to the complexity of this matter, the way that offenders are affected by punishment may be strongly influenced by a number of factors. To this end, the way that sanctioned offenders perceive the fairness of their punishment, the role that social bonds play in the punishment process, the issue of distinguishing specific deterrence from defiance, and the role of situational crime prevention and restorative justice in deterring future crime all promise to be important areas of continued research.

REFERENCES AND FURTHER READING

Beccaria, C. (1986). *Die delitti e delle pene,* 1764, as *On Crimes and Punishments,* translated by D. Young. Indianapolis, IN: Hackett Publishing.

Bentham, J. (1962). An introduction to the principles of morals and legislation, in J. Browning (Ed.), *The Works of Jeremy Bentham,* New York: Russell and Russell.

Braithwaite, J. (1999). Restorative justice: Assessing optimistic and pessimistic accounts, in M. Torny (Ed.), *Crime and Justice: A review of Research,* Vol. 25, Chicago: University of Chicago Press.

Brown, W.K., Miller, T.P., Jenkins, R.L., and Rhodes, W.A. (1991). The human costs of 'giving the kid another chance', *International Journal of Offender Therapy and Comparative Criminology,* 35.

Clarke, R.V., and Homel, R. (1997). A revised classification of situational crime prevention techniques, in S.P. Lab, (Ed.), *Crime Prevention at a Crossroads,* Cincinnati, OH: Anderson Publishing.

Empey, L.T. and Erickson, M.L. (1972). *The Provo Experiment: Evaluating Community Control of Delinquency.* Lexington, MA: D.C. Heath.

Gibbs, J.P. (1975). *Crime, Punishment, and Deterrence.* New York: Elsevier.

Gottfredson, D.C. and Barton, W.H. (1993). Deinstitutionalization of juvenile offenders, *Criminology,* 31.

Jacobs, M.D. (1990). *Screwing the System and Making It Work,* Chicago, IL: University of Chicago Press.

Klein, M.W. (1986). Labeling theory and delinquency policy: An experimental test. *Criminal Justice and Behavior,* 13.

Minor, K.I., Hartmann, D.J., and Terry, S. (1997). Predictors of juvenile court actions and recidivism, *Crime & Delinquency,* 43.

Murray, C.A. and Cox, L.A. (1979). *Beyond Probation: Juvenile Corrections and the Chronic Delinquent,* Beverly Hills, CA: Sage Publications.

Myers, D.L. (2001). *Excluding Violent Youths from Adult Court: The Effectiveness of Legislative Waiver,* New York: LFB Scholarly Publishing.

Paternoster, R. and Iovanni, L.A. (1989). The labeling perspective and delinquency: An elaboration of the theory and an assessment of the evidence, *Justice Quarterly,* 6.

Sherman, L.W. (1993). Defiance, deterrence, and irrelevance: A theory of the criminal sanction, *Journal of Research in Crime and Delinquency,* 30.

Smith, D.A. and Gartin, P.A. (1989). Specifying specific deterrence: The influence of arrest of future criminal activity, *American Sociological Review,* 54.

Smith, D.A. and Paternoster, R. (1990). Formal processing and future delinquency: Deviance amplification as a selection artifact, *Law and Society Review,* 24.

Tonry, M. and Farrington, D.P. (1995). *Building a Safer Society: Strategic Approaches to Crime Prevention.* Chicago, IL: University of Chicago Press.

Wooldredge, J.D. (1988). Differentiating the effects of juvenile court sentences on eliminating recidivism, *Journal of Research in Crime and Delinquency,* 25.

Biological Explanations for Criminal Behavior

4.1 INTRODUCTION: BIOLOGICAL PERSPECTIVES

This chapter explores the roles of biological factors in explaining criminal behavior. Biological theories of crime stress that criminal behavior is a product of a person's physical or biological characteristics. For example, some theories stress the idea that delinquent and criminal behavior may be related to the physical appearance or properties of the individual. Others stress the importance of hereditary and genetic factors (inherited criminal traits) or the influence of biochemical and neurophysiological factors. Some theorists believe certain biological factors increase the probability that a person will act criminally but do not necessarily determine the behavior; that is, to understand criminal behavior, one must consider the interaction between a person's biological makeup and the environment. Scholars of crime term these combination theories **biosocial theories**.[1]

During the past several decades, modern biological research and theory have stressed the importance and influence of these factors on criminal behavior: genetic influences, such as chromosomal abnormalities; biochemical factors, such as dietary and hormonal imbalances; and neurophysiological factors, such as brain-wave abnormalities and brain dysfunction. This chapter examines these and other similar factors in an attempt to provide some degree of insight into different types of delinquent and criminal behavior.

This chapter

- focuses on genetics and its relationship to criminal behavior (section 4.2);
- reports on the history of research on body measurements and other physical characteristics of criminals (section 4.2);
- summarizes research on criminal behavior based on twin studies and adoption studies (section 4.2);
- analyzes biochemical causes of abnormal behavior, including dietary factors, exposure to chemicals in the environment, hormonal changes, and effects of alcohol and drug abuse (section 4.3);
- considers neurophysiological causes such as injuries, abnormalities, or dysfunctions of the central nervous system, as risk factors for violent or criminal behavior (section 4.4).

4.2 CRIMINALITY AND GENETICS

Many studies have uncovered a link between genetic factors and criminal behavior. Early criminologists, who did not have the benefit of modern knowledge about genetics, studied the physical characteristics of criminals in order to identify those features that represented the "criminal type" of person. They believed that a criminal's biological inferiority assuredly produced visible physical characteristics that would distinguish him or her from noncriminals. In other words, according to this perspective, the explanation of criminal and delinquent behavior is in inherited biological inferiority that manifests itself in a variety of physical characteristics.

Recall, for example, Cesare Lombroso's attempt during the late nineteenth century to explain crime on the basis of physical characteristics and heredity.[2] On the basis of various physical and cranial measurements of known criminals, Lombroso developed the theory that certain persons engaged in crime are "born criminals." He believed that criminals resemble lower, apelike ancestors. Examples of physical characteristics that supposedly reflect this atavistic type of individual are an asymmetrical face, a twisted nose, unusually large ears, fleshy lips, and long arms.[3]

Lombroso's theories were eventually disproved, but research into the hereditary and **constitutional** factors of crime continued. A 1938 analysis of studies by thirty-five researchers suggested that there is no relationship between physical characteristics and crime.[4] In addition, Charles Goring studied Lombroso's research and found it unscientific. In his own research, published in 1913, Goring developed the following conclusions, which have been accepted by most modern-day criminologists: "We have exhaustively compared, with regard to many physical characteristics, different kinds of criminals with each other, and criminals, as a class, with the law-abiding public. . . . Our results nowhere confirm the evidence [of a physical criminal type], nor justify the allegation of criminal anthropologists. They challenge their evidence at almost every point. In fact, both with regard to measurements and the presence of physical anomalies in criminals, our statistics present a startling conformity with similar statistics of the law-abiding class. Our inevitable conclusion must be that *there is no such thing as a physical criminal type.*"[5]

Studies of Body Measurements

Researchers such as E. A. Hooton, William Sheldon and Ernst Kretchmer, Sheldon and Eleanor Glueck, and Juan Cortés found links between criminality and body type.

E. A. Hooton did not agree with Goring's conclusion that there is no such thing as a physical criminal type. In his classic study of thousands of criminals and noncriminals, he uncovered a "significant difference between criminals and civilians [noncriminals]" and indicated that "criminals are inferior to civilians in nearly all their bodily measurements." He also believed "the inferiority (probably) is due to heredity and not to situation or circumstance."[6]

There were many criticisms of Hooton's research and position. One criticism centered on his rationale for translating differences between the noncriminal and criminal groups into evidence of inferiority in the criminal group: "Unless there is independent evidence of the inferiority of certain kinds of physical characteristics (for example, low foreheads), conclusions regarding inferiority must be drawn from the association with criminality. This is a nice illustration of circular reasoning—use criminality to discover the inferiority, then turn around and use the inferiority to explain or account for the criminality. . . . [Also] Hooton . . . argued that physical inferiority is inherited, but presented little or no evidence for his claims."[7]

More recent research into the hereditary and constitutional factors of crime is found in the studies of William Sheldon and Ernst Kretchmer. Sheldon and Kretchmer attempted to demonstrate a relationship between certain body types or builds and various aspects of personality. In turn, attempts have been made to demonstrate that some of these body-mind types are particularly prone to crime and delinquency. For example, Sheldon identified three major

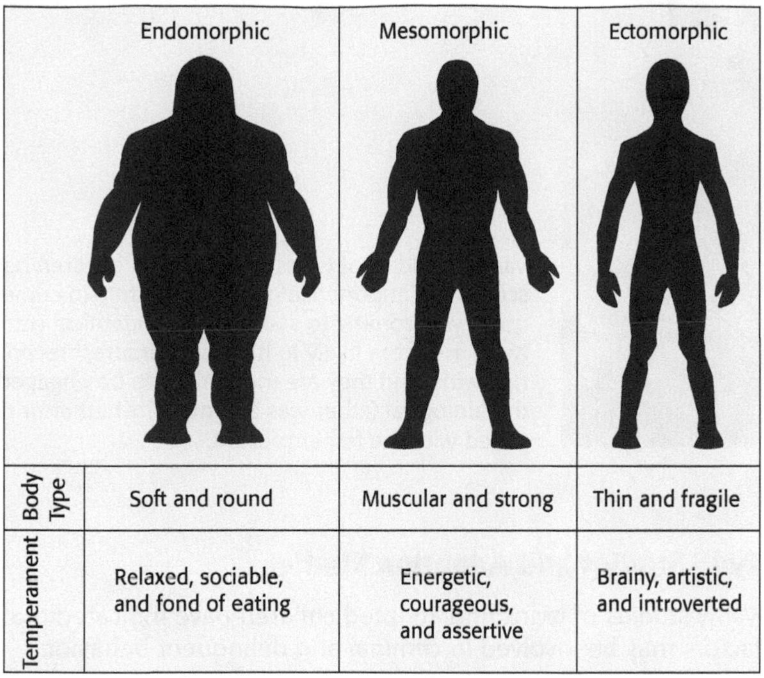

FIGURE 4.1 Sheldon's Types of Physiques. *Source:* W. H. Sheldon, *Varieties of Delinquent Youth: An Introduction to Constitutional Psychiatry,* New York: Harper & Brothers, 1949; see also E. Kretchmer, *Physique and Character,* translated by W. H. J. Sprott, New York: Harcourt Brace, 1925.

types of physiques: *endomorphs*, *ectomorphs*, and *mesomorphs* (see Figure 4.1). Endomorphs have physiques that are heavy, soft, and round in shape. Ectomorphs have physiques that are very tall, lean, and flat-chested. Mesomorphs have physiques that are muscular, heavy-chested, and "athletic." Sheldon believed that this last type, the mesomorph, is the most likely to engage in criminal and delinquent behavior.[8]

Eleanor Glueck and Sheldon Glueck also reported a relationship between delinquency and mesomorphy in their comparative study of 500 proven nondelinquents and 500 persistent delinquents. The Gluecks reported that, in general, mesomorphs are more "highly characterized by traits particularly suitable to the commission of acts of aggression (physical strength, energy, insensitivity, the tendency to express tensions and frustrations in action), together with a relative freedom from such inhibitions to antisocial adventures as feelings of inadequacy, marked submissiveness to authority, emotional instability, and the like."[9]

Studies by Juan Cortés also found that delinquents differ from nondelinquents in being more mesomorphic in body type; delinquents are "more energetic and potentially aggressive temperamentally." However, Cortés, in response to criticism, also recognized the importance of both social and biological factors in explaining human behavior. He stated that "Human behavior is biosocial in nature, that is, it has both biological and social causes. As Hans Eysenck has written, 'It is time the pendulum started swinging back from an exclusive preoccupation with social causes to an appropriate appreciation and understanding of biological causes [of crime].'"[10]

Is there a relationship between physical characteristics and crime? After a thorough review of theories related to physical characteristics, George Vold and Thomas Bernard report that "there is no clear evidence that physical appearance, as such, has any consistent relation to legally defined crime. Improved research techniques may help to clarify this issue in the future, but present findings tend to be negative."[11]

Various studies of twins and adopted children have under-scored the importance of genetic factors in crime and delinquency. According to some studies, identical (monozygotic) twins are more likely to have similar arrest records than fraternal twins, and they are more likely to be engaged in crime if the biological father was a criminal, whether or not they were raised with the father present.

Twin Studies and Adoption Studies

Many studies of twins and adopted children have indicated that genetic factors may be involved in criminal and delinquent behavior.

monozygotic (MZ) twins are genetically identical; that is, they develop from a single fertilized egg that divided into two embryos.

dizygotic (DZ) twins have only half of their genes in common and develop from separate eggs fertilized at the same time.

Some explanations for delinquency and crime stress genetic or hereditary factors. Based on much research data comparing identical and fraternal twins and adoptees, many studies suggest that genetic variables are involved in delinquent and criminal behavior.

One method of determining the impact of genetic factors on criminal behavior is to study relationships between the criminal behavioral patterns of identical twins and those of fraternal twins. Identical or **monozygotic (MZ) twins** are genetically identical; that is, they develop from a single fertilized egg that divides into two embryos. Fraternal or **dizygotic (DZ) twins** have only half of their genes in common and develop from separate eggs fertilized at the same time. Assuming that the environments are much the same for the twins, if heredity does play an important role in determining delinquent or criminal behavior, one should expect to find that MZ twins are more similar in their criminal behavior than DZ twins.

Studies of twins have been conducted all over the world by a number of researchers. In Germany, Johannes Lange, who studied thirteen pairs of identical twins (adult males), reported that when one of the twins had a prison record, the other also did in 77 percent of the researched cases. In a comparable group of fraternal twins (seventeen pairs), when one of the twins had a prison record, the other had a record in only 12 percent of the researched cases.[12]

Twin studies lend support to the hypothesis that identical twins may share genetic characteristics that increase the probability of engaging in criminal activities. However, other researchers report that their findings do not indicate that criminal behavior is genetically determined. Some studies have not reported that DZ pairs are less closely related in their criminal behavior than MZ twin pairs.[13] Thus, although results from many twin studies are impressive, one must be cautious when interpreting them. Vold and Bernard report that the main difficulty with twin studies is that the "greater similarity of behavior noted in the case of the identical twins may be due to the greater similarity of training and environmental experience just as well as to their identical hereditary makeup. There is no certain way of separating environmental and heredity as controlling factors in this situation."[14]

Additional Twin Studies Show Statistical Significance

- Horatio H. Newman, Frank N. Freeman, and Karl J. Holzinger, who studied juvenile delinquents in the United States, reported that when one identical twin (among forty-two pairs) was delinquent, the other twin was also delinquent in 93 percent of the cases. In the fraternal group of subjects, when one twin was delinquent (among twenty-five pairs), the other twin was delinquent in 20 percent of the cases—a statistically significant 73 percent difference.

- Sarnoff A. Mednick and Jan Volavka reviewed a series of studies over a thirty-year period and found that 60 percent of identical twins shared criminal patterns of behavior, compared to 30 percent of fraternal twins— that is, if one twin was criminal, so was the other.

- A U.S. self-reported delinquency study of twin pairs conducted by David C. Rowe and D. Wayne Osgood also underscores the idea that genetic factors are significant in delinquency.

- In a recent study, Wendy Slutske and her associates examined almost 2,700 adult twin pairs. The researchers reported a significant influence on risk for "conduct disorder." The important feature of conduct disorder is a repetitive and persistent pattern of behavior wherein the basic rights of others or societal norms or rules are violated. It includes aggressive conduct that harms people or animals, behavior that causes property damage or loss, deceitfulness or theft, and serious violation of rules.

- Sarnoff Mednick and Karl Christiansen studied more than 3,500 twins in Denmark. They reported in a review of serious cases a 50 percent concordance for MZ twin pairs, compared with only a 20 percent concordance for DZ twin pairs.

- A Canadian study by Philip A. Vernon, Julie M. McCarthy, et al., observed 247 adult female twin pairs. Testing their subjects on eighteen measures of aggression, they reported moderate to large "heritabilities" for aggressive behavior. They also reported an overlap between genes associated with different types of aggression.

- James J. Hudziak and his associates also found a strong genetic component to aggression. Studying 492 monozygotic and dizygotic twin pairs, they reported that estimates of genetic influences on aggression were high (up to 77 percent) for both sexes.

- In a study by Michael Lyons, Judy Silberg et al., the researchers reported that among some twin pairs, their behavior appears to be influenced by their environment. Other twins, however, exhibit behavior disturbances that only can be explained by their genetic similarity.

- A recent British study by Peter McGuffin and Anita Thapar has also reported a genetic basis of "bad behaviour in adolescents."

Sources: H. H. Newman, F. H. Freeman, and K. J. Holzinger, *Twins: A Study of Heredity and Environment,* Chicago: University of Chicago Press, 1937; S. A. Mednick and J. Volavka, "Biology and Crime," in *Crime and Justice: An Annual Review of Research,* N. Morris and M. Tonry, Eds., Chicago: University of Chicago Press, 1980, pp. 85–158; D. C. Rowe and D. W. Osgood, "Heredity and Sociological Theories of Delinquency: A Reconsideration," *American Sociological Review* 49, 1984, pp. 526–540; see also David C. Rowe, "Genetic and Environmental Components of Antisocial Behavior: A Study of 256 Twin Pairs," *Criminology* 24, 1986, pp. 513–532; W. Slutske et al., "Modeling Genetic and Environmental Influences in the Etiology of Conduct Disorder," *Abnormal Psychology* 106, no. 2, 1997, pp. 266–279; *Diagnostic and Statistical Manual of Mental Disorders: DSM-IV,* 4th ed., text revision 2000, Washington, DC: American Psychiatric Association, 2000, p. 48; K. O. Christiansen, "Threshold of Tolerance in Various Population Groups Illustrated by Results from the Danish Criminologic Twin Study," in *The Mentally Abnormal Offender,* A. V. S. de Reuck and R. Porter, Eds., Boston: Little, Brown, 1968; see also *Biosocial Bases in Criminal Behavior,* S. A. Mednick and K. O. Christiansen, Eds., New York: Gardner, 1977; and K. O. Christiansen, "Seriousness of Criminality and Concordance among Danish Twins," in *Crime, Criminology, and Public Policy,* R. Hood, Ed., New York: Free Press, 1974; P. A. Vernon, J. M. McCarthy, A. M. Johnson, K. L. Jang, and J. Aitkin Harris, "Individual Difference in Multiple Dimensions of Aggression: A Univariate and Multivariate Genetic Analysis," *Twin Research* 2, 1999, pp. 1, 16–21; J. J. Hudziak, L. P. Rudiger, M. C. Neale, A. C. Heath, and R. D. Todd, "A Twin Study of Inattentive, Aggressive, and Anxious/Depressed Behaviors," *Journal of the American Academy of Child and Adolescent Psychiatry* 39, 2000, pp. 469–476; M. Lyons, J. Silberg, J. Meyer, A. Pickles, E. Simonoff, L. Eaves, J. Hewitt, H. Maes, and M. Rutter, "Heterogeneity among Juvenile Antisocial Behaviors: Findings from the Virginia Twin Study of Adolescent Behavioral Development," in *Genetics of Criminal and Antisocial Behaviour,* G. R. Bock and J. A. Goode, Eds., Chichester, England: Wiley, 1996; P. McGuffin and A. Thapar, "Genetic Basis of Bad Behaviour in Adolescents," *Lancet* 350, August 9, 1997, pp. 411–412.

FOR YOUR INFORMATION

Adoption Studies Support the Role of Genetic Factors

In a recent study of adoptees, Sarnoff A. Mednick and Barry Hutchings report the following:

- Thirty-six percent of the adoptees had biological fathers with criminal records.
- "Of the boys who had no criminal record, only 31.1 percent had biological fathers with criminal records, whereas 37.7 percent of the boys with minor offenses and 48.8 percent of the boys with criminal records had biological fathers with criminal records."
- "Criminality is more likely to occur in an adopted boy when the biological father has a criminal record."

A longitudinal non-twin adoption study conducted by Donald J. West and David P. Farrington also examines the relationship between parental and child criminality. Their long-term Cambridge Youth Survey studied a group of 1,000 adopted males from the time they were eight years old until they were over thirty years of age. Their data indicated that a significant number of delinquent children had biological fathers who were criminals:

- Thirty-seven percent of the youths who had biological criminal fathers were multiple offenders.
- Only 8 percent of the males of noncriminal biological fathers eventually became chronic offenders.
- The children of criminal parents were more likely to become law violators than the biological children of conventional, law-abiding parents.

Sources: S. A. Mednick, W. Gabrielli, and B. Hutchings, "Genetic Influences in Criminal Behavior: Evidence from an Adoption Cohort," in *Prospective Studies of Crime and Delinquency,* K. Teilmann et al., Eds., Boston: Kluver-Nijhoff, 1983; S. A. Mednick, T. Moffitt, W. Gabrielli, and B. Hutchings, "Genetic Factors in Criminal Behavior: A Review," in *Development of Antisocial and Prosocial Behavior: Research, Theories, and Issues,* D. Olweus, J. Block, and M. Radke-Yarrow, Eds., Orlando, FL: Academic Press, 1986; G. B. Vold and T. J. Bernard, *Theoretical Criminology,* 3rd ed., New York: Oxford University Press, 1986, p. 91; D. J. West and D. P. Farrington, "Who Becomes Delinquent?" in *The Delinquent Way of Life: Third Report of the Cambridge Study in Delinquent Development,* London: Heinemann, 1977; D. J. West, *Delinquency, Its Roots, Careers, and Prospects,* Cambridge, MA: Harvard University Press, 1982.

An additional way to study the effects of heredity on criminal behavior is to study data on the behavior of adopted children. Is their behavior more similar to that of their adoptive parents (findings that would support the importance of environmental factors for criminal behavior) or to that of their biological parents (findings that would support the importance of genetic factors for criminal behavior)?

Many adoption studies indicate that the criminality of the biological parents has greater influence on an adopted person than the behavior of the adoptive parents.[15] The classic and largest such study was conducted by Sarnoff A. Mednick and associates. They studied more than 14,000 adoptees born in Denmark over a twenty-three year period and concluded that the criminality of the biological parents has greater influence on a child than that of the adoptive parents.[16]

Like twin studies, many adoption studies support the possible importance of genetic factors in criminality. Adoption researchers have reported that the criminality of the biological parents has greater influence on an adopted person than that of the adoptive parents.

Adoption studies indicate an important relationship between biological factors and criminal behavior. However, one must not discount the impact of environmental factors on criminality. Many researchers also conclude that both biological and environmental factors influence crime. In other words, much of the research cited in this section also reported that nongenetic variables play an important role in delinquent and criminal behavior. Because no particular genetic structures have been clearly associated with different types of criminal behavior, any hereditary or genetic theory is problematic. However, **biocriminologists** continue to search for factors that could demonstrate an inherited genetic transmission of criminal behavior.[17]

Biocriminologists are scientists and researchers who study the biological factors affecting delinquent and criminal behavior and who develop biological theories to explain it.

Chromosomal Research

Recent research has discounted a relationship between the sex chromosomes and criminal behavior.

Another area of biocriminological research examines the relationship between chromosomal abnormalities, such as mutations at the time of conception that produce extra sex chromosomes—duplicates of the X or Y chromosome—and criminal behavior. Some scholars believe that the XYY chromosomal complement may be associated with criminal behavior—that is, that the existence of an extra Y chromosome in men, the XYY pattern, leads to excessively aggressive behavior. It is theorized that such aggressiveness in turn leads to the predisposition to various types of antisocial behaviors, particularly to crime against persons.

One of the first studies on the XYY pattern was done in a maximum-security mental hospital in Scotland by Patricia Jacobs and associates. They found that a statistically significant percentage of XYY men housed in the "subnormal" wing of the hospital had chromosomal abnormalities. They described these **XYY males** as having "dangerous, violent, or criminal propensities."[18]

However, other studies have shown that XYY prisoners are considerably *less* violent than chromosomally normal inmates. For example, Theodore Sarbin and Miller indicated in 1970 that "males of the XYY type are not predictably aggressive. If anything, as a group they are somewhat less aggressive than comparable XYs."[19] Other, more recent studies have also discounted the relationship between the XYY pattern and criminality.[20] Researchers today recognize that biology and environment, or "nature and nuture," together cause people's characteristics and behaviors. The challenge is to describe the precise relationships between these factors in causing criminal behavior.

XYY males: A chromosomal abnormality thought to be linked to dangerous, violent, or criminal propensities.

The Origins of Violence: Nurturing Nature

Few debates in human biology have been as acrimonious as the one between genetic determinists and social determinists of behavior. But the past few years have seen the emergence of a grudging understanding that although environment—particularly childhood environment—undoubtedly shapes an individual's behavior, how it does so may depend on the individual's genetic makeup. Recent studies by Terrie Moffitt and her colleagues suggest how these factors are related.

- Monoamine oxidase-A (MAOA) is an enzyme that breaks down members of an important group of neurotransmitters, the molecules that carry signals between nerve cells. These neurotransmitters include dopamine, serotonin, and norepinephrine, all of which help to regulate a person's mood.
- There is abundant evidence that a reduced level of monoamine oxidase-A (and therefore an elevated level of these neurotransmitters) results in violent behavior. There is also evidence that chronically low levels early in life result in an individual who is more than averagely predisposed to react violently to any given situation in adulthood, regardless of monoamine-oxidase levels at the time.
- There is considerable variation in the "promoter" on or near the gene itself. This promoter region is responsible for switching the gene on and off, and thus for controlling the amount of monoamine oxidase-A manufactured.
- Moffitt looked at variations in this promoter region in a group of more than five hundred men who are the subject of a long-term research project in New Zealand. The men have been monitored from birth and are now in their late twenties.
- Moffitt and her colleagues grouped the various versions of the promoter region into those that result in low levels of monoamine oxidase-A and those that result in high levels of the enzyme. They also divided their subjects into those who had been maltreated as children and those who had not.
- Only 12 percent of the group had both abused childhoods and low-activity promoter regions, yet this group accounted for 44 percent of those who had criminal convictions for violence. Fully 85 percent of the 12 percent showed some form of routine antisocial behavior. The next most antisocial combination (high-activity promoters and an abused childhood) resulted in only about 45 percent of men showing routine antisocial behavior, while only a quarter of those who had had tranquil childhoods were antisocial in adulthood, regardless of their promoter type.

Source: "Nurturing Nature," *Economist,* August 3, 2002, p. 64.

After reading this section, you should be able to

1. define biocriminology as a field that includes the study of genetic factors to understand criminal behavior;
2. describe the theories of Lombroso, Goring, and Hooton regarding physical characteristics of criminal types;
3. describe the research and conclusions of Sheldon and Kretchmer, the Gluecks, and Cortés regarding body measurements and criminality;
4. summarize the research findings on the criminal behavior patterns of twins and adopted children;
5. evaluate the study of chromosomal abnormalities in research on the causes of crime;
6. explain how a particular gene and a particular environment may interact to produce violent individuals.

4.3 BIOCHEMICAL INFLUENCES ON BEHAVIOR

In addition to studying genetics, biocriminologists have studied the importance of biochemical factors in criminality. This section examines the possible effects that diet, allergies, and environmental conditions may have on body chemistry associated with criminal behavior. For example, hyperactivity, high testosterone levels, and chemical changes caused by alcohol and drug abuse are risk factors for violent and criminal behavior. Neurophysiological factors, such as brain-function abnormalities, also may be linked to criminality. Studies suggest links, for example, between criminal behavior and learning disabilities (such as attention deficit disorder), brain-wave abnormalities, or brain dysfunction.

Dietary Factors

Research reports the importance of biochemical factors in criminal behavior. For example, the foods and chemicals that people ingest may result in undesirable reactions, disorders, and some types of delinquent or criminal behavior.

Many people discount the importance of nutritional and **dietary factors** on human behavior. Others, however, are very much aware of the impact one's diet has on behavior, including delinquent or criminal behavior. Caretakers of children and researchers in the dietary fields have reported significant differences in behavior resulting from food components that people eat. Foods such as wheat, eggs, milk, corn, cocoa, sugar, food dyes, and food components such as tyramine (in cheese and wine), phenylethylamine (in chocolate), MSG (monosodium glutamate, a flavor enhancer), and xanthine (in caffeine) may result in severe allergic reactions and behavioral disorders including criminal behavior.[21]

For example, recent research linked hyperactivity (a risk factor for criminality) to nutritional deficiencies and food intolerance. In a survey of parents of almost 500 hyperactive and 200 nonhyperactive children, the hyperactive children's parents reported that about two-thirds of the children exhibited increased behavior problems when exposed to preservatives, synthetic food colorings and flavorings, certain chemicals, and cow's milk. Only about 12 percent of parents of the children in the control group reported a connection between food additives or colorings and increased behavior problems.[22]

Dietary factors and conditions strongly affected by them, such as **hypoglycemia**, may be related to various types of behavioral disorders and violent behaviors.

Certain foods, such as sugars, food additives, and preservatives, can increase behavior problems in both children and adults. What other dietary factors can directly or indirectly contribute to criminal and delinquent behavior?

Another major study related diets high in sugar to aggression and violence. Stephen Schoenthaler and Walter Doraz studied a group of 276 institutionalized delinquents to determine the effects of sugar on behavior in the institutional setting. Many dietary changes were made, such as replacing sodas with fruit juices, replacing high-sugar cereals with low-sugar cereals, and replacing table sugar with honey. These changes resulted in a significant 45 percent reduction in disciplinary actions, thefts, and aggressive behavior such as fights and assaults.[23]

Hypoglycemia is a diet-related physiological condition that occurs when a person's blood-sugar level falls below an acceptable range. Human brains are particularly sensitive to sugar levels in the blood. Abnormal levels can impair brain functioning, make a person confused and anxious, and cause headaches, fatigue, anger, and aggression. Some researchers have reported a relationship between hypoglycemia and the violent crimes of assault, rape, and homicide. Others have noted a link between hypoglycemic reactions and such crimes as sexual offenses and assault.[24] Prison inmates also have higher levels of hypoglycemia than the noninmate population. In addition, offenders who are anti-

FOR YOUR INFORMATION

Research on Diet and Behavior

- Instituting dietary changes involving almost 8,100 delinquents in juvenile correctional institutions, Stephen Shoenthaler reported a 47 percent reduction in assaultive behavior, insubordination, suicide attempts, and general rule violations. In fact, the more violent the behavior before the dietary intervention, the greater the improvement after intervention.

- J. Breakey reviewed studies conducted from 1985 to 1995 and reported a strong relationship between negative behavior and the food children eat. In almost all the studies reviewed, Breakey found a "statistically significant change in behavior with dietary intervention."

- Aggression and higher levels of violent crime were also linked to a low consumption of the important amino acid tryptophan in a study by Anthony R. Mawson and K. W. Jacobs. They reported that nations whose per capita rates of corn consumption were above the median (corn-based diets are deficient in tryptophan) had significantly higher homicide rates than nations whose diets were based on rice or wheat (which are higher in tryptophan).

- A number of other studies have reported that criminals and juvenile delinquents suffer from vitamin deficiency. For example, studies collected by Leonard J. Hippchen have linked different types of criminal and antisocial behavior with insufficient quantities of the important B_3 and B_6 vitamins in people.

Sources: S. J. Schoenthaler, "Abstracts of Earlier Papers on the Effects of Vitamin and Mineral Supplementation on I. Q. and Behavior," *Personality and Individual Differences* 12, no. 4, 1991, pp. 335–341; J. Breakey, "The Role of Diet and Behaviour in Childhood," *Journal of Pediatrics and Child Health* 33, 1997, pp. 190–194; A. R. Mawson and K. W. Jacobs, "Corn Consumption, Tryptophan, and Cross-National Homicide Rates," *Journal of Orthomolecular Psychiatry* 7, 1978, pp. 227–230; L. J. Hippchen, Ed., *Ecologic-Biochemical Approaches to Treatment of Delinquents and Criminals,* New York: Van Nostrand Reinhold, 1978.

social, habitually violent, and explosive are significantly more hypoglycemic than those in control groups.[25]

Many of the studies that have related aggression and violence to food intake have been criticized for not informing people of either the extent to which nutritional conditions are related to delinquent or criminal behavior, or "the extent to which those behaviors can be reduced through nutritional therapy." In addition, some theorists have indicated that programs using nutritional therapies "may report positive results but generally do not include carefully controlled statistical measures. Proponents argue that these programs offer great promise for the future treatment of criminals and delinquents, but at the present time it is not possible to conclude one way or the other."[26]

Environmental Exposure to Chemicals

Environmental exposure to chemical substances also may contribute to emotional and behavioral disorders that relate to criminal behavior.

Certain chemicals are necessary for thought and other brain processes in humans. Biochemical researchers over many years have developed theories that have attributed many different types of mental illnesses—including behavioral disorders and schizophrenic episodes—to the presence or lack of chemicals in the bloodstream and brain of the mentally ill.

Studies from the 1950s and 1960s have suggested that when too much of a chemical is present in an individual—serotonin, methylated idoleamines, or taraxein, for example—the person will exhibit schizophrenic behavior patterns or other disturbances that may be considered deviant or criminal.[27] Recent studies have reported that low levels of serotonin and high levels of vasopressin, both neurotransmitters, have been linked to higher levels of male and female aggression.[28] For example, a 1998 British study conducted by Terrie Moffitt and associates of almost 800 men and women reported that abnormal levels of serotonin (low brain levels of serotonin but high blood levels) are a risk factor for aggressive behavior in men. No relationship between serotonin levels and aggression was observed among female subjects.[29]

Biochemical changes also may be introduced by **environmental factors** caused by human activities. For example, many of the products and by-products of our technological and industrial processes have been responsible for vast increases in environmental pollution. Toxic substances, such as lead, mercury, cadmium, polychlorinated biphenyls (PCBs), and pesticides, have also found their way into our bodies as a result of complex food-chain activities. In addition, we have introduced more and more pollutants into the air, and the absorption and accumulation of these substances (many of which are toxic) into our bodies can cause severe health problems or death. These and many other environmental contaminants have been linked to severe emotional and behavioral disorders in people.[30]

Allergies related to environmental contaminants that affect the central nervous system and the brain may also contribute to deviant and criminal behavior. Biosocial theorists, in their research on allergies, have reported that chemicals in our environment and in our foods can cause serious allergic reactions in people and can produce physical problems such as brain swelling. Such abnormalities, in turn, may cause emotional and behavioral problems, aggressiveness, and violent behavior in children and adults. Even corn, which some biosocial researchers consider to be a serious cerebral allergen, has been related to homicide rates in a cross-national study.[31]

Environmental factors are products in the environment that have been linked to behavioral disorders.

Hormonal Levels

Hormonal levels in men and women have been linked to various types of criminal behavior.

Several biosocial researchers have studied the relationship between *hormonal levels* and aggressive as well as criminal behavior. Studies have linked androgens—male sex hormones—and testosterone levels to antisocial, aggressive, and violent behavior. For example, several studies have reported that males who exhibit higher levels of dominance, aggression, and violence have higher levels of testosterone in their systems than other men.[32]

- In a study of more than 4,400 men, James Dabbs Jr. reported a positive correlation between high rates of delinquency and high levels of testosterone.
- In a study of young male prisoners, Dabbs also reported that high testosterone levels were associated with increased levels of prison rule violations, parole board decisions against release, and more violent crimes.[33]
- Dabbs and Marian Hargrove reported that among female inmates in a maximum-security prison, there was a relationship between unprovoked crimes of violence, high levels of prior charges, decisions against parole, and high testosterone levels.[34]
- Other studies have noted that testosterone-production levels in men may be strongly related to their criminal aggressiveness; testosterone samples from prison inmates indicated that higher levels of the hormone were more common among the men who committed violent crimes.[35]

As reported in Chapter 2, men are much more likely to engage in criminal behavior than women. Some of the differences in the crime rates between men and women may be accounted for by differences in testosterone levels. A number of researchers believe that testosterone levels are very important to understanding crime-rate differences in not only gender but also the aging-out process. That is, the reason that men become less criminal as they age may be because their testosterone levels decline as they progress through the life cycle.[36] Dabbs and Hargrove also reported that increasing age is linked to reduced criminal violence and aggression in female prisoners "both directly and indirectly through lower levels of testosterone that come with age."[37]

Other research has focused on androgen levels and their effects on brain function and antisocial behavior. This research seems to indicate that hormonal levels affect different types of brain functioning (e.g., arousal levels, seizure thresholds), which can encourage individuals to seek increased levels of environmental stimulation, to tolerate punishment, and to become emotionally volatile, impulsive, antisocial, violent, and perhaps even criminal.[38]

Researchers in Sweden have reported an association between high levels of criminality, delinquency, antisocial behavior, and thyroid hormone levels:

- P. O. Alm and associates reported that delinquents whose criminal activity continued into adulthood had higher T_3 (triiodothyronine, a thyroid hormone) levels than other delinquents or control-group subjects.[39]
- Stalenheim and associates also reported that elevated T_3 levels were associated with psychopathy and criminality in men undergoing forensic psychiatric examinations.[40]

Hormone Studies Have Contradictory Results

Not all studies show a relationship between hormonal levels and aggression or crime:

- Some research studies have indicated there is no link between aggressive and violent behavior and testosterone levels, nor between violent offenders and testosterone levels.[1] Studies have associated antisocial, aggressive behavior and general criminal activities by women offenders to variations in hormonal levels before and during the menstrual cycle.[2]
- Some research has reported a strong link between premenstrual syndrome (PMS) and delinquency. For example, one study showed that women just before and during menstruation tend to be more aggressive, antisocial, and suicidal.[3]
- Other research indicates that the physical and sociopsychological stress of aggression may be the major factor in bringing on menstruation.[4]

One must be cautious with most of these research findings. They do not suggest that variations in hormone levels alone cause delinquent or criminal behavior in men and women. The studies suggest only that different hormonal levels may be one among many contributing factors in crime causation.[5]

1. R. Rubin, "The Neuroendocrinology and Neurochemistry of Antisocial Behavior," in *The Causes of Crime: The New Biological Approaches,* S. Mednick, T. Moffitt, and S. Stack, Eds., Cambridge, England: Cambridge University Press, 1987, pp. 239–262; R. Rada, "Plasma Androgens in Violent and Nonviolent Sex Offenders," *Bulletin of the American Academy of Psychiatry and the Law* 11, 1983, pp. 149–158; R. T. Rada, D. R. Laws, and R. Kellner, "Plasma Testosterone Levels in the Rapist," *Psychosomatic Medicine* 38, 1976, pp. 257–268.

2. S. A. Shah and L. H. Roth, "Biological and Psychophysiological Factors in Criminality," in *Handbook of Criminology,* D. Glaser, Ed., Chicago: Rand McNally, 1974, pp. 124–128.

3. K. Dalton, *The Premenstrual Syndrome,* Springfield, IL: Thomas, 1971.

4. J. Horney, "Menstrual Cycles and Criminal Responsibility," *Law and Human Nature* 2, 1978, pp. 25–36.

5. G. B. Vold and T. J. Bernard, *Theoretical Criminology,* 3rd ed., New York: Oxford University Press, 1986, p. 98.

Alcohol and Drugs

Environmental sources of biochemical changes include alcohol and drug abuse, which have been strongly linked to criminal behavior.

Alcohol and drugs bring about many biochemical changes in the human body. These changes can cause people to be irritable, hostile, agitated, aggressive, violent, depressed, suicidal, and homicidal. With alcohol intoxication, people can experience mood changes and impaired attention or become irritable and violent.

- More than half of all murderers and their victims are believed to be intoxicated at the time of the event.
- Alcohol is also frequently associated with the commission of many other criminal acts.
- About one-quarter of all suicides occur when the person is using alcohol.[41]

In addition, Alphonse J. Sallett reports that

- four out of every ten assaults in the United States occur while the offender is intoxicated;
- almost half of all men arrested for rape are found to have a blood alcohol level of .10 or higher;
- alcohol is involved in at least 29 percent of all other sex crimes.[42]

Obviously, there is a strong relationship between alcohol abuse and violent and criminal behavior. In addition, chemicals in drugs, such as phencyclidine,

This assailant's violent behavior is partly explained by alcohol and drug abuse, which causes biochemical changes in the body and brain. According to research findings, how strong is the relationship between alcohol and drug abuse and criminal behavior? To what extent are crimes by alcoholics and drug addicts a result of biochemical changes, and to what extent are they a result of the need to support their habits?

ketamine (Ketalar), and the thiophene analogue of phencyclidine—commonly called PCP, THC, angel dust, or crystal—can precipitate a wide variety of behaviors in an individual, including irritability, nervousness, hallucinations, paranoid ideation, and bizarre or violent behavior.[43] In 1985, 21 percent of the homicides in the District of Columbia were identified as drug-related. This increased to 34 percent in 1986, to 51 percent in 1987, and to 80 percent or more today.

Incarcerated adults and youths reported high levels of drug use in a 1991 report. Among those incarcerated for violent crimes,

- a third of state prisoners, and more than a third of incarcerated youths, said they had been under the influence of an illegal drug at the time of the offense for which they were incarcerated;
- thirty-nine percent of state prison inmates reported daily drug use;
- sixteen percent reported daily use of a major drug, such as cocaine, heroin, PCP, LSD, or methadone.[44]

After reading this section, you should be able to

1. identify nutritional and dietary factors that may directly or indirectly contribute to criminal behavior;
2. identify environmental factors that may cause biochemical reactions or allergies that contribute to emotional and behavioral disorders;
3. describe possible relationships between hormonal levels and criminal behavior;
4. analyze the relationships between alcohol and drug abuse and criminal behavior;
5. explain why research on biochemical factors must be treated with caution as an explanation of crime.

4.4 NEUROPHYSIOLOGICAL FACTORS

Biological explanations for criminal behavior include theories based on studies of brain damage or dysfunction. Biocriminologists have attempted to explain some criminal behavior in terms of neurophysiological factors, such as brain-wave abnormalities, brain dysfunction, and brain injuries. **Neurophysiology** is the study of the physiology of the central nervous system, which is located in the brain and spinal column. This section summarizes the results of neurophysiological research in relation to criminal behavior.

Brain dysfunction and brain damage can be detected from medical tests such as x-rays, computed tomography (CT) scans, and magnetic resonance imaging (MRI). Using these instruments, researchers have reported that violent patients and incarcerated people suffer from excessive brain dysfunction, especially in the frontal and temporal regions.

Research on neuropsychosocial factors has noted that dysfunction of the temporal and frontal regions of the brain was apparent in more than 75 percent of aggressive and depressed sociopathic patients. Some studies have found high incidence of head injuries with loss of consciousness.[45] Other studies report a high incidence of disturbed central nervous system function in the persistent offender.[46]

As a result of medications, chemicals, drugs, or structural damage to the brain from head trauma, an individual may experience a marked change in personality or behavior. This change may involve

- emotional lability (e.g., sudden tearfulness or explosive temper outbursts);
- impaired impulse control (e.g., shoplifting or poor social judgment);
- suspiciousness.

This type of behavior has been termed *organic personality syndrome* by mental health professionals. The socially unacceptable behavior of individuals with organic personality syndrome "may lead to social ostracism or legal difficulties. Impulsive or explosive behavior may be dangerous to the individual and to others."[47]

Violent behavior in people may also be associated with brain tumors. Studies have reported that previously pleasant and docile people can become aggressive and violent from tumors growing in their brains. If they are fortunate enough to have the tumors surgically removed, their behavior returns to previous docile patterns.[48]

Brain-Wave Abnormalities

Some studies have reported a relationship between abnormal EEG patterns and criminality.

By using an electroencephalograph (EEG) and attaching tiny electrodes to the scalp, researchers can detect electrochemical processes in the brain. For more than fifty years, researchers have been interested in determining whether or not there is a relationship between abnormal brain-wave patterns measured by an EEG and criminality.

- Many studies have reported a significant number of abnormal patterns in 25 to 50 percent of studied criminal groups, compared to abnormal patterns in only 5 to 20 percent of noncriminal populations.[49]
- Criminals who committed homicide have been found to have a disproportionate number of abnormal EEG reports.[50]
- In one of the major studies of **EEG abnormalities** and crime, a group of 355 violent, delinquent youth were divided into two groups. The first group consisted of those who had committed a single violent act; the second group consisted of those who had been habitually violent. The findings indicated that 24 percent of the single-violent-act group had abnormal EEG readings, whereas 65 percent of the habitually violent group had abnormal EEG readings.[51]

Neurophysiology is the study of physiology of the central nervous system. Brain dysfunction and brain damage have been linked to criminality.

EEG abnormalities are the study of the physiology of the CNS.

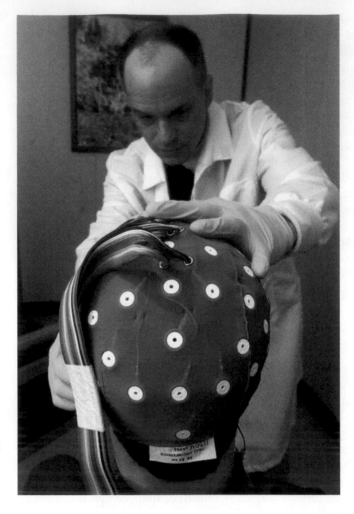

Some researchers believe there may be a relationship between abnormal brain-wave patterns and criminality. In a study involving 1,000 violent criminal offenders, what are the chances that a patient's EEG evaluation would reveal brain-wave abnormalities? What other neurophysiological factors may be linked to violent, criminal, and delinquent behavior?

In 2001, Donald Bars and his associates reported strong evidence that some children may have a predisposition to violent, explosive behavior. The behavior is believed to be an innate characteristic of their central nervous systems. Clinically evaluating more than 325 children with a variety of psychiatric disorders, Bars compared "nonexplosive" children with children exhibiting intermittent explosive-behavior disorder. Each child's brain-wave responses to specific stimuli were measured and his or her EEG was evaluated. The researchers controlled for gender, age, and medication usage. They reported that children with higher amplitudes of certain brain waves were more likely to exhibit explosive behaviors than the other children. The higher the amplitude, the more probable the explosive behaviors. In addition, explosive children exhibited higher brain activity in the right frontal lobe. Bars stressed the important point that these patients constitute a distinct psychiatric population in need of medical treatment provided by the mental health community. They do not need to be identified and incarcerated as sociopaths by the criminal justice system.[52]

Attention Deficit/Hyperactivity Disorder

ADHD is linked to the onset and continuance of criminal careers.

ADHD, or Attention deficit/ hyperactivity disorder, has been linked to delinquency and crime.

Over the past several decades, many names have been attached to what has finally been termed **attention deficit/hyperactivity disorder (ADHD)**. Among other things, it was called attention deficit disorder, hyperkinetic syndrome, hyperactive child syndrome, minimal brain damage, minimal brain dysfunction, and minimal cerebral dysfunction. Following are its essential features, which vary with the function of age, according to the *Diagnostic and Statistical Manual of Mental Disorders IV (DSM-IV)*:

- Developmentally inappropriate lack of attention, impulsivity, and hyperactivity.
- Obstinacy, stubbornness, negativism, bossiness, bullying, rapid mood changes (mood lability), low frustration tolerance, temper outbursts, low self-esteem, and lack of response to discipline.

Predisposing factors include mental retardation, epilepsy, and some types of cerebral palsy, in addition to other neurological disorders. It should be noted that this disorder is ten times more common in boys than in girls, and it occurs in as many as 3 percent of all prepubertal children.[53]

Suspected causes of ADHD include chemicals, food additives, prenatal stress, and neurological damage. It has been medically treated with stimulants, such as Ritalin and Dexedrine, which act to calm ADHD children. Various studies have linked ADHD to the onset as well as the continuance of delinquent and criminal careers.[54]

After reading this section, you should be able to

1. describe ways that brain dysfunction and brain damage may be linked to criminal behavior;
2. identify characteristics of organic personality syndrome;
3. summarize EEG research on brain-wave abnormalities in criminals;
4. list the diagnostic characteristics of ADHD and its links to crime;
5. assess the role of neurophysiological factors in explanations for crime.

CHAPTER SUMMARY

This chapter examines the biological theories of crime, focusing on the idea that to fully understand criminal behavior, we must consider the interaction between a person's biological makeup and the environment. Some of the theories view the criminal as characteristically different from, or biologically inferior to, noncriminals. Others attempt to demonstrate a relationship between body type and certain aspects of personality that are particularly prone to criminal behavior.

Cesare Lombroso developed the theory that certain persons engaged in crime are "born criminals." Charles Goring, however, believed that there is no such thing as a physical criminal type. E. A. Hooton believed that criminals are inferior to noncriminals in their body measurements but there were many criticisms of Hooton. William Sheldon and Ernst Kretchmer presented three major types of physiques, and both Eleanor and Sheldon Glueck and Juan Cortés also reported a relationship between delinquency and body type (pp. 101–103).

Some theories of crime stress genetic and hereditary factors. Many studies have investigated the behavior of twins and adopted children to determine whether or not there is a relationship between heredity and crime. Several twin studies have indicated that genetic factors are significant in criminal and delinquent behavior. Several adoption studies have also reported an important relationship between biological factors and criminal behavior. Another area of research examines the relationship between chromosomal abnormalities and criminal behavior (pp. 104–108).

Researchers have also studied the importance of biochemical factors in criminality, relating different types of criminal behavior to such variables as diet, hypoglycemia, environmental conditions, allergies, hormonal levels, and alcohol and drugs. Biocriminological studies have also linked criminal behavior with neurophysiological factors such as brain-wave abnormality, brain dysfunction, and brain injury (pp. 109–117).

Study Guide

Chapter Objectives

- Describe the findings of Lombroso, Goring, and Hooton.
- Describe the research and conclusions of Sheldon and Kretchmer, the Gluecks, and Cortés.
- Discuss the research findings on the criminal behavior patterns of twins.
- Discuss the findings of adoption studies.
- Examine XYY chromosomal research and its conclusions.
- Examine how a particular gene and a particular environment may interact to produce violent individuals.
- Assess the impact of dietary factors on criminal behavior.
- Discuss the relationship between criminal behavior and hypoglycemia.

- Examine the relationship between criminal behavior and environmental conditions, including allergies.
- Assess the relationship between hormonal levels and criminal behavior.
- Describe the relationship between criminal behavior and alcohol intoxication and drug abuse.
- Examine the link between criminal behavior and neurophysiological factors.
- Describe how brain dysfunction and brain damage are linked to criminal behavior.

Key Terms

Attention deficit/hyperactivity disorder (ADHD) (116)
Biocriminologists (107)
Biosocial theories (101)
Dietary factors (109)

Dizygotic (DZ) twins (104)
Electroencephalograph (EEG) abnormalities (115)
Environmental factors (111)
Hypoglycemia (110)

Monozygotic (MZ) twins (104)
Neurophysiology (114)
XYY males (107)

Self-Test
Short Answer

1. List the physical characteristics of the atavistic type of individual who becomes criminal, according to Lombroso.
2. List Sheldon's three major types of physiques.
3. List mesomorphic traits that the Gluecks argued are particularly suited to the commission of aggressive acts.
4. Define MZ twins and DZ twins.
5. What do twin and adoption studies attempt to find out?

6. List the foods that may be related to behavioral disorders.
7. Define hypoglycemia and cerebral allergies.
8. Alcohol intoxication and drug abuse can bring about what kinds of behavioral changes in people?
9. Define EEG.
10. Define ADHD.

Multiple Choice

1. Goring's research indicated that
   a. nowhere did results confirm evidence of a physical criminal type
   b. results confirmed there is a criminal type
   c. a significant difference exists between criminals and noncriminals
   d. none of the above
2. Which of the following is not one of Sheldon and Kretchmer's body-mind types?
   a. ectomorph
   b. endomorph
   c. mesomorph
   d. mendomorph
3. Mednick and Christiansen, in their study of more than 3,500 twins in Denmark, reported
   a. a 50 percent concordance for DZ twin pairs, compared with a 20 percent concordance for MZ twin pairs
   b. a 50 percent concordance for MZ twin pairs, compared with a 20 percent concordance for DZ twin pairs
   c. findings supporting the hypothesis that identical twins share a genetic characteristic that decreases their probability of engaging in criminal activities
   d. all of the above
4. According to Mednick and Hutchings's study of adopted boys,
   a. criminality is more likely to occur in an adopted boy when the adoptive father has a criminal record
   b. criminality is more likely to occur in an adopted boy when the biological mother has a criminal record
   c. criminality is less likely to occur in an adopted boy when the biological father has a criminal record
   d. criminality is more likely to occur in an adopted boy when the biological father has a criminal record
5. The XYY chromosomal complement
   a. is not associated with criminal behavior
   b. has been proven by researchers to be directly associated with criminal behavior
   c. may be associated with criminal behavior
   d. none of the above
6. Which of the following foods have been linked to severe allergic reactions and behavioral disorders including criminal behavior?
   a. wheat, eggs, and MSG
   b. milk, corn, and cocoa
   c. sugar, food dyes, and xanthines
   d. all of the above
7. Which of the following is not a true statement?
   a. Some research has reported a strong link between PMS and delinquency.
   b. Researchers in Sweden have reported an association between high levels of criminality and thyroid hormone levels.
   c. Hypoglycemia may be related to criminal behavior.
   d. none of the above
8. Which of the following have been linked to higher levels of male and female aggression?
   a. low levels of serotonin
   b. high levels of vasopressin
   c. *a* and *b*
   d. none of the above
9. Which of the following environmental contaminants have not been linked to severe emotional and behavioral disorders in people?
   a. lead
   b. cadmium
   c. PCBs
   d. none of the above
10. Essential features of ADHD include
    a. submissiveness and withdrawal
    b. impulsivity and hyperactivity
    c. high frustration tolerance
    d. high self-esteem

True–False

T F   1. Charles Goring and E. A. Hooton agreed that there is no such thing as a physical criminal type.

T F   2. Many of the twin studies underscore the idea that genetic factors have a significant ability to explain delinquency in individuals.

T F   3. Many adoption studies report that the criminality of the biological parents has less influence on an adopted person than that of the adoptive parents.

T F   4. A longitudinal study by West and Farrington reported that biological children of criminal parents were more likely to become law violators than the biological children of conventional, law-abiding parents.

T F   5. A reduced level of monoamine oxidase-A in people results in violent behavior.

T F   6. There appears to be no relationship between criminality and dietary factors.

T F   7. Many studies report little or no relationship between high rates of delinquency and high levels of testosterone.

T F   8. Alcohol is infrequently associated with the commission of many criminal acts.

T F 9. Criminals who committed homicide have been found to have a disproportionate number of abnormal EEG reports.

T F 10. Violent behavior in people may be associated with brain tumors.

Fill-In

1. Sheldon believed that the person with a _____ body type is most likely to engage in criminal and delinquent behavior.

2. Some scholars believe that the _____ chromosomal complement may be associated with criminal behavior in men.

3. Several studies have reported that men who exhibit higher levels of aggression and violence have higher levels of the hormone _____ in their system.

4. _____ is a diet-related physiological condition that occurs when a person's blood-sugar level falls below an acceptable range.

5. Biocriminologists have explained some criminal behavior in terms of _____ factors, such as brain-wave abnormalities, brain dysfunction, and brain injuries.

6. Many researchers report that crime is the outcome of an interaction between social factors and certain _____ factors.

7. _____ and _____ bring about many biochemical changes in the body. These changes can cause people to be irritable, hostile, agitated, aggressive, violent, depressed, suicidal, and homicidal.

8. Essential features of _____ are developmentally inappropriate lack of attention, impulsivity, and hyperactivity.

9. The scientists who study biological factors affecting criminal behavior and who develop theories to explain it are called _____.

10. _____ theories attempt to explain crime in terms of genetic and hereditary factors, biochemical factors, or neurophysiological factors.

Matching

1. ADHD
2. Sheldon
3. XYY pattern
4. Hooton
5. The Gluecks
6. Testosterone
7. Shonthaler and Doraz
8. Organic personality syndrome
9. Hypoglycemia
10. Alcohol intoxication

A. Low blood-sugar level
B. High sugar levels and aggression
C. Ectomorphs
D. Criminals have inferior bodies
E. Relationship between delinquency and mesomorphy
F. Factor for more than half of all murderers and their victims
G. Occurs in up to 3 percent of prepubertal children
H. Genes and aggression
I. Hormone linked to aggression
J. Socially unacceptable

Essay Questions

1. Compare and contrast the physical theories of Lombroso, Goring, and Hooton.
2. Briefly describe Sheldon's three physique types.
3. What did Eleanor and Sheldon Glueck study? What were their findings?
4. Briefly report Cortés's conclusions.
5. What do the twin studies report regarding the impact of genetic factors on criminal behavior? Be specific.
6. What do the adoption studies report regarding the impact of genetic factors on criminal behavior? Be specific.
7. Describe the relationship, if any, between hormone levels and criminal behavior.
8. Evaluate the impact of alcohol and drugs on criminal behavior.
9. Assess the importance of neurophysiological factors on criminal behavior.

Psychological Explanations for Criminal Behavior

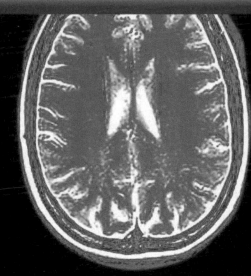

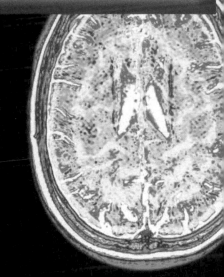

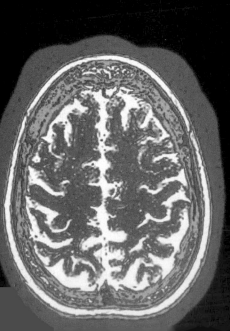

5.1 INTRODUCTION: PSYCHOLOGICAL PERSPECTIVES

In contrast to biological and hereditary theories, there are a variety of psychological explanations for crime that emphasize the importance of personality traits and their role in criminal and delinquent behavior. **Personality** is the organization of attitudes, beliefs, habits, and behavior, in addition to other characteristics, that develop in an individual through social interaction with others. From the psychological perspective, personality is a result of both genetics and socialization through interpersonal relationships with others. Thus, abnormal personalities are not biologically inherited but are developed and are characteristic of persons who have been inadequately socialized to the norms and demands of others and of society.

Some psychological theories stress the importance of mental processes, childhood experiences, and unconscious thoughts. Others stress the importance of social learning or human perception. A review of the relationship between psychological traits and criminality begins with an examination of psychiatric explanations for crime. This chapter

- evaluates both Freud's psychoanalytic theory and mental illness as explanations for criminal behavior (section 5.2);
- considers Bandura's social learning theory (section 5.3);
- presents research on the effects of media violence on people's behavior (section 5.3);
- explores cognitive explanations for crime, including the roles of intelligence and moral judgment (section 5.4);
- analyzes research on links between personality and crime (section 5.5).

5.2 PSYCHIATRIC EXPLANATIONS FOR CRIMINAL BEHAVIOR

Mental health professionals have questioned why some people behave aggressively or violently. Some psychologists and psychiatrists believe that there may be such a thing as a criminal personality. Others stress the importance of early childhood experiences in explaining antisocial or criminal behavior. For example, psychologists and psychiatrists have viewed criminality as the result of an oppressive society or of personalities that seek immediate gratification and pleasure without considering the needs of others.[1] From a psychiatric perspective, criminals are basically viewed as "sick" individuals (either **neurotic**—less seriously mentally ill—or **psychotic**—more seriously mentally ill) whose aberrant behavior (much of which violates the criminal law) is the result of faulty early childhood development or mental illness.

Freudian Explanations for Crime

Sigmund Freud believed that criminals have overdeveloped superegos that lead to guilt, anxiety, and consequent desire for punishment. Sigmund Freud (1856–1939) was the founder of psychoanalysis. He was an important contributor to the theories of the development of personality, which he stressed is the result of social experience. Freud's psychoanalytic approach focused on the importance of early childhood experiences and the conflict between an individual's needs and society's demands.[2] Many of Freud's ideas have been used by some criminologists to explain delinquent and criminal behavior.

Freud believed the following:

- The major work of society is carried on by the superego, in that it molds the individual's personality according to society's dictates.
- It is the superego that permits the expression of impulses that society considers appropriate, and, conversely, it represses asocial (nonsocial and antisocial) instincts.
- The superego is in continual conflict with the desires of the id and provides a guard against the id's impulses.
- The superego provides us with a point of view outside of ourselves from which we can observe our actions and judge them.
- The superego gives us an image of what we ought to be (an ego ideal) according to the demands of society.[3]

Freud believed many criminals have a sense of guilt before they commit a crime. Thus, crime is not the result of guilt but the motive. That is, criminal behavior may be the result of an overdeveloped superego that causes a powerful sense of guilt in the individual. Freud reported that many of his patients who felt guilty committed crimes in order to be caught and duly punished. Guilt feelings were relieved by the punishment.[4]

Personality is the organization of attitudes, beliefs, habits, and behavior, in addition to other characteristics, that develop in an individual through social interaction with others.

A **neurotic** person is a person who is less seriously mentally ill.

A **psychotic** person is a person who is more seriously mentally ill.

Sigmund Freud, the founder of psychoanalysis, believed that crime is the result of an overdeveloped superego.

The **id** is a person's basic biological drives and impulses.

The **ego** is that part of the personality which is conscious and rational.

The **superego** is a morality or "social conscience" learned during childhood.

FOR YOUR INFORMATION

Freud's Id, Ego, and Superego

- According to Freud, the personality is divided into three parts that are always in conflict with one another: id, ego, and superego.
- At birth, we are all **id**; that is, our personality consists of primitive impulses and unconscious drives. It has no sense of time, order, or morals. The id constantly seeks pleasure, is highly charged with energy, and remains unconscious throughout life.
- The **ego** is that segment of the personality which is conscious and rational. It develops as the child begins to realize that he or she is separate from other individuals and objects in the environment. The ego acts as a mediator between the unconscious impulses emanating from the id and the demands of the superego.
- The **superego** is a "social conscience" that embodies society's social restrictions and morality. As an individual interacts with others and is subject to external parental authority, he or she identifies with parent figures and internalizes parental and societal values into his or her own personality. Thus, the superego emerges.

In contrast to Freud, **August Aichorn** believed that criminality is the result of an underdeveloped superego. Aichorn was a psychoanalyst who administered an institution for juvenile delinquents. He observed that many incarcerated youths had underdeveloped superegos, and he attributed their criminality to expressions of an unregulated id. According to Aichorn, "The parents of these children were either absent or unloving, so that the children failed to form the intimate attachments necessary for the proper development of their superegos."[5]

Critics of psychoanalytic perspectives on criminal behavior point out that the theories are untestable and that the psychoanalytic explanations of behavior are "made after the behavior has occurred, and rely heavily on interpretations of unconscious motivations."[6]

Mental Disorders and Crime

Many research studies report that most people who commit crime do not suffer from psychological disorders.

Psychiatric explanations also extend to theories of mental illness as a cause of crime. Research studies on the relationship between mental disorders and crime, however, show conflicting results. From the 1970s through the 1980s, many researchers reported that severely mentally disordered people were no more likely to commit violent crime than those in the general population.[7]

However, recent studies report that the mentally ill who have a minimum of one incident of violent behavior have a high probability of committing another violent act within a year of being released from a hospital. Schizophrenia is the mental disorder most closely associated with violence.[8] A recent Swedish study by Henrick Belfrage has reported a strong association between crime and serious mental disorders. Studying more than a thousand patients diagnosed with schizophrenia, paranoia, and affective psychosis, he concluded that even though most of the mentally ill patients had committed only minor crimes, many (especially schizophrenics) had committed violent acts.[9] In addition, other studies have reported that even when social and demographic factors are

Psychoanalysts Sigmund Freud (seen here) and August Aichorn attempted to explain criminal behavior in terms of unconscious motivations. Prosocial, law-abiding behavior in an individual depended on the strength of the superego in its war with the id, which, in turn, depended on parental influences and other early childhood experiences.

Studies show that as much as 16 percent of all state prison and jail inmates have mental disorders. Were the mental disorders among prisoners present prior to their incarceration, or did the mental disorders develop as a result of their incarceration? Were the crimes for which mentally disordered inmates were incarcerated a direct result of their mental disorders?

controlled for, currently mentally ill patients are more often involved in violent behavior than non–mentally ill people in the general population.[10]

A word of caution is necessary when interpreting the research on mental illness and crime; more than 90 percent of mentally disordered people are not violent. In fact, most studies indicate that most people who commit crimes do not suffer from psychological disorders. For example, a number of criminological studies have consistently indicated that relatively few persons imprisoned for crimes—from 5.0 to 9.5 percent—have been diagnosed as psychotic.[11] However, a survey conducted by the Bureau of Justice Statistics has reported that as much as 16 percent, or about 250,000, of all state prison and jail inmates are mentally disordered.[12]

When reviewing the data on the percentage of prisoners who are diagnosed as mentally ill, one must ask whether the poor conditions in state prisons and local jails have deleterious effects on the mental status of inmates. In addition, studies have reported that when controls are introduced for factors such as gender, age, socioeconomic status, and life history, criminals experience no more mental illness than other, noncriminal groups.[13]

In addition, even when people with psychosis commit crimes, this in itself is not proof that the behavior resulted from the psychosis.[14] A recent study by James Bonta, Moira Law, and Karl Hanson has reported that past or present mental disorder is questionable as a significant predictor of violence and criminal behavior in offenders. Their research concluded not only that offenders with mental disorders were no more violent or prone to crime than offenders without mental disorders, but also that they were less likely to recidivate (reoffend, or commit more crimes) than nondisordered offenders.[15]

Can the presence of mental disorders help in predicting criminal and violent behavior in offenders? In some offenders, it may be possible. However, one must also take into account such factors as a person's family problems, substance-abuse behavior, and criminal history. These and other factors may be more useful in the prediction of criminal and violent behavior among individuals.[16]

After reading this section, you should be able to

1. describe Freud's psychoanalytic explanation for criminal behavior;
2. contrast Aichorn's position with Freud's on the role of the superego in crime;
3. critique psychoanalytic theories as explanations for crime;
4. summarize research on the relationship between crime and mental disorder or mental illness;
5. explain why mental illness is problematic as an explanation for or predictor of crime.

BEHAVIORAL EXPLANATIONS FOR CRIME

Behavioral theories take quite a different approach than psychoanalytic and psychiatric explanations. Behavioral theories do not focus on basic biological drives, child-parent relationships, or unconscious thoughts and drives. **Behavioral theories**, instead, assume that all human behavior is learned:

- They reject the idea that aggression is an innate human drive seeking expression.
- They argue that people learn aggressive behavior as they learn other social behavior—through reward and punishment.
- They view criminal behavior, including aggressive and violent behavior, as a learned response to social conditions and life situations.

Social psychologists have formulated ideas that stress how children learn violence through socialization—the process of learning how to behave in society. These socialization-based ideas are collectively referred to as **social learning theory**.[17]

Bandura and Social Learning Theory

Albert Bandura asserted that children learn violent or aggressive behavior as they observe role models, imitate these models, and act out the roles.

For **Albert Bandura**, a social learning theorist,

- a person is not born with the ability to behave violently; rather, people learn aggressiveness through their life experience;[18]

> **Behavioral theories** assume that all human behavior, including criminal behavior, is learned.

> In criminology, **social learning theory** focuses on the idea that people learn aggressive behavior in the same way they learn other social behavior—through socialization.

> **DID YOU KNOW**
> According to Albert Bandura, children learn aggressiveness through their life experiences with role models.

According to social learning theorists such as Albert Bandura, children are learning violence as a solution to conflict. Treatments of violence based on social learning theory advocate behavioral therapy and behavior modification through reward and punishment. Treatments of criminal offenders based on behavioral theories often emphasize rehabilitation. From what role models and social contexts—other than peers on the playground—do children learn violence?

THEORIST	THEORY
Sigmund Freud	Crime is the result of an overdeveloped superego.
August Aichorn	Crime is the result of an underdeveloped superego.
Albert Bandura	People learn aggressiveness and violent behavior through their life experiences and socialization.

FIGURE 5.1 Psychoanalytic vs. Behavioral Theories of Crime

• children learn violent or aggressive behavior as they observe role models, imitate these models, and act out the roles;
• whether children learn violent behavior depends on the extent to which role models are nonviolent or violent.

Figure 5.1 compares psychoanalytic and behavioral theories of crime.

FOR YOUR INFORMATION

Televisions in America

The great majority of American homes have more than two television sets. The televisions are turned on more than seven hours a day in the average household. Before the average American child finishes elementary school, he or she has viewed more than 8,000 murders and 100,000 other violent acts.[1] Edward Donnerstein reports that in more than three thousand network and cable programs aired during a one-year period, almost six in ten featured violence, three-quarters of which went unpunished.[2] This statistic doesn't even include video games played on television monitors.

A recent review of the nature and extent of violence on television reported that between the hours of 6 AM and 11 PM, movies are the most likely form of program to contain violence (90 percent). Other findings include the following:

• More than two-thirds of children's programs frequently portray violence in a humorous context.
• Only 5 percent of the violent acts in children's programs reflect any long-term negative consequences of the violence.
• Only 18 percent of the programs on public television contain violence.
• Of premium cable programs, 85 percent contain violence; basic cable, 59 percent; independent broadcast stations, 55 percent; and broadcast networks, 44 percent.[3]

From the longitudinal studies of Leonard Eron to the studies of Brandon Centerwall and George Gerbner and Nancy Signorielli, researchers have linked high levels of children's viewing of violence on television to high levels of aggressive attitudes, aggressive behavior, and violence.[4]

1. A. C. Huston, E. Donnerstein, H. Fairchild, N. D. Feshback, P. A. Katz, and J. P. Murray, *Big World, Small Screen: The Role of Television in American Society,* Lincoln: University of Nebraska Press, 1992.

2. E. Donnerstein, "Why Do We Have Those New Ratings on Television?" address to the National Institute on the Teaching of Psychology, 1998.

3. Mediascope, *National Television Violence Study: Executive Summary, 1994–1995,* Los Angeles, 1996.

4. L. D. Eron, "Relationship of TV Viewing Habits and Aggressive Behavior in Children," *Journal of Abnormal and Social Psychology* 67, 1963, pp. 193–196; L. D. Eron, "The Development of Aggressive Behavior from the Perspective of a Developing Behaviorism," *American Psychologist* 42, 1987, pp. 435–442; B. S. Centerwall, "Exposure to Television as a Risk Factor for Violence," *American Journal of Epidemiology* 129, 1989, pp. 643–652; G. Gebner, and N. Signorielli, "Violence Profile, 1967 Through 1988–89: Enduring Patterns," unpublished manuscript, Annenberg School of Communications, University of Pennsylvania, Philadelphia, 1990.

This action video game allows children and youths to create and control lethally violent acts against imaginary persons. According to social learning and behavioral theorists, how might this virtual-reality activity relate to aggression and criminal behavior in real life?

Violence and Crime in the Media

Many studies have linked violence on television to high levels of aggressive activities, aggressive behavior, and violence in people.

It is important to note that aggression and violence are learned not only through interaction with others but also in other social settings that act as learning experiences, such as in the presentation of violence and aggression in films and on television. Children learn violent and aggressive responses from the behavioral models on TV and in movies.[19]

After reading this section, you should be able to

1. explain how behavioral theories approach the problem of crime;
2. compare and contrast behavioral theories with psychoanalytic theories as explanations for crime;
3. apply Bandura's social learning theory to understanding violent crime;
4. summarize research on the relationship between violence and the media.

READING ABSTRACT

Media Violence and Youth

BY JOHN P. MURRAY

This reading carefully examines the relationship between violence in the media and violence in people. Murray reviews results of different research strategies used during the past forty years to study television violence: experimental studies, correlational studies, and field studies. He concludes that the "three rather different approaches to studying 'effects' of violent portrayals in television or film converge on the common conclusion that viewing violence can lead to changes in attitudes, values, and behavior concerning the acceptance and expression of violence."

See reading on page 139.

5.4 COGNITIVE THEORIES AND CRIME

Cognitive theories focus on people's mental processes, including how they perceive the environment and resolve problems.

Cognitive psychologists focus on people's mental processes, including how they perceive and think about the environment; how they learn, remember, and connect information; and how they make decisions and resolve problems. Cognitive scientists also study what goes on in the brain when people are having or thinking about particular experiences. Thus, **cognitive theories** focus on both innate and learned capabilities. Intelligence, for example, which affects the way people think, has basic components that are inherent and others that develop through training and education. Other mental processes, such as learning to make moral judgments as part of one's cognitive development, are mostly learned.

Intelligence and Criminal Behavior

Research does not consistently show a relationship between intelligence and crime.

Many studies have reported strong correlations between low intelligence (IQ) and criminal behavior.[20] Studies have linked IQ and aggression, for example, even in noncriminal males. Peter Giancola and Amos Zeichner have reported that, under conditions of both low and high provocation, there are strong inverse correlations between IQ and aggression.[21] That is, low intelligence and high provocation evoke the greatest likelihood that aggressive behavior will result. Robert Goodman has reported that even when IQs are in the normal range, lower IQs are correlated with larceny-theft, lying, and other symptoms of conduct disorder.[22] Other studies have reported that IQ level has little or no influence on criminal behavior.[23] Is there a direct relationship between criminality or delinquency and mental ability? The answer depends on which studies one examines.

Criminologists do not know the true relationship between intelligence and crime. There are numerous methodological difficulties in research efforts that attempt to study the relationship between these two variables. In addition to the serious criticisms of IQ tests, there is the problem of sampling techniques. As one criminologist reports, "Research using known criminals runs the risk of measuring the intelligence of only those people who have been apprehended, convicted, and sentenced. This group is unrepresentative of the criminal population, since it excludes offenders who escape detection. And, even if it can be shown that known offenders have lower IQs than the general population, this relationship may be more of a result of criminal justice system policy than the propensity of people with low IQs to commit crime. Consequently, the true relationship between intelligence and crime still remains unknown to the criminological community."[24]

Kohlberg and Moral Development

Cognitive development includes the process of learning to make moral judgments. Educational psychologist Lawrence Kohlberg focused on the importance of moral and ethical reasoning.

Lawrence Kohlberg's theory of moral development deals primarily with the development of moral and ethical reasoning. To research and develop this theory, Kohlberg presented to young people a series of "stories with moral dilemmas" and asked the children for an evaluation of the people and their behavior in the stories.

Kohlberg's Moral Dilemmas

The following is an example of Kohlberg's moral-dilemma stories:

> In Europe, a lady was dying because she was very sick. There was one drug that the doctors said might save her. This medicine was discovered by a man living in the same town. It cost him $22 to make it, but he charged $2,000 for just a little of it. The sick lady's husband, Heinz, tried to borrow enough money to buy the drug. He went to everyone he knew to borrow the money. He told the man who made the drug that his wife was dying, and asked him to sell the medicine cheaper or let him pay later. But the man said, "No, I made the drug, and I'm going to make money from it." So Heinz broke into the store and stole the drug.

> Did Heinz do the morally correct thing? Is it always wrong to steal? Do you believe in such a situation the law should be violated? Kohlberg focused on people's logical processes through which they arrived at answers to moral dilemmas such as this one. In his research analyzing those processes, Kohlberg came to the conclusion that moral development could be understood as consisting of three stages, or levels: the preconventional (or premoral) level, the conventional level, and the postconventional (or principled) level.

Sources: L. Kohlberg, *The Philosophy of Moral Development,* vol. 1, San Francisco: Harper and Row, 1981; L. Kohlberg, "Stage and Sequence; The Cognitive-Developmental Approach to Socialization," in *Handbook of Socialization Theory and Research,* D. A. Goslin, Ed., Chicago: Rand McNally, 1969.

Based on the children's responses, Kohlberg developed his *stage theory:* that moral development can be understood as consisting of three successively more advanced stages, or levels, of cognitive development: the preconventional (or premoral) level, the conventional level, and the postconventional (or principled) level:

1. At the *preconventional level,* a child will base his or her moral judgments on the desire to avoid punishment. Later, the child will base his or her moral judgments on the desire to obtain rewards.
2. At the *conventional level,* the child's world expands to include factors such as liking or disliking, approval or disapproval. At this level, the child's moral view is based on what other people will think of him or her. The adolescent will at first define "right behavior" as that which pleases or helps others and is approved by them. Later, at midadolescence, there is a shift toward considering such abstract social virtues as being a "good citizen," doing "one's duty," respecting authority, and maintaining the social order. Obedience to important others (parents and teachers) and others in authority is critical.
3. At the *postconventional,* or *principled,* level, the person judges the rightness or wrongness of actions not according to their consequences but according to ethical principles. At first, the principles are those that are accepted in the person's community. Later, the person acts according to her or his own personal principles.

Some students may perceive that they have an opportunity to cheat on their exam. If they did not cheat, what would be their moral reasoning if they were at the preconventional level? How would their reasoning change if they were at the conventional level? If they rejected the opportunity to cheat at the postconventional level, what might their reasoning be?

At Kohlberg's highest level of moral development, ethical principles may be carefully thought out and may be in conflict with those of the person's community. That is, this level is marked by the person's emphasis on abstract principles apart from his or her concern for existing societal laws and the power of the criminal justice system. Examples of people whom history judges as having functioned at the "high end" of the principled level are Mohandas Gandhi, Eleanor Roosevelt, and Martin Luther King Jr. For them and others at this level, justice, liberty, and equality were the guidelines for determining what was moral and correct—whether or not this corresponded to the laws of a particular time and place.[25]

Some researchers have reported that most people in society never progress beyond Kohlberg's conventional level.[26] Others have criticized Kohlberg's research, indicating that he failed to take into account cultural differences and the effects of gender on moral development.[27] In any event, Kohlberg's theory suggests that a person who obeys the law only to avoid being punished or only because he or she is preoccupied by self-interest is more likely to commit a crime than a person who sees the law as benefiting society and who sympathizes with others' rights.

After reading this section, you should be able to

1. explain why it is difficult to know whether there is a connection between intelligence and criminality;
2. describe Kohlberg's theory of moral development and give examples of each of the three stages of moral reasoning;
3. evaluate the effectiveness of cognitive theories as explanations for crime.

5.5 PERSONALITY THEORIES AND CRIME

Some psychological explanations for crime and other forms of deviant behavior stress the importance of various personality traits in an attempt to explain why some people become delinquents or criminals. **Personality theories**, in general, stress that the possession of certain characteristics predisposes individuals to criminal behavior. When combined, these traits make up what some psychologists term the **criminal personality**. Although personality theories have sparked research into the etiology of criminal behavior, they remain inadequate on a number of counts. For example, there has been little agreement on the part of psychologists, psychiatrists, and other scholars concerning the specific psychological traits that make up the so-called criminal personality, despite the fact that many studies have focused on identifying and describing the personality traits that can be used to predict and possibly prevent tendencies toward crime.

> **Personality theories,** in general, stress that the possession of certain characteristics predisposes individuals to criminal behavior. When combined, these characteristics make up what some psychologists term the **criminal personality.**

Personality Traits

Personality factors or traits—patterned ways of seeing and interacting with oneself and others—are important to any understanding of criminal behavior.

According to the *Diagnostic and Statistical Manual of Mental Disorders (DSM)*, **personality traits** are "enduring patterns of perceiving, relating to, and thinking about the environment and oneself, and are exhibited in a wide range

> **Personality traits** are enduring patterns of perceiving, relating to, and thinking about oneself and others, exhibited in a wide range of social and personal contexts.

FOR YOUR INFORMATION

What Is a Personality Disorder?

Having a personality disorder can negatively affect one's work, one's family, and one's social life. Personality disorders exist on a continuum so they can be mild to more severe in terms of how pervasive and to what extent a person exhibits the features of a particular personality disorder. While most people can live pretty normal lives with mild personality disorders . . . , during times of increased stress or external pressures (work, family, a new relationship, etc.), the symptoms of the personality disorder will gain strength and begin to seriously interfere with their emotional and psychological functioning.

Those with a personality disorder possess several distinct psychological features including disturbances in self-image; ability to have successful interpersonal relationships; appropriateness of range of emotion, ways of perceiving themselves, others, and the world; and difficulty possessing proper impulse control. These disturbances come together to create a pervasive pattern of behavior and inner experience that is quite different from the norms of the individual's culture and that often tend to be expressed in behaviors that appear more dramatic than what society considers usual. Therefore, those with a personality disorder often experience conflicts with other people and vice versa. There are ten different types of personality disorders that exist, which all have various emphases.

Source: Mental Help Net: **http://mentalhelp.net/poc/center_index.php?id=8**

of important social and personal contexts. It is only when personality traits are inflexible and maladaptive and cause either significant impairment in social or occupational functioning or subjective distress that they constitute a personality disorder."[28] Psychological theories of criminality focus on personality disorders that predispose individuals to engage in violent, negligent, or criminal behavior.

Antisocial Personality Disorder

Antisocial personality disorder's essential feature is a history of continuous and chronic antisocial behavior.

Of the ten types of personality disorders, the one of greatest concern to criminologists is antisocial personality disorder. **Antisocial personality disorder (APD)**—at times called the **sociopathic personality**—is characterized by a history of continuous and chronic antisocial behavior that may be criminal and that violates the rights of others. It is estimated that 3 percent of the U.S. male population and less than 1 percent of the female population has APD. A predisposing factor for this disorder is having been diagnosed with a conduct disorder as a child. A **conduct disorder** is characterized by "a repetitive and persistent pattern of aggressive conduct in which the rights of others are violated. . . . The physical violence may take the form of rape, mugging, assault, or, in rare cases, homicide, [while] thefts outside the home may involve extortion, purse-snatching, or holdup of a store."[29]

People with antisocial personality disorder, in addition to exhibiting signs of conduct disorder, often show the following behaviors:

- Inability to sustain consistent work behavior.
- Lack of ability to function as a responsible parent.
- Failure to accept social norms for lawful behavior, for example, through repeated thefts, an illegal occupation (pimping, prostitution, fencing, selling drugs), multiple arrests, or a felony conviction.
- Inability to maintain enduring attachment to a sexual partner.
- Irritability and aggressiveness as indicated by repeated physical fights or assaults.
- Failure to honor financial obligations, failure to plan ahead, disregard for the truth, and recklessness.[30]

Psychiatrists attribute APD to predisposing factors such as having a conduct disorder, experiencing extreme poverty, being removed from the home during childhood, and "growing up without parental figures of both sexes."[31] Antisocial behavior also may be attributed to factors such as parental rejection, inconsistent management with harsh discipline, early institutionalized living, and frequent shifting of parental figures between foster parents, relatives, or stepparents.[32]

Many sociopaths (or psychopaths—the terms are interchangeable) are in continuous conflict with the law, and APD has been linked to crimes such as serial or mass murder. Can psychopaths be rehabilitated through treatment programs? According to R. D. Hare, psychopaths will often pass through many treatment programs without success. He states that psychopaths

- are almost four times more likely to commit a violent crime after release from an intensive therapeutic community program than are other patients;
- are more likely to commit a crime after release from treatment than untreated psychopaths who are otherwise similar;

Antisocial personality disorder (APD)—at times called the **sociopathic personality**—involves a history of continuous and chronic antisocial behavior that violates others' rights and may also be criminal.

Conduct disorders are characterized by a repetitive and persistent pattern of aggressive conduct that violates the rights of others.

- learn enough psychiatric and psychological jargon to convince therapists, counselors, and parole boards that they are making remarkable progress, but use that knowledge only to develop new rationalizations for their behavior and better ways to manipulate and deceive;
- see no reason to change their attitudes and behavior to conform to social standards that they regard as irrelevant.[33]

It must be pointed out, however, that not all people with APD become criminals, and, certainly, the vast majority of criminals do not have antisocial personality disorder.[34]

After reading this section, you should be able to

1. define personality traits;
2. define conduct disorder and describe the characteristics of a person with antisocial personality disorder;
3. explain the connection between sociopaths (or psychopaths) and crime;
4. evaluate the effectiveness of personality theories as explanations for criminal behavior.

CHAPTER SUMMARY

This chapter examines the psychological theories of crime. These theories emphasize the significance of personality and personality traits and their role in criminal behavior. In psychoanalytic theories, Sigmund Freud believed that criminal behavior may be the result of an overactive superego that causes a powerful sense of guilt in the individual. Crime is not the result of guilt, but the motive. August Aichorn, however, believed that criminality is the result of an underdeveloped superego. Psychiatric explanations also extend to theories of mental illness as a cause of crime (pp. 123–126).

Behavioral theories, unlike psychoanalytic theories, assume that criminal behaviors are learned responses to social conditions and life situations. Albert Bandura's social learning theory stresses that violent behavior is learned by people as they observe role models, imitate these models, and act out the roles. Many children learn violence at home, in school, on the playground, and in their neighborhoods. Social learning theorists also believe that children learn violent and aggressive responses from the behavior models on TV, on videos, and in the movies. The reading by John Murray carefully examines the relationship between violence, crime, and the media. Many studies indicate that viewing violence in the media can lead to violent behavior in children and adults (pp. 127–129).

Cognitive theorists, such as Lawrence Kohlberg, focus on the people's mental processes, including how they perceive the environment and resolve problems. Research does not consistently show a relationship between intelligence and crime, but Kohlberg proposed a staged theory of moral development in which moral judgments become part of a more complex system of personal ethics. Personality theories of crime examine links between crime and personality traits and disorders. One of these disorders, antisocial personality disorder, interests criminologists because people with APD exhibit continuous and chronic antisocial behavior that violates others' rights. Nevertheless, not all people with APD become criminals, and the vast majority of criminals do not have APD (pp. 130–135).

Study Guide

Chapter Objectives

- Describe Freud's psychoanalytic approach to crime.
- Examine Aichorn's position on the superego and crime.
- Examine the relationship between crime and mental disorders.
- Describe behavioral theories of crime.
- Examine Bandura's approach to explaining violent behavior.
- Examine the relationship between violence and the media.
- Describe cognitive theory and Kohlberg's theory of moral development.
- Describe the relationship between crime and intelligence.
- Briefly explain what personality theories stress.
- Describe the antisocial personality disorder.
- Discuss the limitations of the psychological explanations for crime.

Key Terms

Aichorn, August (125)
Antisocial personality disorder (APD) (134)
Bandura, Albert (127)
Behavioral theories (127)
Cognitive theories (130)
Conduct disorders (134)

Criminal personality (133)
Ego (124)
Freud, Sigmund (124)
Id (124)
Neurotic (124)
Personality (124)
Personality theories (133)

Personality traits (133)
Psychotic (124)
Social learning theory (127)
Sociopathic personality (134)
Superego (124)

Self-Test
Multiple Choice

1. Personality
   a. is the organization of attitudes, beliefs, habits, and behavior, in addition to other characteristics, that develop in an individual through social interaction with others
   b. is acquired
   c. is genetically inherited
   d. *a* and *b*

2. Freud believed that the major work of society is carried on by the
   a. superego
   b. ego
   c. id
   d. subconscious

3. For Freud, some people are criminal because of
   a. an overdeveloped superego
   b. an underdeveloped superego
   c. a situated superego
   d. a faulty genetic structure

4. With respect to the relationship between mental disorders and crime,
   a. 1970s and 1980s researchers reported that severely mentally disordered people were no more likely to commit violent crime than those in the general population
   b. Belfrage reports a strong association between crime and serious mental disorders
   c. most studies indicate that most people who commit crimes do not suffer from psychological disorders
   d. all of the above

5. Behavioral theories of crime focus on
   a. basic biological drives
   b. child-parent relationships
   c. unconscious thoughts and drives
   d. learned human behavior

6. Over a twenty-two-year period, Gerbner reported in his yearly analysis of violence on television
   a. only a moderate amount of violence
   b. a consistently high level of violence
   c. only a low amount of violence
   d. a sharp increase in violence
7. According to the Murray reading on television and violence, the three major avenues by which we are affected by television violence are
   a. over-the-air broadcasts, cable TV, and satellite TV
   b. indirect effects, sensitization, and infusion
   c. direct effects, desensitization, and the "Mean World Syndrome"
   d. none of the above
8. Kohlberg's three levels of moral development are
   a. preconscious, conscious, and subconscious
   b. precognitive, cognitive, and postcognitive
   c. preconventional, conventional, and postconventional
   d. none of the above
9. People with APD exhibit
   a. inability to sustain consistent work behavior
   b. failure to accept social norms for lawful behavior
   c. irritability and aggressiveness
   d. all of the above
10. Sociopaths
   a. are the same as psychopaths
   b. will often pass through many treatment programs without success
   c. are almost four times more likely to commit a violent crime after release from an intensive therapeutic community program than are other patients
   d. all of the above

True–False

T F 1. Freud linked criminality to a sense of guilt that the person retains because of his or her childhood experiences.

T F 2. Relatively few persons imprisoned for crimes have been diagnosed as psychotic.

T F 3. For Bandura, a person is born with the ability to behave violently.

T F 4. Before the average American child finishes elementary school, he or she has viewed on television more than 18,000 murders and 400,000 other violent acts.

T F 5. According to the National Institute of Mental Health, violence on television does not affect the aggressive behavior of children.

T F 6. Cognitive psychologists focus on people's mental processes and how they perceive the environment and resolve problems.

T F 7. Criminologists do not know the true relationship between intelligence and crime.

T F 8. Personality traits are enduring patterns of perceiving, relating to, and thinking about the environment and oneself, and are exhibited in a wide range of important social and personal contexts.

T F 9. People with APD always become criminals.

Fill-In

1. _____ is the organization of attitudes, beliefs, habits, and behavior, in addition to other characteristics, that develop in the individual through social interaction with others.
2. For Freud, criminal behavior may be the result of an overdeveloped superego that causes a powerful sense of _____ in the individual.
3. _____ is the mental disorder most closely associated with criminal behavior.
4. Bandura and other social psychologists stress that children learn violence through socialization, in what has been termed _____ theory.
5. The _____ process suggests that people who watch a lot of violence on television may become more aggressive.
6. _____ theories focus on the people's mental processes, including how they perceive the environment and resolve problems.
7. For Kohlberg, at the _____ level, a child will base his or her moral judgments on the desire to avoid punishment.
8. Many studies have reported that strong correlations exist between low intelligence and _____ behavior.
9. _____ has as its essential feature a history of continuous and chronic antisocial behavior that violates the rights of others.
10. Many _____ are in continuous conflict with the law.

Matching

1. Bandura
2. Freud
3. Kohlberg
4. Psychotic
5. Principled level
6. APD
7. Television violence
8. Mean World Syndrome
9. Criminal personality
10. Schizophrenia

A. Combination of characteristics predisposing people to criminal behavior
B. Chronic antisocial behavior
C. Criminals have a sense of guilt
D. One of three major effects of TV violence
E. People learn aggression
F. Mental disorder most closely associated with violence
G. Copycat crimes
H. Personal ethical principles
I. More seriously mentally ill
J. Moral development

Essay Questions

1. Assess Freud's psychoanalytic approach to criminal behavior.
2. Describe the relationship between mental disorders and crime.
3. How do behavior theories differ from the psychoanalytic theory of criminal behavior?
4. Do you agree with Bandura's explanation for violence? Why or why not?
5. Examine and assess the relationship between violence on television and violence in children and adults.
6. Do you believe there is a relationship between intelligence and crime? Why or why not?
7. Assess Kohlberg's theory of moral development.
8. Describe and evaluate antisocial personality disorder.

Media Violence and Youth

BY JOHN P. MURRAY

The impact of media violence on youth has been a topic of intense discussion and debate in the United States for the better part of this century. Beginning in the 1920s and '30s, there were questions raised about the influence of crime and violence portrayed in comic books, movies, radio serials, and, by the 1950s, television. For example, the initial studies and concerns about movies were outlined as early as Charters's (1933) monograph *Motion Pictures and Youth: A Summary*. In each instance, the concerns about violence are similar: Does media violence influence the attitudes and behavior of the youngest members of our society? Of course, similar questions could be asked about the influence of media violence on adults, but most of the social concern and much of the scientific research has been focused on children and youth.

Despite almost 70 years of research on media violence, it is still possible to spark a lively discussion of this issue. Moreover, each new form of media—such as video games or the Internet—inspires renewed discussion of the issue of media violence. If the hypothetical "Martian" were to scan the 20th-century discussions of media violence, he/she/it would be appalled by the circularity and indecisiveness of professionals and public policy pundits.

And yet, part of the compelling nature of the media violence discussions is the seemingly transparent relationship between what we see and hear and the way we think and act. Some have argued that this transparent relationship is truly gossamer, whereas others contend that the relationship of media violence and societal violence is substantial and profoundly disturbing. The reason that these two viewpoints can coexist—and have done so for many decades—is the fact that media violence and societal violence are not related in any direct and simple manner, and there are multiple causes for both phenomena. . . .

VIOLENCE IN THE 'HOOD AND IN HOLLYWOOD

In New York, in the fall of 1995, youths set fire to a subway token booth by spraying a flammable substance through the opening for the change and token slot. The booth exploded and burned the subway attendant. The attendant died in December 1995 as a result of extensive burns. This was one of the more dramatic episodes in a series of attacks that seemed to be related to a recently released movie, *Money Train*, in which a similar act occurred.

A few years earlier in Los Angeles, a filmmaker interviewed a young man who was being held in the Los Angeles County Juvenile Detention Center on a charge of attempted murder. The 16-year-old was asked how it happened, and he replied, "The guy came after me and I had a gun. So, I shot him. I shot him twice. It's easy to get a gun in the 'hood." When asked about his favorite television programs, he said, "I like to watch that show, the *Cops*, or *America's Most Wanted*; I might see some of my friends out there, messin up" (Mediascope, 1993).

In the late 1970s, when the movie *The Deerhunter* was released, it contained a very graphic portrayal of Russian roulette. While the film was playing in theaters and in video release, there were numerous reports of adolescents, usually males, imitating the Russian roulette scene, often with tragic results. Of course, there were many additional factors that influenced this result, such as watching the video with a group of young males who were drunk, or a history of depression or suicide attempts. Nevertheless, some incidents of death from this film were simply accidents of imitation gone awry.

In the early 1970s, a made-for-television movie called *The Doomsday Flight* contained an easily imitated bomb threat/hostage plot. When the movie was broadcast in the United States, there were numerous bomb threats directed to various airlines. When the movie was sold to an Australian commercial television network, the result was a ransom of one million dollars paid by Qantas Airlines to save a jetliner en route from Sydney to Hong Kong. (The plot involved a bomb that was activated on takeoff and would detonate when the plane dropped to an altitude of 4,000 feet. In the United States, the bomb threats to the airlines were handled by diverting aircraft to Denver or Mexico City—high-altitude airports. However, Qantas lacked a high-altitude airport for diversion between Sydney and Hong Kong.)

Are these reports of tragic events merely the isolated outcomes of unfortunate circumstances, or are these events simply the more dramatic examples of a subtle and pervasive influence of media violence? What do we know about the nature of the violence on television?

The most extensive analyses of the incidence of violence on television are the studies conducted by a research team at the University of Pennsylvania, directed by George Gerbner. The results of these yearly analyses of the level of violence on American television for the 22-year period 1967–1989 (Gerbner & Signorielli, 1990) indicate a consistently high level of violence. There were some minor fluctuations in the early 1970s, followed by a steady increase to 1976, a sharp decline in 1977, and then a steady climb to an all-time high in 1982–1983. According to Gerbner's initial analysis (Gerbner, 1972), eight out of every 10 plays broadcast during the survey period in 1969 contained some form of violence, and eight episodes of violence occurred during each hour of broadcast time. Furthermore, programs especially designed for children, such as cartoons, were the most violent of all programming. Later analyses by Gerbner and Gross (1974, 1976a, 1976b) indicated that there was some decline in violence levels from 1969 to 1975, at least in terms of the prominence of killing. However, the level of violence dramatically increased in 1976 (Gerbner et al., 1977) and was followed by a decline to one of the lowest levels in the 1977 season (Gerbner et al., 1978). This decline was quite dramatic. From the "bumper-crop violence harvest" of 1976 to the relatively placid 1977, the percentage of programs containing violence fell from 90% to 75.5%; the rate of violent episodes per hour fell from 9.5 to 6.7; and the rate of violence per program fell from 6.2 to 5.0 episodes. However, this downward trend was reversed in 1978 and through the early 1980s, and violence in weekend children's programs reached 30.3 violence episodes per hour in the 1982–1983 season (Gerbner & Signorielli, 1990). Overall, the levels of violence in prime-time programming have averaged about five acts per hour, and children's Saturday morning programs have averaged about 20 to 25 violent acts per hour. Although the 1992–1993 season manifested a sharp decline from those levels, it is not clear whether this will be a permanent change (Gerbner, Morgan, & Signorielli, 1994).

In addition to broadcast television, cable television adds to the level of violence through new, more violent programs, and by recycling older violent broadcasts. A recent survey by the Center for Media and Public Affairs (Lichter & Amundson, 1992) identified 1,846 violent scenes broadcast and cablecast between 6:00 AM to midnight on one day in Washington, DC. The most violent periods were between 6:00 to 9:00 AM, with 497 violent scenes (165.7 per hour) and between 2:00 to 5:00 PM with 609 violent scenes (203 per hour). Most of this violence is presented without context or judgment as to its acceptability. And, most of this violence in the early morning and afternoon is viewed by children and youth. A follow-up study conducted in 1994 found a 41% increase in violence: 2,605 violent acts during one day on the television screens of Washington, DC (Lichter & Amundson, 1994).

In a more recent *qualitative* study of television violence, funded by the commercial television networks (UCLA Center for Communication Policy, 1995), the research team concluded: "The world of television, from broadcast networks, to syndication, to cable, to home videos, is not as violent as we had feared and not as wholesome as we might have hoped. There is room for substantial improvement" (p. 151). However, it is difficult to compare the results of this study with the results of previous research, because its analysis is discursive rather than quantitative as was the evidence found in the reports from the University of Pennsylvania (Gerbner & Signorielli, 1990; Gerbner et al., 1994) or the Center for Media and Public Affairs (Lichter & Amundson, 1992, 1994).

In February 1996, a new report financed by the National Cable Television Association provided a comprehensive review of the nature and extent of violence on commercial and public broadcast television and cable television. The *National Television Violence Study* (Mediascope, 1996) reviewed about 2,500 hours of television involving 2,693 programs by randomly selecting 20 composite weeks of programming on 23 channels, monitoring programs between 6:00 AM and 11:00 PM. The investigators found that the typical perpetrator of violence is adult (76%), male (78%), and Caucasian (76%). Movies are the most likely form of programming to contain violence (90%), although children's programs (67%) frequently portray violence in a humorous context. Also, only 5% of the violent acts on children's programs show any long-term, negative consequences to the violence. Overall, 44% of programs on the broadcast networks contain violence: independent broadcast stations (55%), basic cable (59%), premium cable subscription (85%), and public television (18%).

POTENTIAL EFFECTS OF TELEVISION VIOLENCE

What can be said about violence in society and the relationship to media violence? Is there a rational pattern of relationships; a reasonable level of concern about media violence; a systematic body of evidence from research conducted in various settings? The answer is "yes" to all of these questions. Although there are many causes of violence in society, there are scientifically sound studies from diverse perspectives that link media violence to violence attitudes, values, and behaviors.

One of the suggestions about the way in which media violence affects audiences of all ages is that such depictions transmit a sense of acceptance or normativeness about violence in our lives—a confirmation that violence is an acceptable and usual way to resolve conflicts. This is the sense that Berkowitz (1984) uses when he describes the effects of "thoughts" on the manifestation of antisocial behavior, and it is the sense that is captured in his popular article on gun control entitled "When the Trigger Pulls the Finger" (Berkowitz, 1985).

It is important to note that psychologists and psychiatrists involved in media studies (Donnerstein, Slaby, & Eton, 1994; Menninger, 1995; Murray, 1994, 1995; Murray,

Menninger, & Grimes, 1993) do not suggest that violent media are the only cause of violence in society. Rather there are many wellsprings of violent behavior, such as growing up in an abusive home or a violent neighborhood (Osofsky, 1995). However, media are one component of a potentially toxic environment for youth, and it is important to understand the roles that media play in youth violence and ways to mitigate these harmful influences. So, what do we know, and what can we do about media violence? In particular, since it is the most pervasive form of media violence in the lives of children and youth, what can be done about television violence? . . .

One of the first major reports on media violence was the National Commission on the Causes and Prevention of Violence (Baker & Ball, 1969). The next landmark event occurred when the Surgeon General of the United States released a report in 1972 that concluded that violence on television does influence children who view that programming and does increase the likelihood that viewers will become more aggressive. Not all children are affected, not all children are affected in the same way, but there is evidence that television violence can be harmful to young viewers (Surgeon General's Scientific Advisory Committee on Television and Social Behavior, 1972; Murray, 1973). Ten years later, the National Institute of Mental Health (1982) concluded that violence on television does affect the aggressive behavior of children and there are many more reasons for concern about violence on television. "The research question has moved from asking whether or not there is an effect to seeking explanations for that effect" (p. 6).

In 1992, the American Psychological Association Task Force on Television and Society (Huston et al., 1992) concluded that 30 years of research confirms the harmful effects of television violence. And, these conclusions were reaffirmed by the American Psychological Association Commission on Violence and Youth (1993; Eton, Gentry, and Schlegel, 1994).

How are we affected by television violence? There seem to be three major avenues: direct effects, desensitization, and the Mean World Syndrome:

1. The *direct effects* process suggests that children and adults who watch a lot of violence on television may become more aggressive and/or they may develop favorable attitudes and values about the use of aggression to resolve conflicts.
2. The second effect, *desensitization*, suggests that children who watch a lot of violence on television may become less sensitive to violence in the real world around them, less sensitive to the pain and suffering of others, and more willing to tolerate ever-increasing levels of violence in our society.
3. The third effect, the *Mean World Syndrome*, suggests that children or adults who watch a lot of violence on television may begin to believe that the worls is as mean and dangerous in real life as it appears on television, and hence, they begin to view the world as a much more mean and dangerous place.

CRITICAL THINKING

1. According to social science research, how are media violence and societal violence connected?
2. Why does media violence have the power to inspire copycat crimes, and what are some examples?

Sociological Theories I

Social-Structural Explanations of Criminal Behavior

6

6.1 INTRODUCTION: STRUCTURE-BASED EXPLANATIONS

Previous chapters presented the biological and psychological theories of crime. Those theories are based on the assumption of physical, behavioral, or mental defects in the individual offender. While criminologists recognize that environmental and social factors affect rates of crime, individual acts of crime are attributed to abnormality or inferiority according to biological and psychological perspectives. This chapter focuses on sociological theories that illustrate how social ecology and cultural dynamics, both realities external to individuals, influence crime. These explanations, often called social structural theories, reveal the ways in which culture, values, social class relations, and community stability all impact crime and delinquency.

In some cases, criminal behavior may be a normal response to frustration, strain, and tension generated by pressures and conflict within society itself. In other cases, a criminal or delinquent may be conforming to the deviant norms of the subculture to which he or she has been socialized. Still other theories argue that crime and delinquency are an inevitable result of social and economic inequality and that the law is inherently biased toward the interests of the dominant or ruling groups or classes. This chapter begins our analysis of sociological theories with an examination of social-structural theories of criminal behavior, including

- a review of social disorganization theory (section 6.2);
- an analysis of strain theories (section 6.3);
- an assessment of subcultural theories of delinquency (section 6.4).

6.2 SOCIAL DISORGANIZATION THEORY

The primary focus of **social disorganization theory** is the wide variety of environmental and urban conditions that affect crime rates. It also focuses on the development of high-crime communities, which are associated with the breakdown of conventional norms and values as a result of increased immigration, industrialization, and urbanization. As a theoretical approach to the study of crime, social disorganization theory has its roots in the process of **social change** and is related to the fact that Americans live in a society characterized by **heterogeneity**, various value conflicts, many subcultures, and rapid social change.

Criminologists have observed that social disorganization sometimes results when people attempt to use traditional guidelines to cope with new social conditions and then experience frustration and confusion because the traditional rules are no longer effective or no longer apply. Social disorganization theory examines crime by analyzing the social disorganization that develops with social change.

The major focus of social disorganization theory is environmental and urban conditions and social changes that affect crime rates. How might this neighborhood reflect social disorganization? What social changes and their consequences might account for increased crime rates in this neighborhood? What remedies for crime do you think social disorganization theorists would suggest?

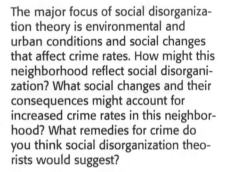

Social disorganization theory stresses that crime increases when traditional social guidelines no longer work or when there is a decline in group unity due to ineffective behavior patterns.

Social change refers to change in the structure and organization of social relationships of a society.

Heterogeneity means mixed, or consisting of different elements or parts.

Social organization is the actual patterning and regulation of people's interactions in society, including social norms.

Social Disorganization and Social Change

One must understand social organization before examining social disorganization, which is a function of social change.

To better understand social disorganization and crime, one must first have a clear conception of what is meant by social organization. **Social organization** is the actual patterning and regulation of human social interaction, whereas

FOR YOUR INFORMATION

On Social Change

- Societies are characterized by different aspects of social change, some of them extensive, some of them minor.
- No society is free from change.
- Change is always present and is manifested by alterations in people's social relationships.
- In societies that experience periods of rapid social change, social disorganization may develop as new attitudes and social norms evolve.
- For some people and social institutions, adjustment to changes in the social structure is not difficult; for others, change may bring many difficulties and problems.

social structure refers to the roles, statuses, and institutions through which societies are organized. Much of what a criminologist terms social organization consists of social norms and expectations that guide human behavior. In all societies

- people depend on one another for their survival and attainment of goals;
- people develop social organization to regulate their own conduct and the conduct of others, and they develop rules for the use of various resources to meet their needs;
- reciprocal expectations are developed as people come to depend on one another.

In other words, people learn what to expect from themselves, what to expect from others, and what others expect from them. In this way, people develop cultural traditions, customs, and complex systems of rules and regulations to guide them in their various actions and activities.

Society's **laws**, which are codified rules of a culture, define which forms of social behavior are acceptable and which are not. The customs, rules, and laws of the society embody social expectations and, to an extent, govern the behavior of society's members. In this manner, society becomes organized around behavior patterns that contribute to human survival, maintenance, and the fulfillment of socially and culturally prescribed **values**.

When traditional social guidelines no longer work, or when there is a decline in group unity due to ineffective behavior patterns, social disorganization results. In every society, then, there exist standards of expected behavior (**social norms**) that guide people in the roles they play. When these norms are functioning efficiently, they go largely unnoticed by most people living in the society. According to social disorganization theory, people internalize the social expectations and rules, facilitating the smooth operation of society. With social change, however, many of society's norms may no longer function effectively. Society may become disorganized when people's norms and laws are no longer appropriate for new social conditions or when social cohesion or unity breaks down because of the ineffectiveness of institutionalized patterns of behavior.

The Chicago School of Criminology

In the 1920s, pioneering criminologists at the University of Chicago studied immigrants to learn how social disorganization and social change can cause criminal behavior.

In the 1920s, two scholars from the University of Chicago, **William I. Thomas** and **Florian Znaniecki**, studied Polish immigrant peasants and the difficulties they encountered in the industrialized, urbanized United States. They found that older Polish immigrants were able to maintain many of the old-world cultural ways in the urban slums. However, the second-generation Poles had a much more difficult time in that they maintained some of the old-world traditions, values, and rules, yet were being raised in a new-world urban American community. Not yet assimilated into the new-world norms and not able to transfer the old customs and norms from their homogeneous European folk community to the anonymous, heterogeneous urban community, this second-generation's rates of delinquency and crime rose. Thomas and Znaniecki attributed this increase to the social disorganization (the breakdown of social controls, bonds, and families) within the second-generation community.[1]

Social structure refers to the roles, statuses, and institutions through which society is organized.

Values are conceptions of worth or desirability, and they make up our judgments of moral and immoral, good and bad, right and wrong, and so forth.

Social norms are standards and rules of accepted behavior; **laws** are the codified rules or norms of a society.

William I. Thomas and **Florian Znaniecki**, theorists of the Chicago school, examined how social disorganization can create personal disorganization and criminal behavior.

Thomas and Znaniecki, then, found the following:

- Social disorganization is a decrease in the influence of existing rules on individual members of a group.
- With social change, there is a breakdown among people in the consensus of social rules, which results in the fragmentation of the social order.
- When people's actions are not oriented by social values, social disorganization develops: people do not know what kind of behavior to expect from others, and they are not sure what others expect from them.
- When this occurs, people's cooperative activities diminish, conflict intensifies, and feelings of fear and uncertainty sometimes are expressed in self-destructive, antisocial, or criminal behavior.
- Social disorganization can create personal disorganization and deviant and criminal behavior.[2]

Clifford R. Shaw and **Henry D. McKay** were also from the Chicago school and helped to popularize the social disorganization approach to crime and delinquency.[3] They began their research in Chicago during the 1920s, when the city was full of newcomers and foreign-born immigrants. Most of the newcomers congregated in the central city area, occupying old, deteriorated housing with many health and environmental hazards. Shaw and McKay scientifically studied crime within this changing urban environment. Rejecting the then-popular racial and cultural explanations of crime, they believed that crime and criminal behavior are very much the product of urban ecological conditions.

Shaw and McKay used a social-ecological zone model, also called a **concentric zone model**, developed by two earlier University of Chicago sociologists, Robert Park and Ernest Burgess, to demonstrate how people were distributed spatially in the urban growth process.[4] They used this concentric zone model (see Figure 6.1) scientifically to study the relationship between crime rates and the various zones.

Shaw and McKay found higher rates of crime and delinquency in the transitional inner-city zones, where high numbers of foreign-born people had recently settled. The highest crime and delinquency rates persisted in Zones I

> **Clifford R. Shaw** and **Henry D. McKay**, of the Chicago school of criminology, popularized the social disorganization approach to crime and delinquency through the study of urban social ecology. Using a **concentric zone model**, they scientifically studied the relationship between crime rates and various community zones.

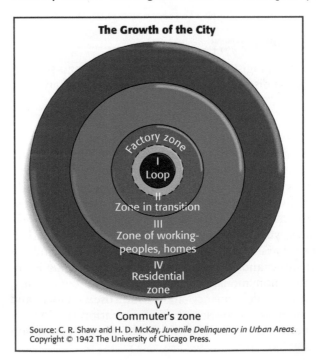

The Growth of the City

Factory zone

I
Loop

II
Zone in transition

III
Zone of working-
peoples, homes

IV
Residential
zone

V
Commuter's zone

Source: C. R. Shaw and H. D. McKay, *Juvenile Delinquency in Urban Areas.*
Copyright © 1942 The University of Chicago Press.

FIGURE 6.1 Shaw and McKay's Concentric Zone Model

and II. These areas retained these rates, even though the ethnic composition of the zones changed over the years. The crime rates dropped significantly as one progressed from the center of the city outward.[5] This finding refuted the assumption (common at the time) that criminality is the property of a specific ethnic or racial minority group. In stressing that neighborhood structure influences criminal behavior, Shaw and McKay also challenged earlier views that criminals were atavistic throwbacks on the Darwinian scale of human evolution or psychologically maladjusted individuals.[6]

Although flawed by modern standards, Shaw and McKay's research laid the groundwork for many community treatment programs over the past sixty years.[7] Shaw and McKay were also among the first scholars to introduce the variable of urban ecology into the study of criminal behavior. Their ideas and ecological perspective are still being applied in today's communities. Studies in the United States, England, and Scandinavia, for example, have reported strong correlations between high crime rates and such social disorganization factors as alienation, poverty, disorder, broken homes, and unemployment, in addition to low organizational participation, unsupervised teens, and sparse friendship networks.[8]

Shaw and McKay specified four key elements of social disorganization: population heterogeneity, transience, poverty, and broken homes.

After reading this section, you should be able to

1. explain the basis of social disorganization theory as an explanation for criminal behavior;
2. describe how social change can lead to social disorganization;
3. summarize the contributions of the Chicago school of criminology to understanding the effects of social organization and disorganization on crime;
4. describe the findings from Thomas and Znaniecki's research on immigrants in Chicago;
5. explain Shaw and McKay's concentric zone model and its relationship to crime.

6.3 STRAIN THEORY

Our society places much emphasis on success. We are all taught to want to be successful in many aspects of our lives. The great majority of Americans want wealth and possessions such as nice clothing, cars, houses, jewelry, and other material comforts. They also want a good education, power, prestige, and status. American society also places great emphasis on the attainment of these goals for all Americans regardless of their economic strata. However, because of their structural position in society, people in certain groups (such as those in the lower classes and in groups against which society discriminates) are not able to achieve these goals or symbols of success through the means available to them. The pressures and frustrations people in this situation experience are often so severe that they cause serious strain and lead or induce the people into deviant or criminal behavior.

Strain theory focuses on the structure of society and the limited means of many Americans to achieve desired goals. In other words, strain theory sees crime and delinquency as a result of the anger and frustration people feel because of their inability to achieve the "American dream." Thus, in this view,

Strain theory views crime and delinquency as a result of the anger and frustration people feel because of their inability to achieve the "American dream."

Strain theorists view crime as a result of anomie and the anger and frustration that people feel due to their inability to achieve the "American dream." What might be some sources of anomie, anger, and frustration for the criminal offenders in this scene from an urban riot?"

socially generated forces and pressures drive people to crime. These "strains," as they are termed, are not evenly distributed in society but are "most severe among the groups with the highest crime rates."[9]

Strain theory, then, is based on the breakdown of social order that can result from unequal access to the means of success. One source of such a breakdown is referred to as **anomie**, or normlessness. The famous sociologist **Émile Durkheim** was the first to develop the concept of anomie to explain increased rates of suicide produced by rapid social change in society. He used the phrase "anomic suicide" to refer to acts of self-destruction resulting from an abrupt breakdown of society's norms, which often occurs during periods of economic depression or political crisis.[10]

Sociologist **Émile Durkheim** introduced the concept of **anomie**, meaning "normlessness," as a source of strain.

Merton's Anomie/Strain Theory

Robert Merton adapted Durkheim's concept of anomie to develop his strain theory.

Robert Merton modified and adapted Durkheim's concept of anomie to explain deviant behavior such as crime and delinquency.

The sociologist **Robert Merton** modified and adapted Durkheim's abstract concept of anomie to explain forms of deviant behavior other than suicide, especially crime and delinquency. Merton formulated his strain theory in the 1930s during the Great Depression, a period of extensive poverty. When the stock market crashed in 1929, the United States, along with most of the world, spiraled into an economic depression, resulting in high unemployment and increased crime. These events influenced Merton's development of the theory in that he associated both anomie and economic deprivation with increased levels of crime.

In 1938, Merton argued that anomie results from a lack of integration between culturally prescribed goals and the availability of legitimate or institutionalized means (norms) for goal attainment. U.S. society places a great deal of emphasis on the attainment of economic as well as material success. However, as a result of their structural positions within society, certain segments of the population (such as the lower classes and certain ethnic and racial groups) have limited opportunities for—and are often denied access to—the legitimate means to achieve this success, such as a good education or a good job. Members of these disadvantaged groups thus experience many pressures, frustrations, and strains, which are often severe enough to cause them to deviate from the legitimate goals and/or means (norms) of the society. Individuals

A TYPOLOGY OF INDIVIDUAL ADAPTATION		
Modes of Adaptation	Culture Goals	Institutionalized Means
Conformity	+	+
Innovation	+	−
Ritualism	−	+
Retreatism	−	−
Rebellion	±	±

Source: Data from R. K. Merton, *Social Theory and Social Structure.* New York: Free Press, 1957, p. 140.

FIGURE 6.2 Figure 6.2 has been adapted from Merton's research. In this figure, a plus sign (+) signifies "acceptance"; a minus sign (−) signifies "rejection"; a plus–minus sign (±) signifies "rejection of prevailing values and substitution of new values."

who are restricted in or denied access to the use of these legitimate means tend to become anomic, or alienated from American society; thus, they have a greater tendency to engage in various types of deviant and criminal behavior.[11]

Merton presented five modes of adaptation in the use of means to attain goals, and for this reason his model is sometimes referred to as the **anomie/strain theory.** Four of these methods of adaptation— **retreatism, rebellion, innovation,** and **ritualism**—occur when legitimate means to goal attainment are blocked. The fifth method of adaptation is **conformity.** Conformity results when the individual accepts both legitimate means and legitimate goals and is in a social position that allows access to both means and goals. As Figure 6.2 illustrates, in other combinations, people might reject legitimate means or legitimate goals or both.

Merton contended that much criminal behavior in society can be explained using his anomie/strain theory, also called his theory of anomie. He argued that offenses such as property crime, robbery, drug selling, and organized crime can all be viewed as forms of anomic response that result when conventional or legitimate means for goal attainment are blocked. Merton also argued that the higher crime rates that exist among particular groups in our society are simply symptomatic of a disjunction between culturally approved goals and opportunities to use culturally approved means to attain them.[12]

The aim of Merton's theory is to discover how "some social structures exert a definite pressure" on certain people to engage in nonconformist, including criminal, behavior. The theory of anomie also provides important insights into the origins and nature of many types of criminal and deviant behavior. However, Merton's theory is much more useful for explaining crimes against property than crimes against persons, such as aggravated assault, forcible rape, and murder. Also, although this theory provides us with an explanation for crime committed by society's lower classes, it inadequately explains crimes committed by affluent people, who typically are neither deprived nor denied the use of legitimate means for goal attainment.[13]

Agnew's General Strain Theory

Robert Agnew's general strain theory stresses the importance of three types of negative relationships in individual strain.

Robert Agnew has developed a new version of strain theory, called **general strain theory (GST).** GST focuses on individual-level influences of strain and

Merton's **anomie/strain theory** argues that anomie results from a lack of integration of culturally prescribed goals (values) and the availability of legitimate or institutionalized means for goal attainment (norms). This discrepancy between goals and means is often addressed through innovative crime adaptations.

According to Merton, **retreatism, rebellion, innovation, and ritualism** are four methods of adaptation, constituting deviant, criminal, or anomic behavior, that occur when legitimate means to goal attainment are blocked.

Robert Agnew proposes a **general strain theory (GST)** to explain criminal and delinquent behavior, defining three major types of strain caused by negative interpersonal relationships.

Retreatism, Rebellion, Innovation, and Ritualism

RETREATISM

Merton suggests that individuals who find themselves blocked in goal attainment may simply decide to give up on conventional goals as well as legitimate means. These people, whom he terms *retreatists*, reject both the goals and means and withdraw from the situation. Vagrancy, drug addiction, alcoholism, and even suicide represent forms of this deviant response.

REBELLION

Merton also believed that people not only may reject goals but also may rebel against the social order and even attempt to introduce new goals and means into the society. This rebellious form of deviant response is typical of various radical or revolutionary groups, or *rebels*, who desire sweeping change in the society.

INNOVATION

Some individuals who encounter limited access to the use of legitimate means frequently adopt a deviant or anomic response that Merton called innovation. The *innovator* is one who rejects only the legitimate means, not the ends or goals. He or she then substitutes illegitimate or criminal means to achieve the goals.

RITUALISM

Ritualism, in Merton's view, occurs when a person fails to achieve the goals and inwardly gives up in his or her efforts to achieve them. The individual nevertheless publicly and strictly conforms to the use of legitimate means that are socially defined as necessary for goal attainment. The *ritualist*, by reducing or ignoring the importance of goals, thereby finds a solution to his or her frustrations and failures. Outwardly, the person manifests a compulsive conformity to legitimate means. For most people, the ritualist's behavior would suggest anything but deviance; however, Merton considers ritualists deviant because they have inwardly withdrawn from the struggle for goal attainment.

Source: R. K. Merton, *Social Theory and Social Structure,* New York: Free Press, 1965, pp. 132–157.

tries to understand why strained individuals are more likely than nonstrained individuals to commit criminal or delinquent acts. Using sociological, psychological, and mental health research, Agnew has expanded on the various adaptations that a person may make in response to strain in the social environment.[14]

Agnew believes that many factors influence one's choice of criminal or noncriminal adaptations to strain, and he focuses on negative interpersonal relationships. GST describes relationships in which people are not treating an individual the way he or she wants to be treated. There are three major types of negative relationships that cause strain:

1. Other people prevent an individual from achieving positively valued goals.
2. Other people remove (or threaten to remove) positively valued achievements or stimuli from the individual.
3. Other people expose (or threaten to expose) the individual to negative or noxious stimuli.

These three strains increase the probability that an individual will experience a range of negative emotions from fear and frustration to anger (see Figure 6.3). The emotions the individual feels may then create pressures or tensions that require corrective action. Criminal behavior is one of the possible responses.

How could you use Merton's strain theory to explain this act of vandalism by a delinquent juvenile gang? Which methods of adaptation in Merton's anomie/strain theory might apply? According to Agnew's general strain theory, what types of negative relationships might have influenced the individual perpetrators to commit such an act? What role might conditioning factors have played?

Individuals who have little power to control or deal with negative stimuli experience more strain than those who have higher degrees of power. This strain increases the probability that individuals will experience various negative emotions. The emotions may then create pressures for corrective action such as delinquent behavior. Anger, for example, may be especially conducive to delinquency, according to Agnew and his associates, "because it energizes the individual for action, lowers inhibitions, and creates a desire for revenge. Delinquency may be used to reduce or escape from strain (e.g., stealing money, running away from abusive parents), seek revenge against those who have inflicted the strain (e.g., assault, vandalism), or reduce the negative feelings that result from strain (e.g., illicit drug use)."[15]

Agnew points out that only some strained individuals turn to delinquency and crime. This means that there must be **conditioning factors** that influence an individual's reaction to strain. Conditioning factors that Agnew identifies include

Various **conditioning factors** affect strain through internal or external constraints on behavior.

- the importance an individual attaches to threatened values, goals, or identities;
- the individual's coping skills;
- resources available to the individual, such as money, self-esteem, social supports, level of social control, and association with delinquent or non-delinquent peers;

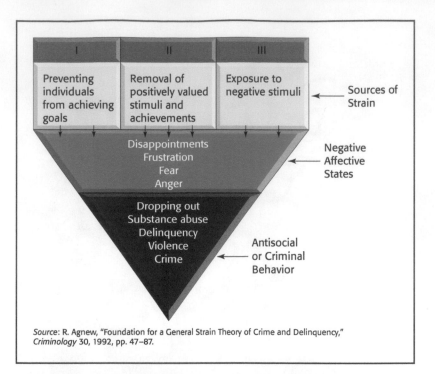

FIGURE 6.3 Elements of Agnew's General Strain Theory (GST)

Source: R. Agnew, "Foundation for a General Strain Theory of Crime and Delinquency," *Criminology* 30, 1992, pp. 47–87.

FOR YOUR INFORMATION

Agnew's Three Types of Strain

(1) The first major type of strain results from ***the failure to achieve goals***. For example, many people in our society aspire to the goals of wealth and status. However, not having the appropriate educational, political, and financial resources, they assume the goals are unachievable. Strain may then result from the disjunction between aspirations and achievements or expectations and achievements. The amount of strain between expectations and achievements may not be as great as between aspirations and achievements, in that most people's expectations are not as lofty or inflated as their aspirations.

(2) The second major type of strain results from ***the removal (or denial) of previously valued stimuli and positive achievements***. For example, the loss or death of a close friend or relative, the loss of a job, and a move to a new community or school are all stressful life events that produce strain in individuals. Losing positive stimuli may lead some individuals to delinquent or criminal behavior as they attempt to salvage their losses, find replacements, or seek revenge against those believed to be responsible for their strain.

(3) The third major type of strain is ***the presentation of or exposure to negative or noxious stimuli***. Abusive and criminal victimization are such negative stimuli. Children who are assaulted at home, adolescents picked on at school, and individuals experiencing violent or property crimes in their communities are all examples of this type of strain.

Source: R. Agnew, "Foundation for a General Strain Theory of Crime and Delinquency," *Criminology* 30, 1992, pp. 47–87.

- the individual's access to alternative (sheltering) values, goals, and identities;
- other coping resources available to the individual, such as intelligence and problem-solving skills.

Conditioning factors constitute internal or external constraints that greatly influence individual responses to strain. For Agnew, then, criminal or delinquent behaviors are not inevitable outcomes of strain. Strain produces only *pressure* toward crime and deviance. There are many ways people adapt to pressure. Some individuals accept responsibility for it; others downplay or ignore it; still others become substance abusers, or they take revenge on those they feel may have caused their anger or strain.

Various studies support general strain theory and report that exposure to strain increases delinquency.[16] Angry and stressed individuals appear to be more likely than other people to interact with delinquent peers and to commit crime.[17] Other studies indicate that strain increases the probability of delinquency but play down the significance of conditioning factors. Paul Mazerolle and Jeff Maahs, for example, report that only three conditioning factors appear to have a significant impact on delinquent behavior outcomes when controlling for strain level: having a disposition toward delinquency, exposure to delinquent peers, and holding deviant beliefs.[18]

Although much research has supported GST, some studies have had trouble explaining why some people are more likely than others to react to strain with criminal behavior. Robert Agnew, Timothy Brezina, John Paul Wright, and Francis T. Cullen have recently used data from the National Survey of Children to address this issue. In their complex study of strain, personality traits, and delinquency, they predicted that juveniles high in negative emotionality and low in constraint would be more likely to react to strain with delinquency and criminal behavior. Their data and results supported their prediction.[19]

After reading this section, you should be able to

1. explain the basis of Merton's strain theory in Durkheim's concept of anomie;
2. list and define Merton's five modes of adaptation to strain in his anomie/strain theory;
3. describe Agnew's general strain theory in terms of his three major sources of strain and the conditioning factors that determine individuals' reactions to strain;
4. evaluate the contributions of strain theory to understanding deviant and criminal behavior.

6.4 SUBCULTURAL DELINQUENCY THEORIES

Robert Merton's strain theory, which focuses on strains caused by differential access to societal goals and means, has been applied to explain lower-class crime and urban-gang delinquency. Subcultural theories, such as those developed by Albert Cohen and by Richard Cloward and Lloyd Ohlin, are based on similar assumptions.[20] **Subcultural theories** focus on the nature and origins of criminal and delinquent groups within society and help to explain variations in

> **DID YOU KNOW**
> Deviant or criminal behavior can be a product of individuals' participation in deviant or criminal subcultures.

Subcultural theories focus on the nature and origins of delinquent subcultures.

Subcultures are diverse subgroups that share the general culture but maintain some unique norms that distinguish them from the wider culture.

rates of delinquency and crime in the United States. When criminologists write about **subcultures**, they are referring to the variety of subgroups (in complex societies such as the United States) that, for the most part, are similar to or share the general culture but that also maintain some unique norms (patterns of expected behavior) that distinguish them from the wider culture. For example, there is a wide variety of ethnic, religious, and occupational subcultures in American society.

The subcultural explanation of deviance stresses that some subcultures contain norms that deviate from and conflict with those of the general society. Conformity to subcultural norms therefore involves deviance from those of the society at large. In this sense, rates of crime and delinquency can be viewed simply as products of deviant subcultures. Subcultural theorists assume that individuals learn deviant or criminal behavior in association with others and that variations in the rates of crime and delinquency reflect the existence of deviant subcultural norms that are learned, shared, and perpetuated over time.[21]

Criminologists have reported on the existence of many types of criminal subcultures, such as those related to professional theft, racketeering, organized crime, prostitution, and the selling of drugs. However, much criminological attention has been focused on analyzing the nature and origins of delinquent subcultures. It is within a **delinquent subculture** that young people, through participation and gradual absorption into group life, become socialized to a variety of norms, beliefs, and skills necessary to the commission of delinquent acts.[22]

Delinquent subculture refers to a subculture within which young people, through participation and gradual absorption into group life, become socialized to a variety of norms, beliefs, and skills necessary for committing delinquent acts.

Studies of Delinquent Gangs

According to Albert Cohen, delinquent gangs consist of working-class boys who scorn middle-class values. Gresham Sykes and David Matza point out that delinquents often seek ways to "neutralize" their misbehavior. Richard Cloward and Lloyd Ohlin propose three types of delinquent gangs.

Albert Cohen believed that a delinquent subculture exists because it offers a solution to the status problems and frustrations that working-class boys experience in their efforts to achieve middle-class success.

Albert Cohen noted relatively high rates of delinquency on the part of working-class youths, and developed a widely respected subcultural theory on delinquent gangs. In his book, *Delinquent Boys: The Culture of the Gang* (1955), he reported the following:

- The delinquent subculture exists because it offers a solution to the status problems and frustrations working-class boys experience in their efforts to achieve middle-class success.
- Although these boys typically aspire to middle-class lifestyles and goals, their early life experiences leave them unprepared to successfully compete in school and other areas necessary for upward mobility.
- Working-class boys are constantly evaluated by "middle-class measuring rods." However, their working-class background does not adequately equip them to practice the middle-class standards necessary for success, such as suppression of aggression, deferral of gratification, self-reliance, self-discipline, ambition, and academic achievement.
- Given this discrepancy, such boys often experience status frustration, which they deal with by developing a **reaction formation**: the youths reject middle-class standards and turn to the delinquent subculture of the gang.
- This subculture provides them with new forms of status achieved through gang membership.

A **reaction formation** occurs when youths reject middle-class standards and turn to the delinquent subculture of the gang.

Albert Cohen was among the first criminologists to study delinquent gangs. How would Cohen have explained the delinquency? Would Sykes and Matza agree? How does strain theory contribute to understanding delinquent subcultures?

Cohen describes this delinquent subculture as malicious, nonutilitarian, and negativistic. It is organized around the need to openly renounce anything suggesting middle-class values, because such lifestyles are largely beyond the hope of attainment.[23]

Cohen's analysis of delinquent gangs has been subject to a number of criticisms and modifications. For example, although agreeing that gang membership is often rooted in status problems, **Gresham Sykes** and **David Matza** argued the following in 1957:

- The delinquent subculture does not totally reject middle-class standards.
- Instead, delinquent boys tend to have ambivalent attitudes toward middle-class standards and conformity to law.
- The delinquent subculture solves this dilemma through its use of "techniques of neutralization," which permit youths to neutralize, or rationalize, their delinquent acts.
- Thus, the boys may deny that their acts really caused anyone harm, or claim that they only "borrowed" rather than stole a car, or assert that the victim of an attack actually deserved it.[24]

Gresham Sykes and **David Matza** argued that the delinquent subculture does not totally reject middle-class standards and attempts to "neutralize" delinquent acts.

Richard Cloward and **Lloyd Ohlin** reported in 1960 in their research on delinquency that three distinct types of delinquent subcultures exist: the **criminal**, **conflict**, and **retreatist subcultures**. From their perspective, even illegitimate means may not always be available to lower-class youths. Thus, the particular type of delinquent subculture that forms depends in large part on whether the youths have access to deviant or criminal opportunities and to adult criminal role models within their neighborhoods. Cloward and Ohlin used the term **differential opportunity** to refer to relative access to criminal role models and opportunities for crime.[25]

Richard Cloward and **Lloyd Ohlin** believed that three distinct types of delinquent subcultures exist: the **criminal, conflict,** and **retreatist subcultures.** The type of subculture that forms depends on members' **differential opportunities** for deviance and support for that deviance.

Cloward and Ohlin's Three Types of Delinquent Subcultures

(1) **Criminal subcultures** develop in areas where opportunities for exposure to adult criminal models are present. It is likely that youths within this type of subculture will learn a variety of criminal roles and will progress to adult criminal careers.

(2) **Conflict subcultures** (gang fighting) arise when access to both illegitimate opportunities and criminal role models is unavailable.

(3) **Retreatist**, or drug-using, **subcultures** exist for those who are "double failures"; they cannot adapt to legitimate conventional means or to illegitimate means and criminal role models.

Source: R. A. Cloward and L. E. Ohlin, *Delinquency and Opportunity: A Theory of Delinquent Gangs,* Glencoe, IL: Free Press, 1960.

Lower-Class Focal Concerns

According to Walter B. Miller, ideas themselves, not social conditions, directly cause criminal behavior. Crime and delinquency stem from lower-class culture with its own values system that evolved in response to living in urban slums.

Subcultural theories such as those of the researchers in the preceding section focus on the role of ideas in causing criminal behavior. These theories "may explore the sources of these ideas in general conditions, but they are characterized by the argument that it is the ideas themselves, rather than the social conditions, that directly cause criminal behavior." In contrast, "the strain theories of Cohen and of Cloward and Ohlin both use the term subculture, but both locate the primary causes of criminal behavior directly in social conditions. There are common thinking patterns that arise among delinquents, but the thinking patterns are not the cause of criminal behavior. In strain theories, both the thinking patterns and the criminal behaviors are caused by the same structural forces."[26]

Illegitimate Means and Delinquent Subcultures

BY R. A. CLOWARD AND L. E. OHLIN

In the short reading at the end of this chapter, Cloward and Ohlin present their insights on the theories of Shaw and McKay and of Sutherland (*The Professional Thief*), and defend their assertion that access to illegitimate roles is not freely available to all. They then present an analysis of their concept of differential opportunity.

See reading on page 165.

Another theorist who maintained that ideas themselves, rather than social conditions, directly cause criminal behavior was **Walter B. Miller**. In his **lower-class focal concerns theory**, he focused on gang delinquency and argued that the lower class "has a separate, identifiable culture distinct from the culture of the middle class."[27]

As you have read, many theorists explain crime and delinquency in terms of subcultural values that have emerged, developed, and been perpetuated from one generation to the next in lower-class urban communities. For Walter B. Miller, however,

- the values of lower-class culture produce crime because they are "naturally" in discord with middle-class values;
- a young person who conforms to lower-class values automatically becomes delinquent;
- crime and delinquency are not based on the rejection of middle-class values; instead, they stem from lower-class culture, which has and maintains its own value system, one that has evolved in response to living in urban slums.[28]

Thus, Miller disagreed with Cohen's contention that lower-class delinquents care about middle-class values and act out their stress and frustration in negativistic crime. Rather, a delinquent subculture stands independently from middle-class culture and draws its ideas from lower-class ways of living.

In his 1958 article, "Lower-Class Culture as a Generating Milieu of Gang Delinquency," Miller developed a set of **focal concerns**, or characteristics of lower-class culture, that tend to foster criminal and delinquent behaviors. He listed six areas that lower-class Americans focus their attention on: trouble, toughness, smartness, excitement, fate, and autonomy. The middle-class, in contrast, has "values," such as achievement. Specifically, Miller's focal concerns are described as follows:

1. *Trouble:* Getting into trouble.
2. *Toughness:* Masculinity, endurance, strength, physical prowess, skill, fearlessness, bravery, and daring.
3. *Smartness:* Ability to dupe, con, or outsmart "the other guy"; shrewdness; ability to gain money by "wits" and street sense rather than by having a high IQ.

Walter B. Miller believed that crime and delinquency stem from lower-class culture, which has its own value system that evolved in response to living in urban slums.

Lower-class focal concerns theory focuses on gang delinquency and argues that the lower class has a separate, identifiable culture distinct from the culture of the middle class.

Miller proposed six **focal concerns** that characterize lower-class culture: trouble, toughness, smartness, excitement, fate, and autonomy.

Miller stressed that boys from lower-income families are concerned with being tough and that this is rooted in the fact that these families are frequently headed by women. Young men, therefore, do not have masculine role models in the family and join delinquent street gangs with whom they can identify. The delinquent nature of gang activity is, then, a consequence of the young men's thinking patterns; that is, of the lower-class culture and its focal concerns. How might you argue against the supposition that boys from female-headed households are more prone to delinquency?

4. *Excitement:* Constant search for thrills, danger, and change as opposed to no risk or just "hanging around."
5. *Fate:* Being lucky and favored by fortune—the perspective that most things that happen to people are beyond their control and nothing can be done about it—as opposed to being "unlucky" and ill-omened.
6. *Autonomy:* Resentment of rules and authority; freedom from external constraint and superordinate authority; independence rather than dependence and the presence of external constraint.[29]

Support for Miller's perspective was found in Oscar Lewis's 1960s study of the **culture of poverty**. Lewis's perspective stresses the idea that the values of the poor are substantially different from the values of people in the mainstream of society. His purpose in developing this perspective was to form a conceptual model of a set of interrelated traits, poverty being the crucial one.[30]

There are, according to Lewis, seventy traits that characterize the culture of poverty. Examples are

- powerless feelings;
- unemployment;
- inability to defer gratification;
- lack of privacy;
- gregariousness;
- a predisposition to authoritarianism.

Many of these traits inhibit the poor from adjusting to a success-oriented, middle-class society and from having upward mobility in that society. Proponents of this viewpoint argue that the poor "do not share the middle-class abhorrence of consensual unions, sexual promiscuity, illegitimacy, and violence in interpersonal relations."[31] From this perspective, the values of the poor reflect both a lack of desire to be a part of or to advance in society's social institutions and a desire to condone behavior regarded by the middle-class as deviant.[32]

The culture of poverty concept summarizes a view of poverty that is shared by consensus theorists. The consensus approach believes a major cause of poverty is the ongoing creation by the poor of a "consensus pattern at odds with the dominant culture," in which the poor adapt to poverty through illegal activities legitimated by their subculture.[33]

Contemporary social scientists who have reacted negatively to the culture of poverty perspective are called situationalists. They believe that the patterns of behavior among the poor are simply a means of adapting to the environment, and they reject the point of view that the poor have a unique set of values. Situationalists such as Lee Rainwater, Elliot Liebow, Hylan Lewis, and Charles Valentine claim that lifestyles among the poor are not mechanically transmitted from one generation to the next; rather, each generation of the poor recreates distinctive lifestyles, ways of thinking, and behaviors as a reaction and an adjustment to living in poverty.[34]

Subcultures of Violence

The subculture of violence, a concept developed by Marvin Wolfgang and Franco Ferracuti, is a set of values, beliefs, attitudes, and expectations that support the use of violence in a variety of social situations.

The *subculture of violence*, a perspective developed by *Marvin Wolfgang* and *Franco Ferracuti* in the 1960s, has its roots in Merton's theory of anomie and Sutherland's theory that criminal behavior is learned behavior. The subculture of violence hypothesizes a subculture that condones violent behavior and claims that recourse to aggressive and violent behavior may be considered

The **culture of poverty** concept, which is widely criticized today, claims that the shared experience of poverty leads to the development of a unique way of life that actively opposes middle-class beliefs and values.

Some people believe that some motorcycle gangs are examples of subcultures that condone violent behavior. If this were true, according to Wolfgang and Ferracuti's theory of the subculture of violence, what characteristics, beliefs, and values would such bikers have?

acceptable within certain groups, particularly lower-class men, African Americans, and Southerners, when such qualities as honor, courage, and manhood are challenged by threats, insults, or weapons.[35]

According to Wolfgang and Ferracuti,

- violence is a learned form of adaptation to particular problematic life circumstances;
- learning occurs in a subcultural environment that supports the advantages of violent behavior over other, nonviolent responses or forms of adaptation;
- the subculture of violence is basically a set of values, beliefs, attitudes, and expectations that are supportive of using violence in various situations;
- included in the subculture of violence is a person's willingness to be involved in violent behavior, expectation of violence from others, and readiness to violently respond to others;
- to maintain one's image and status, one who is insulted or "put down" needs to respond quickly and aggressively;
- disagreements are settled by fighting.

In other words, subcultures of violence expect their members to be violent. Violence is considered necessary and legitimate; violence is the norm. A person who is highly integrated into a subculture of violence is more likely than one who isn't to be violent in his or her responses toward others.[36]

Wolfgang and Ferracuti based their theory of the subculture of violence on their study of homicide between racial groups in Philadelphia. They reported that nonwhite men had a homicide rate twelve times higher than that of white men (and the rate for nonwhite men was twenty-three times higher than for nonwhite women). Most of the homicides studied were committed by a homogeneous group of young, nonwhite, lower-class males. The researchers believed that the value system of this group constituted a subculture of violence.[37]

Critics of the subculture of violence theory cite recent research showing that race does not play a role in violence. Liqun Cao, Anthony Adams, and Vickie J. Jensen reported in 1997 that their own research does not support the notion of a black subculture of violence. They found that white males were actually more likely than black males to respond violently when they encountered defensive situations. No racial differences were observed in responses to offensive situations.[38]

After reading this section, you should be able to

1. define the concepts on which subcultural theories of delinquency and crime are based;
2. compare and contrast Cohen's theory of delinquent subcultures with Sykes and Matza's theory of delinquent subcultures;
3. describe Cloward and Ohlin's three types of delinquent subcultures and the role that differential opportunity plays in the formation of those types;
4. critique Miller's lower-class focal concerns theory and Wolfgang and Ferracuti's subculture of violence theory in relation to Lewis's culture of poverty concept;
5. evaluate subcultural theories overall as explanations for criminal behavior.

CHAPTER SUMMARY

This chapter covers several of the most important social-structural theories of criminal behavior. Social disorganization theory focuses on the wide variety of environmental and urban conditions that affect crime rates. A firm foundation for this theory lies in the analysis of social organization and social disorganization. The social disorganization perspective of William Thomas and Florian Znaniecki examined how social disorganization can create criminal behavior. Clifford Shaw and Henry McKay examined crime in the changing urban environment using their concentric zone model (pp. 143–147).

Strain theory argues that socially generated forces and pressures drive people to crime. Building on Émile Durkheim's concept of anomie, Robert Merton supported this approach in his anomie/strain theory, stressing that much crime in U.S. society—especially property crime, robbery, and drug dealing—can be viewed as an anomic response that results when conventional or legitimate means for goal attainment are blocked. Robert Agnew's general strain theory focuses on the negative relationships that an individual has with others. Agnew believes that many factors influence one's choice of criminal or noncriminal adaptations to strain (pp. 147–153).

Subcultural delinquency theories also attempt to explain crime and delinquency. Albert Cohen's subcultural theory proposed that the delinquent subculture exists because it offers a solution to the status problems and frustrations that working-class boys experience in their effort to achieve middle-class success. Gresham Sykes and David Matza's response to Cohen's theory argued that the delinquent subculture does not reject middle-class standards and attempts to "neutralize" delinquent acts. Richard Cloward and Lloyd Ohlin identified three types of delinquent subcultures and argued that the type of subculture that forms depends on members' differential opportunities for deviance (pp. 153–155).

Walter Miller's lower-class focal concerns theory maintained that a delinquent subculture stands independently from middle-class culture and draws its ideas from lower-class ways of living. Oscar Lewis's study of the culture of poverty supported Miller's perspective. Marvin Wolfgang and Franco Ferracuti developed the idea of a subculture of violence, which is a set of values, beliefs, attitudes, and expectations that support the use of violence (pp. 156–160).

Study Guide

Chapter Objectives

- Write an explanation of the social disorganization approach to crime.
- Briefly describe social change.
- Briefly explain what is meant by social organization.
- Briefly describe what is meant by social disorganization.
- Briefly explain Thomas and Znaniecki's contribution to the social disorganization approach to criminal behavior.
- Describe Shaw and McKay's views on neighborhood structural influences on criminal behavior.
- Briefly explain Merton's anomie/strain theory.
- List and explain Merton's modes of adaptation.
- Briefly explain Agnew's general strain theory.
- Evaluate the contributions of strain theory to understanding deviant and criminal behavior.

- Describe Cohen's theory of delinquent subculture.
- Briefly explain Sykes and Matza's "techniques of neutralization."
- Describe Cloward and Ohlin's types of delinquent subcultures.
- Evaluate Cloward and Ohlin's concept of differential opportunity.
- Describe Miller's lower-class focal concerns theory.
- Describe what Lewis meant by the "culture of poverty" and its relationship to criminal behavior.
- Briefly describe Wolfgang and Ferracuti's "subculture of violence" theory.

Key Terms

Agnew, Robert (149)
Anomie (148)
Anomie/strain theory (149)
Cloward, Richard (155)
Cohen, Albert (154)
Concentric zone model (146)
Conditioning factors (151)
Conflict subculture (155)
Conformity (149)
Criminal subculture (155)
Culture of poverty (158)
Delinquent subculture (154)
Differential opportunity (155)
Durkheim, Émile (148)
Focal concerns (157)

General strain theory (149)
Heterogeneity (143)
Innovation (149)
Laws (145)
Lower-class focal concerns theory (157)
Matza, David (155)
McKay, Henry D. (146)
Merton, Robert (148)
Miller, Walter B. (157)
Ohlin, Lloyd (155)
Reaction formation (154)
Rebellion (149)
Retreatism (149)
Retreatist subculture (155)
Ritualism (149)

Shaw, Clifford R. (146)
Social change (143)
Social disorganization theory (143)
Social norms (145)
Social organization (144)
Social structure (145)
Strain theory (147)
Subcultural theories (153)
Subcultures (154)
Sykes, Gresham (155)
Thomas, William I. (145)
Values (145)
Znaniecki, Florian (145)

Self-Test
Short Answer

1. Define social organization and social disorganization.
2. List Thomas and Znaniecki's findings in regard to social disorganization.
3. Briefly list the major points of Shaw and McKay's study of urban juvenile delinquents.

4. Define anomie according to Durkheim.
5. Define anomie according to Merton.
6. List Merton's modes of adaptation.
7. Define general strain theory.
8. List Agnew's three major types of strain.

9. Define subculture.
10. List Cohen's contributions on gang delinquency.
11. Briefly state Sykes and Matza's critique of Cohen.
12. List Cloward and Ohlin's types of delinquent subcultures.

13. Briefly describe Miller's lower-class focal concerns theory.
14. List the focal concerns that foster criminal behavior, according to Miller.
15. Define the culture of poverty.

Multiple Choice

1. Social disorganization theory has its roots in the process of social change and is related to the fact that Americans live in a society characterized by
   a. heterogeneity
   b. value conflicts
   c. many subcultures
   d. all of the above

2. The social disorganization approach to the study of crime focuses on
   a. the role of social reactions in creating deviant or criminal behavior
   b. the impact of value conflicts on social structure
   c. social change and the breakdown of social norms and rules
   d. the discrepancy between goals and the means to achieve them

3. Which of the following pairs of scholars used a concentric zone model to scientifically study the relationship between crime rates and various community zones?
   a. Shaw and McKay
   b. Sykes and Matza
   c. Cloward and Ohlin
   d. Thomas and Znaniecki

4. According to Robert Merton, the innovator is one who
   a. rejects legitimate means and turns to illegitimate ones in order to achieve approved goals
   b. rejects only the approved goals
   c. rejects both approved goals and legitimate means
   d. rebels against the social order

5. Robert Merton's theory of anomie is most useful in explaining crimes such as
   a. murder
   b. theft
   c. forcible rape
   d. aggravated assault

6. Which of the following is a source of strain in Agnew's GST?
   a. prevention from achieving goals
   b. removal of postively valued stimuli
   c. exposure to negative stimuli
   d. all of the above

7. Which of the following are negative affective states according to Agnew's GST?
   a. innovation, retreatism, and conformity
   b. rebellion, ritualism, and stimulation

c. frustration, fear, and anger
d. none of the above

8. According to Albert Cohen,
   a. every working-class youth develops a "delinquent response"
   b. working-class youths do not typically aspire to middle-class lifestyles
   c. the delinquent subculture provides a solution to the status problems that working-class youths experience
   d. working-class youths do not typically experience status frustration

9. For Sykes and Matza, techniques of neutralization are
   a. stereotypes
   b. subcultures
   c. delinquent acts
   d. rationalizations for delinquency

10. For Cloward and Ohlin, which of the following is not a distinct type of delinquent subculture?
    a. criminal
    b. consensus
    c. conflict
    d. retreatist

11. According to Cloward and Ohlin's subcultural analysis,
    a. conflict subcultures typically become involved in drug use
    b. criminal subcultures arise where opportunities for exposure to adult criminal models are present
    c. both legitimate and illegitimate means are always available to lower-class youths
    d. consensus subcultures usually become involved in violent activities

12. Which of the following theories is not a social-structural explanation for criminal behavior?
    a. labeling theory
    b. theory of anomie
    c. subcultural theory of delinquency
    d. differential opportunity theory

13. Which of the following is not one of Walter B. Miller's focal concerns?
    a. trouble
    b. dependence
    c. excitement
    d. autonomy

14. Proponents of the culture of poverty perspective argue that the poor
    a. do not share the middle-class abhorrence of consensual unions, sexual promiscuity, illegitimacy, and violence in interpersonal relations
    b. have values that are substantially the same as middle-class Americans
    c. will always be with us
    d. none of the above

15. According to Wolfgang and Ferracuti,
    a. violence is a learned form of adaptation to particular problematic life circumstances
    b. the subculture of violence is basically a set of values, beliefs, attitudes, and expections that are supportive of using violence in various situations
    c. in the subculture of violence, violence is considered to be necessary and legitimate
    d. all of the above

True–False

T F 1. The primary focus of social disorganization theory is the wide variety of environmental and urban conditions that affect crime rates.

T F 2. No society is free from change.

T F 3. When people use traditional guidelines that continue to be appropriate for new social conditions, they have social disorganization.

T F 4. Shaw and McKay believed that crime and criminal behavior are very much the product of urban ecological conditions.

T F 5. For Merton, the retreatist form of deviant response is typical of various radicals or revolutionary groups who desire serious change in the society.

T F 6. For Merton, crime rates are symptomatic of anomie.

T F 7. Merton's theory of anomie/strain provides us with a much better explanation for crime committed by the more affluent classes in society.

T F 8. According to Agnew, individuals who have high degrees of power to control or deal with negative stimuli experience more strain than those who have lower degrees of power.

T F 9. Agnew believes that virtually all strained individuals eventually turn to delinquency and crime.

T F 10. According to Cohen, the "delinquent response" is an attempt to cope with status frustration on the part of working-class youths.

T F 11. Sykes and Matza argued that the delinquent subculture totally rejects middle-class standards.

T F 12. For Cloward and Ohlin, criminal subcultures develop in areas where opportunities for exposure to adult criminal models are present.

T F 13. For Miller, crime and delinquency are based on the rejection of middle-class values.

T F 14. The culture of poverty perspective stresses the idea that various social strata manifest distinct cultures, and that there exists among the poor a "culture of poverty."

T F 15. For Wolfgang and Ferracuti, violence is learned in a subcultural environment that supports the advantages of violent behavior.

Fill-In

1. _____ theory focuses on the development of high-crime communities, which are associated with the breakdown of conventional norms and values caused by such factors as increased industrialization, immigration, and urbanization.

2. People create social _____ to regulate their own conduct and the conduct of others, and to provide various resources to meet their needs.

3. The famous sociologist _____ was the first to develop the concepts of anomie to explain suicide.

4. Merton argued that _____ results from a lack of integration between culturally prescribed goals and the availability of legitimate or institutionalized means for goal attainment.

5. According to Merton, _____, as a form of anomic or deviant response, occurs when a person rejects legitimate means and substitutes illegitimate means to achieve culturally approved goals.

6. _____ focuses on individual-level influences of strain and tries to understand why strained individuals are more likely than nonstrained individuals to commit criminal or delinquent acts.

7. _____ may result from a disjunction between aspirations and achievements or expectations and achievements.

8. The _____ explanation of deviance stresses the fact that, given the multitude of subcultures, some invariably contain norms that deviate from and conflict with those of the general society.

9. For Cohen, the delinquent subculture exists because it offers a solution to the _____ problems and frustrations that working-class boys experience in their efforts to achieve middle-class success.

10. For Sykes and Matza, "techniques of _____" permit youths to rationalize their delinquent acts.

11. According to Cloward and Ohlin, _____ subcultures develop in areas where opportunities for exposure to adult criminal models are present.

12. For Cloward and Ohlin, the _____, or drug-using, subculture exists for those who are "double failures"; they cannot adapt to legitimate conventional means or to illegitimate means and criminal role models.

Matching

1. Innovation
2. Differential opportunity
3. Theory of anomie/strain
4. Conformity
5. Cohen
6. Social disorganization
7. Shaw and McKay
8. Retreatist response
9. Rebellious response
10. Sykes and Matza
11. Agnew
12. Anger
13. Miller
14. Lewis
15. Wolfgang and Ferracuti

A. Result of using traditional guidelines no longer appropriate for new social conditions
B. Drug addiction or alcoholism
C. Substitution of illegitimate means to achieve legitimate goals
D. Introduction of new means and new goals
E. Techniques of neutralization
F. Cloward and Ohlin
G. Acceptance of legitimate means and goals
H. Studied urban ecology of newcomers to Chicago
I. Merton
J. A delinquent subculture is malicious, nonutilitarian, and negativistic
K. General strain theory
L. Negative affective state
M. Culture of poverty
N. Lower-class focal concerns theory
O. Subculture of violence

Essay Questions

1. After reviewing the principles of social disorganization theory, do you believe that it is applicable to the study of crime in today's U.S. urban communities? Explain your answer.

2. Do you believe that Merton's or Agnew's theory adequately explains why people are deviant and/or criminal in U.S. society? In explaining your answer, assess the fact that many Americans today have received a good education and might even have experience in their respective fields, but they have not been able to find jobs in the fields for which they have been trained.

3. After reviewing the subcultural theories presented, do you believe that any of these theories adequately explains gang delinquency in a community with which you are familiar? Explain your answer.

4. Delinquent gang behavior can be found in many U.S. communities. After reviewing Miller's focal concerns, select a community or neighborhood with which you are familiar and assess whether or not Miller's concepts, ideas, and explanations apply to that community or neighborhood. If they apply, explain how they apply; if they do not apply, see whether any of the other theories (those of Cohen, Cloward and Ohlin, or Sykes and Matza, for example) apply, and explain why.

Illegitimate Means and Delinquent Subcultures

Source: *Reprinted by permission of The Free Press, a Division of Simon & Schuster Adult Publishing Group from* Delinquency and Opportunity: A Theory of Delinquent Gangs *by Richard A. Cloward and Lloyd E. Ohlin. Copyright © 1960, the Free Press. Copyright renewed © 1988 by Lloyd E. Ohlin. All rights reserved.*

BY RICHARD A. CLOWARD AND LLOYD E. OHLIN

THE AVAILABILITY OF ILLEGITIMATE MEANS

Social norms are two-sided. A prescription implies the existence of a prohibition, and *vice versa*. To advocate honesty is to demarcate and condemn a set of actions which are dishonest. In other words, norms that define legitimate practices also implicitly define illegitimate practices. One purpose of norms, in fact, is to delineate the boundary between legitimate and illegitimate practices. In setting this boundary, in segregating and classifying various types of behavior, they make us aware not only of behavior that is regarded as right and proper but also of behavior that is said to be wrong and improper. Thus the criminal who engages in theft or fraud does not invent a new way of life; the possibility of employing alternative means is acknowledged, tacitly at least, by the norms of the culture.

This tendency for proscribed alternatives to be implicit in every prescription, and vice versa, although widely recognized, is nevertheless a reef upon which many a theory of delinquency has foundered. Much of the criminological literature assumes, for example, that one may explain a criminal act simply by accounting for the individual's readiness to employ illegal alternatives of which his culture, through its norms, has already made him generally aware. Such explanations are quite unsatisfactory, however, for they ignore a host of questions regarding the *relative availability* of illegal alternatives to various potential criminals. The aspiration to be a physician is hardly enough to explain the fact of becoming a physician; there is much that transpires between the aspiration and the achievement. This is no less true of the person who wants to be a successful criminal. Having decided that he "can't make it legitimately," he cannot simply choose among an array of illegitimate means, all equally available to him.... It is assumed in the theory of anomie that access to conventional means is differentially distributed, that some individuals, because of their social class, enjoy certain advantages that are denied to those elsewhere in the class structure. For example, there are variations in the degree to which members of various classes are fully exposed to and thus acquire the values, knowledge, and skills that facilitate upward mobility. It should not be startling, therefore, to suggest that there are socially structured variations in the availability of illegitimate means as well. In connection with delinquent subcultures, we shall be concerned principally with differentials in access to illegitimate means within the lower class.

Many sociologists have alluded to differentials in access to illegitimate means without explicitly incorporating this variable into a theory of deviant behavior. This is particularly true of scholars in the "Chicago tradition" of criminology. Two closely related theoretical perspectives emerged from this school. The theory of "cultural transmission," advanced by Clifford R. Shaw and Henry D. McKay, focuses on the development in some urban neighborhoods of a criminal tradition that persists from one generation to another despite constant changes in population.[1] In the theory of "differential association," Edwin H. Sutherland described the processes by which criminal values are taken over by the individual.[2] He asserted that criminal behavior is learned, and that it is learned in interaction with others who have already incorporated criminal values. Thus the first theory stresses the value systems of different areas; the second, the systems of social relationships that facilitate or impede the acquisition of these values.

Scholars in the Chicago tradition, who emphasized the processes involved in learning to be criminal, were actually pointing to differentials in the availability of illegal means—although they did not explicitly recognize this variable in their analysis. This can perhaps best be seen by examining Sutherland's classic work, *The Professional Thief.* "An inclination to steal," according to Sutherland, "is not a sufficient explanation of the genesis of the professional thief."[3] The "self-made" thief, lacking knowledge of the ways of securing immunity from prosecution and similar techniques of defense, "would quickly land in prison; . . . a person can be a professional thief only if he is recognized and received as such by other professional thieves." But recognition is not freely accorded: "Selection and tutelage are the two necessary elements in the process of acquiring recognition as a professional thief. . . . A person cannot acquire recognition as a professional thief until he has had tutelage in professional theft, *and tutelage is given only to a few persons selected from the total population.*" For one thing, "the person must be appreciated by the professional thieves. He must be appraised as having an adequate equipment of wits, front, talking-ability, honesty, reliability, nerve and determination."

Furthermore, the aspirant is judged by high standards of performance, for only "a very small percentage of those who start on this process ever reach the stage of professional thief. . . ." Thus motivation and pressures toward deviance do not fully account for deviant behavior any more than motivation and pressures toward conformity account for conforming behavior. The individual must have access to a learning environment and, once having been trained, must be allowed to perform his role. Roles, whether conforming or deviant in content, are not necessarily freely available; access to them depends upon a variety of factors, such as one's socioeconomic position, age, sex, ethnic affiliation, personality characteristics, and the like. The potential thief, like the potential physician, finds that access to his goal is governed by many criteria other than merit and motivation.

What we are asserting is that access to illegitimate roles is not freely available to all, as is commonly assumed. Only those neighborhoods in which crime flourishes as a stable, indigenous institution are fertile criminal learning environments for the young. Because these environments afford integration of different age-levels of offender, selected young people are exposed to "differential association" through which tutelage is provided and criminal values and skills are acquired. To be prepared for the role may not, however, ensure that the individual will ever discharge it. One important limitation is that more youngsters are recruited into these patterns of differential associations than the adult criminal structure can possibly absorb. Since there is a surplus of contenders for these elite positions, criteria and mechanisms of selection must be evolved. Hence a certain proportion of those who aspire may not be permitted to engage in the behavior for which they have prepared themselves.

Thus we conclude that access to illegitimate roles, no less than access to legitimate roles, is limited by both social and psychological factors. We shall here be concerned primarily with socially structured differentials in illegitimate opportunities. Such differentials, we contend, have much to do with the type of delinquent subculture that develops.

LEARNING AND PERFORMANCE STRUCTURES

Our use of the term "opportunities," legitimate or illegitimate, implies access to both learning and performance structures. That is, the individual must have access to appropriate environments for the acquisition of the values and skills associated with the performance of a particular role, and he must be supported in the performance of the role once he has learned it.

[Frank] Tannenbaum, several decades ago, vividly expressed the point that criminal role performance, no less than conventional role performance, presupposes a patterned set of relationships through which the requisite values and skills are transmitted by established practitioners to aspiring youth:

It takes a long time to make a good criminal, many years of specialized training and much preparation. But training is

something that is given to people. People learn in a community where the materials and the knowledge are to be had. A craft needs an atmosphere saturated with purpose and promise. The community provides the attitudes, the point of view, the philosophy of life, the example, the motive, the contacts, the friendships, the incentives. No child brings those into the world. He finds them here and available for use and elaboration. The community gives the criminal his materials and habits, just as it gives the doctor, the lawyer, the teacher, and the candlestick-maker theirs.[4]

Sutherland systematized this general point of view, asserting that opportunity consists, at least in part, of learning structures. Thus "criminal behavior is learned" and, furthermore, it is learned "in interaction with other persons in a process of communication." However, he conceded that the differential-association theory does not constitute a full explanation of criminal behavior. In a paper circulated in 1944, he noted that "criminal behavior is partially a function of opportunities to commit specific classes of crime, such as embezzlement, bank burglary, or illicit heterosexual intercourse." Therefore, "while opportunity may be partially a function of association with criminal patterns and of the specialized techniques thus acquired, it is not determined entirely in that manner, and consequently differential association is not the sufficient cause of criminal behavior."[5]

To Sutherland, then, illegitimate opportunity included conditions favorable to the performance of a criminal role as well as conditions favorable to the learning of such a role (differential associations). These conditions, we suggest, depend upon certain features of the social structure of the community in which delinquency arises.

DIFFERENTIAL OPPORTUNITY: A HYPOTHESIS

We believe that each individual occupies a position in both legitimate and illegitimate opportunity structures. This is a new way of defining the situation. The theory of anomie views the individual primarily in terms of the legitimate opportunity structure. It poses questions regarding differentials in access to legitimate routes to success-goals; at the same time it assumes either that illegitimate avenues to success-goals are freely available or that differentials in their availability are of little significance. This tendency may be seen in the following statement by [Robert] Merton:

Several researchers have shown that specialized areas of vice and crime constitute a "normal" response to a situation where the cultural emphasis upon pecuniary success has been absorbed, but where there is little access to conventional and legitimate means for becoming successful. The occupational opportunities of people in these areas are largely confined to manual labor and the lesser white-collar jobs. Given the American stigmatization of manual labor *which has been found to hold rather uniformly for all social classes*, and the absence of realistic opportunities for advancement beyond this level, the result is a marked tendency toward deviant behavior. The status of unskilled labor and the consequent low income cannot readily *compete in terms of established standards of worth* with the promises of power and high income from organized vice, rackets and crime. . . . [Such a situation] leads toward the gradual attenuation of legitimate, but by and large ineffectual, strivings and the increasing use of illegitimate, but more or less effective, expedients.[6]

The cultural-transmission and differential-association tradition, on the other hand, assumes that access to illegitimate means is variable, but it does not recognize the significance of comparable differentials in access to legitimate means. Sutherland's "ninth proposition" in the theory of differential association states:

> *Though criminal behavior is an expression of general needs and values, it is not explained by those general needs and values since non-criminal behavior is an expression of the same needs and values.* Thieves generally steal in order to secure money, but likewise honest laborers work in order to secure money. The attempts by many scholars to explain criminal behavior by general drives and values, such as the happiness principle, striving for social status, the money motive, or frustration, have been and must continue to be futile since they explain lawful behavior as completely as they explain criminal behavior.[7]

In this statement, Sutherland appears to assume that people have equal and free access to legitimate means regardless of their social position. At the very least, he does not treat access to legitimate means as variable. It is, of course, perfectly true that "striving for social status," "the money motive," and other socially approved drives do not fully account for either deviant or conforming behavior. But if goal-oriented behavior occurs under conditions in which there are socially structured obstacles to the satisfaction of these drives by legitimate means, the resulting pressures, we contend, might lead to deviance.

The concept of differential opportunity structures permits us to unite the theory of anomie, which recognizes the concept of differentials in access to legitimate means, and the "Chicago tradition," in which the concept of differentials in access to illegitimate means is implicit. We can now look at the individual, not simply in relation to one or the other system of means, but in relation to both legitimate and illegitimate systems. This approach permits us to ask, for example, how the relative availability of illegitimate opportunities affects the resolution of adjustment problems leading to deviant behavior. We believe that the way in which these problems are resolved may depend upon the kind of support for one or another type of illegitimate activity that is given at different points in the social structure. If, in a given social location, illegal or criminal means are not readily available, then we should not expect a criminal subculture to develop among adolescents. By the same logic, we should expect the manipulation of violence to become a primary avenue to higher status only in areas where the means of violence are

not denied to the young. To give a third example, drug addiction and participation in subcultures organized around the consumption of drugs presuppose that persons can secure access to drugs and knowledge about how to use them. In some parts of the social structure, this would be very difficult; in others, very easy. In short, there are marked differences from one part of the social structure to another in the types of illegitimate adaptation that are available to persons in search of solutions to problems of adjustment arising from the restricted availability of legitimate means.[8] In this sense, then, we can think of individuals as being located in two opportunity structures—one legitimate, the other illegitimate. Given limited access to success-goals by legitimate means, the nature of the delinquent response that may result will vary according to the availability of various illegitimate means.[9]

NOTES

1. See esp. C. R. Shaw, *The Jack-Roller* (Chicago: University of Chicago Press, 1930); Shaw, *The Natural History of a Delinquent Career* (Chicago: University of Chicago Press, 1931); Shaw et al., *Delinquency Areas* (Chicago: University of Chicago Press, 1940); and Shaw and H. D. McKay, *Juvenile Delinquency and Urban Areas* (Chicago: University of Chicago Press, 1942).

2. E. H. Sutherland, Ed., *The Professional Thief* (Chicago: University of Chicago Press, 1937); and *Sutherland, Principles of Criminology*, 4th ed. (Philadelphia: Lippincott, 1947).

3. All quotations on this page are from *The Professional Thief*, pp. 211–213. Emphasis added.

4. F. Tannenbaum, "The Professional Criminal," *The Century,* vol. 110 (May–Oct. 1925): p. 577.

5. See A. K. Cohen, Alfred Lindesmith, and Karl Schussier, eds., *The Sutherland Papers* (Bloomington, IN: Indiana University Press, 1956), pp. 31–35.

6. R. K. Merton, *Social Theory and Social Structure*, rev. and enl. ed. (Glencoe, IL: Free Press, 1957), pp. 145–146.

7. *Principles of Criminology*, op. cit., pp. 7–8.

8. For an example of restrictions on access to illegitimate roles, note the impact of racial definitions in the following case: "'I was greeted by two prisoners who were to be my cell buddies. Ernest was a first offender, charged with being a "hold-up" man. Bill, the other buddy, was an old offender, going through the machinery of becoming a habitual criminal, in and out of jail.... The first thing they asked me was, "What are you in for?"'" (Shaw, *The Jack-Roller*, op. cit., p. 101).

9. For a discussion of the way in which the availability of illegitimate means influences the adaptations of inmates to prison life, see R. A. Cloward, "Social Control in the Prison," *Theoretical Studies of the Social Organization of the Prison*, bulletin no. 15 (New York: Social Science Research Council, March 1960), pp. 20–48.

Sociological Theories II

Social Control, Conflict, Feminist, and Labeling Theories

7

7.1 INTRODUCTION: SOCIOLOGICAL THEORIES II

This chapter examines sociological theories that emphasize the effect of environmental and social factors on crime and delinquency. An analysis of criminal behavior as learned behavior begins the chapter, concentrating on Edwin H. Sutherland's important differential association theory. Later developments based on the concept of differential association included Ronald Aker's social learning theory and identification and anticipation theories proposed by Daniel Glaser. Specifically, this chapter examines

- differential association–based theories (section 7.2);
- Travis Hirschi's control theory and Michael Gottfredson and Hirschi's general theory of crime (section 7.3);
- conflict theory and conflict perspectives on crime, such as Richard Quinney's (section 7.4);
- feminist theories of crime and feminist criminology today (section 7.5);
- labeling theory as an application of social psychology to understand delinquent and criminal behavior (section 7.6).

7.2 DIFFERENTIAL ASSOCIATION THEORY

Before **Edwin H. Sutherland** developed his **differential association theory**,[1] criminology was dominated by medical doctors and psychiatrists who stressed the biological and psychological explanations for crime. More than any other approach, Sutherland's differential association theory was responsible for the decline of biological and psychological perspectives and the genesis of the view that crime is the result of "environmental influences acting on biologically and psychologically normal individuals."[2] Later researchers further developed the theory of differential association. For example, Robert Burgess and Ronald Akers developed differential-association reinforcement theory, and Daniel Glaser developed identification and anticipation theories, all based on the concept of differential association. This section explores these theories, all of which apply the basic assumption of learning theory—that criminal behavior is learned through social observation and social interaction.

Sutherland's Differential Association Theory

Sutherland proposed that individuals learn deviant and criminal behavior in the same way they learn any other social behavior.

Sutherland stressed the influence of learning on crime. He proposed that criminal behavior, like all other social behavior, is learned. This learning occurs through interaction with other people (partners in crime) and, for the most part, occurs within intimate, personal

Edwin H. Sutherland believed that criminal behavior is learned.

Differential association theory stresses the importance of one's associates (or peers) in that learning.

groups (such as a gang). In addition, this learning includes the techniques as well as the motives, attitudes, and rationalizations for committing acts of crime.

The central core of Sutherland's theory is that a person "becomes delinquent because of an excess of definitions favorable to violation of law over definitions unfavorable to violation of law."[3] He argued that everyone has contact with or exposure to both criminal and noncriminal behavior patterns, values, and attitudes. However, as a result of one's associations, one becomes a criminal because one is exposed to and learns more definitions that favor or encourage law violation than definitions that favor or encourage observance of the law. Thus, as Sutherland stated, "When persons become criminal, they do so because of contacts with criminal patterns and also because of isolation from anticriminal patterns."[4] The opposite would hold true for explaining why people conform to laws or legal codes. Sutherland also stressed that the

FOR YOUR INFORMATION

Criminal Behavior as Normal Learned Behavior

1. BASIC PSYCHOLOGICAL ASSUMPTIONS

- One of the oldest formulations about the nature of learning is that we learn by association. Aristotle (384–322 BC) argued that all knowledge is acquired through experience and that none is inborn or instinctive. Basic sensory experiences become associated with each other in the mind because they occur in certain relationships to each other as we interact with an object.
- The behaviorist revolution substituted observable stimuli and responses for the mental images and ideas of earlier times but retained the basic idea that learning is accomplished through association.
- Cognitive theorists retain the original Aristotelian notion that learning takes place because of the association of ideas and factual knowledge. Where behaviorists argue that we acquire habits through the association of stimuli with responses, cognitive theorists argue that we acquire factual knowledge through the association of memories, ideas, or expectations. Behaviorists argue that learning occurs primarily through trial and error, while cognitive theorists describe learning as taking place through insight into problem solving.
- There are three basic ways that individuals learn through association. The simplest way is *classical conditioning*, as originally described by Pavlov. Some stimuli will reliably produce a given response without any prior training of the organism. For example, a dog will consistently salivate when presented with meat. In *operant conditioning*, the organism is active and learns how to get what it wants from the environment. Operant conditioning is associated with B. F. Skinner and is

now probably the dominant learning theory in psychology. Operant conditioning uses rewards and punishments to reinforce certain behaviors. In *modeling* or *social learning* theory, behavior may be reinforced not only through actual rewards and punishments but also through expectations that are learned by watching what happens to other people.

2. TARDE'S LAWS OF IMITATION

- An early criminologist who presented a theory of crime as normal learned behavior was Gabriel Tarde (1843–1904), who argued that criminals were primarily normal people who, by accident of birth, were brought up in an atmosphere in which they learned crime as a way of life. He phrased his theory in terms of three "laws of imitation": First, people imitate one another in proportion to how much close contact they have with one another. Thus imitation is most frequent, and changes most rapidly, in cities. In rural areas, in contrast, imitation is less frequent and changes only slowly. Second, the inferior usually imitates the superior. Crimes such as vagabondage, drunkenness, and murder began as crimes committed by royalty and later were imitated by all social classes. Third, newer "fashions" in crime displace older ones.
- Edwin Sutherland's theory retained some elements of the same basic idea—that criminal behavior is the result of normal learning.

Source: Excerpted from *Theoretical Criminology,* 3rd ed., by George B. Vold and Thomas J. Bernard, pp. 206–209. Copyright © 1985 by Oxford University Press, Inc. Reprinted by permission.

Using Sutherland's differential association theory, one can explain how a young person in a delinquent community may turn to crime, given that it is likely that juvenile delinquents are already present to provide the youth with both example and encouragement. Likewise, adult white-collar corporate employees may learn from other employees the standardized techniques and rationalizations for padding expense accounts and other forms of corporate theft.

greater the duration, frequency, and intensity of associations with criminal behavior, the greater the likelihood that a person will violate the law.

Some research challenges Sutherland's differential association theory. Several criminological studies have reported that the influence of associates in the learning of criminal behavior appears to be minimal. For example, the criminologist Donald Cressey, in his 1952 study of embezzlers imprisoned in California and Illinois, found that the offenders did not necessarily learn the required criminal techniques from their associates. Rather, their previously learned general business skills were sufficient to enable them to commit their crimes.[5]

Criminologist Travis Hirschi also questioned the importance of one's associates. He found in 1969 that, although delinquent boys do tend to associate with other delinquents, they do not generally develop a strong identification with them or hold much respect for their opinions. Hirschi believes that delinquent boys often have delinquent associations only because they manifest similar delinquent backgrounds in the first place.[6]

In spite of these and other criticisms, Sutherland's theory of differential association has been and continues to be held in high regard by criminologists. The theory has been subjected to extensive amounts of empirical testing and research. Most of the evidence derived from this testing lends support to its validity. In general, the theory of differential association has proven to be an important aid in explaining a wide variety of juvenile and adult criminal behavior.

DID YOU KNOW
Behavioral psychology focuses on the way we learn through conditioning—how the consequences of a behavior can cause us to repeat or avoid that behavior.

Reinforcement Theory: Burgess and Akers

Reinforcement theory is a reformulation that links differential association theory with the principles of reinforcement theories in behavioral psychology.

During the past few decades, Sutherland's theory of differential association has undergone a substantial amount of scrutiny. A problem with the theory is that some of its concepts are vaguely worded and phrased so abstractly that precise mathematical testing of the theory is extremely difficult.[7] Some attempts to overcome this problem have reformulated the theory in more empirically

Differential Association

1. *Criminal behavior is learned.* Negatively, this means that criminal behavior is not inherited, as such; also, the person who is not already trained in crime does not invent criminal behavior, just as a person does not make mechanical inventions unless he has had training in mechanics.

2. *Criminal behavior is learned in interaction with other persons in a process of communication.* This communication is verbal in many respects but includes also "the communication of gestures."

3. *The principal part of the learning of criminal behavior occurs within intimate personal groups.* Negatively, this means that the impersonal agencies of communication, such as picture shows and news-papers, play a relatively unimportant part in the genesis of criminal behavior.

4. *When criminal behavior is learned, the learning includes (a) techniques of committing the crime, which are sometimes very complicated, sometimes very simple; (b) the specific direction of motives, drives, rationalizations, and attitudes.*

5. *The specific direction of motives and drives is learned from definitions of the legal codes as favorable or unfavorable.* In some societies an individual is surrounded by persons who invariably define the legal codes as rules to be observed, while in others he is surrounded by persons whose definitions are favorable to the violation of the legal codes. In our American society these definitions are almost always mixed and consequently we have culture conflict in relation to the legal codes.

6. *A person becomes delinquent because of an excess of definitions favorable to violation of law over definitions unfavorable to violation of law.* This is the principle of differential association. When persons become criminal, they do so because of contacts with criminal patterns and also because of isolation from anticriminal patterns. Any person inevitably assimilates the surrounding culture unless other patterns are in conflict. Negatively, this proposition of differential association means that associations which are neutral so far as crime is concerned have little or no effect on the genesis of criminal behavior.

7. *Differential associations may vary in frequency, duration, priority, and intensity.* "Frequency" and "duration" as modalities of associations are obvious and need no explanation. "Priority" is assumed to be important in the sense that lawful behavior developed in early childhood may persist throughout life, and also that delinquent behavior developed in early childhood may persist throughout life. "Intensity" is not precisely defined but it has to do with such things as the prestige of the source of a criminal or anticriminal pattern and with emotional reactions related to the associations.

8. *The process of learning criminal behavior by association with criminal and anticriminal patterns involves all of the mechanisms that are involved in any other learning.* Negatively, this means that the learning of criminal behavior is not restricted to the process of imitation. A person who is seduced, for instance, learns criminal behavior by association but this process would not ordinarily be described as imitation.

9. *While criminal behavior is an expression of general needs and values, it is not explained by those general needs and values since noncriminal behavior is an expression of the same needs and values.* Thieves generally steal in order to secure money, but likewise honest laborers work in order to secure money. The attempts by many scholars to explain criminal behavior by general drives and values, such as the happiness principle, striving for social status, the money motive, or frustration, have been and must continue to be futile since they explain lawful behavior as completely as they explain criminal behavior. They are similar to respiration, which is necessary for any behavior but which does not differentiate criminal from noncriminal behavior.

Source: E. H. Sutherland, *Principles of Criminology,* 4th ed., Philadelphia: Lippincott, 1947, pp. 75–77.

measurable and precise terms. Criminologists **Robert Burgess** and **Ronald Akers** made one such effort. Their **differential-association reinforcement theory** is essentially a reformulation that links differential association with many of the concepts and principles of behavioral psychology, such as the reinforcement of behavior through conditioning. Burgess and Akers held that "criminal behavior is learned both in social and nonsocial situations that are reinforcing or discriminative, and through that social interaction in which the behavior of other persons is reinforcing or discriminative for criminal behavior. . . . The principal part of the learning of criminal behavior occurs in those groups which comprise the individual's major source of reinforcement."[8]

Later, Akers's perspective included the idea of modeling, or **social learning theory**, which argues that much learning occurs by observing the consequences that behaviors have for others. His formulation of social learning theory proposed a particular sequence of events by which the learning of criminal behavior takes place. As George Vold and Thomas Bernard report,

> The sequence originates with the differential association of the individual with other individuals who have favorable "definitions" of criminal behavior, who function as role models for criminal behavior, and who provide social reinforcements for those behaviors. The initial participation of the individual in criminal behavior is explained by those factors. After the person has begun to commit criminal behaviors, the actual consequences of those behaviors determine whether the behaviors are continued or not. Those include the rewards and punishments directly experienced by the individual as a consequence of participating in the criminal behavior, and also the rewards and punishments the person experiences vicariously, by observing the consequences that criminal behavior has for others.[9]

Robert Burgess and **Ronald Akers** developed **differential-association reinforcement theory,** which links differential association with concepts and principles of behavioral psychology.

According to **social learning theory,** people learn vicariously by observing the consequences that behaviors have for others.

Differential Identification and Anticipation Theories: Glaser

Criminal behavior develops because of a person's greater identification with members of criminal groups than with members of noncriminal or conformist groups.

Daniel Glaser's differential identification theory is also rooted in Sutherland's differential association theory but plays down the importance Sutherland gave to the intensity and frequency of association. Instead, Glaser focused on the strength of an individual's identification with associates. **Differential identification theory** basically states the following:

- An individual "pursues criminal behavior to the extent that he identifies himself with real or imaginary persons from whose perspective his criminal behavior seems acceptable."[10]
- Criminal behavior develops because of a person's greater identification with members of criminal groups than with members of noncriminal or conformist groups.
- The process of differential association leads to a personal identification with criminals and results in criminal behavior.

Glaser used the phrase "differential identification" because

- a person identifies with many other people;
- some identifications are weak and some are strong, leading to differential identification;
- identification with an individual, or what one thinks an individual is like, may be more significant in influencing one's behavior than one's associations with actual people.[11]

Various groups in society provide social standards against which people analyze and evaluate themselves and their behavior. These groups are termed **reference groups**. A reference group is any group that a person takes into

Daniel Glaser developed **differential identification theory,** which says that an individual pursues criminal behavior to the extent that he or she identifies with real or imaginary persons who accept his or her criminal behavior.

A **reference group** is a group that a person takes into account when evaluating his or her own behavior or self-concept.

account when evaluating his or her own behavior or self-concept. It is a group that has a strong influence on an individual's values, attitudes, and identity. A person may or may not actually belong to his or her reference group, but it is always a group that the person accepts as a model for his or her judgments and actions. If you know an individual's reference groups, you probably know much about that person's values, attitudes, expectations, and behavior.

In differential identification, delinquency or criminality results when a person develops a greater identification with individuals in criminal groups than with individuals in noncriminal or conformist groups. In his **differential anticipation theory**, Glaser says that a person is likely to behave in ways that will yield the greatest rewards with the least punishment. He believes that a person will "try to commit a crime wherever and whenever the expectations of gratifications from it . . . exceed the unfavorable anticipations from these sources."[12] Glaser provides us with insight with respect to the importance of identification and anticipation in criminal behavior. However, because it is difficult to measure the dimensions of differential identification and differential anticipation, it is difficult to test the validity of these theories.

Differential anticipation theory says that a person is likely to behave in ways that will yield the greatest rewards with the least punishment.

After reading this section, you should be able to

1. define differential association (Sutherland) as the process of social interaction by which an individual acquires definitions unfavorable and favorable to law violation;
2. define differential reinforcement (Burgess and Akers) as the process by which behavior is (a) acquired through social learning and (b) internalized by a person through past and present rewards and punishments;
3. define differential identification (Glaser) as the process by which criminal behavior develops through a person's greater identification with members of criminal groups than with members of other groups;
4. define differential anticipation (Glaser) as the dynamic by which people are likely to engage in behaviors from which they expect to receive the greatest rewards with the least punishment.

7.3 SOCIAL CONTROL THEORY

Many theorists view crime as a morally neutral concept. They view people as being born without any predisposition to commit deviant or criminal behavior. Strain theory, subcultural theories, differential association theories, and others all basically assume that the environments within which people develop create both the motivation and the opportunity to commit delinquent or criminal acts. Many psychological and biological theories of criminal behavior claim that, in addition to social forces, there are psychological or biological forces that drive a person to crime.

Social control theory rejects these ideas and takes a different position. **Social control theory**, also known simply as "control theory," basically assumes the following:

Social control theory stresses the idea that people in society commit delinquent and criminal acts because of the weakness of forces restraining them from doing so, not because of the strength of forces driving them to do so.

- All human beings are, by nature, rule breakers.
- The motivation for delinquent and criminal behavior is "part of human nature."
- All individuals would naturally commit crimes if left to their own devices."[13]

How likely is it that children who frequent neighborhood businesses with their families will one day rob the store? Yet, according to Travis Hirschi, it would be natural for them to do so if left to their own devices. According to Hirschi's control theory, what social factors and personal experiences would account for their not committing crimes?

Travis Hirschi on Control Theory: Elements of the Social Bond

People in society commit delinquent and criminal acts because of the weakness of social bonds restraining them from doing so, not because of the strength of forces driving them to do so.

For **Travis Hirschi**, who originally articulated this perspective, control theory was one "in which deviation is not problematic. The question 'Why did they do it?' is simply not the question the theory is designed to answer. The question is, 'Why don't we do it?' There is much evidence that we would, if we dared."[14] The key question for Hirschi, then, was why most people do not commit crimes. He and other control theorists answered this question by pointing out the following:

- There exist in society restraining or controlling forces that are imposed on people.
- These forces in certain situations break down, resulting in various "uncontrolled" criminal behaviors.
- That is, people in society commit delinquent and criminal acts because of the "weakness of forces restraining them from doing so, not because of the strength of forces driving them to do so."[15]

Hirschi proposed a comprehensive control theory according to which a person who is tightly bonded to such groups as the family, peers, or school is less likely to commit delinquent or criminal acts than a person who is not bonded to such groups. For Hirschi, there exists a bond between the individual and conventional society. The stronger the social bond, the greater the internalization of social norms by the individual and the less likely the individual is to deviate from those norms and laws of the society. Hirschi examined this bond in terms of four components: attachment, commitment, involvement, and belief.[16]

Control theorists, then, believe that all people are potential criminals, but that most individuals do not commit crime because they are sufficiently bonded to society to keep their criminal desires in check. They are kept under control because they fear that criminal behavior would damage their relationships with their families, friends, neighbors, teachers, and employers. Without these social bonds, and in the absence of sensitivity to and interest in other people, an individual is free to be criminal.

Travis Hirschi's control theory states that a person who is tightly bonded to groups such as the family, peers, or school is less likely to commit delinquent or criminal acts than a person who is not bonded to such groups.

Hirschi's Four Elements of the Social Bond

1. **Attachment** refers to an individual's affection for and responsiveness to others, including a sensitivity to others' opinions. If a person has a strong attachment to others, he or she is more likely to internalize society's norms.
2. **Commitment** to the long-term, culturally approved goals of society is another dimension of the social bond. The greater a person's commitment to long-term goals—educational and occupational goals, for example—the less likely it is that person will deviate from those goals.
3. **Involvement** in conventional activities refers to the idea that people who are involved in socially approved activities in community or local institutions are less likely to deviate from social norms or laws. In other words, being busy restricts opportunities for delinquent or criminal activity.
4. **Belief** refers to the social values themselves and consists of things such as respect for those in authority. If this belief is strong, then criminal or delinquent behavior is less likely to occur.

Source: T. Hirschi, *Causes of Delinquency,* Berkeley and Los Angeles: University of California Press, 1969, p. 34.

Although several studies have given support to Hirschi's perspective, others have not.[17] Some critics assess control theories as "generally supported by one type of data—self-report surveys—and . . . they provide a good explanation for one type of crime, the less serious forms of juvenile delinquency. However, they are not as yet supported by studies that focus on more serious delinquency or on adult criminality."[18]

A General Theory of Crime: Gottfredson and Hirschi

Gottfredson and Hirschi's general theory of crime stresses the idea that individuals having low levels of self-control are significantly more likely throughout their lives to engage in criminal behavior.

Michael Gottfredson and Travis Hirschi developed a **general theory of crime (GTC),** which explains crime as the outcome of an individual's low self-control in combination with situational conditions conducive to criminal behavior.

Michael Gottfredson and Travis Hirschi developed a **general theory of crime (GTC)** based on control theory. Defining crime as "acts of force or fraud undertaken in pursuit of self-interest," they believe that deviants and criminals lack self-control.[19] For Gottfredson and Hirschi, high levels of self-control effectively reduce the possibility of crime. Individuals having low levels of self-control are significantly more likely throughout their lives to engage in criminal behavior. Gottfredson and Hirschi state that "people who lack self-control will tend to be impulsive, insensitive, physical, risk-taking short-sighted, non-verbal, and they will tend, therefore, to engage in criminal and analogous acts."[20] For people with low levels of self-control

- crime provides easy and immediate gratification of desires;
- criminal acts provide few or meager long-term benefits;
- criminal acts are exciting, risky, or thrilling.[21]

Gottfredson and Hirschi's general theory of crime explains crime as the outcome of the individual characteristics of low self-control in combination with situational conditions conducive to such behavior. This theory focuses on the idea that crime and criminal behavior are products of a lack of appropriate socialization or learning. That is, low self-control is a result of inadequate or ineffective socialization during child rearing. According to Gottfredson and Hirschi, for adequate child rearing and effective socialization to occur and for high levels of self-control to develop, GTC requires that three basic conditions be met:

1. Someone must monitor the child's behavior.
2. Someone must recognize deviant behavior when it occurs.
3. Someone must punish deviant behavior.

All that is required to activate the system is affection for or investment in the child. The person who cares for the child will watch his or her behavior, see the child doing things he or she should not do, and correct the child. The result is likely to be a child more capable of delaying gratification, more sensitive to the interests and desires of others, more independent, more willing to accept restraints on personal activity, and less likely to use force or violence to attain ends.[22]

Much research tends to support GTC. Research by John Gibbs, Dennis Giever, and Jamie Martin reports that parents who effectively manage their children's behavior help the children to increase their self-control, which helps reduce their delinquent behavior. Carey Herbert reports that individuals who commit workplace crimes have lower self-control levels than nonoffenders. In many juvenile gangs, according to Dennis Giever, Dana Lynskey, and Danette Monnet, gang members have low levels of self-control and parental management compared to the general population.[23] Other studies have been quite critical of GTC. Geis, for example, has criticized GTC, claiming that Gottfredson and Hirschi distorted facts on crime to fit their theory and overlooked data that negate their theory. Others criticize Gottfredson and Hirschi's analysis of homicide, white-collar crime, and other types of criminal behavior.[24] Nevertheless, it appears quite evident that factors and processes such as self-control, the family, socialization, and child rearing are important variables in any understanding of criminal and delinquent behavior.

After reading this section, you should be able to

1. describe and evaluate social control theory as an explanation for crime;
2. identify and define Hirschi's four elements of the social bond as part of his social control theory;
3. describe and evaluate Gottfredson and Hirschi's general theory of crime.

7.4 CONFLICT THEORY

Deviants and criminals, according to **conflict theory**, are the manifestations of the "failure of society to meet the needs of individuals. . . . The sources of crime . . . are found in the laws, customs, and distribution of wealth and power."[25] Conflict theory is based on the idea that, in the United States, many social values conflict with one another, and these value conflicts are the root of

> According to **conflict theory,** the sources of crime are found in conflicts that arise as a result of the laws, customs, and distribution of wealth and power in the society.

Recent high-profile offenses by celeberties like Paris Hilton, Lindsay Lohan, and Nicole Richie have resulted in jail time and challenge the common assumption that the rich and famous receive lenient treatment by the criminal justice system.

DID YOU KNOW
Conflict theory was introduced in Chapter 1 as one of the three basic theoretical orientations in criminology (along with functionalism and interactionism).

much deviance and crime. The conflict perspective assumes that the basic form of social interaction is competition as various segments of society compete for power, wealth, high social status, and scarce resources. The conflict perspective also stresses that one must examine the relationship between the competing values and interests of business, labor, and government to understand society's problems, because this competitive form of interaction can and does lead to conflict, social problems, and deviant or criminal behavior. Thus, conflict theory focuses on such issues as who makes rules and laws, who decides what is deviant or criminal, and which groups in the society gain or lose by these decisions.

Many conflict theorists consider factors such as economics, vested interests, dominance, and power to be important in explaining crime. The dominant segments of society have the power both to decide which rules, norms, and laws govern the society and to ensure that these norms and laws favor their own particular values, interests, and standards of morality. Other segments of society who have conflicting values, interests, and norms, therefore, are judged deviant or criminal and are "subject to punishment by authorities who represent and enforce the views and norms of the dominant groups."[26]

Conflict theorist Eric Goode sums up his assessment of conflict theory as follows:

> Conflict theory . . . abandons the question of why some people break the rules. Instead, it deals with the issue of making the rules, especially the criminal law. Why is certain behavior outlawed? And why is other, often even more damaging behavior, not outlawed? Conflict theorists answer these questions by arguing that laws are passed and rules are approved because they support the customs or the interests of the most powerful members of a society. In a large, complex society, no rule or law is accepted or believed as right by the whole society—only certain segments of it. Likewise, no rule or law protects everybody's rights or interests—again, only those of certain social groups or categories. It is the powerful groups that are able to impose their will on the rest of the society and make sure that laws and rules favorable to themselves, and possibly detrimental to other, less powerful groups, are instituted. That, in a nutshell, is the central concern of conflict theory.[27]

Karl Marx and the Conflict Perspective

Karl Marx's conflict perspective stresses the point that criminal and delinquent behavior is rooted in class conflicts in the capitalist system.

Karl Marx was an early conflict theorist. He wrote that our social reality must be understood in terms of the class struggle for the underlying mode of production. Marx believed that the basic cause of many of our social problems, including criminal behavior, is conflict between the owners of productive property and the workers. As an economic determinist, Marx believed that the entire structure of a society is based on its economic organization and that a person's position in the productive system determines virtually every aspect of his or her life chances, beliefs, behavior, and consciousness. People in similar productive positions (social classes) tend to hold and share similar life chances, consciousness, wealth, power, and prestige. Thus, for Marx, one's social existence determines virtually every aspect of one's life.[28] From this perspective, criminal and delinquent behavior is rooted in class and economic conflicts in the capitalist system.

However, for Marx, crime and delinquency are not simply outcomes of the exploitation of the proletariat by capitalists; they also result when wealthy capitalists define acts as deviant or criminal that threaten their economic interests. For example, Marxist conflict theorists question why acts such as drunkenness, theft, and drug use are defined as crimes but many questionable business procedures and practices are not so defined.

Not all conflict theorists totally agree with the Marxist perspective. Critics of conflict theory exist both within and outside the conflict school. Conflict theorists who consider themselves non-Marxist contend that

- not all conflicts in society are based on economic or class factors;
- deviant behavior and crime will continue to occur regardless of whether a system is capitalist or socialist.

Richard Quinney and the Social Reality of Crime

Richard Quinney is a conflict theorist who argued that the social reality of crime in politically organized society is constructed as a political act.

Influential crime theorist **Richard Quinney** believed that the only solution to crime in the United States lies in the creation of a society based on socialist rather than capitalist principles.[29] In his **social-reality-of-crime theory**, Quinney integrated his ideas—and the ideas of other theorists, such as Vold and Sutherland—about society, power, and criminality. The **six propositions** of his theory are:

1. *Definition of crime.* Crime is a definition of human conduct that is created by authorized agents in a politically organized society.
2. *Formulation of criminal definitions.* Criminal definitions describe behaviors that conflict with the interests of the segments of society that have the power to shape public policy.
3. *Application of criminal definitions.* Criminal definitions are applied by the segments of society that have the power to shape the enforcement and administration of criminal law.
4. *Development of behavior patterns in relation to criminal definitions.* Behavior patterns are structured in segmentally organized society in relation to criminal definitions, and, within this context, persons engage in actions that have relative probabilities of being defined as criminal.

Karl Marx was an early conflict theorist who believed that our social reality must be understood in terms of the class struggle for the underlying mode of production.

Richard Quinney developed the **social-reality-of-crime theory,** which integrates ideas about power and authority in the form of **six propositions** about the social construction of criminality.

Conflict theorists assert that the vested interests of these affluent businesspeople and their corporations determine what is defined and treated as criminal behavior. According to Richard Quinney's social-reality-of-crime theory, by what process is crime socially constructed? How might the conflict perspective be extended to feminist perspectives of crime?

5. **Construction of criminal conceptions.** Conceptions of crime are constructed and diffused in the segments of society by various means of communication.
6. **The social reality of crime.** The social reality of crime is constructed by the formulation and application of criminal definitions, the development of behavior patterns in relation to criminal definitions, and the construction of criminal conceptions.[30]

As you can see, Quinney's propositions derive from earlier theoretical perspectives in criminology and sociology:

- Based on an interactionist perspective, his *first* proposition stresses that deviance is defined by the social reactions to it and that crime is a "definition" of social behavior that is "created" and "developed" by the authorities. In other words, crime is a judgment made by some people about the actions, behavior, and characteristics of others.[31]
- The *second* proposition has its roots in George Vold's ideas that "whichever group interest can marshall the greatest number of votes will determine whether or not there is to be a new law to hamper or curb the interests of some opposition group."[32]
- Proposition *three* is rooted in Vold's statement that "those who produce legislative majorities win control over the police power and dominate the policies that decide who is likely to be involved in violation of the law."[33]
- As analyzed by Vold and Thomas Bernard, Quinney's *fourth* proposition relies on the differential association theory of crime discussed earlier in this chapter: "Different segments of society are said to have different behavior patterns and normative systems, each of which is learned in its own social and cultural setting. The probability that any individual will violate the criminal law depends, to a large extent, on how much power and influence his [or her] segment has in enacting and enforcing laws. Those with little or no power will find many of their normal behavior patterns criminalized, whereas those with great power will find few of their normal behavior patterns criminalized."[34]
- The *fifth* and *sixth* propositions in Quinney's theory are based in contemporary sociology of knowledge, which holds that the world we live in is "primarily subjective and socially constructed."[35]

Quinney argued that "the term 'crime' can be taken to refer to concrete happenings that individuals personally experience, or it can refer to conceptions of reality that are created and communicated to individuals through various forms of interaction, including the media. Different conceptions of crime can be created and communicated as part of the political process of promoting a particular set of values and interests. . . . For example, . . . consumer and ecology groups have argued that the real criminals are in big business. . . . Community organizers in inner-city neighborhoods argue that the real criminals are the absentee landlords and the greedy store owners."[36]

In his book *The Social Reality of Crime*, Quinney sums up this perspective as follows:

> Conceptions of crime . . . are constructed with intentions, not merely to satisfy the imagination. We end up with some realities rather than others for good reason—because someone has something to protect. That protection can be achieved by the perpetuation of a certain view of reality. Realities are, then, the most subtle and insidious of our forms of social control. . . . The reality of crime that is constructed for all of us by those in a position of power is the reality we tend to accept as our own. By doing so, we grant those in power the authority to carry out the actions that best promote their interests. This is the politics of reality. The social reality of crime in politically organized society is constructed as a political act.[37]

The conflict perspective provides a view of crime and deviance quite different from that of other perspectives. Conflict theory challenges the widespread view that a consensus regarding values, morality, and ideas of deviance exists within society and that the law is simply the embodiment of this consensus.[38] As Goode reports, advocates of the conflict perspective also reject the notion that laws serve to benefit and protect everyone in society.[39] Despite valid criticisms of conflict theory, many people believe that it adds a valuable dimension to understanding crime and delinquency in that it stresses the importance of power and political processes in both defining and controlling criminal and deviant behavior.[40]

After reading this section, you should be able to

1. compare and contrast conflict theory with differential association and social control theories as an explanation for crime;
2. trace the development of conflict theory from Marx through Quinney;
3. describe and evaluate Quinney's social-reality-of-crime theory.

7.5 FEMINIST THEORY

Feminism, according to Daniel Curran and Claire Renzetti, is "a school of thought that explains gender in terms of the social structure in which it is constructed and emphasizes the importance of taking collective action to end sexism."[41] Sexism is a system of social, economic, political, and psychological activities and pressures that suppress women and girls because they exhibit certain biologically determined sexual characteristics. Feminist theory is linked to the conflict perspective and focuses on women's experiences and issues that they face in society. Feminists focus on inequalities between

Feminism is a perspective that emphasizes the way gender has been used as a basis for unequal treatment and the importance of collectively ending sexism in America.

Sexism is a system of social, economic, political, and psychological activities and pressures that suppress or discriminate against people because they are female.

Feminist theory focuses on women's experiences and issues that they face in society.

Feminists focus on the various inequalities between women and men.

women and men, which often are configured with factors of social class and race, in addition to the past and present roles of women at home and in the workforce.

Feminist theory examines women's experiences in society and interprets and evaluates these experiences from a woman's perspective or point of view. Feminist theory enhances our understanding of the social world from a gender-focused viewpoint and makes an important and necessary contribution to the field of criminology.

Feminism is rooted in the second feminist movement, which began in the 1960s (the first women's movement in America began in 1848 at Seneca Falls, New York). Several types of feminism have developed in the United States. The three major types that are related to criminology are socialist feminism, radical feminism, and moderate or liberal feminism.

Socialist Feminism

According to socialist feminism, the origin and persistence of women's inferior status can be accounted for by economic factors.

Socialist feminists emphasize women's economic oppression. They believe that the cause of women's subordination is rooted in the institutions of slavery and private property. **Socialist feminism** stresses the necessity of a socialist revolution as a prerequisite to women's complete liberation.

According to socialist feminism, the origin and persistence of women's inferior status can be accounted for by economic factors:

- Many socialist feminists have their ideological roots in the writings of Karl Marx and Friedrich Engels, and they believe that women's oppression stems from the class system.
- Some socialist feminists believe that in primitive cultures women were recognized by men as equals.
- This equality was lost when a class-divided society, with its private property, state power, and patriarchal family, replaced the matriarchal clan commune.[42]
- Women became the breeders and possessions of their husbands as a result.
- Women are also oppressed by a subordinate role in both the family and the work world.

Thus, socialist feminists view sexism and gender inequality as functional for the capitalist system. For example, corporations can make higher profits from poorly paid women workers. Women's work at home is also for the maintenance and reproduction of the workforce. The persistence of sexist ideology and the institution of the family, which maintain the inferior status of women, are an important part of, and perform an important function for, capitalism. According to these feminists, women can be free only through a socialist revolution, because their oppression is useful to a capitalist system.[43]

According to Curran and Renzetti, the criminal justice system and law reflect class interests. In studying crime and criminal justice, socialist feminists examine how gender and class shape criminal opportunities, victimization experiences, and responses by the criminal justice system to both offenders and victims.[44]

James Messerschmidt has contributed to socialist feminist criminology. He focuses on gender and class and explains why males and females commit different crimes. Messerschmidt believes "it is the gendered and class-based

Socialist feminism emphasizes women's economic oppression and believes in the necessity of a socialist revolution as a prerequisite for women's complete liberation.

division of labor coupled with gender and workplace socialization experiences that account for differences in frequency, seriousness, and motivation for offending between men and women in different social classes."[45] According to Curran and Renzetti, Messerschmidt also focuses on women and masculinity: "Masculinity [is] central to understanding crime because males of all social classes commit significantly more crimes than females, a point that underlines the fact that feminist criminological theory is relevant to men's as well as women's experiences. He [Messerschmidt] argues that women are subject to greater controls in society; they are more closely supervised by parents and also by husbands and boyfriends. And . . . they are underrepresented in positions of economic and political power. Both of these factors limit women's opportunities for white-collar, political, and street crime. The crimes they do commit—larceny theft, minor fraud and embezzlement, and drug offenses—reflect their economic marginalization."[46]

Curran and Renzetti report on the strengths of socialist feminist criminology as follows: "The strengths of socialist criminology are its analysis of the dual importance and interactive effects of gender and class inequalities in shaping women's and men's offending and victimization experiences, and its challenges to traditional criminological depictions of victims and offenders as distinct groups; the home as safe and the public world as dangerous; and the legal system as a value neutral protector that acts in females' 'best interests.'"[47]

Nevertheless, some criminologists are critical of the socialist feminist perspective. Some, for instance, maintain that despite socialist feminists' best efforts to equalize gender and class in their analyses, in most cases they fall short and end up giving primacy to one or the other, usually class. Others point out that socialist feminists (as well as other feminists) have overlooked the importance of race and ethnicity in their analyses, treating women as a homogeneous group or as distinguished only by social class.[48]

Radical Feminism

Radical feminism emphasizes the family's role in the personal oppression of women.

Unlike socialist feminism, which emphasizes women's economic oppression, **radical feminism** emphasizes the family's role in the personal oppression of women. Sexism and gender inequality are the most basic forms of oppression. Radical feminists believe that

- the oppression of women is a basic case of domination of one group over another;
- the oppression of women and racism are extensions of male supremacy;
- sexism's function is psychological as well as economic;
- based upon their sex, women are categorized as an inferior class.[49]

Radical feminist Shulamith Firestone believes that women's biologically determined reproductive roles—that is, the bearing and nursing of children—are the roots of America's sex-class system. Until reliable birth-control methods were developed, women were at the mercy of their biology and therefore did not enjoy the same privileges as men. Women are kept in their place and oppressed by institutions such as marriage, motherhood, and love. For women to be free, these institutions and sexist ideology must be destroyed by revolution, and a total restructuring of society must take place.[50]

Some criminologists have pointed out that radical feminist criminologists have focused their research on women as victims rather than offenders, and on

Radical feminism emphasizes the family's role in the personal oppression of women.

the failure of the courts and legal system in their attempts to protect women from male violence. Other critics of radical feminism claim that

- not all men are oppressors of women;
- radical feminists overlook the importance of social class and racial inequalities;
- the legal system is not simply an instrument of male domination.[51]

Moderate or Liberal Feminism

Moderate or liberal feminism stresses that all people are created equal and all should have equal opportunity. Reform, not radical restructuring, will change society.

Moderate or liberal feminism
stresses that all people are created equal and that all people should have equal opportunity.

Moderate or liberal feminism is a less abstract and less theoretical ideological explanation of gender inequality and sexism. Its roots lie in the beliefs that all people are created equal and that all people should have equal opportunity. These principles have not been, but should be applied to women. Other views of this perspective include:

- Sexism is "dysfunctional for society—it deprives society of the talents of half its members."
- Sexism is not helpful to a particular segment of society.
- False consciousness from sexist socialization, not from self-interest, precipitates opposition to feminist demands.
- A sexist society can be eliminated through the current system.
- Reform, not radical restructuring, will change society.[52]

Therefore, a major goal of moderate or liberal feminists is the revamping of society's gender-socialization practices so that men and women learn to be more alike.[53]

Many criminological theorists believe that

- the main goal of liberal feminists is the removal of barriers that women contend with in the labor force, government, and other social institutions;
- the primary strategy for achieving such a goal is legal change;
- the needed changes are (1) abolishing gender-discriminatory laws, and (2) enacting laws that prohibit gender discrimination.[54]

According to Jeanne Flavin, feminist scholarship has strengthed criminological theory in two ways: by pointing out the limitations of applying theories of male criminality to women, and by developing theories of men's and women's criminality. Nevertheless, mainstream criminologists have not been extensively exposed to feminism. This has contributed to the perception that feminism is about women and criminology is about men. Many criminologists do not understand the significance of feminism's contributions to their field and to criminal justice.[55]

After reading this section, you should be able to

1. describe the basis of feminist theory as an explanation of crime;
2. compare and contrast the positions of socialist, radical, and moderate/liberal feminists;
3. identify contributions of feminist scholarship and research to the field of criminology.

LABELING THEORY

Conflict theory asserts that people will be at odds with one another because their values differ and their interests diverge. After gaining power and translating their normative and value preferences into rules governing institutional life, people are then in a position to successfully place negative labels on rule violators. Some theorists have used this perspective to develop what has been termed labeling theory, or the labeling perspective. **Labeling theory** focuses on the process by which some people are defined as deviants, come to think of themselves as deviants, and begin deviant careers. It also stresses that what is deviant is always dependent on, and in a sense created by, group norms and social reactions to human acts.

> **Labeling theory** stresses that what is deviant is always dependent on, and in a sense created by, group norms and social reactions to human acts.

Howard S. Becker on Labeling Theory

Labeling theory, which stresses that deviance depends on and is created by group norms and social reactions to human acts, was popularized by Howard S. Becker.

Proponents of labeling theory include Edwin M. Lemert, **Howard S. Becker**, and Kai T. Erikson. The labeling perspective was popularized, however, by Becker. Labeling theory begins with the basic idea that deviance or criminality is relative, because group norms and laws are relative. Therefore, what is deviant depends not on the act itself nor on a particular attribute of the person who commits the act; what is deviant is always dependent on, and in a sense created by, group norms and social reactions to human acts. In this sense, deviance results from social judgments relative to group norms that are applied to certain forms of behavior. Becker reported: "Social groups create deviance by making the rules whose infraction constitutes deviance, and by applying the rules to particular people and labeling them as outsiders. . . . [Thus,] deviance is not a quality of the act a person commits, but rather a consequence of the application by others of rules and sanctions to an 'offender.' The deviant is one to whom that label has successfully been applied; deviant behavior is behavior that people so label."[56]

> **Howard S. Becker** believed that deviance results from social judgments relative to group norms that are applied as labels to certain forms of behavior.

From the labeling perspective, many persons may be involved, occasionally or regularly, in various forms of deviant behavior without other people's knowledge. However, if their deviance becomes known, others label them deviant. People may become deviant, then, through a process called the **self-fulfilling prophecy,** in which believing a condition to be true (when it is not) actually creates the condition. The process of becoming deviant in this way involves the following steps:

> In a **self-fulfilling prophecy,** one's belief that a condition is true (when it is not) actually creates the condition.

1. The stigma of the deviant label renders people "outsiders," and they are inevitably excluded from participation in more conventional relationships and groups.
2. Their relationships with family and friends are likely to become strained and perhaps severed, and they may be forced into illegitimate types of work and activity because respectable employers may prefer not to hire them.
3. All this leads to the greater probability that they may be forced to associate with other outsiders.

For Becker, deviance is not a quality of the act a person commits but a consequence of the application by others of rules and sanctions to an "offender." Thus, the label "deviant" defines the act. According to this theory, people who wear fur or use animals in laboratory testing are committing offenses, whereas, to many members of the public, it is the protesters whose behavior is offensive. What social factors determine which labels stick?

4. The deviant label increases the chances that others will become suspicious and will keep a "close eye" on an "outsider's" behavior, and, sooner or later, others are likely to find something that will confirm their suspicions.

5. The ongoing process of labeling, stigmatizing, and ostracizing these individuals is bound to deeply influence their self-image to the point where they truly come to identify with and accept the view that others have of them. This deviant self-image ensures the likelihood that they will continue their deviant activities, perhaps even as members of an organized deviant group.[57]

FOR YOUR INFORMATION

Labeling Theorists' Assumptions

1. There are no human acts inherently evil and deviant in themselves.
2. Acts become deviant only when groups define them as such.
3. Deviance is not a quality characteristic of some people and not of others (that is, in truth, we are probably all deviants, because we all violate norms at least some of the time).
4. Whether a person's act or acts will be viewed as deviant depends on what he or she does and on how others respond.
5. Deviance is dependent on (a) which rules society chooses to enforce, (b) in which situations, and (c) for which people (i.e., not all of us get a ticket for speeding, arrested for trespassing, or prosecuted for tax fraud).
6. Labeling a person as deviant has negative consequences in that it sets up social conditions that are conducive to secondary deviance, that is, deviance a person adopts in response to the reactions of others.
7. A person who becomes labeled as a deviant typically is rejected by and isolated from "law-abiding" people.

An Assessment of Labeling Theory

Labeling theory has been criticized for discounting the role of individual choice in deviant and criminal behavior.

In sum, the important questions in labeling theory are whether a person becomes identified and labeled as deviant, whether sanctions are applied to that person by others, and whether that person is cast into a deviant role by others. When these conditions come to pass, a person becomes more isolated from conventional roles, strengthened in his or her self-image as a deviant, and increasingly assimilated into deviant activities and groups.[58]

The labeling approach to crime and deviance, unlike the theory of anomie or cultural transmission theory, discussed in Chapter 6, does not focus on why some people engage in deviant or criminal behavior. Instead, it helps us to understand why a given act or behavior may or may not be considered or labeled deviant, depending on the social situation and the characteristics of the people involved. This theory also provides insight into the process by which individuals become career deviants or criminals.

However, labeling theory has been criticized on at least two counts:

1. The initial labeling of an individual as a deviant, delinquent, or criminal does not automatically necessitate that person's continued involvement in deviant or criminal behavior. For example, many people who are convicted of a crime do not repeat their offense, nor do they adopt criminal lifestyles or criminal careers.
2. Labeling theory deals mainly with the role of social reactions to deviance and crime, especially the long-range consequences of labeling and stigmatization on the individual. However, this still leaves unanswered the question of why the individual committed the deviant or criminal act in the first place. A combination of other theories and perspectives provides an adequate answer to this question.[59]

In general, sociological theories of crime and delinquency provide answers for two interrelated yet analytically distinct questions:

1. They attempt to account for the specific processes by which individuals become criminals (exemplified in the labeling and differential association theories) and to answer the question of how and why a person becomes criminal.
2. They try to explain variations in the rates of crime (e.g., the strain and subcultural theories) and to explore the reasons why different groups and categories of people within society manifest different rates of crime and delinquency.

A substantial number of theories exist to provide answers to questions of crime and delinquency, and the most important ones have been reviewed here and in previous chapters. Still other theories will surface later in the text (e.g., in the review of violent crime—abuse, rape, assault, and homicide). Also, the chapters on social responses to crime will reveal a resurgence of the classical choice and deterrence theories. These theories have serious ramifications in terms of crime-prevention and punishment policies. However, the main focus of the text will now turn to different types of criminal behavior, beginning with a look at violent crime.

After reading this chapter, you should be able to

1. describe the basis of labeling theory as an explanation for crime;
2. describe Becker's contributions to understanding how individuals become deviant or criminal;
3. critique labeling theory as an explanation for delinquent and criminal behavior.

CHAPTER SUMMARY

This chapter examines several major sociological theories: learning, control, conflict, and labeling theories. Edwin Sutherland, a learning theorist, believed that just as a person learns other types of behavior, he or she also learns deviant and criminal behavior. In his theory of differential association, he stressed the importance of one's associates in learning deviance. Robert Burgess and Ronald Akers's differential-association reinforcement theory refers to the process by which conforming or criminal behavior is acquired and internalized by a person through past as well as present rewards and punishments. Daniel Glaser's differential identification theory refers to the process by which criminal behavior develops through a person's greater identification with members of criminal groups than with members of noncriminal or conformist groups. Glaser's differential anticipation theory stresses the idea that people are likely to engage in those types of behavior from which they expect to receive the greatest rewards with the least punishment (pp. 169–174).

Social control theorists, such as Travis Hirschi, believe that people in society commit delinquent and criminal acts because of the weakness of social bonds restraining them from doing so, not because of the strength of forces driving them to do so. Michael Gottfredson and Hirschi, in their general theory of crime, explain crime as the outcome of an individual's low self-control in combination with situational conditions conducive to criminal behavior (pp. 174–177).

For conflict theorists, the sources of crime are found in the society's laws, customs, and distribution of wealth and power. Karl Marx believed that social reality must be understood in terms of the class struggle for the underlying mode of production. According to Richard Quinney, criminal definitions are applied by the segments of society that have the power to shape the enforcement and administration of criminal law (pp. 177–181).

Feminist theory focuses on women's experiences and issues that they face in society and is linked to the conflict perspective. Feminists focus on the various ways inequalities between women and men are often configured with factors of social class and race, in addition to the past as well as present roles of women at home and in the workforce. Unlike socialist feminists, who emphasize women's economic oppression, radical feminists emphasize the family's role in the personal oppression of women. Moderate or liberal feminism stresses that all people are created equal and all should have equal opportunity. Reform, not radical restructuring, will change society.

For Howard S. Becker and other labeling theorists, what is deviant depends not on the act itself nor on a particular attribute of the person who commits the act; what is deviant is always dependent on, and in a sense created by, group norms and social reactions to human acts (pp. 185–187).

Study Guide

Chapter Objectives

- Review the basic assumption of learning.
- Briefly describe Sutherland's differential association theory of crime.
- Write a brief evaluation of the differential association theory of crime.
- Describe differential-association reinforcement theory.
- Briefly describe differential identification theory and differential anticipation theory.
- Review the basic assumptions of social control theory.
- Describe the general theory of crime.
- List and describe the basic assumptions of conflict theory.

- Briefly describe Marx's contributions to the conflict perspective.
- List and explain Quinney's six propositions in his social-reality-of-crime theory.
- Write a brief critique of conflict theory.
- Define feminist theory and describe its contributions to criminology.
- Examine the differences between socialist, radical, and moderate/liberal feminism.
- Briefly describe and explain the basic assumptions of labeling theory.

Key Terms

Akers, Ronald (172)
Becker, Howard S. (185)
Burgess, Robert (172)
Conflict theory (177)
Differential anticipation theory (174)
Differential association theory (169)
Differential-association reinforcement theory (172)
Differential identification theory (173)
Feminism (181)

Feminist theory (181)
Feminists (181)
General theory of crime (GTC) (176)
Glaser, Daniel (173)
Gottfredson, Michael (176)
Hirschi, Travis (175)
Labeling theory (185)
Marx, Karl (179)
Moderate/liberal feminism (184)
Quinney, Richard (179)

Radical feminism (183)
Reference group (173)
Self-fulfilling prophecy (185)
Sexism (181)
Six propositions (179)
Social control theory (174)
Socialist feminism (182)
Social learning theory (173)
Social-reality-of-crime theory (179)
Sutherland, Edwin H. (169)

Self-Test
Short Answer

1. List the nine statements of Sutherland's differential association theory of crime.
2. Define differential-association reinforcement theory.
3. Define differential identification theory.
4. Define differential anticipation theory.
5. Explain what a reference group is and describe its importance.
6. Briefly describe social control theory.
7. List and describe Hirschi's "elements of the social bond."

8. Briefly explain the general theory of crime.
9. List the basic assumptions of conflict theory.
10. Briefly state the Marxist perspective on crime.
11. List and define Quinney's six propositions.
12. Define feminism.
13. Define socialist, radical, and moderate/liberal feminism.
14. List the assumptions of labeling theory.
15. Briefly assess labeling theory.

Multiple Choice

1. Differential association theorists maintain that
   a. criminal behavior is learned behavior
   b. both deviant and nondeviant behavior can be accounted for in terms of personality factors
   c. for the most part, criminal behavior is learned within large, impersonal groups
   d. none of the above
2. Differential identification theory
   a. is the same as differential association theory
   b. is rooted in Sutherland's differential association theory
   c. refers to the process by which criminal behavior develops
   d. *b* and *c*
3. Which of the following is not one of Hirschi's elements of the social bond?
   a. attachment
   b. commitment
   c. reliability
   d. involvement
4. The general theory of crime
   a. stresses the importance of biology in the individual
   b. focuses on the idea that crime is a product of a lack of appropriate socialization and learning
   c. focuses on the genetic factors in criminal behavior
   d. all of the above
5. Conflict theory assumes that criminals
   a. are the manifestations of the failure of society to meet the needs of individuals
   b. make the rules and laws of the society
   c. are the products of conflict in families
   d. all of the above
6. Conflict theory focuses on
   a. who makes the rules
   b. who decides who is deviant or criminal
   c. which groups in society gain or lose by the rules and decisions
   d. all of the above

7. Richard Quinney
   a. integrated his and other theorists' ideas on society, power, and criminality
   b. believed that deviance is defined by the social reactions to it
   c. believed that the social reality of crime is constructed as a political act
   d. all of the above
8. Feminist theory
   a. examines women's experiences in society
   b. evaluates women's experiences from a woman's perspective or point of view
   c. enhances our understanding of the social world from a gender-focused viewpoint
   d. all of the above
9. Critics of radical feminism claim that
   a. not all men are oppressors of women
   b. radical feminists overlook the importance of social class and racial inequalities
   c. the legal system is not simply an instrument of male domination
   d. all of the above
10. Labeling theory stresses that
    a. labeling a person as deviant guarantees that the person will continue in deviance
    b. in general, social reactions have very little influence on a person's self-image
    c. what is deviant depends not on the act itself but on group norms and social reactions
    d. all groups label the same acts as deviant
11. Howard Becker believed that
    a. people become criminal only because they are isolated from anticriminal patterns
    b. many forms of criminal behavior are inborn, or inherited
    c. both deviant and nondeviant behavior can largely be accounted for in terms of personality factors
    d. none of the above

True–False

T F 1. Differential association theorists argue that everyone is exposed to criminal as well as noncriminal behavior patterns, values, and attitudes.

T F 2. Sutherland claimed that endomorphic persons were the most likely to engage in criminal and delinquent acts.

T F 3. For Sutherland, criminal behavior is inherited.

T F 4. For Glaser, the process of differential association involves a personal identification with criminals that results in criminal behavior.

T F 5. Control theory assumes that all human beings by nature are rule breakers.

T F 6. Gottfredson and Hirshi believe that deviants and criminals lack self-control.

T F 7. Conflict theorists play down the importance of such factors as economics, vested interests, and power in explaining crime.

T F 8. All conflict theorists agree with Karl Marx.

T F 9. Feminist theory focuses on women's experiences and issues that they face in society.

T F 10. Radical feminists emphasize the family's role in the personal oppression of women.

T F 11. According to labeling theorists, social groups actually create deviance.

Fill-In

1. _____ theory views criminal behavior as learned through interaction with others, particularly within intimate, personal groups.
2. Sutherland stressed the influence of _____ on crime.
3. For Glaser, criminal behavior develops because of a person's greater _____ with members of criminal groups than with members of noncriminal or conformist groups.
4. _____ theorists start with the assumption that the motivation for delinquent behavior is part of human behavior.
5. For Hirschi, _____ refers to an individual's affection for and responsiveness to others.
6. Control theories assume that delinquent acts result when an individual's _____ bond is weak or broken.
7. The _____ perspective assumes that the basic form of social interaction is competition.
8. For the _____ theorist, criminal and delinquent behavior is rooted in class and economic conflicts in the capitalist system.
9. _____ feminists emphasize women's economic oppression.
10. For Jeanne Flavin, mainstream criminologists have not been exposed to _____.
11. For Howard Becker, _____ results from social judgments.
12. _____ theorists believe that there are no human acts inherently evil and deviant in themselves.

Matching

1. Sutherland
2. Glaser
3. Gottfredson and Hirschi
4. Elements of the social bond
5. Conflict theory
6. Social-reality-of-crime theory
7. Labeling theory
8. Radical feminists
9. Socialist feminists

A. Quinney
B. Differential identification theory
C. Social control theory
D. Marx
E. General theory of crime
F. Differential association theory
G. Becker
H. Women's economic oppression
I. Family and the personal oppression of women

Essay Questions

1. Explain the basic principles of Sutherland's differential association theory of crime. What types of crime or criminal activities does this theory best explain?
2. Examine the basic principles of differential identification theory. How does it differ from differential association and differential anticipation theories?
3. Write a brief critical essay on Travis Hirschi's statement, "Control theories assume that delinquent acts result when an individual's bond to society is weak and broken."
4. Examine the major principles of Gottfredson and Hirschi's general theory of crime. How valid is this theory in explaining crime?
5. Given the major worldwide social, political, and economic changes of the past several years, do you believe that the basic assumptions and perspectives of the conflict approach to crime in the United States are passé? Explain your answer.
6. Examine the influence of feminism on the field of criminology.
7. Do you agree with the premise of labeling theory that states, "There are no human acts inherently evil and deviant in themselves"? Explain and support your position.

On Behalf of Labeling Theory*

BY ERICH GOODE

By the early 1960s labeling theory had become the major approach in the sociology of deviant behavior. But by the early 1970s the antilabeling stance became almost as fashionable as labeling had been a decade earlier. The interim witnessed many dozens of critiques. Most—although not all—share three fundamental flaws. First, they tend to be polemical rather than constructive. Instead of urging labeling theorists to sharpen their conceptual tools with the proffered criticisms, their authors seem intent on *extirpating* labeling theory. A second problem with these critiques is that they rarely render a faithful likeness of the original. The perspective has typically been caricatured, made to affirm principles that no labeling theorist has ever written or believed. Third, and most important: our critics seem incapable of recognizing the crucial difference between what specific labeling theorists have (supposedly) written in specific works and the potential power of the perspective, where future deviance theorists could go with the perspective's root concepts and insights were they to be systematically re-thought and developed.

I would like to re-examine a number of key concepts and assertions made both by critics of labeling theory and by authors seen as labeling theorists. I intend to offer a commentary on the validity of these criticisms, a stock-taking of what has and has not been said by the "reactive" perspective, and some thoughts on where a labeling perspective should take us—even if it has not yet done so.

A convincing case could be made for the assertion that labeling theory does not exist in the first place. A field has been fabricated by observers and critics out of the raw material of a few arresting passages, phrases and concepts. Examined carefully, the ideas of the supposed school's adherents sound increasingly less alike, at times revealing more discord than the harmony marking a genuine tradition of thought.

It has been said that the concept of "secondary deviation" is central to labeling theory (Schur, 1971:10). However, the author of this concept, Edwin Lemert, rejects what may be the key idea in any "reactive" perspective in the study of deviance: that the relationship between action and reaction is problematic. Lemert, in counter-point, invokes "objective aspects of deviance" and "values universal in nature" (1972:22). Consequently, it is difficult to comprehend just what might be meant when it is asserted that Edwin Lemert is a labeling theorist.

Kai Erikson penned what is the single most often quoted article in the labeling tradition, "Notes on the Sociology of Deviance" (1962). But the monograph in which this essay forms the first chapter (Erikson, 1966) rests squarely within the functionalist tradition, as the leading functionalist (Merton, 1971:829) has noted. It may be that there are points of agreement between functionalism and labeling theory (just as there are, say, between functionalism and Marxism), but a theorist whose most important work is primarily functionalist in its orientation cannot be said to be primarily a labeling theorist.

John Kitsuse is the author of "Societal Reaction to Deviant Behavior," (1962) probably the second most frequently quoted paper within the supposed labeling perspective. It is widely regarded as a classic example of labeling theorizing. But Kitsuse is also the co-author of another paper that points to a number of gaps, rigidities and fallacies in current labeling theorists' thinking (Rains and Kitsuse, 1973). Since these criticisms contradict the image of labeling theory that has common currency, it would be difficult to pin the labeling theorist label on John Kitsuse.

Howard Becker's work is more frequently cited than that of any other labeling theorist. Yet Becker has written a number of illuminating comments on the "straw theory" nearly everyone takes to be labeling theory (1973). Labeling theory, Becker writes, is, first of all, not a *theory* in the strict sense of the word as it is generally understood. Second, it wasn't meant to "explain" deviant behavior; it is not the literal "cause" of the acts evaluated in the first place. Third; public stigmatization is neither a necessary nor a sufficient condition

* This paper is part of a larger investigation supported by a fellowship from the John Simon Guggenheim Memorial Foundation; I am grateful for its generous support. In addition, the Research Foundation of the State University of New York permitted me a summer unencumbered by teaching responsibilities by awarding me a Faculty Research Fellowship. I would also like to thank Gerald Suttles, Forrest Dill, Robert Stevenson, and Terry J. Rosenberg for critical comments on an earlier draft of this paper; they have been most helpful.

for an individual's commitment to a career in deviance. Becker agrees with Cohen (1965) in stating that this is an empirical question; no theory can simply assume it. Last, not only should labeling theory not be called a theory, it probably shouldn't be called "labeling" anything. Since the literal application of a negative label to specific individuals committing specific acts is neither the most essential nor even the most fundamental process within the scope of this perspective, perhaps the term "labeling" should be dropped altogether. Becker, along with Rubington and Weinberg (1973), suggests the "interactionist" perspective.

If the four most often invoked figures in labeling theory—Lemert, Erikson, Kitsuse, and Becker—cannot be called labeling theorists (that is, do not accept tenets ascribed as central to labeling theory), who is one? We search in vain for a set of theories, or any systematic, unified body of work to which we can point and say, this is labeling theory, its authors are labeling theorists. There is no real school of labeling theory—outside of the label, the public characterization. We do have a few paragraphs, some insights, a few lines of reasoning aimed at several targets. We have the makings of a perspective, a number of powerful sensitizing concepts that have been inappropriately specified and stereotyped into what appears to be a monolithic edifice.

LABELING: WHAT SOMETHING IS

Early attempts to study deviant behavior made the assumption that acts social scientists attached names to inherently belonged in naturally-occurring categories. Forms of deviance were thought to constitute clinical entities, predefined for the scientist. Attempts to devise theories of deviant behavior had to be based on phenomena having objective, formal, universal features applicable regardless of time and place, perceived by an external observer (the scientist), but not necessarily by the subject scrutinized by the scientist. Just what this scientific quest meant took on a distinctive and even peculiar flavor. After all, the literalminded would say, "subjectivity" is the opposite of "objectivity," Ergo, "subjectivity" has no place in the science of sociology.

Labelists rejected the validity of the necessity for studying "objective" categories of human behavior. "All categories of mankind are phenomenological constructs employed by the members of mankind" (Lofland, 1969:123). Even before we know just what forms of behavior are thought of as deviant, we have to understand how features of those forms of behavior are assembled and categorized, how some specific act comes to be seen as an instance of a larger category of behavior. No class of objects, people, or acts "belongs" together under the same name inherently and automatically. A number of women strolling the beaches of Ipanema, a suburb of Rio de Janeiro, took to wearing topless bathing suits. In the Spring of 1973 the Director of Censorship and Entertainment of the Rio police department ordered topless female bathers to be arrested for "practicing an obscene act." Any woman who bared her breasts, this official declared, committed "violent aggression against society." No doubt the reader does not share this conception of "aggression" or "violence." Is it proper to call same-gender genital contact "homosexuality" when it takes place in one setting devoid of the opposite sex (in prisons, for example), in a society that strongly encourages it—say, among the Siwans of Africa (Ford and Beach, 1951:131–132)—in another subculture of male hustlers who adopt no homosexual self-image, follow a rigid code as to what is permitted with others whom they call homosexuals, have intercourse with their girlfriends, and eventually discontinue the practice (Reiss, 1961)? Sociologically, these acts are "the same behavior" only in the most superficial respect; they might, in fact, be called behavioral analogues. While it is true, as Gibbs points out, arguing for some measure of "objectivism" in studying deviance, that "less than absolute perceptual uniformity within a social unit does not negate the notion of types of acts" (1972: 47), the variations in definitions as to what specific acts fall into what general (deviant) categories are sufficiently great as to treat this as problematic rather than automatic.

This "subjectivistic" view troubles many sociologists. In commenting on the current stress on interpretations of deviant behavior rather than on the behavior itself, Hirschi argues for a return to viewing categories of behavior in terms of objective criteria: "The person may not have committed a 'deviant' act, but he did (in many cases) do *something*. . . . And it is just possible that . . . if he were left alone he would *do it again*" (Hirschi, 1973:169). "Extreme relativism," agrees Edwin Lemert, "leaves the unfortunate impression that almost any meaning can be assigned to human attributes and actions."

> Practically all societies in varying degrees and ways disapprove of incest, adultery, promiscuity, cruelty to children, laziness, disrespect for parents and elders, murder, rape, theft, lying and cheating. Perhaps the point to make is that certain kinds of actions are likely to be judged deleterious in any context. . . . It is not so much that they violate rules as it is that they destroy, downgrade, or jeopardize values universal in nature (Lemert, 1972:22).

One problem with these assertions is that none of the forms of behavior mentioned comprises a universally-agreed-upon category. Just what is regarded as incest isn't the same everywhere; different societies regard different sets of potential sex partners as incestuous. In some civilizations only members of one's immediate family, plus aunts, uncles and grandparents qualify. In others, "the interpretation of incest is so broad as to exclude as potential sex partners half the available population" (Ford and Beach, 1951:113).

The very inclusion of an act within a certain category implies a certain attitude toward it. "Murder," "incest," and "robbery"—terms you and I use to characterize acts we deem to fit—may (or may not) be universally condemned, but if they are, it is because each of these words is already predefined and "loaded with moral disapproval" (Nisbet, 1970:282). In many past societies of the world the "murder" (from our point of view, not theirs) of a commoner by a nobleman did not arouse much moral outrage or even disapproval, Under the reign of King Shaka of the Zulu the king "murdered" citizens at will. His behavior was not only not condemned, but it was applauded, even by his soon-to-be victims, as a sign of the monarch's potency (Walter, 1969).

Thus, when an "objectivist" says of an actor engaged in a given and supposedly deviant form of behavior, "he did do *something*," we can only be left with a feeling of emptiness. *Just what is it, specifically, that he did?* Can we automatically and mechanically equate acts that are externally similar regardless of what they mean to the participants involved?

Everything is not relative, of course; the college sophomore's banalization of a basically powerful idea seems to make a travesty of it. (In fact, a diluted "objectivism," if properly understood, can be seen as a kind of relativism, because looking at categories as having universal properties is only one of many viable, available perspectives that could be adopted by an observer—in this case, someone usually called a "social scientist.") There is a definite utility to looking at social behavior in an "objectivistic" fashion. The point is that while adopting subjective categories and realities will yield crucial consequences and pay-offs, adopting objective categories and realities constructed by social scientists but not seen by participants also has important consequences and pay-offs.

Societies differ significantly in what is considered a normal consumption of alcohol. Heavy drinking in one will be considered average in another. This subjective definition helps us to understand certain things concerning drinking. (For instance, the social organization of the control and condemnation of "excessive" drinking.) But it doesn't help very much in understanding other significant facts. Alcohol does have certain effects on the body. The "objectivistic" view will help discover what these effects will be, while the subjectivistic views constructed by members of the society in which drinking takes place probably will not.

We may simply want to know how frequently and with what consequences intercourse occurs, let's say, between cross-cousins, regardless of how it is seen by the members of the society in which it takes place or by the cousins themselves, regardless of whether it is defined as "incest" in the first place. We may wish to find out how it comes to pass that some men or women do not see themselves, and are not seen by their peers, as engaging in "homosexual" behavior when, to our eyes, they seem to be doing so in the formal, "objective" sense. (As Gerald Suttles pointed out to me, the fact that participants do not share the distinctions sociologists make is itself a problem to be explained. Likewise, I would add, the participants may want to know how sociologists managed to concoct the categories through which *they* see the world.) It is a perfectly legitimate enterprise, this "objectivistic" line of inquiry, but limited. It becomes invalid when investigators: (1) believe it to be the whole story; (2) lose sight of the fact that their categorizations may have nothing to do with those held by participants; (3) wish to understand behavior as it is lived and experienced; or (4) fail to recognize the relevance of subjective distinctions in the sphere they study. In short, we have to know *when whose perspective is relevant*.

EMPATHY

Hirschi (1973) is troubled by the use of empathy in the social sciences. He feels that understanding the world through the eyes of the deviant leads the researcher into an empirical blunder: it blinds the sociologist to the less attractive features of deviance.

Being empathetic means that we have to come as close to the behavior under study as we possibly can, given the limitations of our biography, morality and ideology. Empathy means that the sociologist has mentally, emotionally, and experientially to enter the world of the people he or she wishes to understand. Advocates do not claim that this is the only acceptable means of studying deviance. It does mean that the practitioner of deviant behavior often sees the world in a fairly distinct fashion. It is therefore a crucial and theoretically fruitful dimension of deviance.

This approach has also been called "appreciative" sociology (Matza, 1969:15.40). Perhaps this term is a bit misleading. Deviants may despise what they do or themselves for doing it—witness the child molester (McCaghy, 1967), the stripper (Skipper and McCaghy, 1970), the alcoholic. To assume that prostitutes necessarily enjoy their work would be to fall victim to the "happy hooker" syndrome (Goode and Troiden, 1974:108). In short, deviants may not "appreciate" their own behavior at all. If we were to assume that they do would be anything but empathetic. Their "appreciation" of their deviant behavior is an empirical question.

Empathy does not mean being conned or duped by our subject, by the practitioner of the deviant behavior we study. It does not, above all, indicate a simple-minded gullibility. In fact, it means the reverse: to be conned is to be the victim of an external social facade the deviant presents to the outside world. To empathize is to see the world from a first-hand perspective, to acquire an insider's view. And hence, to recognize the nature of the con job being presented to and believed by those not practiced or adept in the art of empathy. The subject—the deviant—is acutely aware of the fronts he or she presents to the world. Empathy involves knowing just how these fronts operate, not believing in their validity.

An example of this principle may be found in the review of Harold Garfinkel's book, *Studies in Ethnomethodology* (1967), written by the positivistically-inclined sociologist James S. Coleman (1968). Garfinkel describes the case of "Agnes," who was born a biological boy, but passed as a woman for several years after taking female hormones during adolescence, and eventually underwent a sex-change operation. Garfinkel's approach attempts to be empathetic. Since Agnes defined herself as a woman, and successfully "accomplished" womanhood—that is, performed convincingly, and was so regarded by the outside world—the sociologist, too, could regard her, even before her operation, as an accomplished woman.

Coleman takes strong exception to this view. He argues that in adopting the empathetic stance, the researcher becomes "trapped in the confidence game." The "fatal flaw" in identifying with one's subjects, Coleman feels, is that the observer becomes incapable of standing outside the social world described to see it "objectively," as it really is, rather than as our subjects *think* it is.

There are two fallacies underlying Coleman's reasoning. First, Agnes really did know that she was born with the anatomical equipment of a male. She did know that she had been taking hormones to induce female secondary sex characteristics in herself. And she was aware of her lies to the physicians examining her. She knew only too well the fronts, the tricks, the ruses she fabricated to hide her secret from others. So Agnes was fully aware of the leap from being a technically biological male to becoming an hormonally and surgically-induced female. If Garfinkel and his colleagues had really seen the world as Agnes did, they would have been aware of all of this. Their error was not in adopting empathy as an assumption and a research strategy, as Coleman claims, but in *not being empathetic enough*. They had believed in Agnes's front *to* the world, not in her version *of* the world.

And the second flaw in Coleman's "objectivistic" posture toward Agnes is in assuming the unidimensionality of gender, that formal, objective properties determine the essential reality of a phenomenon. It is quite irrelevant exactly how Agnes induced female characteristics in herself. *She truly believed herself to be a woman.* She saw her male sex organs as an excrescence, a pathological growth, much like cancer. Her efforts, she felt, corrected a mistake of nature. Her operation was a vindication of her true sexuality (Garfinkel, 1967:116:185). (Agnes and Coleman agree on the major point: that gender is *essentialistic*, that one has a "true," ultimate, definitive sexuality. They differ only on the criteria. Both versions can be regarded as one out of many ways of looking at gender.) To believe that Agnes "really" was, after all, and above all, a "boy"—as Coleman insists on referring to her throughout his review—is to fail to notice something truly remarkable taking place before one's very eyes. It is to fail as an empiricist.

Empathy does not mean *surrender*, either; it does not mean that the deviant "is always right." Ideological systems describing, explaining and justifying one's own behavior tend to be detailed and subtle. (Although those describing other people's are often shallow and simplified.) Outsiders who are not plugged into what people think and say about what they do, who they are, and what they believe, gloss over the filigcee-like fertility of their subjects' world view.

Deviants do not present an "I am always right" impression to one another, nor to themselves. (Perhaps the paranoid is an exception.) But they do to outsiders. Frequent, heavy users of hard drugs—alcoholics, speed freaks, heroin addicts—do not present the effects of the drug they use in a uniformly positive light, not to insiders, not to themselves, and not to empatbetic researchers who make a genuine effort to understand their world. The closer one comes to that world the more brutally honest they are about what their drug of choice is doing to their mind and body.

Nuts, Sluts, and Preverts

A sizeable proportion of sociological writings on deviance within the labeling tradition has investigated what has come to be called the *nuts, sluts, and deviated preverts* variety of behavior (Liazos, 1972). The study of deviance concentrates on condemned and stigmatized behavior and people; what is studied is specifically only that which is included within these circumscribed boundaries. This means that deviance sociologists have to ignore a great deal of behavior and people that do not fit in with the formal definition, but are similar in interesting ways. This past fascination with dramatic and "immoral" behavior has led to ignoring "the unethical, illegal and destructive actions of powerful individuals, groups and institutions in our society" (Liazos, 1972:111). The "value engaged labelists" express their "class bias" by focusing on the behavior of the powerless and ignoring that of the powerful. In so doing, they avoid examining the workings of the power elite in the drama of deviant behavior, thereby supporting the status quo (Thio, 1973).

This is a valid characterization and criticism of labeling theory as it has been practiced specifically and historically. But critics of this stripe make the assumption that the blunder is inherent to the labeling perspective. In fact, this restriction on what behavior a "reactive" viewpoint can and cannot examine and what levels of society it delves into is entirely self-imposed. I will argue that it is not a logical or a necessary implication of labeling theory. The "interactionist" perspective toward deviance does not automatically restrict our attention to "nuts, sluts, and preverts," to the deviance of the powerless; it can direct our attention to the very phenomena these critics wish to examine. Far from being a kind of ringside seat on a parade of freaks, weirdos, and colorful characters, our perspective should insist on raising the question why certain kinds of acts tend to be condemned while others are not. Inevitably this leads to an examination of the distribution of power in the society under study.

As sociologists further back than Sutherland have pointed out, the thief in the white collar steals far more from the public pocket than the conventional street criminal. If we were to ask a cross-section of the public why crimes such as armed robbery and burglary should receive stiff penalties, the typical reply would be that they represent a great "threat to society." The same public is indifferent toward, fails to condemn—and yet, is being bilked by—the white collar criminal. Why? A recent estimate of bank losses indicated that bank robbers stole approximately 27 million dollars in 1973, while in the same year approximately 150 million was stolen by the bank's own trusted employees. Yet armed robbery was considered significantly more "serious" a crime to a sample of respondents than embezzlement (Rossi, et al., 1974). The public loses incalculably more again from corporate crimes and yet condemns them even less. Which, then, is more deviant?

Consider drug use, possession, and sale. Selling heroin was the third most "serious" crime evaluated by the respondents in the study just cited—ranking below only the planned killing of a policeman and the planned killing of a person for a fee. It was deemed more serious than all forms of forcible rape and the planned killing of a spouse. Even *using* heroin was more strongly condemned than killing someone in a bar-room brawl. Selling marijuana ranked as more serious than the forcible rape of one's former spouse and "killing spouse's lover after catching them together" (Rossi, et al., 1974).

The possession, use, and sale of illegal, recreational drugs is clearly a form of deviant behavior. However, a mechanical and simple-minded interpretation of labeling deviant behavior would be to confine our efforts exclusively to those drug-related forms of behavior that are condemned by the public. A sophisticated interpretation of the labeling perspective would study drug use with the intention of understanding why externally similar forms of behavior are accorded markedly different degrees of condemnation. Certainly legal drug sellers—the alcohol, tobacco, and the pharmaceutical industries—are responsible for far more drug-related deaths, overdoses, medical damage and human misery than purveyors of illegal drugs. Yet we never cast drug manufacturing executives into the role of deviants. Any meaningful examination of drug use is forced to grapple with this paradox (Goode, 1972).

An adequate understanding of labeling theory demands that damaging but respectable (i.e., non-deviant) behavior be studied. These disjunctions between public condemnation and "objective" social damage should intrigue us. If we define deviance by public condemnation, we have to find out both the "why" of it—why some behavior attracts a label of immorality—as well as the "why not": why other forms of behavior are not considered immoral. We can never fully understand what is deviant until we get a good look at what isn't. By looking at both, we realize that it is not "social cost" nor any "objective threat to society" that accounts for behavior labeled as deviant or crystallized into formal law. We couldn't deal with this issue if we concentrated exclusively on deviant (or criminal) behavior itself.

The forms of behavior that Marxists and radicals consider—those they criticize labeling theorists for ignoring—oppression, exploitation, racism, sexism, imperialism,

certainly do far more damage to human life than most (or any) acts of obvious deviance. And yet behavior that falls under their umbrella is not generally regarded as deviant. Many of us might feel that they *should* be condemned by the public. Some no doubt feel that a theory, like labeling theory, should not be taken seriously if we *can't* call such actions deviant. But the fact that they are not deviant in the public mind should excite our curiosity. Deviance is not centrally about oppression, although it overlaps with it in important ways. Oppression is certainly a basic feature in some forms of deviant behavior, just as the quality of deviance is entirely lacking in much oppressive behavior.

This divergence leads to the issue of how definitions of deviance favorable to those in power manage to win out over definitions that would threaten established ideological and material interests. As Marx and Engels pointed out over a century and a quarter ago in *The German Ideology*, the ruling class tends to dominate a society's intellectual and ideological life, its notions of true and false, of good and bad. Consequently it often happens that the relatively powerless in a given society, the economically deprived, are more likely to have their behavior defined as deviant and are less capable of resisting an imputation of deviance than the affluent and powerful. Thus, the study of deviance often parallels the study of powerlessness. Why this essentially Marxist idea should enrage Marxists is puzzling.

WHAT IS DEVIANCE?
WHO IS THE DEVIANT?

Pushed to its logical extreme, the idea of relativity is self-defeating. If what is considered deviant is relative generally to time and place, it is relative even more specifically to each individual instance of time and place. Judgments of the reactions to behavior vary not only across societies and contexts in general, but across specific situations as well. It follows that what is deviance is completely *sui generis* and literally emergent out of actually-occurring instances of behavior and reactions to behavior. This is Pollner's "Model II" version of deviance: "the deviant character of the act . . . depends upon, or more emphatically, is constituted by the subsequent response of the community. . . . There is no deviance apart from the response. . . . If the labeling is constitutive of deviance, then the fact that no one reacts to an act as deviant means that it is not deviant" (Pollner, 1974:29, 33).

It becomes impossible, adopting this view, to predict a priori whether a given act will be judged as deviance until we know whether it already has been so judged. Behavior that has escaped the scrutiny and condemnation by alters is not deviant at all. If act A is identical in all respects to act B, differing only in that A has been observed and condemned while B has not, then A is an instance of deviance and B is not. Becker tried to bridge this chasm by introducing the distinction between *deviance* and *rule-breaking* behavior (1963:14), thereby creating a form of behavior that formally breaks the rules but is not perceived as deviance—"secret deviance" (1963:20). But by employing the dimension of literal condemnation "secret deviance" is not deviant at all; it could not exist within Becker's scheme. Of all aspects of his model, perhaps this conceptual difficulty attracted more criticism than any other. It pleased no one, including Becker himself.

Becker's later formulation attempted to resolve this problem. It is not necessary to call behavior deviant if and only if it has already been condemned. Certain acts can be considered deviant "because these acts are likely to be defined as deviant when discovered" (Becker, 1973:181). Referring to his earlier conceptualization of "secret" deviance, Becker comments: "If we begin by saying that an act is deviant when it is so defined, what can it mean to call an act an instance of secret deviance? Since no one has defined it as deviant it cannot, by definition, be deviant; but 'secret' indicates that *we* know it is deviant, even if no one else does" (1973:187). This difficulty forces us to refer to certain acts as *potentially* deviant. Acts have differing degrees of probability attached to them of being condemned. If we knew the situations in which they occurred and the characteristics of the various actors involved, we would have a clearer idea of just what these probabilities are. This probabilistic conception of deviance permits us to transcend the dilemma that plagued earlier theorists. Behavior is deviant, then, "if it falls within a class of behavior for which there is a probability of negative sanctions subsequent to its detection" (Black and Reiss, 1970:63).

Taken literally, the "everything is relative" vulgarization implies that almost any behavior is deviant—to some people. And that no form of behavior is deviant—that is, to absolutely everyone. This is of course literally true, but not very helpful. The idea of "potential" deviance forces us to recognize that not all groups in a society are equally powerful nor are they equal in the numeric sense. Examining different definitions of evidence as if they all got equal time, as if they operated in a kind of ethical free enterprise system, belies the hierarchical nature of deviance. Most important is the issue of which moral codes are dominant, which forms of behavior stand a high likelihood of condemnation. Different acts command varying probabilities of exciting moral outrage among segments of the community; these probabilities can be determined, even if only approximately. A completely situational view of deviance can be intellectually paralyzing. The probabilistic view rescues us from the solipsistic logical extreme of absolute situational relativity and the empirical obtuseness of behavioral universality.

Does the probabilistic view imply that the deviant shares the majority view of what and who should be condemned? Critics of the labeling theory holding a leftish, conflict viewpoint (Mankoff, 1971; Chambliss, 1974) find "significant traces of consensual thinking" in labelists. "The societal reaction paradigm implies that labelers really share the same *Weltanschauung* as rule-breakers" (Mankoff, 1971:212). This would make labeling theory a variety of a "value con-

sensus" perspective. This position represents a basic misunderstanding.

Several analytically and empirically distinct dimensions are confused in this criticism. It is crucial to separate them. They are:

1. *sharing* the conformist's normative values—that is, believing that rule-breaking (for the deviant, what one is doing) is morally wrong;
2. *knowing* what the majority definition of deviance and conformity actually are;
3. *caring*, in the moral sense, that one will be condemned by the majority's definition of right and wrong;
4. caring about the *consequences* that flow from committing wrong-doing among conformists;
5. taking the negative reactions of conformists to one's own deviance *into account*.

The labelist assumes that rule-breakers and deviants are typically aware of the general society's definitions of right and wrong; most know that what they are doing would be regarded as deviance by a substantial proportion of their fellow members of society. And they are usually motivated to avoid punishment and condemnation, taking care to keep their behavior from public view. The labelist, in other words, *assumes* dimension (2), and takes dimensions (4) and (5) to be an empirical question, although usually true. Dimensions (1) and (3) are usually not true (although they may be). Believing that they are typically the case would make one a "value consensus" theorist. Such assumptions are most decidedly not part of the perspective of anyone known as a labeling theorist. It is necessary, then, to make a distinction between *knowing* and *caring*, and between knowing and caring about how others *feel* and *what they can do to you*, what sanctions they have at their command. Confusing these dimensions mangles one's interpretation of the interactionist perspective.

If we can determine what deviance is a priori (without turning into a value consensus theorist), does the same hold for identifying the deviant? The word "deviant" is, of course, both an adjective and a noun. Used as an adjective, as in "deviant behavior," it has the same meaning as, but is simply grammatically different from, "deviance." "Deviant" takes on a radically different meaning if it is used as a noun. We all know that *doing* deviance is not the same thing as *being a deviant*. And that one possible avenue to becoming "a" deviant is through the application of a stigmatizing label—Tannenbaum's "dramatization of evil" (1938:19). In this sense to be a deviant is to have one's entire character publicly discredited, tainted, and morally damned. A deviant is one who is widely thought to be routinely immoral by others, who is seen to "belong" to a collectively stigmatized group or category, whose behavior has become so scandalous to others that he or she is thought to be the sort of person who is expected to do immoral, evil, disgraceful, diabolical, irritating things. By this definition, one may be a deviant only if one has, in fact, already been collectively condemned by others.

However, this process of public labeling is atypical. Most of the people who would be considered "deviants" were their behavior to become known to the general public do not conform to this definition. Most people who claim affiliation with a stigmatized group or category never themselves literally become publicly stigmatized as deviants. Consider homosexuals. "Most homosexuals live out their lives . . . without their sexual activities ever having been made a public issue. . . . Members of the gay community define themselves as essentially *being homosexual* and tend to organize their lives around the fact of possessing the *symbolic* (as opposed to publicly applied) stigma." Their special claim to being deviant "results *not* from . . . *acts of labeling,* typically at least, but through a more informal and amorphous process of *being-labeled,* or having an identity infused with the cognizance of its public opprobrium" (Warren and Johnson, 1972:76, 77). In short, one can be *a* deviant through the process of *self-labeling*: accepting an identity that one is aware is saturated with public scorn. One may not accept the validity of these public characterizations. One may not even care about them. But one is rarely ignorant of them. This awareness necessitates adjustments, accommodations, and coping mechanisms. In short, one can be committed to a deviant career—and be a deviant—without having been literally so labeled by the public.

Some students of behavior are distressed by the fact that the concepts "deviance" and "deviant" are not precisely parallel. By the definitions I proposed here, it is possible to know in advance (roughly, at any rate) what acts stand a high likelihood of being judged as deviant by specific relevant audiences. This is not acceptable for defining individuals as "deviants," however. Acts can be regarded as potentially deviant; people cannot. When we refer to behavior, contingencies *constitute* the character of the act. When we refer to people, contingencies *qualify* their character. When we think of or refer to behavior, ancillary features may or may not render it an instance of a larger, deviant, form of behavior. (To a specific audience, of course.) "Killing" by itself is not necessarily regarded as deviance; the extenuating circumstances and the contextual features of the act determine whether it is a deviant form of killing, i.e., murder. The many contingencies and auxiliary aspects, its context, the motives regarded as acceptable, are sufficiently qualifying *as to classify it altogether.* These can, however, be spelled out. To cite another instance, one ethnomethodologists are especially fond of, to throw a baby out of a 10-story window is usually taken to be an instance of "insanity." But if the man who does it is a fireman, the building is in flames, and there is a safety net below, it is seen as an instance of "heroism," not madness. The extenuating features of the behavior do not merely qualify it—they constitute it. So that we can refer to murder or incest or homosexuality as deviance in general (given specific audiences) because the referent has *already* been stripped of all qualifying features.

It is quite otherwise with the attachment of a deviant label to specific individuals. People can be many more things than a drunk, an adulterer, an embezzler. Conventional audiences are often willing to admit that, yes, he did a horrible thing—but he's not a horrible *man.* The power of ancillary and contingent features of the individuals in question to determine their deviant status is sufficiently great as to demand that we reserve judgment concerning whether or not a given perpetrator of a clearly deviant act is, in fact, *a* deviant until we know his or her relevant qualifying features, and what they mean to relevant audiences. The escalation from deviant acts to deviant character type is sufficiently problematic that the only way of dealing with the problem is to reserve judgment until learning whether a given individual *has already* been regarded as deviant by relevant audiences— including himself or herself. Specific people live biographical and historical lives; abstract acts are frozen in time. In addition, the passage of time washes many sins away. The compilation of additional features that are conventional or praiseworthy does not render the deviant acts of the past respectable, but they may render the individual respectable.

CONCLUSION

Labeling theory isn't a theory at all. Perhaps it isn't even as grandiose an edifice as a general perspective. It is merely one way of looking not at deviance in general, but at some specific *features* of deviance. Aspects of labeling theory are relevant for some issues in examining deviant behavior and irrelevant for many others. Some of the basic and fundamental issues raised by labeling theorists—what something is, what category it "belongs" to, what is deviant, who is deviant—are always relevant, even when examining deviance in a fairly conventional fashion. But accepting the importance of these issues does not mean, as Hirschi (1973:169–170) seems to have concluded, that this makes deviance "impossible to study." It does mean that the first step in the study of deviance has to be a consideration of these crucial issues. The exquisitely reciprocal relationship between action and reaction makes a simple study of "pure behavior extremely misleading. Included within the scope of what behavior *is* has to be what it *means*—to the various relevant audiences. Hirschi is incorrect in saying that this makes the study of deviance impossible. But what it does mean is that the issues he takes to be "straightforward empirical questions" quite simply aren't.

Beyond this, a number of critics have pointed out labeling theory's limited scope. The question of etiology, for example (Gibbs, 1966) may very well be beyond the scope of labeling theory; it was never intended to be an explanation of causality. Of course, it would help those studying etiology to specify just what they are trying to find the cause of. But no one would hold that labeling creates a given form of behavior de novo. There may be forms of behavior on which labeling has some etiological impact, but generally, this avenue is unlikely to prove fruitful.

Far from a theory of deviance, the major ideas in labeling theory are at the level of what Herbert Blumer (1969:147–151) calls *sensitizing concepts*. The simple fact of the limitations of the scope of labeling theory is rarely recognized; if it is, it is taken as a devastating defect. Commentators discuss the labeling issue as if different theories are in stiff competition, or locked in mortal combat. "Theoretical" discussions degenerate into polemics; making a point is equated with blasting an opponent's arguments into oblivion. Perhaps if there is anything like a universal rule, I suppose it would be this; the bombardier always attracts more attention than the bricklayer.

REFERENCES

Becker, Howard S. (1963). *Outsides: Studies in the Sociology of Deviance*. New York: Free Press.

Becker, Howard S. (1973). "Labeling theory reconsidered." In *Outsiders,* 2nd edition.

Black, Donald J., and Reiss, Jr., Albert J. (1970). "Police control of juveniles." *American Sociological Review 35* (February): 63–77.

Blumer, Herbert. (1969) *Symbolic Interactionism: Perspective and Method*. Englewood Cliffs, NJ: Prentice Hall.

Chambliss, William J. (1974). "Functional and Conflict Theories of Crime." New York: MSS Modular Publications.

Cohen, Albert K. (1965). "The sociology of the deviant act: anomie theory and beyond." *American Sociological Review 30* (February): 5–14.

Coleman, James S. (1968). "Review of Harold Garfinkel's studies in ethnomethodology." *American Sociological Review 30* (February): 126–130.

Erikson, Kai T. (1962), "Notes on the sociology of deviance." *Social Problems 9* (Spring): 307–314.

Erikson, Kai T. (1966) *Wayward Puritans: A Study in the Sociology of Deviance*. New York: John Wiley.

Ford, Clellan S., and Beach, Frank A. (1951). *Patterns of Sexual Behavior*. New York: Harper and Row.

Garfinkel, Harold. (1967). *Studies in Ethnomethodology*. Englewood Cliffs, NJ: Prentice Hall.

Gibbs, Jack P. (1966). "Conceptions of deviant behavior: the old and the new." *Pacific Sociological Review 9* (Spring): 9–14.

Gibbs, Jack P. (1972). "Issues in defining deviance." In Robert A. Scott and Jack D. Douglas (Eds.), *Theoretical Perspectives on Deviance*. New York: Basic Books.

Goode, Erich. (1972). *Drugs in American Society*. New York: Alfred Knopf.

Goode, Erich, and Troiden, Richard R. (Eds.) (1974). *Sexual Deviance and Sexual Deviants*. New York: William Morrow.

Hirschi, Travis. (1973). "Procedural rules and the study of deviance." *Social Problems 21* (Fall): 159–173.

Kitsuse, John I. (1962). "Societal reaction to deviant behavior: problems of theory and method." *Social Problems 9* (Winter): 247–256.

Lemert, Edwin M. (1972). *Human Deviance, Social Problems, and Social Control*. Englewood Cliffs, NJ: Prentice Hall.

Liazos, Alexander. (1972). "The poverty of the sociology of deviance: nuts, sluts, and preverts." *Social Problems 20* (Summer): 103–120.

Lofland, John. (1969). *Deviance and Identity*. Englewood Cliffs, NJ: Prentice Hall.

Mankoff, Milton. (1971). "Societal reaction and career deviance: a critical analysis." *The Sociological Quarterly 12* (Spring): 204–218.

Matza, David. (1969). *Becoming Deviant*. Englewood Cliffs, NJ: Prentice Hall.

McCaghy, Charles. (1967). "Child molesters: a study of their careers as deviants." In Marshall B. Clinard and Richard Quinney (Eds.), *Criminal Behavior Systems: A Typology*. New York: Holt, Rinehart and Winston.

Merton, Robert K. (1971). "Social problems and sociological theory." In Robert K. Merton and Robert Nisbet (Eds.), *Contemporary Social Problems*. New York: Harcourt Brace Jovanovich.

Nisbet, Robert. (1970). *The Social Bond*. New York: Alfred Knopf.

Pollner, Melvin. (1974). "Sociological and common-sense models of the labeling process." In Roy Turner (Ed.), *Ethnomethodology: Selected Readings*. Baltimore: Penguin Books.

Rains, Prudence, and Kitsuse, John I. (1973). "Comments on the Labeling Approach to Deviance." Unpublished manuscript.

Reiss, Albert J. (1961). "The social integration of queers and peers." *Social Problems 9* (Fall): 102–120.

Rossi, Peter H., et al. (1974). "The seriousness of crimes: normative structure and individual differences." *American Sociological Review 39* (April): 224–237.

Rubington, Earl, and Weinberg, Martin S. (Eds.) (1973). *Deviance: The Interactionist Perspective,* 2nd ed. New York: Macmillan.

Schur, Edwin M. (1971). *Labeling Deviant Behavior*. New York: Harper and Row.

Skipper, James K., Jr., and McCaghy, Charles. (1970). "Stripteasers: the anatomy and career contingencies of a deviant occupation." *Social Problems 17* (Winter): 391–405.

Tannenbaum, Frank. (1938). *Crime and the Community*. New York: Columbia University Press.

Thio, Alex. (1973). "Class bias in the sociology of deviance." *The American Sociologist 8* (February): 1–12.

Walter, Eugene Victor. (1969). *Terror and Resistance*. New York: Oxford University Press.

Warren, Carol A.B., and Johnson, John M. (1972). "A critique of labeling theory from the phenomenological perspective." In Robert A. Scott and Jack D. Douglas (Eds.), *Theoretical Perspectives on Deviance*. New York: Basic Books.

Violent Crime I

Assault and Rape

8

8.1 INTRODUCTION: ASSAULT AND RAPE

According to the National Crime Victimization Survey (NCVS), persons age twelve or older living in the United States experience more than 24 million crimes each year.

- Of these victimizations, approximately 5.7 million or one-fourth of all crimes consist of violent offenses such as rape, robbery, aggravated assault, simple assault, and murder.
- For every 1,000 persons age twelve or older, there occur annually one rape or sexual assault, two assaults with injury, and three robberies.
- Murders are the least frequent violent victimizations—about six victims per 100,000 persons.[1]
- About one-half of the violent crimes committed in the United States are reported to the police.[2]

This and the following chapter examine violent crime. This chapter examines assault and rape; Chapter 9 provides a detailed look at robbery, murder, hate crime, and terrorism. Both chapters also discuss the most prominent theories on violent behavior. Specifically, this chapter

- defines three types of assault, rape, and sexual assault, and presents statistics on rates and trends (section 8.2);
- analyzes assault and abuse in the workplace, in American families, and across the world (section 8.3);
- surveys explanations for and responses to assault, abuse, and rape (section 8.4).

8.2 ASSAULT

The law defines and distinguishes three different types of assault (other than sexual assault). It is important to note that different states define the types of assault differently. The following definitions are based on the UCR:

1. **Aggravated assault** is a serious crime of violence and is defined as an attack or attempted attack with a weapon, regardless of whether an injury occurred, or an attack without a weapon when serious injury resulted.
2. **Simple assault** is also a serious crime of violence and is defined as attack without a weapon resulting in no injury, minor injury (for example, bruises, black eyes, cuts, scratches, or swelling), or undetermined injury requiring less than two days of hospitalization. Simple assault also includes attempted assault without a weapon.
3. **Battery** is an attack by one person on another person that results in striking or touching the victim, unlike both simple assault, where an attacker inflicts little or no physical hurt, and aggravated assault, where the perpetrator uses a weapon or inflicts serious harm on the victim.

The NCVS reports that each year about 5 million Americans are assaulted. How are the three types of assault defined? If this victim was assaulted at knifepoint, which type of assault occurred? What are the chances that this victim was in the group of citizens who reported being assaulted that year?

Aggravated assault is an attack or attempted attack with a weapon, regardless of whether an injury occurred, or an attack without a weapon when serious injury resulted.

Simple assault is an attack without a weapon resulting in no injury, minor injury, or undetermined injury requiring less than two days of hospitalization.

Battery is an attack that results in striking or touching the victim.

Assault Rates and Trends

Assault is a serious crime of violence. Each year, millions of Americans experience assault.

According to the Uniform Crime Reporting Program (UCRP), each year there are more than 900,000 aggravated assaults reported to law enforcement in the United States.[3] According to the NCVS, however, there are 1.2 million annual aggravated assaults. These data indicate that many incidents of aggravated assault go unreported to law enforcement each year. In addition, there are 3.5 million simple assaults annually in the United States.[4]

Why do so many assaults go unreported each year? They go unreported because many people consider an assault, whether aggravated or simple, to be a private matter not to be revealed to authorities or outsiders. The NCVS reports that only 58 percent of aggravated assaults are reported to the police.[5]

PROFILES

Assault

- Overall, aggravated assault and simple assault are more likely to be reported to the police when the victim is female (61 percent for females, 52 percent for males).
- Aggravated assaults against black victims (61 percent) are reported to the police at a significantly higher percentage than aggravated assaults against white victims (54 percent).
- In terms of offender characteristics for assaultive behavior, gender makes little difference. That is, the percentage of aggravated assaults reported to the police differs very little when the offender is male (54 percent) or female (55 percent). For simple assaults, the percentage is the same—37 percent.

- In terms of race of the offender, only somewhat higher percentages of aggravated assaults are reported to the police when committed by black offenders (59 percent) than by white offenders (54 percent).
- Simple assault percentages are the same for both white and black offenders (38 percent).
- In terms of age, the younger the offender, the lower the percentage of assaultive behavior reported to the police.

Source: U.S. Department of Justice, Office of Justice Programs, Bureau of Justice Statistics, *Reporting Crime to the Police, 1992–2000*, Washington, DC: Government Printing Office, March 9, 2003, NCJ-195710, pp. 3, 5.

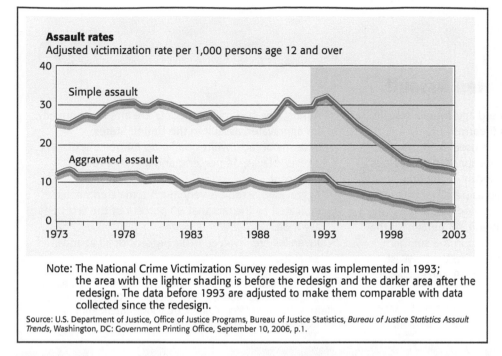

Assault rates
Adjusted victimization rate per 1,000 persons age 12 and over

Note: The National Crime Victimization Survey redesign was implemented in 1993; the area with the lighter shading is before the redesign and the darker area after the redesign. The data before 1993 are adjusted to make them comparable with data collected since the redesign.

Source: U.S. Department of Justice, Office of Justice Programs, Bureau of Justice Statistics, *Bureau of Justice Statistics Assault Trends*, Washington, DC: Government Printing Office, September 10, 2006, p.1.

FIGURE 8.1

As shown in Figure 8.1, between 1994 and today, simple and aggravated assault rates have been declining in the United States. In 1994, there were about twelve aggravated assaults per 1,000 persons twelve years of age and older. Today, there are about five aggravated assaults per 1,000 persons.[6] What factors do you think might account for this decline?

Assaultive Behavior in the Workplace

Assault and violence have become a serious problem in the American workplace.

Workplace violence, or assaultive behavior in the American workplace, has increased over the past decade. One of the most serious problems in the work-place is the escalation of employer–employee conflict and violence. One reason is that many employers have used unpleasant psychological methods to force employees to resign.

- According to the Bureau of National Affairs, about one in four managers abuses employees to the extent that the workers slow productivity, call in sick, or change jobs, costing the economy billion of dollars annually.
- Downsizing in the work world and downturns in the economy have cost hundreds of thousands of people their jobs and have caused a wide-spread malaise among workers.
- These events have engendered a "cycle of vengeful acts by angry and frustrated employees and punitive and abusive acts by management."[7]

Not only do workers steal, commit sabotage, and sell company secrets to their employers' competitors, they also become angry and assaultive. Many employees who have been overlooked for a promotion, restructured, down-sized out, or fired from their jobs have responded with violent acts, even homi-cide. In the United States, homicides account for 17 percent of all occupational deaths. In fact, homicide ranks second only to vehicle accidents as a cause of death on the job.[8]

UCR Data on Aggravated Assault

- Twenty-eight percent of reported aggravated assaults are committed annually with firearms.
- Knives or cutting instruments are used in 18 percent of assaults, and other dangerous weapons, such as clubs or blunt objects, are used 36 percent of the time.
- Hands, fists, and feet, classified as personal weapons, are used in 28 percent of aggravated assaults.
- In terms of geographic distribution, 43 percent of the reported aggravated assaults occur in the southern region of the country. This is followed by the West with 24 percent, the Midwest with 19 percent, and the Northeast with 15 percent.
- Law enforcement agencies have recorded a 56 percent **clearance rate** nationwide for aggravated assault.
- Almost one-half million people are arrested annually for aggravated assault in the United States.
- In terms of race, whites make up 64 percent of arrests; blacks, 34 percent; and all other races, 2 percent.
- Aggravated assault is very much a male crime, as indicated by the fact that 80 percent of the arrestees are men.
- Juveniles are involved in 12 percent of all aggravated assaults.

Source: Federal Bureau of Investigation, Uniform Crime Reports, *Crime in the United States, 2001*, "Section II—Crime Index Offenses Reported," Washington, DC: Government Printing Offices, March 26, 2003, pp. 37–39.

Clearance rate refers to the number of cases solved or closed compared to the number that remain open.

The workplace thus is not a safe place from social or personal tensions. Fortunately, the vast majority of violent workplace incidents are not fatal assaults. Most violence at work consists of harassment, verbal threats, and physical assaults. Nevertheless, one survey reported that 35 percent of respondents stated that someone in their place of work had been harassed, threatened with violence, or assaulted during the previous year.[9]

Harrassment, assault, and other acts of violence are serious problems in the American workplace. Have you ever observed or experienced situations on the job that could lead to violence? What stressors, situations, and conditions do you think contribute most strongly to workplace violence?

In an analysis of violence in the workplace, Detis T. Duhart has reported that during a recent seven-year period,

- an average of 1.7 million violent victimizations were committed against people who were at work or on duty;
- workplace violence accounted for 18 percent of all violent crime;
- the majority of workplace incidents, almost 95 percent (nineteen of every twenty), were aggravated or simple assaults.[10]

Workplace violence appears to result from individual characteristics of offenders and victims, precipitating events, and characteristics of the organization or corporation:

- *Individual characteristics* include feelings of helplessness and isolation, life stressors such as illness and divorce, paranoid personality or thinking patterns, and substance abuse.
- *Precipitating events* include incidents of harassment by fellow workers or supervisors, job change, or job termination.
- *System characteristics* refer to the way the organization characteristically responds to such precipitating events as change, stress, and crisis. According to Mark Braverman and Susan R. Braverman, at-risk organizations ignore early warning signals, are purely reactive in crisis situations, and tend to deny or ignore the work-site and human resource issues that underlie conflict and violence.[11]

After reading this section, you should be able to

1. define aggravated assault, simple assault, and battery;
2. summarize the nature and extent of assault in the United States by type of victim;
3. explain the rise of workplace violence in the United States.

Whether conflict between family members is viewed as a normal, fundamental, and perhaps constructive part of social organization or as a deviant, abnormal situation, social scientists consider conflict and violence to be part of the pattern of American family life. What factors will determine whether a domestic conflict will erupt into violence? What do we know about the effects of spouse assault on children?

8.3 ASSAULT AND ABUSE IN THE AMERICAN FAMILY

Domestic violence is of even greater concern than workplace violence. In American society, many people view the family as characterized by love and affection. However, it is also characterized by assaultive and violent behavior.

Within the structure and processes of all American families, there are stresses, tensions, and various degrees of conflict. These tensions may develop from sources outside family or marital relationships, or from the family or marital relationships themselves. In many cases, family members and couples, after fighting, resolve their respective differences. At times, positive results may develop from the resolution of conflict between family members. Many families and marriages, however, are continuously characterized by unresolved conflicts, and stresses remain as a more or less permanent characteristic of the family relationship(s). These stresses are often manifested in violence.

Unfortunately, in many American families, violence is an everyday occurrence and a fundamental part of family life. This fact may be difficult for many Americans to believe, in that many of us still maintain an idealized image of the family. Before analyzing family violence, it is necessary to first define and examine the relationship between violence and conflict. *Conflict* is a product of social interaction and an effort to resolve a decision-making impasse. *Violence* is any behavior that threatens or causes physical damage to a person or object, and violence can be the product of either an individual characteristic or a social interaction.[12]

Most people view conflict as detrimental to groups, and many family members therefore try to protect the family's cohesiveness from tension and conflict. Unfortunately, much of the time these feelings of tension are simply covered up, not eliminated. This in turn may lead to uncontrollable stress, tension, and conflict.

- Many people stifle emotions that result from conflict, but when these unpleasant emotions finally surface they may cause violence and irreparable damage.[13]
- Violent behavior can, but need not, develop from conflict.
- Violence may or may not characterize individuals who are otherwise involved in extensive conflict-ridden situations.[14]

Spouse Assault

In the United States, one out of six couples experience spouse assault each year.

Spouse assault is assault against one's own spouse—husband or wife. It is rooted in ancient history and sanctioned in many traditional societies. Suzanne Steinmetz notes that, "in ancient societies, laws decreed that a woman who was verbally abusive to her husband was to have her name engraved on a brick that would then be used to knock out her teeth. Euripides, the Greek playwright, argued that women should be silent, should not argue with men, and should not speak first. Roman law even justified a husband's killing of his wife for reasons such as adultery, drinking wine, or other 'inappropriate' behavior."[15]

No one knows the actual extent of violence and assault between husbands and wives in the United States. Estimates of the extent of assaultive behavior between husbands and wives and of wife beating vary. Some researchers believe that estimates of violent and assaultive behavior between spouses is low, because many incidents go unreported. This is because many victims consider assault among family members to be a private matter.

- Even though police departments in the United States classify almost 70 percent of domestic assaults as simple assaults, data reflect that at least half of the assaults inflict injuries equal to or more serious than those inflicted on victims of aggravated assault, robbery, or rape.

> **Spouse assault** is assault against one's own spouse—husband or wife.

FOR YOUR INFORMATION

Women and Men as Victims

- Women are usually on the receiving end of the worst batterings.
- When there is a fight between a husband and wife, or a boyfriend and girlfriend, the wife or girlfriend, on the average, is the loser.
- However, wives or girlfriends are not the only victims of violence. Husband abuse is considered by some criminologists to be one of the most unreported crimes in the nation. It has been estimated that each year at least 250,000 husbands in the United States are severely beaten by their wives.
- Some criminologists see men and women as equal victims of family violence, since the homicides in husband–wife conflicts are fairly equal between the sexes. Other researchers uniformly report that about as many women hit men as men hit women.
- According to some researchers, those who report equal amounts of husband and wife abuse in society overlook two important facts: "*First,* the greater average size and strength of men and their greater aggressiveness means that a man's punch probably produces more pain, injury, and harm than a punch by a woman. *Second,* nearly three-fourths of the violence committed by women is done in self-defense."

Sources: L. Glick and D. Hebding, *Introduction to Social Problems,* Reading, MA: Addison-Wesley, 1980, p. 284; R.J. Gelles and M.A. Straus, *Intimate Violence,* New York: Simon and Schuster, 1988, pp. 77–97; R.J. Gelles and M.A. Straus, "Profiling Violent Families," in *Diversity and Change in Families: Patterns, Prospects, and Policies,* M.R. Rank and E.L. Kain, Eds., Englewood Cliffs, NJ: Prentice Hall, 1995, pp. 370–387; M.A. Straus, "Physical Assaults by Wives: A Major Social Problem," in *Current Controversies on Family Violence,* R.J. Gelles and D.R. Loseke, Eds., Newbury Park, CA: Sage, 1993.

DID YOU KNOW

The assaulting of women by their boyfriends or husbands is not only an American problem. See Reading 8.2 at the end of this chapter, which discusses the international problem of violent crimes against women.

- In a sampling of more than 6,000 U.S. households, researchers reported that one out of six couples experienced assault during the previous year.[16]
- A study in Chicago estimated that more police calls were made for family conflicts than for all other police incidents combined.[17]
- Another Chicago study reported that one in four women attending public health clinics in Chicago had been abused in the previous year. Almost half had experienced domestic abuse at some point in their lives. Although 87 percent of these women lived below the poverty level, this does not mean that only poor women suffer from abuse.[18]
- Husbands who beat their wives and wives who beat their husbands come from all social classes, ethnic and racial groups, and ages.

Intimate Partner Violence

According to both the UCR and the NCVS, the number of violent crimes committed by intimate partners has declined in the United States over the last decade.

Intimate partner violence refers to violent victimizations committed by current or former spouses or sexual partners.

DID YOU KNOW
Reliable and valid statistics on violence and abuse between same-sex couples and intimate partners are not available, mainly because crimes among members of these groups tend to be grossly underreported.

The Bureau of Justice Statistics examines nonfatal and fatal violent victimizations in **intimate partner violence**—violence committed by current or former spouses or heterosexual sexual partners of the victims. The figures are low—so low that researchers conclude that much assaultive behavior goes unreported by victims of assault.[19]

Estimates from the NCVS include the following:

- There were 691,710 nonfatal violent victimizations committed by current or former spouses, boyfriends, girlfriends, or sexual partners of the victims during 2001.
- Intimate partner violence primarily involves female victims. About 588,490, or 85 percent, of victimizations by intimate partners in 2001 were against women.
- The rate of intimate violence against females declined significantly between 1993 and 2001, dropping by nearly half (49 percent), while the rate of intimate violence against males fell 42 percent.
- In fatal intimate partner violence, the number of men murdered by intimates dropped 68 percent between 1976 and 2000, the year of the most recently available data. Between 1976 and 2000 the number of women murdered by intimates fell 22 percent from 1,600 to 1,247.[20]

Tables 8.1 and 8.2 show some of these trends.

Recent data from the Bureau of Justice Statistics indicates:

- Female victims are more likely to be victimized by intimates than male victims. In 2005, of those offenders victimizing females, 18 percent were described as intimates and 34 percent as strangers. By contrast, of those offenders victimizing males, 3 percent were described as intimates and 54 percent as strangers.
- The rate of nonfatal intimate violence against females declined by nearly one-half between 1993 and 2001.
- Between 1976 and 2002, about 11 percent of murder victims were determined to have been killed by an intimate.
- The sharpest decrease in number of intimate murders has been for black male victims. An 81 percent decrease in the number of black men murdered by intimates occurred between 1976 and 2002.

Source: U.S. Department of Justice, Office of Justice Programs, Bureau of Justice Statistics, *Crime characteristics: Intimate violence,* Last revised: September 10, 2006.

TABLE 8.1 INTIMATE PARTNER VIOLENCE—BY CURRENT OR FORMER SPOUSES, BOYFRIENDS, OR GIRLFRIENDS—MADE UP 20 PERCENT OF ALL NONFATAL VIOLENCE AGAINST FEMALES AGE TWELVE OR OLDER IN 2001

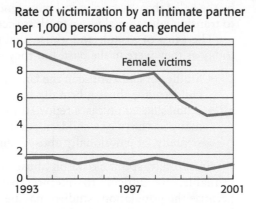

Rate of victimization by an intimate partner per 1,000 persons of each gender

- The number of violent crimes by intimate partners against females declined from 1993 to 2001. Down from 1.1 million nonfatal violent crimes by an intimate in 1993, women experienced about 588,490 such crimes in 2001.

- In 1993 men were victims of about 162,870 violent crimes by an intimate partner. By 2001 that total had fallen to an estimated 103,220 victimizations.

- Intimate partner violence made up 20 percent of all nonfatal violent crime experienced by women in 2001. Intimate partners committed 3 percent of the nonfatal violence against men.

- For intimate partner violence, as for violent crime in general, simple assault was the most common type of crime.

- 1,247 women and 440 men were killed by an intimate partner in 2000. In recent years an intimate killed about 33 percent of female murder victims and 4 percent of male murder victims.

Source: C.M. Rennison, *Intimate Partner Violence, 1993–2001*, crime data brief of the U.S. Department of Justice, Office of Justice Programs, Bureau of Justice Statistics, Washington, DC: Government Printing Office, February 2003, NCJ-197838, p. 1.

TABLE 8.2 RATES OF INTIMATE PARTNER VIOLENCE, BY THE GENDER OF VICTIMS, 1993–2001

Number of nonfatal intimate victimizations per 1,000 persons

Victim characteristics	1993–2001									Percent change (*indicates a significant difference)
	1993	1994	1995	1996	1997	1998	1999	2000	2001	
Total	5.8	5.5	4.9	4.7	4.3	4.8	3.5	2.8	3.0	-48.4*
Male	1.6	1.7	1.1	1.4	1.0	1.5	1.1	0.8	0.9	-41.8*
Female	9.8	9.1	8.5	7.8	7.5	7.8	5.8	4.7	5.0	-49.3*

Note: These rates are based on the data-year only and do not include fatal violence. Nonfatal violence includes rape, sexual assault, robbery, aggravated assault, and simple assault. These rates differ from rates published in *Intimate Partner Violence* (May 2000, NCJ-178247), which included fatal violence and some collection-year data. Percent changes are based on unrounded rates.

Source: C.M. Rennison, *Intimate Partner Violence*, 1993–2001, crime data brief of the U.S. Department of Justice, Office of Justice Programs, Bureau of Justice Statistics, Washington, DC: Government Printing Office, February 2003, NCJ-197838, p. 2.

The Assault and Abuse of Children

As many as 3 million or more children are assaulted each year in the United States.

Because families tend to be viewed as centers of love and gentleness, there is a tendency not to acknowledge the levels of assaultive behavior against children. In previous periods of Western history, children appear to have experienced more assaultive behavior than they do today. Historical analysis of child abuse reveals, for example, that for many centuries the maltreatment of children was justified by the belief that severe physical punishment was needed "to maintain discipline, to transmit educational ideas, to please certain gods, or to expel evil spirits."[21]

The rates of assault and abuse against children are probably not as high today as they were in the past, but they are nonetheless high:

- Studies of child abuse in the United States report that many thousands of children are abused, brutally beaten, or killed by their parents each year.
- Studies based on cases reported to protective agencies have noted that as many as thirty-one children per 1,000 are either neglected or physically, sexually, or emotionally abused annually in the United States.[22]

Even today, specific data on abused children are difficult to obtain and, if available, are difficult to interpret because of variations in definitions or because the populations studied may be unrepresentative of the general population. An example of this difficulty is found in David Gil's estimate that three million cases of child abuse occur every year. The problem with this type of estimate is that it depends on subjective definitions of assault or abuse. For example, "An ordinary spanking or slap by a parent would not be counted as abuse. But if the parties involved were husband and wife, then a spanking or slapping would be considered abuse by most Americans. That has not always been the public attitude. Earlier in American history, it was considered quite appropriate for a husband to physically punish an erring wife. At some future time, we may also come to see what is now regarded as ordinary and permissible spanking of children as abuse. But whether we regard such acts as abuse or not, there is no question that they are violent acts."[23]

Moreover, as with spouse abuse, much child abuse goes unreported, and data on child abuse and assault are often difficult to interpret because of regional and cultural differences in defining abuse.[24] Estimates of the number of cases of varying degrees of child abuse range from one million to three million annually in the United States.[25]

The definition of *child abuse* encompasses a wide variety of behaviors, including

- physical abuse and neglect;
- sexual abuse;
- emotional abuse;
- abandonment or inadequate supervision;
- exploitation.

Very young children are the most likely to be beaten and hurt. According to Richard J. Gelles and Murray A. Straus, however, the myth that "only innocents are victims of abuse hides the teenage victim."[26] Teenagers are just as likely to be assaulted as children under the age of three years. Why? Researchers explain that the youngest children are likely victims of abuse because they are demanding, produce considerable stress, and cannot be reasoned with verbally. Parents of teenagers give the same explanation for why they think teenagers as a group are at equally high risk.[27]

Researchers have found that parents who are abusive to their children demand a much higher performance level from them than do parents who are not abusive. The parents' demands are usually well beyond the children's capacity to understand, much less achieve. In the typical pattern, the parents become upset and angry because the child will not eat, will not stop crying, or will urinate after being told not to do so. The parents then feel righteous about punishing the child and avoid dealing with the abuse and injury they have

Some Facts about Child Abuse

- Mothers tend to be more abusive than fathers to their children. This has been attributed to the fact that the major burden of child-care responsibility falls on women.
- Often, women who assault their children have a history of abuse or are currently in an abusive relationship themselves.
- Fathers who assault their wives are more likely to assault their children.
- A number of factors place younger victims of child assault at risk. According to Richard J. Gelles and Murray A. Straus, "low birth weight babies, premature children, handicapped, retarded, and developmentally disabled children run a high lifelong risk of violence and abuse. In fact, the risk is great for any child who is considered different."[1] The most dangerous period for an abused child is from about three months to three years. A child during this period is "most defenseless and . . . least capable of meaningful social interaction."[2]

Notes:

1. R.J. Gelles and M.A. Straus, *Intimate Violence*, New York: Simon and Schuster, 1988, pp. 77–97; see also R.J. Gelles and M.A. Straus, "Profiling Violent Families," in *Diversity and Change in Families: Patterns, Prospects, and Policies*, M.R. Rank and E.L. Kain, Eds., Englewood Cliffs, NJ: Prentice Hall, 1995, pp. 370–387.

2. R.J. Gelles, "Child Abuse as Psychopathology: A Sociological Critique and Reformulation," in *Violence in the Family*, S. Steinmetz and M.A. Straus, Eds., New York: Dodd, Mead, 1974, pp. 196–197.

caused. The parents then justify their own abusive behavior because they believe that their child has been "bad."[28]

Poverty increases the risk for child assault. David Gil's classic analysis and studies from the past decade indicate that families in which child abuse occurs are generally undereducated, disproportionately poor, and mainly headed by women. The majority receive public assistance. National surveys, case studies, and official and clinical data report that child abuse cases are disproportionately drawn from low-income families.[29] By no means, however, is child assault simply a problem of the lower socioeconomic levels. Middle- as well as upper-socioeconomic-level parents also use violence as a means of controlling their children.[30]

Sibling, Elder, and Parent Assault

Brothers and sisters, grandparents, and parents are also victims of family assault.

Family violence does not occur just between spouses, intimate partners, or parents and children. Because of the intimacy of a brother–sister relationship and because there is a potential for rivalry or competition for care and affection from caregivers, there is a high potential for violence and assault between two or more siblings. Research also indicates that children's aggressive tendencies are probably increased by parents who use physical force to control aggression in their children.[31]

Grandparents and the elderly are also serious victims of family assault More than 2 million elderly are physically or emotionally abused or neglected annually in the United States.

- Many aged husbands and wives are violent with one another.
- Husbands, who are generally older than their wives, are often the recipients of verbal and physical abuse and neglect as they become dependent on their wives for care. This often represents a "turnaround time" for wives who were the recipients of their husband's assaultive behavior in earlier years.
- Many aged are abused by their children and grandchildren.
- Many aged are unable to or do not report their abusive treatment by family members for fear of reprisal such as being placed in a long-term care facility for the aged.
- Some studies have reported that many aged parents who are abused were themselves abusers of their children.[32]

It is estimated that as many as 2.5 million or more parents are physically assaulted by their adolescent children each year. Many are kicked, bitten, physically beaten, or assaulted with weapons. Some are even murdered. Most assaultive children are in their teens or early twenties. Mothers rather than fathers are the primary targets of abuse by children, because they may not be as strong as the fathers and they are a more socially "acceptable" target of abuse.[33]

Family pets and other animals are also targets of abuse. People have left their animals—just as they have left their children—in hot, closed-up cars in summer. *Animal assault* is assault committed against animals. People have beaten, burned, tortured, and mutilated their dogs, cats, horses, or other

FOR YOUR INFORMATION

Family Violence and Animal Cruelty

Backgrounds of violent offenders often reveal the presence of animal cruelty. . . . Animal cruelty, child maltreatment, and domestic violence have been linked as overlapping domains. Most offenders are male and victimize the vulnerable—women, children, and animals. Holding pets hostage is used to control women in domestic violence cases. The link between animal and human violence was ignored by law enforcement, the judicial system, and other agencies until recently. Along a continuum of family violence, strong evidence suggests that animals are the first stage along the path to human violence. Nevertheless, the criminal justice system still largely views animal abuse as a minor offense. . . . Some states have strong misdemeanor laws, whereas others have weak felony laws. Animal cruelty laws may also include provisions for other forms of punishment designed to rehabilitate the offender. . . . No national statistics exist for animal cruelty, so its incidence and prevalence are unknown. (Demographic analysis based on the spatial distribution of reported animal cruelty cases in one county in Georgia showed that the highest incidences occurred in low-income neighborhoods in which people had poor housing conditions and low educational levels.)

Source: L. S. Turnbull, "Animal Cruelty: A Spatial Investigation," in *Atlas of Crime: Mapping the Criminal Landscape*, L. S. Turnbull, E. H. Hendrix, and B. D. Dent, Eds., Phoenix: Oryx, 2000, pp. 113–121.

animals. A neo-Nazi group in Pennsylvania buried a dog up to its neck and exploded firecrackers in its mouth. In the United States, there appears to be a connection between family violence and animal cruelty and violence. It is not uncommon to find the assault and abuse of animals in the histories of people who have committed murder.

After reading this section, you should be able to

1. distinguish between conflict and violence;
2. discuss the incidence and prevalence of violence in American families;
3. analyze patterns of abuse between spouses and intimate partners;
4. identify risk factors in parental abuse of children and profile the typical abuser;
5. describe the dynamics of domestic violence between siblings, toward elders and parents, and toward animals.

8.4 EXPLAINING AND RESPONDING TO ASSAULTIVE AND ABUSIVE BEHAVIOR

Three main types of explanations exist for violent and assaultive behavior in American society:

1. *Psychopathological theories* explain assaultive and abusive behavior in terms of abnormal psychological characteristics among people.
2. *Sociocultural theories* focus on the approval of violence by a society's value system and norms.
3. *Economic or exchange theories* stress the idea that violence is a means that can be used to attain wanted ends. That is, when other resources, such as love, respect, money, or shared goals, are not available or insufficient to achieve desired ends, assaultive behavior—abuse and violence—tends to be employed.[34]

Psychopathological Explanations for Violence

Mental illness may contribute to family violence.

Psychopathological explanations for assaultive and violent behavior involve the idea of mental illness. There is, for example, an assumption that distinctive, psychopathic personality traits are present in an abuser. Psychopathy in child abusers is traced to their childhoods, when they themselves were abused. Ironically, the cause of psychopathy in abusive parents is the fact that they were reared in the same way they re-create with their own children. But are abusers simply insane?

One problem with the psychopathological explanation is the inability to specifically determine what personality traits and mental traits characterize the pathology. Attributing abusive behavior to mental illness also tends to ignore other variables, for example, the cultural, social, economic, and demographic factors that are involved.[35]

Sociocultural Explanations for Violence

American child-rearing practices and childhood socialization contribute to explanations for assault.

When attempting to explain violence in the family, it is important to consider its cultural foundations. Corporal punishment remains a strongly defended right that is rooted in traditional American culture. The family as a social unit rests to a certain degree on the *threat* of force and violence, as well as on their use. American culture, in subtle and not-so-subtle ways, encourages the use of at least a limited degree of physical force in rearing children to discourage anti-social forms of behavior. Furthermore, the norms of society dictate that parents are primarily responsible for the training and socialization of their children. Therefore, parents have a degree of authority over their children. Part of this authority implies the right to punish them if they fail to conform to family norms as well as societal norms.

In the United States, over 90 percent of parents of children ages three and four use physical punishment to correct their children's behavior.[36] Murray A. Straus, who has written extensively on assaultive behavior in families, reports that the links between the corporal punishment of children and child abuse and domestic violence have not been adequately explored, because spanking is such an important, ingrained part of American life: "The universal and chronic use of corporal punishment and its potentially harmful effects on children is the best-kept secret of American child psychology. . . . It is almost as though there were a conspiracy of silence among those who do research on children or write about child rearing."[37]

- National Family Violence surveys and the National Longitudinal Study of Youth report that two-thirds of mothers with children under age six have stated they hit their children an average of three times a week.
- Forty percent of parents report that they still hit their fourteen-year-olds.
- Parents who spank tend to do so often.[38]

Moral authorities and parents warn young children against violence. Adult behavior, however, often runs counter to that advice. Virtually all people in our culture are trained for violence. Children learn that force is an effective means of stopping unpleasant behavior in others and that even its threat affects how others calculate profit and loss. Children "can be persuaded to obey when faced with such consequences. The child experiences this directly, and watches it in others—the fright of his mother when his father is furious, arguments and threats among neighbors, the battles with his own siblings, and so on."[39]

The assaultive behavior of abusive parents and spouses can also be explained by prior socialization, during which they themselves were deprived of tenderness and love from their parents.[40] When children are socialized in a family that uses violence to solve problems, they are learning parental, marital, and other social roles centered on violence. When these children are themselves adults, they reenact the behavior learned in childhood. Adults who are abusive or assaultive to others (for example, men who abuse their girlfriends, husbands who abuse their wives, and parents who abuse their children) have usually had role models who used violence as a method of solving problems. Social learning theorists stress the idea that children learn assaultive, violent behavior as they observe role models, imitate these models, and act out the roles. Furthermore, aggression and violence are learned not only through social interaction with family members but also through the violent, aggressive, and assaultive behavior modeled on TV and in movies.

This perspective underscores the idea that many abusers were themselves abused as children. Some researchers, however, have questioned the intergenerational transmission of abusive behavior. These researchers report that even though many abusers were abused as children, many victims of childhood abuse do not become violent parents.[41]

Childhood Assault and Adult Criminal Behavior

Being abused as a child increases the likelihood of arrest as a juvenile or as an adult.

According to Gelles and Straus, an interesting aspect of the relationship between adult and childhood violence is that *observing* one's parents hit and abuse one another is a "more powerful contributor to the probability of becoming a violent adult than being a victim of violence. The learning experience of seeing your mother and father strike one another is more significant than being hit yourself."[42] Research by Egeland reports that experiencing and, more importantly, observing violence as a child teaches three lessons:

1. Those who love you are also those who hit you, and those whom you love are people you can hit.
2. Seeing and experiencing violence in your home establishes the moral rightness of hitting those you love.
3. If other means of getting your way, dealing with stress, or expressing yourself do not work, violence is permissible.[43]

Do childhood assault and abuse lead to adult criminal behavior? Will today's abused children become the violent offenders of the future? Cathy Spatz Widom reported in her study *The Cycle of Violence* that childhood assault and abuse increase the odds of future crime (delinquency and adult criminality) by 40 percent. Widom followed almost 1,600 cases from childhood through young adulthood and compared arrest records of abused and nonabused children. She reported that, although "most members of both groups had no juvenile or adult criminal records, being abused or neglected as a child increased the likelihood of arrest as a juvenile by 53 percent, as an adult by 38 percent, and for a violent crime by 38 percent."[44]

Economic Explanations for Violence

Economic factors produce stresses and strains that play an important role in explaining assaultive and violent behavior.

There appear to be a wide variety of stress-producing situations that generally occur just prior to assaultive acts against children and wives. Economic stressors, for example, are triggering factors. Data on unemployment strongly suggest that economic conditions produce or increase frustration and stress levels, which are then vented on spouses and children. In an analysis of battered children (those who are bruised, drastically injured, or physically and psychologically malnourished), H. C. Raffali noted the presence of financial and marital difficulties among 90 percent of the most abusive families.[45]

Richard J. Gelles and Murray A. Straus have profiled violent families and have explained violence by examining their economic adversity, stressful life circumstances, violent parents, and isolation from the community.[46] Money worries and economic adversity pervade the typical violent family. For example, a thirty-four-year-old wife of an assembly-line worker and her husband have both beaten, kicked, and punched their children. The wife explained their economic stress:

"He worries about what kind of job he's going to get, or if he's going to get a job at all. He always worries about supporting the family. I think I worry about it more than he does. . . . It gets him angry and frustrated. He gets angry a lot. I think he gets angry at himself for not providing what he feels we need. He has to take it out on someone, and the kids and me are the most available ones."[47]

Stressful life circumstances, according to Gelles and Straus, are "at the hallmark" of the violent family, and include problems at work, the death of a family member, and problems with children. They report that the greater the number of stressful events experienced, the greater the rate of abusive violence toward children in the home.[48]

Like other researchers, Gelles and Straus focus as well on violent parents. They report that violent parents are likely to have been exposed to or experienced violence as children. They stress that although being exposed to violence as a child does not predetermine that a person will be violent (some abusive parents grew up in nonviolent households), there is the heightened risk that a violent past will lead to a violent future. In addition, violent parents are almost always cut off from the community in which they live. Gelles and Straus's research reports that the most violent parents have lived in the community for less than two years, tend to belong to few, if any, community organizations, and have little contact with relatives and friends.[49]

Social scientists such as Gelles have developed what has been termed the "exchange/control theory" of family violence. The first part of this perspective, *exchange theory*, stresses the point that in our social interactions with others, we continually weigh the perceived rewards against the perceived costs. Exchange theory says that the social expectation is that people "will use violence toward family members only when the costs of being violent do not outweigh the rewards."[50] Getting one's own way, getting revenge, or relieving stress may be the rewards of violent behavior. Getting beaten by a family member, losing social status in the community, or being arrested may be the costs of violent behavior. The second part of this perspective, *social control theory*, points out that social controls such as arrest, imprisonment, loss of status, and loss of income increase the costs of violent behavior.[51]

Bryan Strong and Christine DeVault have identified the following three characteristics of families as factors that may reduce social control and increase the likelihood of family violence:

1. *Inequality.* Men are stronger than women and often have more economic power and social status. Adults are more powerful than children.
2. *Family privacy.* People are reluctant to look outside the family for help, and outsiders (the police or neighbors, for example) may hesitate to intervene in private matters. The likelihood of family violence goes down as the number of nearby friends and relatives increases.
3. *"Real man" image.* In some American subcultures, aggressive male behavior brings approval. The violent man in these groups may actually gain status among his peers for asserting his "authority."[52]

Other social scientists believe that the root of violence and abuse in families is in the structure of society itself and that such factors as child-rearing practices, parental socialization experiences, and values play only a supplementary role in abuse and merely "individualize what is essentially a social problem."[53] According to a structural theory of "angry aggression," the causes are factors such as an urban environment, low social position, racial and ethnic discrimination, and social isolation. Thomas Bernard, for example, reports that, in such an environment, each person's rules for anger tend to expand, so that people become angry in a greater range of situations and, when angry, respond with more violence.[54]

The relationship between substance abuse (alcohol and drugs) and assaultive behavior in families has also been studied. Researchers have reported that men with severe substance-abuse problems are much more likely to be violent and to inflict greater injury on their spouses or girlfriends when intoxicated than when sober.[55]

No one theory or approach can adequately explain assaultive or violent behavior in the family or in the community. Each theory discussed here and in earlier chapters emphasizes different factors. Assaultive behavior is a complex phenomenon consisting of diverse social, cultural, individual, and economic elements; no single explanation can account for all such behavior.

Responses to the Problem of Family Violence

Responses to family violence include prevention, intervention, and criminalization through the passage and enforcement of civil and criminal laws.

Historically in America, people have been opposed to punishing parents who assault their children and have usually opposed the removal of abused children from the home unless no other alternative is possible. Similar attitudes have existed in regard to abused wives.[56] These attitudes, and the fact that child-care facilities and shelters for abused wives are inadequate, have left many spouses and children in need of protective services. This situation has led to alternatives other than removal as a solution to assault. Responses have taken the form of prevention and intervention through individual, family, and group counseling programs and therapies such as behavior modification. Many of these responses reflect an attempt to treat rather than punish assaultive family members, in the hope of keeping families intact. Recently, there have been broader efforts to deal with the social, environmental, and legal dimensions of the family assault problem.

Two basic prevention strategies deal with family violence:

1. Supporting and strengthening families
2. Facilitating social change and reducing social stress[57]

During the past decade, many communities have responded to assaultive behavior at home and in the community through a third strategy—by arresting and vigorously prosecuting the abusive offender. However, in the United States, the responsibility for developing adequate supportive programs for assaulted families continues to fall through the bureaucratic cracks between

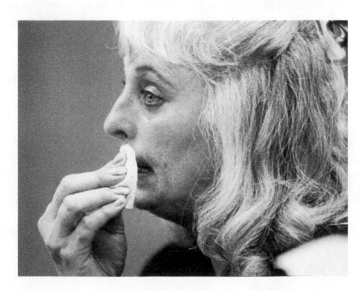

The criminalization of domestic violence is an effort to deal with the incidence of domestic violence and assault through the enactment and enforcement of criminal and civil laws. Making family abuse a punishable offense rather than a matter for private judgment is thought to act as a deterrent. What are some other approaches to dealing with the problem of domestic violence?

Explaining and Responding to Assaultive and Abusive Behavior **217**

READING ABSTRACT

The Criminalization of Domestic Violence

BY FRAN S. DAVIS

This reading examines various domestic violence interventions; theoretical foundations and effectiveness of police interventions; protective orders, prosecution, and victim advocacy; court responses and batterers' intervention programs as a condition of probation; and coordinated community responses. Davis also presents a summary of implications for social work and criminal justice practice.

See reading on page 227.

social welfare agencies and criminal prosecution departments. Complicating the situation is the fact that the problem occurs in the home, which in America is a private sanctuary protected by custom and law.

Some child advocates, such as the organization Justice for Children, believe the solution to the problem of child assault is to remove child protection from social service agencies and place it in the criminal justice system. Social service agencies receive federal funding that places emphasis on keeping the family system together rather than protecting children from violence. These child advocates, however, believe that child abuse is assaultive, criminal behavior against children. When an adult gets beaten, the police should be called, not adult protective services.

According to Suzanne Steinmetz, the devastating, long-term effects of being raised in a family in which violent behavior occurs can be seen in the media's coverage of violent crimes and in prisoners' abusive histories. Fortunately, she states, this is an area where "intervention in terms of legislation, education, crisis lines and shelters, and programs to improve individuals' parenting and partnering skills have had an impact. A comparison of the levels of family violence in two national surveys found a nearly 50 percent decrease in child abuse and over a 25 percent decrease in wife abuse in a decade. The authors of these studies suggest that these reductions were directly the result of policy and legislative changes as well as prevention and intervention programs."[58]

Another response is the *criminalization of domestic violence*—the process of dealing with assaultive behavior in families through the passage and enforcement of civil and criminal laws.

After reading this section, you should be able to

1. give examples of psychopathological and sociocultural explanations for assaultive and abusive behavior;
2. explain the relationship between childhood assault and adult criminal behavior;
3. analyze economic factors, exchange theory, and social control theory in explaining family violence;
4. give examples of prevention, intervention, and criminalization as three responses to the problem of family violence;
5. use information in Reading 8.1 to argue for or against greater criminalization of domestic violence.

Rape is another serious crime of violence and is defined in many ways:

- *Black's Law Dictionary* defines **rape** as "unlawful sexual intercourse with a female without her consent" and "the unlawful carnal knowledge of a woman by a man forcibly and against her will."[59]
- The UCR defines **forcible rape** similarly but also includes assaults or attempts to commit rape by force or threat of force.[60]
- Basically, rape occurs when one person imposes a sexual act on another person by force or the threat of force.

Americans regard rape as a very serious crime.[61] What makes the crime so reprehensible is its violent nature. Susan Brownmiller, in her classic analysis, views rape as an act of humiliation, aggression, trespassing, and possession that is committed as an expression against women in general or a woman in particular.[62]

- Rape is an act of aggression and should not be viewed simply as a sexual offense.
- It is violent and coercive, and it doesn't discriminate on the basis of age or gender. Infants, children, the aged, women, and men are raped.
- Rape can occur between two strangers or between friends or family members. It may be a marital rape or a date rape.
- Some rapists attack without warning, whereas others carefully and slowly, through friendliness and encouragement, entice their victims into harmful situations.
- There are one-time, occasional, and serial rapists.
- Rape varies by region, race, and age.

Because of the women's movement and a variety of U.S. groups' efforts to inform the public about rape, the average person is much more aware of its seriousness and the importance of adequately helping victims than in past years. Many believe that we continually need to rework the legal definition of this crime to better facilitate the prosecution of rapists.

Rape is unlawful sexual intercourse with a female without her consent and the unlawful carnal knowledge of a woman by a man forcibly and against her will. The UCR defines **forcible rape** similarly but also includes assaults or attempts to commit rape by force or threat of force.

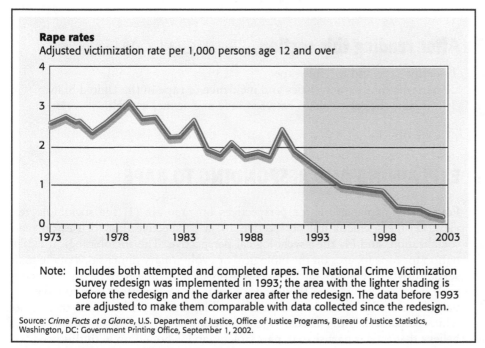

Rape rates
Adjusted victimization rate per 1,000 persons age 12 and over

Note: Includes both attempted and completed rapes. The National Crime Victimization Survey redesign was implemented in 1993; the area with the lighter shading is before the redesign and the darker area after the redesign. The data before 1993 are adjusted to make them comparable with data collected since the redesign.

Source: *Crime Facts at a Glance*, U.S. Department of Justice, Office of Justice Programs, Bureau of Justice Statistics, Washington, DC: Government Printing Office, September 1, 2002.

FIGURE 8.2

According to the UCR, an estimated 91,000 forcible rapes are reported annually to law enforcement agencies across the United States. This figure does not include the many tens of thousands of rapes that go unreported.[63] According to the NCVS, there are more than 143,000 rape victims in the United States each year.[64] Even this figure is considered low by some criminologists who believe that the actual number of rapes may be several times higher.[65] Rape is one of the most unreported crimes in the United States. Many victims do not report being raped because they do not think others will believe them or they do not want to be embarrassed or stigmatized by others.

The forcible rape rate in the United States is about 65 per 100,000.[66] As Figure 8.2 shows, NCVS data indicate a decrease in the volume of reported rapes since 1991.

According to the Bureau of Justice Statistics, *sexual assault* includes a wide range of victimizations that are separate from rape or attempted rape. These crimes include attacks or attempted attacks generally involving unwanted sexual contact between victim and offender. Sexual assaults may or may not involve force and include such things as grabbing or fondling. Sexual assaults also include verbal threats.[67]

Recent statistics from the 2005 Uniform Crime Report indicate:

- There were an estimated 93,934 forcible rapes reported to law enforcement in 2005, a 1.2 percent decrease when compared to the 2004 estimate.
- When compared to 2001 data, the number of forcible rapes increased an estimated 3.4 percent, but when compared to the 1996 data, the number of forcible rape offenses declined 2.4 percent during the ten-year period.
- The rate of forcible rapes in 2005 was estimated at 62.5 offenses per 100,000 female inhabitants, a 2 percent decrease when compared to the 2004 estimate of 63.8 forcible rapes per 100,000 female inhabitants.
- Based on rape offenses actually reported to the UCR Program in 2005, rapes by force comprised 91.8 percent of reported rape offenses, and assaults to rape attempts accounted for 8.2 percent of reported rape offenses. This equated to 48.4 rapes by force per 100,000 female inhabitants and 4.3 assaults to rape attempts per 100,000 females in 2005.

After reading this section, you should be able to

1. define rape and forcible rape;
2. describe the characteristics and incidence of rape in the United States;
3. examine the relationship between rape and sexual assault.

8.6 EXPLAINING AND RESPONDING TO RAPE

Four major explanations for perspectives on rape are (1) the sociobiological view, (2) the sociocultural perspective, (3) a perspective that focuses on male socialization, and (4) the psychological perspective. The sociobiological explanation for rape focuses on the biological or evolutionary dimensions of the male sexual drive. The **sociobiological view** stresses that rape may be an instinctive male drive developed over thousands of years that encourages men to have sexual relations with as many women as possible, as a way of favoring their genes while perpetuating the human species. Scientist Donald Symons and others believe that rape is part sexual, part violent, and is bound up with this need.[68]

The **sociobiological view** stresses that rape may be an instinctive male drive developed over thousands of years that encourages men to have sexual relations with many women as a way of favoring their genes while perpetuating the human species.

A prominent explanation for rape is based on the **sociocultural view**. This view stresses that rape is a part of a cultural configuration that includes male dominance and interpersonal violence. Cross-cultural research by Peggy Reeves Sanday supports this view. Sanday challenged the perspective that rape is an inherent male tendency. She sampled a variety of tribal societies throughout the world and studied the incidence, meaning, and function of rape in those societies. Her guiding hypotheses were that rape varies cross-culturally and that a high incidence of rape will occur in cultural configurations distinguishably different from societies with a low incidence of rape. Her results were as follows:

- In almost one hundred societies studied, 47 percent were rape-free, 35 percent were intermediate, and 18 percent were rape-prone.
- In societies that were rape-prone, women had low status and little decision-making power and lived apart from men.

Sanday's research thus supported her hypotheses, indicating that violence is not biologically determined but socially programmed.[69]

Researchers such as Diana Russell believe that rape is a function of **male socialization** in our culture. That is, rape can be seen as an act that conforms to masculine qualities and expectations, such as dominance, aggressiveness, toughness, and forcefulness, that little boys are taught from an early age. According to Russell, women are taught to want to be dominated, just as men are taught to be dominating. Women who are sexually aggressive with men frighten some of them, who may then doubt their own masculinity. This insecurity, in turn, may cause some men to commit rape to uphold their masculine identity and self-image.[70]

Other researchers come from a **psychological perspective** and believe that rapists are mentally ill or have a serious personality disorder. For example, Paul H. Gebhard and associates reported in their 1965 study of imprisoned rapists that a significant percentage exhibited psychotic tendencies. Many also had histories of violent behavior and sadistic, hostile feelings toward women.[71] In another study of rapists, Richard Rada reported in 1978 that many convicted rapists were psychotic, others were sociopathic, and still others had serious masculine identity problems.[72]

A. Nicholas Groth and Jean Birnbaum studied five hundred convicted rapists in Connecticut in the 1970s. They believed that each rape contains elements of power, anger, and sexuality. They developed a three-fold classification system: the power rape, the anger rape, and the sadistic rape.

(1) In the **power rape**, the rapist is usually insecure about his masculinity. The rape is his attempt to show he is master over his victim, a form of domination. In that the goal is sexual conquest, he does not want to harm his victim and uses only the minimal amount of force necessary to achieve his objective. He wants to be in control, to have women at his mercy. He will often hold his victim captive over a period of time, controlling her and raping her repeatedly.

(2) In the **anger rape**, the rapist expresses his hostility toward women in general by selecting a victim and raping her. Long-term, pent-up feelings of rage are discharged in an extremely physical, brutal attack. This type of rapist will act on a moment's notice after an upsetting incident where he has become irritated, aggravated, or conflicted.[73] The assault goes far beyond the level of violence necessary to subdue the victim; the rapist's goal is to hurt the victim as much as possible. The sexual aspect may be an afterthought. This type of rapist is not sexually excited and may even be impotent during the attack. He will then attempt to degrade and humiliate his victim by forcing her into such acts as fellatio and sodomy.

READING ABSTRACT

Violence Against Women: A Cross-Cultural Perspective

BY TONI NELSON

In this reading, Toni Nelson carefully examines violence and assault against women across cultures. She examines female genital mutilation, rape, physical assault, domestic violence, and violent crimes against women in many parts of the world, from the Middle East, Africa, and India to South America, the United States, and Canada.

See reading on page 234.

In **sadistic rape**, anger and power over the victim become eroticized.

(3) In a **sadistic rape**, anger and power over the victim become eroticized. This type of rapist gets sexual satisfaction and pleasure out of tormenting, humiliating, and sadistically maltreating his victim. He achieves orgasm by cutting, burning, or flagellating her. This type of rapist is mentally ill. His victims often represent someone who he believes has persecuted or hurt him; thus, he wants to severely harm his victim and, in many cases, murder her. Groth and Birnbaum's research indicated that about 5 percent of their sample were sadistic rapists, approximately 40 percent were anger rapists, and about 55 percent were power rapists.[74]

In summary, there are many theories to explain rape. Some are biosocial or sociocultural; others emphasize psychological factors. Some criminologists and social and behavioral scientists view rape as a product of an abnormal social environment, whereas others view it as a product of a psychologically sick mind and deviant social experiences. No matter how it is explained, forcible rape is one of the most vicious crimes in the criminal repertoire.

FOR YOUR INFORMATION

Rape and Sexual Assault: Reporting to Police and Medical Attention, 1992–2000

BY CALLIE MARIE RENNISON

- Persons age twelve or older experienced an average annual 140,990 completed rapes, 109,230 attempted rapes, and 152,680 completed and attempted sexual assaults, according to the NCVS. Most rapes and sexual assaults were committed against females: female victims accounted for 94 percent of all completed rapes, 91 percent of all attempted rapes, and 89 percent of all completed and attempted sexual assaults.

- Because of the small number of sample cases of rape and sexual assault against males, analysis in the remainder of this report relates to female victims only. Data are aggregated across nine years to produce average annual estimates.

INJURIES

- All victims of completed rape are considered to have been injured, by NCVS definition. Thirty-eight percent of female rape victims sustained an injury in addition to the rape. Thirty-nine percent of attempted rape victims and 17 percent of sexual assault victims were injured during their victimization. Nonfatal injuries from any crime range from bruises and chipped teeth (minor) to broken bones and gunshot wounds (serious).
- Among completed rape victims, 33 percent had additional minor injuries, and 5 percent suffered additional serious injuries. Two-thirds of attempted rape victims also suffered minor injuries, and 3 percent of injured victims were seriously injured during an attempted rape. Fifty-four percent of injured sexual assault victims reported receiving minor injuries, and 5 percent were seriously injured.

REPORTING TO POLICE

- Most rapes and sexual assaults were not reported to the police. Sixty-three percent of completed rapes, 65 percent of attempted rapes, and 74 percent of completed and attempted sexual assaults against females were not reported to the police. When the police were notified about a rape or sexual assault, the victim most often made the report.

TREATMENT OF INJURIES

- Most injured rape and sexual assault victims were not treated for their injuries. Treatment for injuries ranged from receiving care at the scene or in the victim's home to being admitted to a hospital. Thirty-two percent of completed rape victims, 32 percent of injured attempted rape victims, and 27 percent of injured sexual assault victims were treated. Forty-eight percent of female rape victims who received treatment for their injuries were treated at, but not admitted to, a hospital. An additional 24 percent of treated rape victims were cared for at home or at the scene, and 20 percent were treated at a doctor's office or clinic. Injured victims of attempted rape were equally likely to be treated at the scene, at home, or at a hospital. Of injured female attempted rape victims, 44 percent were treated at but not admitted to the hospital, and

39 percent were treated at the scene or at home. Injured victims of completed and attempted sexual assault received treatment at the scene or at home (20 percent), at a doctor's office or clinic (31 percent), or at the hospital (24 percent).

REPORTING VIOLENCE TO THE POLICE AND TREATMENT OF INJURIES SUSTAINED

- An annual average of 131,950 completed rapes were committed against females age twelve or older in the United States. By definition, all 131,950 victimizations resulted in an injured victim, but only 36 percent (or 47,960) of these victimizations were reported to the police. A greater percentage of reported victimizations, compared to nonreported victimizations, involved medical treatment of the victims. Fifty-nine percent of victims of a reported completed rape, compared to 17 percent of victims of an unreported completed rape, received medical attention.
- U.S. females age twelve or older were victims of an estimated 98,970 attempted rapes, annually. Thirty-nine percent of attempted rape victims were injured. Among injured victims, 42 percent stated the violence was reported to police. Among injured victims, a higher percentage of reported attempted rapes (45 percent), compared to unreported attempted rapes (22 percent), received medical treatment.
- Seventeen percent (or 23,020) of the 135,550 completed or attempted sexual assaults annually against females age twelve or older resulted in an injury. Most sexual assault victims were not injured (83 percent). Most uninjured sexual assault victims stated that the violence went unreported to the police (77 percent). Of those victims injured during a sexual assault, 41 percent of the violence was reported to police, and 57 percent went unreported. Among injured sexual assault victims, a higher percentage of those whose assault was reported (37 percent), compared to victims of unreported crimes (18 percent), received treatment.

Source: C. M. Rennison, *Rape and Sexual Assault: Reporting to Police and Medical Attention, 1992–2000,* selected findings of the U.S. Department of Justice, Office of Justice Programs, Bureau of Justice Statistics, Washington, DC: Government Printing Office, August 2002, NCJ-194530.

After reading this section, you should be able to

1. discuss explanations for rape based on sociobiological, sociocultural, male socialization–oriented, and psychological views;
2. distinguish among power rape, anger rape, and sadistic rape as three classifications of rape;
3. relate explanations for rape to explanations for assault and violence discussed earlier in the chapter;
4. give examples from cross-cultural research of violence against women, based on Reading 8.2.

CHAPTER SUMMARY

This chapter on violent crime begins with an examination of assault, particularly in the American family. Aggravated assault accounts for the majority of all violent crimes reported in the United States.

- There are 1.2 million annual aggravated assaults in the United States.
- Aggravated and simple assault rates have been declining.
- Almost 95 percent of the annual 1.7 million violent workplace incidents are for aggravated or simple assault (pp. 201–205).
- In the United States, there are about 700,000 annual nonfatal violent victimizations committed by current or former spouses, boyfriends, girlfriends, or sexual partners of the victims.
- Child assault cases run as high as 3 million or more annually.
- Research has indicated that teens are just as likely to be assaulted as children under the age of three years.
- Siblings, grandparents, and parents are also victims of family assault (pp. 206–213).
- Assaultive behavior is explained by psychopathological, sociocultural, and economic approaches.

- Responses to assault and violence have varied. Today, many more people than ever before believe that American communities must deal with domestic violence and assault by enacting and enforcing criminal and civil laws (pp. 213–218).

The second part of the chapter focuses on the nature and extent of rape and sexual assault.

- Rape is a crime of violence.
- Rape is one of the most unreported crimes in the United States. The official figures of annual rapes are significantly underestimated and underreported (pp. 219–220).
- Explanations for rape vary from sociobiological and sociocultural perspectives to theories that focus on male socialization and psychological factors.
- A. Nicholas Groth and Jean Birnbaum developed a threefold classification of rape: power rape, anger rape, and sadistic rape.
- Women throughout the world encounter many forms of violence (pp. 220–222).

Study Guide

Chapter Objectives

- Distinguish between aggravated assault, simple assault, and battery.
- Describe the nature and extent of assault in the United States.
- Describe the nature and extent of assault and violence in the American workplace.
- Make a distinction between conflict and violence.
- Examine the nature and extent of spouse assault in the United States.
- Describe the dimensions of intimate partner violence in the United States.
- Examine the nature and extent of child assault and abuse in America.
- Describe sibling, elder, and parent assault in the United States.
- Present and describe the primary explanations for assaultive behavior in American society.
- Describe the relationship between childhood assault and adult criminal behavior.
- Explain how America has responded to family violence.
- Define rape.
- Describe the nature and extent of rape in the United States.
- Examine the relationship between rape and sexual assault.
- List and describe the major explanations for rape.
- Examine the different types of rape identified by Groth and Birnbaum.

Key Terms

Aggravated assault (201)
Anger rape (221)
Battery (201)
Clearance rate (204)
Forcible rape (219)
Intimate partner violence (208)

Male socialization (and rape) (221)
Power rape (221)
Psychological perspective (on rape) (221)
Rape (219)
Sadistic rape (222)

Simple assault (201)
Sociobiological view (of rape) (220)
Sociocultural view (of rape) (221)
Spouse assault (207)

Self-Test
Short Answer

1. Write definitions for aggravated assault, simple assault, and battery.
2. Briefly describe the rates and trends of assault in the United States.
3. Briefly examine violence and assault in the American workplace.
4. Define the terms *conflict* and *violence*.
5. Briefly describe the nature and extent of spouse assault in America.
6. Define intimate partner violence.
7. Define child abuse and describe the extent of child assault and abuse in the United States.
8. Define sibling, elder, and parent assault.
9. Briefly examine the major explanations for assaultive behavior in American society.
10. Briefly describe the relationship between childhood assault and adult criminal behavior.
11. List and briefly describe three major responses to family violence.
12. Define rape and forcible rape.
13. Briefly describe the incidence and characteristics of rape.
14. Describe the issues around the reporting of rape.
15. Briefly describe three explanations for rape.
16. List and briefly describe three classifications of rape.
17. Define and explain female genital mutilation.
18. Briefly describe how violence against women is an international problem.

Multiple Choice

1. Which of the following is not true?
   a. Assault is different from battery.
   b. Assault has been on the decrease over the last decade.
   c. Assault is primarily a female crime.
   d. Assault is a crime of violence.

2. In the United States during the past decade, the rates of aggravated assault have
   a. steadily increased
   b. steadily decreased
   c. basically stayed the same
   d. increased dramatically

3. In the United States, aggravated assault
   a. is very much a female crime
   b. is very much a male crime
   c. is equally committed by men and women
   d. is basically the same as battery

4. Workplace violence appears to be the result of such factors as
   a. individual characteristics
   b. precipitating events
   c. system characteristics
   d. all of the above

5. Conflict is
   a. a product of social interaction and an effort to resolve a decision-making impasse
   b. any behavior that threatens or causes physical damage to a person or object
   c. basically the same as violence
   d. none of the above

6. Which of the following statement(s) is(are) false?
   a. No one knows the actual extent of violence and assault between spouses in the United States.
   b. The estimates of assault between spouses is low, because many incidents go unreported.
   c. Husbands and wives who beat their spouses come from all social classes, ethnic and racial groups, and ages.
   d. all of the above

7. The definition of child abuse includes
   a. physical abuse and neglect
   b. emotional abuse
   c. abandonment or inadequate supervision
   d. all of the above

8. Gelles and Straus explain violence by examining
   a. sociocultural, economic, and psychological factors
   b. the factors of economic adversity, stressful life circumstances, violent parents, and isolation from the community
   c. psychopathological, genetic, and biochemical factors
   d. none of the above

9. During the past decade, according to NCVS data, U.S. rape rates have
   a. declined
   b. increased
   c. stayed about the same
   d. have increased and decreased many times

10. The most often-cited reason for rape victims not reporting the crime is that
    a. the victimization is considered a personal matter
    b. the victim wants to protect the offender
    c. the victim believes that he or she deserved to be raped
    d. the victim fears reprisal from the offender

11. Which perspective stresses that rape is a part of a cultural configuration that includes male dominance and interpersonal violence?
    a. sociobiological
    b. psychological
    c. sociocultural
    d. male socialization–oriented

12. In which classification of rape do anger and power over the victim become eroticized?
    a. power
    b. anger
    c. sadistic
    d. ritualistic

True–False

T F   1. Simple assault is a serious crime of violence.

T F   2. More than half of reported aggravated assaults are committed annually with firearms.

T F   3. In the United States, all people are trained for violence.

T F   4. Husband abuse is one of the most unreported crimes in the nation.

T F   5. Teenagers are just as likely to be assaulted as children under the age of three.

T F   6. Children's aggressive tendencies are decreased by parents who use physical force to control aggression in their children.

T F   7. Money worries and economic adversity rarely pervade the typical violent family.

The Criminalization of Domestic Violence

Source: Reprinted by permission of the National Association of Social Workers from Social Work, *vol. 48, no. 3, 2003, pp. 237–246.* "The Criminalization of Domestic Violence: What Social Workers Need to Know" *by F.S. Davis. Copyright (c) 2003, National Association of Social Workers, Inc. Social Work.*

BY FRAN S. DAVIS

Domestic violence is a crosscutting issue that affects the daily lives of people seeking social work services. During the past 20 years, the social science and criminal justice fields developed interventions designed to deter abuse and rehabilitate abusers so they will not abuse again. Central to these interventions has been the increasing role of the criminal justice system to enforce laws that regard the use of violence against one's intimate partner as a criminal act. Thus, domestic violence is viewed as not only a social problem, but a criminal justice problem. The criminalization of domestic violence (Fagan, 1996) refers to efforts to address the issue of domestic violence through the passage and enforcement of criminal and civil laws.

Based on a literature review from social science, legal, and criminal justice fields, this article provides an overview of criminal justice interventions to deter male batterers from abusing their female partners and to rehabilitate batterers found guilty of abuse. It reviews the effectiveness of police arrest, protective orders, prosecution, victim advocacy, court responses, batterers' intervention programs as a condition of probation, and domestic violence coordinated community responses. It also provides practical suggestions for practice with victims of domestic violence. Although same-sex and female-to-male violence does occur, interventions reviewed in this article focus on male-to-female violence.

OVERVIEW OF DOMESTIC VIOLENCE

Definitions of domestic violence usually are worded broadly to encompass a pattern of behaviors used by people who abuse their intimate partners, including physical, sexual, and emotional abuse. However, from the criminal justice perspective, *domestic abuse* is more narrowly defined as "an act by a member of a family or household against another member that is intended to result in physical harm, bodily injury, assault, or a threat that reasonably places the member in fear of imminent physical harm" (Texas Department of Public Safety, 1998, p. 47). People who commit domestic abuse may be arrested and charged with numerous offenses, including homicide, assault and battery, criminal trespass, terroristic threats, stalking, and sexual assault (Miller, 1998). Depending on the severity of injuries or the use of a weapon, charges can be either misdemeanors or felonies. Research on the characteristics of batterers is focused on developing typologies so that interventions and resources can be matched appropriately to offenders (see Gondolf, 1988, and Jacobson & Gottman, 1998). Risk factors for men who batter their partners include prior domestic violence or assault and battery arrests, prior arrests involving the same victim, and drug involvement (Healey, Smith, & O'Sullivan, 1998).

Official estimates of the incidence and prevalence of domestic violence have yielded consistent and troubling results. The National Violence Against Women Survey (Tjaden & Thoennes, 1998) estimated 5.9 million incidents of physical assaults against women annually, with approximately 76 percent of those incidents perpetrated by current or former husbands, cohabiting partners, or dates. Women's lifetime prevalence rate of male-to-female partner abuse is estimated at 14 percent to 50 percent (Straus, Gelles, & Steinmetz, 1980). The National Crime Victimization Survey (Bachman & Saltzman, 1995) found that nearly 30 percent of all female homicide victims were killed by their husbands, former husbands, or boyfriends in contrast with just over 3 percent of male homicide victims killed by their wives, former wives, or girlfriends. Women of all races were equally vulnerable to attacks by intimates (Bachman & Saltzman). Domestic violence incidents needing emergency room treatment were four times higher than the estimates of domestic violence that came to the attention of law enforcement agencies (Rand, 1997).

Links between domestic violence and public assistance (Brandwein, 1998) and child welfare (Bennett, 1999; Edleson, 1999) have been established. As battered women come into contact with health, education, legal, and social institutions (Peled & Edleson, 1994), they are more likely to contact social workers for help (Hamilton & Coates, 1993). It is important for all social workers to understand the array of interventions that exist to deter and change violent behavior and the strategies that maximize victim safety.

From the first law of marriage proclaimed by Romulus in 75 BC through the early 20th century, legal and institutional support for wife beating can be found (Dobash & Dobash, 1979). The feminist movement starting in the 1960s

(Schechter, 1982), the victim witness movement of the 1970s, and the availability of empirical evidence (Straus et al., 1980) accelerated public attention to the legal and procedural barriers that existed between safety for women and the de facto right to beat one's wife (Fagan, 1996). These barriers included informal and formal police and prosecution policies of nonintervention, misinformation and myths about domestic violence, inability of police to arrest on misdemeanor offenses, and limitations of restraining orders only to people filing for divorce (Fagan; Zorza, 1992).

Beginning in the late 1970s, advocates for battered women established partnerships with feminist, liberal, and conservative lawmakers for a "get tough" approach to domestic violence that yielded criminal justice reforms (Fagan, 1996; Zorza, 1992). By 1980, 47 states had passed legislation that allowed police to make misdemeanor arrests without warrants and to enforce civil restraining orders, called protective orders in many jurisdictions (Fagan; Zorza). Court challenges helped to change nonintervention police policies. In a 1984 landmark case, *Thurman v. City of Torrington*, the courts found the lack of action by police negligent and awarded the plaintiff $2.3 million (Wallace, 1996). Other legal challenges resulted in changes in policies, mandatory training in the dynamics of domestic violence, and requirements for police to provide information and referrals for victim services (Zorza).

THEORETICAL FRAMEWORKS

Because there is no single recognized causal theory for domestic violence, criminal justice interventions are based on four theories: social exchange/deterrence, social learning, feminist theory, and the ecological framework.

A key assumption of social exchange theory (Blau, 1964) is that human interaction is guided by the pursuit of rewards and the avoidance of costs and punishments. Gelles and Cornell (1985, 1990) posited that people use violence against family members when the costs of being violent do not outweigh the rewards. They define the costs of being violent as the potential that someone would hit back, the potential for arrest and imprisonment, the loss of status, and the dissolution of the family. One way to reduce domestic violence is to increase societal sanctions, thereby increasing the costs of violent behavior. This is the basic concept underlying the enforcement of laws against domestic violence, as a deterrent against future abuse. *Deterrence* is defined as the "state's ability to diminish the incidence of a prohibited action through legal threats which clearly indicate that the cost of the action would be greater than would any benefits that might derive from it" (Dutton, 1995, p. 242). Thus "a man who batters his partner and is punished by harsh criminal sanctions or even by arrest only will be less likely to batter again than if he experienced milder sanctions or no arrest" (Ford, 1991, p. 192).

According to social learning theory (Bandura, 1973), people learn to be violent through being directly rewarded or punished immediately after aggressive behavior takes place (reinforcement) and vicariously through watching other people's experiences (modeling). This approach is also referred to as the intergenerational transmission of violence (Mihalic & Elliott, 1997; Widom, 1989). A correlation exists between being an abusive partner and having witnessed abusive behavior by fathers toward mothers (O'Leary, 1987). Many batterers' programs are founded on the basic premise of social learning theory: What is learned can be unlearned.

Feminist theory views domestic violence as an expression and consequence of a patriarchal social system that gives men responsibility for control and management of their female partners (Dobash & Dobash, 1979; Yllo, 1993). Domestic violence is considered a problem rooted in the structure of society rather than the pathologies of individual men. A feminist orientation is used in curricula for psychoeducational groups for batterers (Healey et al., 1998). Feminist theory also underlies advocacy interventions that use an empowerment approach with battered women (Gutierrez, Parsons, & Cox, 1998).

The National Research Council's panels on violence against women (Crowell & Burgess, 1996) and on violence in the family (Chalk & King, 1998) proposed adopting an ecological framework in recognition that no one theory can explain or predict domestic violence. The ecological model is familiar to social workers as the basis for generalist practice (Germain, 1991) and has been proposed as an approach to understand domestic violence since the mid-1980s (Carlson, 1984; Edleson & Tolman, 1992; Heise, 1998). The ecological framework includes risk factors and interventions at the micro, meso, and macro system levels. The coordinated community approach is a macro system intervention; batterer programs fit into both the micro and meso levels, whereas police, prosecution, and court interventions are considered part of the meso system.

Each of these theories contributes to interventions designed for abusers. Social exchange/deterrence theory provides the framework for interventions such as arrest, conviction, and punishment. Social learning theory contributes the belief that if violence is learned, it can be unlearned, to provide the basis for batterer's intervention programs. Feminist theory influences the curricula for batterer's intervention as well as victim advocacy programs, and the macro level of the ecological framework provides the foundation for coordinated community approaches.

CRIMINAL JUSTICE INTERVENTIONS FOR DOMESTIC VIOLENCE

During the past 20 years, the effectiveness of criminal justice system components to deter abusive behavior has been examined. A typical domestic violence case moves through the system starting with intervention by police, the granting of a protective order, prosecution either on initial criminal charges or on violation of the protective order, court response, and if the perpetrator is found guilty, sentencing the offender to a batterers' intervention program as a condition of probation. Although victims may apply for a protective order before police intervention, many victims first learn about protective orders as a result of police intervention. The violation of a protective order is a criminal act that moves the case to the criminal prosecution phase. Many communities have adopted a comprehensive strategy referred to as coordinated community responses, which combine criminal justice interventions, batterers' intervention, and victim advocacy (Hart, 1995).

POLICE INTERVENTIONS

Police are the gatekeepers to the criminal justice system. Subsequent interventions hinge on the attitudes of police toward domestic violence (Buzawa, 1988; Buzawa & Austin, 1998) and options of police to make arrests (Schmidt & Sherman, 1996). Sherman and Berk's (1984) Minneapolis Domestic Violence Experiment is the first study testing the effectiveness of police intervention strategies on domestic violence misdemeanor cases (Fagan, 1996). In this study, police were randomly assigned to arrest the suspect, order the suspect out of the house, or provide advice to the couple. Arrest was found to be the most effective strategy in reducing subsequent police involvement. Replication studies conducted in five communities had mixed results, leading to the conclusion that arrest per se would not stop subsequent assaults (Sherman, 1992). Arrest by itself may also be considered a "weak dose" of punishment as few offenders were prosecuted (Sherman). Although there is currently no consensus among researchers and advocates regarding the effectiveness of arrest as a deterrent (Bowman, 1992; Stark, 1996), many state and local communities have adopted mandatory arrest policies requiring police to arrest if there is probable cause to believe an assault has taken place (Miller, 1998).

Serious unintended consequences can occur as a result of police interventions, including retaliation against victims by their abusers, dual arrests, and the potential lack of cultural sensitivity to victims and perpetrators. Ford (1991) found that on-the-scene arrests resulted in higher risks of retaliation compared with warrants for arrest based on victim complaints. Partners of enraged batterers may be less safe after an arrest than before the arrest. Another unintended consequence has been a rise in dual arrests. Police trained to respond to crime as single discrete incidents and not as a pattern of behavior may arrest both batterers and victims, even though the victims may have used violence as an attempt to defend themselves (Martin, 1997). Racist attitudes by some police officers may result in slow response to 911 calls in communities of color or overly aggressive response to offenders, including police brutality (Wright, 1998). The historic conflict and mistrust between the police and communities of color has its roots in U.S. slavery and is evidenced by the disproportionate number of people of color arrested and convicted of crime in this country. Therefore, women of color may be reluctant to request police intervention because

it may be viewed as disloyalty to their race, and they often feel obligated to protect their batterers from police and the criminal justice system (Richie, 1996; Williams, 1998). Latino and immigrant women also face language barriers to seeking help from the criminal justice system. Police often use family members or neighbors as interpreters, thus further embarrassing the victim and potentially angering the abuser. Women without official immigrant status may fear deportation for themselves and their families if the police are called. (For the relationship among domestic violence, race, and the criminal justice system see Richie and Williams.)

PROTECTIVE ORDERS

Protective orders are civil court orders that prohibit the offender from contacting the victim or their children, using physical abuse and the threat of physical abuse, or damaging personal property of the victim (Wallace, 1996). The order may provide for custody, visitation, support of minor children, and living arrangements (Wilson, 1997). The violation of a protective order is now a criminal offense in 43 states and the District of Columbia (Miller, 1998). As a tool to keep women and children safe, the use of protective orders has had mixed results. Protective orders are successful in deterring repeated incidents of physical and psychological abuse among offenders who do not have a history of violent crime (Keilitz, Hannaford, & Efkeman, 1998). However, Harrell and Smith (1996) found that 60 percent of women with protective orders reported violations during the year after they were issued. (For a discussion of the lack of legal protections for battered lesbians and gay men see Fray-Witzer [1999].)

PROSECUTION AND VICTIM ADVOCACY

Serious obstacles to victim participation in prosecution of domestic violence are strong emotional, familial, and financial ties between the victim and offender. Ongoing, unsupervised contacts between victim and perpetrator are common, especially when the presence of children requires arrangements for visitation. Furthermore, there are differences in desired outcomes between the victim and criminal justice system, such as wanting partners to get counseling instead of incarceration (Hart, 1993). Prosecutors use varied strategies to overcome the reluctance of victims to participate, including taking the onus of filing charges away from the woman by having police file charges against the abuser, adopting no-drop policies, pursuing victimless prosecution, and using victim advocates to help women through the process (Mills, 1998).

Ford and Regoli (1993) tested the effectiveness of prosecutorial policies that allowed a victim to stop prosecution by dropping charges against her abuser versus no-drop policies that threatened victims with subpoenas if they failed to testify against their abusers. Regardless of the policies used, considerable reabuse occurred in the six months following case settlement. However, victims who were allowed to drop complaints but elected to go forth with prosecution were significantly less likely to be reassaulted (13 percent) than those who did not drop their complaints. Some jurisdictions now use victimless prosecution without victim testimony (Rebovich, 1996). This strategy requires extensive evidence gathering at the crime scene by police. It is uncertain whether victimless prosecution is a more effective deterrence than prosecution with victim participation.

Many prosecutors also employ victim advocates to provide services to victims. Advocates help apply for protective orders; gather information regarding the nature, severity, and prior violence by the offender; provide information about the criminal justice system; notify victims of key events; accompany victims to courtroom events; link victims with community resources; and help file claims for crime victim compensation (Wallace, 1996). The presence of advocates can help victims feel empowered to pursue prosecution (Weisz, 1999). However, prosecution policies that force women to testify against their abuser can be disempowering and may lead to feelings of being revictimized by the criminal justice system (Mills, 1998; Hanna, 1996).

COURT RESPONSES

Judges have significant influence, and a judge without appropriate training in domestic violence can undermine all earlier efforts at deterrence (Ford, Rompf, Faragher, & Weisenfluh, 1995). Specialized courts have been created to centralize dockets, expertise, and the accessibility of court based victim services (Fagan, 1996; Healey et al., 1998). Specialized courts reduce processing time by half, increase convictions, and show a slight reduction in subsequent felony arrests (Davis, Smith, & Nickles, 1997). Judges prefer mandating batterers' intervention as a condition of probation, with little interest in incarceration as a possible deterrent (Hanna, 1998).

BATTERERS' INTERVENTION PROGRAMS AS A CONDITION OF PROBATION

Despite court reliance and the victims' hope (Hanna, 1998), the short- and long-term effectiveness of counseling for batterers remains undear, with reabuse rates ranging from 3 percent to 33 percent (Chalk & King, 1998; Fagan, 1996; Tolman & Edleson, 1995). Most intervention programs are either pro-feminist, family systems, or psychotherapeutic (Healey et al., 1998) and use social learning or cognitive behavioral approaches (Tolman & Edleson). Regardless of the approach, programs need to reduce dropout and no-show rates of 25 percent to 50 percent (Chalk & King), tailor interventions for cultural differences (Williams & Becker, 1994), develop consistent outcome measures (Tolman & Edleson), match interventions for different batterer profiles (Fagan, 1996), develop program standards (Healey et al., 1998), and improve outcomes. Required periodic court appearances can

reduce the dropout rates from 50 percent to 35 percent and no-shows from 36 percent to 6 percent (Gondolf, 2000). First-time offenders mandated into counseling for longer periods were significantly less likely to reassault their partners than those who were not arrested the first time or who were mandated into shorter counseling programs (Syers & Edleson,1992). It is unclear what linkages exist among the overall deterrent effect, the length of the counseling program, subsequent abuse, and the function of surveillance. Research is being conducted to track the behavior of completers of a batterers' intervention program four years after the intervention (Gondolf).

COORDINATED COMMUNITY RESPONSES

The coordinated community response strategy involves coordination to protect battered women, hold abusers accountable, deter future abuse, and coordinate the flow of information so that neither party gets lost in the cracks of a multifaceted system (Hart, 1995; Pence, 1983). This approach brings together criminal justice, health, and human services providers to adopt common policies, procedures, and tracking systems and delivers a communitywide message that domestic violence is taken seriously. Coordinated responses can lead to increases in arrest, prosecution, and mandated counseling (Gamache, Edleson, & Schock, 1988). Men arrested and court ordered to treatment were least likely to repeat their violence, followed by those who were not arrested, and then by those who were arrested but not ordered to treatment (Syers & Edleson, 1992). Lower recidivism rates are associated with the degree of sanctions levied by the court and the compliance with those sanctions (Murphy, Musser, & Maton, 1998). Higher numbers of program sessions are associated with fewer subsequent arrests (Babcock & Steiner, 1999). These findings also support earlier studies, which found that batterers who completed intervention programs were likely to be first-time offenders, reported a higher income, and were more educated than batterers who dropped out of treatment.

SUMMARY OF CRIMINAL JUSTICE INTERVENTIONS

Research addressing the effectiveness of the criminalization of domestic violence has yielded inconsistent and inconclusive results (Fagan, 1996). Police interventions may be the first step in establishing a safe environment, but they may also result in unintended consequences of more violence to both victims and offenders. Although the majority of protective orders may be violated, protective orders taken as a proactive step by the victim may be more effective. Successful prosecution will not necessarily stop abusive behavior, and various prosecution strategies may empower or disempower victims. The role of the victim in taking proactive steps to involve the criminal justice system is an important issue, although the linkage between a stronger deterrent effect, victim empowerment, and specific legal intervention is not known. When a guilty verdict is obtained, judges prefer mandating batterers to intervention programs as a condition of probation, the success of which has been for the most part unproven. The coordinated community response strategy has had preliminary success in showing that a combination of legal interventions has better outcomes than the use of one strategy alone.

IMPLICATIONS FOR SOCIAL WORK PRACTICE

Because domestic violence affects many clients, all social workers need some fundamental knowledge about criminal justice interventions and options available for clients. Because no one intervention has been proven effective, social workers need to be realistic. There are no simple answers to getting the batterer to stop his abusive behavior or to ensuring client safety.

For clients whose lives may be in danger, safety issues must take precedence over all considerations. A thorough risk assessment should consider severity and frequency of abuse, access to firearms, and use of alcohol. Social workers should document past and current client injuries, the nature of threats, current level of fear, and criminal justice interventions previously tried. Discussions about the limits of confidentiality and state statutes regarding privileged communication should occur. If working with batterers, social workers should pay attention to duty-to-warn issues. It may also be appropriate to establish relationships with local police, prosecutor, and probation offices to exchange appropriate information about the criminal record of the batterer. Although social workers are obligated to report suspected child abuse, few states have mandatory reporting laws regarding domestic abuse.

Despite the debate about the effectiveness and risks of police interventions, particularly for communities of color, social workers should not hesitate to tell clients to contact police if they believe their lives are in danger. They should develop culturally appropriate safety plans with clients that identify safe places to go to for protection. The National Domestic Violence Hotline at 1–800–799–SAFE provides referrals to local specialized services, maintains Spanish-speaking advocates on all shifts, and has access to interpreters for a wide variety of languages. It is important to respect a client's decision to pursue other options, even if that means staying with an abusive partner until she believes she is safe enough to leave (Peled, Eisikovits, Enosh, & Winstok, 2000). She knows her abuser best. Risk is greater if her abuser has been previously arrested, but if the abuser holds a steady job and has never been arrested before, he may be a viable candidate for successful criminal justice deterrents and batterers' intervention programs.

Protective orders can be used as proactive options for women. Social workers should know where clients can apply for a protective order, what information they need to present, and what options exist regarding the waiving of filing fees. Many states allow for pro se protective orders that allow applications without an attorney. Clients should be advised to give a copy of their protective order to a friend for safekeeping and to keep a copy with them at all times. Some police still want to see the protective order before arresting an abuser for violating the order. Social workers must caution their clients that a protective order does not guarantee their safety. It is only a mechanism that potentially holds a batterer accountable if he violates the order.

During prosecution, accompaniment through the court system is a tool that helps battered women feel more empowered. If a client has to appear in court, it is important to find out if the prosecutor's office has its own victim advocates or if the local domestic violence program provides this service. It is important to know the prosecution policies in your local jurisdiction. Does the office use victimless prosecution or have a no-drop policy? No-drop policies create challenges for social workers in reconciling social work values regarding client self-determination and the criminal justice system's value on gaining convictions. A no-drop policy may trigger revictimization issues for clients and may influence the level of support that clients may need. Social workers should caution their clients that participation in prosecution is no guarantee of their safety or behavior change of the batterer.

If the court finds the batterer guilty and sentences him to an intervention program, there is no guarantee that the violence will stop. It is important to learn how individual programs measure success, what contact the program has with the victim, how often the program communicates with the referring court or probation office, criteria for program completion, program length, and the ability of the program and its staff to provide culturally sensitive services. The lengthier the program, the more effective it may be. Again, social workers should not raise false hopes regarding the effectiveness of batterers' intervention programs.

Agencies or practitioners that provide services to significant percentages of battered women should participate in their community's domestic violence coordinating council or task force. As case managers, social workers can identify gaps in services, advocate for individual cases, and propose policy and procedural changes to increase victim safety. Social workers should also advocate for linguistically and culturally appropriate services for both victims and batterers. If a community does not have a coordinating council, social workers should encourage the appropriate agencies and personnel to work together to promote collaboration.

Social workers can support changes in laws to increase victim safety and hold batterers accountable for their behavior. State domestic violence coalitions are important sources of information about current laws and potential changes. Feed-back to these organizations about local practices can be useful. Although it is important to advocate for individual women, participation in institutional advocacy efforts also is important.

CONCLUSION

During the past 20 years, there has been an explosion of knowledge about domestic violence, its prevalence, and its linkage with other social problems. Although a number of criminal and civil justice tools exist to stop abuse and hold batterers accountable for their behavior, no one tool has been proven effective in all situations. Social workers need an understanding of both the tools that work best in specific situations and the potentially dangerous consequences resulting from the use of these tools.

CRITICAL THINKING

1. Which criminal justice interventions to deter rape do you favor, and why?
2. What rape-offender rehabilitation measures do you think the public should support?
3. What do you think should be the features of an effective rape-victim advocacy program?

REFERENCES

Babcock, J. C., & Steiner, R. (1999). The relationship between treatment, incarceration, and recidivism of battering: A program evaluation of Seattle's coordinated community response to domestic violence. *Journal of Family Psychology, 13*(1), 46–59.

Bachman, R., & Saltzman, L. E. (1995). *Violence against women: Estimates from the redesigned survey* (Bureau of Justice Statistics Special Report). Washington, DC: U.S. Department of Justice.

Bandura, A. (1973). *Aggression: A social learning analysis.* Englewood Cliffs, NJ: Prentice Hall.

Bennett, A. (1999). *Child welfare and domestic violence: A review of recent literature* (Prevention Report No. 2). Iowa City: National Resource Center for Family Centered Practice.

Blau, P. M. (1964). *Exchange and power in social life.* New York: John Wiley & Sons.

Bowman, C. G. (1992). The arrest experiments: A feminist critique. *Journal of Criminal Law and Criminology, 83,* 201–208.

Brandwein, R. (Ed.). (1998). *Battered women, children, and welfare reform: The ties that bind.* Thousand Oaks, CA: Sage Publications.

Buzawa, E. (1988). Explaining variations in police responses to domestic violence: A case study in Detroit and New England. In G. T. Hotaling, D. Finkelhor, J. T. Kirkpatrick, & M. A. Straus (Eds.), *Coping with family violence: Research and policy perspectives* (pp. 169–182). Newbury Park, CA: Sage Publications.

Buzawa, E. S., & Austin, T. L. (1998). Determining police response to domestic violence victims. In *Legal interventions in family violence: Research findings and policy implications* (p. 58). Washington, DC: National Institute of Justice.

Carlson, B. E. (1984). Causes and maintenance of domestic violence: An ecological analysis. *Social Service Review, 38,* 569–587.

Chalk, R., & King, A. (1998). (Eds.). *Violence in families: Assessing prevention and treatment programs.* Washington, DC: National Research Council/National Academy of Sciences.

Crowell, N. A., & Burgess, A. W. (1996). (Eds.). *Understanding violence against women.* Washington, DC: National Academy Press.

Davis, R. C., Smith, B. E., & Nickles, L. (1997). *Prosecuting domestic violence cases with reluctant victims: Assessing two novel approaches in Milwaukee* (Final Report, American Bar Association's Criminal Justice Section). Washington, DC: National Institute of Justice.

Dobash, R. E., & Dobash, R. (1979). *Violence against wives: A case against the patriarchy.* New York: Free Press.

Dutton, D. G. (1995). *The domestic assault of women: Psychological and criminal justice perspectives.* Vancouver: University of British Columbia Press.

Edleson, J. L. (1999). The overlap between child maltreatment and woman battering. *Violence Against Women, 5,* 134–154.

Edleson, J., & Tolman, R. M. (1992). *Intervention for men who batter: An ecological approach.* Newbury Park, CA: Sage Publications.

Fagan, J. (1996). *The criminalization of domestic violence: Promises and limits.* Washington, DC: National Institute of Justice.

Ford, D. (1991). Preventing and provoking wife battery through criminal sanctioning: A look at the risks. In D. D. Knudsen & J. L. Miller (Eds.), *Abused and battered: Social and legal responses to family violence* (pp. 191–209). New York: Aldine de Gruyter.

Ford, D. A., & Regoli, M. J. (1993). The Indianapolis Domestic Violence Prosecution Experiment. (1998). In *Legal interventions in family violence: Research findings and policy implications* (pp. 62–64). Washington, DC: National Institute of Justice.

Ford, D. A., Rompf, E. L, Faragher, T., & Weisenfluh, S. (1995). Case outcomes in domestic violence court: Influences of judges. *Psychological Reports, 77,* 587–594.

Fray-Witzer, E. (1999). Twice abused: Same-sex domestic violence and the law. In B. Leventhal & S. E. Lundy (Eds.), *Same-sex domestic violence: Strategies for change.* Thousand Oaks, CA: Sage Publications.

Gamache, D. J., Edleson, J. L., & Schock, M. D. (1988). Coordinated police, judicial and social service response to woman battering: A multiple-baseline evaluation across three communities. In G. T. Hotaling, D. Finkelhor, J. T. Kirkpatrick, & M. A. Straus (Eds.), *Coping with family violence: Research and policy perspectives* (pp. 193–209). Newbury Park, CA: Sage Publications.

Gelles, R. J., & Cornell, C. P. (1985). *Intimate violence in families*. Newbury Park, CA: Sage Publications.

Gelles, R. J., & Cornell, C. P. (1990). Intimate violence in families (2nd ed.). Newbury Park, CA: Sage Publications.

Germain, C. B. (1991). *Human behavior in the social environment: An ecological view*. New York: Columbia University Press.

Gondolf, E. W. (1988). Who are those guys? Toward a behavioral typology of batterers. *Violence and Victims*, 3, 187–203.

Gondolf, E. W. (2000). Mandatory court review and batterer program compliance. *Journal of Interpersonal Violence*, 15, 437–438.

Gutierrez, L. M., Parsons, R. J., & Cox, E. O. (1998). *Empowerment in social work practice: A sourcebook*. Pacific Grove, CA: Brooks/Cole.

Hamilton, B., & Coates, J. (1993). Perceived helpfulness and use of professional services by abused women. *Journal of Family Violence 8*, 313–324.

Hanna, C. (1996). No right to choose: Mandated victim participation in domestic violence prosecutions. *Harvard Law Review*, 109, 1850–1910.

Hanna, C. (1998). The paradox of hope: The crime and punishment of domestic violence. *William & Mary Law Review*, 39, 1505–1584.

Harrell, A., & Smith, B. E. (1996). Effects of restraining orders on domestic violence victims. In E. Buzawa & C. G. Buzawa (Eds.), *Do arrests and restraining orders work?* (pp. 214–242). Thousand Oaks, CA: Sage Publications.

Hart, B. (1993). Battered women and the criminal justice system. *American Behavioral Scientist*, 36, 624–638.

Hart, B. (1995). Coordinated community response research themes. Paper presented at the Strategic Planning Workshop on Violence Against Women, National Institute of Justice, Washington, DC.

Healey, K., Smith, C., & O'Sullivan, C. (1998). *Batterer intervention: Program approaches and criminal justice strategies*. Washington, DC: National Institute of Justice.

Heise, L. L. (1998). Violence against women: An integrated, ecological framework. *Violence Against Women, 4*, 262–290.

Jacobson, N., & Gottman, J. (1998). *When men batter women: New insights into ending abusive relationships*. New York: Simon & Schuster.

Keilitz, S., Hannaford, P., & Efkeman, H. S. (1998). The effectiveness of civil protective orders. In *Legal interventions in family violence: Research findings and policy implications* (pp. 47–49). Washington, DC: National Institute of Justice.

Martin, M. E. (1997). Double your trouble: Dual arrest in family violence. *Journal of Family Violence*, 12(2), 139–157.

Mihalic, S. W., & Elliott, D. (1997). A social learning theory model of marital violence. *Journal of Family Violence*, 12(1), 21–47.

Miller, N. (1998). *Domestic violence legislation affecting police and prosecutor responsibilities in the United States: Inferences from a 50-state review of state statutory codes* [Online]. Retrieved January 14, 2003, from **www.ilj.org/dv/vawa1.html**.

Mills, L. G. (1998). Mandatory arrest and prosecution policies for domestic violence: A critical literature review and the case for more research to test victim empowerment approaches. *Criminal Justice and Behavior*, 25, 306–319.

Murphy, C. M., Musser, P. H., & Maton, K. I. (1998). Coordinated community intervention for domestic abusers: Intervention system involvement and criminal recidivism. *Journal of Family Violence*, 13, 263–284.

O'Leary, K. D. (1987). Physical aggression between spouses: A social learning theory perspective. In V. B. Van Hasselt, R. L. Morrison, A. S. Bellack, & M. Hersen (Eds.), *Handbook of family violence* (pp. 31–55). New York: Plenum Press.

Peled, E., & Edleson, J. L. (1994). Advocacy for battered women: A national survey. *Journal of Family Violence*, 9, 285–296.

Peled, E., Eisikovits, Z., Enosh, G., & Winstok, Z. (2000). Choice and empowerment for battered women who stay: Toward a constructivist model. *Social Work*, 45, 9–25.

Pence, E. (1983). The Duluth domestic abuse intervention project. *Hamline Law Review*, 6, 247–275.

Rand, M. R. (1997). *Violence-related injuries treated in hospital emergency departments*. Washington, DC: U.S. Department of Justice.

Rebovich, D. J. (1996). Prosecution response to domestic violence: Results of a survey of large jurisdictions. In E. Buzawa & C. G. Buzawa (Eds.), *Do arrests and restraining orders work?* (pp. 176–191). Thousand Oaks, CA: Sage Publications.

Richie, B. E. (1996). *Compelled to crime: The gender entrapment of battered black women*. New York: Routledge.

Schechter, S. (1982). *Women and male violence: The visions and struggles of the battered women's movement*. Boston: South End Press.

Schmidt, J. D., & Sherman, L. W. (1996). Does arrest deter domestic violence? In E. Buzawa & C. G. Buzawa (Eds.), *Do arrests and restraining orders work?* (pp. 43–53). Thousand Oaks, CA: Sage Publications.

Sherman, L. W. (1992). The influence of criminology on criminal law: Evaluating arrests for misdemeanor domestic violence. *Journal of Criminal Law and Criminology*, 83(1), 1–45.

Stark, E. (1996). Mandatory arrest of batterees: A reply to its critics. In E. Buzawa & C. G. Buzawa (Eds.), *Do arrests and restraining orders work?* (pp. 115–149). Thousand Oaks, CA: Sage Publications.

Straus, M., Gelles, R., & Steinmetz, S. (1980). *Behind closed doors: Violence in the American family*. Garden City, NY: Doubleday/Anchor.

Syers, M., & Edleson, J. L. (1992). The combined efforts of coordinated criminal justice intervention in woman abuse. *Journal of Interpersonal Violence, 7,* 490–502.

Texas Department of Public Safety. (1998). *Crime in Texas 1998: The Texas crime report*. Austin: Texas Department of Public Safety.

Tjaden, P., & Thoennes, N. (1998). *Prevalence, incidence, and consequences of violence against women: Findings from the National Violence Against Women Survey*. Washington, DC: National Institute for Justice and Centers for Disease Control and Prevention.

Tolman, R. M., & Edleson, J. L. (1995). Intervention for men who batter: A review of research. In S. R. Stith & M. A. Straus (Eds.), *Understanding partner violence: Prevalence, causes, consequences and solutions* (pp. 262–273). Minneapolis: National Council on Family Relations.

Wallace, H. (1996). *Family violence: Legal, medical and social perspectives*. Needham Heights, MA: Allyn & Bacon.

Weisz, A. N. (1999). Legal advocacy for domestic violence survivors: The power of an informative relationship. *Families in Society 80,* 138–147.

Widom, C. S. (1989). Does violence beget violence? A critical examination of the literature. *Psychological Bulletin, 106,* 3–28.

Williams, O. J. (1998). Healing and confronting the African American male who batters. In R. Carrillo & Tello (Eds.), *Family violence and men of color: Healing the wounded male spirit* (pp. 74–94). New York: Springer.

Williams, O., & Becker, L. (1994). Domestic partner abuse treatment programs and cultural competencies: The results of a national survey. *Violence and Victims, 9,* 287–296.

Wilson, K. J. (1997). *When violence begins at home: A comprehensive guide to understanding and ending domestic abuse*. Alameda, CA: Hunter House.

Wright, E. A. (1998). Not a black and white issue. *On the Issues: The Progressive Woman's Quarterly, 7*(1), 42–47.

Yllo, K. A. (1993). Through a feminist lens: Gender, power, and violence. In R. J. Gelles & D. R. Loseke (Eds.), *Current controversies on family violence* (pp. 47–62). Newbury Park, CA: Sage Publications.

Zorza, J. (1992). The criminal law of misdemeanor domestic violence, 1970–1990. *Journal of Criminal Law and Criminology, 83*(1), 46–72.

READING 8.2

Violence Against Women: A Cross-Cultural Perspective

Source: T. Nelson, "Violence against Women: Mutiliation, Assault, and Rape: A Cross-Cultural Perspective," World Watch, July/August 1996, pp. 33–38. Copyright © 1996 by the Worldwatch Institute www.worldwatch.org. Reprinted by permission.

BY TONI NELSON

It is not a ritual that many people would expect—much less want—to witness. Yet in the fall of 1994, the television network CNN brought the practice of female genital mutilation (FGM) into living rooms around the world, by broadcasting the amputation of a young Egyptian girl's clitoris. Coinciding with the United Nations International Conference on Population and Development in Cairo, the broadcast was one of several recent events that have galvanized efforts to combat the various forms of violence that threaten women and girls throughout the world. The experience suffered by 10-year-old Nagla Hamza focused international attention on the plight of the more than 100 million women and girls in Africa victimized by FGM. In doing so, it helped spur conference delegates into formulating an official "Programme of Action" that condemned FGM and outlined measures to eliminate the practice.

Euphemistically referred to as female circumcision, FGM encompasses a variety of practices ranging from excision, the partial or total removal of the clitoris and labia minora, to infibulation, in which all the external genitals are cut away and the area is restitched, leaving only a small opening for the passage of urine and menstrual blood. Nagla's mutilation, performed by a local barber without anesthesia or sanitary precautions, was typical. Although the physical and psychological consequences of FGM are severe and often life-threatening, the practice persists due to beliefs that emerged from ancient tribal customs but which have now come to be associated with certain major religions. In Israel, for instance, FGM is practiced by Jewish migrants from the Ethiopian Palasha community; elsewhere in Africa, it is found among Christian and Islamic populations. But FGM has no inherent association with any of these religions. Although some Islamic scholars consider it an important part of that religion, FGM actually predates Islam, and neither the Qur'an, the primary source for Islamic law, nor the Hadith, collections of the Prophet Mohammed's lessons, explicitly require the practice.

Justifications for FGM vary among the societies where it occurs (FGM is practiced in 28 African nations, as well as in scattered tribal communities in the Arabian Peninsula and various parts of South Asia). But most explanations relate in some way to male interest in controlling women's emotions and sexual behavior. One of the most common explanations is the need to lessen desire so women will preserve their virginity until marriage. The late Gad-Alhaq Ali Gad-Alhaq, Sheik of Cairo's al-Azhar Islamic University at the time of the CNN broadcast, explained it this way: the purpose of FGM is "to moderate sexual desire while saving womanly pleasures in order that women may enjoy their husbands." For Mimi Ramsey, an anti-FGM activist in the United States who was mutilated in her native Ethiopia at age six, FGM is meant to reinforce the power men have over women: "the reason for my mutilation is for a man to be able to control me, to make me a good wife." Today, migrants are bringing FGM out of its traditional societies and into Europe, North America, and Australia. Approximately 2 million girls are at risk each year.

As in other countries where the practice is commonplace, Egypt's official policy on FGM has been ambiguous. Although a Ministry of Health decree in 1959 prohibited health professionals and public hospitals from performing the procedure, and national law makes it a crime to permanently mutilate anyone, clitoridectomies and other forms of FGM are not explicitly prohibited. An estimated 80 percent of Egyptian women and girls, or more than 18 million people, have undergone some form of FGM, which is often carried out by barbers in street booths on main squares of both small towns and large cities.

Before the CNN broadcast, Egyptian public opinion seemed to be turning against the practice. In early 1994, activists founded the Egyptian Task Force Against Female Genital Mutilation. Later that year, during the population conference, Population and Family Welfare Minister Maher Mahran vowed to delegates that "Egypt is going to work on the elimination of female genital mutilation." Plans were even laid for legislation that would outlaw FGM. But some members of Egypt's religious community saw the broadcast as a form of Western imperialism and used it to challenge both the secular government of Hosni Mubarak and the conference itself.

In October 1994, Sheik Gad-Alhaq ruled that FGM is a religious obligation for Muslims. The same month, Minister of Health Dr. Ali Abdel Fattah issued a decree permitting the practice in selected government hospitals. The Minister's directive came just 10 days after a committee of experts convened by him condemned FGM and denied that it had any religious justification. Fattah affirmed his personal opposition, but insisted that the decree was necessary to "save those victimized girls from being 'slaughtered' by unprofessionals."

In the wake of the Minister's decision, plans for the bill outlawing FGM were postponed. Contending that Fattah had effectively legalized the procedure, national and international nongovernmental organizations sought to reverse the decision through petition drives, public education initiatives, and lawsuits. And on October 17, 1995, Fattah reversed his decision, and the Ministry of Health once again banned FGM in public hospitals. The anti-FGM legislation, however, remains on hold.

Egypt's confused and ambivalent response to FGM mirrors in many ways the intensifying international debate on all forms of violence against women. And even though FGM itself may seem just a grotesque anomaly to people brought up in cultures where it isn't practiced, FGM is grounded in attitudes and assumptions that are, unfortunately, all too common. Throughout the world, women's inferior social status makes them vulnerable to abuse and denies them the financial and legal means necessary to improve their situations. Over the past decade, women's groups around the world have succeeded in showing how prevalent this problem is and how much violence it is causing—a major accomplishment, given the fact that the issue was not even mentioned during the first UN Women's Conference in 1975 or in the 1979 UN Convention on All Forms of Discrimination Against Women. But as the situation in Egypt demonstrates, effective policy responses remain elusive.

Violence stalks women throughout their lives, "from cradle to grave"—in the judgment of *Human Development Report 1995*, the UN's annual assessment of social and economic progress around the world. Gender-specific violence is almost a cultural constant, both emerging from and reinforcing the social relationships that give men power over women. This is most obvious in the implicit acceptance, across cultures, of domestic violence—of a man's prerogative to beat his wife. Large-scale surveys in 10 countries, including Colombia, Canada, and the United States, estimate that as many as one-third of women have been physically assaulted by an intimate male partner. More limited studies report that rates of physical abuse among some groups in Latin America, Asia, and Africa may reach 60 percent or more.

Belying the oft-cried cliché about "family values," studies have shown that the biggest threat to women is domestic violence. In 1992, the *Journal of the American Medical Association* published a study that found that women in the United States are more likely to be assaulted, injured, raped, or murdered by a current or former male partner than by all other types of attackers combined. In Canada, a 1987 study showed that 62 percent of the women murdered in that year were killed by an intimate male partner. And in India, the husband or in-laws of a newly married woman may think it justified to murder her if they consider her dowry inadequate, so that a more lucrative match can be made. One popular method is to pour kerosene on the woman and set her on fire—hence the term "bride burning." One in four deaths among women aged 16 to 24 in the urban areas of Maharashtra state (including Bombay) is attributed to "accidental burns." About 5,000 "dowry deaths" occur in India every year, according to government estimates, and some observers think the number is actually much higher. Subhadra Chaturvedi, one of India's leading attorneys, puts the death toll at a minimum of 12,000 a year.

The preference for sons, common in many cultures, can lead to violence against female infants—and even against female fetuses. In India, for example, a 1990 study of amniocentesis in a large Bombay hospital found that 95.5 percent of fetuses identified as female were aborted, compared with only a small percentage of male fetuses. (Amniocentesis involves the removal of a sample of amniotic fluid from the womb; this can be used to determine the baby's sex and the presence of certain inherited diseases.) Female infanticide is still practiced in rural areas of India; a 1992 study by Cornell University demographer Sabu George found that 58 percent of female infant deaths (19 of 33) within a 12-village region of Tamil Nadu state were due to infanticide. The problem is especially pronounced in China, where the imposition of the one-child-per-family rule has led to a precipitous decline in the number of girls: studies in 1987 and 1994 found a half-million fewer female infants in each of those years than would be expected, given the typical biological ratio of male to female births.

Women are also the primary victims of sexual crimes, which include sexual abuse, rape, and forced prostitution. Girls are the overwhelming target of child sexual assaults; in the United States, 78 percent of substantiated child sexual abuse cases involve girls. According to a 1994 World Bank study, *Violence Against Women: The Hidden Health Burden*, national surveys suggest that up to one-third of women in Norway, the United States, Canada, New Zealand, Barbados, and the Netherlands are sexually abused during childhood. Often very young children are the victims: a national study in the United States and studies in several Latin American cities indicate that 13 to 32 percent of abused girls are age 10 and under.

Rape haunts women throughout their lives, exposing them to unwanted pregnancy, disease, social stigma, and psychological trauma. In the United States, which has some of the best data on the problem, a 1993 review of rape studies suggests that between 14 and 20 percent of women will be victims of completed rapes during their lifetimes. In some cultures, a woman who has been raped is perceived as having violated the family honor, and she may be forced to marry her attacker or even killed. One study of female homicide in Alexandria, Egypt, for example, found that 47 percent of women murdered were killed by a family member following a rape.

In war, rape is often used as both a physical and psychological weapon. An investigation of recent conflicts in the former Yugoslavia, Peru, Kashmir, and Somalia by the international human rights group Human Rights Watch found that "rape of women civilians has been deployed as a tactical weapon to terrorize civilian communities or to achieve ethnic cleansing." Studies suggest that tens of thousands of Muslim and Serbian women in Bosnia have been raped during the conflict there.

A growing number of women and girls, particularly in developing countries, are being forced into prostitution. Typically, girls from poor, remote villages are purchased outright from their families or lured away with promises of jobs or false marriage proposals. They are then taken to brothels, often in other countries, and forced to work there until they pay off their "debts"—a task that becomes almost impossible as the brothel owner charges them for clothes, food, medicine, and often even their own purchase price. According to Human Rights Watch, an estimated 20,000 to 30,000 Burmese girls and women currently work in brothels in Thailand; their ranks are now expanding by as many as 10,000 new recruits each year. Some 20,000 to 50,000 Nepalese girls are working in Indian brothels. As the fear of AIDS intensifies, customers are demanding ever younger prostitutes, and the age at which girls are being forced into prostitution is dropping; the average age of the Nepalese recruits, for example, declined from 14–16 years in the 1980s, to 10–14 years by 1994.

Whether it takes the form of enforced prostitution, rape, genital mutilation, or domestic abuse, gender-based violence is doing enormous damage—both to the women who experience it, and to societies as a whole. Yet activists, health officials, and development agencies have only recently begun to quantify the problem's full costs. Currently, they are focusing on two particularly burdensome aspects of the violence: the health care costs, and the effects on economic productivity.

The most visible effects of violence are those associated with physical injuries that require medical care. FGM, for example, often causes severe health problems. Typically performed in unsterile environments by untrained midwives or barbers working without anesthesia, the procedure causes intense pain and can result in infection or death. Long-term effects include chronic pain, urine retention, abscesses, lack of sexual sensitivity, and depression. For the approximately 15 percent of mutilated women who have been infibulated, the health-related consequences are even worse. Not only must these women be cut and stitched repeatedly, on their wedding night and again with each childbirth, but sexual dysfunction and pain during intercourse are common. Infibulated women are also much more likely to have difficulties giving birth. Their labor often results, for instance, in vesico-vaginal fistulas—holes in the vaginal and rectal areas that cause continuous leakage of urine and feces. An estimated 1.5 to 2 million African women have fistulas, with some 50,000 to 100,000 new cases occurring annually. Infibulation also greatly increases the danger to the child during labor. A study of 33 infibulated women in delivery at Somalia's Benadir Hospital found that five of their babies died and 21 suffered oxygen deprivation.

Other forms of violence are taking a heavy toll as well. A 1994 national survey in Canada, for example, found that broken bones occurred in 12 percent of spousal assaults, and internal injuries and miscarriages in 10 percent. Long-term effects may be less obvious but they are often just as serious. In the United States, battered women are four to five times more likely than non-battered women to require psychiatric treatment and five times more likely to attempt suicide. And even these effects are just one part of a much broader legacy of misery. A large body of psychological literature has documented the erosion of self-esteem, of social abilities, and of mental health in general, that often follows in the wake of violence. And the problem is compounded because violence tends to be cyclical: people who are abused tend to become abusers themselves. Whether it's through such direct abuse or indirectly, through the destruction of family life, violence against women tends to spill over into the next generation as violence against children.

Only a few studies have attempted to assign an actual dollar value to gender-based violence, but their findings suggest that the problem constitutes a substantial health care burden. In the United States, a 1991 study at a major health maintenance organization (a type of group medical practice) found that women who had been raped or beaten at any point in their life-times had medical costs two-and-a-half times higher during that year than women who had not been victimized. In the state of Pennsylvania, a health insurer study estimated that violence against women cost the health care system approximately $326.6 million in 1992. And in Canada, a 1995 study of violence against women, which examined not only medical costs, but also the value of community support services and lost work, put the annual cost to the country at Cdn $1.5 billion (US $1.1 billion).

One important consequence of violence is its effect on women's productivity. In its *World Development Report 1993*, the World Bank estimated that in advanced market economies, 19 percent of the total disease burden of women aged 15 to 44—nearly one out of every five healthy days of life lost—can be linked to domestic violence or rape. (Violence against women is just as pervasive in developing countries, but because the incidence of disease is higher in those regions, it represents only 5 percent of their total disease burden.) Similarly, a 1993 study in the United States showed a correlation between violence and lower earnings. After controlling for other factors that affect income, the study found that women who have been abused earn 3 to 20 percent less each year than women who have not been abused, with the discrepancy depending on the type of sexual abuse experienced and the number of perpetrators.

Violence can also prevent women from participating in public life—a form of oppression that can cripple Third World development projects. Fear may keep women at home; for example, health workers in India have identified fear of rape as an impediment to their outreach efforts in rural sites. The general problem was acknowledged plainly in a UN report published in 1992, *Bartered Dreams: Violence Against Women as an Obstacle to Development*: "Where violence keeps a woman from participating in a development project, force is used to deprive her of earnings, or fear of sexual assault prevents her from taking a job or attending a public function, development does not occur." Development efforts aimed at reducing fertility levels may also be affected, since gender-based violence, or the threat of it, may limit women's use of contraception. According to the 1994 World Bank study, a woman's contraceptive use often depends in large part on her partner's approval.

A recurrent motive in much of this violence is an interest in preventing women from gaining autonomy outside the home. Husbands may physically prevent their wives from attending development meetings, or they may intimidate them into not seeking employment or accepting promotions at work. The World Bank study relates a chilling example of the way in which violence can be used to control women's behavior: "In a particularly gruesome example of male backlash, a female leader of the highly successful government sponsored Women's Development Programme in Rajasthan, India, was recently gang raped [in her home in front of her husband] by male community members because they disapproved of her organizing efforts against child marriage." The men succeeded in disrupting the project by instilling fear in the local organizers.

"These women are holding back a silent scream so strong it could shake the earth." That is how Dr. Nahid Toubia, Executive Director of the U.S. based anti-FGM organization RAINBO, described FGM victims when she testified at the 1993 Global Tribunal on Violations of Women's Human Rights. Yet her statement would apply just as well to the millions of women all over the world who have been victims of other forms of violence. Until recently, the problem of gender-based violence has remained largely invisible. Because the stigma attached to many forms of violence makes them difficult to discuss openly, and because violence typically occurs inside the home, accurate information on the magnitude of the problem has been extremely scarce. Governments, by claiming jurisdiction only over human rights abuses perpetrated in the public sphere by agents of the state, have reinforced this invisibility. Even human rights work has traditionally confined itself to the public sphere and largely ignored many of the abuses to which women are most vulnerable.

But today, the victims of violence are beginning to find their voices. Women's groups have won a place for "private sphere" violence on human rights agendas, and they are achieving important changes in both national laws and international conventions. The first major reform came in June 1993, at the UN Second World Conference on Human Rights in Vienna. In a drive leading up to the conference, activists collected almost half a million signatures from 124 countries on a petition insisting that the conference address gender violence. The result: for the first time, violence against women was recognized as an abuse of women's human rights, and nine paragraphs on "The equal status and human rights of women" were incorporated into the Vienna Declaration and Programme of Action.

More recently, 18 members of the Organization of American States have ratified the InterAmerican Convention on the Prevention, Punishment and Eradication of Violence Against Women. Many activists consider this convention, which went into effect on March 5, 1995, the strongest existing piece of international legislation in the field. And the Pan American Health Organization (PAHO) has become the first development agency to make a significant financial commitment to the issue. PAHO has received $4 million from Sweden, Norway, and the Netherlands, with the possibility of an additional $2.5 million from the InterAmerican Development Bank, to conduct research on violence and establish support services for women in Latin America.

National governments are also drawing up legislation to combat various forms of gender violence. A growing number of countries, including South Africa, Israel, Argentina, the Bahamas, Australia, and the United States, have all passed special domestic violence laws. Typically, these clarify the definition of domestic violence and strengthen protections

available to the victims. In September 1994, India passed its "Prenatal Diagnostic Techniques (Regulation and Prevention of Misuse) Act," which outlaws the use of prenatal testing for sex-selection. India is also developing a program to eradicate female infanticide. FGM is being banned in a growing number of countries, too. At least nine European countries now prohibit the practice, as does Australia. In the United States, a bill criminalizing FGM was passed by the Senate in May, but had yet to become law. More significant, perhaps, is the African legislation: FGM is now illegal in both Ghana and Kenya.

It is true, of course, that laws don't necessarily translate into real-life changes. But it is possible that the movement to stop FGM will yield the first solid success in the struggle to make human rights a reality for women. Over the past decade, the Inter-African Committee on Traditional Practices Affecting the Health of Women and Children, an NGO dedicated to abolishing FGM, has set up committees in 25 African countries. And in March 1995, Ghana used its anti-FGM statute to arrest the parents and circumciser of an eight-year-old girl who was rushed to the hospital with excessive bleeding. In Burkina Faso, some circumcising midwives have been convicted under more general legislation. These are modest steps, perhaps, but legal precedent can be a powerful tool for reform.

In the United States, an important precedent is currently being set by a 19-year-old woman from the nation of Togo, in west Africa. Fleeing an arranged marriage and the ritual FGM that would accompany it, Fauziya Kasinga arrived in the United States seeking asylum in December 1994. She has spent much of the time since then in prison, and her request for asylum, denied by a lower court, is at the time of writing under appeal. People are eligible for asylum in the United States if they are judged to have a reasonable fear of persecution due to their race, religion, nationality, political opinions, or membership in a social group. However, U.S. asylum law makes no explicit provision for gender-based violence. In 1993, Canada became the world's first country to make the threat of FGM grounds for granting refugee status.

Whichever way the decision on Kasinga's case goes, it will be adopted as a binding general precedent in U.S. immigration cases (barring the passage of federal legislation that reverses it). But even while her fate remains in doubt, Kasinga has already won an important moral victory. Her insistence on her right not to be mutilated—and on the moral obligation of others to shield her from violence if they can—has made the threat she faces a matter of conscience, of politics, and of policy. Given the accumulating evidence of how deeply gender-based violence infects our societies, in both the developing and the industrialized countries, we have little choice but to recognize it as the fundamental moral and economic challenge that it is.

CRITICAL THINKING

1. What was the outcome of Kasinga's case? What did she decide to do, and why? (Find out online.)
2. Cross-culturally, what forms of violence against women seem to reflect their political status?
3. What forms of violence against women seem to reflect their economic status?
4. What is being done internationally to oppose violence against women?

9

Violent Crime II

Robbery, Murder, Hate Crime, and Terrorism

9.1 INTRODUCTION: DEFINING VIOLENT CRIMES AGAINST PERSONS

This chapter on violent crime examines the crimes of robbery, murder, hate crime, and terrorism. How are these crimes defined? What is their nature and extent? How are these crimes classified into types, and what are the patterns and trends? Why do people commit these crimes? How does society respond?

A reading by James A. Fox and Jack Levin in this chapter examines the phenomenon of serial killing. Serial killing and mass murder, as portrayed in the popular HBO documentary "The Ice Man," captures attention and fascinates the public, although it is actually rare.

In particular, this chapter examines

- the nature and extent of robbery, types of robbers, robbery patterns, and reasons for committing robbery (section 9.2);
- the nature and extent of murder in the United States, including homicide trends and homicidal relationships and transactions (section 9.3);
- several important theories on the causes of murder (section 9.4);
- hate crime, including victim, offender, and incident characteristics, followed by a description of three types of offenders (section 9.5);
- various organized hate groups and responses to hate crime (section 9.6);
- terrorism, including the goals and methods of terrorists and an examination of the relationship between terrorism and hate crimes (section 9.7);
- cyberterrorism, a growing crime in the United States and the world (section 9.8).

9.2 ROBBERY

The Uniform Crime Report (UCR) defines **robbery** as the taking or attempt to take anything of value from the care, custody, or control of a person or persons by force or the threat of force or violence and/or by putting the victim in fear.[1] Although the object of robbery is to obtain money or property, the crime always involves force or its threat, and many victims suffer serious personal injury.

- A robbery occurs in the United States every minute.
- Robbery is usually perpetrated by a stranger in a highly threatening manner.
- Material reward or money is the primary goal of robbery.
- Many psychological factors motivate people to rob, including thrill seeking, control, revenge, and street justice.[2]

In an analysis of more than 14 million robbery victims, the Bureau of Justice Statistics reported that two-thirds of robbery victims had property stolen. One-third of the victims were injured, and one-quarter suffered both property loss and personal injury.[3]

Robbery accounts for almost one-third of all violent crime. How prevalent is robbery today in the United States? How is robbery different from other kinds of theft? What is the crime profile for robbery?

Robbery is the taking or attempt to take anything of value from the care, custody, or control of a person or persons by force or the threat of force or violence and/or by putting the victim in fear.

The UCR reports that robbery accounts for about 30 percent of all violent crimes in the United States. There are approximately 450,000 robberies reported annually to our nation's police departments. The National Crime Victimization Survey (NCVS), however, reports about 900,000 annual robbery victims. This indicates that a significant percentage of robberies goes unreported to the police each year.[4] As Figure 9.1 shows, the number of reported robbery offenses has declined since 1994. In 1992, the national robbery rate was 264 per 100,000 people. Today, it is about 149 per 100,000 people.[5]

Robbery rates vary depending on the time of year and the region of the country in which robberies occur. They occur in public places, commercial places, and victims' residences. Almost half of robberies involve the use of firearms. The clearance and arrest rates for robbery vary with the offender's age, gender, and race.

The UCR data from 2005 indicates:

- Nationwide in 2005, there were an estimated 417,122 robbery offenses.
- In terms of robbery trends, robbery had the largest percentage increase, 3.9 percent, in the estimated number of offenses when compared with

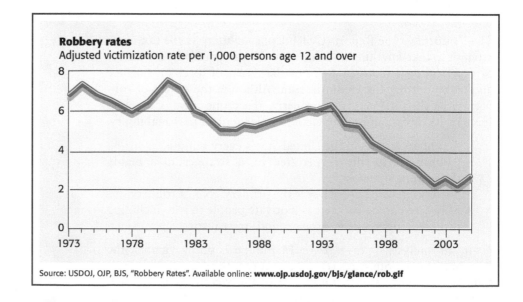

FIGURE 9.1

the 2004 estimate. The estimated number of robbery offenses declined 22.1 percent in comparison with the data from 10 years earlier (1996 and 2005).

- By location type, most robberies (44.1 percent) were committed on streets or highways.
- Firearms were used in 42.1 percent of reported robberies.
- The average dollar value of property stolen per robbery offense was $1,230. By location type, bank robbery had the highest average dollar value taken—$44,169 per offense.

A Typology of Robbers

According to criminologist John Conklin, there are four types of robbers: professional, opportunistic, addict, and alcoholic.

A typology of robbers was developed by John Conklin in his classic text, *Robbery and the Criminal Justice System* (1972). Conklin developed the following four types of robbers: the professional, the opportunist, the addict, and the alcoholic.

(1) The **professional robber** has a long-term commitment to robbery as a source of livelihood. He or she organizes and plans the robberies carefully, often in concert with other professionals. He, or they, steal large sums of money perhaps three or four times a year to support what Conklin calls a "hedonistic lifestyle." Professional robbers are committed to robbery because it is fast, direct, and quite profitable.

> A **professional robber** has a long-term commitment to robbery as a source of livelihood.

(2) The **opportunistic robber** is the most common type of robber. He or she does little planning and makes no long-term commitment to robbery. Perpetrators are usually young and steal to obtain small amounts of cash from vulnerable, accessible targets such as older people, cabdrivers, and drunks.

> An **opportunistic robber** does little planning and has no long-term commitment to robbery.

(3) The **addict robber** is dependent on drugs and steals to support his or her habit. He or she has a high level of commitment to theft, because it supplies money, but a low commitment to robbery, because of its danger. He or she does not plan the crime as much as the professional robber but is generally more cautious than the opportunistic robber. If addict robbers are not too desperate "for a fix," they will choose victims who present a minimum of risk. At times, they carry weapons. Their main goal is to obtain money quickly to support their habit.

> The **addict robber** is dependent on drugs and steals to support his or her habit.

(4) The **alcoholic robber** has no commitment to robbery as a way of life, does not plan out robberies, and steals for reasons related to excessive alcohol use. This type of robber steals when he or she is disoriented or when drinking keeps him or her from being employed and money for alcohol is needed. This type of robber usually steals from people he or she has first assaulted. Because little planning and few precautions are taken, alcoholic robbers are more frequently apprehended by the police than other types of robbers.[6]

> The **alcoholic robber** steals for reasons related to excessive alcohol use.

Robbery Patterns, Choices, and Motives

Studies of robberies reveal a wide variety of patterns, choices, and motives.

Robberies can occur in a wide variety of open areas, on streets, in parks, and in parking lots. Victims may be mugged or grabbed from behind, and their belongings, such as pocketbooks or jewelry, are stolen. Other robberies occur in stores, banks, offices, and other places where people handle money or valuables such as securities, jewelry, or electronic equipment. Robberies of banks, commercial businesses, and convenience stores have increased during the past decade.[7] Still other robberies occur in such private places as people's homes (i.e., breaking and entering, or burglary); about one-third of all robberies occur at a victim's home.[8] Less often, robberies occur after a preliminary association of short duration between the offender and victim, such as after a brief sexual encounter, at a party, or in a bar or club.[9]

Studies of robbery by Ira Sommers and Deborah R. Baskin indicate that offenders make a number of decisions as a way of minimizing risks.[10] They make strategic choices regarding targets, escape plans, and witnesses. The victim is viewed as the least predictable and least controllable threat. Therefore, according to Robert Lejeune, the robber focuses much of his or her attention on selecting the "right" victim.[11]

Robbers also make choices "according to (a) their own potency in generating a convincing threat and overcoming the victim's resistance, and (b) their perception of the vulnerability and attractiveness of the victim."[12] Dermot Walsh reports that although robbers can expect less resistance from vulnerable targets, such as young or old victims, the payoff or rewards from those targets tend to be low. Robbers who select relatively well-defined targets with high payoffs may seek to increase their firepower by acquiring weapons or accomplices.[13]

In terms of motive, robbery is typically characterized as an "instrumental" offense.[14] That is, its principal motive is to obtain money or some other desired valuable.[15] In a study of violent female offenders, Sommers and Baskin reported that

- eighty-nine percent of respondents indicated they committed robbery "for the purpose of obtaining money";
- eighty-one percent of those seeking money "wanted it for drugs";
- for 66 percent of the women interviewed, the perpetration of robbery "occurred in the course of and subsequent to a criminal career that included involvement in other offenses such as nonviolent theft or vice."[16]

According to Doug Williamson, a large proportion of robbers report that they prey on individuals who are themselves involved in illegal activities, especially low-level drug activity. The main reason for choosing criminals as victims is that they are less likely to report their victimizations to the police. Williamson states, "There is a high correlation between robberies and illicit drug activity."[17]

After reading this section, you should be able to

1. describe the nature and extent of robbery and profile robbery as a crime;
2. categorize the four different types of robbers defined by Conklin;
3. describe a robber's choices and patterns of behavior;
4. explain what motivates people to commit robbery.

9.3 MURDER

Most people know what is meant by the term *homicide,* or murder. Each day, many of us read about homicides in newspapers or watch news about homicides on TV. We may even know someone who has been murdered. The United States has the world's highest murder rate. Before examining this deadly form of violence, the term *homicide* must be carefully defined. According to *Black's*

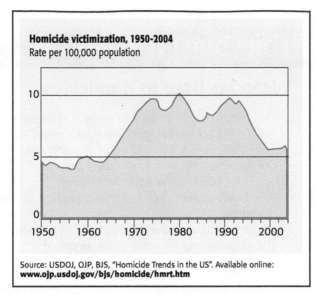

Homicide victimization, 1950–2004
Rate per 100,000 population

Source: USDOJ, OJP, BJS, "Homicide Trends in the US". Available online:
www.ojp.usdoj.gov/bjs/homicide/hmrt.htm

FIGURE 9.2

Law Dictionary, **homicide** is "the killing of one human being by the act, procurement, or omission of the other. [It is] the act of a human being . . . taking away the life of another human being." To be guilty of *criminal homicide*, a person must "purposely, knowingly, recklessly, or negligently cause the death of another human being. Criminal homicide is murder, manslaughter, or negligent homicide." **Murder** is defined as the "unlawful killing of a human being by another with malice aforethought, either expressed or implied." **Manslaughter** is the "unlawful killing of another without malice, either expressed or implied." There are two types of manslaughter, voluntary and involuntary. According to *Black's Law Dictionary*, and the *Model Penal Code*, *voluntary manslaughter* is manslaughter that is "committed voluntarily upon a sudden heat of the passions; as if, upon a sudden quarrel, two persons fight, and one of them kills the other (210.3(1)(b))."[18] *Involuntary manslaughter*, on the other hand, occurs when a "person in committing an unlawful act not felonious or tending to great bodily harm, or in committing a lawful act without proper caution or requisite skill, unguardedly or undesignedly kills another (210.3(1)(a))."[19] **Negligent homicide** is a criminal offense "committed by one whose negligence is the direct and proximate cause of another's death."[20]

In addition to these distinctions, most states divide murder into two degrees. Murder of the first degree, or **first-degree murder**, awards a more severe penalty for "all murder which shall be perpetrated by means of person, or by lying in wait, or by any other kind of willful, deliberate, and premeditated killing, or which shall be committed in the perpetration of, or attempt to perpetrate, any arson, rape, robbery, or burglary."[21] All other types of murder are deemed murder of the second degree, or **second-degree murder**. This pattern is followed by most states.[22]

According to the Uniform Crime Reports, the annual total number of murders in the United States is more than 15,000. This is down from more than 23,000 in 1980 and in 1991. As Figure 9.2 shows, the nation's homicide rate today is about 5.6 per 100,000 people.[23]

In the United States, murder rates are lowest in the northeastern states and highest in the southern states. The Northeast, with 19 percent of the nation's population, accounts for about 14 percent of murders annually. This is followed by the Midwest (23 percent of population, 21 percent of murders), the West (23 percent of population, 22 percent of murders), and the South (36 percent of population, 42 percent of murders).[24]

Homicide is the killing of one human being by the act, procurement, or omission of the other. [It is] the act of a human being . . . taking away the life of another human being.

Murder is the unlawful killing of a human being by another with malice aforethought, either expressed or implied.

Manslaughter is the unlawful killing of another without malice, either expressed or implied.

Negligent homicide is a criminal offense committed by one whose negligence is the direct and proximate cause of another's death.

First-degree murder is all murder perpetrated by means of person, or by lying in wait, or by any other kind of willful, deliberate, and premeditated killing, or committed in the perpetration of, or attempt to perpetrate, any arson, rape, robbery, or burglary.

Second-degree murder is all types of murder other than first-degree murder.

FOR YOUR INFORMATION

Weapons Used in Homicides

- In 2001, nearly 70 percent of homicides involved the use of a firearm.
- Within the firearm category, handguns were used in 77.9 percent of homicides, shotguns were used in 5.7 percent, and rifles in 4.5 percent.
- Knives or cutting instruments were employed in 14.3 percent of homicides for which the weapon was known.
- Personal weapons such as hands, fists, or feet were used in 7.4 percent of murders.
- Blunt objects were the weapon used in 5.3 percent of murders.
- Other dangerous weapons (such as poison or explosives) accounted for the remainder.

Source: Federal Bureau of Investigation, Uniform Crime Reports, *Crime in the United States, 2001*, "Section II—Crime Index Offenses Reported," Washington, DC: Government Printing Office, April 1, 2003, p. 27.

Characteristics of Murderers and Their Victims

Murder victims and offenders vary by gender, age, race, and other characteristics.

The following section reports some of the major findings on homicide data and trends.[25]

GENDER

- Males are most often the victims and the perpetrators in homicides. Homicide victims are most often male (77 percent) and adult (90 percent).
- Males are ten times more likely than females to commit murder.
- Both male and female offenders are more likely to target male than female victims.

RACE

- Fifty percent of murder victims are white, and 48 percent are black.
- Blacks are six times more likely to be homicide victims than whites and seven times more likely than whites to commit homicides.
- Eighty-six percent of white murder victims are killed by whites, and 94 percent of black victims are killed by blacks.
- Among homicides in which the victim is killed by an acquaintance, one in ten is interracial, whereas when the killer is a stranger, three in ten are interracial.

AGE

- In 2000, persons age 18–24 were murdered at a rate higher than all other age categories, the highest rates since 1986. Prior to 1986, persons age 25–34 had the highest rate.
- Since 1991, murder rates of persons age 25–34 have decreased to the current rate—the lowest rate recorded for this age group.

- Homicide rates for those age 35–49, 50–64, and 65 or older have declined steadily since 1976.
- The most dramatic change in homicide rates occurred for those age 18–24, which increased to the peak rate of twenty-four murders per 100,000 persons in the early 1990s. Since 1995, murder rates of persons in this age group declined steadily.
- Homicide rates for persons age 12–17 peaked in the early 1990s. Since 1996, homicide rates for this age group have fallen and are currently at levels that were seen in the 1970s.
- The number of *infanticides* (murders of victims under age five) has grown roughly in proportion to the number of young children in the population, with most perpetrators being a parent.
- The number of *eldercides* (homicides of persons age 65 and over) has been decreasing. Yet, among all age groups, the elderly have the highest percentage of homicides that occur during the commission of a felony.

Factors of age, race, and gender often combine to form patterns of crime and criminal victimization. For example, there were dramatic increases in both homicide victimization and offending rates among young black males in the late 1980s and 1990s before recent declines in both categories. From 1999 to 2000, older teens and young adults and older adults from all race and gender groups were no longer experiencing double-digit declines in homicide rates. The rates for older black males and older teen and young adult black females increased slightly. The offending rates displayed similar patterns. About 90 percent of murderers are male, and more than 92 percent are over the age of eighteen. Fifty percent of murder offenders are black, and 47 percent are white.[26]

A majority of homicide victims know their assailants. As Figure 9.3 shows, of homicides committed in 2001, about 42.3 percent of the victims knew their assailants (29.2 percent were acquainted with their killers and 13.1 percent were related to them). Another 13.1 percent of murder victims were known to have been murdered by a stranger. About one-third of female victims were slain by a husband or boyfriend. Male homicide victims were killed by a wife or girlfriend in about 3 percent of all murders. For 44.6 percent of the victims, the victim–offender relationship was unknown.[27]

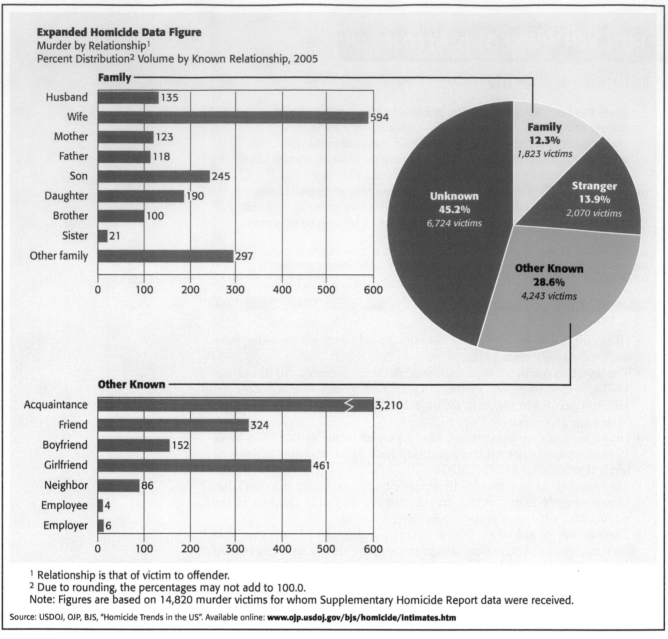

Expanded Homicide Data Figure
Murder by Relationship[1]
Percent Distribution[2] Volume by Known Relationship, 2005

Family

Husband	135
Wife	594
Mother	123
Father	118
Son	245
Daughter	190
Brother	100
Sister	21
Other family	297

Pie chart:
- Unknown 45.2% — 6,724 victims
- Family 12.3% — 1,823 victims
- Stranger 13.9% — 2,070 victims
- Other Known 28.6% — 4,243 victims

Other Known

Acquaintance	3,210
Friend	324
Boyfriend	152
Girlfriend	461
Neighbor	86
Employee	4
Employer	6

[1] Relationship is that of victim to offender.
[2] Due to rounding, the percentages may not add to 100.0.
Note: Figures are based on 14,820 murder victims for whom Supplementary Homicide Report data were received.

Source: USDOJ, OJP, BJS, "Homicide Trends in the US". Available online: **www.ojp.usdoj.gov/bjs/homicide/intimates.htm**

FIGURE 9.3 Expanded Homicide Data Figure

Figures 9.4 and 9.5 illustrate recent trends in the homicides of intimates by race and gender.

Some criminologists believe the figures on stranger murders in Figure 9.3 are understated. Marc Riedel reports that the true stranger homicide rate is in the 14 to 29 percent range. He also believes that the impact of stranger murder on the quality of urban living and the fear of crime it causes is much greater than statistics suggest.[28]

In recent years, attention has been drawn to children who murder their parents, or commit *parricide*. Years ago, children who committed parricide were considered evil or mentally ill. Today, some people are changing their views, especially if the children have been victims of serious child abuse.

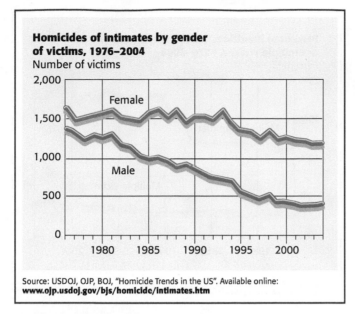

FIGURE 9.4 Homicides of Intimates by Gender of Victims, 1976–2004

According to the National Center for Prevention of Child Abuse, each year, more than 2.7 million children are physically, mentally, or sexually assaulted by their parents. Some of these children murder their parents. Parricide accounts for about 2 percent of all U.S. homicides (about three hundred annually). Most involve teens who kill abusive parents.[29]

According to the Bureau of Justice Statistics (BJS), few homicides involve multiple offenders and fewer involve multiple victims. Figure 9.6 illustrates the following data:

- Homicides are more likely to involve multiple offenders than multiple victims.
- The percentage of homicides involving multiple offenders rose dramatically in the late 1980s and early 1990s, increasing from 10 percent in 1976 to 18 percent in 2000.
- The percentage of homicides involving multiple victims increased gradually during the last two decades from just under 3 percent of all homicides in 1976 to 4.1 percent in 2000.[30]

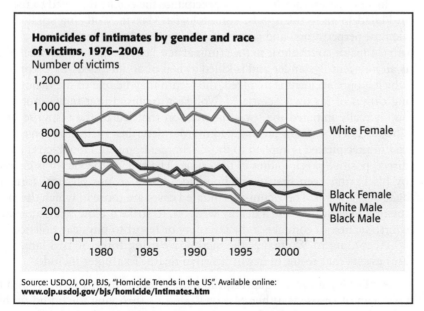

FIGURE 9.5 Homicides of Intimates by Gender and Race of Victims, 1976–2004

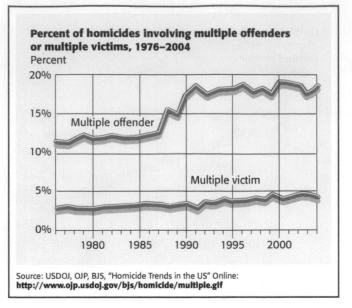

Percent of homicides involving multiple offenders or multiple victims, 1976–2004

FIGURE 9.6 Percent of Homicides Involving Multiple Offenders of Multiple Victims, 1976–2004

Source: USDOJ, OJP, BJS, "Homicide Trends in the US" Online:
http://www.ojp.usdoj.gov/bjs/homicide/multiple.gif

Circumstances That Lead to Murder

Felonious activities, arguments, and intoxication or narcosis are among the situations that lead to murder; some murders are victim-precipitated, whereas others are without apparent motive.

According to the UCR, there are many conditions and circumstances that lead to murder.

- Seventeen percent of murders occurred as a result of felonious activities such as robbery or arson in 2001.
- Arguments resulted in almost 28 percent of murders.
- Three percent of murders were committed during brawls while offenders were under the influence of alcohol or narcotics.[31]

Examples of murder patterns are victim-precipitated murder, homicide without apparent motive, gang murder, and cult murder.

In some cases, murder victims precipitate the events that lead to their demise. In Philadelphia in the 1950s, criminologist Marvin Wolfgang studied homicide victims, perpetrators, and situations. He reported that, in murders, the victim is often a major contributor to the criminal act: "except in cases in which the victim is an innocent bystander and is killed in lieu of an intended victim, or in cases in which a pure accident is involved, the victim may be one of the major precipitating causes of his own demise."[32] Wolfgang reported that many murder victims had actually initiated the social interaction that led to the response of murder. The category of **victim-precipitated murder** describes such situations: "The term victim-precipitated is applied to those criminal homicides in which the victim is a direct, positive precipitation in the crime. The role of the victim is characterized by his having been first in the homicide drama to use physical force directed against the slayer. The victim-precipitated cases are those in which the victim was the first to show and use a deadly weapon, to strike a blow in an altercation—in short, the first to commence the interplay or resort to physical violence."[33]

According to Wolfgang, the victim, by using force or bad language, initiates events that result in her or his own death. Examples include:

- "During a lovers' quarrel, the male (victim) hit his mistress and threw a can of kerosene at her. She retaliated by throwing the liquid on him, and then tossed a lighted match in his direction. He died from burns.

Victim-precipitated murder is applied to criminal homicides in which the victim contributes directly to precipitating the crime.

- A drunken husband, beating his wife in their kitchen, gave her a butcher knife and dared her to use it on him. She claimed that, if he should strike her once more, she would use the knife, whereupon he slapped her in the face and she fatally stabbed him.”[34]

In the conclusion of his research on homicide victims, Wolfgang reported that in many cases the victim had most of the characteristics of an offender. In some cases, “two potential offenders come together in a homicidal situation and it is probably often only chance which results in one becoming a victim and the other an offender.” He also challenged the stereotypes many of us have of victims: “Connotations of a victim as a weak and passive individual, seeking to withdraw from an assaultive situation, and of an offender as a brutal, strong, and overly aggressive person seeking out his victim, are not always correct. Societal attitudes are generally positive toward the victim and negative toward the offender, who is often feared as a violent and dangerous threat to others when not exonerated. However, data in the present study—especially that of previous arrest records—mitigate, destroy, or reverse these connotations of victim-offender roles in one out of every four criminal homicides.”[35]

Homicide without apparent motive is another murder pattern. In the great majority of murders, the perpetrator has a motive, or reason, for killing a person. Researchers such as William R. Holcomb and Anasserile E. Daniel, however, indicate that, in as many as one-quarter of all homicides, the motive remains unclear. In many respects, murderers who do not have apparent motives have similar profiles to those who do have motives, but, according to Holcomb and Daniel, they are more likely to have “no history of alcohol abuse; a recent release from prison; claims of amnesia for the crime; denial of the crime; and a tendency to exhibit psychotic behavior following the crime and to be assessed not guilty of the crime due to mental illness.”[36]

Gang and cult murders have different patterns. In recent years, gang and cult killings have become more frequent and have received greater publicity in the media. **Gang murder** involves gang members who, as part of their group organization and activities, include the murder of rival gang members, people who “do not cooperate” in the trafficking of drugs, and enemies or innocent strangers—including children—who get caught in the crossfire (e.g., “drive-by” shootings).[37] **Cult murder** occurs when members of a cult—a religious or satanic cult, for example—kill strangers (as a show of loyalty or because of a perceived threat) or other cult members (who deviate from the cult’s teachings).[38] One cult killing involved a young college student who was murdered as part of a black-magic rite—*palo mayombe*—practiced by a Mexican drug ring to ward off bullets and criminal prosecution by the authorities.[39]

Gang murder involves gang members who, as part of their group organization and activities, murder others.

Cult murder occurs when members of a cult kill strangers or other cult members.

Serial and Mass Murder

Serial and mass murders involve multiple victims and can be a grave threat to public safety.

In recent years, the media have given more and more attention to serial and mass murder. **Serial murder** involves the killing of several victims over a period of time—from days or weeks to months or years. **Mass murder** involves the killing of several victims in one event. A well-known serial killer was the law student Theodore “Ted” Bundy, who killed between nineteen and thirty-six young women over a period of many months, in Florida and the Northwest. A well-known mass murderer was James Huberty, who one day in 1984 went into a McDonald’s restaurant in California and shot forty men, women, and children, killing twenty-one.

Serial murder involves the killing of several victims over a period of time.

Mass murder involves the killing of several victims in one event.

READING ABSTRACT

Mass Murder

BY JAMES A. FOX AND JACK LEVIN

The authors of this reading focus on six factors that contribute to the phenomenon of mass murder: the killer's frustration, externalization of responsibility, and fears of contagion; a catastrophic loss; social isolation; and possession of a weapon of mass destruction.

See reading on page 270.

The FBI estimates that, at any time, there may be from thirty-five to one hundred serial killers operating in the United States. These killings account for about 1 to 2 percent of known murders annually. Jack Levin and James Allan Fox propose three types of serial killers, based on their motivations to kill:

- "*Profit-driven* serial killers kill their victims in connection with other crimes, such as robbery. Profit-driven serial killers believe that killing is a requirement for their survival—either to keep their victims from identifying them or to keep from being apprehended and prosecuted.
- *Mission-oriented* serial killers are fanatically engaged in a social, political, or religious quest to rid the society of evil, deviance, and immorality. They target 'unacceptable' people, such as prostitutes, drug abusers, the homeless, or homosexuals.
- *Thrill-oriented* serial killers kill for fun and derive great satisfaction over controlling and torturing their victims."[40]

Serial killers come from all ethnic, racial, and religious groups and from all age categories. Much of the time, however, they are white males in their late twenties and early thirties.

Explaining Criminal Homicide

There are subcultural, structural, social disintegration–oriented, and learning violence-oriented explanations for criminal homicide.

There are many reasons why one person murders another person, and several of the theories discussed in earlier chapters can help us understand those reasons. Four types of theories about the causes of this violent crime are presented here: the subculture of violence, structural adaptation, social disintegration, and learning violence.

Subculture of violence theories focus on the approval of violence in a subculture's value system and social norms. Social norms include guidelines indicating the socially appropriate times for the use of violence. As discussed in Chapter 7, Clifford Shaw and Henry McKay assumed that criminal attitudes, values, and traditions develop in socially disorganized areas or communities and are self-perpetuating.[41] These ideas have been more recently expressed in the subcultural approach to violent behavior. Marvin Wolfgang and Franco Ferracuti argue that such behavior, as manifested in such criminal acts as assault and homicide, is part of a more general subculture of values and norms

Subculture of violence theories focus on the approval of violence, and the use of violence to resolve interpersonal conflicts, in a subculture's value system and social norms.

that legitimate the use of violence. Certain societal subcultures, in other words, are prone to violence.[42] The relationship between a violent cultural orientation and murder is summarized by Kirk R. Williams and Robert L. Flewelling in their study of homicide rates: "Antagonistic interactions (i.e., intense interpersonal conflicts) are more accepted among some groups or within some regions of society. People in such groups or regions are more likely to endorse the use of force in settling quarrels or in simply 'getting one's way.' Consequently, the more a violent cultural orientation penetrates social relationships, the greater the intensity of interpersonal conflicts and the greater the likelihood that some of those conflicts will result in criminal homicide."[43]

Several theorists have applied this idea to explain higher homicide rates among certain groups and in certain regions of the country. For instance, some believe that, because of historical conditions, "Southerners have a cultural orientation that encourages the use of violence to resolve interpersonal conflicts."[44] This "regional culture of violence" perspective has been used to explain the persistence of high homicide rates in the South and among blacks.[45]

Other researchers have questioned the subculture of violence approach to regional and racial homicide patterns and have expressed doubt as to whether variations in assault and homicide rates are a "consequence of differential exposure to such cultures."[46] These criminologists view violence as an "adaptive response to the structural conditions under which people live . . . variation in the homicide rate is a function of other social and economic factors that vary by race or region in the United States." In their **structural adaptation theories**, these researchers emphasize the factors of inequality and poverty (measures of economic deprivation) and divorce and mobility (indicators of social disintegration).[47]

Social disintegration is often cited as a factor in violent crime. For example, Shaw and McKay reported that deterioration of community integration can weaken institutional as well as informal types of social control, which in turn increases the likelihood of criminal behavior in the community.[48] Robert D. Crutchfield and associates applied this idea to homicide: "An integrated social system provides (1) a high degree of consensus in norms, values, and goals; (2) cohesiveness, or social solidarity; and (3) a sense of belonging or 'we feeling' among persons living in the community in question."[49] Williams and Flewelling concur with this view, stating that "factors which impede the maintenance of an integrated social system create a social context conducive to homicide."[50]

A fourth type of explanation emphasizes childhood socialization, or **learning violence**. This approach focuses on the idea that children learn, even into adulthood, violent or aggressive behavior as they observe and imitate role models. These role models are provided by family members, friends, neighbors, and actors on TV and in films.[51] Moreover, studies have reported a high level of serious abuse among children who have committed murder.[52] There have been many cases of children who were violently or sexually abused by their parents later killing them.[53]

Other explanations for homicide, as discussed in Chapters 6 and 7, include biochemical factors, such as those produced by environmental conditions or diet. Neurophysiological conditions such as brain tumors—as in the case of Charles Whitman, who killed over a dozen people at the University of Texas—can also be a major factor.[54] Some homicides can be explained only by serious personality or mental disorders, as illustrated so well by the serial killer Hannibal "the Cannibal" Lecter, played by Anthony Hopkins in the 1991 film *Silence of the Lambs*. Other homicides can best be attributed to environmental and psychological stressors that are increasingly more common in the lives of many Americans, such as anger, unemployment, family stress, anxiety, poverty,

Structural adaptation theories view violence as an adaptive response to the social-structural conditions under which people live.

Social disintegration theories explain violent crime as a product of the deterioration of community integration.

Learning violence theory stresses the idea that violent behavior is learned from the family and society.

agitation, homelessness, work stress, insecurity, drug and alcohol abuse, marital problems, and economic stress. These and other factors can combine in an individual's life at a particular time, causing the person to become violent against others.

School Violence and School Shootings

Violence and crime are major problems among the youth and in our nation's schools.

Crimes of violence are heavily concentrated among young people in the United States. This behavior not only occurs in neighborhoods and communities but also is brought into schools. Violence and crime are a problem, not only in high schools and junior high schools but also in elementary schools and colleges. One report on *school violence* and crime states: "Destructive behaviors and aggressive attitudes come with troubled children into classrooms. Confrontations with peers, drug deals, or parental conflicts may originate in homes or on the streets, but too often reach unhappy resolutions during the school day. Debilitating poverty and complicated family relationships that result in little parenting, alienation, and anger serve as kindling for a fire that burns within. . . . Such fundamental breakdowns of society that contribute to violence permeate schools and must be dealt with daily by educational personnel. As violence has escalated in the larger society, it has spilled over into the schools as well."[55]

Combating crime and violence in schools has been difficult. Specific safety initiatives developed in public schools have included violence-prevention programs, collaborative efforts among schools and communities, conflict resolution, peer counseling, administrative and instructional initiatives, and school violence-prevention curricula. Attempts to decrease weapons in schools have ranged from the use of metal detectors at school entrances to open cubbyholes instead of lockers. In order to cope with such school problems as delinquency, crime, gangs, weapons, violence, drug trafficking and abuse, vandalism, schoolyard bullying, and crisis management, a "School Safety Leadership Curriculum"—a model for the development of a school violence-prevention curriculum—has been developed to train teachers at Pepperdine University's Graduate School of Education and Psychology.[56]

The federal response to violence in America's schools has come primarily from the Goals 2000: Educate America Act and the Safe Schools Act of 1994. The Goals 2000: Educate America Act is a set of nationwide educational standards that attempts to create a comprehensive approach to education that "will improve learning at every level—from early childhood to adulthood," according to the U.S. secretary of education.[57] Part of the Goals 2000 Act is the *Safe Schools Act*. This act authorizes the U.S. education secretary to award grants to our nation's school districts to help reduce violence in schools. Grants are to be used for

- "implementing violence-prevention efforts that include the training of school personnel;
- coordinating violence-prevention efforts with related community efforts;
- counseling victims and witnesses of school violence and crime;
- acquiring metal detectors, hiring security personnel, and developing safe zones of passage to school (not more than 5 percent of grant funds may be used for these activities)."[58]

In 1995, the Safe Schools Act was combined with the Drug-Free Schools and Community Act to encourage a comprehensive effort to eliminate drugs

In the twenty-first century, keeping schools, students, and teachers safe is a challenge. Although school shootings are very rare, violent and criminal behavior may be common, especially in large urban public schools. Anticrime and antidrug measures increasingly involve police raids and weapons inspections in the schools, in addition to special curricula. Some critics say that students' rights to privacy should be balanced against the need for public safety. What do you think?

and violence in schools.[59] School administrators have been criticized for failing to prevent violence and shootings. Community boards of education and state legislators have also been criticized for not passing sufficient procedures and laws to deal with school violence and crime. With each outbreak of violence and murder, there are pressures for better school security and weapon controls. The media give the average American the impression that there is an epidemic of school violence. Statistics, however, indicate that there is no such epidemic. In fact, there has been no significant increase in school violence over the past thirty years, according to some researchers.[60]

After reading this section, you should be able to

1. define criminal homicide and describe the extent of homicide in the United States;
2. list characteristics of and relationships between murder offenders and victims;
3. identify types of murder and circumstances that lead to murder;
4. analyze factors that contribute to multiple, serial, and mass murder;
5. summarize four prominent theories that attempt to explain homicide;
6. describe school violence in the United States.

9.4 HATE CRIME

The Community Relations Service of the U.S. Department of Justice defines *hate crime* as "the violence of intolerance and bigotry, intended to hurt and intimidate someone because of [his or her] race, ethnicity, national origin, religion, sexual orientation, or disability."[61] In other words, hate crimes—or bias crimes, as they are sometimes called—are criminal offenses that are motivated by an offender's bias against a race, religion, sexual orientation, or ethnicity.

The FBI reports that about 10,000 hate crime incidents are reported annually to law enforcement agencies nationwide. Criminal incidents may involve more than one offense, victim, and/or offender. A breakdown of more than 12,000 victims and more than 9,000 offenders reflects that about two-thirds of hate crimes are against persons and one-third are against property.[62]

Examples of crimes that were motivated by hatred and bigotry include:

- "In Springfield, Missouri, a black male in the company of a white female was stabbed at a local Denny's restaurant by a group of white males.
- Near San Diego, California, elderly immigrant workers were attacked by white youths. The body of a Latino immigrant youth was also discovered in the same vicinity.
- In Modesto, California, an interracial couple reported a firebomb thrown through their bedroom window.
- In Duxbury, Vermont, an interracial family reported harassment of their children at a local school.
- A Jewish synagogue was vandalized by four Arab Americans in the Bronx, New York."[63]
- After the 9/11 terrorist attacks on the World Trade Center in New York City and the Pentagon in Washington, DC, hate crimes against Arab Americans proliferated across the nation.

Of all crimes, hate crimes

- "are most likely to create or exacerbate tensions;
- can trigger larger community-wide racial conflict, civil disturbances, and even riots;
- put cities and towns at risk of serious social and economic consequences."[64]

To create fear in their victims, hate crime offenders use physical violence, verbal threats, weapons and explosives, and arson. The Community Relations Service reports that some hate crime offenders commit their crimes in concert with their peers as a "thrill," while under the influence of drugs or alcohol, as a reaction against a perceived threat or to preserve their "turf," or out of resentment over the growing economic power of a particular racial or ethnic group. Their behaviors instill feelings of alienation, helplessness, suspicion, and fear, which leaves hate crime victims vulnerable to further attacks.[65]

Hate Crime Victim, Offender, and Incident Characteristics

Hate crimes tend to have a unique profile for victims, offenders, and incidents, compared to other violent crimes.

Are hate crimes motivated more by race, religion, ethnicity, or sexual orientation? Which groups are primarily targeted by religious and racial hatred? What are the ages of victims and offenders? These and other questions are

Although the majority of hate crime incidents are motivated by race, violent crimes relating to the sexual orientation and reproductive rights of individuals, many motivated by religious hatred, often are just as sensational. Examples include cases of predatory murder of homosexuals, the bombing of abortion clinics, and the assassination of doctors who perform abortions. How do criminologists classify this type of hate crime?

answered by data gathered in the FBI's National Incident-Based Reporting System (NIBRS). The following facts are from a 2001 report evaluating a three-year period of hate crimes in the United States:

- In 60 percent of hate crime incidents, the most serious offense was a violent crime, most commonly intimidation or simple assault. (Intimidation is defined as verbal or related threats of bodily harm.)
- In nearly four out of ten incidents, the most serious hate crime was a property offense. Seventy-three percent of these involved damage, destruction, or vandalism of property.
- Sixty-one percent of hate crime incidents were motivated by race, 14 percent by religion, 13 percent by sexual orientation, 11 percent by ethnicity, and 1 percent by victim disability.
- The majority of incidents motivated by race, ethnicity, sexual orientation, or disability involved a violent offense, whereas two-thirds of incidents motivated by religion involved a property offense, most commonly vandalism.
- Of incidents motivated by hatred of a religion, 41 percent targeted Jewish victims and 31 percent were directed at other unspecified religious groups.
- Racially motivated hate crimes most frequently targeted blacks: six in ten racially biased incidents targeted blacks, and three in ten targeted whites.
- Younger offenders were responsible for most hate crimes: 31 percent of violent offenders and 46 percent of property offenders were under age eighteen.
- Thirty-two percent of hate crimes occurred in a residence, 28 percent in an open space, 19 percent in a retail/commercial establishment or public building, 12 percent at a school or college, and 3 percent at a church, synagogue, or temple.[66]

Types of Hate Crime Offenders

Criminologists classify hate crime offenders as thrill-seeking, reactive, or mission types.

Researchers have attempted to explain the reasons behind hate crime in the United States. What motivates this kind of crime, and what types of people commit hate crimes? According to Levine and McDermitt, hate or bias offenders can be classified into thrill-seeking, reactive, and mission types.

Thrill-seeking offenders are groups of teenagers who go outside their "turf" and spontaneously vandalize property or attack members of groups they consider to be inferior to them (as well as vulnerable). These offenders are not typically associated with a hate group, and their manifested hatred of the victim is superficial. Such offenders may often be deterred from repeating the crimes if the community responds with a strong condemnation of their actions.

Reactive offenders have a sense of entitlement with regard to their rights and privileges that does not extend to their victims. They victimize individuals or groups of individuals on their own "turf" whom they consider to be a threat to their way of life, community, place of work, or privilege and then apply the rationale that their aggression is a justifiable defensive action. Rarely are they affiliated with an organized hate group, although they may approach such a group for assistance in mitigating the perceived threat. If the perceived threat subsides, the criminal behavior generally subsides.

Mission offenders are often psychotic and suffer from mental illnesses that cause them to hallucinate and impair their ability to reason. They typically perceive their victim groups as evil or subhuman, believe that they have been empowered by a higher force to rid the world of evil, and feel intense paranoia and a sense of urgency that they carry out their mission. They generally operate alone, committing crimes that are violent in nature and that may be carried out indiscriminately against any member of the target group in the community.[67]

A fourth type of offender is the member of an organized hate group. As the following section suggests, there are many self-legitimating organized hate groups in the United States, and many of these groups have active web sites.

Organized Hate/Bias Groups

In the United States, hate/bias groups have recently escalated their attacks on minorities.

"Hate or bias groups typically develop during a period of intense immigration, such as the 1920s; periods when disenfranchised groups try to increase their political and economic power, such as the civil rights movement; and periods of economic instability during which people seek scapegoats to blame for high unemployment, such as the recession of the late 1980s. Although hate/bias groups have, at times, been powerful forces in American political life—generally through violence and intimidation—they have a tendency to fragment because of internal dissension. Explicitly racist, traditional white supremacist groups consider all people of color to be subhuman (although homophobia has been added to their agenda). They blame the federal government, communism, and international conspiracies for the nation's problems.

"Although hate/bias crimes have predominately been directed at African Americans, hate/bias crimes *committed* by African Americans have been 'escalating at an alarming rate,' according to Klanwatch, a project of the Southern Poverty Law Center. From 1991 to the end of 1993, 46 percent of all racially motivated homicides tracked by Klanwatch were committed by African Americans on white, Asian, or Hispanic victims. Statistics that would demonstrate that African American hate/bias crime offenders operate in organized groups like their Caucasian counterparts are not available; however, it is clear that in the incident-provoked Los Angeles riots of 1992 and the attacks on Hasidic Jews in Crown Heights, Brooklyn, racially motivated groups were responsible for the violent attacks on Caucasians and other minorities.

"In 1995, it was estimated that no fewer than 20,000 and possibly as many as 50,000 members of white supremacist groups in the United States who fell into the overlapping categories of Ku Klux Klan groups, neo-Nazi groups, Christian-identity groups, and skinheads. Among the white teenagers and young adults called 'skinheads,' Wooden found that they could be divided into two groups: racist skinheads, who were considered bullies in grammar school, were abused as children, and favored violence in the lyrics of their music; and teenage Satanists, who were products of strict religious upbringing. Only 15 percent of bias crimes are committed by organized hate groups, and most of them can be attributed to skinheads who use self-identity tactics such as their fists, boots, bats, and knives. Although their attacks appear to be spontaneous, law enforcement agencies have recently implicated skinheads in organized violence involving firearms and bombs against selected targets."[68]

Responses to Hate Crime

There are many anti–hate crime laws and programs to combat hate crime in the United States.

To combat hate crime in the United States, Congress has enacted legislation that has formed, and will continue to form, the future of hate crime initiatives in addition to preventive measures. Anti–hate crime laws and programs include:

- **The Hate Crime Statistics Act of 1990.** This act requires the U.S. Department of Justice to collect data on hate crimes.
- **The Violent Crime Control and Law Enforcement Act of 1994.** This act provides for longer sentences when the offense is determined to be a hate crime.
- **The Church Arson Prevention Act of 1996.** This act created the National Church Arson Task Force to oversee the investigation and prosecution of arson at houses of worship.
- **The Hate Crimes Prevention Act of 1999.** This act prohibits persons from interfering with an individual's federal right (e.g., voting or employment) by violence or threat of violence due to his or her race, color, religion, or national origin.[69]

The U.S. Congress and the U.S. Department of Justice have taken additional steps to combat hate crimes. The 1992 Juvenile Justice and Delinquency Prevention Act required that each state's juvenile delinquency prevention plan include measures to combat hate crimes.

The act also required the U.S. Department of Justice, Office of Juvenile Justice and Delinquency Prevention (OJJDP) to conduct a national assessment of youth that commit hate crimes. The resulting Juvenile Hate Crime Study of 1993 found that only six states and seven cities had collected data specifying the age of hate crime offenders. On the basis of this data, the Bureau of Justice Statistics nevertheless estimated that 17 to 26 percent of all recorded hate crime could be attributed to juveniles.[70]

The OJJDP also supported the development of a school-based curriculum for dealing with the problem; *Healing the Hate: A National Crime Prevention Curriculum for Middle Schools* was released in 1997. Other measures included the Violence Against Women Act of 1994, which allowed victims of gender-based crimes to sue the perpetrator in either federal or state court, and the Hate Crime Sentencing Act, which increased penalties for perpetrators of hate crimes.[71]

In addition to the major legislative and public policy initiatives at the federal level, the great majority of states have enacted hate crime laws. Many of these laws were based on models developed by the Anti-Defamation League. Most states now have statutes that mandate the collection of hate crime data. In addition, the National Victim Assistance Academy (NVAA) reports that dozens of law enforcement agencies across the nation promulgated new policies and procedures addressing hate/bias crimes. Many of these were based on model policies developed by the International Association of Chiefs of Police and The National Organization of Black Law Enforcement Executives.

The act also required the U.S. Department of Justice, Office of Juvenile Justice and Delinquency Prevention (OJJDP) to conduct a national assessment of youth that commit hate/bias crimes. As a result, OJJDP funded a national study in 1993 entitled the *Juvenile Hate Crime Study*. The study found that at that time, only six states and seven major cities within those states collected offense data that specified the age of hate/bias crime offenders. However, from the data collected, BJS estimated that 17 to 26 percent of all hate/bias crime incidents recorded by law enforcement could be attributed to juveniles.[72]

According to the NVAA, "The Bureau of Justice Assistance (BJA) of the U.S. Department of Justice (DOJ) has developed four pilot programs to enhance the ability of law enforcement and prosecutorial agencies to recognize, respond to, investigate, prosecute, and prevent hate crimes. Each program includes material to assist in the development of victim sensitive hate crime scene response, and victims' assistance and support throughout the criminal justice process."[73]

The Community Relations Service (CRS), a division of the DOJ, was established to combat hate crimes. The CRS helps local and state officials resolve and prevent hate crimes, racial and ethnic conflict, and violent and civil disorders. The CRS also helps officials and community residents develop locally defined resolutions when communities are threatened by conflict and violence. The CRS offers the following services:

- "Mediation and conciliation to help communities resolve tensions and conflicts arising from hate crimes
- Technical assistance to assist officials and community leaders in developing and implementing policies, practices, and procedures to respond to hate crimes and obtain community support
- Training to teach police and residents how to recognize hate crime, gain community support, and identify victims of and witnesses to hate crime
- Public education and awareness to conduct hate crime prevention and education programs in schools, colleges, and the community
- School-based conflict resolution and prevention programs."[74]

After reading this section, you should be able to

1. define hate crime and list five of its characteristics;
2. profile types of hate crime offenders and victims;
3. give examples of federal and state responses to hate crimes in America.

9.5 TERRORISM

Interpol, one of the world's preeminent international police organizations, defines **terrorism** as the "premeditated use or threatened use of violence by an individual or group in order to gain a social or political objective."[75] The FBI defines terrorism as the "unlawful use of force or violence against persons or property to intimidate or coerce a government, the civilian population, or any segment thereof, in furtherance of political or social objectives."[76]

Terrorism has been used by various individuals and by terrorist groups to promote an ideological position, to publicize a cause, to rebel against a government, or to achieve religious and/or political goals. Terrorists use various methods to achieve their ends or goals, such as hotel and airport bombings, skyjacking and using planes as bombs, armed attacks and assassinations, and kidnapping and hostage taking.

Two types of terrorism are domestic and transnational. **Domestic terrorism** involves attacks that originate and end within the same country. An example of domestic terrorism is the 1995 Oklahoma City bombing of a federal office building, which injured more than 200 people and killed 168. *Transnational terrorism* involves attacks that originate in one country but take place in another. Examples of transnational terrorism are the two attacks on New York's World Trade Center (in 1993 and 2001), the attack on the Pentagon (2001), and the bombing of the USS *Cole* (2000). Transnational terrorists may live in one country and strike in another, as occurred in 1988 when Libyan terrorists downed Pan American Flight 103 over Lockerbie, Scotland. Or, terrorists may be born and socialized in one nation and then move to another nation in which they commit terrorist acts, such as those that occurred in the United States on September 11, 2001.

Terrorist Goals and Means

Terrorists favor weapons of mass destruction to enact revenge, eliminate perceived threats, or bring about social or political change.

Domestic and transnational terrorists believe their attacks are justified because they believe they have been alienated and excluded from the political and social processes that have been established by those in power. Both domestic and transnational terrorist groups are interested in gaining power. *Power* is the ability to realize one's own will even against the resistance of others. By obtaining power, terrorist groups believe they can then force others to submit or agree to their demands. Terrorist groups gain power through terrorist attacks that generate publicity and focus attention on their organizations. Terrorist attacks also foster environments of intimidation and fear that terrorists can then manipulate to achieve their desired goals.

What do terrorist groups expect to achieve with their firearms, chemical and biological weapons, and bombs? Spain's Basque separatists want to establish their own homeland in Spain. The goal of radical Islamic groups is to develop devoutly religious governments that operate under divine guidance termed theocracies. Examples are the Islamic Abu Sayyaf terrorist group in the Philippines and Osama bin Laden's al-Qaeda organization.

The Abu Sayyaf militant Islamic organization operates in the southern Philippines, where it has been active for the past three decades. Its goal has been to establish an Islamic state that is independent of the Christian Philippines. The terrorists have bombed a Philippine Airlines plane and attacked towns and department stores.[77] Osama bin Laden and his terrorist organizations have been linked to the "1993 World Trade Center Bombing; the 1996 killing of nineteen U.S. soldiers in Saudi Arabia; the 1998 bombings in Kenya and Tanzania; the 2000 attack on the USS *Cole* in Yemen; and the September 11, 2001, attacks on the World Trade Center and Pentagon."[78]

Some observers hypothesize links between hate groups in the United States and international terrorist groups. For example, in an article entitled "The Swastika and the Crescent," Martin A. Lee points out possible ties between

Interpol is one of the world's preeminent international police organizations.

Terrorism is the use or threatened use of violence to gain a political objective.

Domestic terrorism is terrorism that originates and is carried out within one country.

The September 11, 2001 attack on the World Trade Center marks a day never to be forgotten by Americans. What type of terrorism and terrorist goals does this event demonstrate? What has been America's response to terrorism?

neo-Nazi extremists in the United States and Muslim nationalists engaging in transnational terrorism.[79]

Overlaps between hate crime and acts of domestic terrorism have led political leaders and scientists to develop a new definition of hate crime. This new definition, according to the National Victim Assistance Academy, "might include crimes motivated by a hatred of people, not because of their race, national origin, sex, sexual preference, [or] religion but because of their affiliations or occupation."[80]

Cyberterrorism

Terrorists use the Internet and computers to plan, coordinate, and commit their crimes.

Cyberterrorism is the premeditated misuse or threatened misuse of computers, the internet, and information technology to gain a political or social objective.

Computers and the Internet have been used by terrorists to achieve their political and social goals. **Cyberterrorism** is the premeditated misuse or threatened misuse of computers, the Internet, and information technology to gain a political or social objective. Over the past few years, the al-Qaeda terrorist group, according to federal law enforcement authorities, has planned cyberattacks on commercial and banking networks and U.S. defense department computers.[81]

A recent analysis of high-tech terror reports, "The Internet is a likely means of attack, because it can provide easy access to computer systems and data. Hackers can spread computer viruses or access and corrupt information and processes. A cyber-terrorist who, by becoming a government employee or contractor, gains access to systems, networks and data, is even a greater threat."[82]

In addition,

- ninety percent of government agencies and U.S. corporations detected security breaches in their computer systems during the past year;

- only 26 percent of all U.S. cities have developed cyberterrorism safeguards;
- the Computer Emergency Response Team at Carnegie Mellon University in Pittsburgh reported more than 42,000 computer security breaches in the first three months of 2003, up from more than 82,000 in *all* of 2002;
- experts call for security policies to include antivirus software, firewalls, intrusion detection, and data-backup systems.[83]

According to researchers Clifford E. Simonsen and Jeremy R. Spindlove, cyberterrorism is complex, multifaceted, and often baffling. Terrorists may rise to prominence, disappear for years, and then reappear. In addition, terrorist incidents proliferate across the world. They can trigger chains of events that would destabilize a whole region and bring nations to the edge of ruin.[84]

Responding to Terrorism

The FBI, Department of Homeland Security, and many other government agencies are in a fight against terrorism.

Since September 11, 2001, Americans have been deeply concerned about the U.S. government's efforts to combat terrorism in the United States. The FBI is a "part of a national and international campaign dedicated to terrorism's defeat. Working with law enforcement partners, intelligence, the military, and diplomatic circles," their job is to neutralize terrorist cells and operatives at home and to help abroad.

The FBI claims that since September 11, 2001, more than 3,000 al-Qaeda leaders and foot soldiers have been taken into custody around the globe, nearly two hundred suspected terrorist associates have been charged with crimes in the United States, and as many as one hundred terrorist attacks or plots have been broken up worldwide.[85]

According to terrorist expert Deborah J. Daniels, to improve the sharing of information to fight terrorism, the Office of Justice Programs (OJP) works with the FBI to expand access to the Regional Information Sharing System and the FBI's Law Enforcement Online (LEO) System, and to coordinate the operation of these two systems. The Department of Justice also deals with communication problems encountered by public safety personnel when different government departments and agencies converge on a crime scene. Daniels stresses that the OJP is at the forefront of ensuring that criminal justice practitioners have information and resources needed to fight terrorism while fighting other crimes in their communities.[86]

The *Department of Homeland Security (DHS)* was established to coordinate the U.S. government's efforts against terrorism. The *Homeland Security Act of 2002* created the DHS. The department's major goal is the establishment of a single contact point for local and state government officials to address equipment, emergency planning, training, and other needs for emergency response.[87]

According to the U.S. General Accounting Office (GAO), the DHS has brought together twenty-two diverse organizations to help prevent terrorist attacks in the United States, reduce the vulnerability of the nation to terrorist attacks, minimize damage, and assist in the recovery from attacks that do occur. To accomplish these four goals, the Homeland Security Act established specific homeland security responsibilities for the department, which include sharing information among its own entities and with other federal agencies, state and local governments, the private sector, and others.[88]

The GAO has examined and evaluated the DHS's efforts at sharing information. It found that although improvements have been made, more efforts are needed to address the following challenges, among others, that the GAO has identified:

- developing a comprehensive and coordinated national plan to facilitate information sharing on critical infrastructure;
- developing productive information-sharing relationships between the federal government and state and local governments and the private sector;
- providing appropriate incentives for nonfederal entities to increase information sharing with the federal government and to enhance other critical infrastructure-protection efforts.[89]

In an attempt to prevent further terrorist attacks in the United States, the U.S. Congress passed the *USA PATRIOT Act* in October, 2001. H.R. 3162 was sent to the President who signed it on October 26, 2001.

Federal officials are given, by the USA PATRIOT Act, greater authority to track as well as intercept communications both for foreign intelligence gathering and law enforcement purposes.

The USA PATRIOT Act

- seeks to further close U.S. borders to foreign terrorists and to detain, as well as remove, terrorists that are within our borders;
- vests the secretary of the treasury with regulatory powers to deal with corruption of U.S. financial institutions for foreign money-laundering purposes;
- creates new crimes, penalties, and procedural efficiencies for use against international and domestic terrorists.[90]

The America Civil Liberties Union (ACLU) is quite critical of the USA PATRIOT Act. It believes that the Act threatens American's civil liberties. They believe the Executive Branch of the U.S. government now has sweeping new powers that undermine the Bill of Rights. They state that the Act violates our rights under the First, Fourth, Fifth, Sixth, Eighth, and Fourteenth Amendments.

According to a recent report by Charles Lewis and Adam Mayle, there are efforts to expand the USA PATRIOT Act even further. According to David Cole of Georgetown University, the proposed legislative draft of an expanded USA PATRIOT Act—called the Domestic Security Enhancement Act—raises even more civil rights concerns. He believes that it "would radically expand law enforcement and intelligence gathering authorities, reduce or eliminate judicial oversight over surveillance, authorize secret arrests, create a DNA database based on unchecked executive 'suspicion,' create new death penalties, and even seek to take American citizenship away from persons who belong to or support disfavored political groups."[91]

Virtually every American wants the U.S. government and its various agencies and law enforcement departments to be successful at the societal or macro level in dealing with and preventing terrorism. For many Americans, however, terrorism affects them on a more personal, or micro, level. The events of 9/11 brought the reality of terrorism into the homes of all Americans.

After reading this section, you should be able to

1. define terrorism and identify two types of terrorism;
2. describe terrorists' goals and methods;
3. explain how cyberterrorism and links between terrorism and hate crime pose special risks;
4. summarize the government's responses to terrorism;
5. distinguish between macro- and microlevel responses to terrorism

CHAPTER SUMMARY

This chapter examines robbery, murder, hate crime, and terrorism. The object of robbery is to obtain money or property. This crime always involves force or its threat. Many victims suffer serious personal injury. Robbery accounts for about one-third of all violent crimes in the United States. John Conklin identified four types of robbers: professional, opportunistic, addict, and alcoholic. Robbers attempt to minimize risks when committing their offenses. Their primary motive is to obtain money or some other desired valuable (pp. 241–244).

Murder is the unlawful killing of a human being. Males are most often the perpetrators and victims in homicides. More than 42 percent of murder victims know their assailants. Victim-precipitated murder occurs when the murder victim is a direct, positive precipitator in the crime. In most murders, the perpetrator has a motive for killing a person, but in about 25 percent of homicides, the motive for murder is unclear. Serial murders involve the killing of several victims over a period of time. Mass murders involve the killing of several victims in one event. The reading by Fox and Levin examines the six factors that contribute to mass murder (pp. 244–252).

There are many explanations for murder. Subcultural violence theories focus on the approval of violence in a subculture's value system and social norms. Other theories focus on structural factors, social disintegration, and learning violence in families and society. Still others focus on biochemical factors, personality or mental disorders, or environmental and psychological stressors (pp. 252–254).

School violence and shootings have also become a serious problem in the United States. More than 100,000 guns are brought to school each day in the United States. About 300,000 high school students are attacked each month in school. Schools, communities, and the federal government have developed a variety of responses to school crime and violence (pp. 254–255).

Hate crime is violence of intolerance and bigotry intended to hurt and intimidate a person or persons because of their race, ethnicity, national origin, religion, sexual orientation, or disability. In 60 percent of hate crime incidents, the most serious offense is a violent crime. Targets of hate crimes are mostly individuals. Younger offenders are responsible for most hate crimes. There are three types of hate crime offenders: thrill-seeking, reactive, and mission. There are different types of organized hate groups, and both the federal and state governments have enacted legislation and programs to combat hate crime (pp. 256–260).

Terrorism is the use or threatened use of violence by an individual or a group in order to gain a social or political objective. Terrorists favor weapons of mass destruction to gain power. There is some overlap between hate crime and acts of domestic terrorism. Cyberterrorism is the premeditated misuse or threatened misuse of computers, the Internet, and information technology to gain a political or social objective. During the past year, 90 percent of government agencies and U.S. corporations detected security breaches in their computer systems. The government response to terrorism is complex and multifaceted, involving efforts of the FBI, the Department of Justice, the Department of Homeland Security, and various other agencies (pp. 260–264).

Study Guide

Chapter Objectives

- Describe the nature and extent of robbery.
- Categorize the different types of robbers identified by Conklin.
- Describe a robber's choices and patterns of behavior.
- Explain what motivates people to commit robbery.
- Define criminal homicide.
- Describe the nature and extent of criminal homicide in the United States.
- Describe the characteristics of murder offenders and victims.
- List and explain the different types of homicidal relationships and transactions.
- Define and describe victim-precipitated murder.
- Describe homicide without apparent motive.

- Examine the factors that contribute to mass murder.
- Describe three major theories that explain homicide.
- Describe school violence in the United States.
- Examine the issue of school shootings in the United States.
- Define and give three examples of hate crime.
- Examine the major characteristics of hate crime incidents.
- Examine organized U.S. hate groups.
- List and describe responses to hate crime.
- Define terrorism and name its two types.
- Describe the goals and methods of terrorists.
- Describe the possible link between terrorism and hate groups.
- Define and explain cyberterrorism.
- Describe the responses to terrorism.

Key Terms

Addict robber (243)
Alcoholic robber (243)
Cult murder (251)
Cyberterrorism (262)
Domestic terrorism (261)
First-degree murder (245)
Gang murder (251)
Homicide (245)

Interpol (260)
Learning violence (253)
Manslaughter (245)
Mass murder (251)
Murder (245)
Negligent homicide (245)
Opportunistic robber (243)
Professional robber (243)

Robbery (241)
Second-degree murder (245)
Serial murder (251)
Social disintegration (253)
Structural adaptation theories (253)
Subculture of violence (252)
Terrorism (260)
Victim-precipitated murder (250)

Self-Test
Short Answer

1. Define robbery.
2. List the different types of robbers.
3. Briefly describe a robber's choices and patterns of robbery.
4. Briefly examine what motivates robbers.
5. Give a clear definition of murder.
6. Briefly describe how murder offenders vary by gender, race, and age.
7. Define victim-precipitated murder.

8. List and briefly define the factors that contribute to mass murder.
9. Briefly explain why people commit murder.
10. Briefly describe the issues around school shootings.
11. Define and list five characteristics of hate crime.
12. Briefly describe the characteristics of hate crime offenders and victims.
13. Briefly examine the federal responses to hate crimes.

14. Define terrorism and its methods.
15. Briefly examine the relationship between terrorism and hate groups.
16. Define cyberterrorism.
17. Briefly examine the government's responses to terrorism.
18. Examine talking to children about terrorism as a microlevel response to terrorism.

Multiple Choice

1. Robbery
   a. is usually perpetrated by a stranger in a highly threatening manner
   b. always involves actual or threatened force
   c. occurs most frequently during the months of October and December
   d. all of the above
2. Which of the following is not one of Conklin's types of robbers?
   a. amateur
   b. opportunist
   c. professional
   d. addict
3. Robbers focus on
   a. escape plans
   b. witnesses
   c. selecting the "right" victim
   d. all of the above
4. Robberies
   a. are primarily committed by people familiar to the victim
   b. are primarily committed at or near a victim's home
   c. are characterized as instrumental offenses
   d. none of the above
5. The annual total number of murders in the United States is about
   a. 200,000
   b. 100,000
   c. 40,000
   d. 15,000
6. Homicide victims are
   a. most often female
   b. most often male
   c. most often teens
   d. most often black
7. Of homicide offenders,
   a. 90 percent are male
   b. 92 percent are over age eighteen
   c. 50 percent are black
   d. none of the above
8. Marvin Wolfgang reported that, in murders,
   a. the victim is often a major contributor to the criminal act
   b. the victim is always a major contributor to the criminal act
   c. the victim is never a major contributor to the criminal act
   d. none of the above

9. In the reading "Mass Murder," which of the following do Fox and Levin not include in their list of factors that contribute to mass murder?
   a. frustration
   b. contagion
   c. social isolation
   d. social engagement
10. The subculture of violence theories focus on
   a. socially disintegrated subcultures
   b. the approval of violence in a subculture's value system and social norms
   c. biochemical factors in ethnic subcultures
   d. none of the above
11. With respect to school violence,
   a. more than 100,000 guns are brought to school each day in the United States
   b. about 300,000 high school students are attacked in school each month
   c. inside schools, or on school property, about 3 million assaults, robberies, thefts, and rapes occur each year
   d. all of the above
12. Hate crime offenders use the following behaviors to create fear in their victims:
   a. physical violence and verbal threats
   b. weapons and explosives
   c. arson
   d. all of the above
13. According to the NIBRS, from 1997 to 1999,
   a. the targets of hate crimes were most commonly businesses and religious organizations
   b. the majority of persons suspected of committing hate crimes were black
   c. more than half of persons arrested for hate crimes were over twenty-five
   d. none of the above
14. Terrorism has been used by individuals and groups to
   a. publicize a cause
   b. promote an ideological position
   c. achieve religious and/or political goals
   d. all of the above
15. Osama bin Laden has been linked to
   a. the 1993 and 2001 World Trade Center bombings
   b. the 1998 bombings in Kenya and Tanzania
   c. the 2000 attack on the USS *Cole* in Yemen
   d. all of the above

True–False

T F 1. A robbery occurs in the United States every minute.

T F 2. The UCR indicates that robbery accounts for about 50 percent of all violent crimes in the United States.

T F 3. July and August are the months when robberies are most frequent.

T F 4. The opportunistic robber is dependent on drugs and steals to support his or her habit.

T F 5. Robbery is typically characterized as an instrumental offense.

T F 6. To be guilty of criminal homicide, a person must purposely, knowingly, recklessly, or negligently cause the death of another human being.

T F 7. Females are most often the victims and the perpetrators in homicides.

T F 8. Blacks are six times more likely to be homicide victims than whites and seven times more likely than whites to commit homicides.

T F 9. Handguns are used in only about 40 percent of homicides.

T F 10. Homicides are more likely to involve multiple victims than multiple offenders.

T F 11. The firearm is the weapon of choice in mass murder incidents.

T F 12. Mass murderers are often characterized in the popular press as loners.

T F 13. Social disintegration is rarely cited as a factor in violent crime.

T F 14. Some researchers believe that there has been no significant increase in school violence over the past thirty years.

T F 15. Hate crimes are criminal offenses that are motivated by an offender's bias against a race, religion, or sexual orientation, but not ethnicity.

T F 16. Some hate crime offenders commit their crimes in concert with their peers out of resentment over the growing economic power of a particular racial or ethnic group.

T F 17. According to NIBRS, 61 percent of hate crime incidents are motivated by race.

T F 18. Terrorist groups gain power through terrorist attacks that generate publicity and focus attention on their organizations.

T F 19. There appear to be few, if any, links between hate groups and terrorist groups.

Fill-In

1. Although the object of _____ is to obtain money or property, the crime always involves force or its threat.

2. The _____ robber has a long-term commitment to robbery as a source of livelihood.

3. The _____ robber is the most common type of robber.

4. Robbery is typically characterized as an _____ offense.

5. _____ is the unlawful killing of a human being by another with malice aforethought, either expressed or implied.

6. The term _____ is applied to criminal homicides in which the victim is a direct precipitation in the crime.

7. In the great majority of murders, the perpetrator has a _____, or reason, for killing a person.

8. _____ involves the killing of several victims in one event.

9. According to Fox and Levin, mass killers generally do not select their victims on a _____ basis.

10. According to the _____ theory, a person's aggressive, violent behavior is learned from the family and society.

11. Guns in schools are referred to as _____.

12. The media give the average American the impression that there is an _____ of school violence.

13. _____ hate crime offenders have a sense of entitlement with regard to their rights and privileges that does not extend to their victims.

14. There are basically two types of terrorism: domestic and _____.

15. _____ attacks foster environments of intimidation and fear.

Matching

1. Object of robbery
2. Grants for reducing school violence
3. Professional robber
4. Learning violence theory
5. Criminal homicide
6. Innocent strangers caught in crossfire
7. Contagion
8. Opportunistic robber
9. Serial murder
10. Mass murder
11. Oklahoma City bombing
12. Firebombing of a black church

A. Long-term commitment to robbery
B. Killing of several victims in one event
C. Safe Schools Act
D. Most common type of robber
E. Gang murder
F. Killing of several victims over a period of time
G. Mass killers inspire one another
H. Aggression and violence are learned from family and society
I. To obtain money or property
J. Murder, manslaughter, or negligent homicide
K. Hate crime
L. Domestic terrorism

Essay Questions

1. After assessing the chapter materials on robbery, select a friend or relative who has been a victim of robbery and analyze and evaluate the incident in terms of what you have learned about the crime.
2. Examine Conklin's typology of robbers. Do you believe his typology adequately describes most robbers? Why or why not?
3. Review the data on murder in the United States, and write an essay, using the theories on homicide, explaining why the United States has one of the highest homicide rates in the world.
4. Do you agree that some victims precipitate their own homicide? Explain your answer.
5. Why do you think men commit murder much more often than women in American society? Explain your answer.
6. Evaluate the reading on mass murder. Can we as a society reduce the number of mass murders in the United States?
7. Examine a recent hate crime that has been committed in your community or a neighboring one. How do you explain it? How has the community responded to the crime?
8. What was your impression of, and reaction to, the September 11, 2001, attacks on the World Trade Center and the Pentagon? Do you think our government responded well to the events? Explain your answer.
9. What recent terrorist attacks have caused problems in the United States? How has the government responded to those attacks?

Mass Murder

Source: J. A. Fox and J. Levin, "Mass Murder: An Analysis of Extreme Violence," Journal of Applied Psychoanalytic Studies, vol. 5, issue 1, Jan. 2003, pp. 47–64. Reprinted by permission of Springer Science + Business Media.

BY JAMES A. FOX AND JACK LEVIN

Mass murder is that form of multiple homicide in which four or more victims are slain during a single episode. In December 2000, for example, Michael McDermott, a 42-year-old employee of Edgewater Technology in Wakefield, Massachusetts, opened fire on his co-workers, killing seven of them. In June 2001, Andrea Yates drowned her five children in Houston, Texas.

We can derive some sense of the prevalence of mass killing from the FBI's Supplementary Homicide Reports, an incident-level database of over 92% of the murders committed in the United States each year (see Fox 2000). For the years 1976 through 1999, an estimated 497,030 people were murdered in the United States. Of these, 3,956 were slain in incidents claiming four or more victims. Still, many of these mass killings involve circumstances in which the homicide may not have been intentional—most notably arson resulting in the deaths of large numbers of people. Although occasionally mass killers specifically use fire as their weapon of choice, most of these cases entail unplanned fatalities, and should arguably be eliminated from consideration. After this exclusion, the 24-year-period yields 599 mass killings, involving 2,800 victims and 826 killers.

On average, therefore, two incidents of mass murder occur per month in the United States claiming more than 100 victims annually. Most incidents, of course, are not as widely publicized as the horrific slaughters of 14 postal workers in an Oklahoma post office in 1986, or of 23 customers in a Texas restaurant in 1991. Still, the phenomenon of the massacre or mass murder, although hardly of epidemic proportions, is not the rare occurrence that it is sometimes assumed to be.

Also based on these FBI homicide data, we have determined that the popular image of mass murder differs in significant ways from the reality. While the most heavily publicized type of mass murder involves the indiscriminate shooting of strangers in a public place by a lone gunman, other kinds of mass killing are actually far more common. Included within this scope are, for example, the disgruntled employee who kills his boss and co-workers after being fired, the estranged husband/father who massacres his entire family and then kills himself, the band of armed robbers who slaughter a roomful of witnesses to their crime, and the racist hatemonger who sprays a schoolyard of immigrant children with gunfire. Thus, the motivations for mass murder can range from revenge to hatred, from loyalty to greed; and the victims can be selected individually, as members of a particular category or group, or least often on a purely random basis.

The location of mass murder differs sharply from that of homicides in which a single victim is slain. First, mass murders do not tend to cluster in large cities as do single-victim crimes, but are more likely to occur in small town or rural settings. Moreover, while the south (and the deep south in particular) is known for its high rates of murder, this does not hold for mass murder. In comparison to single-victim murder, which is highly concentrated in urban areas populated by poor blacks and in the deep south where arguments are often settled through gunfire (see, for example, Doerner 1975), mass murder more or less reflects the geographic distribution of the general population.

Not surprisingly, the firearm is the weapon of choice in mass murder incidents, even more than in single-victim crimes. Clearly, a handgun or rifle is the most effective means of mass destruction. By contrast, it is difficult to kill large numbers of people simultaneously with physical force or even a knife or blunt object. Furthermore, although an explosive device can potentially cause the death of large numbers of people (as in the 1995 bombing of the Oklahoma City federal building), its unpredictability would be unacceptable for most mass killers, who target their victims selectively.

The findings regarding victim-offender relationship are perhaps as counter-intuitive as the weapon-use results may be obvious. Contrary to popular belief, mass murderers infrequently attack strangers who just happen to be in the wrong place at the wrong time. In fact, almost forty percent of these crimes are committed against family members, and almost as many involve other victims acquainted with the perpetrator (e.g., co-workers). It is well-known that murder often involves family members; but this is especially pronounced among massacres.

The differences in circumstance underlying these crimes are also quite dramatic. While more than half of all single-victim homicides occur during an argument between the victim and offender, it is relatively rare for a heated dispute to escalate into mass murder.

Some of the most notable differences between homicide types emerge in the area of offender characteristics. Compared to those assailants who kill but one, mass murderers are overwhelmingly likely to be male, are far more likely to be white, and are somewhat older. Typically, the single-victim offender is a young male, slightly more often black than white, whereas the massacrer is typically a middle-aged white male (this profile comes into sharpest focus for those mass killers who are motivated by something other than robbery).

Victim characteristics are, of course, largely a function of the offender patterns noted above, indicating that mass killers generally do not select their victims on a random basis. That is, for example, the victims of mass murder are usually white simply because the perpetrators to whom they are related or with whom they associate are white. Similarly, the youthfulness and greater representation of females among the victims of mass murder, as compared to single-victim homicide, stem from the fact that a typical mass killing involves the breadwinner of the household who annihilates the entire family—his wife and his children.

Media accounts of mass murderers tend to focus on killers who suddenly "go berserk" or "run amok"—on the likes of George Hennard, Jr., who, in 1991, opened fire in a crowded Killeen, Texas, restaurant, killing twenty-three victims at random. Or, those old enough to remember may recall Charles Whitman, the ex-marine who, in 1966, killed 14 and wounded 30 others while perched atop a tower at the University of Texas.

These sudden, seemingly episodic and random incidents of violence are as atypical as they are extreme. A majority of mass killers have clear-cut motives—especially revenge—and their victims are chosen because of what they have done or what they represent. Even cases that would seem indiscriminate to the casual observer often involve a process of selection. In August 1999, for example, Mark Barton killed nine people and wounded a dozen more during an afternoon shooting spree at two Atlanta day-trading offices. Hardly random, these were the very locations where Barton had lost nearly a half-million dollars in stock trades. Moreover, his not-so-sudden and not-so-random assault had begun days earlier when he murdered his wife and then his two children. Despite the popular image, therefore, the indiscriminate slaughter of strangers by a "crazed" killer is the exception to the rule (Levin and Fox 1985; Dietz 1986; Fox and Levin 1994a).

Finally, the more specific and focused the element of revenge, the more likely the outburst is planned and methodical rather than spontaneous and random (see Kinney and Johnson 1993; and Fox and Levin 1994b, for a discussion of workplace avengers). Also, the more specific the targets of revenge, the less likely it is that the killer's rage stems from psychosis.

When then do they kill? Why would a 31-year-old former postal worker, Thomas McIlvane, go on a rampage in Royal Oak, Michigan, killing four fellow postal workers before shooting himself in the head? And, what would cause a 28-year-old graduate student, Gang Lu, to execute five others at the University of Iowa before taking his own life? Finally, why would a 55-year-old Missourian, Neil Schatz, fatally shoot his wife, two children, and two grandchildren before committing suicide?

An analysis of numerous case studies (see Levin and Fox 1985; Fox and Levin 1994a) suggests that the following factors contribute to mass murder.

1. *Frustration.* In his early book, *The Psychology of Murder*, Stuart Palmer (1960) studied 51 convicted killers, most of whom had experienced severely frustrating childhood illnesses, accidents, child abuse, physical defects, isolation, and poverty. The mass murderer similarly suffers from a long history of frustration, humiliation, and failure, concomitant with a diminishing ability to cope and increasingly negative self-image, which begin early in life but which continue well into adulthood (Hale 1994; Goldberg 1996). As a result, he may also develop a condition of profound and unrelenting depression, although not necessarily at the level of psychosis. This in fact explains why so many mass killers are middle-aged; it usually takes years to accumulate the kinds of childhood and adulthood disappointments that culminate in this kind of deep sense of frustration. For example, 41-year-old James Ruppert, who slaughtered his eleven relatives in Hamilton, Ohio, on Easter Sunday, 1975, had been extremely incompetent in school, friendships, and sports throughout his youth, lost his father at an early age, suffered from debilitating asthma and spinal meningitis, was so uncomfortable around women that he never experienced a sexual relationship, and was unable to hold a steady job as an adult (Levin and Fox 1985). By focusing on frustration, we do not rule out the possibility in a few cases that the depression may have a biological or organic foundation. For example, Joseph Wesbecker, who murdered eight co-workers in a Louisville, Kentucky, printing plant, was being treated for depression, which itself could have been linked to his own history of failure.

2. *Externalization of responsibility.* Many people who suffer from frustration and depression over an extended period of time may commit suicide without physically harming anyone else. Part of the problem is that they perceive themselves as worthless, and as responsible for their failures in life. Their aggression is intropunitive (Dollard et al. 1939; Henry and Short 1954).

Thus, a critical condition for frustration to result in extrapunitive aggression is that the individual perceives that others are to blame for his personal problems and failures (Henry and Short 1954). As a response-style acquired through learning, the mass killer comes to see himself *never* as the culprit but always as the victim behind his disappointments. More specifically, the mass murderer externalizes blame; it is invariably someone else's fault.

3. *A catastrophic loss.* Given both long-term frustration and an angry, blameful mind-set, certain situations or events can precipitate or trigger violent rage. In most instances, the killer experiences a *sudden loss* or the threat of a loss, which from his point of view is catastrophic. The loss typically involves an unwanted separation from loved ones or termination from employment.

In 1991, for example, thirty-nine-year-old James Colbert of Concord, New Hampshire, killed his estranged wife and three daughters. Learning that his wife had started a new relationship, Colbert reasoned, "if I can't have her and the kids, then no one can." James Ruppert, by contrast, was facing eviction by his mother from the only house in which he had ever lived. Either he stopped his drinking and paid his debts, or he would have to leave.

Employment problems are even more frequently found to precipitate mass killing. In 1991, for example, postal worker Thomas McIlvane was fired from his job and lost his appeal for reinstatement just prior to his Royal Oak rampage, while Patrick Sherrill's supervisor threatened to fire him just two days before the 1986 Edmond, Oklahoma, Post Office massacre (Fox and Levin 1994b).

The overabundance of men among mass killers, even more than among murderers generally, may stem in part from the fact that men are more likely to suffer the kind of catastrophic losses associated with mass murder. Following a separation or divorce, it is generally the husband/father who is ejected from the family home. Furthermore, despite advances in the status of women in America, males more than females continue to define themselves in terms of their occupational role ("what they do" defines "who they are") and therefore tend more to suffer psychologically from unemployment (Campbell 1991).

4. *Contagion.* Although not as common as the loss of a relationship or employment, certain external cues or models have also served as catalysts or inspiration for mass murder. While the so-called "copycat" phenomenon is difficult to document scientifically (however, see Phillips 1983), the anecdotal evidence is at least highly suggestive. For example, the rash of schoolyard slayings—beginning with Laurie Dann's May 1988 shooting at a Winnetka, Illinois, elementary school and ending with Patrick Purdy's January 1989 attack in Stockton, California—suggests the possibility of a "fad" element in which mass killers inspire one another. Most striking was the case of James Wilson of Greenwood, South Carolina, a "fan" of Laurie Dann. Much like his hero, Wilson, in September 1988, sprayed a local elementary school with gunfire, killing two children. When police searched Wilson's apartment, they found the *People* magazine cover photo of Laurie Dann taped to his wall. They also learned in subsequent interviews with those who knew James Wilson that he talked about Dann incessantly (Fox and Levin 1994a).

The more recent string of teenaged school massacres also illustrates the power of imitation to inspire mass murder. On February 2, 1996, in the first of a series of school shootings, 14-year-old Barry Loukaitis burst into his math class at the Frontier High School in Moses Lake, Washington, removed a high-powered rifle from beneath his long overcoat, and started firing. After killing the teacher and two classmates, he remarked, "this sure beats Algebra," a line drawn from his favorite Stephen King novella about a school shooting.

The Moses Lake school tragedy was then followed by schoolyard multiple killings in Pearl, Mississippi; West Paducah, Kentucky; Jonesboro, Arkansas; Springfield, Oregon; and Littleton, Colorado. Unlike the series of school attacks in 1988–89, the newest breed of avengers are teenagers and pre-teenagers—one as young as 11 years old. Apparently, copycat effects can be so strong as to mitigate the necessity of a *long-term* frustration factor.

5. *Social isolation.* Mass murderers are often characterized in the popular press as "loners." It is indeed true that many of them are cut off from sources of comfort and guidance, from the very people who could have supported them when times got tough. Some live alone for extended periods of time. Other mass killers relocate great distances away from home, experiencing a sense of anomie or normlessness. They lose their sources of emotional support. It is no coincidence that mass murders tend to concentrate in areas of the nation where there are large numbers of drifters, transients, newcomers, and migrants—individuals who lack family, friends, and fraternal organizations to get them through bad times. Many Americans have, for the sake of a new beginning or a last resort, migrated to such states as California, Texas, Florida, Alaska, New York, and Illinois. These states have had more than their share of mass murders.

6. *A weapon of mass destruction.* Even when people feel angry, hopeless, and isolated, they don't necessarily commit mass murder. In many cases, they simply don't have the means. It is almost impossible to commit a massacre with a knife or a hammer. Such weapons are potentially destructive, but are not *mass* destructive. Killers like James Ruppert and James Huberty were well-trained in the use of firearms and owned quite a few of them. Ruppert often went target shooting on the banks of the Great Miami River; Huberty practiced at the firing range in his own basement. Moreover, both of them were armed with loaded firearms at the very time they felt angry enough to kill.

Explosives are potentially another effective means of mass destruction, as was tragically shown in Timothy McVeigh's April 1995 bombing of the federal building in Oklahoma City in which 168 innocent people lost their lives. In reality, however, the lack of knowledge of the construction of powerful bombs has limited their role in perpetrating mass murder in the United States. By contrast, in agricultural societies where dynamite is readily available and firearms are not (e.g., rural China), massacres are usually committed by means of explosives, not semiautomatic rifles. Moreover, the

September 11th attack on America illustrated in a particularly tragic way that terrorists who are willing to take their own lives in order to maximize their body count can make jet aircraft into powerful weapons of mass destruction.

REFERENCES

Campbell, A. 1991. *Men, Women, and Aggression.* New York: Basic Books.

Dietz, P.E. 1986. "Mass, Serial and Sensational Homicides." *Bulletin of the New York Academy of Medicine* 62:477–491.

Doerner, W.G. 1975. "A Regional Analysis of Homicide Rates in the United States." *Criminology* 13:90–101.

Dollard, J., L. Doob, N. Miller, O.H. Mowrer, and R.R. Sears. 1939. *Frustration and Aggression.* New Haven: Yale University Press.

Fox, J.A. 2000. *The Supplementary Homicide Reports, 1976–1999.* Ann Arbor, MI: Criminal Justice Archive, Inter-University Consortium of Political and Social Research.

Fox, J.A., and J. Levin. 1994a. *Overkill: Mass Murder and Serial Killing Exposed.* New York: Plenum.

Fox, J.A., and J. Levin. 1994b. "Firing Back: the Growing Threat of Workplace Homicide." *The Annals of the American Academy of Political and Social Science* 536:15–30.

Goldberg, C. 1996. *Speaking with the Devil.* New York: Viking.

Hale, R. 1994. "The Role of Humiliation and Embarrassment in Serial Murder." *Psychology: A Journal of Human Behavior* 31:17–22.

Henry, A., and J.F. Short. 1954. *Suicide and Homicide.* Glencoe, IL: Free Press.

Kinney, J.A., and D.L. Johnson. 1993. *Breaking Point: The Workplace Violence Epidemic and What to Do about It.* Chicago: National Safe Workplace Institute.

Levin, J., and J.A. Fox. 1985. *Mass Murder: America's Growing Menace.* New York: Plenum Press.

Palmer, S. 1960. *The Psychology of Murder.* New York: Crowell.

Phillips, D.P. 1983. "The Impact of Mass Media Violence on U.S. Homicides." *American Sociological Review* 48:560–568.

CRITICAL THINKING

1. According to Fox and Levin, what is the actual prevalence of mass murder in the United States?
2. How does the popular image of mass murder differ from the reality?
3. Why do mass murderers kill?

10

Property Crimes

10.1 INTRODUCTION: DEFINING PROPERTY CRIMES

In the United States, people are more tolerant of property crimes than they are of crimes of violence. This is not to say that Americans are not concerned about theft, fraud, burglary, fencing, and arson—especially when it is their cars that get stolen, their homes that are burglarized, or their family members who lose money or property through some fraudulent scheme. Today, these schemes are becoming increasingly complex and often involve using the Internet to scam people.

At times, people may be ambivalent about property crimes because "the car was insured," "the store can pass the cost of shoplifting on," and "the big corporation can absorb the losses." However, Americans do end up paying for these crimes; the average citizen, for example, pays through his or her taxes, insurance premiums, and the costs of goods and services for the billions of dollars that are lost each year to fraud alone.

This chapter begins with an analysis and profile of property crime in general and then goes on to examine

- types of larceny–theft, including motor vehicle theft, carjacking, shoplifting, and identity theft (section 10.3);
- fraud, including confidence games, Internet fraud, and disaster fraud (section 10.4);
- burglary and antiburglary efforts (section 10.5);
- fencing of stolen property (section 10.6);
- the crime of arson (section 10.7).

10.2 AN OVERVIEW OF PROPERTY CRIMES

According to the Uniform Crime Report (UCR), **property crimes** include larceny–theft, burglary, motor vehicle theft, fencing, fraud, and arson. The object of these offenses is taking money or property, but there is no force or threat of force against the victims.

Property crime makes up about three-quarters of all crime in the United States, and the annual estimated dollar loss attributed to property crime is about $20 billion. The UCR estimates there are about 14 million property crimes annually reported to the police in the United States. The annual overall reported property crime rate is about 4,000 per 100,000 inhabitants. However, the National Crime Victimization Survey (NCVS) reports that in the United States there are about 19 million annual property crimes. The difference between the UCR and the NCVS figures is significant. This difference (5 million) indicates that much property crime goes unreported to the police. From 1990 to 2000, property crimes in the United States declined by about 20 percent. However, since 2000, the rates have been increasing at about 2 percent per year.[1]

Property Crimes in the United States

- Larceny–theft accounts for the highest volume of offenses: about 68 percent of the nation's estimated property crimes and 60 percent of the Crime Index offenses.
- In general, the lowest number of property crimes occurs in February. The highest number of property crimes occurs during the months of July and August.
- In terms of regional differences, the Northeast accounts for 13 percent of the annual total of property crimes reported; the Midwest, 22 percent; the West, 24 percent; and the South, 41 percent.
- Property crimes generally have the lowest clearance rates: only about 16 percent.
- Juveniles account for about 21 percent of the overall property crime clearances.
- In terms of victim characteristics, persons age sixty-five and older are disproportionately affected by property crimes. Annually, on average, 2.5 million

property crimes against seniors occur in the United States. More than 90 percent of the crimes against the elderly are property crimes.
- In relation to race, per 1,000 persons in each category, 180 black and 164 white households are victims of a property crime annually.
- Regardless of the type, property crime occurs more frequently to people living in rented properties. In addition, urban households historically have been and continue to be the most vulnerable to property crime.

Sources: U.S. Department of Justice, Federal Bureau of Investigation, Uniform Crime Reports, *Crime in the United States, 2001,* "Section II—Crime Index Offenses Reported," Washington, DC: Government Printing Office, October 28, 2002, pp. 1–52; U.S. Department of Justice, Office of Justice Programs, Bureau of Justice Statistics, *Sourcebook of Criminal Justice Statistics, 2001,* April 2003.

After reading this section, you should be able to

1. define and characterize property crime;
2. contrast UCR and NCVS statistics on property crime and explain the reason for data differences;
3. summarize property crimes in the United States in a crime profile.

10.3 LARCENY-THEFT

Property crimes include larceny–theft, burglary, motor vehicle theft, fencing, fraud, and arson.

Larceny–theft is the unlawful taking, carrying, leading, or riding away of property from the possession or constructive possession of another.

About 68 percent of the nation's estimated property crimes and 60 percent of the Crime Index offenses are larceny–theft. **Larceny–theft** is defined in the UCR as "the unlawful taking, carrying, leading, or riding away of property from the possession or constructive possession of another. It includes crimes such as shoplifting, pocket-picking, purse-snatching, thefts from motor vehicles, thefts of motor vehicle parts and accessories, bicycle thefts, etc., in which no use of force, violence, or fraud occurs. In the Uniform Crime Reporting Program, this crime category does not include embezzlement, confidence games, forgery, and worthless checks. Motor vehicle theft is also excluded from this category inasmuch as it is a separate Crime Index offense."[2] A

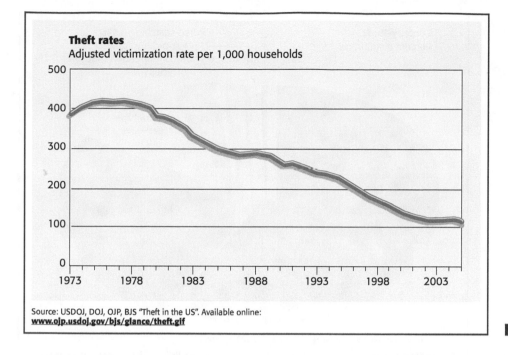

Theft rates
Adjusted victimization rate per 1,000 households

Source: USDOJ, DOJ, OJP, BJS "Theft in the US". Available online:
www.ojp.usdoj.gov/bjs/glance/theft.gif

FIGURE 10.1 Theft Rates

personal larceny is defined in the NCVS as the theft or attempted theft of property or cash by stealth, either with contact (but without force or the threat of force) or without direct contact between the victim and the offender.[3]

Larceny–theft accounts for the highest volume of offenses. According to the UCR, an estimated 7.2 million larceny–theft offenses are reported annually in the United States. They make up almost 70 percent of all property crimes and 60 percent of all crime index offenses. Reported larceny–theft offenses cost the United States about $6 billion annually. Although larceny–thefts have recently risen by about 2 percent per year, they have generally declined over the past two decades (see Figure 10.1). The United States annually experiences larceny–thefts at the rate of 2,500 per 100,000 population. The South, as the most populous region, has about 41 percent of all larceny offenses; the West and Midwest, 23 percent each; the Northeast, almost 14 percent.[4]

The distribution of types of larceny–theft in the United States is as follows (see Figure 10.2):

- Thefts from autos account for 26 percent and shoplifting for 14 percent of annual larcenies.
- Thefts from buildings account for 13 percent of the total.
- Thefts of auto accessories account for 10 percent of the total.
- Stolen bicycles make up 4 percent of larcenies.
- The remainder of larceny–thefts are purse snatchings, pocket pickings, theft of coin-operated machines, and all other thefts.[5]

The average value of property stolen in larceny–theft is about $740 per crime, according to the UCR. The annual loss to victims nationally is more than $5.2 billion. This is considered a conservative amount, because many offenses in this category never come to the attention of law enforcement officials.[6] Estimates based on the NCVS are much higher: The NCVS reports that about 15 million personal larceny offenses occur annually in the United States.[7]

The difference in findings between the UCR (7.2 million annual larcenies) and the NCVS (15 million) can be explained by the fact that only about one-half

DID YOU KNOW
In the UCR, motor vehicle theft is treated as a separate category rather than included in larceny–theft.

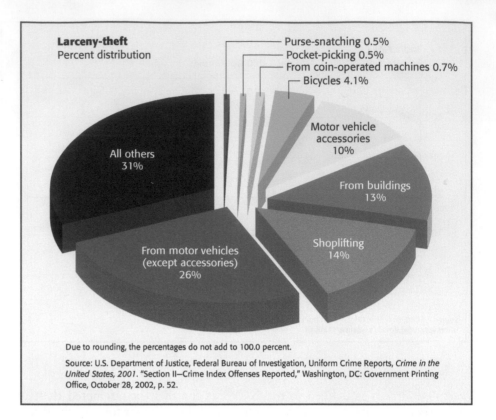

Larceny-theft
Percent distribution

Purse-snatching 0.5%
Pocket-picking 0.5%
From coin-operated machines 0.7%
Bicycles 4.1%

Motor vehicle accessories 10%

From buildings 13%

Shoplifting 14%

From motor vehicles (except accessories) 26%

All others 31%

Due to rounding, the percentages do not add to 100.0 percent.

Source: U.S. Department of Justice, Federal Bureau of Investigation, Uniform Crime Reports, *Crime in the United States, 2001*. "Section II—Crime Index Offenses Reported," Washington, DC: Government Printing Office, October 28, 2002, p. 52.

FIGURE 10.2 Types of Larceny–Theft and Rates of Distribution

of all larceny victims report the incident to the police. Only about one-third of personal thefts are reported to the police; in fact, personal theft is the least likely crime in the major categories (the others being violent and household crimes) to be reported to the police. The most common reasons for not reporting a theft to law enforcement are that the object was recovered or the crime

FOR YOUR INFORMATION

UCR larceny–theft statistics in 2005 indicate:

- There were an estimated 6.8 million larceny–theft offenses nationwide during 2005.
- An examination of two- and ten-year trends revealed a 2.3 percent decrease in the estimated number of larceny–thefts compared with the 2004 figure, and a 14.3 percent decline from the decline from the 1996 estimate.
- Two-thirds of all property crime in 2005 were larceny–thefts.
- During 2005, there were an estimated 2,286 larceny–theft offenses per 100,000 inhabitants.
- From 2004 to 2005, the rate of larceny–thefts declined 3.2 percent, and from 1996 to 2005, the rate declined 23.3 percent.
- The average value for property stolen during the commission of a larceny–theft was $764 per offense.

Source: FBI, 2005 Uniform Crime Reports, Release date: September 2006.

was not successful. Two other common reasons for not reporting are that the crime was reported to some other official or there was a lack of proof. Victims who do report crimes of theft to the police give the following reasons: to recover property (31 percent), because it was a crime (14 percent), to collect insurance (10 percent), and out of a sense of duty (10 percent).[8]

Types of Thieves: Amateur and Professional

Most larceny–thefts are committed by amateurs. Professional thieves regard their crimes as a full-time occupation.

The **amateur thief** is an occasional criminal uncommitted to a criminal value system. He or she makes the decision to steal with little or no planning. Amateur thieves are opportunists who steal when the risks are low and there exists an opportunity or situational inducement to commit the crime.

For criminologist John Hepburn, a **situational inducement** is a short-run influence on a person's behavior that increases his or her risk taking, such as peer influence and pressures (social factors) or financial problems (psychological factors). An amateur criminal, in an unplanned, unskilled manner, commits a crime in response to a pressing situation such as a need to get food, pay the rent, or pay off a gambling debt. For Hepburn, situational inducements and opportunities do not cause the crimes; rather, they are the occasions for crime.[9]

The professional criminal regards crime as a career. He or she is committed to a criminal value system and way of life. These thieves rely on their acquired skills, techniques, and knowledge to commit their crimes. Career criminals are usually quite good at avoiding detection and apprehension when committing crime, unlike amateurs. As we have seen in Reading 2.1, according to Edwin Sutherland, the **professional thief** "devotes his entire working time and energy to larceny. . . . Every act is carefully planned. . . . The professional thief has technical skills and methods . . . is generally migratory and may work in all the cities of the United States . . . [and] has nothing in common with the amateur thief. The professional thief has status [and] is part of an underworld [that] defines its own membership."[10]

The professional thief's status is based on his or her technical skills, power, financial standing, connections, dress, manners, and experience. According to Sutherland, professionals such as forgers, shoplifters, confidence men, extortionists, pickpockets, jewel thieves, and hotel thieves depend on their well-developed skills and wits. They are organized and learn from one another. They are also

> The **amateur thief** is an occasional criminal uncommitted to a criminal value system.
>
> A **situational inducement** is a short-run influence on a person's behavior that increases risk taking, such as peer influence (social factors) or financial problems (psychological factors).

> The **professional thief** devotes his or her entire working time and energy to larceny, in which every act is carefully planned.

DID YOU KNOW
Review Reading 2.1, "The Professional Thief," by Edwin Sutherland.

FOR YOUR INFORMATION

Amateur Thieves

- Amateur thieves are not adept at perpetrating crimes, nor are they very skilled in the avoidance of detection and apprehension.
- Amateur thieves do not consider themselves criminals and view their criminal behavior as being "out of character" with their conventional lives (going to work or school, being with friends, going to church, etc.).
- Amateur thieves are not considered professionals by career criminals; professional thieves hold themselves aloof from amateurs and have little regard for them.

protective of one another and bound by a consensus—a sharing of values with their peers. Accorded to their own peer subculture and to law enforcement personnel, professional thieves enjoy a status or position above that of "common criminals," and they pride themselves in this. Sutherland reported that, in the world of the professionals, the title "thief" is worn with much pride.[11]

There is debate in the field of criminology as to whether or not the professional criminal is a dying breed. According to Sheldon Messinger, professional criminals are growing increasingly rare as a result of weakening loyalty to other criminals and a decline in professionalism among persons who engage in criminal activities to make money.[12] Gresham M. Sykes reports, "Instead of being a full-time occupation, part of a life-style set off sharply from the law-abiding world, much criminal activity appears to be a form of moonlighting, in which crime is used to supplement the income from low-paying work."[13] Criminals today are more often working alone, are untutored when young, and do not belong to any criminal subculture. However, other researchers have reported that many of Sutherland's principles are still very much alive in a wide variety of professional crimes, such as stooping (picking up accidentally discarded winning racetrack tickets) and fencing (buying and selling stolen merchandise).[14] In any event, there continue to be thieves who are amateurs and thieves who are professionals.

Motor Vehicle Theft

Motor vehicle theft is one of the most common larceny offenses.

Motor vehicle theft (MVT) is the theft or attempted theft of a motor vehicle, including automobiles, trucks, buses, motorcycles, motor scooters, and snowmobiles.

One of the most common larceny offenses is **motor vehicle theft (MVT)**, defined by the FBI as the theft or attempted theft of a motor vehicle, including automobiles, trucks, buses, motorcycles, motor scooters, and snowmobiles. In the United States, about 1.2 million motor vehicles are annually stolen from streets, parking lots, malls, garages, and driveways. The national annual MVT rate is about 450 per 100,000 people. As Figure 10.3 shows, after declining since 1992, MVT rates have recently begun to increase. Regionally, the MVT rates are highest in the South and West.[15]

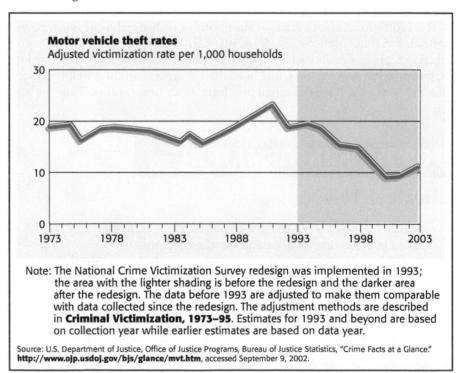

Note: The National Crime Victimization Survey redesign was implemented in 1993; the area with the lighter shading is before the redesign and the darker area after the redesign. The data before 1993 are adjusted to make them comparable with data collected since the redesign. The adjustment methods are described in **Criminal Victimization, 1973–95**. Estimates for 1993 and beyond are based on collection year while earlier estimates are based on data year.

Source: U.S. Department of Justice, Office of Justice Programs, Bureau of Justice Statistics, "Crime Facts at a Glance." **http://www.ojp.usdoj.gov/bjs/glance/mvt.htm**, accessed September 9, 2002.

FIGURE 10.3 Motor Vehicle Theft Rates

Car thieves steal for a variety of reasons: joyriding, short-term or long-term transportation, or profit. Thus, there are many different types of car thieves.

(1) Most young people steal cars to go out "*joyriding.*" This type of car thief is motivated by a need for the power, status, and recognition associated with having a car in our society. This type of theft, according to Charles McCaghy and fellow researchers, is not for financial profit or gain but for the short-term thrill of experiencing an American status symbol.[16]

(2) A second type of car thief is the *short-term transportation* thief. He or she uses the car only to go from one place to another. These thieves also steal cars in order to commit another crime, such as robbery or burglary.

(3) A third, usually older type of car thief, is the *long-term transportation* thief. This thief intends to keep the car for his or her personal use after repainting and disguising it.

(4) Some thieves steal cars for *profit*. Many of these are amateurs who steal parts such as tires, batteries, and wheel covers for a quick sale. Others are more organized, with highly sophisticated **chop shops** where new cars are quickly broken down into their component parts and resold at a high profit. Still other car thieves are highly organized professionals who steal high-priced cars on consignment and resell them after altering vehicle identification numbers and falsifying registration papers.[17] Parts from stripped and dismantled stolen cars, often targeted by specific make and model, are then sold on the black market. Researchers on chop shops and MVT have recently reported that border states, such as Texas, have higher MVT rates because of the ease with which stolen cars and car parts can be exported to other parts of the world.[18]

To combat the crime of MVT, insurance companies and auto-alarm manufacturers have developed a wide variety of antitheft devices to make it more difficult to steal cars. Some of the antitheft devices in use today are armored

A **chop shop** is a garage where stolen cars are broken down into their component parts for resale.

FOR YOUR INFORMATION

UCR motor vehicle theft statistics in 2005 show that:

- Nationwide in 2005, there were an estimated 1.2 million motor vehicle thefts, or approximately 416.7 motor vehicles stolen for every 100,000 inhabitants.
- The estimated volume and rate of motor vehicle thefts in 2005 decreased 0.2 percent and 1.1 percent respectively, when compared with data for 2004.
- When considering data for ten years earlier, the estimated volume and rate of motor vehicle thefts in 2005 decreased 11.4 percent and 20.7 percent, respectively, when compared with estimates for 1996.
- An estimated 93.3 percent of the nation's motor vehicle thefts occurred in Metropolitan Statistical Areas in 2005.
- Property losses due to motor vehicle theft in 2005 were estimated at $7.6 billion, averaging $6,173 per stolen vehicle.
- Among vehicle types, automobiles comprised 73.4 percent of the motor vehicles reported stolen in 2005.

Source: FBI, 2005 Uniform Crime Reports, Release date: September 2006.

Each year, about 1.2 million motor vehicles are stolen in the United States. According to criminological research, what are the three main reasons for stealing cars? How is carjacking different from motor vehicle theft?

ignition or starter cut-off switches, steering-column armored collars, fuel cut-off devices, steering-wheel locks, alarm systems, and auto tracking-transmitting systems. Unfortunately, as fast as many antitheft devices are employed, thieves are devising methods of disarming them. Over the past decade, however, better parking facilities and guarded lots have helped to make it more difficult for the car thief.

In tracking down chop shops and MVT, geographic information systems (GIS) have proved particularly useful in identifying MVT patterns, distances, and directions. According to Nancy G. LaVigne, Jill K. Fleury, and Joseph Szakas,

> Geographic Information Systems allow law enforcement agencies to establish a platform for automated mapping and to undertake more advanced analysis of spatial components. The distance-decay theory suggests that if a person is searching for a target and several targets are in his or her proximity, then, all else being equal, the person will choose the closest target. It is suggested that the location of chop shops from which the majority of vehicles are recovered will be closest in distance to the point from which the car was stolen. Data for analysis contained information on stolen automobiles over a 7 year period. . . . Results indicated that where the car was stolen and its recovery were valuable in determining two potentially important spatial components: distance and direction.[19]

Carjacking: From Nonviolent to Violent Crime

Carjacking can be easier than motor vehicle theft for criminals but is regarded as a more serious crime.

Because of the increasing difficulty in stealing a car due to antitheft devices, some thieves have increasingly been resorting to carjacking. *Carjacking* is a serious crime in which, instead of breaking into parked vehicles, thieves force drivers out of their cars at stop signs, parking lots, and red lights to steal their cars. A Los Angeles police detective believes that some criminals "are lazy." He indicated in an interview that "if you point a weapon and take a car, you don't have the hassle of breaking the window or popping the ignition, and the car's not damaged."[20] However, as one news article states, "A crime once considered 'victimless' is turning up casualties": "Kimberly Horton was waiting at a red light on the way home one July night when some young men decided they wanted her car. The twenty-one-year-old college student ended up on the sidewalk, shot in the head and dying. Her Honda Accord was pulled over two hours later, thirty-five miles away.... 'It's just beyond comprehension,' her father, the Rev. Richard Horton, said. 'All her hopes and dreams gone, and for such an inconceivable reason.'... And in a highly publicized carjacking [in 1992], a Maryland woman was dragged to her death."[21] Carjacking, therefore, is a good example of how the crime of theft, a nonviolent crime, can turn into a crime of violence. Currently, law enforcement personnel and political leaders are developing legislation and laws to help curb this serious crime.[22]

Shoplifting

Shoplifting accounts for 14 percent of all larcenies in America.

Shoplifting is the stealing or theft of goods from retail stores and merchants. The theft can take place in a small shop or in a large department or discount store. The goods stolen can range from toothpaste and laxatives to meat, clothing, and jewelry.

Studies report that one out of every eight or nine shoppers is a shoplifter. They come in all sizes, shapes, and colors: rich, middle-class, and poor; young, middle-aged, and old. They are out of work or employed, unskilled workers or professionals. They come from all racial and ethnic groups and are just as likely to be a man as they are to be a woman.[23] Shoplifters will steal when store clerks are occupied with customers or are busy elsewhere in the store, taking items from shelves and counters and shoving them into their pockets, between their legs, and into their baby carriages, underwear, or mouths—a method recently used by diamond thieves. Shoplifting accounts for 14 percent of all larcenies and costs several billion dollars each year. These costs, and the costs of security measures—guards and electronic security devices, for example—are then passed on to consumers in the form of higher prices.[24]

A major, now-classic study on shoplifting was conducted by Mary Owen Cameron in the 1960s. She divided shoplifters into professionals and amateurs. According to her report, most shoplifters are amateurs, or snitches. Her findings about amateurs include:

- A snitch does not believe himself or herself to be a criminal.
- Amateurs may be otherwise "respectable" people who systematically shoplift merchandise for their own use.
- Amateurs are prepared to steal when shopping and are not merely responding to a sudden urge to take something.
- When caught, amateurs usually have no record of a previous shoplifting apprehension.[25]

Professional shoplifters, by contrast, share the following characteristics:

- They make up about 10 percent of all shoplifters.
- They derive most of their income from the sale of stolen goods.

Shoplifters are male or female, rich or poor, young or old. Shoplifters also are amateur or professional. What proportion of shoplifting is conducted by professionals? What most likely will happen to the items a person steals?

Many professional shoplifters can be distinguished from amateurs by the use of mechanical devices. For example, a professional shoplifter may carry a "booster box," which is wrapped to suggest that it will be sent through the mail. Built into the box is a trapdoor that opens to receive stolen items. The "booster coat" is constructed with a loosened lining that permits stolen items to be dropped into the billowy bottom. These coats may also be lined with hooks to hold concealed items.[26] Cameron's research indicated that professional shoplifters share the characteristics of professional thieves as reported by Sutherland.

Amateur shoplifters, on the one hand, steal out of greediness or because they need the merchandise. A good opportunity may also precipitate a theft. Sometimes people will shoplift because they are depressed, under great stress, or have psychological problems. *Professional shoplifters,* on the other hand, steal for profit. They resell the stolen goods to fences and pawnshops.[27]

To combat heavy losses from shoplifting, retailers have increasingly employed a wide variety of technologically advanced security devices. These devices range from elaborate video systems to electronic tags and magnetic clips and strips. This type of theft, however, is very difficult to control.

- Research by criminologists has shown that only about 10 percent of shoplifting incidents are detected by store employees.
- When customers observe other people shoplifting (the great majority go unobserved), they are usually unwilling to report the behavior to store managers.

- Even when stores maintain strong antishoplifting policies and employees report shoplifters to management, they will rarely prosecute.

Some studies have found that those previously arrested for shoplifting were more likely to shoplift than those who had never been arrested. Other studies have found that shoplifters who had been arrested were traumatized by the apprehension and would not risk a second offense.[28]

Identity Theft

Identity theft has risen significantly in the United States in the past five years and causes many serious problems for victims.

People steal many things besides cars and merchandise. Almost anything that one can think of has been stolen at one time or another, including boats, planes, manhole covers, street signs, credit cards, checks, works of art, and musical instruments. People steal computers, databanks, and information. They also steal pets, clothing, and books. Thieves also steal people's identities.

Identity theft is the theft of a person's identity for the purpose of stealing property. Identity theft is becoming much more common in the United States. Each year, several hundred thousand people have their identity stolen, up from about 10,000 annual thefts in the mid-1990s. Identity thieves obtain information from a person's credit reports and mail. They use information such as account numbers and social security numbers to open new accounts in the victim's name, run up charges, and withdraw cash from these new accounts. Many identity thieves also use another person's identity when they are arrested for other crimes. Months may pass before an identity-theft victim discovers the crime and finds that his or her credit is ruined or that there is an outstanding arrest warrant in his or her name.

It is a federal crime to steal an individual's identity. The Identity and Assumption Deterrence Act of 1998 (the Identity Theft Act) made it a crime to knowingly use or transfer (without legal authority) the identification documentation of another person with the intent to aid (or abet) any unlawful activity that constitutes a felony.

After reading this section, you should be able to

1. define and describe the nature and prevalence of five types of larceny;
2. profile the crimes of larceny–theft, motor vehicle theft, carjacking, shoplifting, and identity theft;
3. explain the differences between an amateur and a professional thief in each type of larceny;
4. analyze offenders' motivations and the public's responses to larceny in the United States.

10.4 FRAUD

Fraud is defined in *Black's Law Dictionary* as "an intentional perversion of truth for the purpose of inducing another in reliance upon it to part with some valuable thing belonging to him or to surrender a legal right."[29] Fraud, or false pretenses, involves the acquiring of another person's property through deception

> **Fraud,** or false pretenses, involves the acquiring of another person's property through deception or cheating.

READING ABSTRACT

Crimes of Fraud

BY JAMES A. INCIARDI

This reading, an excerpt from James A. Inciardi's book *Careers in Crime,* examines the swindle or confidence game. Inciardi writes that this form of fraud is well-documented throughout history.

See reading on page 300.

or cheating. Because the victim of fraud willingly gives his or her goods or money to the offender, it is not considered to be theft. Larceny–theft involves a "trespass in the taking," whereas fraud does not.

Examples of fraud abound in our society. They range from such activities as selling vitamin pills and calling them a cure for AIDS, to defrauding coin dealers by purchasing coins with worthless checks, to elaborate schemes that bilk insurance companies out of billions of dollars. Many types of fraud exist, such as confidence games or swindling, forgery, and counterfeiting.

In spite of the efforts of law enforcement and the education of targeted individuals, such as the elderly, fraud and the opportunity to defraud others abound in our society. New areas to perpetuate fraud are continually opening. The Internet, for example, has provided an abundant means for fraud, including identity fraud. *Disaster fraud,* although not a new phenomenon, has recently been brought to the public's attention because of its proliferation following the September 11, 2001, World Trade Center disaster.

> **DID YOU KNOW**
> Chapter 11, on white-collar and organized crime, examines other types of fraud, such as securities and investment fraud and corporate fraud.

After reading this section, you should be able to

1. define and describe three major types of fraud;
2. use examples from Reading 10.1 on page 300 to explain how confidence games have a long history;

10.5 BURGLARY

According to the UCR, **burglary** is the unlawful entry of a structure to commit a felony or theft. The use of force to gain entry is not required to classify an offense as a burglary.[30] The word *burglar* comes from the two German words *berg,* meaning "house," and *laron,* meaning "thief" (literally, "house thief").

The NCVS makes note of the fact that burglary usually, but not always, involves theft. The illegal entry may be by force (cutting a screen or breaking a window or lock) or without force (entering through an open window or unlocked door). As long as a person has no legal right to be present in the structure (e.g., house, garage, hotel room), a burglary has occurred.[31]

> According to the UCR, **burglary** is the unlawful entry of a structure to commit a felony or theft.

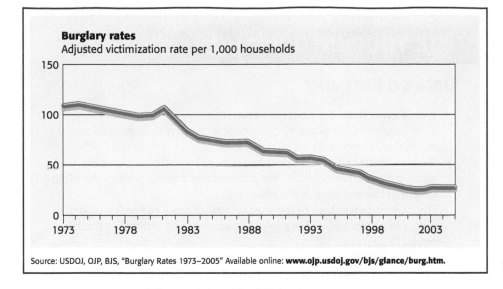

Burglary rates
Adjusted victimization rate per 1,000 households

Source: USDOJ, OJP, BJS, "Burglary Rates 1973–2005" Available online: **www.ojp.usdoj.gov/bjs/glance/burg.htm.**

FIGURE 10.4 Burglary Rates

- Americans are frightened by burglary. Many report that they feel personally violated when their houses or apartments have been burglarized. Victims are angry and resentful of the fact that someone invaded the privacy of their homes.
- Many people feel that their houses and apartments are extensions of themselves and report distressing feelings of emptiness, especially if items of personal importance have been stolen during the burglary.
- People fear personal harm from burglars; during one-third of burglaries, someone is at home.
- The majority of rapes in the home are committed by burglars.[32]

The UCR indicates that about 2.1 million burglaries are reported annually to the police. They make up about one-quarter of reported property crimes in the United States. The reported burglary rate is about 678 per 100,000 inhabitants.[33] As Figure 10.4 shows, the burglary rates have been steadily declining since 1981.[34]

PROFILES

Burglary

- The majority of U.S. burglaries occur from July through December; the minority occur from January through June.
- The peak month is August, when many people are vacationing, whereas the fewest are reported in February.
- Distribution figures by region indicate that the lowest volume of burglaries occurs in the northeastern states, with 12 percent (the rate is about 470 for every 100,000 in the population). This is followed by the midwestern states, with 21 percent (678 per 100,000); the western states, with 23 percent (736 per 100,000); and the southern states, which are the most populous, with 45 percent (927 per 100,000).

Source: U.S. Department of Justice, Federal Bureau of Investigation, Uniform Crime Reports, *Crime in the United States, 2001,* "Section II—Crime Index Offenses Reported," Washington, DC: Government Printing Office, October 28, 2002, pp. 44–47.

Burglary **287**

FOR YOUR INFORMATION

Data on Burglary

- Two of every three burglaries are residential.
- Most burglaries (61 percent) occur during the day. Most nonresidential burglaries (58 percent) occur at night.
- Burglary clearances occur either by arrest or by exceptional means (i.e., when circumstances beyond law enforcement control prevent the placing of formal charges against the offender).
- The highest percentage of reported annual clearances involve unlawful entry (14 percent); forcible entry (12 percent); and attempted forcible entry (11 percent).
- The estimated number of annual arrests nationwide for burglary is 300,000, an arrest rate of 103 per 100,000 inhabitants.
- In terms of age, 31 percent of annual burglary arrestees are juveniles (under age eighteen; 12 percent are under age fifteen).
- In terms of gender, males account for 86 percent of arrestees. Of these arrests, 32 percent are males under the age of eighteen.
- Fourteen percent of those arrested for burglary are females. Of those females arrested, 27 percent are juveniles.
- In terms of race, 69 percent of annual burglary arrestees are white. About 30 percent of burglary arrestees are black.

Source: U.S. Department of Justice, Federal Bureau of Investigation, Uniform Crime Reports, *Crime in the United States, 2001,* "Section II—Crime Index Offenses Reported," Washington, DC: Government Printing office, October 28, 2002, pp. 44–47.

According to the NCVS, there are about 3.5 million household burglaries each year in the United States. This figure is about 1.4 million burglaries higher than that reported in the UCR, reflecting that many victims are not reporting victimizations to the police. Nevertheless, the NCVS data, like the UCR data, show that burglary rates are down from earlier levels. Reasons given by victims for not reporting burglaries include:

- the object was recovered, or the offender was unsuccessful;
- there was a lack of proof;
- they were not aware a crime had occurred until later;
- they thought police would not want to be bothered; and
- they reported the theft to another official.

Victims *did* report burglaries for the following reasons:

- to recover property (the most frequent reason given);
- because it was a crime;
- to prevent further crimes against themselves by the offender.[35]

Types of Burglars and Their Methods

Most burglars are amateurs. Some are professionals who progress through a series of career stages.

Most burglars throughout the United States are amateurs, sharing the following characteristics:

- *Amateur burglars* tend to be relatively unskilled and commit only occasional burglaries along with a variety of other crimes.
- Most amateur burglars tend to live near or in the places they burglarize.
- Amateurs are in search of immediate economic rewards.
- Upon entering an apartment or house, amateurs search for cash, jewelry, or other items that can readily be converted to cash by a fence.
- Unlike the professional burglar, the amateur is noisier and more forceful in methods of entry.[36]

Professional burglars, or what Neal Shover calls "good burglars," are quite different from amateurs. In his research, Shover found that professionals shared the following characteristics:

- They have technical competence and specialty in their field.
- They maintain a sense of personal integrity.
- They have financial success in their criminal behavior.
- They have an ability to avoid imprisonment.[37]

Like any other professionals, many burglars go through a series of career-development stages. Paul F. Cromwell and associates report that the results of a study in which they used the interview method of data collection reflect a three-stage career progression: the novice, the journeyman, and the professional stages.

(1) During the *novice stage,* the young burglar learns burglary methods and techniques from the older, more experienced practitioner. Provided they find their own markets for their stolen goods, the novices will be tutored by the older professionals.

(2) During the *journeyman stage,* the developing young burglar is permitted to take part when the professional is planning and searching for new opportunities and targets. He (the great majority of burglars are men) is also now allowed by the elders to "partake in hits" and to develop his expertise and reputation as a trustworthy, experienced burglar. The status of professional burglar is achieved when the journeyman burglar can maintain a high level of organizational skill and ability that enables him to carefully plan and carry out the crime, and when he is recognized by his peers as such.[38]

(3) Being a burglar in the *professional stage* is not easy. This burglar chooses targets that he has very carefully "cased." Many work in teams with a complex division of labor wherein each member, with his own area of expertise, is assigned a particular task that must be precisely executed. The professional burglar is expert in the disarming of alarm systems; in fact, this skill is what primarily distinguishes the professional from novice and journeyman burglars.[39]

Many criminologists have become increasingly interested in how burglars choose their targets. Why do they pick one community over another? Why do they pick one house over another? What conditions and factors does a burglar take into consideration when choosing a target? Some of these questions were answered by George Rengert and John Wasilchick in their interview-survey research on suburban burglary.[40]

In Rengert and Wasilchick's study, burglars reported the following information regarding their decision-making patterns, methods, and techniques. These results reveal differences in the way burglaries are planned, targets are selected, and situational cues are noted:

- "A professional burglar is involved in extensive planning before taking any action. Amateurs plan much less.
- Before targeting a home, the less experienced burglar will examine some of the more obvious clues that no one is there, such as newspapers piled high on a doorstep, excessive mail in the mailbox, and an active burglar-alarm system. The more experienced professional will assess these clues, but he will also evaluate more subtle clues, such as whether air-conditioning systems are shut down in homes with closed, locked windows.
- A more experienced burglar will pay close attention to situational clues that the amateur may miss, such as choosing a house located on a corner, because it offers more opportunities for escape, has fewer adjoining properties, and offers greater visibility.
- Burglars select particular communities over others, where they are familiar with the area, are less likely to be recognized by someone, and are not going to stand out as someone who doesn't belong.
- Time is a major factor in burglary. Many burglars have only a limited number of hours available for committing burglary; that is, they may

Neighborhood crime-watch groups may involve residents in patrolling their neighborhoods and reporting to the police any unusual or suspicious activities. Many criminal-investigation studies have underscored the citizens' important role in effective local crime prevention and law enforcement, especially against the crime of burglary. What should neighborhood crime-watch participants watch out for? What else can they do to prevent burglaries?

have other commitments, such as a legitimate job or family obligations, that limit their 'working hours.' In addition, the burglar must minimize the time spent in the targeted area(s) in order not to reveal his criminal intentions."[41]

A recent study by Susan M. Walcott stresses individual and community characteristics in addition to the factors of place and time. She reports the following:

> The best approach to predicting place vulnerability combines individual and community characteristics. Young, unmarried males experience the highest rates of victimization. Burglaries of residential property usually occur by entry through a door. Visibility or "surveillability" is the key factor affecting susceptibility of a structure to burglary. Areas of highest unemployment and transience are key burglary sites. Lowest rates are guarded entry areas, where security guards, dogs, or alarm systems present obstacles to entry. Homes with children or elderly residents also seem to provide deterrence. Suburban burglaries are characterized by planning rather than passion. Situational opportunities aside, sites falling along a home-work-leisure path are the most likely targets. Timing patterns vary depending on the occupation pattern of residents.[42]

Responses to Burglary

Many new procedures and technologies have been developed to fight the crime of burglary.

A number of new techniques and approaches have been developed to curb burglaries. Lewis Yablonsky reports that sophisticated portable crime-lab kits and computers have reduced crime in some communities: "In one district in San Francisco, specialized units with portable crime-lab kits respond immediately to obtain physical evidence. Arrests increased substantially, and reported burglaries declined 25 percent over the year. . . . In some communities, police have fed information on past burglaries into computers. They claim that the computer gives them information that helps them predict when and where burglaries are likely to occur. In one computer experiment, the rate of reported burglaries dropped 25 percent."[43]

Other research, conducted by Lawrence Sherman and associates, has shown that during a one-year period in Minneapolis, 324,000 calls to the police came in from 155,000 addresses and city intersections. Of the total calls, 16,000 were burglary calls that came from only 11 percent of the city's addresses and street intersections. With this information, police and other law enforcement agencies could target high-rate burglary areas and employ prevention strategies that might reduce criminal opportunities.[44]

Many communities throughout the United States have developed what have been termed "neighborhood crime-watch" programs, in which neighbors keep a close eye on each other's houses and apartments. Research has shown that citizen-provided information leads to far more crimes solved and criminal perpetrators apprehended than extensive police detective work. Citizen involvement, awareness, and "prompt, complete, and accurate reports to the police, not magical genius and superweapons, are instrumental in apprehending and convicting suspects."[45]

10.6 FENCING

What becomes of property that is stolen through larceny–theft or burglary? Thieves and burglars usually want to dispose of stolen merchandise quickly, so they will seek out a fence. A *fence* is a receiver of stolen goods who operates in conjunction with thieves and burglars to dispose of those goods. Fences are an important part of the trade in stolen property. Many fences are "legitimate" businesspeople who "have a retail outlet for specific articles, and maintain regular contact with thieves."[46]

Criminologist Carl B. Klockars spent several hundred hours in Philadelphia interviewing and studying a professional fence known as Vincent Swaggi. Klockars reported three criteria that distinguish a fence from other people who trade in stolen goods:

(1) "The fence must be a dealer in stolen property; that is, a buyer and seller with direct contact with thieves (sellers) and customers (buyers), not simply a member of a burglary gang charged with selling what is stolen, nor a thief hustling his own swag, nor an 'in-between man' or 'piece man' trading on his knowledge of where certain types of property can be sold.

(2) The fence must be successful: he must buy and sell stolen property regularly and profitably, and have done so for a considerable period of time, perhaps years.

(3) The fence must be public: he must acquire a reputation as a successful dealer in stolen property among lawbreakers, law enforcers, and others acquainted with the criminal community. He must arrive at a way of managing the full-time significance of that reputation.[47]

To be a successful fence, according to a professional fence interviewed and studied by Darrell Steffensmeier,

- one must have plenty of up-front cash to buy stolen goods and merchandise quickly;
- one must have the extensive knowledge base to "wheel and deal"; that is, to buy at very low prices, sell at a good profit, and not get caught;
- one must have excellent long-term connections and relationships with honest and stable suppliers and buyers of stolen merchandise and goods;
- one must have complicity with cooperative law enforcement people through bribery with cash or merchandise.[48]

After reading this section, you should be able to

1. define fencing;
2. explain what it takes to succeed as a professional fence.

Fires that are intentionally set endanger lives as well as property. According to criminological research, what are the three main motivations for arson? Arson is a unique offense because it is not always investigated by law enforcement. Why is that the case?

10.7 ARSON

As defined by the UCR, **arson** is "any willful or malicious burning or attempt to burn, with or without intent to defraud, a dwelling house, public building, motor vehicle or aircraft, personal property of another, etc. . . . Only fires determined through investigation to have been willfully or maliciously set are classified as arsons."[49] Since 1979, arson has been a Part I index crime. It causes much property damage and also threatens life. Under common law, arson was considered to be the willful, malicious burning of another person's house or outbuilding; the penalty was death. Today, arson laws now extend to cover "other buildings, personal property, crops, and

Arson is "any willful or malicious burning or attempt to burn, with or without intent to defraud, a dwelling house, public building, motor vehicle or aircraft or personal property of another."

FOR YOUR INFORMATION

Arson

- About 69,000 arson offenses are annually reported by U.S. law enforcement agencies.
- The annual reported arson rate is about thirty-six offenses per 100,000 population.
- Structures are the most frequent targets of arsonists, accounting for about 42 percent of reported incidents.
- Mobile property such as motor vehicles and trailers account for 33 percent, and other types of property such as crops and timber account for 25 percent of reported incidents.

- Residential property is involved in about 61 percent of the annual structural arsons.
- Structural losses annually average about $20,000. Mobile property losses annually average about $7,000 per incident.

Source: U.S. Department of Justice, Federal Bureau of Investigation, Uniform Crime Reports, *Crime in the United States, 2001,* "Section II—Crime Index Offenses Reported," Washington, DC: Government Printing Office, October 28, 2002, pp. 56–58.

the burning of one's own property. . . . The elements of the crime of arson include: Willful, malicious burning of a building or property of another; or one's own to defraud; or causing to be burned, or aiding, counseling, or procuring such burning."[50]

According to the UCR, only fires determined through investigation to have been willfully or maliciously set are classified as arson. Fires of suspicious origins are excluded. The UCR states the following: "Arson is a unique offense because it is not always investigated by law enforcement. In some communities, arson offenses are investigated by fire marshals within the local fire department. In such cases, the incidents are less likely to be reported to the UCR Program. Because the level of reporting may be lower than for the other Crime Index offenses, arson data should not be regarded as a comprehensive accounting of the national arson problem. Rather, these statistics serve as an indicator of the types of arson incidents occurring in the Nation."[51]

Some studies report that incendiary and suspicious fires in the United States annually result in about $1.3 billion in property damage and several hundred deaths. Other research indicates annual property losses run as high as several billion dollars with several thousand deaths. According to the National Fire Protection Association (NFPA), the number of incendiary and suspicious structure fires in the United States has decreased 57 percent since 1977. Related deaths have dropped 42 percent. In seventeen of twenty-two years studied by NFPA from 1977 to 1999, the number of these fires either fell or remained the same.[52]

There are several explanations for why people commit arson. Some fires are set by people who have a psychological disorder. Others are set out of anger, a desire to vandalize, or a desire to "get even" with another person. Still other fires are set simply for profit. There are even professional arsonists (called "torches") who, for a fee, will burn down any structure. Concealment is another motive. The Law Enforcement Assistance Administration's arson-investigation department reports the following common motives for the crime: revenge, spite, and jealousy; vandalism and malicious mischief; crime concealment and diversionary tactics; profit and insurance fraud; intimidation, extortion, and sabotage; and psychiatric afflictions, pyromania, alcoholism, and feeblemindedness.[53]

Some people recurrently fail to control or resist impulses to set fires. They have an intense fascination with setting fires and watching them burn. These people are considered by psychologists and psychiatrists to have the impulse disorder termed *pyromania*. Psychiatrists believe that before setting the fire, the arsonist with pyromania experiences a buildup of tension and that once the fire has started, he or she experiences intense pleasure or release.

- Individuals with the diagnosis of pyromania are "often recognized as regular 'watchers' at fires in their neighborhoods, frequently set off false alarms, and show interest in fire-fighting paraphernalia."
- People with pyromania may be "indifferent to the consequences of the fire for life or property, or they may get satisfaction from the resulting destruction."
- Cases of pyromania have been described in which the person was sexually aroused by the fire.[54]

In dealing with pyromania, mental health professionals have developed counseling and therapeutic techniques to provide treatment and rehabilitation for these troubled children and adults. Community and school educational and counseling programs also have been developed to provide early identification and treatment of young, psychologically troubled would-be arsonists.[55]

Some arsons are for profit. There are a number of financial reasons why people will burn down, or will have someone else burn down, their property. A businessperson, for example, may turn to arson to collect fire insurance because business is bad or because he or she is deeply in debt and sees no other way out. People will also commit arson to destroy old inventories of equipment and machinery, to profitably remodel their place of business, or to destroy a competitor.[56]

According to criminal investigators, concealment motivates many criminals to commit arson to destroy evidence of a crime or evidence connecting themselves to the crime. For example, in murder cases, arson may make victim identification impossible. In other cases, people set fires to destroy records that contain evidence of fraud, forgery, or embezzlement. Arson is also used to "divert attention while a criminal commits another crime or covers his escape."[57]

Criminal-investigation specialists experience some problems in investigating and dealing with arson. As Wayne Bennett and Karen Hess report, these problems include coordinating efforts with the fire department and others, "determining if a crime has been committed, finding physical evidence and witnesses, and determining if the victim is also a suspect."[58]

After reading this section, you should be able to

1. define arson and describe the nature and extent of arson in the United States;
2. explain the reasons that people commit arson.

This chapter discusses property crimes, primarily focusing on the crimes of larceny–theft, fraud, burglary, fencing, and arson. The object of property crime is the taking of money or property; there is no force or threat of force against the victims. Most larceny–thefts are committed by amateur criminals. The professional thief, by contrast, devotes his or her entire working time and energy to larceny—every act is carefully planned (pp. 276–280).

One of the most common larceny offenses is auto theft. There are many different types of car thieves and reasons for stealing cars, the most common of which are young people who steal cars to go out "joyriding." Because of the increasing difficulty in stealing a car due to antitheft devices, some thieves have increasingly resorted to carjacking. This crime, once considered victimless, is now turning up casualties (pp. 280–283).

Shoplifting is another type of theft. People shoplift for a wide variety of reasons. Amateurs shoplift out of greediness or because they need the merchandise. A good opportunity may also motivate an individual to shoplift. Some people shoplift because they are depressed, under great stress, or have psychological problems. Professional shoplifters, by contrast, steal for profit. Thieves also steal people's identities. The crime of identity theft has grown considerably during the past five years (pp. 283–285).

Fraud, or false pretenses, involves the acquiring of another person's property through deception or cheating. There exist many types of fraud, including confidence games or swindling, forgery, and counterfeiting. The extent of fraud in the United States is enormous. The chapter readings focus on the crimes of Internet fraud and disaster fraud. A greater number of criminals are now using the Internet to commit business opportunity scams, credit card fraud, and investment and other types of fraud. Disaster fraud occurs when the government, individuals, or insurance companies are defrauded after a natural or human-made disaster (pp. 285–286).

Burglary is the unlawful entry or attempted entry of a residence. Most burglars in the United States are amateurs. They tend to be relatively unskilled and commit only occasional burglaries along with a variety of other crimes. Professional burglars, by contrast, have technical competence and specialty in their field, maintain a sense of personal integrity, have financial success in their criminal behavior, and have an ability to avoid imprisonment. Many communities throughout the United States have developed neighborhood crime-watch programs in which neighbors keep a close eye on each other's houses and apartments (pp. 286–291).

A fence is a receiver of stolen goods who operates in conjunction with thieves and burglars to dispose of such goods for profit. Fences are an important part of the trade in stolen property (p. 292).

Arson is a major crime that causes much property damage and also threatens life. Some arsons are committed by people who have a psychological disorder (pyromania); others are set out of anger, a desire to vandalize, or a desire to get even with another person. Still other fires are set for profit or concealment (pp. 293–295).

Study Guide

Chapter Objectives

- Define and describe the nature of property crimes.
- Describe the nature and extent of larceny–theft in the United States.
- Explain the differences between an amateur and a professional thief.
- Describe the nature and extent of motor vehicle theft in the United States.
- List the different explanations for and responses to car theft.
- Describe the nature of carjacking.
- Describe the nature and extent of shoplifting in the United States.
- Explain the differences between an amateur and a professional shoplifter.

- Briefly explain why people shoplift and how to combat shoplifting.
- Briefly describe and examine three major types of fraud.
- Describe the nature and extent of burglary in the United States.
- List the different types of burglars and their methods.
- Describe the techniques and approaches that have been developed to curb burglary in the United States.
- Describe the crime of fencing.
- Describe the nature and extent of arson in the United States.
- Explain the reasons why people commit the crime of arson.

Key Terms

Amateur thief (279)
Arson (293)
Burglary (286)
Chop shop (281)

Fraud (285)
Larceny–theft (276)
Motor vehicle theft (MVT) (280)
Professional thief (279)

Property crimes (275)
Situational inducement (279)

Self-Test
Short Answer

1. Write a definition of property crimes.
2. Describe the professional thief.
3. Briefly describe MVT in the United States.
4. Write a short list of reasons why people shoplift.
5. Briefly describe three different types of fraud.
6. Describe Internet fraud.

7. List and briefly describe the professional burglar's three-stage career progression.
8. Briefly describe how burglars choose their targets.
9. Write a brief paragraph describing the crime of fencing.
10. Briefly describe arson. List three motives for committing arson.

Multiple Choice

1. Which of the following property crimes is excluded from the UCR?
   a. burglary
   b. motor vehicle theft
   c. arson
   d. none of the above
2. For Sutherland, professional thieves
   a. are organized and learn from one another

b. are protective of one another

c. enjoy a status above that of "common criminals"

d. all of the above

3. Thieves steal cars

a. in order to commit another crime or crimes

b. for profit

c. for parts

d. any of the above

4. Shoplifting accounts for what percentage of all larcenies?

a. 14 percent

b. 34 percent

c. 54 percent

d. 74 percent

5. Which of the following crimes does not come under the category of fraud?

a. fencing

b. forgery

c. confidence games

d. counterfeiting

6. Which of the following is not a type of Internet crime?

a. business opportunity scheme

b. identity theft

c. credit card fraud

d. boat theft

7. Approximately how many household burglaries occur annually in the United States, according to the NCVS?

a. 2 million

b. 3.5 million

c. 8.5 million

d. 12 million

8. For Shover, professional burglars

a. are not that different from amateurs and have little integrity

b. have technical competence in their field

c. have little financial success in their criminal behavior

d. none of the above

9. For Klockars, in order to be called a fence, a person must

a. deal in stolen property

b. be successful

c. be public

d. all of the above

10. Which of the following elements is not included in the crime of arson?

a. willful, malicious burning of a building or property

b. defrauding insurance companies

c. entering with the intent to commit a crime

d. causing property to be burned, or aiding, counseling, or procuring such burning

Fill-In

1. _____ is the unlawful taking, carrying, leading, or riding away of property from the possession or constructive possession of another.

2. The _____ criminal regards crime as a full-time career.

3. _____ are very helpful in identifying MVT patterns, distances, and directions.

4. A crime once considered victimless that is now turning up casualties is _____.

5. According to Mary Owen Cameron, most shoplifters are amateurs, also called _____.

6. Counterfeiting and forgery are crimes of _____.

7. The professional _____ is expert in the disarming of alarm systems.

8. Many communities throughout the United States have developed _____ programs to combat burglary.

9. In the United States, arson is a major crime that can be triggered by an impulse disorder called _____.

Matching

1. Property crimes

2. Amateur thief

3. Professional thief

4. Professional shoplifter

5. Fraud

6. Fence

7. Professional burglar

8. Carjacking

9. Motor vehicle theft

A. Identity theft

B. Receives stolen goods

C. Uses a booster box or coat

D. Carefully plans thefts

E. Crime increasing as a result of antitheft devices

F. Steals spontaneously

G. No use of force

H. Carefully "cases" targets

I. Crime most likely to be reported to police

True–False

T F 1. The object of property offenses is to take money or property, but there is no force or threat of force against the victim.

T F 2. Personal theft is the most likely crime in the major categories of the NCVS to be reported to the police.

T F 3. Shoplifters are more likely to be women than men.

T F 4. The rates of identity theft have dramatically decreased in the past five years.

T F 5. Fraud is basically a crime of theft.

T F 6. Much disaster fraud occurred after the September 11, 2001 catastrophe.

T F 7. Burglary always involves theft.

T F 8. In the United States, most burglars are professionals.

T F 9. Arson is the malicious, unwillful burning of a building or property.

Essay Questions

1. After reading the material on larceny, do you believe that larceny–theft will increase or decrease in the near future? Why?

2. After reviewing the reading on motor vehicle theft, assess the problem of auto theft in your community. Have the rates of auto theft increased or decreased in recent years? Why? Is teen joyriding a problem in your neighborhood?

3. Review the text materials on shoplifting. Investigate and evaluate the level of the problem in your local community.

4. Check with your family members and friends to determine whether any of them have been a victim of fraud. Briefly describe and assess the crime using the information provided in this chapter. What could the victim have done, if anything, to prevent the crime?

5. Some communities have high rates of arson. Search out the statistics on arson in your community. Are they high or low? Why? If they are high, what, if anything, is your community doing about it?

Crimes of Fraud

Source: J.A. Inciardi, Careers in Crime, *Chicago: Rand McNally, 1975, pp. 22–28.*
Copyright © James A. Inciardi. Reprinted by permission.

BY JAMES A. INCIARDI

Swindling or confidence games refers to any operations in which advantage is taken of the confidence placed by the victim in the swindler or confidence man. A swindle or confidence game is fraud: any misrepresentation by trickery or deceit, any false representation by word or conduct.

CONFIDENCE SWINDLING

Activities of confidence swindlers have been known for centuries, perhaps even before the efforts of the Elizabethan rogues. The varieties and types of this form of criminality are as numerous as social situations, for a con game can be accomplished under any circumstances where one individual may place trust in another. The confidence operator is a smooth, adroit talker and has the ability to "size up" and manipulate people. Furthermore, he has a winning personality, is shrewd and agile, and is an excellent actor. The two classes of confidence games, the *big con* and the *short con,* are differentiated by the amount of preparation needed and the quantity of benefits reaped. . . . All confidence operations, whether large or small, usually involve the following steps:

1. Locating and investigating the victim *(putting up the mark)*
2. Gaining the victim's confidence *(playing the con)*
3. Steering him to meet the inside man *(roping the mark)*
4. Showing the victim how he can make a large amount of money, most often dishonestly *(telling the tale)*
5. Allowing the victim to earn a profit *(the convincer).* This is not always present in short-con games
6. Determining how much the victim will invest *(the breakdown)*
7. Sending the victim for his money *(putting him on the send)*
8. Fleecing him *(the touch)*
9. Getting rid of him *(the blowoff)*
10. Forestalling action by the law *(putting in the fix)*

THE SHORT CON

The short con is designed to obtain whatever money the victim may have on his person at the time he is approached. It can be operated at almost any place, and in a short period of time. Virtually thousands of rackets of this type have been undertaken over the years, but most of these have been variations of a few basic ideas. The success of the short-con racket depends upon a combination of four factors: (1) the existence of an opportunity, namely, a victim with money; (2) the easy, convincing manner of the confidence operator; (3) the gullibility of the victim; and (4) the desire of the victim to gain something dishonestly. Numerous writers suggest that it is the intrinsic dishonesty of the victim that makes the confidence game possible. Maurer maintained that the success of a confidence scheme depended upon the "fundamental dishonesty" of the victim, or as Chic Conwell, a professional thief, indicated, "it is impossible to beat an honest man in a confidence game." All professional thieves seem to agree on this point: the victim must have "larceny in his heart" before a swindle can be effected. [Edwin] Sutherland cites numerous comments by professional criminals on this point, and "Yellow Kid" Weil, perhaps the most famous of con men, stated that the men he fleeced were no more honest than he was.

One of the more common rackets, called *ring falling* by John Awdeley in his *The Fraternity of Vagabonds,* published in 1552, was reported again by Egan in the early nineteenth century as *ring-dropping.* A variety of ring-dropping might involve a pair of female victims and two swindlers. One operator would converse with the ladies as they walked, and after a short period he would find a pair of earrings, a ring, or some other jewelry along their path. After informing them that they were entitled to half the value of the articles, since they were in his presence when he found them, a second operator would appear, observe the goods, and declare that they were pure gold. The ensuing conversation would induce the women to provide money to the first operator for his share. When offered later to a jeweler, the women would learn that the jewelry was worthless. Another variation of this same idea exists now as the *pigeon drop.* This short con is similar to high-pressure salesmanship. After securing the victim, his gullibility is played upon by the manipulative abilities of the operator. And as many observers have indicated, con men are usually well dressed, exuding an air of real or fictitious prosperity, and their smooth flow of conversation is wonderfully soothing to the vanity of the proposed victim.

The number of swindles would be difficult to calculate, yet in every arena of social activity, numerous varieties exist. In 1873, sixty-four different types of swindles were listed by Lening, and some years later, MacDonald described no less than one hundred varieties. The more common short-con rackets include the selling of worthless articles, allegedly stolen or of a high value but "discounted"; the legitimate purchase of goods with worthless checks; and swindles with dice or cards. Descriptions and explanations of numerous short-con enterprises in all types of literature in the last few centuries indicate a fascination with the offense. In 1841, Douglas Jerrold, a journalist for *Punch* magazine, described the offense as it appeared in England at that time. Much of the antiurban literature, which launched a hostile attack upon city life from 1850 through the turn of the century, explored every phase of swindling and confidence operations. Greiner wrote an illustrated guidebook specifically designed as a warning to rural folk. It outlined more than two hundred and fifty swindles, the majority of which continue to exist.

THE BIG CON

Big-con games involve greater preparation than the short con, and the profits reaped are larger. The big-con men are uppermost in the professional underworld, and appear to be businessmen of the highest caliber. Their rackets include stock and real estate swindles, fraudulent business deals, and securing money under false pretenses from wealthy people. The three major big-con games are *the rag, the wire,* and *the payoff,* all of which follow the basic framework of confidence swindling in general. Perhaps the most well known of the big-con men was "Yellow Kid" Weil, mentioned earlier, who is said to have acquired about $8 million in various swindles and was a master at taking an everyday situation and turning it into a lucrative swindle.

Confidence men often dream about the rarely obtained "big one." It may be the fixed telegraph message that delays the results of a horse race, allowing one to bet heavily on a "sure thing"; it may be a land swindle that permits thousands of acres of worthless desert to earn millions of dollars; or it may be a fraud that disposes of millions of shares of worthless stock. This confidence game usually enables the professional to leave the rackets, and the execution of any such elaborate scheme is possible only with the accumulated wealth of knowledge obtained as a long-term operator. Among the more unique examples was the perpetual motion machine of John Ernest Worrell Keely. Keely, an ex-carnival pitchman, began a hoax in 1874 that reaped many fortunes and lasted for a quarter of a century. His nonexistent perpetual motion machine, "which would produce a force more powerful than steam and electricity," involved the financiers of many cities, the public of two continents, and the United States secretary of war. Before his career ended, Keely had a 372-page volume written on his "discovery," over a million dollars in cash, a life of luxury for twenty-five years, and an international reputation.

The story of John Keely is an unusual one, but the methods of his operation were not. The basic ingredients of the con were at work, a complex of factors that are still present in our social system. The practitioners of such operations may be less colorful than Keely, but the profits of many stock and land swindles often approach the size of his earnings.

CRITICAL THINKING

1. Have you ever been the victim of a con? How does this reading help to shed light on what happened?
2. What are the differences between a short and a big con?

Ex-Enron boss fights 11 charge[s]

By Marilyn Geewax
Cox News Service

INDICTED: Former Enron CEO Kenneth Lay is led into federal court in Houston.

Associated Press

Lay Hears Federal Charges in Court

By Dana Calvo AND DAVID STREITFELD

Adelphia founder, son are convicted

Result may boost civil suit

By David Lieberman and Michael McCarthy
USA TODAY

NEW YORK — Adelphia Communications founder John Rigas became the first former CEO of a major company to be convicted of accounting fraud in the post-Enron era Thursday.

A U.S. District Court jury here found Rigas and his son and former CFO, Timothy, guilty of conspiracy and bank and securities fraud. They were acquitted of wire fraud.

Prosecutors say they bilked shareholders of the No. 5 cable operator $3.2 billion while siphoning millions for personal use.

John Rigas, 79, and Timothy, 47, each could be sentenced to as many as 25 years in jail. They and their lawyers wouldn't comment on the decisions.

Also among four executives on trial was another son, Michael, 50, the former exec[utive]...

John Rigas: Adelphia founder.

D. Acker, Bloomberg News

...chairman holds ...sky news conference

By Greg Farrell
USA TODAY

Former Enron chairman and chief executive Kenneth Lay, charged with 11 criminal counts of fraud and conspiracy, launched a robust defense Thursday of his role in the energy company's meltdown, holding a news conference in Houston to proclaim his innocence and asking for a speedy trial.

"As CEO...

court: Ken Lay wea[rs] [ha]ndcuffs Thursday.

By Michael Stravato...

Media meeting: Ken Lay show[ed] [c]onfidence, 1...

defense in m[...]

premised on a complete absen[ce] and reliance on others," says Jac[k] Gambrell & Russell. "What Ken La[y] that in his own wor[ds]
▶ To catch prosec[utors]

Jur[y] 2 in A[...] Fraud

Founder John Rigas and his [son] guilty of looting the cable TV f[irm] acquitted of some charges in a pa[...]

By THOMAS S. MULLIGAN AND SALLIE HO[...]
Times Staff Writers

NEW YORK — In a big win for corporate crim[e] York federal jury Thursday convicted Adelphia Corp. founder John J. Rigas and his son Timothy of insolvent cable TV company and lying to investors abo[ut]

The jury of seven women and five men found John Rigas, 79, and Timothy J. Rigas, 48, guilty of conspiracy, bank fraud and securities fraud after eight days of deliberations that followed a laborious 18-week trial. The two face prison terms of as many as 30 years.

In a partial verdict, the jury acquitted Michael J. Rigas, 50, another of John Rigas' sons, of conspiracy and wire fraud but was undecided on charges of securities fraud and bank fraud. U.S. District Judge Leonard...

11.1 INTRODUCTION: WHITE-COLLAR CRIME DEFINED

In formulating his differential association theory of crime, Edwin H. Sutherland was attempting to explain a wide variety of crime, particularly what is termed "white-collar," or occupational, crime. In his study *White-Collar Crime*, Sutherland defined **white-collar crime**, or **occupational crime**, as "crime committed by a person of respectability and high social status in the course of his occupation."[1] This now-classic study of officially recorded corporate violations in the 1940s constitutes one of the most widely known and comprehensive research reports on white-collar crime to date. Sutherland revealed that corporate white-collar crime was extensive in seventy of the largest mining, manufacturing, and mercantile corporations in the United States. Included were 222 cases of patent infringement, 307 cases of restraint of trade, 158 cases of unfair labor practices, 97 cases of false advertising, 66 cases of illegal rebates, and 130 cases of miscellaneous corporate offenses.[2]

Since Sutherland coined the concept (in his presidential address to the American Sociological Society in 1940), white-collar crime has expanded to include a wide variety of occupational crimes in the business world, the government, and the professions. Numerous types of fraud (such as health-care fraud), embezzlement, kickbacks for political favors, illegal campaign contributions, illegal acts of high political officials, fee splitting, padding expense accounts, price-fixing, antitrust violations, and employee theft are all types of white-collar crime.

No one knows the true extent of or the actual cost to society of white-collar crime today. According to the U.S. Department of Justice *Report to the Nation on Crime and Justice*, few data are available on its extent. The report also indicates that measuring white-collar crime presents the following special problems:

- "No *uniform definitions exist* for either the overall scope of white-collar crime or individual criminal acts.
- *Wide variations in commercial record-keeping procedures* make it difficult to collect and classify data on the loss.
- *Uncertainty over the legal status* of financial and technical transactions complicates the classification of data.
- *Computer technology* can conceal losses resulting from computer crimes.
- *Crimes may not be reported* to protect consumer confidence."[3]

Despite these problems, estimated costs of white-collar crime run into the hundreds of billions of dollars.[4] The following examples are only a small sample of such crimes:

- Chrysler sold a number of 1987 cars as new when they actually had been used as demonstration models or as transportation for company executives. (The odometers had been turned back to zero.)[5]

- In 1988, the Hertz Corporation pleaded guilty to defrauding 110,000 customers, motorists, and insurance companies from 1978 to 1985 by charging them inflated and sometimes fictitious repair costs.[6]
- From 1985 to 1993, John Morrell and Company dumped slaughterhouse waste into the Big Sioux River in Sioux Falls, South Dakota. In 1996, the company pleaded guilty to these unlawful discharges and paid a $2 million criminal fine.[7]
- Several managers from GTE embezzled $1.3 million between 1992 and 1998.[8]
- In 1999, Sears Bankruptcy Recovery Management Services, a unit of Sears, Roebuck and Company, pleaded guilty to fraud. It paid a $60 million fine.[9]
- WorldCom admitted to inflating revenues by $11 billion beginning in 2000, and in 2003 agreed to pay a $500 million fine imposed by the Securities and Exchange Commission.[10]

Without a doubt, the economic cost to society of white-collar crime is far greater than that of property crime. Moreover, according to David R. Simon and D. Stanley Eitzen, street crime is "minuscule in terms of economic costs when compared to illegal activities by corporations. . . . The $2 to $3 billion lost in [just one equity funding fraud] involved more money 'than the total losses of all street crimes in the United States for one year.'"[11]

The money lost in this equity funding fraud does not even compare to the more recent losses due to the white-collar crimes committed by top executives at companies such as Enron and WorldCom. Before its collapse in 2001, Enron was the seventh-largest corporation in the United States. WorldCom, before its demise in 2002, was the second-largest long-distance calling service in the United States. It was also a major player in the Internet and in electronic commerce. Both Enron's and WorldCom's fraud and accounting scandals ran into the tens of billions of dollars. Hundreds of thousands of investors, consumers, and employees were victims of the white-collar crimes committed by top executives at these two companies.[12]

There are additional serious costs to our society from white-collar crime. August Bequai states, "White-collar crime poses a threat not only in terms of its impact on the thousands of victims that are defrauded of their hard-earned money, but also in terms of what the average citizen thinks of our system of justice. In a democracy, where consensus is the key stabilizing element, a cynical citizenry may signal the decay of that system. White-collar felons largely escape punishment because of the antiquated legal apparatus that is brought to bear against them . . . . A dual system of justice has come into being—one for the masses, who commit traditional offenses, and another for a small select group of white-collar felons."[13]

White-collar crime, according to the DOJ, refers to a group of nonviolent crimes that generally involve deception or abuse of power.

According to the U.S. Department of Justice, **white-collar crime** refers to a group of nonviolent crimes that generally involve deception or abuse of power, including the following:

- business-related crimes;
- abuse of political office;
- some aspects of organized crime;
- the newly emerging area of high-technology crime.[14]

White-collar crimes often involve the deception of a gullible victim and generally occur where a person's job, power, or personal influence provides the access and opportunity to abuse lawful procedures for unlawful gain. Specific white-collar crimes include the following:

- embezzlement;
- fraud (including procurement, stock, government-program, and investment fraud);

www.mycrimekit.com

- theft of services;
- theft of trade secrets;
- tax evasion;
- obstruction of justice.[15]

In addition, in white-collar and occupation-related criminal activities, one usually finds either of two underlying motives: some white-collar criminals use their position of trust for private or personal gain; others use their position in the corporate world to improve their company's power and profits illegally. Bank employees who embezzle money for gambling debts or overspending seek private gain. Corporate employees who are involved with price-fixing, theft of trade secrets, or illegal takeovers seek corporate power and profit gains.

After reading this section, you should be able to

1. define and give examples of white-collar crime;
2. explain the reasons for difficulties in measuring white-collar crime;
3. identify six specific white-collar crimes.

11.2 EMBEZZLEMENT AND CONSUMER FRAUD

White-collar crimes for private gain include embezzlement. According to *Black's Law Dictionary,* to embezzle means "willfully to take, or convert to one's own use, of another's money or property, of which the wrongdoer acquired possession lawfully, by reason of some office or employment or position of trust."[16] **Embezzlement**, then, is the taking or converting to one's own use money or property with which one has been entrusted. It is the *violation of trust* between the owner of the property or money and the offender that distinguishes embezzlement from other categories of theft. Embezzlement was not considered a crime in the United States until the late 1700s. It became a crime in response to the increased problem of employee theft.

> **Embezzlement** is the taking or converting to one's own use money or property with which one has been entrusted.

According to the *National White Collar Crime Center (NW3C),* two factors affect the ways that employees embezzle from an organization:

1. the type of property or money entrusted to the employee;
2. the employee's access to company funds (or property).

For example, "a department store cashier might steal from a cash register, fail to ring up purchases and pocket the money, give purchases to friends and family for considerable discounts, or take merchandise from storage rooms or receiving areas. Other employees with more access within the company might cheat on expense accounts, or misappropriate funds through billing, inventory, or payroll schemes."[17]

Even though the number of embezzlements is low compared to many other crimes, the financial impact is great. A single case may involve tremendous amounts of money. (One European bank lost $100 million to three officers.) The problem is greatly exacerbated by the use of computers to embezzle, making the crime "fast, easy (with the use of a personal computer and a modem), and very difficult to discover and prove."[18] Embezzlement and employee-related thefts of money and property are responsible for tens of billions of dollars in industrial losses each year.

Bank employees and other insiders have become quite sophisticated in their criminal activities. For example, if banking authorities had not been tipped off, a group of computer hackers could have bilked a cash-machine network out of as much as $14 million in one weekend. These insiders made up phony cards to steal cash from ATMs (automated teller machines). Federal agents stated that the insiders "pulled the personal ATM code numbers from GTE phone lines. The lines transmit transactions from accounts at Bank of America and thousands of other banks linked to the Plus System, a national network of shared ATMs. . . . [Those charged with these activities] then put the data in magnetic strips on 5,500 pieces of cardboard. They allegedly planned to use the bogus cards to make withdrawals around the country. Were it not for the tip, the plan 'would have worked,' says Richard J. Griffin, head of the Los Angeles office of the Secret Service."[19] In another incident, someone used a Security Pacific National Bank ATM master-access card that could tap into any account at the bank to steal $237,000, and precipitated the American Bankers Association to urge its members to strictly limit access to ATM master cards and personal identification codes.[20]

Banks are not the only target of embezzlers and white-collar thieves. The following are additional cases in which trusted white-collar employees have embezzled money:

- Corporate employees have used computers to print up paychecks to fictitious people, and department-store employees have credited their charge accounts with thousands of dollars and then gone shopping.[21]
- The former supervisor of accounts receivable of a major U.S. insurance company was convicted of embezzling more than $200,000 from the firm by putting false vouchers through the main computer, then programming it to issue checks to fictitious companies he owned. The fraud was discovered when a clerk noticed that one of the checks was for an unusually large amount.[22]
- Over an eight-year period, two women stole $400,000 from a union pension fund. One woman worked for the company that administered the fund; she ran false claims for pension benefits through the computer. Her accomplice cashed 600 of the fraudulent checks.[23]

In what ways could bank managers and tellers embezzle money from the bank? How might the computer make their crimes of embezzlement easier to commit? Why might you never find out if your bank lost millions to embezzlement?

- Over a seven-year period, several managers from GTE embezzled $1.3 million. They submitted bogus expense reports and bills from a fictitious contractor. After being found guilty of embezzlement in May 2002, one of the perpetrators was sentenced to forty-one months in federal prison and had to pay restitution. Another perpetrator was sentenced to two years and also required to pay restitution.[24]
- Between 1997 and 2000, an American Red Cross Society executive stole more than $7 million. He was the organization's chief financial officer and a computer expert who used his skills to embezzle the money. After being found guilty, he was sentenced to more than thirteen years in prison and required to pay restitution.[25]

Embezzlement is not easy to control, in that it is often committed in "labyrinthine ways to avoid detection." For example, "a hospital administrator netted $500,000 over five years in an elaborate scheme in which he laundered hospital funds through a dozen bank accounts, then paid 'supply' firms he controlled for nonexistent products and services provided the hospital."[26]

Embezzlement: Explanations and Responses

Many embezzlers are driven simply by avarice and temptation.

Why do people embezzle? In the 1950s, criminologist Donald Cressey studied embezzlers in prisons throughout the United States. He reported that embezzlers committed their crimes when they

1. came up against a "nonshareable" financial problem—one they felt could not be resolved with the help of another (e.g., a gambling debt or unusual family expense);
2. recognized that they could secretly resolve their problem by taking advantage of their positions of financial trust;
3. found ways to justify and rationalize their acts to retain self-concepts in which they were still worthy of financial trust.[27]

Cressey reported that embezzlers made a set of rationalizations for their criminal behavior that allowed them to view themselves as trustworthy, law-abiding people whose actions were morally and ethically justified. For example, embezzlers claimed that they were underpaid and taken advantage of for many years by their employers. This served as an excuse for embezzlement as fair retaliation.[28]

Some criminologists question Cressy's explanation for embezzlement and report that embezzlers justify their crimes not in terms of nonshareable problems but in terms of family needs. Other criminologists point out that many embezzlers are driven simply by avarice and temptation. These factors, combined with being in an appropriate job position, provide the opportunity and the means for embezzlement.[29]

Rod Willis recommends three rules that can help prevent businesses from becoming victims of embezzlement:

1. Keep tight, accurate, up-to-date business records.
2. Don't let any individual control or have access to the entire disbursement or accounts-receivable process.
3. Investigate all irregularities and complaints from vendors or suppliers quickly and thoroughly.[30]

Employee Pilferage and Theft

Forty percent or more of employees may be involved in theft from their employers.

Employee-related pilferage, theft, and fraud cost tens of billion dollars annually. From 35 to 40 percent or more of all employees may be involved in the theft of products, services, or time. In industries such as air-cargo handling and freight shipping, *employee thefts* may account for 80 percent of the losses. Internal losses were also blamed for the Federal Department Stores chains going out of business.[31]

Other things besides goods and materials are stolen. According to Rod Willis, employees and vendors steal time and services by

- putting friends or relatives on company payrolls;
- padding overtime records;
- making false claims on travel-expense forms;
- charging for services not rendered or goods never delivered;
- changing high-risk customers' ratings for kickbacks;
- creating false credit accounts.[32]

Simple pilferage—for example, when a sales clerk rings up a $200 sale as one for $100, or stealing from inventory and falsifying the records—is rampant in many industries.[33] Many of the incurred costs are then passed on to the consumer through higher prices for goods and services.

According to John P. Clark and Richard C. Hollinger, much employee theft and pilferage can best be explained by factors related to the thief's work setting. They downplay the importance of economic factors in an employee's decision to steal or pilfer. Instead, they report that factors such as job dissatisfaction and workers feeling exploited by their supervisors and employers more accurately explain employee theft.[34]

According to the NW3C, a major difficulty in responding to employee theft and embezzlement and developing policy to deal with it is that the reasons or rationales behind the offenses vary: "While a large number of crimes can be attributed to opportunity or the economic need of the offender, loss incurred through the actions of employees can also be a response to poor working conditions, dissatisfaction with management or compensation, or pressure from co-workers. The subsequent measures that organizations need to take, therefore, include not only deterrence-based security technology, but also a comprehensive program of proactive initiatives to ensure employees are generally satisfied with their environments."[35]

Consumer and Business-Opportunity Fraud

Americans lose billions of dollars from consumer and business-opportunity fraud.

Consumer fraud occurs when a consumer of goods and services surrenders his or her money through a misrepresentation of a material fact or through deceit. American consumers annually lose about $40 billion to telemarketing fraud, which is one type of consumer fraud.[36] In business-opportunity fraud, the consumer is persuaded by the perpetrator to invest money in a business that is worth much less than is indicated or stated. Examples include scams that promise you can "work out of your home" or "make big money" by stuffing envelopes or selling water filters. Consumers have lost millions of dollars through these and other types of false or inflated business opportunities and ventures.

Home-Improvement and Real Estate Fraud

Other kinds of consumer fraud include home-improvement fraud and real estate and land fraud.

Each year in the United States, many home owners become victims of home-improvement fraud, in which the sales pitch is that renovation of their property is a very worthwhile investment. At highly inflated prices, the home owner is sold a product or service, such as aluminum or vinyl siding, storm doors and windows, a driveway recoating, a roof repair, or a paint job. The consumer finds himself or herself paying three to four times what the product or service is worth. To make it worse, the home owner is persuaded to make a large downpayment for work that will be done poorly or not at all. The contractor, in other words, does a shoddy job, "goes out of business," or leaves the community.

Many Americans have also lost millions in fraudulent real estate "investments." In real estate and land frauds, consumers are led to believe that the property or land being sold is a once-in-a-lifetime, wise investment of their money that will grow in value and provide them with vacation or retirement fun and security. Unfortunately, many investors soon find out that the land is not to be improved or that the property is worth very little money.

Health-Care Fraud

Each year, health-care fraud costs Americans up to $50 billion.

Consumers are also victims of health-care fraud. Annual health care in the United States costs over $1 trillion annually, and it is expected to more than double in the next decade. At current expenditure levels, fraud losses range from $30 billion to $50 billion annually in the United States.

Securities and Investment Fraud

Securities and investment fraud amounts to about $40 billion a year.

Consumer securities and investment fraud is also a problem. U.S. investors are often baited through the promise of a very high return and shelter from tax collection. A classic example is the Ponzi scam, which was used in the famous

---

Consumer fraud occurs when a consumer of goods and services surrenders his or her money through a misrepresentation of a material fact or through deceit. In business-opportunity fraud, the consumer is persuaded by the perpetrator to invest money in a business that is worth much less than is indicated or stated.

In home-improvement fraud, consumers are persuaded to pay inflated prices for home improvements. In real estate and land fraud, consumers are persuaded to pay inflated prices for property or land of much less value.

A Ponzi scam is a classic fraudulent pyramid scheme in which early investors are paid off with proceeds from sales to later participants. It is called a pyramid scheme because in the business structure, which resembles a pyramid, a small number of people at the top receive payments from a broad base of investors who never see returns on their investment.

Health-care fraud runs up to $50 billon annually in the United States, and the biggest victim is the Medicare system and the taxpayers who support it. Of the many types of health-care fraud, one of the most common is billing for health-care services that were never rendered. This is done by adding claims charges for services never performed to otherwise legitimate bills, or by using genuine patient names and health-insurance information as the basis for fabricating false claims. For example, a doctor could order a patient's bill to be charged for tests that were not conducted or could bill for appointments that the patient never attended.

oil-well-exploration "Home-Stake swindle" of the 1960s and early 1970s. As Simon and Eitzen report, many fraudulent schemes are based on this classic **pyramid scheme**, developed by Charles Ponzi in 1920. In this system,

early investors are paid off handsomely with proceeds from sales to later participants. The result is often a rush of new investors, greedy for easy profits. An example of the Ponzi scam was the Home-Stake swindle perpetrated by Robert Trippet, which consisted of selling

FOR YOUR INFORMATION

Investment Fraud

- Investment, securities, and commodities fraud amounts to about $40 billion a year or more.
- In September 2000, the Securities and Exchange Commission instituted legal action against thirty-three companies and individuals who were involved in online stock scams. The companies on the Net inflated the prices of more than seventy microcap stocks and netted $10 million in illegal profits.
- Executives at Enron Corporation received $744 million in payments and stock during the year leading up to its bankruptcy filing.
- Hundreds of thousands of American investors and thousands of Enron employees lost billions of dollars (and their jobs) when Enron stocks collapsed.
- In 2002, Enron's head of electricity trading pleaded guilty to the charge of conspiracy to commit white-

collar fraud by manipulating California's energy market to drive up power prices.
- In 2003, bankrupt WorldCom agreed to pay a record $500 million fine for the largest accounting fraud ever in the United States. The company admitted to inflating its revenues by $11 billion. It is the most dramatic example of corporate abuse of investor trust during a year of many high-profile white-collar business scandals.

Sources: National White Collar Crime Center, *Securities/Investment Fraud,* Fairmont, WV: NW3C, September 2002; U.S. Department of Justice, Federal Bureau of Investigation, Economic Crimes Unit, "Securities/Commodities Fraud," Washington, DC, June 2003, **http://www.fbi.gov/hq/cid/fc/ec/about/about_scf.htm**; R. Davies, "2002 Classic Financial Scandals," BBC, October 17, 2002; "WorldCom to Pay Record Fine," *Houston Chronicle,* May 20, 2003.

participation rights in the drilling of sometimes hypothetical oil wells. The beauty of this plan was that, since oil exploration was involved, it provided a tax shelter for investors. Thus, the plan especially appealed to the wealthy. As a result, many important persons were swindled of a good deal of money, including the chairman of Citibank, the head of United States Trust, . . . [and] entertainers such as Jack Benny, Candice Bergen, Faye Dunaway, Bob Dylan, and Liza Minnelli.[37]

According to Kent Brunette, a representative of the American Association of Retired Persons, stock-investment fraud is a new peril for older Americans: "Although there are no firm statistics, we know that countless numbers of older persons are being bilked out of millions of dollars each year—dollars that often represent the savings of a lifetime."[38] As witnesses at a hearing of the Senate Special Committee on Aging reported, fraud and deceptive practices against the elderly are increasing as retirees cash in lower-yield investments for those with higher yield. For example, Senator William Cohen (R-Maine) reported that, in the state of Maine alone, about 5,000 people "opened accounts with First Investors Corp. . . . Client losses nationwide have been estimated as high as $400 million. . . . The upshot [is], the Federal Securities and Exchange Commission (SEC) fined First Investors [only] $25 million . . . charging that it misled investors [by steering them into high-risk junk-bond funds]."[39]

According to Robert Lewis, in his analysis of stock-fraud schemes, Maine and several other states filed administrative, civil, or criminal charges against First Investors, who then "reached settlements with fifteen other states. In agreeing to the settlement[s], First Investors neither admitted nor denied wrongdoing." Lewis also cites Prudential Securities Inc., a division of Prudential Insurance Company, as being a defendant in a class-action suit brought by 130,000 clients who "bought $1.4 billion in energy-limited partnerships in the 1980s . . . a high-risk security with poor liquidity, meaning the investment would be hard to sell."[40]

Many organizational white-collar criminals, then, have used their positions in the corporate world to illegally improve their companies' power and profits. Corporate executives and employees who are involved with stock-investment fraud, stock-fraud schemes, price-fixing, and accounting fraud seek corporate power and increased profitability for their companies.

In spring 2004, a guilty verdict was handed down in the case against celebrity Martha Stewart. She was accused of insider trading. On a private ("inside") tip she ordered her broker to sell off her majority shares of stock in ImClone—just before their price fell drastically. ImClone, along with the other stockholders, suffered the losses. Stewart claimed that she had a prior agreement to sell the shares when their price fell to a certain value, but her broker admitted to a cover-up.

Tax and Insurance Fraud

Well over $100 billion in federal taxes is uncollected annually in the United States. Insurance fraud occurs in many contexts other than health care.

In **tax fraud**, a taxpayer underreports or does not report taxable income; purposely attempts to evade or defeat a payment of owed taxes; and is willful, i.e., voluntarily and intentionally violates a known legal duty.

"Under penalties of perjury, I declare that I have examined this return and accompanying schedules and statements, and to the best of my knowledge and belief, they are true, correct, and complete." Each year, millions of Americans pay their federal income taxes and sign below this statement on their income tax forms. The Internal Revenue Service (IRS) has the legal right to impose substantial penalties for negligence, substantial understatement of tax, and tax fraud. It may also impose severe criminal penalties—heavy fines and imprisonment—for willful failure to file, tax evasion, or making a false statement. The purposeful filing of a fraudulent tax return is a felony. For the IRS to prove **tax fraud**, it must prove that the taxpayer underreported or did not report taxable income; purposely attempted to evade or defeat a payment of owed taxes; and was willful, that is, the taxpayer voluntarily and intentionally violated a known legal duty.[41]

Each year, many taxpayers fail to report taxable income. It is estimated that well over $100 billion in federal taxes is uncollected annually due to fraud. The IRS audits many taxpayers each year, especially those in the middle classes, but many taxpayers, especially the wealthy, manage to avoid this process.[42]

Other federal agencies investigate *insurance fraud,* which occurs in many contexts other than health care. For example, insurance policyholders may file false claims on a homeowner's policy or auto or marine insurance policy for nonexistent damage to their house, car, or boat. Other policy owners have faked injuries from falls or auto accidents and have filed fraudulent claims.

Businesses have also committed insurance fraud. In the 1980s, two criminologists, Paul E. Tracy and James E. Fox, conducted a field experiment on insurance fraud in the auto-body repair industry. They presented two autos—one with superficial and one with moderate damage—to almost two hundred auto-body repair shops for estimates. At times, they claimed the autos were covered by insurance policies that would pay for the repairs. At other times, they claimed the autos were uninsured. Their findings strongly suggested fraudulent practices, in that repair estimates for the "insured" autos were significantly higher than those for the "uninsured" cars.[43]

Not only do policyholders and third parties defraud insurers; insurers also defraud the public (see Figure 11.1).

After reading this section, you should be able to

1. define embezzlement and discuss the reasons that people embezzle or steal from their employers;
2. describe measures for preventing embezzlement and employee theft;
3. identify six types of consumer fraud;
4. give examples of business-opportunity fraud, home-improvement and real estate fraud, and health-care fraud;
5. give examples of securities and investment fraud and tax and insurance fraud.

Type of Crime: Fraud
Criminal Fine: $4 million
12 Corporate Crime Reporter 29(1), July 20, 1998

Health Care Service Corporation (HCSC), also known as Blue Cross Blue Shield of Illinois, pled guilty to eight felony counts and agreed to pay $144 million after admitting it concealed evidence of poor performance in processing Medicare claims for the federal government.

HCSC, the Medicare contractor for Illinois and Michigan, also admitted obstructing justice and conspiring to obstruct federal auditors.

The company agreed to pay $4 million in criminal fines and $140 million in a civil settlement to resolve its liability under the False Claims Act.

"Medicare fraud and abuse is always a serious matter but it is particularly grievous when the abuse involves a contractor entrusted to protect the financial integrity of the program," said June Gibbs Brown, the Inspector General at the Department of Health and Human Services. "In this case, the trust was flagrantly violated by a prestigious nationally known company. It engaged in unconscionable conduct that adversely affected Medicare beneficiaries, providers and the program itself."

Brown said the company "comprised protections by artificially inflating performance results."

"It also falsified and destroyed documents for the purpose of disguising its shortcomings," Brown said.

FIGURE 11.1

11.3 COMPUTER CRIME

Many types of consumer fraud once occurred primarily over the telephone and through the mail. The computer has now changed the methodology of many white-collar criminals. You have read how a thief can quickly embezzle or steal large sums of money from his or her company with a password, a modem, and a personal computer. According to the NW3C, many white-collar crimes are being committed on the Internet because of the potential for economic gain combined with the ease of commission. Many of the old white-collar fraud schemes that existed before the Internet are now online.[44]

Examples of online white-collar crimes, according to the NW3C, are

- fraudulent marketing schemes
- online auctions
- work-at-home schemes
- gambling operations
- spam

The Internet provides criminals with a quick and efficient means of communicating large quantities of information to a wide range of victims via chatrooms, e-mail, message boards, and web sites. In addition, the Internet allows for anonymity, whereby a victim may know the offender only by an e-mail address or web site.[45]

In addition to the use of computers as a weapon to commit crimes, computers also can be the targets of crime. Computer criminals use many techniques, ranging from the setting up of fake accounts and transferring into those accounts a few pennies from thousands of legitimate customer accounts, to the planting of viruses and logic bombs that can systematically destroy valuable data. According to Rod Willis, "The introduction of fast, inexpensive microcomputers is one of the most important phenomena of our time. Along with giving managers instant access to information and making their jobs easier, it has made it relatively easy for a skilled bandit or dishonest employee with a personal computer and a modem to obtain confidential data—or millions of dollars—from unwitting companies, banks, and government agencies."[46]

The main categories of **computer crime** include

Computer crime is the use of computer hardware or software in property crimes against others and includes vandalism, information theft, unauthorized personal use, burglary by modem, and financial fraud.

- vandalism
- theft of information
- use of computers for personal benefit
- "burglary by modem"
- financial fraud[47]

(1) In *vandalism,* the criminal damages or destroys the computer, its components, or its software. The motive may be a grudge, a labor-management dispute, terrorism, market competition, or random mischief. In any case, the crime may cause excessive delay and expense. One employee erased computer tapes worth $192,000 because, he said, "I just didn't feel like working." In another case, "a saboteur removed the labels from 1,500 reels of computer tape. It was incredibly expensive and time-consuming to reidentify all the data."

(2) In *theft of information,* insiders steal computer data or programs and sell them to the competition. For example, one employee stole a company's master tape file of more than 2 million customers and sold it to a competitor.

(3) *Unauthorized personal use* of computers includes employees' "moonlighting on an employer's computer" and government officials' "using taxpayers money to run out lists for campaign mailings on municipal equipment."[48]

(4) *Burglary by modem* occurs when "criminals place a large order directly into the computer over the phone lines. They ask for delivery on a given day at a specific location, then pick up the goods and take them away for sale."[49]

(5) *Financial fraud* usually occurs when a start-up or economically troubled company's top management "creates" false company earnings and assets to entice or please investors. Examples are the WorldCom accounting fraud and the famous Equity Funding Case, in which officials falsified 60,000 of the company's 97,000 insurance policies: "They assigned a secret computer code to all fake policies: 'Dept. 99.' This code made the computer skip those policies for billing purposes. When the federal investigators asked to audit those files, the company said they weren't immediately available, then forged hard-copy files complete with health reports, contracts, and supporting documents. A discharged official tipped off authorities while they were concocting [these documents], and the management was caught red-handed. Their fraud ultimately cost investors $1 billion [now revised to between $2 to $3 billion]."[50]

After reading this section, you should be able to

1. evaluate the role of the Internet in consumer fraud;
2. identify and describe five main categories of computer crime.

11.4 ENVIRONMENTAL CRIME

By contaminating air, water, or land, environmental crimes victimize entire communities. In the United States, environmental crimes are considered *mala in se* (intrinsically or morally wrong) by environmentalists and most Americans. Environmental crimes are also considered to be *mala prohibita* (prohibited by statute because they infringe upon the rights of others).[51] *Environmental crimes* are acts or omissions that violate federal, state, or local environmental standards by endangering human health and the environment. According to the NW3C, criminal violations of environmental regulations and laws "range from record keeping errors to illegal dumping of hazardous wastes."[52]

Environmental crimes victimize large segments of a community or even an entire community. The magnitude and damages caused by environmental crimes may be difficult to detect and determine, because it usually takes years or decades before ecological effects on the land, air, or water pollution appear. Even biological effects of pollution (e.g., cancer from chemical contamination or lung diseases from exposure to asbestos) may take years to become apparent.[53]

People depend on air as well as water for survival. Yet, each day, many tons of pollutants are discharged by U.S. industries into the atmosphere, resulting in *air contamination*. Estimates indicate that in recent years more than 100 million tons of pollutants have been released into the air annually. These pollutants include nitrogen and sulfur oxides, particulate matter, carbon monoxide, hydrocarbons, and volatile organic compounds. Air pollution from carbon monoxide, sulfur oxides, and volatile organic compounds comes from industrial processes.[56] Nitrogen oxides and sulfur dioxide from industrial and power plants are sources of acid rain, which causes damage to streams, lakes, aquatic life, forests, monuments, and buildings.[57]

There are many EPA and state laws that attempt to protect air quality in the United States. However, many American companies continue to pollute the air in spite of these laws. Several years ago, a former Louisiana Pacific Corporation (LPC) supervisor filed a lawsuit against LPC, the largest producer of

FOR YOUR INFORMATION

Water Contamination

Corporate America has been responsible for a wide variety of environmental crimes involving *water contamination*. According to the Environmental Protection Agency (EPA), about one-half of all U.S. streams, rivers, and lakes are either threatened or damaged by pollution.[54] Typical water contaminants include many toxic chemicals and substances, nitrates, and oils, many of which come from our nation's industries. Emissions from industrial plants, in addition to those from sewage-treatment facilities, have greatly contributed to the process of eutrophication (the excessive buildup of phosphates and nitrates in our nation's bodies of water).[55]

- The Allied Chemical Corporation was fined $13.2 million for discharging chemical wastes, including the pesticide kepone, into Virginia's James River.
- For many years, a number of Youngstown, Ohio, industries dumped approximately 158 tons of grease, cyanide, oil, and metal particles into the Mahoning River on a daily basis.
- One of the most striking examples of water contamination occurred in 1989 off the coast of Alaska. The tanker *Exxon Valdez* ran aground on a reef, tore apart, and dumped more than 10 million gallons of crude oil that polluted several hundred miles of coastline and killed millions of fish and waterfowl. In 1993, Exxon paid $1 billion in criminal and civil fines.
- HAL Beheer BV, the Dutch company that operated the Holland America Line cruise ship SS *Rotterdam,* illegally discharged oily mixtures from the bilges of the *Rotterdam.* As part of its guilty plea, the corporation paid a $2 million fine and was placed on probation for five years.
- A 1999 report stated the Colonial Pipeline Company (CPC) had spilled about 1 million gallons of oil into South Carolina's Reedy River. CPC operated the largest hazardous-liquid pipeline in the world. After pleading guilty to criminal charges in connection with the spill, CPC was fined $7 million and put on five years' probation.

Sources: "$13 Million Reminder," *Time,* October 18, 1976, p. 83; "Safe Water or Jobs? A Classic Confrontation," *U.S. News & World Report,* February 7, 1977, p. 47; "Massive Oil Slick Spreading over Alaskan Water," *Philadelphia Inquirer,* March 26, 1989; *In re Exxon Valdez,* 270 F.3d 1215 (9th Cir. 2001); *Corporate Crime Reporter,* 12, no. 39, October 12, 1998; *Corporate Crime Reporter,* 13, no. 9, March 1, 1999; R. Mokhiber and R. Weissman, "The 100 Top Corporate Criminals," AlterNet.org, April 26, 2000, **http://www.alternet.org/story.html?storyid=1075**.

oriented strand board (laminated structural wood panels) in the country. The former supervisor alleged that the company fired him because he refused to tamper with the company's pollution-monitoring equipment. The investigation expanded, and environmental- and consumer-fraud charges were brought against LPC. In 1998, as part of a plea agreement, LPC pleaded guilty to eighteen felonies for such crimes as conspiring to violate the Clean Air Act and the False Statement Act, and tampering with air-pollution monitors. The company was fined $37 million and placed on five years' probation.[58]

Air pollution adversely affects our personal well-being as well as the environment. Dust and dirt in the air make our throats burn and eyes water.

In December 1984, methyl isocyanate leaking into the air from a Union Carbide plant killed 8,000 people at once and injured another 12,000 people in Bhopal, India. The company admitted that the plant had not been operating safely, blamed the negligence on local officials, and stated that the plant should have been closed. In 2003, the survivors of Bhopal and environmental activists still sought justice, as the plant, now owned by Dow Chemical, continued to pollute water and soil.

Nitrogen and sulfur-dioxide fumes cause coughing and make breathing more difficult. Carbon-monoxide pollution impairs the flow of oxygen in our bodies, thus placing increased stress on the coronary and central-nervous systems. Many volatile organic compounds can cause cancer.[59]

Given the presence of certain atmospheric conditions, such as temperature inversions, air pollution can have sudden catastrophic effects. Thermal inversions occur when a layer of warm air traps a layer of cooler air underneath it, closer to the earth's surface. If that air is polluted, this condition can sicken and even kill large numbers of people. This occurred in Denora, Pennsylvania, in 1948, killing twenty people and sickening or severely affecting the health of 6,000 other residents. A similar incident occurred in London, England, in 1952—approximately 4,000 people died.[60] Over the past few decades, cities such as Los Angeles, New York, and Birmingham, Alabama, have experienced dense industrial-pollution stagnation, resulting in increased rates of respiratory irritation, sickness, and death among area residents.[61]

Today, people are more aware of the fact that long-term exposure to high levels of toxic substances in the air poses a far greater and more widespread menace to public health than do the type of atmospheric disasters just described. However, disasters give us the clearest and most alarming signals of the threat that toxic chemicals in the air pose for us all.

According to the EPA, approximately 102 million Americans are breathing air that is unsafe. Researchers have reported that industrial air pollution in the

United States has directly contributed to increased rates of emphysema, chronic bronchitis, chronic asthma, pneumonia, lung cancer, and heart disease.[62] Health-care expenses and lower work productivity due to air pollution are estimated to cost our nation a minimum of $110 billion annually.[63] Criminal sanctions against corporations that contaminate our environment have increased, but they still fall well below needed levels of enforcement and punishment.[64]

After reading this section, you should be able to

1. define environmental crime and give examples of its main types;
2. describe the economic, health, and human costs of environmental crimes.

11.5 EXPLANATIONS FOR AND RESPONSES TO WHITE-COLLAR CRIME

The explanations for white-collar crime are varied. As is briefly reported at the beginning of this chapter, Edwin H. Sutherland developed the theory of differential association to explain a wide variety of criminal behavior, particularly white-collar crime. He believed that, just as we learn other social behavior, we learn criminal behavior—including white-collar criminal behavior. Sutherland theorized that this learning occurs through interaction with others in the streets (conventional crimes) or in the suites (white-collar crimes) and, for the most part, within intimate primary groups. Among white-collar criminals, this learning includes acquiring the techniques as well as the motives, attitudes, and rationalizations for committing crimes. For example, adult white-collar employees may learn from other employees the standardized techniques and rationalizations for padding expense accounts and for other forms of corporate theft.[65]

John Braithwaite maintains a corporate cultural perspective on white-collar crime. He views white-collar organizational crime as a function of the existing corporate climate. That is, where one finds an employee subculture that dislikes and resists any governmental regulation and socializes its new employees in the values, attitudes, and skills needed to violate the law, one finds ongoing organizational crime. Many corporate enterprises in a sense "cause" crime by making great demands on their employees while maintaining a corporate cultural atmosphere that is tolerant of white-collar deviant and criminal behavior. Many businesspeople find themselves in positions where organizational goals cannot be achieved through legitimate or conventional practices, so they view illegitimate opportunities as the only solution to this problem.[66]

Travis Hirschi and Michael Gottfredson disagree with this view. They believe white-collar criminal behavior is motivated by the choice of an offender who lacks self-control and views the violation of law as a means of obtaining rewards. That is, the motives that produce white-collar crime are the same motives that produce conventional crime—the desire for quick rewards and benefits with little effort. Thus, white-collar criminals are inclined to follow their impulses without taking into consideration the long-term effects or costs.[67]

Prosecution of White-Collar Offenders

White-collar criminals have been increasingly reported, prosecuted, and convicted.

However one explains white-collar crime, research indicates that many offenders engage in criminal behavior because they are able to rationalize its effects. White-collar criminals simply say to themselves, "We're not street criminals." They believe that people who are not in business or are in government do not really understand the business world. White-collar criminals view their behavior as "normal business practice" and feel that no one "really gets hurt."[68]

White-collar criminals have been increasingly reported, prosecuted, and convicted. For example,

> government surveys have reported that white-collar crime accounted for 6 percent of all arrest dispositions in 1986 and that 88 percent of those arrested for white-collar crime were prosecuted. Seventy-four percent of those prosecuted were subsequently convicted in a criminal court. However, although 60 percent of those convicted in state court were imprisoned for their crimes, only a small proportion (18 percent) received a prison term exceeding one year.[69]

In the United States, however, there is a wide disparity in white-collar crime sentences. Some U.S. federal courts are much more likely than others to send convicted white-collar criminals to prison. Many white-collar crimes are never officially reported, and offenders who are reported are rarely prosecuted. In the 1960s, criminologist Gerald Robin studied 1,600 employees who stole from their companies. Over 99 percent were terminated from their jobs, but only 17 percent were prosecuted. Robin also reported that a higher percentage of lower-level versus higher-level employees were prosecuted and convicted.[70] However, more recent research indicates no association between sentencing policy and socioeconomic status; that is, lower-level employees are no more likely to be prosecuted and convicted than upper-level managers, except when offenses are "more serious."[71] Criminologists Marshall Clinard and Peter Yeager studied almost 500 U.S. corporations and reported in 1980 that only 20 percent of moderate corporate violations and only 10 percent of serious violations resulted in government sanctions. In addition, when the laws were enforced, companies that were more powerful were treated with greater leniency.[72]

There are a number of reasons for the infrequent prosecutions of white-collar offenders:

- Occupational offenses are not highly publicized.
- Many white-collar criminals have a high social status.
- The public tends to view these offenders as essentially respectable people rather than as criminals.
- There is little organized public resentment against many harmful white-collar crimes.
- Without political pressure from the general public, it is quite difficult to develop criminal laws against this type of behavior.

One should also keep in mind that many socially harmful corporate practices were not always against the law. For example, the sale of fraudulent securities, false advertising, the misuse of trademarks, and restraint of trade, in addition to other types of business activities, were not considered criminal acts until the late nineteenth or twentieth century. Also, because corporations are regarded as legal entities under federal law, it is still more common for criminal actions to be handled by administrative agencies, such as the Federal Trade Commission or the Internal Revenue Service, than by the criminal courts.

Controlling White-Collar Crime

Effective defensive, deterrent, and demotivating strategies exist to combat white-collar crime.

The American Management Association (AMA) received a grant from the Law Enforcement Assistance Administration to carefully research and plan ways of controlling white-collar crime. Its recommendations fell into three strategy categories: defensive, deterrent, and demotivating programs.

(1) *Defensive programs* would protect assets by making it more difficult to steal them. *Recommendation:* Educate and train management in the systems approach to loss prevention.

(2) *Deterrent programs* would make it more costly to steal assets. *Recommendation:* Accelerate the development of specialized economic crime units within the offices of district attorneys.

(3) *Demotivating programs* would decrease the motivation to steal company assets. *Recommendation:* Launch a joint community effort by schools, businesses, civic groups, and law enforcement agencies to demotivate young people from employee theft and computer crime.[73]

Many of the AMA's recommended strategies have been implemented over the past decade by law enforcement agencies and companies. For example, deterrence strategies—those that involve the detection of white-collar violations, the determination of responsibility, and the punishment of violators to deter future violations—provide a warning to potential white-collar violators "who might break rules if other violators had not already been penalized."[74] Some criminologists have reported a decline in white-collar crime when such criminals have been imprisoned.[75] In their analysis of the deterrent effect of perceived certainty and severity of punishment, Steven Klepper and Daniel Nagin report that one's perceptions of "detection and punishment for white-collar crimes appear to be a powerful deterrent to future law violations."[76] Some criminologists believe that government should adopt deterrence strategies involving harsh punishments more often.[77]

Compliance strategies have also been implemented to control white-collar crimes. These strategies aim for "conformity without the necessity of detecting, processing, or penalizing violators. . . . [they] attempt to create conformity by providing economic incentives or by using administrative efforts to prevent unwanted conditions before they occur . . . [and] rely on the threat of economic sanctions to control violators."[78] The effectiveness of compliance strategies has been limited, however. Criminologist Larry J. Siegel reports that "economic sanctions have limited value in controlling white-collar crime because economic penalties are imposed only after crimes have occurred, require careful governmental regulation, and often amount to only a slap on the wrist."[79] Siegel also makes clear that compliance is difficult to achieve if the government "adopts a pro-business, antiregulation fiscal policy that encourages economic growth by removing controls over business."[80]

Although these strategies may work in controlling or reducing many types of white-collar criminal activities, alternative methods must also be considered. In the case of environmental crimes, for example, Murray Weidenbaum believes that society can motivate people and companies not to pollute the environment by using economic incentives. He believes people should view corporate environmental pollution not merely as a sinful act but also as an "activity costly to society and susceptible to reduction by means of proper incentives": "The most desirable approach is to reduce the generation of pollutants in the first place. Economists have an approach that is useful—providing incentives to manufacturers to change their production processes to reduce the amount of wastes created or to recycle them in a safe and productive manner."[81] An additional alternative, according to Weidenbaum, is to tax the generation and disposal of wastes. The object is not to punish the polluters but to have them change their ways: "If something becomes more expensive, business firms have a natural desire to use less of the item. In this case, the production of pollution would become more expensive."[82]

Strategies for reducing white-collar crime also can be applied from within. To reduce corporate and white-collar theft, fraud, and computer crime, for example, Rod Willis recommends that companies observe the golden rule of security—the separation of duties. That is, one person in the organization should never have responsibility for a whole function, such as payment approval, inventory, or accounts receivable: "No matter how long the person has worked for the organization, no matter how 'nice' he or she is, if the opportunity for theft is present and the employee has a strong enough motive, a theft is likely."[83] Willis also recommends that

- outside accountants should audit a company's financial records at least quarterly, because many thefts and frauds are committed in organizations with the help of company bookkeepers and accountants;
- to avoid hiring criminals, companies should carefully screen all job applicants;
- regarding computer security, companies should control remote access by outsiders, protect the input and output from tampering, and monitor the erasure and disposal of computer disks, tapes, and so on;
- above all, companies should create a corporate culture that values integrity and enforces security.[84]

Norman Jaspan, a security consultant, addresses some practical ways of dealing with white-collar crime and criminals. He notes five "false assurances of safety" that corporate managers should not trust:

1. Don't try to justify some employee theft as a "cost of doing business."
2. Don't believe in "foolproof" security methods.
3. Don't assume that your company's team spirit will ensure the loyalty of all your employees.
4. Don't assume that a long-time friend or employee would never steal from the company.
5. Don't assume uniformed guards are uniformly trustworthy.[85]

Jaspan also recommends the following five ways to help create and maintain a healthy, honest organizational climate:

1. *Estimate employee capabilities and set realistic performance standards.* Setting unrealistic performance goals leaves employees with a choice between failing or resorting to dishonest measures.
2. *Don't just announce operating rules for security; communicate them.* Enforce the rules, make sure all levels of company hierarchy obey them, and make sure they are properly understood by everyone.
3. *Be unpredictable in establishing and enforcing controls.* Spot checks are very effective in uncovering theft, as is introducing occasional deliberate errors to test the system's controls.

4. *Maintain uniform policies.* Don't show favoritism or use double standards in judging or supervising favored employees. Favoritism ruins morale and lessens respect for management procedures.

5. *Measure work output and evaluate employee performance regularly.* Employees need and want to know how they're doing and what management thinks of their productivity. Supervisors have the responsibility to let them know.[86]

Thus, the most effective solutions to many types of white-collar crime—especially employee theft, fraud, and computer crimes—will come, as Willis suggests, not from the "state-of-the art technological advances and the leading-edge management theories, but from the application of commonsense security policies and a work environment that supports and rewards honest behavior."[87]

After reading this section, you should be able to

1. evaluate three theories attempting to explain white-collar crime;
2. give reasons for the difficulties in prosecuting this kind of crime;
3. describe four approaches to responding to or preventing white-collar crime;
4. identify ways that corporations can control corporate and white-collar crime from within.

11.6 ORGANIZED CRIME

Organized crime in America is as structured and complex as corporate America. Much of what the average American knows about organized crime has come from the mass media. Successful films such as *The Godfather, Goodfellas,* and *The Firm,* in addition to television shows such as *The Untouchables, Miami Vice,* and *The Sopranos,* have provided us with an entertaining and colorful picture of organized-crime activities in the United States. Although there are elements of truth in these films and TV shows, much of the information is misleading, fragmented, and even false. For example, much of the media's focus is on organized criminal groups that are of Italian or Sicilian descent, yet much organized-crime activity in this country involves Chinese triads, Japanese yakuza, Vietnamese gangs, Colombian cocaine cartels, Jamaican posses, "Russian" gangs, biker gangs, and prison gangs.[88]

According to the *Report to the Nation on Crime and Justice,* there is no universally accepted definition of the term *organized crime.*[89] The President's Commission on Organized Crime defines **organized crime** as a "continuing, structured collectivity of persons who utilize criminality, violence, and a willingness to corrupt in order to gain and maintain power and profit."[90] It has also been defined as "business enterprises organized for the purpose of making economic gain through illegal activities."[91]

The U.S. Task Force on Organized Crime reports that organized crime in the United States has economic gain as its primary goal, which is achieved through illegal goods and services such as drugs, gambling, prostitution, and pornography. Crime organizations

Organized crime is a "continuing, structured collectivity of persons who utilize criminality, violence, and a willingness to corrupt in order to gain and maintain power and profit."

Characteristics of Organized Crime Groups

- **Hierarchical structure:** All organized crime groups are headed by a single leader and structured into a series of subordinate ranks, although they may vary in the rigidity of their hierarchy. Nationwide organizations may be composed of multiple separate chapters, or "families." Each unit is generally headed by its own leader, who is supported by the group's hierarchy of command. Intergroup disputes, joint ventures, and new membership are generally reviewed by a board composed of the leaders of the most powerful chapters.

- **Organizational continuity:** Organized crime groups ensure that they can survive the death or imprisonment of their leaders and can vary the nature of their activities to take advantage of changing criminal opportunities.

- **Restricted membership:** Members must be formally accepted by the group after a demonstration of loyalty and a willingness to commit criminal acts. Membership may be limited to race or common background and generally involves a lifetime commitment to the group, which can be enforced through violent group actions.

- **Criminality, violence, and power:** Power and control are key organized crime goals and may be obtained through criminal activity of one type or through multiple activities. Criminal activity may be designed directly to generate "income" or to support the group's power through bribery, violence, and intimidation. Violence is used to maintain group loyalty and to intimidate outsiders and is a threat underlying all group activity. Specific violent criminal acts include, murder, kidnapping, arson, robbery, and bombings.

- **Legitimate business involvement:** Legitimate businesses are used to launder illegal funds or stolen merchandise. For example, illegal profits from drug sales can be claimed as legitimate profits of a non-criminal business whose accounting records have been appropriately adjusted. Legitimate business involvement also elevates the social status of organized crime figures.

- **Use of specialists:** Outside specialists, such as pilots, chemists, arsonists, and assassins, provide services under contract to organized crime groups on an intermittent or regular basis.

Sources: F. A. J. Ianni and E. Ianni, Eds., *The Crime Society: Organized Crime and Corruption in America,* New York: New American Library, 1976, p. xvi; U.S. Department of Justice, Office of Justice Programs, Bureau of Justice Statistics, *Report to the Nation on Crime and Justice,* 2nd ed., M. W. Zawitz, Ed., Washington, DC, 1988, NCJ-105506, p. 8.

- use predatory techniques and tactics such as corruption, intimidation, and violence;
- do not limit activities to providing illicit goods and services but also commit computer crimes, land fraud, and money laundering through legitimate businesses such as banks;
- enter into conspiratorial activities that involve the coordination of many people in the planning, development, and execution of illegal acts;
- control and discipline their members, associates, and victims through punishment.[92]

The highly organized and powerful *La Cosa Nostra* (the Mafia) is the most experienced and diversified of all organized crime groups in the United States. Criminologist Donald Cressey views the Mafia as a formally organized national network of twenty-four tightly knit "families" who are Italian or of Italian descent.[93] Other criminologists, such as Francis Ianni and Elizabeth Reuss-Ianni, disagree with the perspective that organized crime fits the formal organizational model followed by business corporations or governments. Ianni and Reuss-Ianni view the Sicilian Mafia families as "traditional social systems, organized by action and by cultural values. . . . Like all social systems, they have no structure apart from their functioning; nor do they have structure independent of their current 'personnel.'"[94]

FOR YOUR INFORMATION

Organized Crime Activities

Organized crime activities are varied and have infiltrated many segments of society. Whatever perspective one takes on their structure, organized crime groups have an estimated gross income as high as $100 billion annually.

- Over one-third of organized crime income comes from the distribution of narcotics.
- Other income comes from loan-sharking, prostitution, pornography, gambling, and theft.
- Organized crime has infiltrated legitimate industries such as construction, waste removal, wholesale and retail distribution of goods, hotel and restaurant operations, liquor sales, motor vehicle repairs, real estate, and banking.
- The indirect costs of organized crime are also very high, especially for the consumer. Kickbacks, protection payments, increased labor and material costs, and lack of competition in industries controlled by organized crime all increase consumer prices and costs.
- In addition, unpaid taxes on illegal activities result in higher tax burdens for legal wage earners.

Sources: President's Commission on Organized Crime, *The Impact: Organized Crime Today; Report to the President and the Attorney General,* Washington, DC, April 1986; U.S. Department of Justice, Office of Justice Programs, Bureau of Justice Statistics, *Report to the Nation on Crime and Justice,* 2nd ed., M. W. Zawitz, Ed., Washington, DC, 1988, NCJ-105506.

Peter Reuter, another criminologist, also disagrees with the perspective of a centrally directed, formally organized, bureaucratic, national alliance of *La Cosa Nostra* families. Relations among the various Mafia groups are, in his opinion, a result of venture partnerships, exchanges of services, and a way of avoiding uncertainty when "doing business" in an unfamiliar territory.[95] Still other researchers question any centralized direction and domination by local organized criminal gangs.[96]

The government has many tools with which to fight organized crime, including witness-protection programs, electronic-surveillance procedures, and immunity statutes. Besides the USA PATRIOT Act, an additional key tool in the fight against organized crime is the **Racketeer Influenced and Corrupt Organizations (RICO) Act**. The federal RICO statutes were enacted in 1970 and amended in 1986.[97] Most states have also enacted RICO statutes that are similar to the federal statutes.

The RICO Act was specifically designed to target the overall, continuing operations of organized crime organizations, unlike other existing statutes that addressed only individual criminal acts, such as robbery or murder. Specifically, the act prohibits the use of racketeering activities or profits to acquire, conduct, or maintain the business of an existing organization or enterprise. Racketeering activities are defined as any acts or threats involving murder, kidnapping, gambling, arson, robbery, extortion, drug dealing, fraud, or other crimes. The act also provides for forfeiture of illegally obtained gains and interests from such enterprises.[98] To some extent, the RICO Act has weakened organized crime in America.

RICO, or the Racketeer Influenced and Corrupt Organizations Act, is the government's principal weapon against organized crime.

After reading this section, you should be able to

1. define organized crime and discuss public perceptions of organized crime groups;
2. profile the characteristics of organized crime groups in the United States;
3. identify the income-generating activities of organized crime groups;
4. assess impacts of organized crime activities on society and efforts to combat organized crime groups.

CHAPTER SUMMARY

This chapter discusses the nature and extent of white-collar and organized crime. The cost of white-collar crime runs into the hundreds of billions of dollars. It includes a wide variety of criminal behavior. Embezzlement is one of the more serious white-collar crimes, in that a single case may involve many millions of dollars. People embezzle because of financial problems, as a form of retaliation, out of family need, or out of simple greed (pp. 303–308).

Employee pilferage, theft, and fraud are also serious forms of white-collar crime. Consumer fraud occurs in such areas as business opportunities, home improvement, real estate, health-care services, and investing. Tax and insurance fraud are also widespread in the United States (pp. 308–312).

White-collar computer theft continues to be a serious crime in this country, as criminals develop new and more sophisticated techniques to steal. There are many types of computer crimes, ranging from vandalism to financial fraud (pp. 313–315).

Environmental crimes range from record-keeping errors to illegal dumping of hazardous wastes and may take years or even decades before they become apparent. The primary types of environmental crime involve water or air contamination (pp. 315–318).

Explanations for white-collar crime range from Sutherland's differential association theory to theories that stress the choice of an offender. Many white-collar crimes are never officially reported, and the offenders who are reported are rarely prosecuted. Controlling white-collar crime continues to be a difficult task, but four types of methods have had some success (pp. 318–322).

The chapter concludes with an examination of organized crime in the United States. Organized crime consists of business enterprises organized for the purpose of making economic gain through illegal activities. Gross income from organized crime is estimated to be as high as $100 billion annually. This income comes from activities ranging from the distribution of narcotics, to loan-sharking and prostitution, to the infiltration of legitimate industries such as construction and liquor sales. Responses to organized crime involve the use of the Racketeer Influenced and Corrupt Organizations (RICO) Act, which prohibits the use of racketeering activities or profits to acquire, conduct, or maintain the business of an existing organization or enterprise (pp. 322–324).

Study Guide

Chapter Objectives

- Define white-collar crime.
- Explain the difficulties in measuring white-collar crime.
- Describe three examples of white-collar crime.
- Briefly describe the major types of white-collar crime.
- Define and discuss the crime of embezzlement.
- Explain why people embezzle.
- Examine how embezzlement may be prevented.
- Describe four types of consumer fraud.
- Examine health-care fraud in America.
- Describe tax fraud.
- Describe the main categories of computer crime.
- Describe the three classes of crime in which a computer is used as a weapon.
- Examine corporate water and air contamination.
- Describe the health costs of environmental contamination.
- Briefly describe three major theories that explain white-collar crime.

- Explain the wide disparity in white-collar crime sentences.
- Explain four ways of controlling white-collar crime.
- Describe Norman Jaspan's five false assurances of safety, and five ways of creating and maintaining a positive organizational climate.
- Define organized crime.
- Describe six characteristics of organized crime in the United States.
- Briefly describe how organized crime is structured in the United States.
- Describe the three categories of illicit behavior that constitute organized crime activity.
- Examine the true extent of organized crime and efforts to combat organized crime.

Key Terms

Business-opportunity fraud (309)
Computer crime (314)
Consumer fraud (309)
Embezzlement (305)
Home-improvement fraud (309)
Occupational crime (303)

Organized Crime (322)
Ponzi scam (309)
Pyramid scheme (310)
Racketeer Influenced and Corrupt
  Organizations (RICO) Act (324)

Real estate and land fraud (309)
Tax fraud (312)
White-collar crime (303, 304)

Self-Test
Short Answer

1. Write a definition of white-collar crime.
2. List the special problems one encounters when trying to measure white-collar crime.
3. List six specific white-collar crimes.
4. Write a brief paragraph describing the crime of embezzlement.

5. List and define the many types of consumer fraud.
6. Write a brief paragraph describing health-care fraud.
7. List and define the main categories of white-collar computer crime.
8. List and define the three classes of crime in which a computer is used as a weapon.

9. Give an example of corporate water and air contamination and their health costs.
10. List and describe three explanations for white-collar crime.
11. Write a definition of organized crime.
12. Write a brief paragraph describing the activities of organized crime in the United States.

Multiple Choice

1. Which of the following is not a white-collar crime?
   a. tax evasion
   b. embezzlement
   c. theft of art
   d. theft of trade secrets
2. White-collar crime refers to a group of nonviolent crimes that generally involve deception or abuse of power and include the following:
   a. business-related crimes and abuse of political office
   b. some aspects of organized crime
   c. the newly emerging areas of high-technology crime
   d. all of the above
3. Much embezzlement goes unreported because
   a. many banks and other organizations do not want the public to become aware of crimes that may undermine public confidence
   b. a bank or other business is willing to prosecute the offender
   c. most cases involve very little money
   d. none of the above
4. Employees and vendors steal time and services by
   a. putting friends or relatives on company payrolls
   b. padding overtime records and making false claims on travel-expense forms
   c. charging for services not rendered or goods not delivered
   d. all of the above
5. Which of the following is not a main category of computer crime?
   a. vandalism
   b. burglary by modem
   c. theft of information
   d. none of the above

6. The American Management Association recommends the following three categories for strategies to control white-collar crime:
   a. offensive, defensive, and controlling
   b. defensive, deterrent, and demotivating
   c. deterrent, decisive, and demanding
   d. detective, deriding, and definitive
7. Which of the following is not a characteristic of organized crime in the United States?
   a. hierarchical structure
   b. organizational discontinuity
   c. restricted membership
   d. legitimate business involvement
8. According to the U.S. Task Force on Organized Crime, organized crime in this country
   a. has economic gain as its secondary goal
   b. is synonymous with *La Cosa Nostra*
   c. limits its activities to providing illicit goods and services
   d. uses predatory techniques and tactics
9. Annual gross income from organized crime is estimated to be as high as
   a. $10 billion
   b. $25 billion
   c. $100 billion
   d. $1 trillion
10. Which of the following is not a major category of organized crime activity?
    a. the provision of legitimate services
    b. the provision of illicit services
    c. the provision of illicit goods
    d. the infiltration of legitimate business

True–False

T F 1. According to Sutherland, white-collar crime is crime committed by a person of respectability and high social status in the course of his or her occupation.

T F 2. According to the U.S. Department of Justice, uniform definitions now exist that define the overall scope of white-collar crime.

T F 3. Some criminologists report that many embezzlers are driven to their criminal activities simply by avarice and temptation.

T F 4. Many of the old white-collar fraud schemes that existed before the computer and the Internet are now online.

T F 5. The least common type of health-care fraud scheme is billing for services never rendered.

T F 6. Environmental crimes are considered both *mala in se* and *mala prohibita*.

T F 7. Braithwaite portrays white-collar crime as motivated by the choice of an offender who lacks self-control and views the violation of law as a means of obtaining rewards.

T F   8. Some U.S. federal courts are more likely to send convicted white-collar criminals to prison than others.

T F   9. Organized crime is defined as business enterprises organized for the purpose of making economic gain through legal activities.

T F   10. Because of the success of the RICO statutes, legitimate businesses are no longer used by organized crime to launder illegal funds or stolen merchandise.

Fill-In

1. _____ crime includes such crimes as tax evasion and obstruction of justice.

2. _____ is the taking or converting to one's own use money or property with which one has been entrusted.

3. _____ fraud occurs when a consumer of goods and services surrenders his or her money through a misrepresentation of a material fact or through deceit.

4. In a _____ scam, early investors are paid off with proceeds from sales to later participants.

5. _____ bombs are small amounts of computer code placed within larger programs.

6. The golden rule of security is the _____ of duties.

7. _____ is a continuing, structured collectivity of persons who use criminality, violence, and a willingness to corrupt in order to gain and maintain power and profit.

8. Organized crime uses _____ to maintain group loyalty and to intimidate outsiders.

9. _____ , or the _____ , is the most experienced and diversified of all organized crime groups in the United States.

10. _____ is one of the key tools in the fight against organized crime in the United States.

Essay Questions

1. How has the definition of white-collar crime changed since 1940, when Sutherland first presented the concept at the American Sociological Society? How do you think it will change in the next several decades? Explain your answer.

2. After reviewing the material on embezzlement, assume you are the chief executive officer of a midsize company or bank and you uncover the fact that one of your employees has embezzled more than $1 million from the organization over the past two years. How will you respond to such a situation? Why will you respond in this way and not in another manner?

3. Consumer and other types of fraud are common in many U.S. communities. After rereading the material on fraud, examine two incidents of fraud that have occurred in your community. What happened to the perpetrators? How were they punished? What, if anything, could have prevented these crimes?

4. After carefully rereading the material on white-collar computer crime, briefly describe this crime, discuss whether or not the crime is getting worse, and explain how you believe it can be better controlled.

5. After rereading the chapter material on corporate white-collar crimes, go to your library and review your local newspaper's business pages over the past several months. Write a short essay (two to four pages) on a recent example of corporate white-collar crime in the United States. How did it affect its victims? Do you think the company will be punished? Who will pay for the crime?

6. After rereading the material on corporate environmental contamination, choose a large corporation within fifty miles of your house or apartment and assess how much pollution it has been responsible for during the past twenty-five years. What type of contamination occurred? How extensive was it? Was the corporation or its executives prosecuted? If so, what was the outcome?

7. Many white-collar criminals are never prosecuted. Why does this occur? What societal conditions and law enforcement policies must change in order for there to be a significant increase in white-collar criminal prosecutions?

8. You have just been appointed chief of security in your business or corporation. What changes will you make in your organization to combat its white-collar crime problem? Do you believe you can eliminate virtually all the white-collar crime in your company? Why or why not?

9. Describe the image of organized crime that you have developed from the media. How, if any, does it differ from the information you have read in the text?

10. Describe organized crime activities that you know of in your community or in a community with which you are familiar.

Two Enron Chiefs Are Convicted in Fraud and Conspiracy Trial

Source: Alexei Barrionuevo, Vikas Bajaj, and Kyle Whitmire, "The Enron Verdict: The Overview; Two Enron Chiefs Are Convicted in Fraud and Conspiracy Trial," May 26, 2006, The New York Times. Copyright © 2006 by The New York Times Co. Reprinted with permission.

HOUSTON, May 25. Kenneth L. Lay and Jeffrey K. Skilling, the chief executives who guided Enron through its spectacular rise and even more stunning fall, were found guilty Thursday of fraud and conspiracy. They are among the most prominent corporate leaders convicted in the parade of scandals that marked the get-rich-quick excesses and management failures of the 1990s.

The eight women and four men on the jury reached the verdicts after a little more than five days of deliberations. Mr. Skilling was convicted of 18 counts of fraud and conspiracy and one count of insider trading. He was acquitted on nine counts of insider trading. Mr. Lay was found guilty on six counts of fraud and conspiracy and four counts of bank fraud.

The conspiracy and fraud convictions each carry a sentence of 5 to 10 years in prison. The insider trading charge against Mr. Skilling carries a maximum of 10 years.

Both men are expected to appeal. Judge Simeon T. Lake III, the judge in the case, set sentencing for Sept. 11. Until then, the two men are free on bail. If they lose their appeals, Mr. Skilling and Mr. Lay face potential sentences that experts say they believe will keep them in prison for the rest of their lives. Mr. Skilling, who had few family members in attendance, reacted with little emotion as the verdict was read, briefly searching the audience's faces and later striding confidenlty alone out of the courtroom ahead of his lead lawyer, Daniel Petrocelli.

"Obviously, I'm disapointed," Mr. Skilling said as he left the courthouse, "but that's the way the system works."

Once jurors and the judge cleared out of the courtroom, Mr. Lay's family members huddled around him. Elizabeth Vittor, Mr. Lay's daughter and a lawyer who had worked on his defense team, sobbed uncontrollably. Two local ministers also leaned in and hugged Mr. Lay, whose family members soon formed a circle in the courtroom, with arms over shoulders, and cried together. "I know, I know," Mr. Lay said in a soothing voice to several of them, as they clutched at his suit coat.

After he emerged from court, Mr. Lay said, "I firmly believe I'm innocent of the charges against me."

In televised remarks he said, "We believe that God in fact is in control and indeed he does work all things for good for those who love the Lord."

For a company that once seemed so complex that almost no one could understand how it actually made its money, the cases ended up being simpler than most people envisioned. Mr. Lay, 64, and Mr. Skilling, 52, were found guilty of lying to investors, employees and regulators in an effort to disguise the crumbling forutunes of their energy empire.

The 12 jurors and 3 alternates, who all agreed to talk to about 100 reporters at a news conference after the verdict, said they were persuaded by the volume of evidence the government presented and by Mr. Skilling's and Mr. Lay's own appearances on the stand that the men had perpetuated a far-reaching fraud by lying to investors and employees about Enron's performance.

The panel rejected the former chief executives' insistence that no fraud occured at Enron other than that committed by a few underlings who stole millions in secret side deals. And the jurors said they did not believe that negative press and failing market confidence combined to sink the company.

"The jury has spoken and they have sent an unmistakable message to boardrooms across the country that you can't lie to shareholders, you can't put yourself in front of your employees' interests, and no matter how rich and powerful you are you have to play by the rules," Sean M. Berkowitz, the director of the Justice Department Enron Task Force, said outside the courthouse.

For years, Enron's gravity-defying stock price made it a Wall Street darling and an icon of the "New Economy" of the 1990s. But its sudden collapse at the end of 2001 and revelation as little more than a house of cards left Enron, with its crooked E logo, the premier public symbol of corporate ignominy. Investors and employees lost billions when Enron shares became worthless.

Enron's fall had a far greater impact than on just the energy industry by heightening nervousness among average investors about the transparency of American companies. "The Enron case and all the other scandals and cases that trailed after it may have finally punctured that romance with Wall Street that has been true of American culture for a while now," said Steve Fraser, a historian and author of *Every Man a Speculator: A History of Wall Street in American Life.*

At Enron, Mr. Skilling was the visionary from the world of management consulting who spearheaded the company's rapid ascent by fastening on new ways to turn commodities, like natural gas and electricity, into lucrative financial instruments.

Mr. Lay, the company's founder, was the public face of Enron. Known for his close ties to President Bush's family, he built Enron into a symbol of civic pride and envy here in its hometown of Houston and throughout the financial world.

The verdicts are a vindication for federal prosecutors, who had produced mixed results from their four-year investigation of wrongdoing at the company. The investigation resulted in 16 guilty pleas by Enron executives, and four convictions of Merrill Lynch bankers in a case involving the bogus sale of Nigerian barges to the Wall Street firm.

Last year, however, the Supreme Court, blaming flawed jury instructions, overturned the obstruction-of-justice verdict that sounded the death knell for the accounting firm Arthur Anderson, Enron's outside auditor. And a jury either acquitted or failed to agree on charges in the fraud trial of former managers of Enron's failed broadband division.

In the 56-day trial, defense lawyers repeatedly criticized prosecutors for bringing criminal charges against Mr. Skilling and Mr. Lay, saying the government had set out to punish the company's top officers regardless of what the facts might be. The lawyers said the government was criminalizing normal business practices and accused prosecutors of pressuring critical witnesses to plead guilty to crimes they did not commit.

The defense lawyers also complained about a lack of access to witnesses who they contended could have corroborated their clients' versions of events. Several jurors said they would have liked to hear from more witnesses, in particular Richard A. Causey, the chief accounting officer, whom neither side called. "To me, he was a missing link," said a juror, Douglas Baggett, an administrative manager for a corporate legal department at Shell.

The Enron trial, more than any other, punctuates the era of corporate corruption defined by the failure of WorldCom, the telecommunications giant whose bankruptcy following revelations of $11 billion in accounting fraud exceeded even Enron's in size; the prosecution of Frank P. Quattrone, the technology industry banker; and scandals at Tyco, Adelphia and HealthSouth.

Mr. Lay was forced to remain in the courthouse for more than three hours after the verdict was announced for a hearing on securing a $5 million bond, which will come from a mix of financial pledges from his children, and to surrender his passport.

Judge Lake will have broad discretion in determining the former executives' sentences.

He is not known for his leniency. Two years ago he sentenced Jamie Olis, a former midlevel executive at Dynegy, an Enron competitor, to 24 years for his role in a scheme to disguise the company's finances. An appeals court last year ordered the judge to revise the sentence. A hearing is set for June 9. The guilty verdicts could have limited impact on a spate of civil cases. "They are not the ones who are going to pay the billions of dollars in additional recoveries that we hope to obtain on top of the $7.2 billion we already have from banks in our previous settlements," said William S. Lerach, the lead lawyer in the largest civil case, set to go to trial in October.

From the beginning, the Enron leaders' trial was not what many people expected after revelations of secret off-the-books schemes that earned a small fortune for Andrew S. Fastow, Enron's former chief financial officer, and his cadre of co-conspirators. Some of those transactions were used by Mr. Fastow without approval by anyone to enrich himself at Enron's expense; others were used to manipulate Enron's financial reports with what Mr. Fastow testified was the full knowledge of his bosses.

Rather than delve into those intricate structures, prosecutors focused on what they cited as the false statements Mr. Skilling and Mr. Lay made to employees and outside investors.

The "lies and choices" theme transformed the case into a test of credibility between the former chief executives and the more than half a dozen witnesses from inside Enron who testified for the government.

During the trial, the government called 25 witnesses and the defense called 31, including Mr. Skilling and Mr. Lay. Government witnesses, including the former Enron treasurer, Ben F. Glisan Jr., testified that the executives had sanctioned or encouraged manipulative accounting practices and then crossed the line from cheerleading into outright mirepresentations of financial performance.

Mr. Fastow's emotional turn on the stand offered some of the most devastating evidence against Mr. Skilling, and to a lesser extent, Mr. Lay. He said he had struck "bear hug" side deals with Mr. Skilling guaranteeing that his off-the-books partnerships, called LJM, would not lose money in their dealings with Enron. Mr. Fastow also described how Mr. Skilling had bought into using the LJM's to bolster earnings.

But Mr. Fastow's own admitted history of extensive crimes at Enron was dissected by Mr. Petrocelli, and jurors said they did not find Mr. Fastow particularly persuasive. "Fastow was Fastow," said a juror, Donald Martin, shaking his head. "We knew where he was coming from."

The jurors said they were moved, in contrast, by the testimony of Mr. Glisan. "We kept on going back to that testimony to corroborate things," said one juror, Freddy Delgado, a school principal.

The surprise testimony of David W. Delainey, the former chief of a retail unit called Energy Services, also helped pave the way for Mr. Skilling's conviction. Mr. Delainey, who pleaded guilty to fraud, said that Mr. Skilling took part in a decision to shift some $200 million in losses from Energy Services to the more profitable wholesale energy division to avoid having to admit to investors that Energy Services was failing.

On the stand, Mr. Skilling offered differing and confusing explanations for the shift. He proved evasive and sometimes forgetful, and he revealed a highly emotional demeanor rarely seen among the stoic class of chief executives.

His resignation in August 2001, after only six months as chief executive, led to a bout of heavy drinking as a depressed Mr. Skilling watched in horror as the company he helped build edged closer to the brink.

For Mr. Lay, a turning point came when Sherron S. Watkins, the former Enron vice president, took the stand to describe how she confronted him with concerns about Enron's accounting. Ms. Watkins suggested that the subsequent investigation Mr. Lay ordered was intentionally limited in scope to conclude that there were no problems.

Other issues plagued Mr. Lay's defense, most notably his own testiness on the stand and the sudden illness of his lead lawyer, Michael W. Ramsey, a well-regarded criminal defense lawyer who was forced to miss more than a month of the trial because of coronary disease that required two operations. Mr. Lay, in part because of his own strained finances, decided to carry on without Mr. Ramsey rather than seek to delay the trial and fight another day.

Morality Crimes

Drugs, Alcohol, and Sex

12

12.1 INTRODUCTION: DRUG PROHIBITION

Some drug use in the United States is viewed by the majority of Americans as acceptable behavior. Many adults and children believe that there is nothing wrong with taking certain drugs to lose weight; drinking several cups of coffee, tea, or cola each day; smoking cigarettes; having one or two cocktails before or after dinner; or using an over-the-counter or prescription drug to get rid of a headache. Most Americans have tried marijuana and many have shared prescription drugs with others. Americans spend many billions of dollars each year on prescription drugs, caffeinated drinks, cigarettes, and various alcoholic beverages.[1]

Such drug use tends to be seen as legitimate and acceptable—a matter of individual freedom of choice. In fact, the use of some drugs is so common that many of these substances are not even thought of as drugs.[2] For example, most Americans do not think of tobacco products as drugs, even though they account for more deaths than result from the combined total of illicit drugs, alcohol, toxic agents, microbial agents, firearms, auto accidents, and AIDS.[3]

Although many drugs and the reasons for taking them are socially sanctioned, the use of cocaine, heroin, crack, and other substances that society terms "hard drugs" or "street drugs" meets with much social disapproval and is considered criminal. Although we tend to exclusively define our drug problem in terms of these disapproved substances, it is important to recognize that the use and abuse of many legal and socially acceptable drugs can be just as dangerous to society and individuals as the use of the illicit or street drugs.

Why, then, do we tend to define the drug problem in the United States only in terms of specific drugs? Also, why are other drugs and certain other reasons for drug use viewed as acceptable? Many factors underlie this selective acceptability. One factor is tradition. For example, drugs such as alcohol, tobacco, and caffeine have a long history of use in our society. Other drugs have a stamp of approval because they are legal, or broadly defined as medicines, or prescribed by physicians. In addition, the alcohol, tobacco, and pharmaceutical industries annually spend millions of marketing dollars to convince Americans of the legitimacy of their respective products. The acceptability of drug use, then, is related to the ways in which drugs are acquired, the reasons for their use, and the kinds of people who take them.

In many instances, drugs with a widespread use by dominant groups in society tend to be both legal and acceptable. Conversely, other drugs have been termed unacceptable, problematic, or criminal because they are associated with a lifestyle that flouts conventional middle-class values.[4] As the U.S. Commission on Marihuana and Drug Abuse stated in 1973, "This society is not opposed to all drug taking but only to certain forms of drug use by certain persons. Self-medication by a [homemaker or businessperson] with amphetamines or tranquilizers, for example, is generally viewed as a personal judgment of little concern to the larger society. On the

Most Americans do not think of tobacco products as drugs, even though they account for more deaths than result from the combined total of illicit drugs, alcohol, toxic agents, microbial agents, firearms, auto accidents, and AIDS. Legislation banning smoking in public places—including airplanes, office buildings, and restaurants—is a recent development based on medical research. But whereas smoking is becoming criminalized nationwide, some states have moved closer to decriminalizing the smoking of marijuana. What determines whether drug use is regarded as legitimate or illicit?

other hand, use of such drugs by a college student or other young person to stay awake for studying or simply to experience the effect of such drugs is ordinarily considered a matter of intense community concern extending even to legal intervention."[5]

This chapter addresses the following questions:

- How are illegal drugs defined and classified (section 12.2)?
- What are the facts of drug abuse, drug and alcohol addiction, and illegal drug use (section 12.3)?
- What are the links between drugs and alcohol and crime (section 12.4)?
- How can alcohol abuse and illegal drug use be explained (section 12.5)?
- How has society responded to illegal drug use and other public-order crimes (section 12.6)?
- How do sex-related crimes threaten the public order, and should they be regarded as victimless (section 12.7)?

12.2 DRUGS DEFINED

The term *drug* is used in a variety of ways. Scientifically defined, a **drug** is "any substance other than food which by its chemical nature affects the structure or function of the living organism."[6] This is obviously a very broad definition under which could be included thousands of substances. From a medical perspective, a drug refers to any substance prescribed by a physician to treat or cure illness.

The term is also subject to a social or popular definition independent of the pharmacological and medical contexts. In a social sense, a **drug** is any substance that has been "arbitrarily defined by certain segments of society as a drug. . . . [Thus,] society defines what a drug is, and the social definition shapes our attitudes toward the class of substances so described."[7] Although we cannot ignore the importance of this definition or the real consequences it has for shaping public opinion on drugs, we must be aware that the popular definition typically involves certain prejudgments and stereotypes. In effect, social definitions tend to label as drugs only those chemical substances that are socially disapproved and illicit.

Cocaine, heroin, barbiturates, amphetamines, alcohol, and tobacco are termed **psychoactive drugs** by social scientists. For our purposes, this term

> Scientifically, a **drug** is "any substance other than food which by its chemical nature affects the structure or function of the living organism." Socially, a **drug** is any substance that has been "arbitrarily defined as a drug by certain segments of society."

> **Psychoactive drugs** are chemical substances that affect the user's central nervous system and thus influence mood, perceptions, emotions, and behavior.

emphasizes the fact that there is a wide range of chemical substances capable of affecting the user's central nervous system and thus influencing thought processes, perceptions, emotions, and behavior—criminal as well as noncriminal. Psychoactive drugs are usually divided into three categories: depressants, stimulants, and hallucinogens.

Depressants decrease (or depress) the functioning of a person's central nervous system, reducing anxiety, stress, and tension. Some depressants also tend to produce a sense of well-being or euphoria.

- Examples include narcotics or opiates (opium, heroin, morphine, and codeine) and sedatives (barbiturates and tranquilizers).
- In spite of what most people believe, alcohol is also classified as a depressant, because its overall effect is to depress activities of the central nervous system, which decreases motor activity, inhibitions, and alertness.

Stimulants generally increase the functioning of a person's central nervous system. They tend to decrease appetite and fatigue and heighten mood, alertness, and general motor activity.

- Stimulants of the natural variety include nicotine (found in cigarettes), caffeine (found in coffee and tea), and cocaine.
- Use of stimulants such as crack (a cheap, potent, crystalline form of cocaine) has become widespread in the past fifteen years.
- Cocaine and crack users can exhibit paranoid, erratic, hallucinatory, and violent behavior. Frequent use can induce personality changes, confusion, anxiety, depression, and even psychosis.[8]
- Synthetic stimulants are termed amphetamines, examples of which are Benzedrine, Dexedrine, and Methedrine.

Hallucinogens and marijuana are more difficult to classify, in that their effects on the user vary widely depending on the hallucinogen used and the dose taken. In general, hallucinogens cause a mild to intense distortion of visual and auditory functions. Users have a tendency to experience changes in mood and stepped-up thought processes. Long-term use often results in impaired judgment, delusions, and even acute psychosis.

- Lysergic acid diethylamide (LSD), psilocybin, and mescaline are examples of hallucinogens being used today.
- Marijuana, or pot, can either depress or stimulate a person. Although the effects of marijuana are highly variable as well as subjective, in most cases the user tends to experience mild euphoria, relaxation, decreased alertness, and some confusion in time perspective.[9]

In spite of these general categories and descriptions, the actual effect of a drug on a user is not always fixed. Users have had widely different responses and reactions, even when using the same drug. Thus, although the type of drug taken and the frequency and dose are important, other elements are also important. Factors such as body size, weight, age, health, personality, prior drug involvement, and the conditions under which the drug is used help determine its full effects.[10]

Depressants are psychoactive substances that decrease or depress the functioning of the central nervous system.

Stimulants are psychoactive substances that increase the functioning of the central nervous system.

Hallucinogens are psychoactive substances that cause mild to intense distortions of visual and auditory functions.

After reading this section, you should be able to

1. identify factors related to the acceptability of certain drugs and drug use in American society;
2. define the term *drug* scientifically and socially;
3. briefly define and compare depressants, stimulants, and hallucinogens.

Many people equate drug abuse with using socially disapproved-of and typically illegal psychoactive substances, such as heroin, cocaine, and LSD. In the United States, patterns of drug abuse include, but are not necessarily limited to, the use of these illegal substances. In this chapter, *drug abuse* is defined as the excessive or compulsive use of a drug to the degree that it is harmful to the user's health or social functioning, or to the extent that it can result in harmful consequences to others.[11] With **addiction**, the person becomes physically dependent on a drug and so will go through withdrawal if drug use ceases. The drug itself may be socially acceptable and legal (caffeine or nicotine), or it may be socially unacceptable and illegal (heroin or crack). With this definition, any drug, including aspirin, has the potential for being abused. Alcohol, barbiturates, and narcotics run a high risk for abuse, given that their regular and continued use results in addiction. Milder tranquilizers, antidepressants, and amphetamines do not necessarily create a physical dependence; however, the potential for abuse is still present, because their constant use or overuse can lead to psychological dependence or habituation.[12]

Addiction is the condition in which a person becomes physically dependent on a drug and so will go through withdrawal if drug use ceases.

What is illicit drug use? According to the U.S. Department of Justice, **illicit drug use** is the use of prescription-type psychotherapeutic drugs for nonmedical purposes or the use of illegal drugs. Some people define any illicit drug use as drug abuse. For others, drug abuse is any illicit drug use that results in social, economic, psychological, or legal problems for the user.[13]

Illicit drug use is the use of prescription-type psychotherapeutic drugs for nonmedical purposes or the use of illegal drugs.

As is examined in previous chapters, the incidence of violent crime and property crime has decreased over the past decade or so. However, the incidence of illegal drug use has increased. About 16 million Americans are regular illicit drug users. This trend is occurring despite increased federal funds, higher levels of drug arrests, and higher incarceration rates.[14]

Illicit Drug Use and Crime

There is a strong relationship between illicit drug use and crime in the United States.

According to the National Crime Victimization Survey, in 2001,

- there were about 7.4 million annual violent victimizations of U.S. residents age twelve or older;
- when victims were asked to describe whether they perceived the offenders to have been using drugs or alcohol, 28 percent believed their assailants were under the influence of drugs or alcohol;
- based on the perceptions of crime victims, about 1.2 million violent crimes occurred each year in which victims were certain that the offenders had been using alcohol;
- for one in four victimizations involving the offender's use of alcohol, the victim believed the offender was also using drugs at the time the offense occurred.[16]

Concerning the workplace, drugs, and crime, the NCVS reported that

- 35 percent of violent-crime victims in the workplace believed the offenders were using alcohol or using drugs at the time of the incident;
- 36 percent did not know if the offenders had been drinking or using drugs at the time of the incident;
- victims of workplace violence differed, by occupation, in their perception of whether the offenders used drugs or alcohol;
- 47 percent of victims in law enforcement perceived the offenders to be using drugs or alcohol, 35 percent in the medical fields, and 31 percent in retail sales.[17]

DID YOU KNOW

The NSDUH is the National Survey on Drug Use and Health. See http://www.oas .samhsa.gov/nhsda.htm.

National Survey on Drug Use Findings

Findings from the 2005 National Survey on Drug Use and Health are described here and shown in Figure 12.1.

- In 2005, an estimated 19.7 million Americans age twelve or older were current (past month) illicit drug users, meaning they had used an illicit drug during the month prior to the survey interview. This estimate represents 8.1 percent of the population age twelve or older.
- The overall rate of current illicit drug use among persons age twelve or older in 2005 (8.1 percent) was similar to the rate in 2004 (7.9 percent), 2003 (8.2 percent), and 2002 (8.3 percent).
- Marijuana was the most commonly used illicit drug (14.6 million past month users). In 2005, it was used by 74.2 percent of current illicit drug users. Among current illicit drug users, 54.5 percent used only marijuana, 19.6 percent used marijuana and another illicit drug, and the remaining 25.9 percent used only an illicit drug other than marijuana in the past month.
- In 2005, there were 2.4 million persons who were current cocaine users, which is more than in 2004 when the number was 2 million. However, the change in the rate of current use of cocaine between 2005 and 2004 (1.0 and 0.8 percent, respectively) was not statistically significant.

- The number of current crack users increased from 467,000 in 2004 to 682,000 in 2005. However, the change in the rate of current use of crack between 2004 and 2005 (0.2 and 0.3 percent, respectively) was not statistically significant.
- Hallucinogens were used in the past month by 1.1 million persons (0.4 percent) in 2005, including 502,000 (0.2 percent) who had used Ecstasy. These estimates are similar to the corresponding estimates for 2004.
- There was no significant change in the number of current heroin users in 2005 (136,000), nor in the rate of heroin use (0.1 percent), compared with estimates from 2004.
- The rates for past month and past year methamphetamine use did not change between 2004 and 2005, but the lifetime rate declined from 4.9 to 4.3 percent. From 2002 to 2005, decreases were seen in lifetime (5.3 to 4.3 percent) and past year (0.7 to 0.5 percent) use, but not past month use (0.3 percent in 2002 vs. 0.2 percent in 2005). Although the number of past month users has remained steady since 2002, the number of methamphetamine users who were dependent on or abused some illicit drug did rise significantly during this period, from 164,000 in 2002 to 257,000 in 2005.[15]

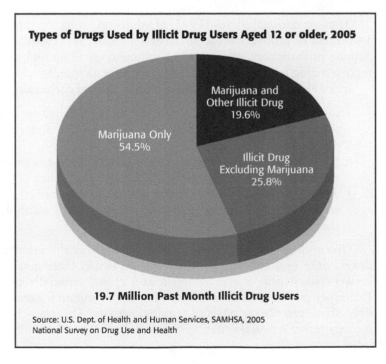

Types of Drugs Used by Illicit Drug Users Aged 12 or older, 2005

Marijuana and Other Illicit Drug 19.6%

Marijuana Only 54.5%

Illicit Drug Excluding Marijuana 25.8%

19.7 Million Past Month Illicit Drug Users

Source: U.S. Dept. of Health and Human Services, SAMHSA, 2005 National Survey on Drug Use and Health

FIGURE 12.1 Types of Drugs Used by Illicit Drug Users Age Twelve or Older, 2005

Alcohol and Crime

VICTIM AND OFFENDER SELF-REPORTS OF ALCOHOL INVOLVEMENT IN CRIME

Research suggests that a decreasing share of violent crime is attributable to offenders who had been drinking alcoholic beverages. Surveys of victims indicate that the rate of alcohol-involved violent crimes (i.e., crimes in which the perpetrators had been drinking, as perceived by the victims) decreased 34 percent from 1993 to 1998, whereas the rate of non-alcohol-involved violence decreased 22 percent. Surveys of some offenders also suggest that alcohol's role in violence is decreasing. The decrease in alcohol-involved violence is consistent with declines in other measures of alcohol use and misuse, including per capita alcohol consumption and alcohol involvement in traffic crashes. In contrast, violent offenders in State prisons are increasingly likely to report having used alcohol before committing their offenses, possibly illustrating the effect of more severe sanctions for alcohol-involved offenses.

Researchers face significant limitations in measuring the role of alcohol use in criminal behavior, because most alcohol consumption does not result in crime. In addition, nonoffending behavior is not typically measured; therefore, limited statistical information exists on which to estimate the likelihood that a person will commit a criminal act during or following alcohol consumption. . . . [There are] two major sources of information on alcohol's involvement in crime: (1) victim surveys and (2) offender surveys. A study reported by BJS in 1998, which used both of these resources, found that they yielded similar estimates regarding the involvement of alcohol and other drug use in crime. The investigators evaluated victim, offender, and law enforcement data from 1992 through 1995 and estimated that offenders had used either alcohol alone or alcohol with other drugs in approximately 37 percent of violent victimizations in which victims were able to describe substance use by the offenders (Greenfeld, 1998). The study also found that in regard to violent offenders, 41 percent on probation, 41 percent in local jails, and 38 percent in State prisons reported that they had been using alcohol when they committed their offenses (Greenfeld, 1998).

Sources: L. A. Greenfeld and M. A. Henneberg, **http://www.niaaa.nih.gov/publications /arh12–1/ 20–31.htm**, May 17, 2003; L. A. Greenfeld, *Alcohol and Crime: An Analysis of National Data on the Prevalence of Alcohol Involvement in Crime,* Washington, DC: Bureau of Justice Statistics, 1998.

The first national survey (1995) of adults on probation reported that about 14 percent of probationers were on drugs when they committed their offense. Among probationers, 49 percent of the mentally ill and 46 percent of others reported drug or alcohol use at the time of the offense.[18]

In a 1999 survey of inmates in state and federal correctional facilities,

- one-third of state and 22 percent of federal prisoners reported that they had committed their current offense while under the influence of drugs;
- forty-two percent of drug offenders and 37 percent of property offenders reported the highest incidence of drug use at the time of the offense;
- almost two-thirds of mentally ill and more than half of other inmates in state prison were under the influence of drugs or alcohol at the time of their current offense.[19]

Given all of this information, what exactly is the relationship between drugs, drug use, and crime? More specifically, is there a strong association between illicit drug use in America and crime, especially predatory crime? *Predatory crimes* are instrumental offenses committed for material gain. Does drug abuse precede the onset of criminal activity? Do research studies in criminology report a causal ordering between drug use and criminality?

This law enforcement officer is investigating a break-in and burglary at a pharmacy. Drugs were the principal target of this crime. In general, criminological research suggests a strong relationship between illicit drug use and crime in the United States. The term *crime–drug link* has been used to refer to the positive correlation between drug abuse, drug trafficking, and crime. What data support this link?

Alcohol Abuse

Alcohol continues to be the most widely used and abused drug in the United States.

Alcohol is a central nervous system depressant. Many people, however, believe it is a stimulant in that, in limited quantities, it tends to make the user more sociable, lively, and talkative. Actually, these mild effects are only by-products of its depressant action; the drug depresses areas in the brain that normally control inhibitions.

READING ABSTRACT

Drugs and Predatory Crime

BY JAN M. CHAIKEN AND MARCIA R. CHAIKEN

The authors of this reading answer numerous questions relating to crime and drugs and review the implications of their research for the U.S. justice system.

See reading on page 369.

Alcohol abuse, or a pattern of frequent and excessive alcohol consumption, leads to many devastating long-term consequences, both physical and mental. These consequences include:

- impairment of learning
- memory loss
- impotence and testosterone deficiency in men
- loss of appetite, leading to malnutrition and increased susceptibility to disease, mental disorders
- heart disease
- cirrhosis of the liver
- irreversible neurological and brain damage
- shorter life expectancy.[20]

Multiple-Drug Use

In multiple-drug use, a user takes additional drugs to either dampen or heighten the effects of another drug.

Multiple-drug use in the United States is increasingly common, according to the Department of Justice, and is becoming an important problem. Such use is dangerous because of the interactive effects of some drug combinations.

- Sometimes a particular drug is used to moderate the effects of another drug; for example, heroin or alcohol may be used to dampen the high produced by cocaine.
- At other times, a drug is used to enhance the effects of another drug, such as in "speedballing," or the use of both cocaine and heroin intravenously. This combination results in many hospital emergency-room visits.[21]

FOR YOUR INFORMATION

The Effects of Alcohol

The effects of alcohol vary according to the user's personality, present expectations, prior involvement with alcohol, and the amount of alcohol absorbed and concentrated in the blood. In turn, the level of blood-alcohol concentration is affected by body size and weight, the type of beverage consumed, the speed of consumption, and the presence of food in the stomach.

- With a blood-alcohol level of .08 percent (about four 12-ounce beers or four other standard drinks on an empty stomach for a person weighing 160 pounds), a user experiences slurred speech, decreased alertness, impaired judgment, and a noticeable lack of coordination.
- A blood-alcohol level between .13 and .15 leads to gross motor impairment, lack of physical control, blurred vision, and major loss of balance. Judgment and perception are severely impaired.
- With a continued increase in the level of blood-alcohol concentration, a user experiences stupor, coma, the loss of breathing and heartbeat, and eventually death.

According to the NSDUH, more than 100 million Americans drink alcoholic beverages, and alcohol is the most widely used and abused drug in the United States. Of the 8 million persons who have driven a vehicle under the influence of illicit drugs during the past year, 77 percent of them have also driven under the influence of alcohol. Excessive alcohol consumption is a problem on many college campuses nationwide. What consequences of alcohol abuse are these students risking?

FOR YOUR INFORMATION

Research on Substance Abuse

- Research has shown that about 18 million Americans have alcohol problems.
- About 6 million Americans have drug problems (other than alcohol).
- There are more annual deaths and disabilities from substance abuse than from any other cause.
- Substance abuse costs the American economy about $276 billion per year. These losses are from crime, health-care expenditures, lost productivity, and other conditions.

Sources: National Council on Alcoholism, *Facts on Alcoholism and Alcohol-Related Problems,* 1987; National Council on Alcoholism and Drug Dependence, "Facts and Information: Alcoholism and Drug Dependence Are America's Number One Health Problem," June 2002, **http://www.ncadd.org/facts/numberoneprob.html**; Brandeis University, Schneider Institute for Health Policy, *Substance Abuse: The Nation's Number One Health Problem; Key Indicators for Policy,* Princeton, NJ: Robert Wood Johnson Foundation, 2001; J. Fort and C. Cory, *American Drugstore,* Boston: Educational Associates, 1975; E. Goode, *Drugs in American Society,* New York: Knopf, 1972; L. Glick and D. E. Hebding, *Introduction to Social Problems,* Reading, MA: Addison-Wesley, 1980.

After reading this section, you should be able to

1. define drug abuse and illicit drug use;
2. profile illicit drug use in the United States;
3. explain the link between substance abuse and crime;
4. define alcohol abuse and list the effects of alcohol on the user;
5. draw conclusions about the role of multiple-drug use in the U.S. drug problem.

12.4 ILLEGAL DRUGS

The following several sections focus on the most widely used illicit psychoactive drugs—cannabis (marijuana), amphetamines, barbiturates and narcotics (heroin), and cocaine. Each section examines the nature and consequences of the illicit use of, and identifies the trafficking patterns for, each drug.

Cannabis (Marijuana)

Marijuana, after alcohol, is the most widely used mind-altering drug.

Marijuana, after alcohol, is the most widely used mind-altering drug.

There are several million daily users of **marijuana** in the United States. Many people use marijuana to produce feelings of relaxation and euphoria. One-quarter to one-third of the U.S. population has tried this drug at least once.[22] It is usually smoked, but it may also be swallowed. In user slang, to smoke marijuana is to "blast," "blast a roach," "blow," "hit," "mow the grass," "poke," "puff the dragon," or "have a tea party."[23] Medically, marijuana has been used to treat glaucoma, asthma, epilepsy, post-polio syndrome, cancer, bacterial infections, anxiety, pain, and depression.[24]

According to the NSDUH, "More than 10,000 metric tons of domestic marijuana and more than 5,000 metric tons of marijuana are annually cultivated and harvested in Mexico and Canada and marketed to more than 20 million users in the United States. Smaller quantities of marijuana are also produced in Colombia, Jamaica, Paraguay, and other countries.[25]

Amphetamines and Other Stimulants

Amphetamines (e.g., speed) are synthetic stimulants.

Amphetamines are synthetic stimulants, including substances such as Methedrine, Dexedrine, and Benzedrine.

The use of amphetamines is a major drug problem in the United States. **Amphetamines,** initially developed in the 1920s, are synthetic stimulants that include such substances as Methedrine (speed, ice, meth), Dexedrine (dex), and Benzedrine (bennies). Amphetamine use began to increase rapidly during the 1930s and 1940s, as physicians prescribed these drugs for medical problems such as depression and respiratory ailments. Amphetamines were also frequently given to military personnel during the Second World War to reduce fatigue and keep them awake for extended periods of time.[26] During the past several decades, the availability and use—both legal and illegal—of amphetamines has grown substantially.[27]

- Some of the effects of amphetamines are euphoria, excitement, increased alertness, and wakefulness.
- Amphetamines and other stimulants are usually taken orally or injected.

Marijuana Trafficking

According to 2000 Domestic Cannabis Eradication/ Suppression Program (DCE/SP) statistics, the five leading states for indoor growing activity were California, Florida, Oregon, Washington, and Wisconsin. DCE/SP statistics indicate that the major outdoor growing states in 2000 were California, Hawaii, Kentucky, and Tennessee; these states accounted for approximately three-quarters of the total of eradicated outdoor cultivated plants.

Organized crime groups operating from Mexico have smuggled marijuana into the United States since the early 1970s. These groups maintain extensive networks of associates, often related through familial or regional ties to associates living in the United States, where they control polydrug smuggling and wholesale distribution from hub cities to retail markets throughout the United States.

Groups operating from Mexico employ a variety of transportation and concealment methods to smuggle marijuana into the United States. Most of the marijuana smuggled into the United States is concealed in vehicles—often in false compartments—or hidden in shipments of legitimate agricultural or industrial products. Marijuana also is smuggled across the border by rail, horse, raft, and backpack. Shipments of twenty kilograms or less are smuggled by pedestrians who enter the

United States at border checkpoints and by backpackers who, alone or in groups ("mule trains"), cross the border at more remote locations. Jamaican organizations also appear to be involved in dispatching Mexican marijuana via parcel carriers. . . .

Besides overland smuggling, drug traffickers use ocean vessels to move Mexican marijuana up the coast of Mexico to U.S. ports, drop-off sites along the U.S. coast, or to rendezvous points with other boats bound for the United States.

Canada is becoming a source country for indoor-grown, high-potency (15 to 25 percent THC) marijuana destined for the United States. Canadian law enforcement intelligence indicates that marijuana traffickers there are increasingly cultivating cannabis indoors. Such indoor-grow operations have become an enormous and lucrative illicit industry, producing a potent form of marijuana that has come to be known as "BC Bud." Canadian officials estimate that cannabis cultivation in British Columbia is a billion-dollar industry, and that traffickers smuggle a significant portion of the Canadian harvest into the United States.

Source: U.S. Department of Justice, U.S. Drug Enforcement Administration, "Drug Trafficking in the United States," May 12, 2003, **http://www.usdoj.gov/dea/concern/drug_trafficking.html**.

- Students may take them to remain alert through long periods of study.
- Truck drivers often take them to stay awake during long-distance driving.
- They also have been used for weight reduction.

Thus, amphetamines affect physiological function, cognitive ability, and mood. These effects can increase the likelihood that users will act violently. In addition, high-dose or long-term use tends to be more hazardous to the user's health. Among the effects of excessive use are:

- malnutrition
- susceptibility to disease, resulting from severe appetite loss
- extreme sleeplessness
- delusions
- irritability

All estimates indicate that the use and abuse of amphetamines is widespread within our society. Fourteen million Americans have reported using stimulants at least once during their lifetime. Many others have used stimulants but have never reported this usage.[28] The illegal use of amphetamines is a major crime problem in the United States.

According to the Department of Justice, "the stimulant **methamphetamine** is one of the drugs most commonly produced in illegal labs in the U.S. Phenyl-2-propanone (P2P) is an immediate precursor that is easily synthesized into

Methamphetamine is a stimulant that is synthesized from phenyl-2-propanone (P2P), an immediate precursor chemical.

methamphetamine. The production of methamphetamine is fairly easy and cheap. Setting up a lab to produce a substantial amount of the drug may cost less than $2,000 and be enormously profitable—one day's production may be worth $70,000."[29]

A very popular amphetamine-like drug in the United States today is Ecstasy, an amphetamine analog. **Ecstasy** is the common name for 3–4 methylenedioxymethamphetamine, or **MDMA**. Ecstasy's stimulant properties provide a chemical high allowing users to dance for hours at "raves," or all-night dance parties. Researchers indicate that MDMA's most pernicious quality is that many of its users see it as a performance enhancer. However, it is a very dangerous drug.

> **Ecstasy** is an amphetamine analog and is the common name for 3–4 methylenedioxymethamphetamine, or **MDMA**.

MDMA Trafficking

MDMA is popular among middle-class adolescents and young adults. MDMA is increasingly becoming an abuse problem because many users view it as nonaddictive and benign. MDMA is sold primarily at legitimate nightclubs and bars, at underground nightclubs sometimes called "acid houses," or at all-night parties known as "raves."

MDMA tablets range in weight from 150 to 350 mg and contain between 70 to 120 mg of MDMA. The profit margin associated with MDMA trafficking is significant. It costs as little as 25 to 50 cents to manufacture an MDMA tablet in Europe, but the street value of that same MDMA tablet can be as high as $40, with a tablet typically selling for between $20 and $30.

Although the vast majority of MDMA consumed domestically is produced in Europe, a limited number of MDMA laboratories operate in the United States. Law enforcement seized seven clandestine MDMA laboratories in the United States in 2000 compared to nineteen seized in 1999. It should be noted that these laboratories were primarily capable of limited drug production. While recipes for the clandestine production of MDMA can be found on the Internet, acquiring the necessary precursor chemicals in the United States is difficult.

MDMA is manufactured clandestinely in Western Europe, particularly in the Netherlands and Belgium. Much of the MDMA is manufactured in the southeast section of the Netherlands near Maastricht. Despite the Dutch Government's efforts to curtail MDMA trafficking, the Netherlands remains a primary source country for the drug. International MDMA traffickers based in the Netherlands and Belgium, and a significant number of U.S.-based traffickers who coordinate MDMA shipments to major metropolitan areas of the United States, often use Montreal and Toronto as transit points. In December 2000, the Royal Canadian Mounted Police (RCMP) seized approximately 150,000 MDMA tablets in Toronto that had been shipped via DHL from Brussels, Belgium, by an Israeli MDMA trafficking organization. The shipment was destined for distributors in the United States.

Due to the availability of precursor chemicals in Canada, a number of MDMA laboratories have been discovered operating near metropolitan areas such as Vancouver, Toronto, and Montreal. Such laboratories continue to supply U.S.-based MDMA trafficking organizations. According to the RCMP, the total potential yield of MDMA from laboratories uncovered in Canada since 1999 is in excess of 10 million tablets.

Another emerging trend is the use of Mexico as a transit zone for MDMA entering the United States. During 2000, several seizures were reported in or destined for Mexico. In September 2000, Dutch authorities seized a 1.25 million-tablet shipment of MDMA destined for Mexico. Previously, in April 2000, a shipment of 200,000 MDMA tablets was seized at the airport in Mexico City. The MDMA was discovered in an air cargo shipment manifested as aircraft parts sent from the Netherlands and destined for the United States.

USCS statistics show a dramatic increase in seizures of MDMA tablets. In FY 1997, approximately 400,000 MDMA tablets were seized compared to approximately 9.3 million tablets seized in FY 2000. On July 22, 2000, approximately 2.1 million tablets were seized in Los Angeles. To date, this is the largest seizure of MDMA tablets in the United States.

Source: U.S. Department of Justice, U.S. Drug Enforcement Administration, "Drug Trafficking in the United States," May 12, 2003, **http://www.usdoj.gov/dea/concern/drug_trafficking.html**.

Barbiturates

- Barbiturates and other depressants are taken orally.
- Barbiturates have a high potential for abuse, and addiction is more common in the United States than heroin addiction.
- In small to moderate doses, they have an effect on the user similar to that of other depressants, such as alcohol.
- The user experiences mild euphoria, impairment of reflexes, and lessening of tension, anxiety, and inhibitions.
- The possibility of violent behavior and of unplanned overdose also poses problems.
- With larger doses, the user experiences slurred speech, a noticeable loss of physical coordination, drowsiness, and sleep.
- Heavy or long-term use causes severely impaired coordination and a slowing of many bodily functions, such as respiration and heart rate. It can also ultimately lead to coma and death.
- Barbiturates are the primary cause of death resulting from drug overdoses. Some overdoses are accidental; others result from combined use of barbiturates and alcohol; still others represent suicides.

Sources: J. Fort and C. Cory, *American Drugstore*, Boston: Educational Associates, 1975; Drugs and Crime Data Center and Clearinghouse, *Drugs, Crime, and the Justice System: A National Report from the Bureau of Justice Statistics*, M. W. Zawitz, Ed., Washington, DC: U.S. Department of Justice, Bureau of Justice Statistics, 1992; S. Cohen, *The Substance Abuse Problems*, New York: Haworth, 1981.

According to the NSDUH, brain-imaging research in humans indicates that MDMA/Ecstasy causes injury to the brain.

- It affects neurons that use the chemical serotonin to communicate with other neurons. The serotonin system regulates a person's sensitivity to pain, mood, aggression, sexuality, and sleep.
- The National Institute for Drug Abuse has linked MDMA use to possible long-term damage to the brain's thought and memory pathways.
- A study with primates reported that a four-day exposure to Ecstasy caused brain damage that was apparent six years later.[30]

Barbiturates and Other Depressants

Barbiturate addiction is more common than heroin addiction in the United States.

Barbiturates are depressant drugs. They include substances such as phenobarbital, Amytal, Nembutal, Amtal, and Seconal. In the illegal marketplace, barbiturates may be called downers, rainbows, goofballs, reds, or blue dragons. Two depressants of the central nervous system are gamma hydroxybutyrate (*GHB*) and gamma butyrolactone (*GBL*).

The first barbiturate was created in 1903 and was called barbital (Veronal). A decade later, phenobarbital (Luminal) was introduced. Since then, a couple of thousand different barbiturates have been manufactured, even though only a dozen or so are in frequent use today.[31]

GHB/GBL Trafficking

GHB (gamma hydroxybutyrate), a central nervous system depressant, was banned by the FDA in 1990. . . .

GHB generates feelings of euphoria and intoxication. It is often combined in a carbonated, alcohol, or health food drink, and is reportedly popular among adolescents and young adults attending raves and nightclubs. At lower doses, GHB causes drowsiness, nausea, and visual disturbances. At higher dosages, unconsciousness, seizures, severe respiratory depression, and coma can occur.

GHB has been used in the commission of sexual assaults because it renders the victim incapable of resisting, and may cause memory problems that could compli-

cate case prosecution. GHB recipes are accessible over the Internet; the drug is simple to manufacture, and can be made in a bathtub or even a Pyrex baking dish. DEA, along with state and local law enforcement agencies, seized seventeen GHB laboratories in 2000, ten of which were located in California.

GBL (gamma butyrolactone), an analog of GHB, is also abused. GBL is a chemical used in many industrial cleaners and it also has been marketed as a health supplement. GBL is synthesized by the body to produce GHB. One 55-gallon drum yields 240,000 capfuls of GBL. One capful sells for $8.00, potentially yielding 1.9 million dollars per 55-gallon drum.

Source: U.S. Department of Justice, U.S. Drug Enforcement Administration, "Drug Trafficking in the United States," May 12, 2003, **http://www.usdoj.gov/dea/concern/drug_trafficking.html**.

Heroin and Other Narcotics

More than one hundred thousand Americans are addicted to the popular narcotic heroin.

Narcotics are depressants that include opiates such as opium, morphine, heroin, and codeine, and synthetic drugs such as methadone and Demerol. **Opium** is a narcotic/depressant drug of which **morphine** is a derivative.

Narcotics are depressants that include opiates such as **opium**, **morphine**, *heroin*, and *codeine*, and synthetic drugs such as methadone and Demerol. Medically, narcotics are used to relieve pain. When used in small to moderate doses, narcotics cause drowsiness, a reduction of pain, euphoria, a lessening of inhibitions and general alertness, and loss of appetite. Occasionally, nausea and vomiting can occur.

Heavy narcotics use over an extended time period brings about sharp decreases in appetite, weight loss that frequently leads to malnutrition, temporary impotency in men, sterility, and increased possibility of overdose that may lead to death. Narcotics, especially opiates, are highly addictive, and the narcotics user develops a tolerance for them rather quickly. With frequent use, the user may become addicted within a short period of time. Withdrawal symptoms vary with the person and the narcotic and may include such symptoms as anxiety, restlessness, tension, headache, body twitching, chills, cramps, and vomiting.[32]

Heroin addiction is a major problem in the United States. About 3 million Americans have reported having used heroin at least once during their lifetime; more than one hundred thousand of these people are addicted. The prevalence of heroin use and addiction in our society is relatively small compared to that of alcohol, barbiturates, and cocaine; however, heroin use results in a number of seriously detrimental effects on the body. For example, it accounts for several thousand deaths each year. Most deaths do not result from the chemical properties of the drug itself; rather, they are related to the conditions under which the drug is taken. Most heroin deaths are due to overdose, malnutrition, hepatitis, AIDS, or other infections resulting from unsterilized needles previously used by an infected person. Nineteen percent of adult and adolescent AIDS cases have been solely attributed to intravenous (IV) drug use.[33]

Heroin and Crime

Research studies consistently indicate a strong relationship between heroin use and crime.

- Most of the crimes committed by heroin addicts are property offenses rather than violent crimes.
- Estimates indicate that addicts steal hundreds of millions of dollars in goods each year in order to support a habit that costs up to several hundred dollars a day.
- The chemical properties of heroin in itself do not lead people to commit crime; the relationship between its use and crime is basically explained by the fact that the drug is illegal and therefore expensive to obtain.

Source: J. Fort and C. Cory, *American Drugstore,* Boston: Educational Associates, 1975.

Heroin can be injected, sniffed (snorted), or smoked. Many heroin users who once used the drug intravenously are now smoking or "snorting" it to avoid the risk of contracting AIDS from shared needles. Combined with increases in heroin production in the 1990s and the higher purity of street samples, this shift in method of administration may attract both new and former users to the drug.[34]

U.S. involvement with opiates actually began prior to the discovery of heroin. In the nineteenth and early twentieth centuries, opium or its derivatives were widely available in over-the-counter patent medicines or in prescriptions. They were used to treat all kinds of physical complaints and illnesses, ranging from headaches and insomnia to cancer. Morphine, a derivative of opium, was used in many patent medicines. Its administration to injured Civil War soldiers resulted in the addiction of thousands of military personnel. At the beginning of the twentieth century, addiction to opium and its derivatives was widespread in the United States. Estimates of the addict population ranged from several hundred thousand to several million. Many of these people had become inadvertently addicted through medical use and, although addicts came from every segment of society, they tended to be white, middle-aged women from urban and rural communities.[35]

Around the turn of the twentieth century, two changes occurred that had significant consequences for the scope of opiate addiction:

1. The development of heroin in 1898. Heroin, a more powerful substance than morphine, became the opiate of addiction in the twentieth century.
2. The recognition of a growing "opiate problem" in the United States, resulting in the passage of restrictive legislation such as the Harrison Act of 1914. This act prohibited the sale and use of opiate substances. Thus, the process of defining addiction as criminal began.[36]

Cocaine and Crack

Cocaine use has decreased in the United States, but millions of Americans use its derivative, crack, on a daily basis.

Cocaine (coke) is a stimulant that is processed from the leaves of coca plants. It is designated as a narcotic under the Controlled Substances Act. In the user, cocaine produces increased alertness, excitement, euphoria, and feelings of great power. A person becomes hyperstimulated when snorting, smoking, swallowing,

PROFILES

Heroin Trafficking

Criminals in four foreign source areas produce the heroin available in the United States: South America (Colombia), Southeast Asia (principally Burma), Mexico, and Southwest Asia/Middle East (principally Afghanistan). While virtually all heroin produced in Mexico and South America is destined for the U.S. market, each of the four source areas has dominated the U.S. market at some point over the past thirty years. Over the past decade, the United States has experienced a dramatic shift in the heroin market from the domination of Southeast Asian heroin to dominance of the wholesale and retail markets by South American heroin, especially in the East. In the West, by contrast, "black tar" and, to a lesser extent, brown powdered heroin from Mexico have been, and continue to be, the predominant available form. . . .

Since the mid-1990s, [South American] heroin traffickers have diversified their methods of operation. Couriers still come into Miami, New York City, San Juan, and other U.S. cities on direct commercial flights from Colombia. Increasingly, however, Colombian traffickers are smuggling heroin from Colombia into the United States through such countries as Costa Rica, the Dominican Republic, Ecuador, Panama, Mexico, Argentina, and Venezuela. . . .

Mexican heroin has been a threat to the United States for decades. It is produced, smuggled, and distributed by polydrug trafficking groups, many of which have been in operation for more than twenty years. Nearly all of the heroin produced in Mexico is destined for distribution in the United States. . . . Although illegal immigrants and migrant workers frequently smuggle heroin across the U.S./Mexico border in 1- to 3-kilogram amounts for the major trafficking groups, seizures indicate that larger loads are being moved across the border, primarily in privately owned vehicles. Once the heroin reaches the United States, traffickers rely upon well-entrenched polydrug smuggling and distribution networks to deliver their product to the market, principally in the metropolitan areas of the midwestern, southwestern, and western United States with sizable Mexican immigrant populations. . . .

Southeast Asian (SEA) heroin shipments destined for U.S. markets may transit through China, Japan, Malaysia, the Philippines, Singapore, Taiwan, or South Korea. Largely independent U.S.-based ethnic Chinese traffickers control distribution within the United States, principally in the Northeast and along the East Coast. During the late 1990s, Vancouver, British Columbia, emerged as a key operational headquarters for ethnic Chinese criminal elements. These criminal groups were enmeshed with North American gangs of Asian descent in transporting SEA heroin to the United States, mainly to the East Coast. A DEA New York Field Division investigation led to the seizure, in January 2001, of 57 kilograms of SEA heroin from a container ship docked at the port in Elizabeth, New Jersey.

Trafficking groups composed of West African criminals also smuggle SEA heroin to the United States. Nigerian criminals have been most active in U.S. cities and areas with well-established Nigerian populations, such as Atlanta, Baltimore, Houston, Dallas, New York City, Newark, Chicago, and Washington, D. C. Over the past several years, Chicago has become a hub for heroin trafficking controlled by Nigerian criminals who primarily deal in SEA heroin.

While a large portion of Southwest Asian (SWA) heroin is consumed in Western Europe, Pakistan, and Iran, traffickers operating from Middle Eastern locations smuggle SWA heroin to ethnic enclaves in the United States. Criminal groups composed of ethnic Lebanese, Pakistanis, Turks, and Afghans are all involved in supplying the drug to U.S.-based groups for retail distribution. SWA heroin traffickers and wholesale distributors generally have been consistently cautious, rarely conducting heroin business with persons not of Southwest Asian or Middle Eastern ethnicity. Therefore, the ethnic aspect of SWA heroin importation and distribution has made SWA heroin more prevalent in areas with large Southwest Asian populations.

West African traffickers, who primarily smuggled SEA heroin to the United States in the 1990s, now also deal in SWA heroin.

Source: U.S. Department of Justice, U.S. Drug Enforcement Administration, "Drug Trafficking in the United States," May 12, 2003, **http://www.usdoj.gov/dea/concern/drug_trafficking.html**.

or injecting cocaine. Sniffing, or snorting, has been the primary way to use cocaine. However, ingestion by smoking powdered cocaine and crack has increased. In user terms, to inhale cocaine is to "blow," "blow a coke," "do a line," "geeze," "hitch up the reindeer," "pop," "sniff," "snort," or "toot." Smoking cocaine is "chasing," "freebasing," or "ghost busting."[37]

In the United States, the consumption of cocaine has declined. However, cocaine still poses a major drug threat.

- An estimated 300 metric tons of coke annually enter the United States primarily from Colombia, Peru, and Bolivia.
- According to the NSDUH, Colombia is the world's leading producer and distributor of cocaine to the United States.
- About 80 percent of the world's cocaine hydrochloride (HCL) is processed in Colombia.[38]

Cocaine and heroin revenues fuel terrorism and the decades-old civil war in Colombia. All the insurgent and paramilitary groups depend upon them. They fund the Revolutionary Forces of Colombia (FARC), the hemisphere's largest and oldest terrorist group; the National Liberation Army (ELN); and the paramilitary United Self-Defense Forces of Colombia (AUC). The AUC and the FARC control areas that have the densest levels of coca and poppy cultivation in the country.[39]

Crack cocaine is a stimulant derived from cocaine. According to the U.S. Department of Justice, crack is easily manufactured by heating powdered cocaine and baking soda on a stove top—a much less dangerous procedure than freebasing (smoking cocaine).

- Heavy crack and cocaine use leads to weight loss, insomnia, and anxiety.
- Oversuspiciousness and paranoia with hallucinations and delusions are frequent.[40]
- Evidence indicates a tendency for crack cocaine and cocaine users to increase the frequency of use over time.[41]
- According to Sidney Cohen, crack and cocaine tolerance and withdrawal symptoms occur at high doses and, therefore, it is "correct to speak of cocaine addiction. It is the craving to repeat the experience for long periods in high doses."[42]
- Some 24 million people have reported using cocaine once during their lifetime.[43]
- The number of reported lifetime crack cocaine users, about 4 million, probably underestimates the number of actual users, in that certain segments of the population are not included in household surveys.[44]
- The easy availability of crack and the low cost of single doses have stimulated greater use of the drug, contributing to its threat.[45]

LSD, PCP, and Other Drugs

Hallucinogens (such as LSD and PCP), flunitrazepam, and steroids are also drugs that are abused. Lysergic acid diethylamide *(LSD)* and phencyclidine *(PCP)* are manufactured hallucinogens. *Flunitrazepam* is a central nervous system depressant. *Steroids* are manufactured drugs used in bodybuilding and to enhance athletic performance.

After reading this section, you should be able to

1. discuss the trafficking and use of marijuana;
2. describe the effects of amphetamines and other stimulants on the user;
3. profile methamphetamine and MDMA trafficking in the United States;
4. describe the history and effects of barbiturates and other depressants;
5. compare the effects of heroin, cocaine, and crack;
6. profile narcotics trafficking in the United States;
7. discuss the use of hallucinogens and steroids.

Trafficking LSD, PCP, Flunitrazepam, and Steroids

LSD production reportedly is centered on the West Coast, particularly in San Francisco, northern California, the Pacific Northwest, and recently the Midwest. Since the 1960s, LSD has been manufactured illegally within the United States. LSD production is a time-consuming and complex procedure. Several chemical recipes for synthesizing LSD are on the Internet, but clandestine production requires a high degree of chemical expertise. . . . LSD is produced in crystal form that is converted to liquid and distributed primarily in the form of squares of blotter paper saturated with the liquid. To a lesser extent, LSD is sold as a liquid, contained in breath mint bottles and vials; in gelatin tab form ("window panes") of varying colors; and in pill form known as "microdots."

Distribution of LSD is unique within the drug culture. A proliferation of mail order sales has created a marketplace where the sellers are virtually unknown to the buyers, giving the highest-level traffickers considerable insulation from drug law enforcement operations. The vast majority of users are middle-class adolescents and young adults attracted by its low prices. Rock concerts continue to be favorite distribution sites for LSD traffickers; however, distribution at raves throughout the United States is becoming more popular. Contacts made at raves and concerts are used to establish future transactions and shipments of larger quantities of LSD.

PCP production is centered in the greater Los Angeles metropolitan area. During the late 1980s and early 1990s, the widespread availability and use of crack cocaine displaced demand for PCP. More recently, however, reporting suggests that PCP abuse is increasing slightly in many cities, as some crack addicts return to the use of this drug. DEA reporting indicates that PCP is being encountered with greater frequency along the Southwest border, particularly in Texas. . . .

Flunitrazepam is sold under the trade name Rohypnol. . . . Flunitrazepam is manufactured worldwide, particularly in Europe and Latin America, where it is sold legally by prescription. This drug is neither manufactured nor approved for medical use in the United States. Distributors in Texas allegedly travel to Mexico to obtain the drug. In addition, Colombian sources of supply smuggle flunitrazepam into South Florida via international mail services and/or couriers using commercial airlines.

According to law enforcement officials in south Florida, flunitrazepam is routinely referred to as a "club drug," since it is popular in local nightclubs. It is also referred to as the "date rape drug," characteristically causing the victim to experience short-term memory loss after ingestion. It is ingested orally, frequently in conjunction with alcohol or other drugs. High school and college students are the most frequent users of flunitrazepam which is unadulterated, and, therefore, "safe" because of pre-sealed bubble packaging. . . .

Fitness clubs have been, and continue to be, the primary distribution centers of steroids, because bodybuilders and weightlifters comprise a predominant portion of the user population. Once viewed as a problem strictly associated with professional athletes, a recent survey of students indicates increased steroid use among boys in the eighth and tenth grades. . . . Anabolic steroids are illicitly smuggled from Mexico and European countries to the United States. Recent DEA reporting indicates that Russian and Romanian nationals are significant traffickers of steroids and are responsible for substantial shipments of steroids entering the United States. The lack of international control over foreign sources of supply, however, makes it impossible to attack the trafficking at its source.

Source: U.S. Department of Justice, U.S. Drug Enforcement Administration, "Drug Trafficking in the United States," May 12, 2003, **http://www.usdoj.gov/dea/concern/drug_trafficking.html**.

12.5 EXPLANATIONS FOR ILLICIT DRUG USE AND ADDICTION

Given all the research data on the effects of drug and alcohol abuse, why do so many Americans use and abuse legal and illicit drugs? Why do so many individuals become involved with, and sometimes addicted to, drugs and alcohol? The reasons are complicated, because there are physiological, psychological, and sociological explanations for illicit drug use. Certainly, the physiological effects of drugs and alcohol on the human body cannot be ignored. Yet scientific research reports that neither the chemical attributes of drugs nor the physiological response of the human organism to drugs can sufficiently explain the process and patterns of addiction. To adequately explain how drugs influence people's behavior and why people become addicted to drugs, one must recognize that, in addition to the physiological factor, many social, situational, and psychological factors are involved.

Physiological Explanations

Addiction may result from biological or physiological characteristics.

Physiological theories of addiction and alcoholism generally focus on the assumption that addiction results from some biological or physical characteristic of the person.

- Some explanations emphasize a genetic theory that stresses, for example, the idea that alcoholism is inherited and passed directly from parents to children.
- Some studies have reported that the biological children of alcoholics raised by nonalcoholic adoptive parents more frequently develop alcohol problems than the natural children of the adoptive parents.[46]
- Other explanations stress genotrophic origins of alcoholism, that is, the theory that alcoholism comes from a hereditary flaw that necessitates an exceptionally high need for a number of basic vitamins. Persons with this defect develop nutritional and vitamin deficiencies, which in turn bring about an insatiable desire for alcohol.[47]
- Although the results are inconclusive, studies that have compared alcoholism among identical and fraternal twins have reported that the degree of concordance (both siblings behaving identically) is twice as high among the identical-twin groups, suggesting some genetic basis.[48]
- Still other physiological theories stress that addiction is caused by certain hormone imbalances triggered by glandular problems.

In general it appears that these theories have only a limited potential for explaining addiction and its sociocultural variations. It is true, for example, that alcoholism is often found in the children of alcoholics, but it is found in the children of nonalcoholics as well. Likewise, the nutritional deficiencies and hormone imbalances often observed among alcoholics may well be the effects of drinking rather than the cause of the problem.[49]

Purely physiological explanations of the effects of drugs on the human organism were once very popular. This view is similar to what Erich Goode terms the *chemicalistic fallacy*, or the "view that drug A causes behavior X, [and] that what we see as behavior and effects associated with a given drug are solely a function of the biochemical properties of that drug."[50] In this view, the person plays a purely passive role. Behavior, including whether the user becomes addicted, is entirely dependent on the influence of the specific drug on that person's body. This view is called a fallacy because it has come under serious attack by many medical experts and other authorities in the drug field.[51]

People tend to view drug and alcohol use solely in terms of their effects on the human organism. The popular beliefs still hold, for example, that if people use drugs they will inevitably become addicted. Once in the "clutches of addiction," one is powerless to control the situation. A single dose of certain drugs will automatically lead to lifelong addiction. These beliefs are particularly widespread with respect to the opiates (such as heroin), but even the power of these chemical substances to permanently influence behavior is exaggerated.[52]

FOR YOUR INFORMATION

The Limits of Physiological Explanations

- The effect of drug and alcohol use on the human organism is relative.
- Physiological explanations of drug use and addiction fail to account for the role that social and psychological factors play.
- They do not specify what the individual experiences as a result of drug use, or what the effects of drugs on the person's behavior and social functioning—whether noncriminal or criminal—will be.
- These theories are limited in their ability to explain why people become involved with drugs in the first place, and why some but not all people persist in drug use to the point of addiction.
- Physiological theories cannot account for the discrepancies in behavioral effects and patterns of drug use found among drug users and addicts.
- The physiological approach is unable to explain why some addicts return to drug or alcohol use after withdrawal or detoxification, when obviously there can be no physiological basis for such behavior.

As discussed earlier, drugs vary in their ability to influence behavior and produce physical dependence. Chemicalistic interpretations of the effects of drugs on humans fail to take into account the important roles of personality and situation in drug abuse. As Peter Laurie reports, "Drugs are used quite differently in different social situations; very often the situation and the expectations of the user have far more effect than the chemical."[53]

Studies document that the effects of drugs such as marijuana, LSD, heroin, and alcohol depend on the personal characteristics of the user and the context of drug use. For example, street users experience morphine as pleasurable; most hospital patients do not. The importance of psychological and situational factors in drug use is also attested to by the frequent use of placebos in medical therapy and in scientific research.[54]

The context of drug use, then, has as much to say about a drug's long-term behavioral effects on the user as the drug itself. One of the best examples of this is found in Charles Winick's study of physicians addicted to narcotics. The study revealed some significant contrasts to street patterns of addiction. Physician addicts did not incur the availability and cost problems of supporting their habit. They were able to self-administer high-quality narcotics under sanitary conditions, and they guarded against nutritional deficiencies. As a result, even with many years of narcotic abuse, their physical health was not affected. Moreover, as far as could be determined, they were able to function within a demanding profession.[55]

Psychological Explanations

Reinforcement theory and personality theory offer psychological explanations by looking at the people who use drugs rather than the drugs themselves.

In contrast to physiological explanations, psychologists and social scientists have stressed the importance of investigating the people who use drugs rather than the drugs themselves. From this perspective, psychologists have attempted to explain addiction in terms of what drugs do *for* people rather than *to* them.

What is it about people that attract them to drug use, particularly excessive drug use and addiction? In attempting to answer such questions, psychologists have developed a number of theories, the most popular of which are the reinforcement and personality theories.

Reinforcement theory is based on a basic principle of conditioned learning, namely, that people (and other animals) tend to continue in activities that are reinforced (i.e., they bring pleasure) and will likewise refrain from behaviors that bring about unpleasantness, pain, and punishment. In terms of this principle, psychologists emphasize that, for many people, the use of drugs and alcohol constitutes a rewarding and pleasant activity, because these substances may relieve depression, anxiety, tension, and boredom. Many people in our society develop a pattern of frequent and excessive drinking and drug use to lessen tensions and anxieties produced by life's stressful problems and situations.

In the 1960s, Alfred Lindesmith developed one of the more important theories on drug addiction (particularly opiate addiction). His perspective was consistent with the reinforcement principle. For Lindesmith, the development of physical dependence is a necessary precondition, but not in itself a sufficient explanation, for addiction. In other words, in order for addiction to actually occur, the person must first begin to experience withdrawal distress. In addition, the individual must link this distress with the absence of the drug. It is only under this circumstance that the individual will become addicted, subsequently actively engaging in the habitual use of drugs for the primary purpose of avoiding withdrawal. Thus, in Lindesmith's view, it is not the euphoric or pleasurable aspects of drug use that produce addiction; on the contrary, addiction ultimately results from the person's overwhelming need to avoid withdrawal distress.[56]

There are a number of deficiencies in the reinforcement theory. For example, it ignores the important role that group and sociological factors play in drug use and the development of addiction. In addition, research with respect to psychological factors in alcoholism has shown that, contrary to reinforcement theory, alcohol tends to increase stress, anxiety, and depression, at least in chronic drinkers. That is, although people may initially turn to alcohol to relieve their anxieties and problems, once the stage of chronic drinking is reached, alcohol no longer serves this purpose.[57]

Personality theories stress the importance of various personal traits in an attempt to explain why some people become addicted to drugs and alcohol and others do not. These explanations stress that the possession of certain personality characteristics predisposes individuals to addiction. When combined, these traits make up what some psychologists term the addict or alcoholic-personality type. Many researchers agree that both the addict and alcoholic-personality types tend to share certain psychological similarities, especially high dependence needs and an extreme sense of personal inadequacy. The addict, according to Laurie, is unable to deal with anxiety, never feels self-satisfaction, and is plagued with conflicts over sexuality and aggression.[58] From the standpoint of personality, alcoholics have frequently been described as emotionally immature, highly self-indulgent, sexually maladjusted, unable to tolerate frustration, and unable to relate to others.[59]

Jerome Platt and Christina Labate's research in the 1970s studied the personality characteristics of drug abusers. They reported that there exists a significant degree of personal pathology among drug abusers. Drug abusers tend to have personality disorders characterized by a weak ego, anxiety, fantasies of omnipotence, and a low tolerance for frustration. Their research also reported that many addicts exhibit sociopathic behavior that forms an addiction-prone personality.[60]

Often, psychologists and psychiatrists trace the origins of these traits to inconsistent and unstable family relationships. This inadequate socialization in the family leads to a lack of maturity, deep feelings of insecurity, and other personality maladjustments in later adult life.[61]

A research study of more than 20,000 people in several U.S. cities reported on the personality characteristics of drug abusers. Results, published in 1990, indicated a significant relationship between drug abuse and mental illness. For example, over one-half of drug abusers and over one-third of alcohol abusers had at least one type of serious mental disorder. In addition, almost one-third of those diagnosed as mentally ill in the survey had substance-abuse problems.[62]

Although personality theories have generated a considerable amount of research into the etiology of drug addiction and alcoholism, they also have their inadequacies:

- There has been little agreement on the part of mental health professionals concerning the specific psychological traits that make up the addict personality.
- Even though psychologists tend to assert that certain personality traits cause drug addiction or alcoholism, it may well be that such traits are actually a result of drug addiction or excessive drinking rather than its cause.
- Personality theories of addiction are unable to explain why many people who also exhibit high dependence needs, chronic anxiety, and strong feelings of personal insecurity do not become drug addicts or alcoholics. Addicts and nonaddicts alike sometimes manifest similar personality characteristics.[63]

Sociological Explanations

Group factors and the social environment are important variables in explaining addiction.

Sociological theories of addiction stress the importance of group factors and the influence of a person's social environment and social situations in attempting to explain drug addiction and alcoholism. In general, sociological explanations view drug use and addiction as products of *social learning*. For example, Sutherland's theory of *differential association* can help us explain drug use and abuse.[64] According to this theory, people learn drug use and addiction through interaction with others who exhibit such behavior.

In addition, Ronald Akers, applying *differential-association reinforcement theory*, reports that people are often introduced to and encouraged in drug and alcohol use by friends or others in the surrounding environment. In part, this process operates through a system of positive reinforcements—such as rewards—from others in the form of social status, praise, social approval, or comradeship.[65]

Howard Becker used a learning perspective in his classic analysis, "Becoming a Marijuana User." Becker stated that marijuana smoking tends to be a social and group-supported activity. Typically, people are initially exposed to marijuana use through their associations with others. In order to continue using marijuana, the individual must first learn certain things from other users. According to Becker, "No one becomes a user without learning to smoke the drug in a way which will produce real effects; learning to recognize the effects and connect them with drug use (learning, in other words, to get high); and learning to enjoy the sensations he perceives. Without the example and guidance of other users, such learning would be extremely difficult."[66]

The Development of Drug Use and Addiction

Theories such as those of Sutherland and Akers assign much importance to a person's environment and associations and to the influence these social factors play in the development of drug use and addiction.

- In the great majority of cases, people are "turned on" to drugs by their acquaintances, friends, or others in their environment. This is true even for such commonplace drugs as alcohol and nicotine; many people initially use these drugs for social and recreational purposes when they are with other people.
- In many instances, the initial use of these substances is not pleasurable. Often people must learn to enjoy drinking alcohol, for example.

- In other instances, the initial use may be pleasurable; young people who learn from their peers that drugs cause pleasurable experiences may be the most likely to experiment with various illegal substances.
- Studies have shown that if the user experiences a lessening of anxiety, tension, and fear, he or she may develop a drug habit.

Sources: R. Akers, *Deviant Behavior: A Social Learning Approach,* Belmont, CA: Wadsworth, 1973; G. T. Wilson, "Cognitive Studies in Alcoholism," *Journal of Consulting and Clinical Psychology* 55, 1987, pp. 325–331; L. T. Winfree, C. Griffiths, and C. Sellers, "Social Learning Theory, Drug Use, and American Indian Youths: A Cross Cultural Test," *Justice Quarterly* 1989, pp. 393–417.

Sociological explanations include subcultural theories. *Subcultural theories of substance abuse* view drug use and addiction as the product of a drug subculture. From this perspective, people become involved in drug use and addiction as a result of social-reinforcement processes that occur through their participation with and gradual absorption into the subculture (i.e., through socialization). Sociologists have noted subcultural patterns of drug use for many illegal substances, including marijuana, LSD, and some amphetamines, particularly Methedrine.[67]

The existence of a drug subculture is apparent in the use of cocaine and the opiates, particularly heroin. Criminologist Richard Quinney describes the subcultural aspects of drug use and addiction in the following terms:

> Drug addiction involves participating in an elaborate subculture supported by group norms, which one writer has called a "survival system." This involves justifying the ideology for drug usage and the "reproductive" system: that addicted persons must continually recruit new members in order to sell them drugs to support their habit. There is also a defensive communication, with its own argot for drugs, suppliers, and drug users, which must be learned by the initiates, and the "neighborhood warning system," in which addicts are protected by others. Supporting the habit requires a complex distribution network of the illegal drugs, a "circulatory" system that teaches addicts how to secure illegal drugs. Drugs are imported and wholesale distribution is made mostly by crime syndicates or other highly organized groups.[68]

In other words,

- the subculture itself maintains distinctive norms, values, beliefs, and ways of acting specific to drug use, which individuals come to learn and accept;
- subcultures provide the person with opportunities to learn the techniques and skills for using drugs, ideologies and interpretations for drug use and

the drug experience, and sets of rationalizations and social encouragement for continuing the use;

- the person also acquires knowledge of the drug distribution and supply network.[69]

After reading this section, you should be able to

1. evaluate physiological explanations for addiction and alcoholism, and explain the chemicalistic fallacy;
2. contrast reinforcement theory and personality theories as psychological explanations of addiction;
3. explain social learning theory and subcultural theories of drug use and abuse;
4. give an example of how physiological, psychological, and sociological factors might interact in substance abuse.

12.6 RESPONDING TO THE DRUG PROBLEM

The criminalization of addiction and the punitive handling of drug offenders have paradoxically added to the growth of drug use and related crime problems in the United States. The government spends an enormous amount of money on drug-control programs that attempt to deal with the U.S. drug problem. According to the Office of National Drug Control Policy,

> federal spending on drug-control programs increased from $1.5 billion in 1981 to about $20 billion in 2003. The National Center on Addiction and Substance Abuse at Columbia University has reported that, at the state levels, more than $81 billion is annually spent on substance abuse and addiction programs. Today, the figure is approaching $100 billion.[70]

Local, state, and federal agencies share the responsibility for enforcing our nation's many drug laws. Most arrests in the United States are made by local and state authorities. Annually, there are about 1.6 million state and local arrests for drug abuse violations.

Drug abuse violations are defined in the UCR as local and/or state offenses "relating to the unlawful possession, sale, use, growing, manufacturing, and making of narcotic drugs including opium or cocaine and their derivatives, marijuana, synthetic narcotics, and dangerous non-narcotic drugs such as barbiturates."[71] More than 80 percent of drug law violation arrests are for possession violations.[72]

Society has responded in a number of ways to the phenomena of drug addiction and alcoholism. Concerning drugs, public policy has focused largely on narcotics use and addiction. For the most part, societal reaction toward addiction has stressed a punitive and legally suppressive approach.

Throughout the twentieth century, emphasis was on developing laws to restrict and ultimately eliminate narcotics trafficking, while addicts as well as users were stereotyped primarily as criminals. Alcoholics, although not usually labeled as criminals, nevertheless have often been treated as social outcasts and have been stereotyped as undependable, morally corrupt, and dishonest. Strauss reports that, up until the 1940s, imprisonment or some other form of institutionalization was the only method available for dealing with alcoholics.[73]

In the past, a punitive and largely criminalistic method was the dominant approach to dealing with the drug addict as well. During the 1970s and 1980s, however, addiction to alcohol and other drugs was increasingly viewed as a sickness rather than as a crime or a sign of immorality. Consistent with this view, there has been an ever-increasing call for treatment and rehabilitation in the form of medical, psychiatric, or social therapy for addicts and alcoholics.

What were the nature, origins, and consequences of twentieth-century governmental policy on narcotics use and addiction? The legislative response was primarily one of criminalization. Governmental control of addictive drugs began with the **Harrison Narcotics Tax Act of 1914**, a revenue measure limiting possession of opiates to particular registered parties. Responsibility for the act's enforcement was assigned to the Narcotics Division of the Treasury Department. This act instituted strict regulations of the use and sale of opiates and, in essence, criminalized their possession for other than "legitimate medical purposes." In effect, the Harrison Narcotics Tax Act cut off over-the-counter supplies of opiates, but the question as to whether a medical prescription constituted a "legitimate medical purpose" remained. Regardless of the actual scope or intent of the act, officials of the narcotics division were opposed to the medical administration of opiates in the treatment of addiction, and a series of criminal prosecutions of physicians was instituted. In addition, the Supreme Court made several decisions that, in effect, prohibited opiate prescriptions.

Drug use and addiction were becoming subject to governmental and legal regulation and were no longer solely issues of medical treatment. The Treasury Department's Narcotics Division, committed to an enlargement of its own power, organized a successful effort to transfer control of narcotics from physicians to law enforcement and federal authorities. The narcotics division engaged in a number of attempts to increase public fear and hostility toward drugs and drug users. Addicts were often branded as "worthless criminals" and "moral degenerates." The result has been a punitive rather than a rehabilitative and treatment-based policy toward addiction.

In the years that followed, the U.S. Supreme Court, in the Linder case, reversed its earlier rulings and actually upheld the medical approach to addiction—but by this time, it was too late. Drug use and addiction had come to be viewed as police and penal matters, not as medical cases. In addition, faced with frequent prosecution and police harassment, most physicians ceased prescribing narcotics. These factors provided fertile ground for the rise of illicit narcotics trafficking in the United States.[74]

Over the years, the government's punitive drug policies have not solved the problem of drug use in the United States. According to Erich Goode, the development of restrictive drug legislation over the decades has largely been responsible for the widespread growth of the current "street" addict population, which, by necessity, has become intimately linked with and dependent on the criminal underworld.[75]

There have been indications of a shift toward a rehabilitative and treatment-centered approach to drug abuse on the part of the federal government (see Figure 12.2).[76] Rehabilitation programs have received much more emphasis today than in previous years. However, it appears that the punitive approach will remain the dominant method of dealing with the U.S. drug problem, shaped by law enforcement personnel and societal conceptions of the drug user.[77]

The criminalization of addiction and the punitive handling of the drug offender have, paradoxically, added to the growth of drug use and related crime problems.

(1) One of the most important consequences of the punitive approach has been the *creation of an addict subculture*. In the late nineteenth and early

The **Harrison Narcotics Tax Act of 1914** limited possession of opiates to particular registered parties and assigned enforcement responsibility to the Narcotics Division of the Treasury Department.

twentieth centuries, people could legally purchase narcotics; thus, there was no need for addicts to unite. However, when drugs became illegal, addicts were faced with the necessity of coming together in order to purchase drugs from one another and to acquire knowledge regarding other illegal means of supply. The growth of this subculture brought about vigorous recruitment efforts aimed at perpetuating its existence. In fact, Goode links the continuous rise in narcotics addiction to the recruitment powers of the addict subcultures.[78]

(2) Another important consequence of the punitive approach to addiction has been the *growth of crime* on the part of addicts, as reported earlier. Prior to the criminalization of opiate use, addicts could obtain narcotics easily and at a comparatively low cost. With the Harrison Narcotics Tax Act and other subsequent restrictive drug legislation, however, addicts were forced to resort to illegal means of supply. As discussed earlier, there is a significant relationship between addiction and crime, but the vast majority of addict crime is economically motivated.

Continued addiction vastly increases the probability of the addict's arrest and imprisonment for some type of drug-related crime. In most cases, prisons provide merely a custodial environment where little in the way of treatment and rehabilitation is offered to deal with the addict's drug problems. In fact, rather than providing rehabilitation, some experts believe that prisons partly serve as subcultural "breeding grounds" for continued addiction. Many inmates in our state and federal prisons have major drug or alcohol problems.[79]

(3) The third major consequence of our legally suppressive drug policy has been the *growth of an extensive illegal drug market*. Many parallels can be seen between antidrug legislation today and Prohibition. In the long run, Prohibition failed; more importantly, Prohibition laws had disastrous side effects. The most important of these was the development of a black market for alcoholic beverages. Similarly, many of our drug laws have given rise to a vast organized crime industry that perpetuates itself by supplying goods that cannot be obtained through other channels. In turn, the high price of such illegal goods frequently forces addicts to become involved with other forms of crime.

To summarize: the punitive and legally suppressive orientation toward drug and alcohol abuse has not worked. It has neither eliminated nor even significantly curtailed the use of these substances; in fact, this approach has probably had the opposite effect. There has been an increased awareness of the necessity for alternative approaches to dealing with drug addiction and alcoholism. In recent years, a number of public and private agencies, organizations, and programs have been formed to provide various forms of treatment for the relief or elimination of addiction.

After reading this section, you should be able to

1. trace the history of public policy and social responses to drug addiction and alcoholism;
2. summarize the 2004 U.S. National Drug Control Strategy and recent trends in response to drug offenders;
3. give three major reasons that criminalization and punitive policies have increased rather than decreased the drug problem in the United States.

12.7 SEX-RELATED CRIMES

Alcohol and drugs are often involved in sex-related crimes such as prostitution. There is continuing debate, however, over the enforcement of moral laws such as those that attempt to regulate sexual behavior. Not all laws receive uniform public support. Behaviors in violation of certain laws such as murder, rape, and aggravated assault are, for the most part, strongly condemned by the public, but other types of violations may be ignored, tolerated, or even condoned. Some of the latter types of behavior are often referred to as **victimless crimes**, which include homosexuality, gambling, marijuana use, prostitution, and pornography.

The persistence, prevalence, and, at times, demand for such activities well illustrate the lack of uniform public support for a variety of existing laws and the conflict between subcultural norms and legal regulations in our society. Some have argued that the attempt to enforce moral laws—those enacted to control victimless crimes—has many negative consequences.

- A. B. Smith and H. Pollack report that the existence and enforcement of such laws can conflict with civil liberties, contribute to the pervasiveness of organized crime, and often create more crime and corruption than the laws prevent.[80]
- Others have argued that moral laws must be enforced, and that many of the so-called victimless crimes are in fact dangerous to people (as illustrated by the high death rate among drug abusers, the high rates of venereal disease, AIDS, and tuberculosis among prostitutes, etc.).
- Many feel such crimes destroy the moral fabric of the community and, therefore, should be punished by the criminal law.
- Many think victimless crimes should be prohibited in that a major function of criminal law is to express public morality.[81]

Two sex offenses that are considered victimless are prostitution and pornography. These offenses occur between consenting adults who voluntarily engage in the illegal behavior. They are considered public-order and *mala prohibita* crimes—that is, behaviors that are criminal because they conflict with prevailing moral rules, public opinion, and current social policy.

Prostitution

Prostitution—sex for hire—is a growing problem in the United States.

Prostitution has been defined as "performing an act of sexual intercourse for hire, or offering or agreeing to perform an act of sexual intercourse or any unlawful sexual act for hire."[82] An act of prostitution has also been defined as "an exchange of sex for money or some other commodity."[83] It is difficult to assess the amount of prostitution or the number of prostitutes in the United States; estimates range from 250,000 to more than 1 million part-time or full-time male and female prostitutes working at any given time.[84]

Many prostitutes are termed *streetwalkers,* because they are found on the streets of our communities. They are considered to be the lowest-paid and most vulnerable category of prostitutes. They operate in view of customers, citizens, and the police. Researchers report that many are runaway, minority teens who were often sexually abused as children and who come from impoverished homes.[85] Many streetwalkers abuse drugs and work where

Sex-related and other crimes based solely on moral laws are often referred to as **victimless crimes**.

Prostitution is "performing an act of sexual intercourse for hire, or offering or agreeing to perform an act of sexual intercourse or any unlawful sexual act for hire."

risks are great—on street corners and in bus terminals, vehicles, and cheap hotel rooms.

Slightly higher in the prostitution hierarchy are the *brothel prostitutes*. Brothels—also called cathouses, whorehouses, bordellos, and houses of ill repute—were a major outlet for prostitution in the United States for many decades until after World War II, when they declined in popularity and importance. Brothel prostitutes generally work in a house or building with several dozen other women under the supervision of a *madam*—usually a retired prostitute—who owns or manages the operation.[86] Brothels exist legally in the state of Nevada and illegally in many other large cities in the United States. A million-dollar bordello was operated in New York City by the socialite Sydney Biddle Barrows during the early to mid-1980s. Her business catered to an elite city clientele. In 1993, a Hollywood brothel established for celebrities was uncovered by the media. Nationwide, the number of brothels has declined as a result of pressure from church groups and community organizations. According to Kathleen Daly, the closedown of U.S. brothels has made the prostitution business more unpleasant and dangerous for both clients and prostitutes.[87]

Still higher in the prostitution hierarchy are the *call girls*. These women are among the elite of prostitutes and can command up to $2,000 an evening. They are usually middle-class women who maintain their own apartments and keep a private list of client names and phone numbers (hence the term "little black book"). They may entertain in their own apartment or at their client's hotel or apartment. Howard Greenwald's 1958 study of call girls reported that many are rejected as children by their parents and that this strongly accounts for their choice of profession. He believed that call girls are attempting to replace the affection and love that they missed during their childhood.[88]

There are also *massage parlor prostitutes*. The massage parlors of today are a type of illegal brothel. Located in a wide variety of communities throughout the United States, these parlors offer clients a wide variety of sexual services.

The explanations for why people go into the field of prostitution varies. As discussed, some stress parental rejection, sexual abuse, and exploitation. Others stress a dislike of more conventional jobs, broken homes, poverty, or the desire for material things and money.[89]

Despite claims to the contrary, there are many victims of this "victimless crime"—the children who are drawn into prostitution and the women and men who are exploited, used, and abused in the course of their work. Many clients are also victims, contracting venereal diseases, tuberculosis, and AIDS from this unregulated profession. The only people who appear to profit from prostitution are the pimps (the prostitutes' managers and bosses) and members of organized crime.

Prostitution is a global problem. According to a recent study by Jacqueline Boles, the distribution of sex workers around the globe is related to a number of factors:

1. The laws and law enforcement practices of a country are determined by those in power and by the income of the citizens.
2. Those countries with the highest rates of prostitution are generally poor, give low status to women, and have politicians that encourage prostitution for economic reasons.
3. Prostitution is competitive; therefore, political jurisdictions may offer different services to attract customers.
4. Southeast Asia and South America are tolerant of child prostitution.
5. Religious or ideological beliefs strongly curtail prostitution.
6. Islam condemns prostitution, so most Muslim countries have low rates.[90]

READING ABSTRACT

Sex-Slave Trade Enters the U.S.

BY CATHERINE EDWARDS AND JAMES HARDER

In this reading, the authors describe how international crime syndicates are abducting women and children from various countries around the world. The women and children are then sold by these crime rings as prostitutes and sex slaves in the United States.

See reading on page 374.

Pornography

Pornography, especially on the Internet, is a multi-billion-dollar-a-year industry in the United States.

The word *pornography* is derived from the Greek word *pornographos* (*porne,* a prostitute, and *graphein,* to write). Pornography is defined as any medium "intended primarily to arouse sexual desire."[91] It has also been defined as anything that is "of or pertaining to obscene literature; obscene; [or] licentious."[92] This definition is rooted in the Supreme Court's famous 1973 *Miller v. California* decision, which stated that obscenity (i.e., pornography) falls outside the U.S. Constitution's protection. The decision provided the following standard for judging something as pornographic or obscene: "Material is pornographic or obscene if the average person, applying contemporary community standards, would find that the work taken as a whole appeals to the prurient interest, and if it depicts in a patently offensive way sexual conduct, and if the work taken as a whole lacks serious literary, artistic, political, or scientific value."[93]

Under the *Miller* decision, in order for an individual to be convicted of a pornographic crime, a community must statutorily define "obscene conduct" and the pornographer must engage in that conduct. A major question, however, is, "How are community standards determined?" In 1987, the Supreme Court attempted to deal with this issue with its *reasonableness doctrine* in the *Pope v. Illinois* decision, which basically states that a work is considered obscene if a reasonable individual applying objective, nationally developed standards would consider the material in question lacking in any social value.[94]

A wide variety of materials, such as photographs and videotapes that depict nudity and sex, are typically legal in the United States. They are also protected by the First Amendment provision that limits governmental control of freedom of speech. In the United States, however, a majority of criminal codes prohibit the production, distribution, display, and sale of obscene materials. In addition, federal law prohibits the use of the mail, television, telephone, and radio for disseminating pornographic materials, and they are also prohibited from being transported through interstate commerce.

Major questions that invariably arise when discussing pornography are, "What materials are obscene?" and "Who judges and determines what is obscene?" These are important questions considering that law enforcement personnel can legally seize only those materials judged to be obscene, and there are no easy answers.

Many years ago, D. H. Lawrence's novel *Lady Chatterley's Lover* was considered obscene. In 1990, many people considered Robert Mapplethorpe's photographic exhibition of nude children and men in homoerotic poses obscene. This brought about obscenity charges against the exhibit's director at the Cincinnati Contemporary Arts Center, who was later declared not guilty. The relationship between the law and pornographic materials is complex, especially in light of our First Amendment right to free speech.

Much research has been conducted on the relationship between pornography, crime, and violence. In 1970, the National Commission on Obscenity and Pornography funded more than eighty research projects to study pornography. After assessing research results on the effects of pornography, the commission concluded that there was no clear relationship between pornography and violence in American society. With respect to the relationship between pornographic materials and criminal behavior, the commission "found no evidence . . . that exposure to explicit sexual materials plays a significant role in the causes of . . . criminal behavior among youth or adults." As for pornography and sex crimes, the commission "[could not] conclude that exposure to erotic materials is a factor in the causation of sex crimes or sex delinquency."[95]

Although studies report little, if any, relationship between violence and pornography, some criminologists view a relationship between rates of rape in various countries and pornography consumption as evidence that obscenity may, in fact, have a strong influence on criminality.[96] Still other evidence exists that people who are exposed to erotic materials that portray sadism, violence, or women enjoying being degraded and raped are likely to be sexually aggressive toward women.[97]

The Attorney General's Commission on Pornography analyzed many studies in the 1970s and 1980s. In 1986, it reported that nonviolent, nondegrading pornography is not significantly related to crime and aggression. However, the commission did find a causal link between exposure to violent pornographic materials and sexual violence.[98] According to the commission, exposure to sexually degrading and violent materials

1. leads to a greater acceptance of rape myths and violence against women;
2. results in pronounced effects when the victim is shown enjoying the use of force or violence;
3. is arousing for rapists and for some males in the general population;
4. has resulted in sexual aggression against women in the laboratory.[99]

Moreover, many of the subjects in pornographic material are victims of physical and psychological coercion and violence. Some are children who are manipulated and forced into child-pornography rings. As a result of these findings, the commission called for serious legal attacks on hard-core pornography in the United States.[100]

The "kiddy porn" industry is a billion-dollar-a-year business. Estimates are that more than one million children in the United States are used in the pornography and prostitution business. Needless to say, the sexual exploitation of children is psychologically and physically devastating for them.[101] Most states have introduced severe penalties for pornography that depicts children. In addition, in 1982 the U.S. Supreme Court, in *New York v. Ferber,* ruled in favor of local and state laws that ban sexually explicit materials involving children.[102]

Pornography has become much more common on the Internet during the past ten years. As a result, in 1996 President Clinton signed the Communications Decency Act (CDA) into law. The CDA was a legislative attempt to ban the transmission of pornography and other obscene materials across the Internet. The CDA made all Internet service providers, online services, or mail providers, criminally liable if their services were used to transmit materials considered obscene or indecent. Violators could spend up to two years in prison and/or pay fines up to $100,000. The American Civil Liberties Union (ACLU), Microsoft, the American Library Association, and other plaintiffs filed lawsuits to stop enforcement of the new law. The suits questioned the CDA's constitutionality on the grounds that it violated the First Amendment right to free speech.[103]

In June 1996, three federal judges, in a major decision reaffirming guarantees of free speech, blocked the enforcement of CDA. They ruled that the Internet is protected by the First Amendment. The U.S. Supreme Court, in 1997, upheld the ACLU's claim (*Reno v. ACLU*). The Court ruled that the CDA unconstitutionally restricted free speech. The ACLU also successfully challenged the Child Online Protection Act, which attempted to ban web postings of materials considered to be harmful to minors.[104]

In December 2000, President Clinton signed into law the Children's Internet Protection Act (CIPA). The law requires that public libraries that are receiving federal funds meet two requirements:

1. they adopt Internet safety policies;
2. they use mandatory filtering programs to block Internet access to materials that are considered to be obscene, deemed harmful to minors, or contain child pornography.

In May 2000, the U.S. District Court in Philadelphia struck down the second requirement of the CIPA as unconstitutional. The federal government filed an appeal of this decision with the U.S. Supreme Court. The CIPA was argued before the U.S. Supreme Court in 2003. Its requirement that public libraries adopt Internet safety policies was not challenged, and it remains in effect.[105]

After reading this section, you should be able to

1. define prostitution and evaluate it as a victimless crime;
2. describe the sex-slave trade in the United States, based on Reading 12.2;
3. define pornography and trace its legal history in America;
4. explain the relationships between sex-related crimes and criminal violence according to criminological research.

This chapter examines morality crime. One focus of the chapter is drugs, illicit drug use, and the illegal drug market. Although various drugs are socially approved and their use is even encouraged in the United States, heroin, cocaine, and other "hard drugs" or "street drugs" meet with social disapproval and are illegal.

In a strict scientific sense, a drug is a substance other than food that, by virtue of its chemical nature, affects the functioning or structure of living organisms. Social scientists use the more specific term *psychoactive drug* to refer to substances that in some way affect the user's central nervous system. Psychoactive drugs are divided into three general categories: depressants, stimulants, and hallucinogens (pp. 334–335).

Illicit drug use is the use of prescription-type psychotherapeutic drugs for nonmedical purposes or the use of illegal drugs. Drug abuse is the excessive or compulsive use of a drug to the degree that it harms the user's health or social functioning or results in harmful consequences to others. Thus, any drug can be abused, although certain drugs—those capable of producing physical dependence—run the highest risk for abuse. Illicit drug use has been on the rise in the United States. Various studies reflect statistically recent increases in the use of marijuana, cocaine, pain relievers, and tranquilizers. The nature and consequences of the use of certain drugs (alcohol, marijuana, amphetamines, barbiturates, narcotics, cocaine, and others) are varied and potentially harmful. The illegal drug market and drug trafficking in the United States are complex and well organized (pp. 336–349).

Physiological, psychological, and sociological theories all try to explain drug addiction and alcoholism. Physiological theories generally focus on the assumption that addiction results from some biological or physical characteristic of the person. Psychological theories attempt to explain addiction in terms of what drugs do *for* people rather than *to* them. Sociological theories focus on the importance of group factors and the influence of the social environment (pp. 350–356).

Another focus of the chapter is the relationship between crime and drugs. A significant percentage of violent-crime victims report that their assailants were under the influence of drugs or alcohol at the time of the offense. Chaiken and Chaiken examine the relationship between illicit drug use and predatory crime in Reading 12.1 (pp. 336–338).

There have been a number of societal responses to drug addiction, illicit drug use, and trafficking. In general, governmental and public policies have stressed a punitive and legally suppressive approach to these problems. Many drug users have been stereotyped and labeled as criminals. The criminalization of addiction and the punitive handling of the drug offender have resulted in an addict subculture, a generally growing increase in crimes committed by addicts, and the continued growth of an extensive and powerful illegal drug market (pp. 356–358).

The final section of the chapter examines sex-related crimes, including prostitution and pornography. There may be more than a million prostitutes operating in the United States. There are four types of prostitutes and a variety of reasons men and women go into this criminal field. The powerful reading on the sex-slave trade and prostitution describes one of the world's most lucrative illegal activities (pp. 359–361).

Pornography involves the distribution and sale of sexually explicit materials that are intended to sexually arouse the consumer. In the United States, depicting nudity and sex is not illegal; however, it violates the law when it is judged obscene based on community standards. According to the U.S. Supreme Court, local communities have the right to pass statutes prohibiting sexually explicit materials. Many studies deny any relationship between aggression, crime, and pornography. However, some research reports that violent sexual material is related to sexually violent behavior in those who have viewed it. Many people, including children, are victims of pornography. Pornography has become much more common on the Internet in the last ten years (pp. 361–363).

Study Guide

Chapter Objectives

- Identify the factors related to the acceptability of certain drugs in American society,
- Define the term *drug* scientifically and socially.
- Briefly define and compare depressants, stimulants, and hallucinogens.
- Define drug abuse and illicit drug use.
- Briefly analyze the patterns of illicit drug use in the United States.
- Examine the relationship between drug use and crime.
- Describe the relationship between predatory crime and drugs.
- Briefly describe the effects of alcohol on the user and define alcohol abuse.
- Describe multiple-drug use.
- Examine marijuana—its use and trafficking.
- Describe (1) the effects of amphetamines on the user; and (2) methamphetamine trafficking in the United States.
- Examine MDMA, its effects, and its illegal trafficking in the United States.
- Describe the effects on the user of barbiturates and GHB/GBL.
- Examine heroin, its effects on users, and its trafficking.
- Describe cocaine, its effects on users, and its trafficking.
- Describe LSD, PCP, and flunitrazepam.
- Examine and assess physiological explanations for addiction and alcoholism.
- Contrast the reinforcement and personality theories and the social learning and subcultural theories of drug use and abuse.
- Examine and assess public policy and social responses to the drug problem.
- Analyze the major consequences of criminalization and punitive policies with respect to drug offenders.
- Define and evaluate the crime of prostitution in the United States.
- Describe the sex-slave trade in the United States.
- Define pornography and assess its relationship to crime in America.

Key Terms

Addiction (336)
Amphetamines (342)
Depressants (335)
Drug (334)
Ecstasy (344)
Hallucinogens (335)
Harrison Narcotics Tax Act of 1914 (357)
Illicit drug use (336)

Marijuana (342)
MDMA (344)
Methamphetamine (343)
Morphine (346)
Multiple-drug use (336)
Narcotics (346)
National Survey on Drug Use and Health (NSDUH) (336)

Opium (346)
Prostitution (359)
Psychoactive drugs (334)
Psychological theories of addiction (348)
Stimulants (335)
Victimless crimes (359)

Self-Test
Short Answer

1. List the major types of psychoactive drugs and their characteristics.
2. Write a definition of drug abuse.
3. Briefly describe the relationship between drug use and crime.
4. Briefly examine the relationship between drugs and predatory crime.
5. Briefly describe drug trafficking in the United States.
6. Briefly describe the physiological and psychological explanations of drug use and addiction.
7. Write a paragraph that describes the sociological perspective on drug use and addiction.
8. Briefly examine how our society has responded to the drug problem.
9. Describe the crime of prostitution.
10. Briefly describe the issues surrounding pornography and the Internet.

Multiple Choice

1. The acceptability of certain drugs in our society is related to
   a. the length of time the drug has been used in our society
   b. how the drug is obtained and who takes the drug
   c. the reason why the drug is used
   d. all of the above
2. Psychoactive drugs
   a. do not affect the central nervous system
   b. influence one's behavior, perceptions, and emotions
   c. are also known as "dangerous drugs"
   d. none of the above
3. Stimulants include
   a. heroin
   b. morphine
   c. crack cocaine
   d. all of the above
4. The excessive or compulsive use of a drug to the degree that one's health or ability to function socially is harmed or that harm can occur to others is termed
   a. illegal drug use
   b. drug abuse
   c. drug dependence
   d. withdrawal
5. Which of the following statements is not true?
   a. There appears to be no simple relationship between high rates of drug use and high rates of crime.
   b. Among predatory offenders, the high-frequency drug users are also likely to be high-rate predators.
   c. In drug trafficking, violence is rarely used to gain competitive advantage.
   d. Most people who use illicit drugs do not commit predatory crimes.
6. Large amounts of illegal drugs made from agricultural crops are smuggled into the United States from
   a. Central and South America
   b. Southeast and Southwest Asia
   c. Asia and the Middle East
   d. all of the above
7. According to Erich Goode, the "chemicalistic fallacy" refers to the notion that
   a. the effect of a drug on a person's behavior is solely a function of the biochemical properties of the drug
   b. "once an addict, always an addict"
   c. habituation is the same as physical dependence
   d. none of the above
8. The criminalization of addiction and the punitive handling of drug offenders have resulted in
   a. the creation of an addict subculture
   b. the growth of an extensive and illegal drug market
   c. an upsurge in crime on the part of addicts
   d. all of the above
9. Which of the following terms is not related to prostitution?
   a. call girl
   b. brothel
   c. streetwalker
   d. stomper
10. Which of the following U.S. Supreme Court decisions stated that obscenity falls outside the Constitution's protection?
    a. *Miller v. California*
    b. *Pope v. Illinois*
    c. *New York v. Ferber*
    d. *Roe v. Wade*

True–False

T F 1. Most Americans do not use drugs.
T F 2. Some research suggests that an increasing share of violent crime is attributable to alcohol-drinking offenders.
T F 3. There is a strong relationship between high-frequency drug use and high-frequency criminality.
T F 4. Alcohol is the most widely used and abused drug in the United States.
T F 5. The illegal use of amphetamines is a major crime problem in the United States.
T F 6. Ecstasy causes injury to the brain.

T F 7. Statistics show a dramatic increase in U.S. seizures of MDMA tablets.
T F 8. Psychologists are in strong agreement as to the specific psychological traits that comprise the "addict personality."
T F 9. The criminalization of addiction and the punitive handling of drug offenders have led to the growth of drug use and related crime problems.
T F 10. In the United States, there exists a strong link between violence and pornography.

Fill-In

1. _____ are a category of drugs that decrease or depress the functioning of the central nervous system.
2. An individual will experience _____ if he or she ceases to use a drug for which a physical dependency has developed.
3. The _____ Narcotics Tax Act of 1914 regulated the sale and use of opiate substances.
4. In general, sociological theories view drug use and addiction as products of _____.
5. _____ used a learning perspective in his well-known analysis, "Becoming a Marijuana User."

6. _____ theories view drug use and drug addiction as an outgrowth or product of a drug subculture.
7. According to Chaiken and Chaiken, no single sequential or causal relationship is now believed to relate drug use to _____ crime.
8. Brothel prostitutes work under the supervision of a _____ , who owns or manages the operation.
9. According to the _____, a work is considered obscene if a reasonable individual applying objective, nationally developed standards would consider the material in question lacking in any social value.

Matching

1. Linder case
2. Harrison Narcotics Tax Act
3. Stimulants
4. Barbiturates
5. Cocaine
6. Marijuana
7. Alcohol
8. Addiction
9. Prostitute
10. Obscenity

A. Depressant drugs
B. Increase the functioning of the central nervous system
C. Regulated the sale and use of opiate substances
D. Upheld a medical approach to addiction
E. Most abused drug in the United States
F. Physical dependence
G. Communications Decency Act
H. Drug that impairs memory
I. Stimulant processed from coca leaves
J. Massage parlor

Essay Questions

1. Many Americans incorrectly believe they understand the physical and behavioral properties and effects of a wide variety of drugs. After carefully reading section 12.2, write a brief essay that demonstrates an adequate understanding of basic psychoactive substances.
2. Drug use and abuse is largely a matter of social and legal definition. After assessing the materials presented in this chapter, how do you personally view the use and abuse of various drugs in American society?

3. After reviewing the major explanations for drug use and addiction, select a particular type of addiction and write a brief analysis of how each of these theories would explain such use or abuse. Compare your analysis with those of other students in the class. This form of applied exercise should aid in your understanding of the various theoretical perspectives as well as the strengths and weaknesses of each.

4. Problems of substance abuse exist in all American communities. How serious is the drug problem in your neighborhood? How much crime in your community might be related to its drug problem?

5. After reviewing the wide variety of governmental policies, strategies, and tactics that have been applied to the drug problem in the United States, how would you, if you were the U.S. chief administrator in charge of fighting drug abuse and crime, go about dealing with the drug problem?

6. Are there any victims in "victimless" crimes? Explain your answer.

7. What would happen if the Mapplethorpe photo exhibit were presented in your local museum or arts center? How would you feel about it? Why?

8. What is your opinion on controlling pornography on the Internet? Explain your answer.

Drugs and Predatory Crime

Source: J. M. Chaiken and M. R. Chaiken, "Drugs and Predatory Crime," in Drugs and Crime, M. Tonry and J. Q. Wilson, Eds., vol. 13 of Crime and Justice: A Review of Research, Chicago: University of Chicago Press, 1990, pp. 203–207, 210–216, 218–221, 234–235. Reprinted by permission of The University of Chicago Press. © 1990 by The University of Chicago. All rights reserved.

BY JAN M. CHAIKEN AND MARCIA R. CHAIKEN

A strong association has long been surmised between illicit drug use and predatory crime. Almost twenty years ago, Sutherland and Cressey (1970:164) pointed out that in the United States "felons are overrepresented in the addict population, [and] crime rates are increased considerably by drug addiction." But, although they proposed several hypotheses to explain the relationship, they summarized the state of knowledge at the time by saying that "a precise definition of the process by which narcotic drugs are related to criminal behavior has not been made" (p. 167).

Ten years later, numerous studies of incarcerated or addicted populations had increased knowledge of the drug/crime nexus; but the information was still complex and incomplete. Only in regard to heroin addiction did a coherent viewpoint prevail, but it was not universally accepted. The prevailing view, summarized by Gandossy et al. (1980), was that drug use propelled income-producing crime primarily because addicts required money to buy drugs. This view was supported by the following findings: many serious offenders were drug users and had started using drugs as juveniles; not all drug users became addicts, but continued drug use frequently led to heroin addiction; minority group members were proportionately more likely than nonminority group members to be drug users and to be arrested for crimes; many (although not all) drug users became addicted before they were involved in criminal pursuits or arrest; among arrestees and prisoners, drug users were more likely than nondrug users to have been arrested for income-generating crimes rather than crimes of violence; drug users in treatment were more likely to have been arrested for property crimes than for violent crimes; and the drug users who were most likely to commit numerous crimes were heroin addicts.

At the time, some researchers and many policymakers were convinced from this evidence that a fairly simple causal relation existed between drug use and criminality, especially for minority group members who were disproportionately likely to become involved in drug use: first came some form of drug use as juveniles, then drug use progressed to heroin addiction, and, as heroin addicts, these users committed many nonviolent income-producing crimes to support their habits. But many countervailing facts were already known, such as that a substantial number of casual users of heroin (nonaddicts) existed and were not heavily involved in crime (e.g., Robins, Davis, and Wish, 1980).

The picture available from today's research indicates that, while the progression to heroin addiction and income-producing crimes may apply to some drug users, other behavioral sequences also occur often (even *more* often), for example, patterns involving drugs other than heroin, or predatory crime before drug addiction, or violent rather than nonviolent criminality. Some patterns are applicable only in particular subgroups of the population.

In short, no single sequential or causal relationship is now believed to relate drug use to predatory crime. When the behaviors of large groups of people are studied in the aggregate, no coherent general patterns emerge associating drug use per se with participation in predatory crime, age at onset of participation in crime, or persistence in committing crime. Rather, different patterns appear to apply to different types of drug users (Chaiken and Johnson, 1988). But research does show that certain types of drug abuse are strongly related to offenders' committing crimes at high *frequencies*—violent crimes as well as other, income-producing crimes. The observed relationship applies to various population subgroups, including groups defined by age, race, or sex.

This essay summarizes the known research information—with emphasis on quantitative research—about the association between drug use and *predatory crime*. The association between drug dealing and predatory crime is also discussed, because it is often more pertinent or stronger than the association between drug use and crime.

In discussing predatory crime, we have in mind instrumental offenses committed for material gain. We do not include aggressive crimes such as marital violence, homicide, or assault unrelated to robbery or burglary; public disorder crimes; driving under the influence of alcohol or drugs; or consensual crimes such as prostitution. However, in reviewing the results of published works, some nonpredatory crimes may be included with predatory crimes if they were studied together or summarized together by the original authors.

In summarizing and commenting on the literature on drug use and predatory crime, we use a specialized vocabulary that has been developed in the study of criminal careers (Blumstein et al., 1986). The terms *onset, participation, frequency, desistance,* and *persistence* are drawn from the concept of a criminal career as a sequence of crimes committed by an *individual offender* (Blumstein et al., 1986). A person's criminal career has its *onset* when he or she commits a crime for the first time, at which time the offender is said to be *participating* in crime. A *participation rate* is the proportion of a group of people who engage in crimes during a specified period. The *frequency* or *rate of* crime commission is the number of crimes committed per year when the offender is free to commit crime (that is, unincarcerated). *Desistance* is the end of the criminal career, and *persistence* refers to a career that lasts a long time between onset and desistance.

Since this essay focuses on predatory crime and not on assault or other destructive behavior resulting from physiological effects of drugs, we do not distinguish among pharmacological classes of drugs such as amphetamines, barbiturates, or hallucinogens. However, as shown in the sections that follow, the types of drugs used by offenders and the frequency with which they use them are important in understanding the connections between drug abuse and predatory crime. Most drug users abuse at least two types of substances; therefore many research studies summarized in this essay categorize types of *drug abuse* rather than types of *drugs abused*. Commonly employed categories of drug abuse, in order of increasing seriousness, are: marijuana and alcohol abuse; use of other nonopiate illicit drugs (possibly in addition to marijuana and alcohol); and opiate or cocaine use, including various derivative forms of those substances.

People are generally considered to be involved in a specific category of drug abuse if they have a sustained pattern of involvement. For example, most researchers would not classify as a drug abuser a person who has used marijuana two or three times. Similarly, a person who frequently drinks and also smokes marijuana would be classified by most researchers as involved in marijuana use; this would be the case even if he or she is also known to have used cocaine on one occasion. However, people who have a sustained pattern of relatively serious drug abuse would be classified as involved in that form of drug abuse even though they were more likely to indulge in less serious forms of abuse. For example, people who use heroin every week would be classified as heroin users even if they drank alcohol and smoked marijuana every day.

Almost all the studies discussed in this essay were based on self-reports of drug use and crime. Self-reports are less likely than criminal justice system records or other forms of agency records to underestimate study subjects' involvement in crime, delinquency, or drug use. However, the validity of self-report information about drug abuse and criminality is questionable because respondents may have had difficulty recalling past behavior, may not have understood the questions they were asked, or may either have concealed or exaggerated their illegal activities. Researchers who conduct these studies are aware of these validity issues and use methods that minimize the possible distorting effects on their findings.

The studies most likely to avoid problems of recall are those in which subjects are interviewed at set intervals over a period of time. These studies provide valuable information on the relationships between predatory crime and drug use over the life course. However, many other studies learn about respondents' past behavior retrospectively. When findings from prospective and retrospective studies are similar, they reinforce each other.

The methods used for collecting data about drug use and criminality range from relatively large national surveys to indepth interviews and observations of small groups. The study subjects include random samples of the nation's youth, groups of school children, addicts in treatment centers, inmates in prisons and jails, defendants whose cases had been just concluded, samples of inner-city youth, probationers, and adult street populations. Aside from studies of addicts in treatment, important data sources drawn on in this essay are the National Youth Survey, a Rand Corporation inmate survey, and interview data from street addicts in New York City. . . .

I. SUMMARY OF FINDINGS FROM RECENT RESEARCH

People who commit predatory crimes over long periods tend also to commit other crimes and to have begun their criminal careers at young ages. Similarly, people who use illicit drugs often or in large quantities tend to use a variety of drugs and to have begun using drugs during adolescence. These seemingly similar groups of persistent offenders and persistent drug users are not necessarily the same people. There appears to be no simple general relation between high rates of drug use and high rates of crime.

A. Patterns of Criminal Behavior and Drug Use

Research on criminal behavior over the past decade has demonstrated strong interrelationships among age at onset of a criminal career, persistence of criminal activity, rates of committing offenses, and types of offenses committed. In any population of offenders, most commit nonviolent offenses and at low rates. Even adult offenders who were incarcerated for violent crimes such as robbery or assault typically committed only one or two of these offenses in the year preceding their incarceration (Chaiken and Chaiken, 1982; Visher, 1986; Mande and English, 1988; Chaiken and Chaiken, 1989). However, a relatively small group of offenders commits crimes at very high rates—hundreds of crimes per year when they are free to do so (Chaiken and Chaiken, 1982; Ball, Shaffer, and Nurco, 1983; Johnson et al., 1985; Ball, 1986; Mande and English, 1988; Chaiken and Chaiken, 1989). Those who frequently commit violent crimes also are very likely to commit other crimes, such as burglary and theft, and to commit one or more of these types of crimes at high rates (Chaiken and Chaiken, 1982; Chaiken and Chaiken, 1985; Johnson et al., 1985). Moreover, this small group of adult offenders is likely to have started committing crimes as young adolescents (Chaiken and Chaiken, 1982; Hanson et al., 1985; Johnson et al., 1985).

Studies of patterns of drug use have produced parallel findings. Most people who use illicit drugs confine their use to sporadic use of marijuana, while relatively few use other illicit drugs such as barbiturates, amphetamines, cocaine, or heroin (Miller et al., 1983; Johnston, O'Malley, and Bachman, 1985, 1986). An even smaller number of people use these drugs frequently (e.g., daily or more often); and those who use any drug in high quantities or at high frequencies are likely to be using also several other types of illicit drugs frequently, often in combination with alcohol (Elliott and Huizinga, 1985; Wish and Johnson, 1986; Elliott, Huizinga, and Menard, 1989). The high-frequency users are also more likely than other users to have started using drugs as adolescents (Newcomb and Bentler, 1988).

While these parallel patterns of criminal behavior and drug abuse are strongly interrelated, research does not support the view that they are basically overlapping descriptions of the same people. There are a few severely addicted people who commit no crimes aside from illegal possession of drugs (Collins et al., 1982); and there are criminals who commit numerous serious crimes but are not involved in drug use (Chaiken and Chaiken, 1985; Innes, 1988). Moreover, for most people, changes over time in individuals' use or nonuse of drugs are not systematically related to changes in their participation or nonparticipation in criminal activity (Kandel, Simcha-Fagan, and Davies, 1986; Newcomb and Bender, 1988). One exception is a repeated finding that, among heroin-using high-rate offenders, intensity of offending appears to vary directly with intensity of drug use (e.g., Anglin and Speckart, 1986; Nurco et al., 1988).

Research does not support the view that drug abuse necessarily precedes onset of criminal activity, nor does it demonstrate a causal ordering between drug use and criminality. A more coherent interpretation is that drug abuse and participation in crime coexist in some social groups. Rather than having a cause-and-effect relationship, the onset of drug use, the onset of predatory crime, or both, can occur in early puberty as products of similar external factors. Fagan and others have found that both or either of these behaviors can be explained by intervening variables such as destructive factors in the environment (e.g., physical abuse or criminal siblings) or the absence of traditional social controls (e.g., lack of parental attention or participation in rewarding school activities) (White, Pandina, and LaGrange, 1987;

Fagan and Weis, 1990). The more deviant the environment, the more likely an adolescent is to perform poorly in school, to use multiple forms of illicit drugs frequently, and to participate frequently in predatory crime (Williams and Kornblum, 1985; Simcha-Fagan and Schwartz, 1986).

From analysis of self-report surveys of male prison and jail inmates in three states in the late 1970s, we concluded that predatory criminals may be involved in drug use as a part of their nontraditional lifestyle, which in most instances is also evidenced by other factors such as irregular employment and absence of marital ties (Chaiken and Chaiken, 1982). However, many long-term offenders in these inmate surveys had never used drugs; in fact, nearly half (47 percent) of inmates who had never used drugs were persistent offenders (they had committed crimes for more than five years prior to their arrest). Generally, older criminals are less likely than younger offenders to use illicit drugs (Wish and Johnson, 1986); but even among young delinquents who committed crimes such as robbery, burglary, or serious assaults in inner-city areas, most have been found not to use drugs (Fagan and Weis, 1990).

Where, then, lies the strong relationship between drug use and criminality? A large body of research, discussed in the remainder of this essay, shows that, among predatory offenders, the ones who are high-frequency drug users are also very likely to be high-rate predators and to commit many different types of crimes, including violent crimes, and to use many different types of drugs. This finding has been confirmed for adolescents and adults, across states, independent of race, and in many countries. It also is the same for both males and females with one notable exception: females who use drugs frequently are less likely than males to commit violent crimes (but women drug users are more likely to resort to prostitution, shoplifting, and similar covert, nonviolent crimes at high rates [Sanchez and Johnson, 1987]).

The relationship between high-frequency drug use and high-frequency criminality is intensified by long durations of involvement in drug use and predatory crime (Nurco et al., 1988). Adult offenders who commit robbery and burglary at the highest rates typically have been persistent offenders and drug users since they were juveniles, for example, using heroin as juveniles and starting to commit predatory crimes before they were sixteen years old (Chaiken and Chaiken, 1982). The earlier the age of onset of cocaine or heroin use, the more likely persistent offenders are to be serious predatory offenders as adults (Chaiken and Chaiken, 1985; Collins and Bailey, 1987).

B. Drug Sellers

In all studies that have examined the issue, the relationship between drug use and criminality has been found to be substantially weaker than the relationship between drug sales and other forms of criminality (Chaiken and Chaiken, 1982; Johnson et al., 1985; Chaiken, 1986). Most people who sell drugs do so occasionally and privately and are not likely to be involved in predatory crimes. But those who sell drugs publicly, for example, in parks, streets, or back alleys, are likely to commit predatory crimes and to commit them at higher rates than people who commit the same type of offenses but do not sell drugs (Johnson et al., 1985; Williams and Kornblum, 1985).

Based on surveys of inmates and interviews with other offenders, adult robbers who sell drugs on average report committing many more robberies than robbers who do not sell drugs; these robbers also report committing more burglaries than many other burglars, especially burglars who do not distribute drugs (Johnson et al., 1985; Chaiken, 1986). Among urban youth, drug sales were also found to have a strong association with committing numerous serious crimes, including armed robbery (Fagan and Weis, 1990).

While many public drug dealers are themselves frequent users of various types of drugs, others are careful not to mix business with pleasure; they only sporadically use their own illicit merchandise. Yet these nonuser drug dealers still commit predatory crimes, including numerous robberies and burglaries (Chaiken and Chaiken, 1982; Williams and Kornblum, 1985; Mieczkowski, 1986).

Some of the robberies and other assaultive crimes committed by offenders who also sell drugs are systemic aspects of the drug trade (Johnson et al., 1985). Given the highly competitive nature of drug distribution (Kleiman and Smith, 1990; Moore, 1990) and the obvious lack of official regulation, violence and robbery are sometimes used to drive competitors out of business or to protect a dealer's money, supplies, and connections (Adler, 1985; Johnson et al., 1985). Other assaults and predatory crimes committed by drug dealers arise from their need for money for drugs and are opportunistically focused on the first available target (Williams and Komblum, 1985)—although many addicts are able to sustain their use by committing less serious crimes (Goldstein, 1985; Hunt, 1990). However, many predatory crimes are committed by dealers who find vulnerable victims with cash, follow them to a secluded area, threaten or actually injure them, and take their money (Chaiken and Chaiken, 1985; Hanson et al., 1985). . . .

II. Chronology of Participation in Use of Illegal Drugs and Predatory Crime

The criminal careers model provides a useful framework for organizing the discussion of research on the relationship between drug use and predatory crime. Similarities and differences between the onset and persistence of these two types of behaviors are discussed in this section. Particular emphasis is given to research on the interrelatedness of the onset and persistence of drug use and predatory crime.

A. Onset of Criminal Behavior

Research does not support the hypothesis that use of illicit drugs ultimately results in the user's involvement in predatory crime, or even that this is a predominant pattern. Studies of

youths' drug use and crime that refute this hypothesis have included repeated interviews with over 1,500 youngsters selected as a representative sample for a National Youth Survey (Elliott and Huizinga, 1985); in-depth interviews with 100 youngsters in a medium-size upstate city in New York (Carpenter et al., 1988); surveys of over 800 inner-city youth including almost 200 school dropouts (Fagan and Weis, 1990); repeated surveys from age fifteen to age twenty-five with a sample of over 1,000 youths selected to be representative of students enrolled in New York State secondary schools (Kandel, Simcha-Fagan, and Davies, 1986); and repeated interviews over a period of eight years with a sample of 1,000 youths who originally attended Los Angeles County schools (Newcomb and Bentler, 1988).

Virtually all these studies have found that many more youngsters use illicit drugs than are involved in predatory crime. As youthful users of illicit substances approach adulthood, they are likely to continue to use drugs, but they are less likely—not more likely—to commit predatory crimes (Kandel, Simcha-Fagan, and Davies, 1986). Moreover, youths who commit serious predatory crimes are more likely to use illicit drugs frequently than are youthful users of illicit drugs to engage in predatory crime (Fagan and Weis, 1990).

Research evidence provides little support for the popular conception that most drug-involved offenders begin committing predatory crimes because they want money to buy drugs. In fact, many of them were involved in juvenile delinquency, including minor forms of predatory crime, before they were involved in illicit drug use. The data are more consistent with the commonsensical notion that minor predatory crime is a precursor to serious predatory crime. Prospective longitudinal self-report data from the National Youth Survey (Elliott and Huizinga, 1985) and studies based on a sample of New York youngsters (Kandel, Simcha-Fagan, and Davies, 1986) demonstrate that, among youngsters who both use drugs and commit nondrug offenses, delinquency is about as likely to begin before as after initial use of illicit drugs. . . .

In sum, use of illicit drugs may be a primary cause for initial participation in predatory crime for some offenders; however, for the vast majority of offenders who commit predatory crimes, use of illicit substances appears to be neither a necessary nor a sufficient cause of onset of predatory criminal behavior. Even onset of narcotic addiction often does not appear to be causally related to onset of involvement in property crime. Rather, the onset of heroin addiction is often a key point in accelerating an existing criminal career.

B. Persistence of Drug Use and Predatory Crime

Studies that have followed the behavior of youngsters over the span of early adolescence to young adulthood indicate that drug use is more likely to persist over this life span than is involvement in predatory crime (Kandel, Simcha-Fagan, and Davies, 1986; Newcomb and Bentler, 1988). Further, continued criminality is more predictive of future drug use than is drug use predictive of criminality. Although over two-thirds of youthful users of drugs are likely to continue use as adults, as they approach their late teens and early twenties, half of the juveniles who commit crimes stop (Elliott and Huizinga, 1985; Kandel, Simcha-Fagan, and Davies, 1986). As they grow older, delinquents are likely to use more addictive drugs—starting with marijuana, progressing to hallucinogens, sedatives and analgesics, and then to cocaine and heroin (Inciardi, 1987). Delinquents most likely to engage in drug use are those who have been sexually abused as children (Dembo et al., 1987). Moreover, almost all persistent serious delinquents are likely eventually to use drugs. Only 18 percent of chronic, serious offenders in the National Youth Survey remained drug free as they aged (Elliott and Huizinga, 1985).

A review of cohort studies covering nearly 12,000 boys in Philadelphia, London, Racine (Wisconsin), and Marion County (Oregon) suggests that youngsters are most likely to continue committing serious crimes as adults if they behave badly in school, come from poor families, have other criminals in their immediate family, have a low IQ, and receive inadequate parental attention (Blumstein, Farrington, and Moitra, 1985). Retrospective studies of the careers of predatory adult offenders suggest that essentially the same factors are characteristic of persistent offenders who commit the most serious predatory crimes (robbery and burglary) at high rates (Chaiken and Chaiken, 1985). While drug abuse may often be concomitant with these predictive factors, it generally has not been shown to have independent value as a predictor of persistent offending.

Although sustained drug use cannot, in general, be considered a cause of predation, involvement in predatory crime increases the probability of serious forms of drug use which in turn enhance continuation and seriousness of a "predatory career." This self-reinforcing relationship has been demonstrated by interviews conducted with patients in methadone treatment about their "addiction careers"; in these studies, Anglin and Speckart (1986) found that theft precedes addiction more frequently than it follows addiction; however, burglary and robbery are more likely to follow than precede addiction; and there is positive covariation between the levels of narcotics use and the numbers and seriousness of crimes committed.

Ethnographic studies of street addicts suggest that these relationships may be explained by involvement in a lifestyle of "taking care of business" in which "the hustle" is any legitimate or illegal activity that can generate income (Hanson et al., 1985). Theft and other minor predatory crimes become a "normal" activity for relatively many elementary school-aged boys raised on inner-city streets. As they approach adolescence, boys in many major cities have the opportunity to participate in the drug trade (Mieczkowski, 1986; Hunt, 1990). Part of the street drug trade often involves keeping a small amount of drugs for personal use and robbing street drug distributors or other community residents of drugs or cash (Johnson et al., 1985). As adults, heroin use may continue as part of this lifestyle, but even regular users of heroin may abstain for relatively long periods in the absence of a safe and lucrative hustle (Hanson et al., 1985). Among hustlers, robbery is not generally considered a safe means of obtaining money; however, a relatively small proportion of adult hustlers like to do "stick-ups" (robberies) because they consider the activity adventuresome and exciting (Hanson et al., 1985).

Little is known about the end of hustling lifestyles or the termination of predatory careers among drug-involved persistent offenders. Recent research suggests that addicted adult offenders often continue to use drugs and commit crimes for twelve or more years in the absence of effective treatment and supervision (Anglin, Piper, and Speckart, 1987). There is some evidence that mortality rates are relatively high for this population and that almost half of the deaths are due to drug use (Joe and Simpson, 1987). There is also evidence, based on in-depth interviews with over 100 ex-addicts, that the end of a hustling lifestyle can be self-initiated because of a personally negative incident endemic to hustling, such as a threat of bodily harm from another dealer, and can take place in the absence of formal treatment (Biernacki, 1986).

Future research is urgently needed on the causes and reasons for desisting from a life of drug use, crime, or both. Most pertinent for policy purposes will be improved information on the manner and extent to which drug addiction extends an addict's criminal career. . . .

III. CONCLUSIONS AND IMPLICATIONS FOR THE JUSTICE SYSTEM

Use of illicit drugs does not appear to be strongly related to onset and participation in predatory crime; rather, drug use and crime participation are weakly related as contemporaneous products of factors generally antithetical to traditional United States lifestyles. Most of the underlying causative factors, such as irregular employment or weak attachment to school or parents, are not amenable to intervention by the justice system. Moreover, general prevalence figures for drug use do not give much hope that even major reductions in the numbers of people who use illicit drugs could significantly reduce the numbers of incidents of predatory crime.

More specifically, among adolescents and adults who use illicit drugs, most do not commit predatory crimes. Reducing the number of adolescents who are sporadic users of illicit drugs, especially marijuana, may possibly affect the incidence and prevalence of some types of crime, such as disorderly conduct and driving under the influence of controlled substances, but not predatory crime. In addition, most adults who sporadically use drugs such as hallucinogens, tranquilizers, or cocaine do not commit predatory crimes. Therefore, reducing the number of adults who are sporadic users of these types of drugs may also affect the incidence and prevalence of some types of crime, but is unlikely to affect the incidence of predatory crime.

About 50 percent of delinquent youngsters are delinquent before they start using drugs; about 50 percent start concurrently or after. Reducing the number of adolescents who sporadically use illicit drugs may potentially reduce the incidence and prevalence of minor predatory crime; but these types of crime are more likely to be reduced through comprehensive delinquency prevention measures which do not focus exclusively or particularly on drug abuse.

Persistent use of drugs other than heroin (and perhaps also excluding cocaine) appears to be unrelated to persistence in committing predatory crimes. Among youngsters who use drugs and commit theft or other predatory crimes, most continue to use drugs as adults but stop committing crimes at the end of adolescence. Moreover, almost half of convicted offenders who are persistent offenders never used drugs. Therefore preventing persistent use of drugs other than heroin and cocaine is not likely to reduce the numbers of persistent predatory offenders.

However, there is strong evidence that predatory offenders who persistently and frequently use large amounts of multiple types of drugs commit crimes at significantly higher rates over longer periods than do less drug-involved offenders, and predatory offenders commit fewer crimes during periods in which they use no heroin.

These findings suggest that criminal justice programs that focus resources on high-rate predatory offenders should include among their selection criteria evidence of persistent, frequent use of multiple types of illicit drugs. In addition, criminal justice system programs that effectively prevent addicted predatory offenders from using heroin appear promising when measured against the goal of reducing the incidence of predatory crime.

CRITICAL THINKING

1. What is meant by predatory crime?
2. How does predatory crime relate to substance abuse?
3. Why is the relationship between drugs and crime so difficult to pin down?

READING 12.2

Sex-Slave Trade Enters the U.S.

Source: C. Edwards and J. Harder, "Sex-Slave Trade Enters the U.S.," Insight on the News, November 27, 2000. Copyright © 2000 News World Communications, Inc. Reprinted with permission of Insight.

BY CATHERINE EDWARDS AND JAMES HARDER

The profits from a growing global sex trade in women and children soon will be the world's most lucrative illegal activity if a new U.S. law doesn't change the situation. "Human trafficking is the third-highest illegal-income source in America today behind drug- and gunrunning," notes Sen. Sam Brownback, R-Kan. "The dark side of human trafficking is that, unlike drugs, [sexually enslaved] human beings can be resold and reused, thus making them a more profitable commodity."

The alarming growth of the sex trade prompted Brownback and Democratic colleague Paul Wellstone of Minnesota in the Senate, and House members Chris Smith, R-N.J., and Sam Gejdenson, D-Conn., to sponsor legislation to monitor and combat such trafficking worldwide. The measure, known as the Victims of Trafficking and Violence Protection Act of 2000, overwhelmingly passed the House in May and

the Senate in July. A bipartisan conference report was published in early October and the president signed it into law three weeks later.

In recent years most government agencies and nongovernmental organizations (NGOs) have used the term "trafficking" to refer to all acts involved in the movement of women and children from one country to another or within national borders for sexual exploitation or forced labor. The new law prohibits both. According to a spokesman for Wellstone, profits from this trade top $7 billion annually.

"These girls are not living the life of Julia Roberts in the film *Pretty Woman*," says Rachel Lloyd, the director of the New York–based Girls Education and Mentoring Service. "We work with kids who have really been abused. Not many have ever been given a chance to make something of themselves."

Smuggled into brothels in the United States with fake visas or hidden in packing cases, they often have been kidnapped, bought or lured by false employment opportunities. Beaten and raped, some do not survive even the initial brutality. Removed from even the hope of protection by family and friends, locked in airless, dark rooms, starved and beaten, they often are forced to engage in unspeakable sex acts with people whose language they don't understand.

While there is nothing new about what once was called white slavery, the last two decades have seen sex trafficking turned into a well-organized international criminal enterprise corrupting whole countries. Such traffic began to flourish in the Philippines and Thailand after the Vietnam War—first catering to soldiers and then to sexual holidays for Japanese, American, Canadian and European men frequenting brothels in Southeast Asia. After the collapse of the Soviet Union, Russian women were targeted by these criminal enterprises.

Prior to the 1990s, many of the women trafficked into the United States came from Asia. While the nationality and character of victims now varies greatly, researchers cite a common socioeconomic profile of the women caught up in this trade. Often they are desperate young people in search of opportunity, livelihood and sometimes even a means to survive. The breakup of the Eastern bloc, for instance, created economic dislocation and destitution for many young women that made them vulnerable to the ploys and schemes of brothel owners and traffickers. Porous borders, globalization and cooperation among criminal syndicates also contributed to the explosive growth during the last decade, say leading experts.

Marie Jose Ragab sees the fall of the Berlin Wall and the ensuing growth of organized crime in Eastern Europe as landmark events in the proliferation of sex trafficking. As the international director for a dissident chapter of the National Organization for Women, she has spent years looking at issues related to sex trafficking. "Before, it was through mail-order brides and making trips to Thailand and Asia," Ragab says of the international sex trade. "Once the Soviet Union collapsed, organized crime took over and there was a new market. Suddenly there were all of these Western-looking girls on the market."

Ian Vasquez, director of the Project on Global Economic Liberty at the libertarian Cato Institute in Washington, acknowledges that globalization may have played a role in facilitating sex traffic, but he is quick to point out that the development of the global economy is not the issue. Vasquez says Communist policies in Eastern Europe largely were responsible because "past policies have impoverished people and taken away many or all the benefits" of their industry and savings, creating the desperation and criminality from which this traffic springs. As a result the Russian Federation, Ukraine and Hungary have been producing a flood of desperate victims for the sex traffickers.

Laura Lederer of the Protection Project, a program affiliated with Johns Hopkins University, has been organizing international police records and tracking the main routes of the sex trade for the last three-and-a-half years. When charted, the maps look like flight routes for a major airline, covering much of Africa, Southeast Asia, Eastern Europe and South America. But shutting down those routes has been extremely difficult, says Lederer, because of hesitancy by many countries even to acknowledge the problem. "We mainly track through police and journalistic reports, and if the police don't ask the right questions during the investigation it's that much more difficult to know what's going on," says Lederer.

A report being prepared by the National Center for Missing and Exploited Children (NCMEC), which is due out early next year, may help shed light on how trafficking in children as sex slaves has been added to this international trade. Christine Dolan, a Washington-based freelance journalist, recently was commissioned by NCMEC to spend nine weeks investigating the trafficking of children in Europe, especially in the Balkans. "I hung out with pimps, whores, kids, transvestites and police. I walked the streets and I saw this stuff firsthand. It's a huge, huge problem," Dolan tells *Insight*.

THE SEX TRADE AND **HIV/AIDS**

International Justice Mission investigator Bob Mosier met the 17-year-old in Bombay. A virgin kidnapped from her village in West Bengal at age 14, she was drugged and woke up in a brothel where she was beaten and forced to have sex as many as 25 times a day. By age 17 she had undergone three abortions, which she had to pay for with tips from the long lines of clients she was made to service.

For three years the teen-ager repeatedly tried to escape. Now she has AIDS and will be allowed by the traffickers to go home to die, Mosier tells *Insight*.

"A virgin like her can cost a customer more than $10,000," he says. "Some mistakenly assume that sex with a virgin can purify them of AIDS. Other customers with AIDS do not like to use condoms and spread the disease that way. Governments need to be concerned about this trade from a humanitarian point of view but also from a public-health point of view—and I don't see that happening."

—CE

After a close look at the situation, Dolan is adamant that government bureaucracies and research institutions have a long way to go before they even have a remote grasp of the magnitude and volume of the problem. But it is the age of the children being trafficked and forced into prostitution that she finds most shocking. "What's nearly impossible for people to understand," she says, is that even "toddlers and infants are being kidnapped and sexually molested"—as a business.

Ernie Allen, president of NCMEC, tells *Insight* that kids increasingly are being used for sexual activity and trafficking because even perverts fear HIV/AIDS. "The profile that we have developed on this," he says, "is that we have seen kids exploited and in the stream of child trafficking as young as 3 and 4 years old. This is not just a by-product of pedophilia or some sort of sexual attraction to younger kids. Part of this is that because of the AIDS epidemic there is a demand for younger and younger kids because of the thought that they would be less likely to be HIV-positive." Allen likens the magnitude of sex trafficking to the Holocaust, noting that it has spread throughout the world.

The new U.S. law proposes to address part of this problem. It will require the State Department to expand the annual human-rights reports to cover severe forms of trafficking in persons, and an interagency task force chaired by the secretary of state will coordinate antitrafficking efforts nationally and internationally. The law also provides for allied public-awareness campaigns at home and abroad through NGOs.

"The biggest thing this law does is say to the world that the United States sees this as a serious human-rights issue. It raises public awareness about the dangers of trafficking and the protections available for victims," Brownback tells *Insight*.

A more controversial provision addresses the immigration status of trafficked victims. As many as 5,000 aliens trafficked into the United States by organized-crime syndicates will be permitted to remain on a new nonimmigrant visa provided they assist in the investigation of their perpetrators, are younger than age 15 or can demonstrate that they would suffer severe harm if returned to their country of origin. The president also can impose nontrade, nonhumanitarian sanctions against countries that do not comply with minimum standards to eliminate trafficking. The countries that currently have no laws against forced labor and prostitution will have four years to enact such laws before application of sanctions, but all sanctions can be waived by the president at any time.

Finally, the new law provides for stiff punishment of traffickers who in the past have received light sentences. As Wellstone put it on the Senate floor: "In Los Angeles, traffickers kidnapped a Chinese woman, raped her and forced her into prostitution, posted guards to control her movements and burned her with cigarettes. Nevertheless, the lead defendant received only four years and the other defendants received only two to three years."

The maximum sentence for dealing in small quantities of the drug LSD is life in prison. Under the new law, the penalty for trafficking kids younger than age 14 is life; if caught trafficking a person ages 14 to 18, the perpetrator faces at least 20 years behind bars. The penalty for traffickers who kill or attempt to kill a victim is life in prison.

Rep. Smith was adamant that the law be given the teeth to bite the big players who are facilitating this international shame. "We have to put these mafioso types away for life. Get some high-level convictions . . . and throw away the key. They're facilitating the rape of these young girls, sometimes 10, 15 times a day," he tells *Insight*.

Congress has appropriated almost $100 million to various government agencies to implement the new law. And Janis Gordon, assistant U.S. attorney for the Organized Crime Strike Force in Atlanta, tells *Insight* that this indeed will help her prosecute the traffickers more effectively.

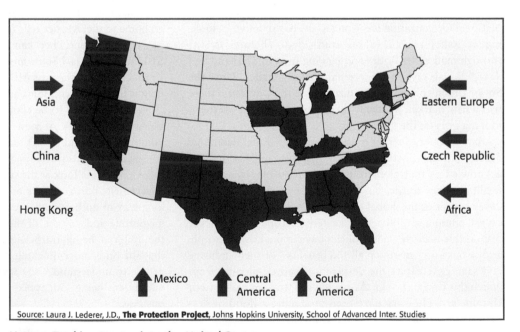

Source: Laura J. Lederer, J.D., **The Protection Project**, Johns Hopkins University, School of Advanced Inter. Studies

Human Tracking Routes into the United States
Where they come from and where they go: Points of entry of sex-slaves sent into the U.S.

Last summer Gordon's office busted an Asian smuggling and prostitution ring. Women and girls as young as age 13 had been trafficked as sex slaves to Atlanta from China, Thailand, Korea, Malaysia and Vietnam. Before she had time to question the girls about their detention, however, the Immigration and Naturalization Service (INS) had deported them to their countries of origin. "Because all my witnesses were gone, I was not able to prove coercion," Gordon tells *Insight*. "The INS wouldn't let me hold them here, so the maximum sentence any of the traffickers got was 33 months." Gordon says the new immigration provisions in the trafficking legislation allow witnesses to remain in the United States to assist with investigations.

"This is big business for the traffickers who don't get caught," says Gordon. "After examining one brothel's records, I was able to show that it grossed $1.5 million over a two-year period. The girls were shuttled around the country to other brothels, forced to work in dire conditions, only allowed to run errands if accompanied by armed guards until they paid off their contracts to their captors, which could be as much as $30,000 in value."

As more women are trafficked into the United States every year, they not only violate U.S. immigration, labor and prostitution laws, but also can become a national-security threat by strengthening corrosive elements abroad, says former CIA director James Woolsey. "Trafficking is a lucrative source of income for organized crime, often less risky than drug smuggling," Woolsey tells *Insight*. "If countries do not effectively prosecute [slave] traffickers, organized crime assumes a stronger role which in turn corrupts law enforcement and the rule of law—which is not good for the overall economic stability of these countries, thus creating a national-security threat to the United States."

One human-rights group that is working to help free trafficked women and children from brothels abroad and to put their traffickers behind bars is the International Justice Mission (IJM), which works with police, NGOs and faith-based groups at the local level to document abuses and assist in conducting the raids. IJM investigator Bob Mosier is a former police officer and served with the international police task force in Bosnia. He and his team have participated in more than 12 raids since January 1999 and assisted in 25 raids on brothels in Asia. Women trafficked against their will from Nepal to India or from Burma to Thailand were found by Mosier's team locked by their captors in dark rooms.

"Some of these women had been sold into prostitution by their own families and were afraid to return home," Mosier tells *Insight*. "The problems we face when freeing some of these girls is that, unless there is a church or NGO willing to take them in, there is nowhere for them to go. They don't speak the language in order to find work, and often they are poor, uneducated and lack skills. Out of fear some return to the brothel simply because they have food and shelter there."

Mosier says he sees a great deal of government corruption at the national and local levels concerning sex trafficking. "But most international governments are concerned that children are being sexually exploited and want to do something to stop it. Even so, most of the in-country laws still do not treat human traffickers as harshly as drug smugglers," he says. Mosier, who recently returned from the Philippines, opens a file and points to a Filipino immigration card. Written on it in red letters are the words: "Drug Trafficking in the Philippines is punishable by death." Not so for traffickers in human beings.

Meanwhile, in October, a U.N. Crime Commission finished negotiations on a new international treaty to combat trafficking in slaves. Delegates wrangled for months over language and the definition of treaty terms. The outcome changed little of the existing 1949 U.N. treaty that condemns trafficking with or without individual consent for sexual purposes, and national laws regarding prostitution will not be affected. Countries may sign the new document starting in December.

Meanwhile, the independent action taken in the United States is likely to have more effect. Smith says the new law marks a historic day in the struggle to protect women from violence. The 10-term Republican says he saw the problem of sex trafficking begin exploding in the 1980s, but it wasn't until he attended a Commission for Cooperation and Security in Europe, held in St. Petersburg, Russia, two years ago that he realized the severity of the problem. "Just looking in the eyes of those girls . . . ," says Smith, breaking off his thought in mid-sentence. Momentarily flustered, he pauses before launching back into the opportunities for prosecution afforded under the new law he helped write.

Lederer is similarly touched by the great outrage. She says that the number of women and children who have been trafficked for sexual exploitation during the last 10 years already is on a par with estimates of the number of Africans who were enslaved for sale in the United States during the 16th and 17th centuries. "The minimum number of African slaves transported here was between 5 million and 6 million," says Lederer. "There is no doubt that world trafficking [in sex slaves] now is around that number."

Reprinted by permission of *Insight*, November 27, 2000, pp. 14–17. © 2000 by News World Communications, Inc. All rights reserved.

CRITICAL THINKING

1. What factors do you think account for recent increases in sex slavery globally and in the United States?
2. Why are children targeted for this crime?
3. What measures do you think should be taken against human trafficking?

13

Responding to Crime

The Police and the Courts

13.1 INTRODUCTION: THE CRIMINAL JUSTICE SYSTEM

The government responds to crime through the **criminal justice system**, which consists of the police, the courts, and the correctional system. Criminal offenders in the United States are apprehended, tried, and punished in a loose confederation of multilevel government agencies. The U.S. criminal justice system evolved from the English common law into a complex series of procedures and decisions. In the United States, there is no single criminal justice system.[1]

Most people enter the criminal justice system through arrest. Sometimes a suspect is apprehended at the scene. At times, however, extensive investigations may be required to identify a suspect. To arrest a suspect properly, law enforcement agencies must get an arrest warrant from the court prior to the arrest, or they must be able to show that at the time of arrest they had probable cause to believe that the suspect committed the crime. A suspect who is taken into custody, or arrested, must then be booked, which involves the official recording of the suspect's identity and alleged offenses.[2]

Because many crimes are not discovered or reported to the police, the U.S. justice system does not respond to most crime. Police agencies learn about crime from citizens who report crime, police officers who uncover crime in the field, and criminal investigators.[3]

The response to crime in the United States is complex. It is a process that involves citizens; local, state, and federal agencies; and various branches of government. Part of this process also involves the private sector of our society. In fact, the U.S. Department of Justice believes that the first response to crime may come from parts of the private sector such as

- individuals and families;
- neighborhoods and neighborhood associations;
- business, industry, and agriculture;
- educational institutions and the news media;
- any other private service to the public.[4]

According to the Bureau of Justice, the private response to crime involves

> crime prevention as well as participation in the criminal justice process once a crime has been committed. Private crime prevention is more than providing private security or burglar alarms or participating in neighborhood watch. It also includes a commitment to stop criminal behavior by not engaging in it or condoning it when it is committed by others.
>
> Citizens take part directly in the criminal justice process by reporting crime to the police, by being a reliable participant (for example, witness, juror) in a criminal proceeding, and by accepting the disposition of the system as just or reasonable. As voters and taxpayers, citizens also participate in

The **criminal justice system** consists of the police, the courts, and the correctional system.

criminal justice through the policy-making process that affects how the criminal justice process operates, the resources available to it, and its goals and objectives. At every stage of the process, from the original formulation of objectives to the decision about where to locate jails and prisons and to the reintegration of inmates into society, the private sector has a role to play. Without such involvement, the criminal justice process cannot serve the citizens it is intended to protect.[5]

Many services needed to make our communities safer and to prevent crime are supplied by noncriminal justice agencies, such as

- public health agencies;
- educational agencies;
- welfare agencies;
- public works agencies;
- housing agencies.[6]

To fully understand the United State's response to crime, one must examine the entire criminal justice system.

This chapter addresses the following questions:

- What are the historical roots of policing in the United States (section 13.2)?
- What are the structures and functions of law enforcement in the United States (section 13.3)?
- What does research suggest are the most effective policing strategies for crime prevention (section 13.4)?
- How does the U.S. court system work, and what is the judicatory process (section 13.5)?
- What are the facts and issues surrounding capital punishment (section 13.6)?
- How does the juvenile justice system differ from the adult criminal court system (section 13.7)?

13.2 THE POLICE

The **police** are an organized civil force that has the important functions of law enforcement and the control of crime. The police

- identify criminal activities and suspects, and investigate crimes;
- apprehend offenders and participate in subsequent court trials;
- have the important role of deterring crime and reducing the opportunities for the commission of crime through preventive patrol and other methods;
- have an important order-maintenance function. They resolve conflicts in the community, promote civil order and peace, and maintain a sense of community security.

The **police** are an organized civil force that has the important functions of law enforcement and the control of crime.

The role of a police officer is complex and stressful. In performing duties, the police officer must deal with difficult situations and cope with a variety of political, social, and economic issues. The officer must also make the "correct" response according to his or her needs and the needs and demands of others, such as police administrators, political and community leaders, and the public.

Research studies on police stress usually make a distinction between two categories of police work. The first category is *operational stressors*, or

The first component of the criminal justice system is the police. The roles and functions of the police are complex and stressful. According to criminological research, what realities of police work might law enforcement officers find even more stressful than confrontations such as this one?

dimensions of police work such as facing the unknown, exposure to danger, physical threats, and violence.

The second category of police work is *organizational stressors*, which may include a difficult management style, poor communication, and lack of support. Research studies indicate that organizational stressors with the highest levels of associated stress are staff shortages, work overload, inadequate resources, time pressures, and lack of communication. In other words, job stress in police work is primarily produced by management and the organization, and to a lesser degree by routine operational duties or task-related factors.[7]

Historical Roots of U.S. Policing

U.S. policing and U.S. police departments are rooted historically in the British system.

To understand modern police organization, the role of the police in the criminal justice system, and policing issues, we must first examine the historical roots and foundations of modern professional policing. Policing in the United States was modeled after the British system. In 1285, England developed what was termed the *parish constable watch system*. The parish was the smallest unit of government in England and would appoint, by election or lot, two constables without pay. These constables would select watchmen who would patrol community streets all night long as part of their civic duty. They made sure strangers were not at large and that townspeople were in their houses. They were also responsible for tending to trash in the streets, lighting street lamps, and putting out fires if needed. In addition to acting as a deterrent force, watchmen looked out for any criminal activities that might be taking place and chased criminal suspects out of the parish.[8]

The American colonies adopted a system of policing similar to the early English watch system. However, in the mid-nineteenth century, with increasing population growth, industrialization, immigration, and crowded cities resulting in social disorder, urban unrest, mob violence, and crime, the constable watch system was replaced with a police system modeled after the centralized, publicly funded "New Police" in England. The *New Police*, or "bobbies," were the first paid uniformed police. The New Police met the demand for crime control using increased numbers of policemen, a highly organized chain of command, and increased training and pay.[9]

In 1845, the City of New York organized a police force that paralleled the British model. The New York police patrolled twenty-four hours a day, controlling social conflict, keeping the peace, and preventing crime. Throughout the 1850s and 1860s, other cities, such as San Francisco, St. Louis, Cleveland, and Detroit, established their own police departments administered by a board of police commissioners. These cities and others, such as Boston and Philadelphia, had police departments organized by a hierarchy of command consisting of a chief, a deputy, and city departments with subdivided precincts. The precincts were patrolled by paid police officers who were eventually issued uniforms and weapons. Policing became a job and not merely a civic duty.[10]

Despite these developments, from the mid-nineteenth century to the beginning of the twentieth century, policemen were called on to fight fires and clean streets in addition to keeping the peace and fighting crime. City police departments came to be controlled by local politicians as part of "machine" politics. Police appointments and promotions were made by political bosses on the basis of party loyalty. When political parties changed in an election, new police commissioners and many new officers were appointed to replace those of the old party.[11]

Throughout much of the nineteenth and early twentieth centuries, many U.S. police departments were characterized by graft and corruption. Numerous efforts to reform police departments through state legislative control or the creation of police administrative boards to reduce local political influence failed. In most cities at the turn of the twentieth century, one would often find the police not only powerful and corrupt but also unsupervised, abusive, and poorly trained. For example, Chicago's 3,200 police had no organized training; new police officers "heard a brief speech from a high-ranking officer, received a hickory club, a whistle, and a key to the call box, and were sent out on the street to work with an experienced officer."[12]

Police Reform and Professionalism

Professionalism in policing began in the early twentieth century.

In the early twentieth century, policing in the United States came under the scrutiny of progressive reformers and saw the advent of a police-professionalism movement rooted in the writings of **August Vollmer**, regarded by many as the father of modern professional police practices in the United States. Progressives at the time were interested in uncovering and eliminating corruption in U.S. society, particularly in politics and government. Finding corruption in our nation's police departments, the progressives focused on professionalizing the police by taking them out of politics and by taking politics out of the police.

Among many others, three major proposals for police departments were advocated by middle-class progressive reformers:

1. Centralization by concentrating authority in an autonomous police chief.
2. Upgrading police personnel by means of selection, training, and discipline.
3. Restricting the police role to enforcing criminal law.

However, these and many other reforms proposed by the progressives failed.[13] Real reform has been traced to August Vollmer and his model of police organization and activity, which was based on the police's crime-fighting role in the community. Vollmer was head of the police department in Berkeley, California,

August Vollmer was the father of police reform and professionalism in the United States.

for more than twenty-five years. Between 1905 and 1932, he played a major role in making California a leader in police innovation and professionalism.[14] In 1908, he began the first police school, which taught a wide variety of subjects related to police work. By 1914, he had his entire force operating out of police cars.

Much of Vollmer's reputation rests on his concern with the social dimensions of police work. In an address to the International Association of Police Chiefs in 1919, entitled "The Policeman as a Social Worker," he urged that the police "develop crime-prevention programs that would attack crime at its sources." Specifically, Vollmer called for "organized cooperation between police and other social agencies to reduce juvenile delinquency." By the late 1920s, he became the leader of a movement to establish police schools in universities. Vollmer also initiated scientific crime-detection procedures and a wide variety of crime-solving methods.[15]

Another advocate of modern, professional policing was Orlando W. Wilson, a student and protégé of Vollmer's. Wilson was well-known for pioneering advanced training methods for police officers. He also developed and applied many modern managerial and administrative techniques to policing.[16]

A second major reform movement occurred in the 1960s. According to some scholars, "liberal reformers called for formalizing the criminal process, particularly the whole range of police-citizen encounters beginning with street contacts to interrogation and other procedures in police departments."[17] The President's Commission on Law Enforcement and the Administration of Justice was formed by President Lyndon Johnson. This commission focused on "the complex police role in American society; the fragmented nature of law enforcement; the poor training and minimum education of police officers; police corruption, brutality, and prejudice; the separation of police from the communities they served; and the consequent diminution in the public support on which effective policing ultimately depends."[18]

Also in the 1960s, the government formed the **Law Enforcement Assistance Administration (LEAA)** to achieve a high level of criminal justice reform in the United States. Because of political controversy and its ineffectiveness in reaching the goals for which it was established, the agency was dissolved in 1980.[19] Throughout the past two decades, police departments across the nation have become increasingly professionalized. Many departments have instituted innovations in police education and training that show promise in improving police effectiveness. Much government funding has also been funneled toward the development of sophisticated police hardware, including computers and advanced technologies to fight crime.[20]

> The **Law Enforcement Assistance Administration (LEAA) was** created in the 1960s to achieve a high level of criminal justice reform in the United States.

After reading this section, you should be able to

1. define police and generally identify the key roles and functions of the police in the criminal justice system;
2. analyze types of police stress;
3. trace the roots of U.S. policing and early police departments in the British system;
4. evaluate the influence of August Vollmer and his followers on U.S. policing;
5. examine the two major waves of police reform during the twentieth century and their effects on police professionalization.

13.3 POLICE ORGANIZATION

In the United States, law enforcement agencies operate at the local, state, and federal levels. More than fifty organizations at the federal level and two hundred organizations at the state level are involved in law enforcement duties. About 18,000 separate law enforcement agencies exist at the state, county, and local levels. Law enforcement agencies in the United States employ more than 1 million full-time sworn officers and civilians.[21]

FEDERAL LAW ENFORCEMENT

Federal law enforcement consists of several important law enforcement agencies and bureaus, including the FBI.

The United States has an extensive, complex network of federal organizations involved in nationwide criminal law enforcement. Perhaps the most widely known federal law enforcement agency is the **Federal Bureau of Investigation (FBI)**. The FBI is considered by many Americans to be the most important federal law enforcement agency.

The FBI's role as an investigative agency has greatly expanded over the years. Its jurisdiction includes all federal statutes that are not specifically assigned to other government agencies. Among other areas, the FBI is involved in investigating sabotage, civil rights violations, bank robberies, kidnappings, interstate transportation of stolen property, mail fraud, treason, and the assault or murder of federal employees.[22]

In recent years, the FBI has increased its focus on such areas as organized and white-collar crime, drug crime, public corruption, and terrorism. With thousands of agents and workers, today's FBI maintains the National Police Academy in Virginia; field offices in all states; the Laboratory and Forensic Science Research and Training Center; and the **National Crime Information**

> The **Federal Bureau of Investigation (FBI)** is the most important federal law enforcement agency.

> The **National Crime Information Center (NCIC)** provides information on criminals to law enforcement agencies in all fifty states.

FOR YOUR INFORMATION

The FBI

The FBI originated in 1870 when the U.S. Department of Justice hired private investigators to enforce the Mann Act, which prohibited the transportation of women across state lines for "immoral purposes" ("white slavery"). In 1908, President Theodore Roosevelt formally established the FBI (then called the Department of Justice's Bureau of Investigations) to deal with political and business corruption, antitrust violations, bankruptcy fraud, and a variety of other federal law violations. President Calvin Coolidge appointed J. Edgar Hoover as the bureau's deputy director in 1924, and the bureau's jurisdiction and power expanded with congressional legislation passed in 1934. The following year, Hoover's organization was renamed the Federal Bureau of Investigation.

In its early years, the FBI was involved with the investigation of subversion, radicalism, and espionage. Under Hoover's direction, the FBI became famous for its campaigns against organized crime and the capture of such criminals as John Dillinger, "Baby Face" Nelson, and Bonnie Parker and Clyde Barrow ("Bonnie and Clyde").

Center (NCIC), which provides information on criminals to law enforcement agencies in all fifty states.[23]

The FBI is not without its detractors. In the past, it was criticized for harassing civil rights leaders and burglarizing the offices of radical groups. Today, it has been criticized for its handling of domestic and transnational espionage, intelligence gathering, ability to deal with terrorism in the United States, and treatment of terrorism suspects.[24]

In addition to the FBI, the U.S. Department of Justice maintains other federal law enforcement agencies. These include the U.S. Marshal Service, the U.S. Citizenship and Immigration Services, the Drug Enforcement Administration, and the Organized Crime and Racketeering Unit.

- The *U.S. Marshal Service,* established by Congress in 1789, was our nation's first federal law enforcement agency. Marshals provide security services for the federal courts. They are also responsible for federal prisoners, investigating federal fugitive-law violations, and providing protection services for relocated witnesses.
- The function of the *U.S. Citizenship and Immigration Services* (formerly the *Immigration and Naturalization Service*) is to patrol and protect our nation's borders and to administer immigration laws (i.e., to naturalize legal and deport illegal aliens).
- In 1973, earlier federal drug agencies were combined to form the *Drug Enforcement Administration (DEA).* The DEA assists state as well as local authorities in their investigations of illegal drug trafficking and use. In addition, the DEA is charged with the enforcement of laws dealing with narcotics and other controlled substances.
- The *Organized Crime and Racketeering Unit (OCRU)* of the U.S. Justice Department directs investigations of racketeering and organized crime in the United States.

The U.S. Treasury Department also administers a number of law enforcement bureaus, including the *Secret Service,* which has the responsibility of protecting government officials such as the president and his staff. The Secret

These DEA agents and U.S. customs agents work for different branches of the federal government, but they have shared jurisdiction in this case of drug smuggling and are cooperatively seizing an illegal shipment aboard a vessel. Communication and cooperation among federal law enforcement agencies and between federal and state agencies are goals of the Homeland Security Act. Which branches of government may be involved in this seizure?

The U.S. Customs and Border Protection is a federal agency in charge of examining all cargo entering the country and investigating smuggling, cargo, and criminal frauds, and currency violations.

The Internal Revenue Service (IRS) is the federal agency in charge of investigating violations of federal taxes, such as income, stamp, and excise taxes.

The Department of Homeland Security (DHS) is a federal agency with law enforcement functions related to the war on terrorism.

Service also investigates counterfeiting and forgery crimes and matters relating to national security. The Treasury Department operates the *Bureau of Alcohol, Tobacco, Firearms and Explosives (ATF)* as well, which enforces federal laws regulating the importation, distribution, and use of these products. A major focus of the ATF is arson and the criminal use of explosives. The U.S. Treasury Department also maintains the **Internal Revenue Service (IRS)**. **U.S. Customs and Border Protection**, formerly a Treasury Department agency, was moved to the Department of Homeland Security on March 1, 2003. It examines all cargo entering the country and also investigates smuggling, cargo, and criminal frauds, and currency violations. The IRS investigates violations of income, stamp, and excise taxes, and a variety of other tax laws.

Finally, the **Department of Homeland Security (DHS)**, created in 2003, is a federal umbrella agency under the direct control of the executive branch of government. The DHS has law enforcement functions in connection with its primary mission, which is to help prevent, protect against, and respond to acts of terrorism.

State Law Enforcement

State law enforcement in the United States began in 1835 and reflects America's traditional concern with states' rights.

The first U.S. state police were the Texas Rangers, founded in 1835. The Rangers protected early Texas settlements and controlled the border with Mexico. In the late nineteenth and early twentieth centuries, Connecticut, Massachusetts, Pennsylvania, and other states created their own law enforcement agencies to deal with problems ranging from vice and corruption to labor-management conflicts.

With the enormous growth in the number of automobiles in the country and the ability of criminals to drive from one community or county to another quickly, the need for a law enforcement agency with statewide jurisdiction became apparent. Today, each state maintains its own state police department.

The authority of highway patrol officers varies from state to state. In some states, their function is limited to highway patrol. In others, they may have more general law enforcement and investigative roles. The state police also help with crowd control, trace stolen cars, give laboratory assistance, and provide police services to communities between rural and suburban areas that have little or no police force of their own.

County and Local Law Enforcement

Local or municipal police departments make up the majority of U.S. law enforcement agencies.

Outside the cities and towns of this country, in the unincorporated or rural sections of the states, the sheriff's department is responsible for enforcing criminal law. In addition to county law enforcement, sheriff's departments also administer and maintain county jails, serve court papers (such as eviction notices, summonses, and court judgments), and assess and collect taxes.

Local or municipal police departments are more common than sheriff's departments and make up the majority of U.S. law enforcement agencies. There are more than 17,000 municipal or town law enforcement agencies in the United States.[25] Generally, large municipal police departments are organized by a hierarchical, military-style command structure, with the scope of each officer's responsibilities clearly defined. As in other government bureaucracies, the police department has a formal system of rules and regulations that govern departmental decisions and actions. Most cities have adopted the prototype of a well-organized municipal police department that was developed by the President's Commission on Law Enforcement and the Administration of Justice.[26]

A municipal police department has an operations bureau, where line functions are performed, and administrative and services bureaus, where nonline service functions are performed.

- *Line functions*, to which most police officers are assigned (under the operations bureau), include patrol assignments, traffic control, investigation, and other specialized services including juvenile, vice, and domestic disputes.
- *Administrative functions* include planning and research, personnel and training, intelligence, inspections, public relations, and legal affairs.
- *Nonline service functions* include the support of line functions via computerized identification and records systems, advanced communication systems, high-tech laboratory services, jail facilities, and supply and building-maintenance services.[27]

After reading this section, you should be able to

1. compare and contrast police organization at the federal, state, and local levels;
2. identify the important federal law enforcement agencies and list their functions;
3. evaluate the FBI and the DHS as powerful federal agencies with law enforcement functions;
4. explain the origins of state and local law enforcement agencies;
5. describe how a well-organized municipal police department operates.

13.4 POLICE ROLES AND THE FUTURE OF POLICING IN THE UNITED STATES

The complex organizational structure of local police departments reflects the many roles and functions with which municipal police are entrusted. According to the *Report to the Nation on Crime and Justice*, the roles and functions of police officers are as follows:

1. *Law enforcement*—applying legal sanctions (usually arrest) to behavior that violates a legal standard.
2. *Order maintenance*—taking steps to control events and circumstances that disturb or threaten to disturb the peace. For example, a police officer may be called on to mediate a family dispute, to disperse an unruly crowd, or to quiet an overly boisterous party.
3. *Information gathering*—asking routine questions at a crime scene, inspecting victimized premises, and filling out forms needed to register criminal complaints.
4. *Service-related duties*—a broad range of activities, such as assisting injured persons, animal control, and fire calls.[28]

Police officers have the important functions of law enforcement and the control of crime. Criminologists such as James Q. Wilson and George Kelling believe that the police should maintain a presence in the community and get to know the people by walking the beat and enhancing harmonious relationships. This style of policing inspires feelings of public safety, reduces the fear of crime, and stimulates cooperation between the police and citizens. For Wilson and Kelling, the primary focus of the police should not be crime fighting but public safety, order maintenance, and the preservation of the community.[29]

FOR YOUR INFORMATION

Discretion Is Exercised throughout the Criminal Justice System

Discretion is "an authority conferred by law to act in certain conditions or situations in accordance with an official's or an official agency's own considered judgment and conscience."[1] Discretion is exercised throughout the government. It is a part of decision making in all government systems from mental health to education, as well as criminal justice. The limits of discretion vary from jurisdiction to jurisdiction.

Concerning crime and justice, legislative bodies have recognized that they cannot anticipate the range of circumstances surrounding each crime, anticipate local mores, and enact laws that clearly encompass all conduct that is criminal and all that is not.[2] Therefore, persons charged with the day-to-day response to crime are expected to exercise their own judgment within limits set by law. Basically, they must decide

- whether to take action;
- where the situation fits in the scheme of law, rules, and precedent;
- which official response is appropriate.[3]

To ensure that discretion is exercised responsibly, government authority is often delegated to professionals. Professionalism requires a minimum level of training and orientation, which guide officials in making decisions. The professionalism of policing is due largely to the desire to ensure the proper exercise of police discretion.

The limits of discretion vary from state to state and locality to locality. For example, some state judges have wide discretion in the type of sentence they may impose. In recent years other states have sought to limit the judges' discretion in sentencing by passing mandatory sentencing laws that require prison sentences for certain offenses.

1. Roscoe Pound, "Discretion, dispensation and mitigation: The problem of the individual special case," *New York University Law Review* (1960) 35:925, 926.

2. Wayne R. LaFave, *Arrest: The decision to take a suspect into custody* (Boston: Little, Brown & Co., 1964), pp. 63–184.

3. Memorandum of June 21, 1977, from Mark Moore to James Vorenberg, "Some abstract notes on the issue of discretion."

Source: U.S. Department of Justice, Bureau of Justice Statistics, "The Justice System," August 6, 2001, **http://www.ojp.usdoj.gov/bjs/justsys.htm**.

The police also have an important service function whereby they help individuals who are in danger or in need of assistance and provide emergency services to members of the community. For example, they help return lost or runaway children, help accident or crime victims, and provide immediate assistance for a wide variety of other personal, economic, and social problems. Studies indicate the majority of an officer's time is spent on social service and administrative tasks and not on fighting crime.[30] The police officer's role changed in the 1990s, however. Although police continue to perform the service functions previously described, research conducted by such criminologists as Jack Greene and Carl Klockars reports that a larger proportion of police work is crime-related than has been claimed in previous studies.[31]

Police Discretion

The police in the United States have important discretionary powers in carrying out their duties.

Police *discretion* is the implicit authority that a law enforcement officer has to act on the basis of his or her professional judgment and personal conscience. Although there are strict rules for police procedures, discretionary powers enter into officers' decisions about when to conduct a search, for example, or whether or not to detain a potential suspect, whether or not to make an arrest, or how far to go in collecting evidence. As Table 13.1 shows, discretion is exercised throughout the criminal justice system—by police, judges, correctional officials, and parole authorities.[32]

TABLE 13.1 WHO EXERCISES DISCRETION?

These criminal justice officials . . .	must often decide whether or not or how to . . .
Police	Enforce specific laws Investigate specific crimes Search people, vicinities, buildings Arrest or detain people
Prosecutors	File charges or petitions for adjudication Seek indictments Drop cases Reduce charges
Judges or magistrates	Set bail or conditions for release Accept pleas Determine delinquency Dismiss charges Impose sentences Revoke probation
Correctional officials	Assign to type of correctional facility Award privileges Punish for disciplinary infractions
Paroling authorities	Determine date and conditions of parole Revoke parole

Source: U.S. Department of Justice, Bureau of Justice Statistics, "The Justice System," August 6, 2001, **http://www.ojp.usdoj.gov/bjs/justsys.htm**.

Policing for Crime Prevention

Policing for crime prevention is a complex social and political process.

Discretion contributes to making the police officer's role complex and stressful. In performing their duties, police officers deal with difficult situations and cope with many social and political issues. They must also make the "correct" response to a wide variety of demands and situations. Crime prevention is foremost among those demands, but responding to crime and preventing crime are two different matters. As Lawrence Sherman points out, three decades of research has shown that hiring more police to provide rapid 911 responses, more random patrols, and more reactive arrests does not prevent serious crime, "but directed patrols, proactive arrests and problem-solving at high-crime 'hot spots' has shown substantial evidence of crime prevention."[33] Policing that is focused on risk factors at high-crime hot spots is called **problem-oriented policing.**

Figure 13.1 lists eight major hypotheses about the relationships between policing and crime prevention. According to research sponsored by the National Institute of Justice, "One of the most striking recent findings is the extent to which the police themselves create a risk factor for crime simply by using bad manners. Modest but consistent scientific evidence supports the hypothesis that the less respectful police are towards suspects and citizens generally, the less people will comply with the law. Changing police 'style' may thus be as important as focusing on police 'substance.' Making both the style and substance of police practices more 'legitimate' in the eyes of the public, particularly high-risk juveniles, may be one of the most effective long-term strategies for crime prevention."[34]

Problem-oriented policing is policing for crime prevention through a focus on risk factors in the community.

Eight Major Hypotheses About Policing and Crime

1. *Numbers of Police.* The more police a city employs, the less crime it will have.

2. *Rapid Response to 911.* The shorter the police travel time from assignment to arrival at a crime scene, the less crime there will be.

3. *Random Patrols.* The more random patrol a city receives, the more a perceived "omnipresence" of the police will deter crime in public places.

4. *Directed Patrols.* The more precisely patrol presence is concentrated at the "hot spots" and "hot times" of criminal activity, the less crime there will be in those places and times.

5. *Reactive Arrests.* The more arrests police make in response to reported or observed offenses of any kind, the less crime there will be.

6. *Proactive Arrests.* The higher the police-initiated arrest rate for high-risk offenders and offenses, the lower the rates of serious violent crime.

7. *Community Policing.* The more the quantity and better the quality of contacts between police and citizens, the less crime.

8. *Problem-Oriented Policing.* The more police can identify and minimize proximate causes of specific patterns of crime, the less crime there will be.

Source: Lawrence W. Sherman, "Policing for Crime Prevention," in *Preventing Crime: What Works, What Doesn't, What's Promising,* a report to the United States Congress prepared for the National Institute of Justice by L. W. Sherman, D. Gottfredson, D. MacKenzie, J. Eck, P. Reuter, and S. Bushway, n.d., **http://www.ncjrs.org/works/chapter8.htm**.

FIGURE 13.1

The conclusions from the research on varieties of police crime prevention, including a report entitled *Preventing Crime: What Works, What Doesn't, What's Promising*, prepared for the National Institute of Justice, are that the more focused the police strategy is, the more likely it is to prevent crime. Thus, "what works" includes

- increased directed patrols on street-corner hot spots of crime;
- proactive arrests of serious repeat offenders;
- proactive drunk-driving arrests;
- arrests of employed suspects for domestic assault.

"What doesn't work" includes

- neighborhood block watch;
- arrests of some juveniles for minor offenses;
- arrests of unemployed suspects for domestic assault;
- drug-market arrests;
- community policing with no clear crime-risk-factor focus.

"What's promising" in crime-prevention strategies includes

- police traffic-enforcement patrols against illegally carried handguns;
- community policing with community participation in priority settings;
- community policing focused on improving police legitimacy;
- zero tolerance of disorder, if legitimacy issues can be addressed;
- problem-oriented policing generally;
- adding extra police to cities, regardless of assignments;
- warrants for arrest of suspects absent when police respond to domestic violence.

Other measures that might be promising but need to be researched further include gang prevention, police curfews, truancy programs, police recreation activities with juveniles, automatic identification systems, and in-cruiser computer terminals.[35]

After reading this section, you should be able to

1. trace recent trends in the specific roles and functions of the police;
2. define and illustrate the concept of police discretion;
3. summarize eight major hypotheses about relationships between policing and crime prevention;
4. give examples of "what works," "what doesn't work," and "what is promising" in policing for crime prevention.

13.5 THE COURTS

The second important component of the U.S. criminal justice system is the courts. The United States has a dual-court system, that is, a separate court system in each of the states in addition to a complete federal system of trial and appellate (appeals) courts. **State courts** administer the laws of the states within which they operate, while **federal courts** administer federal laws. The **U.S. Supreme Court** interprets the terms of the U.S. Constitution and any conflicts between state and federal laws, and acts on issues that pose a threat to constitutional order.

State courts administer the laws of the states within which they operate. **Federal courts** administer federal laws. The **U.S. Supreme Court** interprets and applies the U.S. Constitution and decides conflicts between state and federal laws.

The courts in the United States and the law and procedures they use are rooted in the English common law and equity traditions. But unlike the English courts with their executive origins, the American courts were created by statute or constitution and make up the dual-court system. The state and federal court systems coexist with little difficulty. According to N. Gary Holten and Lawson L. Lamar, the authority of the U.S. Supreme Court links the court systems and also interprets and enforces "the terms of the Constitution—the 'Supreme Law of the Land.'"[36]

Criminal cases arise when agents of government bring lawsuits against persons alleged to have committed crimes or a variety of other offenses as defined in the statutes or codes (all other cases or matters brought before the court are termed "civil").[37] The **judicatory process** that follows involves prosecuting and defending the accused in a criminal trial and determining the outcome, for example, by acquitting or sentencing. Criminal cases in the United States are filed and pursued by the state, not by a private party. **Prosecution** refers to the process by which one institutes or conducts criminal proceedings against a defendant. **Adjudication** refers to the decision making that occurs in formal court proceedings. Adjudication is the determination of guilt or innocence— the judgment concerning criminal charges—and the process of attaining finality in litigation. If the defendant is found guilty, the court imposes the sentence. A **sentence** is a criminal sanction, such as a fine, probation, incarceration, or the death penalty that is imposed by the court on a convicted defendant. For the defendant, no decision made by criminal justice system officials is more important than that made by the judge (or in some states, the jury) at sentencing. It is through sentencing that society attempts to express its goals for the correctional process.[38]

> **Criminal cases** arise when agents of government bring lawsuits against persons alleged to have committed crimes or a variety of other offenses as defined in the statutes or codes. The **judicatory process** involves prosecution, defense, and sentencing or other outcome of a criminal trial.
>
> **Prosecution** is criminal proceedings against a defendant.
>
> **Adjudication** is the decision making that occurs in formal court proceedings.
>
> A **sentence** is a criminal sanction issued against a convicted defendant.

The Funneling Effect

The court's processing of defendants has a funneling effect in the criminal justice system.

In the United States, only about 12 percent of the felony arrestees brought in by police for prosecution are sentenced to prison for more than one year.[39] What happens to the remaining 88 percent of those arrested? In the U.S. criminal court system, a "funneling effect" or "sorting operation" occurs. The *funneling effect* moves some people along for further criminal processing while it releases others from the process. Which behavior and which people come within the scope of the criminal justice system are questions defined and determined by criminal law and procedure:

- Police sort out (through police discretion) those individuals who will continue to have contact with the criminal justice system (by arresting them) from those who will not have this contact (by not arresting them).
- Criminal prosecutors continue this funnel effect by not charging those arrested with crimes (through prosecutorial discretion).
- The courts reject or dismiss cases (through judicial discretion) for a wide variety of reasons, including insufficient evidence, witness or due-process problems, or pretrial diversion.

In the judicatory process, the adjudication follows the decision to charge a person with a crime. Adjudication proceeds according to formal rules by which judges oversee the proceedings. Adjudication, public and visible, accounts for only a small percentage of criminal case dispositions. This low disposition of criminal cases occurs because the outcome in the majority of cases is determined by "informal, low-visibility, private negotiations between prosecutors for the government and defense counsel for the defendant."[40] An example is **plea bargaining**. Adjudicative outcomes (public and formal) merely ratify "what the parties decided informally outside the courtroom."[41]

Participants in the Judicatory Process

Participants in the judicatory process include the prosecutor, defense counsel, judge, and others.

In the United States, criminal cases are filed and pursued by the state in a prosecution. The purpose of prosecution is to "deal with the question of guilt or innocence of the persons accused and to seek the appropriate disposition of the persons found guilty."[42] The **prosecutor** is a government attorney who represents the state and the people against persons who have been accused of committing criminal acts. Some observers believe that the prosecutor, in terms of the control he or she has over cases and the defendants, is the most influential participant in the criminal justice system.[43]

The **defense counsel** (or attorney) represents the accused in the criminal process, acting on behalf of the defendant when he or she is arrested, interrogated, and arraigned. The defense attorney investigates matters and interviews witnesses and law enforcement officers. He or she also meets with the prosecutor, enters into plea negotiations, and prepares the case for trial.

The **judge** is the senior officer in a court of criminal law. For many observers, the judge is the most powerful official in the entire criminal justice system. He or she has the power to terminate a criminal case at virtually any point in the court proceedings by "granting a motion for dismissal, for suppression of key evidence, or for a judicial acquittal." The judge may also find persons in contempt of court and order them to jail.[44]

Sentencing of Criminals

Courts, legislatures, and administrative agencies exercise sentencing power. It is through sentencing that society attempts to express its goals—retribution, incapacitation, deterrence, rehabilitation, and restitution—for the correctional process. As you can imagine, the sentencing of criminals often reflects conflicting social goals. According to the Bureau of Justice Statistics, these objectives are basically the following:

1. *Retribution*—giving offenders their "just deserts" and expressing society's disapproval of criminal behavior.
2. *Incapacitation*—separating offenders from the community to reduce the opportunity for further crime while they are incarcerated.
3. *Deterrence*—demonstrating the certainty and severity of punishment to discourage further crime by the offender (specific deterrence) and by others (general deterrence).
4. *Rehabilitation*—providing psychological or educational assistance or job training to offenders to make them less likely to engage in future criminality.
5. *Restitution*—having the offender repay the victim or the community in money or services.[45]

Plea bargaining is negotiating an agreement between the prosecution and the defense in which a criminal case is decided outside of the courtroom, which thus has a funneling effect.

The **prosecutor** is a government attorney who represents the state and the people against persons who have been accused of committing criminal acts.

The **defense counsel** or attorney represents the accused in the criminal process.

The **judge** is the senior officer in a court of criminal law.

Attitudes about Sentencing

ATTITUDES ABOUT SENTENCING REFLECT MULTIPLE GOALS AND OTHER FACTORS

Research on judicial attitudes and practices in sentencing reveals that judges vary greatly in their commitment to various goals when imposing sentences. Public opinion also has shown much diversity about the goals of sentencing, and public attitudes have changed over the years. In fashioning criminal penalties, legislators have tended to reflect this lack of public consensus.

Sentencing laws are further complicated by concerns for

- **Proportionality**—severity of punishment should be commensurate with the seriousness of the crime
- **Equity**—similar crimes and similar criminals should be treated alike
- **Social debt**—the severity of punishment should take into account the offender's prior criminal behavior.

JUDGES USUALLY HAVE A GREAT DEAL OF DISCRETION IN SENTENCING OFFENDERS

The different sentencing laws give various amounts of discretion to the judge in setting the length of a prison or jail term. In a more fundamental respect, however, the judge often has a high degree of discretion in deciding whether or not to incarcerate the offender. Alternatives to imprisonment include

- probation
- fines
- forfeiture or the proceeds of criminal activity
- **restitution** to victims
- **community service**
- **split sentences,** consisting of a short period of incarceration followed by probation in the community.

Often, before a sentence is imposed a presentence investigation is conducted to provide the judge with information about the offender's characteristics and prior criminal record.

STATES USE A VARIETY OF STRATEGIES FOR SENTENCING

Sentencing is perhaps the most diversified part of the nation's criminal justice process. Each state has a unique set of sentencing laws, and frequent and substantial changes have been made in recent years. This diversity complicates the classification of sentencing systems. For nearly any criterion that may be considered, there will be some states with hybrid systems that straddle the boundary between categories.

Source: U.S. Department of Justice, Bureau of Justice Statistics, "The Response to Crime: An Overview of the Criminal Justice System," in *Report to the Nation on Crime and Justice*, 2nd ed., March 1988, NCJ-105506, pp. 90–93, 96–97, 100–101.

Different states have different systems for sentencing, based on the sharing of discretion between the judge and parole authorities. There are five basic types of sentencing:

1. *Indeterminate,* in which the judge specifies minimum and maximum sentence lengths and parole boards have discretion to determine the time of release.
2. *Determinate,* in which the judge sets a fixed prison term with no discretionary parole release.
3. *Mandatory,* in which the law requires a certain sentence of a certain length for certain crimes with no option of probation or suspended sentence.
4. *Presumptive,* in which the judge can shorten or lengthen sentences within specified boundaries set by law.
5. *Sentencing guidelines,* in which the judge's decision can be based on circumstances such as the nature of the offense and the number of prior offenses.[46]

Mandatory sentencing has been criticized, because first-time offenders can receive the same sentence as repeat offenders and can serve serious time for lesser offenses, such as possessing a small quantity of marijuana. Some critics have called for sentencing reform to ensure that punishments fit the crimes. Others call for different sentencing reform in response to judges' abuses of their discretionary powers.

After reading this section, you should be able to

1. describe the U.S. dual-court system and the judiciary process;
2. explain the funneling effect of the U.S. court system and its impact on the criminal justice system;
3. explain the judiciary process in terms of the roles of its participants;
4. discuss the five conflicting purposes of sentencing and identify five major types of sentencing in the United States.

13.6 THE DEATH PENALTY

The United States is among one hundred nations that use **capital punishment**, or the death penalty. About fifty nations have abolished capital punishment, and about sixteen others have abolished it for all but "exceptional crimes," such as wartime crimes. About twenty countries that have the death penalty have not carried it out during the past decade or so. The United States is the only Western democratic country that has not abolished capital punishment.[47] About seventy-five criminals are executed annually in the United States. Three times as many whites are executed as blacks. Only about 3 percent are women. Lethal injections account for virtually all executions. Currently thirty-eight states and the federal government have capital statutes.[48] Figure 13.2 reflects capital punishment's use from the 1930s to today.

Capital punishment refers to the death penalty.

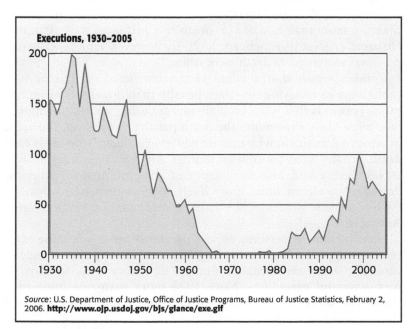

Executions, 1930–2005

FIGURE 13.2 Executions, 1930–2005

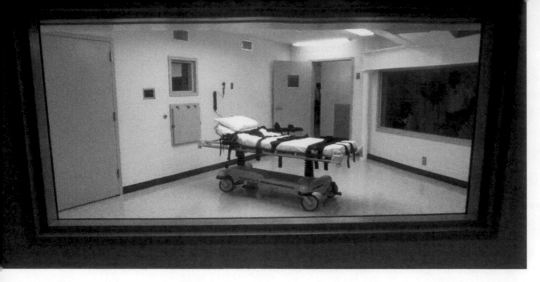

This lethal-injection chamber is being readied for use. What is the likely profile of an inmate slated for execution? What model of criminal sanctioning does capital punishment reflect? Why has the death penalty been controversial in the United States, and what are the arguments for and against capital punishment?

The death penalty has been used against convicted criminals in most societies for thousands of years. In the United States its use has been controversial: some criminologists and others have developed strong arguments for the death penalty; others have argued against it.

Sometimes the same arguments can be made for and against capital punishment, such as those based on religious scriptures, which contain both views. There are other contradictions. Some proponents of the death penalty argue, for example, that it is more economical than keeping an inmate in prison for life, but opponents of the death penalty point out that the cost of maintaining a prisoner during the death-row appeals process and the cost of the appeals are actually much greater than maintaining a prisoner sentenced to a life term.

Many opponents of capital punishment charge that it is discriminatory. For example, researchers reported that of the 3,859 people executed since 1930, almost 55 percent were African American or members of other minority groups—a percentage out of proportion with the number of capital crimes committed by African Americans. In 1990, this trend did not appear to have changed: more than half of U.S. death-row prisoners were African American, Hispanic, or Native American. In 2002, however, almost 75 percent of U.S. prisoners sentenced to death were white.[49]

Studies report that a white person convicted of murder has a higher probability of receiving the death penalty than does an African American. A major reason is that whites mainly murder other whites; the murder victim's race more likely determines the death penalty conviction. Individuals (white or African American) who murder whites are much more likely to receive the death penalty than those who murder African Americans.[50] One study by David Baldus and associates reported that an African American murder defendant is eleven times more likely to be sentenced to death for killing a white person than a white murder defendant is for killing an African American.[51]

Finally, some Americans oppose the death penalty because of evidence of errors in applying it uncovered by DNA analyses, police scandals involving cases of planted evidence, and findings of wrongful convictions. There have been wrongful executions. Since 1973 more than one hundred death-row inmates have been exonerated through evidence and released.[52]

Arguments For and Against the Death Penalty

FOR THE DEATH PENALTY:

- As a criminal sanction, the death penalty prevents many potential criminals from killing other innocent human beings. Isaac Ehrlich's research reflects that each execution results in seven or eight fewer murders. Steven Layson studied homicide data for a forty-one-year period and concluded that each execution prevented almost twenty murders. In addition, many criminals are so dangerous that they can be kept from killing others only by being put to death. The U.S. Department of Justice reported in 1991 that one in twelve of the prisoners then under the death penalty had a prior homicide conviction. If these killers had been executed when they first committed murder, about 250 murder victims would be alive today.
- The death penalty has an economic benefit, in that it is much more cost-effective to use the death penalty in capital offenses than to maintain murderers in prison for the rest of their lives.
- Religious leaders and moral philosophers throughout history were not all against the death penalty; supporters cite the Old Testament passages "an eye for an eye" (Exodus) and "whoever sheds the blood of man, by man shall his blood be shed" (Genesis) in support of their view.
- Proponents believe it is morally right to despise and execute criminals who have committed heinous criminal acts against innocent men, women, and children; if a person murders another person, he or she deserves to be condemned to death by society.

AGAINST THE DEATH PENALTY:

- With respect to the deterrent effect of the death penalty, a number of studies in the past four decades have reported that homicide rates are not at all affected by executions. Thorsten Sellin and associates, for example, compared capital crime rates in states that had the death penalty with states that did not and found no significant differences. Sellin concluded that capital punishment was not a significantly greater deterrent to murder than life imprisonment. Hans Zeisel, William Bailey, and Brian Forst have also seriously questioned the ability of executions to deter murder in our society.
- In many cases (such as Sacco and Vanzetti, and Ethel and Julius Rosenberg), innocent people have been wrongly convicted and put to death. Michael Radelet and Hugo Bedeau report that there have been about 350 wrongful convictions during the past one hundred years, and twenty-three of these led to executions.
- Some research studies question the high rates of recidivism among death-row inmates, pointing out that convicts who are released (because of legal changes, etc.) rarely recidivate and pose little threat to society.

Sources: I. Ehrlich, "The Deterrent Effect of Capital Punishment: A Question of Life and Death," *American Economic Review* 65, 1976, pp. 397–417; S. K. Layson, "Homicide and Deterrence: A Reexamination of the United States Time-Series Evidence," *Southern Economics Journal* 52, 1985, p. 68; L. A. Greenfield, *Capital Punishment*, 1991, Bulletin of the Bureau of Justice Statistics, Washington, DC, 1992, p. 1; E. Van Den Haag, "The Ultimate Punishment: A Defense," in *Taking Sides*, R. C. Monk and S. Dock, Eds., Guilford, CT: Dushkin Publishing, 1991, pp. 214–225; T. Sellin, *The Penalty of Death*, Beverly Hills, CA: Sage, 1980; T. Sellin, *The Death Penalty*, Philadelphia: American Law Institute, 1959; H. Zeisel, "The Deterrent Effect of the Death Penalty: Facts v. Faith," in *The Supreme Court Review*, P. E. Kurland, Ed., Chicago: University of Chicago Press, 1976, pp. 317–343; W. C. Bailey, " A Multivariate Cross-Sectional Analysis of the Deterrent Effect of the Death Penalty," *Sociology and Social Research* 64, 1980, pp. 183–207; B. Forst, "The Deterrent Effect of Capital Punishment: A Cross-State Analysis of the 1960s," in *The Death Penalty in America*, 3rd ed., H. A. Bedeau, Ed., New York: Oxford University Press, 1982, pp. 131–132; M. Radelet and H. Bedeau, "Miscarriages of Justice in Potentially Capital Cases," *Stanford Law Review* 40, 1987, pp. 21–181; H. A. Bedeau and M. Radelet, "The Myth of Infallibility: A Reply to Markman and Cassell," *Stanford Law Review* 42, 1989, pp. 161–170; J. Marquart and J. Sorensen, "Institutional and Post-release Behavior of Furman-Commuted Inmates in Texas," *Justice Quarterly* 26, 1988, pp. 677–693.

READING ABSTRACT

Reasonable Doubts

BY STEPHEN POMPER

In this reading, the author critically examines problems plaguing America's criminal justice system and makes recommendations to correct them. Topics include criminal procedures, the exclusionary rule, DNA evidence, witness intimidation and protection, policing prosecutors, and the insanity defense.

See reading on page 405.

After reading this section, you should be able to

1. define capital punishment and describe its place in the U.S. system of criminal justice;
2. give arguments for and against the death penalty;
3. identify and discuss three issues or problems in the U.S. criminal justice system, based on Reading 13.1.

13.7 THE JUVENILE JUSTICE SYSTEM

Juvenile delinquency refers to illegal acts committed by young people, usually sixteen to eighteen years of age or younger.

Status offenses are criminal offenses that apply specifically to youths.

An important area of law violation is termed *juvenile delinquency*. **Juvenile delinquency** refers to illegal acts committed by young people, usually sixteen to eighteen years of age or younger. Juvenile delinquency does not come under the area of criminal law or under the jurisdiction of criminal courts. Delinquency cases involve a separate area of law and are specifically dealt with by juvenile courts. As reported earlier in the text, from a legal perspective, delinquency pertains to all acts that, if committed by adults, would be considered crimes. Delinquency also refers to various additional offenses, termed **status offenses**, that apply specifically to youths. Examples of status offenses are incorrigibility, truancy, and running away.

Distinct from the adult criminal code, the juvenile laws and court system emphasize the notions of protection, guidance, and rehabilitation of juveniles rather than their punishment and incarceration. This philosophy is based on the idea that, in general, juveniles are too young to be capable of having the criminal intent necessary to commit malicious crime. The perspective also stresses the notion that young people can be helped and redirected from a life of crime. This philosophy was first expounded by a nineteenth-century American social movement know as the child-saving movement.

The *child-saving movement* of the late 1800s was spearheaded by a number of people who were committed to the idea of saving "wayward youth" from the effects of a "bad environment" in the home and in the community. The child savers argued that youths were basically "good" rather than "bad." Therefore, a revised system of juvenile justice and corrections was needed. In this revised system, the state would act as parent to the young offender. If needed, removal of the child from the home or community should be undertaken

This youth is in juvenile court. How will his experience in the juvenile justice system be different from that of adults in the criminal court system? Many more juveniles are being tried as adults in American courts today than in the past.

for the youth's protection and reform rather than for punishment and incarceration with hardened adult criminals.

The child-saving movement was largely responsible for the passage of the *Juvenile Court Act of 1899*. This act paved the way for the establishment of the first juvenile court (in the same year), in Illinois. The Juvenile Court Act of 1899 laid the foundation for the juvenile court system that is present within the United States today. In addition, the child-saving movement was partly responsible for the development of new types of correctional institutions for handling young offenders.[53]

According to the U.S. Department of Justice, although the juvenile courts remain separated from criminal processing, the concepts on which they are based have changed. The U.S. Department of Justice states: "Today, juvenile courts usually consider an element of personal responsibility when making decisions about juvenile offenders. Juvenile courts may retain jurisdiction until a juvenile becomes legally an adult. This limit sets a cap on the length of time juveniles may be institutionalized that is often much less than that for adults who commit similar offenses. Some jurisdictions transfer the cases of juveniles accused of serious offenses or with long criminal histories to criminal court so that the length of the sanction cannot be abridged."[54]

Nevertheless, today the philosophy of juvenile law still basically emphasizes the ideas of protection and guidance rather than punishment. The young offender receives a "hearing" rather than a "trial." Judges, for the most part, are permitted wide discretion in deciding upon a course of action that would be most beneficial for the young person. In addition, the language used in juvenile courts is less harsh. For example, "juvenile courts accept 'petitions' of 'delinquency' rather than criminal complaints; 'adjudicate' juveniles to be 'delinquent' rather than find them guilty of a crime; and order one of a number of available 'dispositions' rather than sentences. Despite the wide discretion and informality associated with juvenile court proceedings, juveniles are protected by most of the due-process safeguards associated with adult criminal trials."[55] A Supreme Court decision in 1969, the Gault case, has helped to ensure the legal rights of the juvenile offender. According to this decision, juveniles who are likely to be committed to state correctional institutions are granted the same legal rights to "due process under the law" as adults.

FOR YOUR INFORMATION

Processing of Juveniles

The processing of juvenile offenders is not entirely dissimilar to adult criminal processing, but there are crucial differences in the procedures. Many juveniles are referred to juvenile courts by law enforcement officers, but many others are referred by school officials, social services agencies, neighbors, and even parents, for behavior or conditions that are determined to require intervention by the formal system for social control.

When juveniles are referred to the juvenile courts, their intake departments, or prosecuting attorneys, determine whether sufficient grounds exist to warrant filing a petition that requests an adjudicatory hearing or a request to transfer jurisdiction to criminal court. In some states and at the federal level prosecutors under certain circumstances may file criminal charges against juveniles directly in criminal courts.

The court with jurisdiction over juvenile matters may reject the petition or the juveniles may be diverted to other agencies or programs in lieu of further court processing. Examples of diversion programs include individual or group counseling or referral to educational and recreational programs.

If a petition for an adjudicatory hearing is accepted, the juvenile may be brought before a court quite unlike the court with jurisdiction over adult offenders. In disposing of cases juvenile courts usually have far more discretion than adult courts. In addition to such options as probation, commitment to correctional institutions, restitution, or fines, state laws grant juvenile courts the power to order removal of children from their homes to foster homes or treatment facilities. Juvenile courts also may order participation in special programs aimed at shoplifting prevention, drug counseling, or driver education. They also may order referral to criminal court for trial as adults.

Despite the considerable discretion associated with juvenile court proceedings, juveniles are afforded many of the due process safeguards associated with adult criminal trials. Sixteen states permit the use of juries in juvenile courts; however, in light of the U.S. Supreme Court's holding that juries are not essential to juvenile hearings, most states do not make provisions for juries in juvenile courts.

Source: U.S. Department of Justice, Bureau of Justice Statistics, "The Response to Crime: An Overview of the Criminal Justice System," in *Report to the Nation on Crime and Justice,* 2nd ed., March 1988, NCJ-105506, pp. 71–82.

In theory, the young offender, as noted previously, is not "tried" or "sentenced." Often, however, actual practice falls short of this philosophy, with juveniles being handled as adults. To an extent, this situation has resulted from the fact that delinquency encompasses a much wider range of behaviors than the adult criminal code, and the number of judicial and correctional personnel are inadequate to deal with the large number of juvenile offenders.

In the United States today, politicians and the public view juvenile crime differently than they did just a few years ago. Because of this change in perception, there have been many new policies and new justice procedures developed for the treatment of juvenile offenders. Today, society is much more likely to have juvenile offenders tried as adults.

After reading this section, you should be able to

1. describe the roots and goals of the United State's juvenile justice system;
2. explain how adult criminal courts and juvenile courts differ;
3. examine the issues involved in trying juveniles as adults.

CHAPTER SUMMARY

This chapter examines the first two components of the U.S. criminal justice system—the police and the courts. The response to crime is an intricate, multifaceted process. It involves citizens as well as many agencies of government (pp. 379–380).

A major agency of the government is the police. Policing in the United States is modeled after the British system. Early U.S. police departments controlled social conflict, kept the peace, and prevented crime. From colonial times into the early twentieth century, the police also fought fires and cleaned the streets. Throughout much of the nineteenth and early twentieth centuries, many police departments were characterized by graft and corruption, and the police officers were poorly trained (pp. 380–382).

In the early part of the twentieth century, policing in the United States was influenced by progressive reformers and the advent of police professionalism rooted in the theories and writings of August Vollmer. Policing was later influenced by a second reform movement that occurred in the 1960s (pp. 382–383).

Various law enforcement agencies (federal, state, county, and local) play important roles in fighting crime. Local or municipal police departments make up the majority of U.S. law enforcement agencies (pp. 384–387).

Today, police perform many important functions in the areas of law enforcement, order maintenance, information gathering, and service-related duties. Discretion is exercised throughout the criminal justice system—the police, prosecutors, judges, correctional officers, and paroling authorities. Research on varieties of crime prevention reveal what works and doesn't work, and what's promising (pp. 387–391).

The dual-court system of the United States consists of state courts and federal courts, including the U.S. Supreme Court. The judiciary process involves prosecuting and defending accused persons in a criminal trial and determining the outcome. The funneling effect moves some people along for further criminal processing while it releases others from the process. Participants in the judiciary process include the prosecutor, the defense counsel, and the judge. It is through sentencing that society expresses its goals for the correctional process (pp. 391–395).

Capital punishment, or the death penalty, has been controversial in the United States. Arguments for the death penalty focus on its deterrent effect, the economic benefits and moral rightness of its use, and passages of religious scriptures. Arguments against the death penalty focus on its lack of deterrent effect, the wrongful conviction and execution of innocent people, its discriminatory nature, and passages of religious scriptures (pp. 395–398).

The juvenile justice system emphasizes protection, guidance, and rehabilitation rather than punishment and incarceration. The public view of juvenile crime has changed over the years, and today juvenile offenders are much more likely to be tried as adults (pp. 398–400).

Study Guide

Chapter Objectives

- Define the criminal justice system.
- Describe how citizens take part in the criminal justice system.
- Define police.
- Briefly describe the parish constable watch system.
- Describe early police departments in the United States.
- Examine how progressives focused on police professionalization.
- Describe August Vollmer's influence on U.S. policing.
- Briefly describe the second major police-reform movement of the 1960s.
- Describe the functions of the FBI.
- Briefly examine three federal law enforcement agencies other than the FBI.
- Describe the prototype of a well-organized municipal police department.
- Define and briefly explain police discretion.
- List eight major hypotheses about policing and crime.
- List "what works" in policing for crime prevention.
- List "what is promising" in crime-prevention efforts.
- Briefly describe restorative justice.
- Briefly describe the U.S. dual-court system.
- Describe the funneling effect.
- Briefly describe the roles of prosecutor, defense counsel, and judge.
- Explain what a sentence is, and list the different types of sentencing in the United States.
- Define capital punishment.
- Briefly examine the arguments for and against the death penalty.
- List and briefly examine three problems in the U.S. criminal justice system.
- Describe the roots and goals of the U.S. juvenile justice system.
- Explain how criminal courts and juvenile courts differ.
- Examine the issues involved in trying juveniles as adults.

Key Terms

Adjudication (392)
Capital punishment (395)
Criminal cases (392)
Criminal justice system (379)
Defense counsel (393)
Department of Homeland Security (DHS) (386)
Federal Bureau of Investigation (FBI) (384)
Federal courts (391)

Internal Revenue Service (IRS) (386)
Judge (393)
Judicatory process (392)
Juvenile delinquency (398)
Law Enforcement Assistance Administration (LEAA) (383)
National Crime Information Center (NCIC) (384)
Plea bargaining (393)
Police (380)

Problem-oriented policing (390)
Prosecution (392)
Prosecutor (393)
Sentence (392)
State courts (391)
Status offenses (398)
U.S. Customs and Border Protection (386)
U.S. Supreme Court (391)
Vollmer, August (382)

Self-Test
Short Answer

1. Write a definition of the criminal justice system.
2. List three characteristics of early U.S. police departments.
3. Define and give an example of police discretion.
4. List and briefly examine three methods of policing that "work."
5. Briefly describe the funneling effect.

6. Describe the roles of prosecutor and judge.
7. List two arguments for and two arguments against the death penalty.
8. Describe two criticisms of the criminal justice system.
9. Describe the juvenile justice system in the United States.

Multiple Choice

1. In most U.S. cities at the turn of the twentieth century, one would find the police
   a. powerful and corrupt
   b. unsupervised and poorly trained
   c. frequently abusive
   d. all of the above
2. Reform and professionalization of the police has been largely attributed to whom?
   a. Robert Merton
   b. August Vollmer
   c. Calvin Coolidge
   d. J. Edgar Hoover
3. Which of the following law enforcement agencies is not maintained by the U.S. Department of Justice?
   a. FBI
   b. Secret Service
   c. DEA
   d. U.S. Marshal Service
4. The functions of police officers include which of the following?
   a. law enforcement
   b. order maintenance and information gathering
   c. service-related duties
   d. all of the above
5. Discretion is exercised by
   a. police and correctional officers
   b. prosecutors and paroling authorities
   c. judges and magistrates
   d. all of the above
6. According to the report *Preventing Crime*, which of the following "works"?
   a. neighborhood block watch
   b. drug-market arrests
   c. proactive arrests of serious repeat offenders
   d. arrests of unemployed suspects for domestic abuse
7. Prosecution is
   a. the process by which one institutes or conducts criminal proceedings
   b. the decision-making process that occurs in formal court proceedings
   c. the determination of guilt
   d. a criminal sanction
8. About how many persons are annually executed in the United States?
   a. 75
   b. 175
   c. 575
   d. 1,575
9. According to the reading "Reasonable Doubts,"
   a. courts are supposed to be finders of fact
   b. DNA evidence can keep innocent people from going to death row and guilty people from going free
   c. we need to abolish the insanity defense
   d. all of the above

True–False

T F 1. The justice system does not respond to most crime, because so much of it is undiscovered or not reported to the police.
T F 2. The response to crime is mainly a federal function.
T F 3. More than one agency has jurisdiction over some criminal events.
T F 4. Policing in the United States was modeled after the French and British systems.
T F 5. The FBI limits its jurisdiction to federal laws, including all federal statutes that are not specifically assigned to other government agencies.
T F 6. Local or municipal police departments make up the majority of U.S. law enforcement agencies.
T F 7. The more respectful police are toward suspects and citizens generally, the less people will comply with the law.
T F 8. Gun buyback programs have been found to be effective in reducing U.S. crime.
T F 9. The United States has a dual-court system.

Fill-In

1. _____ is an authority conferred by law to a law enforcement officer to act under certain conditions or situations in accordance with his or her own judgment and conscience.
2. Most people enter the criminal justice system through _____.
3. _____ refers to the process by which one institutes or conducts criminal proceedings against a defendant in court.
4. _____ refers to the decision making that occurs in formal court proceedings and is the determination of innocence or guilt.

5. The most widely known federal law enforcement agency is the _____.
6. _____ is giving offenders their "just deserts" and expressing society's disapproval of criminal behavior.
7. _____ is having the offender repay the victim or the community in money or services.
8. The _____ represents the accused in the criminal process.
9. A _____ is a criminal sanction.
10. _____ evidence can help to correct past mistakes in identifying criminals.

Matching

1. Welfare agency
2. Criminal justice system
3. August Vollmer
4. Reliable tool for identifying criminals
5. Crime-prevention strategy that doesn't work
6. Municipal police departments
7. Senior officer in a court of criminal law
8. Federal courts
9. Police
10. Crime-prevention strategy that works

A. Component that identifies criminal activities and suspects, and investigates crimes
B. Proactive drunk-driving arrests
C. The majority of U.S. law enforcement agencies
D. Component that administers federal laws
E. Judge
F. DNA evidence
G. Noncriminal justice agency
H. Drug-market arrests
I. Police reform
J. Police, courts, and the corrections system

Essay Questions

1. Carefully describe your local police department. How does it compare, in terms of organization and functions, to other local police departments in the nation as described in this chapter? What have been some of the major issues or problems facing your local department during the past five years? Are your police officers under much stress when on duty? Is your local police department involved in the community? How?

2. Select a recent criminal incident in your community and follow—through newspaper articles, news broadcasts, and so on—the accused person's processing through the criminal justice system from arrest to sentencing. Was the defendant an adult or juvenile? What kinds of issues and problems developed? Was the case rejected or dismissed? Was the defendant released pending trial? Be detailed and specific.

3. Review the arguments for and against the death penalty. Write a brief essay on your personal opinion of the death penalty. Are you for it or against it? Why?

Reasonable Doubts

Source: Reprinted with permission from the Washington Monthly, June 2000, pp. 21–26.
© 2000 by The Washington Monthly Publishing, LLC, 733 15th Street, N.W., Suite 520,
Washington, D.C. 2005 (202) 393-5155,
http://www.washingtonmonthly.com

BY STEPHEN POMPER

Crime may be down but the criminal justice system remains something of a mess. If you've ever spent time on a jury, if you've worked in a criminal court, or if you caught even 10 minutes of the O. J. trial on TV, you've seen some of the problems. The system has an Alice-in-Wonderland quality: The guilty are over-protected, the innocent are under-served, and much of the time the public interest simply fails to enter the picture. Jurors spend days in court dozing through endless delays and witnesses who dare come forward find their lives imperiled. When all is said and done, too many violent and dangerous felons wind up with Get-Out-of-Jail-Free cards and too many nonviolent and just-plain-innocent people wind up doing time.

How do we make it better? Read on for the *Monthly*'s guide to criminal justice reform.

GET THE TRUTH OUT

Courts are supposed to be finders of fact. Yet there's an awful lot about the criminal justice system that keeps them from ever getting to those facts. Some of the obstacles are straight-forwardly bad laws. Others are more a question of resources and oversight. We could help our courts get past some of these obstacles and here's how:

(1) *End "Two Wrongs Make a Right" Criminal Procedure.* The judicial system labors under rules crafted by the Warren Court, which protect defendants even if it's at the expense of the truth. In a 1997 law review article, University of Minnesota law professor Michael Stokes Paulsen casts this as the "Dirty Harry" problem. In the movie of the same name, Detective Harry Callahan gets increasingly violent as he goes after a serial murderer named "Scorpio." He busts into his place without a warrant, nabs the murder rifle, and savages Scorpio until he spits out the location of a kidnap/rape/murder victim. But here's the kicker: Although Scorpio is a monster, and Harry does some monstrous things, neither of them is actually punished. Scorpio goes free because all the evidence against him is tainted by Harry's antics, and Harry slides by because cops get away with stuff.

Decades later, this lose-lose approach is still at the heart of criminal procedure. To be sure, the failing has noble origins.

Back in the Civil Rights era, the Supreme Court, concerned about segregationist states deploying policemen to harass and imprison minorities, developed a set of constitutional principles that stopped them from doing that: Ill-gotten evidence was treated like fruit from a poisoned tree and had to be discarded. If the police ransacked your car without a warrant, the resulting evidence could not be produced at trial.

But the days of officially-sponsored police racism are over. And while there's still racism and police abuse on a different scale, it's hard to see why they are best dealt with by excluding otherwise helpful evidence. It's one thing to say that forced confessions should not be considered: That protects innocent people who might be beaten into confessing crimes they did not commit. But what kind of protection does an innocent person get from an "exclusionary rule" that prevents a court from considering ill-gotten evidence? If Harry busts into an innocent person's apartment and doesn't find anything to seize, then there won't be any evidence for a court to exclude, and there won't be any negative consequence for the police. Not that exclusion is such a negative consequence anyway: when police are evaluated in cities like New York, the emphasis is on the number of arrests to their credit, not convictions. If Scorpio goes free because Harry trashes his place, Harry still may be eligible for a promotion.

Part of the problem with the exclusionary rule is that it assumes that the Bill of Rights is focused on protecting the guilty rather than the innocent. But some leading constitutional scholars have begun to suggest that this assumption is backwards—protecting the innocent is in fact the top priority. The correct way to control police abuse is not by tossing potentially useful evidence onto the compost pile. It is by punishing the policeman or the police department through a lawsuit or through criminal charges. But the court should, by all means, be allowed to consider Scorpio's rifle and any other relevant evidence that Harry has managed to dig up.

In 1995 Congress considered a bill that would have gone in this direction—by getting rid of the exclusionary rule and making it easier to sue delinquent cops—but it fizzled. Supporters of the status quo argue that it doesn't really matter: There are so many exceptions to the exclusionary rule that only a small percentage of arrests are lost as a result. They also argue that the rule is useful because it provides at least some check on police abuse—and that creating an alternate system of checks would be a real challenge. This, however, ignores the problems in the current system. Read the recent coverage about the Los Angeles and New York police departments and you will see that the exclusionary rule is not an especially effective mechanism for controlling police brutality. Meanwhile, courts and lawyers waste their time on motions to suppress evidence that can only undermine the truth-seeking process.

Getting to the truth should be the court's foremost objective. And this principle doesn't apply just to the exclusionary rule. For example, a majority of states have deadlines after which a convict cannot introduce new evidence to prove his innocence. In Virginia, the deadline is a scant 21 days after trial. The idea is to keep appeals from dragging out endlessly, but that's not a good rationale for keeping innocent people in jail. If a convict can present credible new evidence, then a court should review it. But if a case reopens for this reason and the state has come up with new evidence of guilt, the court should look at that too.

It's time to end the lose-lose cycle that we create by excluding evidence. A court must get the information it needs to send Scorpio to Alcatraz. If he can prove his innocence later, it must hear the evidence it needs to spring him. And the Harrys of this world must pay for their brutality through some mechanism that punishes them directly—rather than one that punishes the community by putting guilty people back on the street.

(2) *Create a Universal DNA Database.* This is an idea that Rudy Giuliani has endorsed and the ACLU has said could usher in a "brave new world" of genetic discrimination—but looking past the rhetoric, it's a winner.

The idea is to take full advantage of the enormous power of DNA evidence. Because it's so much more reliable at identifying people than eyewitnessing, DNA evidence can keep innocent people from going to death row and guilty people from going free. And because it is such powerful proof, it can help shorten trials, relieve problems with witness intimidation, and generally lend itself to a more efficient and reliable criminal justice system. But in order to maximize its usefulness, you need to be able to check crime scene DNA samples against the biggest possible database. The government is already coordinating a database that will include mostly convicted felons' DNA samples. That's a decent start: Convicted felons have a high probability of returning to their old ways when released from prison. Still, plenty of crime is committed by people who have never spent time behind bars. So why not do it right and create a database that includes everybody?

The idea is simple and nondiscriminatory. Upon the birth of any child, a hospital would take a DNA sample using a simple procedure that involves swabbing cells off the inside of a cheek with a bit of cotton and then analyzing their genetic material for patterns at 13 separate points,

called loci. The information recorded at these loci is referred to as "junk" by geneticists because it doesn't say anything interesting about whether a person is likely to be an insurance risk, is likely to win a Nobel Prize, is a cat or a dog person, or anything of the sort. Like a finger-print, it would simply identify who a person is. This information would be sent to a federal database where it could be used only by law enforcement authorities when trying to establish the identity of a criminal.

Civil libertarians get hysterical over the privacy issues, but where's the beef? Given the restricted information that we're talking about, and the limited access that would be afforded, the main privacy right at stake is the right to commit crimes anonymously. It's also worth noting that millions of hospital patients leave blood and tissue samples when they come for treatment. Some hospitals keep these on file. So if your local homicide chief decides that he wants to get a DNA profile on you, he may very well be able to go down to City General, retrieve some old cells of yours, and do his own genetic analysis. This analysis could wind up furnishing information that is much more sensitive than the information that would be recorded in the national database. Wouldn't it be preferable to require the police to limit their DNA sleuthing to one tightly controlled source?

One more point on DNA evidence: It can help us correct past mistakes, and we should use it to do so. States should be required to take DNA samples from all convicts in all cases where it could prove their innocence and the prisoner wants it. Given that no fewer than 67 prisoners have already been found innocent using DNA testing, states should be working overtime to find other innocents who have been wrongly imprisoned. The flip side of this position is that states and courts should do whatever it takes to make certain that statutes of limitations don't stop victims and prosecutors from going after violent offenders where DNA technology for the first time allows guilt to be established.

(3) *Save the Witnesses.* If you watch too many movies of the week, you can get a highly distorted view of what this country does to protect its witnesses. There is a romantic idea that once you agree to testify in a dangerous case, the FBI rushes in with a team of plastic surgeons, draws up new papers, and moves you to the furthest corner of the furthest possible state—where it continues to keep a watchful eye on you for the rest of your natural born days. But there's a problem: The FBI program is for federal witnesses—it was designed to help U.S. attorneys bust up organized crime. It doesn't do a thing to help out at the state and local levels where most crime, and most witness intimidation, occurs.

And a shocking amount of witness intimidation does occur at those levels. According to a 1995 report published by the National Institute of Justice (their latest on this subject), some prosecutors were able to identify gang-dominated neighborhoods where between 75 and 100 percent of violent crimes involved intimidation—from knee capping potential witnesses to staring them down in court to actually rubbing them out. That's an unsettling figure when you consider that a court's fact-finding machinery can grind to a halt without witnesses.

Consider the following example: A Baltimore jury recently acquitted three men who had been accused of shooting one Shawn L. Suggs in a street fight that spilled out into rush hour traffic. At first, the prosecution seemed to have a good case—but then the key witnesses started dropping out of the picture: The first was killed in his home. Another disappeared without a trace. And the third (Suggs' former girlfriend) claimed at the last moment to have lost her memory to heroin addiction. "I think she is afraid to tell the truth," Suggs' mother told the *Baltimore Sun*. "I think I would be afraid too."

How do you fight that kind of fear? Many states and communities have created their own witness protection programs that try to offer some measure of security—from posting police cars outside witnesses' homes to moving witnesses out of their old neighborhood until the trial is over. But the programs often lack adequate funding. And on top of that, it can be a lot tougher to protect state and local witnesses than it is to deal with mob rats. Street and gang crime witnesses are frequently reluctant to abandon their homes and neighborhoods. They get bored, lonely, and afraid when they're pulled away from their families. And even if they can be persuaded to move a short distance—say a few towns away—the temptation to look in on friends and relatives back in the old neighborhood can be both irresistible and dangerous.

More could be done. Improving funding and stiffening penalties would be a good start. When prosecutors can persuade a witness to cooperate, they should have the money they need to pay for motel bills, replace locks on doors, and pick up the tab for gas and groceries. Because it can be tough to come up with the scratch to do this on short notice, some states, like California, have set aside funds that communities can use to foot the bill. Other states should follow their lead, and the federal government should set up an emergency fund to help communities pick up the slack when there's a shortfall. And with regard to penalties, states should rank intimidation right up there with the gravest noncapital offenses. Under Washington, D.C., law, intimidators can get up to life imprisonment. That sounds about right.

(4) *Police the Prosecutors—as Well as the Police*. Police and prosecutors are the gatekeepers of the criminal justice system. But although police brutality gets a lot of attention—as it has recently in New York and Los Angeles—prosecutors tend to escape scrutiny.

We should pay closer attention to the prosecutors. They, after all, are the ones who decide which cases go to trial and how they're presented. If they misrepresent the facts, they can wind up sending innocents to jail. And that's a problem for two reasons. First, there are a lot of powerful incentives that make prosecutors want to win—sometimes even at the expense of the truth. ("Winning has become more important than doing justice," complained Harvard Law School

professor Alan Dershowitz in a 1999 *Chicago Tribune* interview. "Nobody runs for Senate saying 'I did justice.'") Second, when a prosecutor does step over the line, he rarely faces serious punishment.

How do we know? In 1999, the *Chicago Tribune* published a nationwide survey. They looked at all the murder cases in the past 40 years that had to be retried because a prosecutor hid evidence or permitted a witness to lie. They found 381 in all. What happened to the prosecutors in those cases? Almost nothing. About a dozen were investigated by state agencies, but only one was actually fired—and he was eventually reinstated. And not a single one of the offending prosecutors was ever convicted of either hiding or presenting false evidence. Indeed, not a single prosecutor in the history of the Republic has ever been convicted on those grounds—even though they're both felony offenses. As Pace University law professor Bennett Gershman told the *Tribune*: "There is no check on prosecutorial misconduct except for the prosecutor's own attitudes and beliefs and inner morality."

But isn't the defense bar a check on prosecutorial misconduct? Don't count on it. In December 1999, the *New York Times* noted that the number of legal aid lawyers in New York City's Criminal Court had dropped from 1,000 a decade ago to 500 today. And it quoted Manhattan defense attorney Ronald Kuby as saying that "No competent criminal defense lawyer zealously representing his clients can make a living on [legal aid rates]." This problem is obviously not limited to New York.

All this suggests that if we want to make certain prosecutors are doing the right thing, we have to police them more aggressively. That means creating well-muscled independent agencies that have strong incentives to find out when prosecutors misbehave—and to fine, press charges, and/or fire them when they do. Judges should help them out by publishing the names of prosecutors who commit misconduct in their orders and opinions (not a common practice)—and circulating them to the independent watchdogs. And while we're on the subject, states should also set up similar watchdogs to police the police—both for abuse and sheer incompetence. There should be independent civilian commissions that not only have responsibility for overseeing police departments, but that also have the power to impose discipline on the departments when they stray.

(5) *Abolish the Insanity Defense*. It is true that you have to be a bit crazy to shoot the President like John Hinckley, or to cut off your husband's penis like Lorena Bobbit—but should that affect the state's ability to keep you separated from the rest of society, where you might do further harm? If you are rich or high profile or just plain lucky enough to find a defense lawyer who can successfully argue the insanity defense on your behalf, it can.

Consider the case of Tomar Cooper Locker, who opened fire on a crowded D.C. hospital ward—killing a boxer named Ruben Bell and wounding five bystanders. The apparent motive for the shooting was that Locker had a vendetta against Bell, who he thought had killed his girlfriend. But Locker pled insanity based on the claim that he was suffering from a momentary attack of posttraumatic stress disorder—a claim endorsed by the same psychiatrist who testified in the Lorena Bobbit incident. The jury bought it. Locker was then committed to St. Elizabeth's Hospital, where he was treated for two whole months until, earlier this spring, doctors declared him fit to reenter society.

Michael Lazas is another example of someone who slipped through the system as a result of the insanity defense. In 1993, Lazas was found not guilty by reason of insanity for strangling his infant son and sent to Maryland's Perkins Hospital Center. It was his second violent assault; two years earlier he had stabbed a picnic companion in the throat. In 1998, Perkins officials thought Lazas was ready for a group home, so they moved him to an essentially zero-security facility in Burtonsville, Maryland. In February of this year, Lazas simply walked away from the Burtonsville facility. He was reportedly gone for four days before anyone notified the authorities he was missing.

In both cases, the public would have been better served if there were no insanity defense. There is no dispute that Locker and Lazas did what they were accused of doing. As a society, we've made a judgment that people who do these things need to be separated from the rest of us for a certain amount of time. Locker and Lazas should each have been found guilty and served the requisite time for his offenses—in an appropriate treatment facility to the extent necessary. The law should not force chronic schizophrenics to do hard time in maximum-security prisons. But it should be adamant about finding ways to keep those who commit violent crimes at a safe distance from the rest of society.

LOCK UP THE RIGHT PEOPLE

Politicians who vote for mandatory minimum sentences stake a claim to being tough on crime. Politicians who vote against them run the risk of appearing weak. Of course in a perfect world, "toughness" would be assessed by whether you put the right (i.e., most dangerous) people in jail—rather than how many people you put in jail. But the world of sentencing statutes is far from perfect.

The political blindness that surrounds these laws can be partly traced to the death of Len Bias—a Maryland basketball star who had been the Celtics' first pick in the NBA draft. When Bias overdosed on cocaine in his college dorm room in 1986, he become an overnight poster child for the war on drugs. It was an election year and Beltway legislators, who were close enough to Maryland to be caught up in the public horror at Bias' death, wanted to make a statement. So they replaced a set of temporary federal sentencing guidelines that had been in place with permanent "mandatory minimum" sentencing requirements. States followed suit with their own iterations of these requirements. And in 1994, California and Washington added a new wrinkle when they passed so-called "three strikes laws" that require courts to give 25-year minimum sentences to any two-time felony offender who steps out of line a third time—even if to commit a misdemeanor offense.

These laws have generated some spectacularly unfair results. For example, a California court recently sentenced Michael Wayne Riggs, a homeless man, to 25 years in jail for stealing a bottle of vitamins. His most serious prior offense was snatching a purse.

But if Riggs' story is maddening at the individual level, the major concern at the policy level is what all this chest-thumping legislation is doing to our nation's prison system. There are roughly 2 million Americans behind bars, of whom more than half are there for nonviolent (in most cases drug-related) crimes. The country spends $31 billion per year on corrections—twice what it spent 10 years ago. There is still not enough room in America's prisons.

Even looking past the overcrowding issues, however, sentencing laws have proven to be losers. Sending minor drug offenders to jail exposes them to hardened criminals and increases the risk of them committing more serious felonies when they get out. The Rand Corporation has found that mandatory minimums are the least cost-effective way to reduce drug use and crime—as compared to treatment programs and discretionary sentencing. Even White House Drug Czar Barry McCaffery has acknowledged that "we can't incarcerate our way out of the drug problem." It is therefore unsurprising that a dozen or so states have formed commissions to reconsider their rigid sentencing policies and several, like Michigan, have begun to repeal them. And on the progressive front, Arizona recently became the first state to offer the option of drug treatment, rather than prison to its nonviolent offenders convicted on drug charges.

Arizona's program is both cost efficient and makes sense. A California study found that one dollar spent on drug treatment saves seven dollars in reduced hospital admissions and law enforcement costs. These savings can be put to better use elsewhere in the criminal justice system. For example, they can be used to help communities develop facilities to siphon off nonviolent offenders from the heart of the system. Roughly two percent of the nation's drug offender traffic is processed in special "drug courts," which dole out a combination of light sentencing—such as short jail terms, community service, and probation—plus mandatory drug treatment. More drug courts would almost certainly be a good thing.

Communities also do themselves a service when they set up tough probation programs that actually help minor offenders steer away from trouble. Orange County, California, has had substantial success with a program that involves 6 a.m. inspection visits to all participants from program officers, surprise drug testing, counseling, and monthly evaluations by the supervising judge. Anecdotal evidence suggests that in order to work these programs have to be ready to dish out real discipline to participants who fail to live up to their end of the bargain. Orange County participant Dale Wilson, who had been addicted to cocaine for three decades before joining the program, told the *Los Angeles Times* that he was sent to jail for nine days when he had a relapse. "It's a strict program," he said. "But I never would've gotten to the point to keep me sober if I hadn't been faced with these punishments."

PUT MORE ORDER IN THE COURTS

Finally, we shouldn't forget that the best laws and policies in the world aren't going to do a whole lot of good unless we have reliable, industrious, and smoothly administered courts. And while there are lots of hardworking judges with the same objective, there are also plenty of clunkers.

In a 1996 San Francisco case, for example, two municipal court judges batted a domestic violence case back and forth on an October Friday. According to the *Recorder*, a legal newspaper, Judge Wallace Douglass was supposed to hear the case—but he double-booked another trial for the same day. So he sent it across the hall to Judge Ellen Chaitin, who held a mid-day conference—and then sent it back to Douglass when it failed to settle by the early afternoon. Douglass then said that he couldn't find a jury to hear the case (it was Friday afternoon, after all) and, because a delay would have violated the defendant's speedy trial rights, he dismissed it. This calls to mind the story of the Manhattan judge who in 1971 adjourned a robbery trial to catch a flight to Europe. Another trial would have violated the defendant's constitutional rights, so he walked away scot-free.

The problem is two-fold. One is that judges don't always push themselves that hard. In 1989, *Manhattan Lawyer* correspondents observed that, on average, the judges in Manhattan's criminal court were in session about four and a half hours a day. Sixty-two percent spent less than five hours in session, and 42 percent started after 10 a.m. In Baltimore, which has more than 300 homicides per year, you can sometimes walk through a criminal courthouse around 3:30 or 4:00 p.m. and find courtrooms that have adjourned for the day.

But the additional problem is that judges are too often inclined to schedule things first for their own convenience, second for the convenience of lawyers, and last of all for the convenience of the people the system should be bending over to accommodate—jurors and witnesses. One prosecutor said that there are days in D.C. Superior Court that unfold as follows: The jury is instructed to arrive at 10 a.m. and sits for hours while the judge kibbitzes with the lawyers over technical legal issues. Sometimes the kibbitzing runs right into lunch. Then everybody trundles off for a two hour break. The trial starts in earnest at 3 p.m. And court adjourns between 4:30 and 5 p.m.—sometimes earlier.

Lack of organization is another problem. Washington D.C.'s Superior Court has no central scheduling mechanism. Judges control their own dockets and are allowed to book two or three trials for the same day, anticipating that there will be pleas and continuances. Policemen who are supposed to testify wind up milling around the courthouse for days on end, waiting for their trials to be called, and—if they otherwise happen to be off-duty—collecting overtime.

It has to be possible to run a tighter ship because some judges already do. As noted in last month's "Tilting at Windmills," for example, a Tennessee judge named Duane Slone has adopted a policy that he won't hear plea bargains on the day a trial is scheduled to begin. This saves the jury from having to sit and wait while lawyers haggle over a plea and allows trials to start promptly at 9 a.m. Common sense courtesies like this could kill a lot of the inefficiencies that you see in courtrooms today. But more importantly, disciplinary panels need to keep better tabs on the courts and punish (by fines or demotions if necessary) those judges who fail to show up on time, stay all day, and run an orderly docket.

CRITICAL THINKING

1. Which of the problems identified in this article concern you the most, and why?
2. Which solutions proposed in the article appeal to you the most, and why?
3. What might you add to the discussion of what's wrong with the U.S. criminal justice system?

14

Responding to Crime

Corrections

14.1 INTRODUCTION: CORRECTIONS

Corrections involve the treatment, incapacitation, and punishment of criminal offenders who have been convicted in a court of law. The criminal court convicts and sentences those defendants who are found guilty of crimes. Upon sentencing, the corrections component of the criminal justice system begins to function. In the United States, there are about ten thousand correctional agencies—residential facilities, juvenile and adult probation and parole agencies, and so on—established to correct, treat, and administer postadjudicatory care to convicted criminal offenders. Reference to these facilities typically suggests incarceration, but as the system both deals with overcrowding and attempts to divert offenders from correctional facilities, community corrections is becoming a larger aspect of managing offenders.

A few decades ago, there was a significant change in the field of corrections from the mere institutionalization of criminal offenders to the increased use of community-based correctional alternatives, such as probation, parole, and reentry programs. Today, corrections in the United States consist of many areas including jails, prisons, and a wide variety of community-based programs. This chapter discusses these important areas, beginning with an analysis of the public responses to crime, which have included retribution and deterrence at one extreme and rehabilitation and restorative justice at the other.

For centuries, retribution was the major social response to criminal behavior. **Retribution** is the notion that a wrongdoer should be punished to "pay back" or compensate for his or her criminal acts. Retributive forms of punishment can be traced to ancient times. For example, the famous Code of Hammurabi stressed the doctrine of *lex talionis*, "an eye for an eye." This penal practice was based on the motive of reciprocal revenge for crime: murderers were to be murdered themselves; those who caused physical injury to others were to be harmed in a like manner.

During the feudal period of European history, trial by "ordeal" was quite common. For example, the accused were bound and cast into a stream of water; those who remained afloat were considered guilty. This period of history witnessed an increase in the severity of retributive punishments and a growth in the number of offenses to which such punishments applied. Punishment by death was the most prevalent, followed by mutilation, corporal punishment, and banishment. In addition, a number of lesser offenses were punishable by fines; it was common practice to levy severe fines against fraudulent businessmen and unscrupulous landlords.[1]

This chapter addresses the following questions:

- How and why have penal sanctions changed (section 14.2)?
- What are the differences between modern models of rehabilitation, retributive justice, and utilitarianism (section 14.2)?
- What are the origins, types, and conditions of jails and prisons (section 14.3)?

Corrections involve the treatment, incapacitation, and punishment of criminal offenders who have been convicted in a court of law.

- What are some characteristics and problems of prison inmates (section 14.3)?
- What are the forms of community-based and alternative corrections, and to what extent are they effective (sections 14.4 and 14.5)?
- What facts and issues surround the practices of probation, parole, and prison release (sections 14.6 and 14.7)?

14.2 DETERRENCE AND IMPRISONMENT

Retribution is the notion that a wrongdoer should be punished to "pay back" or compensate for his or her criminal acts. *Lex talionis* ("an eye for an eye") was an ancient penal practice that was based on the motive of reciprocal revenge for crime.

Beccaria and Bentham argued that the proper objective of punishment should be to protect society and its laws and that punishment should be inflicted for its deterrent effect, not for vengeance. **Deterrence** refers to demonstrating the certainty and severity of punishment to discourage further crime by the offender (specific deterrence) and by others (general deterrence).

It was not until the late eighteenth century that Cesare Beccaria and Jeremy Bentham advocated a new philosophy and system of legal and penal reform. They argued that the proper objective of punishment should be to protect society and its laws; punishment should not be inflicted for vengeance—rather, the primary purpose of punishment should be the reduction or deterrence of crime. **Deterrence** refers to demonstrating the certainty and severity of punishment to discourage further crime by the offender (specific deterrence) and by others (general deterrence).

Beccaria and Bentham also advocated that the excessively brutal punishments of death and mutilation be abolished and that penal reforms be introduced so that "the punishment fit the crime." The punishments inflicted should be just severe enough to outweigh any pleasures, either contemplated or actually experienced, that could be derived from the commission of a criminal act. In this way, the threat of punishment would deter most people from committing crimes in the first place, and the actual infliction of punishment would deter the offender from committing additional criminal acts. Beccaria, in addition, presented convincing arguments for imprisonment as a form of punishment, believing it to be the most effective and efficient method for carrying out these new penal reforms. The more-than-adequate number of preexisting jails in Europe were easily adapted for use in implementing Beccaria's programs.[2]

The Solitary System and the Silent System

The Quakers believed that imprisonment should reform and rehabilitate prisoners.

By the turn of the nineteenth century, imprisonment had become a major form of punishment. In the United States, the Quakers of Pennsylvania spearheaded the movement to have imprisonment take the place of other, harsher forms of punishment. The Quakers believed that imprisonment should have a deterrent function, but, more importantly, it should also serve the purpose of reforming and rehabilitating the inmate.

Quakers of Pennsylvania spearheaded the movement to have imprisonment take the place of other forms of punishment. They started the **solitary system** (or **Pennsylvania system**), a system of imprisonment in which each prisoner was required to live and work in solitary confinement throughout the entire sentence.

The Quakers were also concerned with the potential detrimental effects of prisoner contact and association. Therefore, the two major penitentiaries built in Pennsylvania used what has come to be known as the **solitary system**. Under this system, each prisoner had a personal prison cell and exercise area. In effect, each prisoner was required to live and work in solitary confinement throughout the entire sentence. This system solved the problem of prisoner contact, provided prisoners more time and opportunity to learn a trade, and also gave them more time to think over their "evil ways" and practice penitence—hence the name *penitentiary*.[3]

The Quakers were satisfied with the solitary system, but others were concerned with the detrimental effects resulting from extended periods of physical

In 1821, Pennsylvania's legislature approved funding to build this prison, Eastern State Penitentiary, now a museum, in Philadelphia. The architecture of Eastern State reflected the "Pennsylvania system" of solitary confinement, which was based on Quaker philosophy. What was that philosophy, and what was the solitary system intended to accomplish? How was New York's silent system different from the solitary system?

and social isolation. Hence, in the decades that followed, few states adopted the "Pennsylvania system." Instead, most states opted for an alternative plan of administration. This plan became known as the **silent system**, or the **Auburn system** (it was first introduced at the penitentiary in Auburn, New York, in 1823).

Under the silent system, prisoners were permitted to work side by side, but at no time were they allowed to speak or even glance at one another. For example, when passing one another outside their cells, prisoners had to keep their eyes downcast. When moving about in the company of others, prisoners were required to walk in lockstep formation—that is, in single file, facing the back of the person immediately ahead. Infraction of these rules brought swift and severe disciplinary action.[4]

> The **Auburn system** or **silent system** was a system of imprisonment within which prisoners were permitted to work side by side, but at no time were they allowed to speak or even glance at one another.

Rehabilitation, Retributive Justice, and the Utilitarian Model

In the 1970s, after decades of focus on the rehabilitation of criminals, corrections shifted to retributive justice and utilitarian models.

During the late nineteenth and early twentieth centuries, many repressive disciplinary measures began to fade. New regulations allowed prisoners to talk and associate with one another in a comfortable, open manner in all spheres of activity. However, even during the twentieth century, prisons were not in the forefront of movements for correctional innovations. Change in the prison system has occurred only slowly; some of the older, more repressive methods are still being used in some institutions.[5]

From the 1940s to the 1960s, **rehabilitation** of offenders, at least in theory, was a dominant goal of imprisonment and other forms of correction. The aim was to help the offender become a useful and productive member of society by instilling the appropriate standards, attitudes, and skills necessary for the offender to live a more acceptable life upon release. The rehabilitation philosophy was clearly emphasized by the National Advisory Commission on Criminal Justice Standards and Goals in 1973:

> **Rehabilitation** is a goal of imprisonment; its aim is to help offenders become useful and productive members of society by instilling the appropriate standards, attitudes, and skills necessary for an acceptable life after release.

> A rehabilitative purpose is or ought to be implicit in every sentence of an offender unless ordered otherwise by a sentencing court. The correctional authority . . . should give first priority to implementation of statutory specifications or statements of purpose on rehabilitative services. A correctional authority's rehabilitation program should include a mixture of educational, vocational, counseling, and other services appropriate to offender needs. Correctional authorities regularly should advise courts and sentencing judges of the extent and availability of rehabilitative

READING ABSTRACT

The Goals of Punishment: The Return to Retributivism and the Utilitarian Model

BY CLEMENS BARTOLLAS AND JOHN P. CONRAD

In this reading, the authors examine the changing goals of punishment in the United States.

See reading on page 438.

Retributivism ("justice model") is a goal of punishment that stresses the idea that offenders are responsible people and, therefore, deserve to be punished if they violate the law.

The **utilitarian punishment model** is a philosophy of punishment based on the assumption that punishment is necessary to protect society from crime and also to deter offenders.

services and programs within the correctional system to permit proper sentencing decisions and realistic evaluation of treatment alternatives.[6]

During the 1970s and into the 1980s, there was a return to **retributivism**, or the **justice model**, which stresses the idea that offenders must take responsibility for their actions and, therefore, deserve to be punished if they violate the law. The United States also reverted to a utilitarian model to deal with crime. The **utilitarian punishment model** is based on the assumption that punishment is necessary to protect society from crime and also to deter offenders.

Today retribution (giving offenders their "just deserts" and expressing society's disapproval of criminal behavior) and incapacitation (separating offenders from the community to reduce opportunity for further crime while they are incarcerated) are the primary justifications for imprisonment in the U.S. criminal justice system. This shift in philosophy and goals for crime prevention and the correctional process—from rehabilitation to retribution and incapacitation—has been accompanied by a dramatic increase in the offender population in the United States. The following section examines U.S. jails and prisons and the increase in U.S. offender populations.

After reading this section, you should be able to

1. define the concepts of corrections and retribution;
2. summarize Beccaria and Bentham's views on punishment and deterrence;
3. compare and contrast the solitary system and the silent system;
4. give examples of how prisons and prison life have reflected different correctional models;
5. trace and evaluate the trends in corrections from the rehabilitation of offenders to the use of retributive justice;
6. explain how incapacitation is an expression of the utilitarian punishment model.

14.3 CORRECTIONS TODAY: JAILS AND PRISONS

A **jail** is a secured government institution used to retain arrested individuals who are awaiting arraignment, or trial, conviction, or sentencing. They are locally operated facilities, and they confine individuals before or after adjudication.

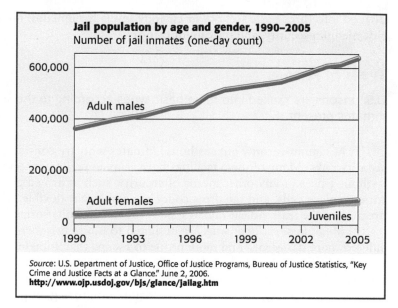

Jail population by age and gender, 1990–2005
Number of jail inmates (one-day count)

Source: U.S. Department of Justice, Office of Justice Programs, Bureau of Justice Statistics, "Key Crime and Justice Facts at a Glance." June 2, 2006.
http://www.ojp.usdoj.gov/bjs/glance/jailag.htm

FIGURE 14.1   Jail Population by Age and Gender, 1990–2005

Jails are also used to house convicts who are usually serving sentences of one year or less.

Data reported by the Bureau of Justic Statistics for 2005 indicated:

A **jail** is a secured local detention facility used to retain arrested individuals who are awaiting arraignment, trial, conviction, or sentencing.

- At mid-year 2005, 747,529 inmates were held in the nation's local jails, up from 713,990 at mid-year 2004.
- From 1995 to 2005, the number of jail inmates per 100,000 U.S. residents rose from 193 to 252.
- Almost nine out of every ten jail inmates were adult males (see Figure 14.1). However, the number of adult females in jail increased faster than males.
- Blacks were almost three times more likely than Hispanics and five times more likely than whites to be in jail (see Figure 14.2).

In contrast to jails, **prisons** are state or federal correctional institutions for the incarceration of felony offenders for terms longer than one year. There are well over five hundred state and federal prisons in the United States. They are

A **prison** is a state or federal correctional institution for the incarceration of felony offenders for terms of longer than one year.

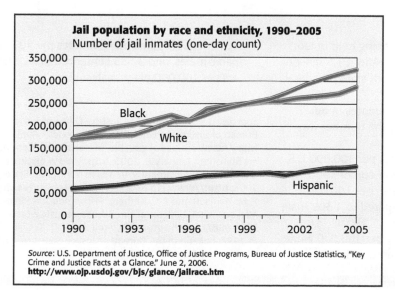

Jail population by race and ethnicity, 1990–2005
Number of jail inmates (one-day count)

Source: U.S. Department of Justice, Office of Justice Programs, Bureau of Justice Statistics, "Key Crime and Justice Facts at a Glance." June 2, 2006.
http://www.ojp.usdoj.gov/bjs/glance/jailrace.htm

FIGURE 14.2   Jail Population by Race and Ethnicity, 1990–2005

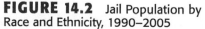

divided into three basic security or custody levels for inmates: minimum security, medium security, and maximum security.[8]

Types of Prisons

U.S. prisons are ranked into three basic types according to the security risks inmates present.

Minimum-security prisons house inmates who are considered to be low security risks.

Medium-security prisons are designed to house prisoners who are considered more dangerous and more prone to escape.

Maximum-security prisons have been carefully designed to house the most dangerous and most violent inmates.

(1) **Minimum-security prisons** house inmates who are considered to be low security risks. Many of these facilities have relaxed perimeter security, at times without fences or any other means of security, such as armed guards. Dormitories replace cells, and the dress codes are somewhat flexible. The prisoners are among the least violent inmates; many are white-collar offenders.

(2) **Medium-security prisons** are designed to house prisoners who are considered more dangerous and more prone to escape than inmates in minimum-security facilities, but less violence-prone than those in maximum-security facilities. Unlike a minimum-security prison, a medium facility will have single or double fencing, closed-circuit television monitoring, or guarded towers.

(3) **Maximum-security prisons** have been carefully designed to house the most dangerous and most violent inmates. They are typically surrounded by very high walls, multiple-perimeter fences, armed guards, and elaborate security measures including electronic monitoring systems. The governing principle and assumption underlying maximum security is that the "physical characteristics of the prison will be such that complete control of any and all prisoners can be realized at any time."[9]

Boot camps are forms of imprisonment that are styled after the U.S. military basic-training model.

In the late 1980s and into the 1990s, correctional **boot camps** styled after the U.S. military basic-training model were increasingly employed in about twenty states to deal with the ever-increasing problem of prison overcrowding and the public demand for more severe treatment of prisoners.[10] Unlike many more

PROFILES

Prisoners

- More than 2 million prisoners are being held in federal or state prisons or in local jails. About 1.5 million prisoners are under the jurisdiction of state or federal correctional authorities.
- In 1980, there were only 329,821 inmates in our state and federal prisons. In 1992, the number was 883,593.
- There are about 500 prison inmates per 100,000 U.S. residents. This is up from 292 at the end of 1990.
- There are about 113 female inmates per 100,000 women in the United States, compared to 1,309 male inmates per 100,000 men.
- There are 462 white male inmates per 100,000 white males in the United States, compared to 1,117

sentenced Hispanic male inmates per 100,000 Hispanic males, and 3,535 sentenced black male prisoners per 100,000 black males.

Sources: U.S. Department of Justice, Office of Justice Programs, Bureau of Justice Statistics, "Prison Statistics," April 6, 2003, **http://www.ojp.usdoj.gov/bjs/prisons.htm**, "Criminal Offenders Statistics," January 8, 2003, **http://www.ojp.usdoj.gov/bjs/crimoff.htm**, and "Reentry Trends in the United States," June 13, 2003, **http://www.ojp.usdoj.gov/bjs/reentry/reentry.htm**; P. M. Harrison and J. C. Karberg, *Prison and Jail Inmates at Midyear 2002*, bulletin of the Bureau of Justice Statistics, NCJ-198877, Washington, DC, April 2003; D. K. Gilliard, *Prisoners in 1992*, bulletin of the Bureau of Justice Statistics, NCJ-141874, Washington, DC, May 1993, pp. 1–11.

traditional correctional facilities, boot-camp programs are typically characterized by physical training, strict discipline, military bearing and courtesy, drill and ceremony, physical labor, and summary punishment for minor violations of rules.[11]

Prisoners and Prison Populations

Incarceration rates greatly increased during the 1980s and 1990s, especially for violent crimes, and more women served time than in the past.

- According to the Bureau of Justice Statistics, lifetime chances of an individual going to prison are higher for men (9 percent) than for women (1.1 percent); higher for blacks (16.2 percent) and Hispanics (9.4 percent) than for whites (2.5 percent); based on current rates of first incarceration, an estimated 28 percent of black males will enter state or federal prison during their lifetime, compared to 16 percent of Hispanic males and 4 percent of white males.
- Between 1990 and 2000, an increasing number of violent offenders accounted for 53 percent of the total growth of the state prison population; 20 percent of the total growth was attributable to an increasing number of drug offenders (see Figure 14.3).
- If recent incarceration rates remain unchanged, an estimated one of every twenty persons (5.1 percent) will serve time in a prison during his or her lifetime.
- After dramatic increases in the 1980s and 1990s, the incarceration rate has recently leveled off (see Figure 14.4).[12]

Prison Conditions

Prison conditions in the United States are generally poor and may contribute to "prison pathology."

In general, conditions in U.S. prisons are much better than in jails. The majority of prisons have better management policies than jails and generally maintain educational, recreational, employment, and other supportive programs.[13]

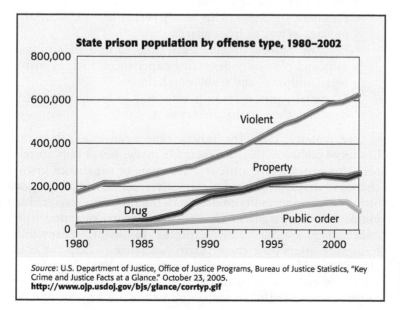

Source: U.S. Department of Justice, Office of Justice Programs, Bureau of Justice Statistics, "Key Crime and Justice Facts at a Glance." October 23, 2005.
http://www.ojp.usdoj.gov/bjs/glance/corrtyp.gif

FIGURE 14.3 State Prison Population by Offense Type, 1990–2002

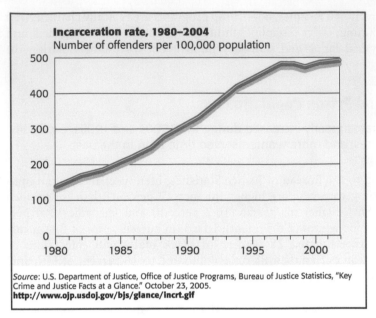

 is a figure above the caption. The figure itself contains:

Incarceration rate, 1980–2004
Number of offenders per 100,000 population

Source: U.S. Department of Justice, Office of Justice Programs, Bureau of Justice Statistics, "Key Crime and Justice Facts at a Glance." October 23, 2005.
http://www.ojp.usdoj.gov/bjs/glance/incrt.gif

FIGURE 14.4 Incarceration Rate, 1980–2004

More advanced prison systems apply a variety of treatment modalities, ranging from different types of therapies (reality therapy, behavior modification, drug and alcohol counseling, and skill-development programs) to self-help programs such as Alcoholics Anonymous, Narcotics Anonymous, and Gamblers Anonymous.[14] Many correctional institutions provide nutritional food services, good medical care, libraries, and visiting and recreational facilities. However, some state prisons continue to provide inadequate to poor food and medical services.[15]

Despite the many positive goals, programs, and services in the majority of our nation's correctional facilities, the reality of the prison experience is often quite different for prisoners. Researchers report the following:

- Many prison atmospheres are oppressive and punitive, and many prisoners are subject to harsh discipline and repressive policies.
- Elaborate systems of regulation circumscribe much of a prisoner's daily behavior: how and when to eat, work, sleep, and so forth.
- Violence, including organized violence, is a way of life in many prisons.
- Prisoners are exposed to much verbal and physical abuse from other inmates as well as from guards.
- In many prisons, offenders are exposed to a wide range of psychologically and physically degrading experiences, such as strip searches, numbered uniforms, and regulation haircuts.
- Ultimately, prisons punish offenders in many ways other than simply depriving them of their freedom.[16]

For inmates, then, the prison experience is a dehumanizing, punitive, hostility-building experience that, for many, serves only to reinforce criminal behavior patterns and attitudes. This type of experience gives offenders little chance to develop respect for themselves, for others, or for society and offers little, if any, opportunity to deal with the problems responsible for their commitment in the first place. The system segregates offenders from the society to which they are ultimately expected to adapt; meanwhile, that society frequently offers little constructive assistance to help the offenders function effectively and acceptably in the community when released.[17]

Additional indicators of the oppressive atmosphere of some correctional institutions in the United States can be obtained by examining the quality of the prisoners' living facilities. Many prisons lack adequate living space due to overcrowding caused by the significant increases in incarceration. Researchers have associated prison overcrowding with increased violent behavior, increased disciplinary infractions, suicide, and violent deaths.[18]

According to psychologist Philip G. Zimbardo, prison conditions may contribute to a "pathology of imprisonment." What happens to people when they are labeled as "outsiders," "worthless animals," and "criminals," and are placed in a situation where they have to live with these labels? What happens to those who are given virtually total power over the actions and lives of these "outsiders"? How do both groups react when told that it is only an experiment and they are only playing roles? What actually happens in the American prison system?[19]

Despite generally poor conditions in U.S. prisons, some prisons in a few states have been described as "country clubs," with swimming pools and tennis courts on prison grounds, VCRs, DVDs, cable TV, and computers connected to the Internet, phones, and fax machines in prisoners' cells. In various parts of the country, some prisoners in minimum-security facilities are allowed to have full clothing wardrobes in their cells, work all day in the community and return to the prison at night, have weekend conjugal visits with their spouses, are permitted to have weekend visits at home, and attend college and obtain undergraduate degrees or degrees in law and other fields at no cost to themselves. Critics of lenient prison policies and those who advocate the "get tough on crime" approach have questioned why we bother to send convicts to prison when conditions in some prisons are better than those "on the outside."

Releases from State Prisons, Rearrests, and Reentry Trends

In America, over two-thirds of released prisoners are rearrested within three years.

Almost 600,000 state prison inmates are annually released to the community after serving time in prison. According to the Bureau of Justice Statistics, these releases represent about a 45 percent increase over the 405,400 offenders released in 1990. The *release rate* is the number of releases per 100 sentenced prisoners at the beginning of each year, plus the number admitted during the year. The release rate of state prisoners declined from 37 percent in 1990 to 31 percent in 1994. Since 1994, the rate of release has remained stable: it is about 31 to 32 percent today. About 33 percent of annual state prison releases are for drug offenders (up from 26 percent in 1990). Twenty-five percent are violent offenders (the same as 1990), and 31 percent are property offenders (down from 39 percent in 1990).[20]

In terms of method of release, since 1990 mandatory parole releases have increased, while discretionary releases have decreased. *Discretionary parole* exists when a parole board has authority to conditionally release prisoners based on a statutory or administrative determination of eligibility. *Mandatory parole* generally occurs in jurisdictions using determinate-sentencing statutes, in which inmates are conditionally released from prison after serving a specified portion of their original sentence minus any "good time" earned.[21]

Results of a fifteen-state study indicate that over two-thirds (67.5 percent) of released prisoners were rearrested within three years. In fact, almost 52 percent of the prisoners released during the year studied returned to prison either because of a new crime (for which they received another sentence) or because of a parole violation.[22] Herein lies the chief failure of the U.S. correctional system, according to its critics.

After reading this section, you should be able to

1. define *jail* and *prison* and distinguish between the types of prisons;
2. summarize facts about prison populations, rates, characteristics, and trends;
3. characterize prison conditions in the United States;
4. evaluate statistics on rates of prison release, rearrest, and reentry in the United States.

14.4 COMMUNITY-BASED CORRECTIONS: PROBATION

Community-based corrections are correctional measures that are applied in the community rather than in jails and prisons. Types of community-based corrections include the following:

- *Pretrial release,* the release of an individual from pretrial detention or jail pending case adjudication.
- *Diversion,* the development of alternatives to the formal justice system such as resolution of citizen disputes.
- *Probation,* the correctional service that allows an offender, under the supervision of a probation officer, to remain in the community while complying with court-imposed conditions.
- *Reentry programs* (work-release centers, halfway houses, etc.).
- *Parole,* the release—under the custody of the state—of an offender after the offender has served a portion of his or her sentence.

Community-based corrections are rooted in the nineteenth century, began to grow in the early twentieth century, and blossomed in the 1960s and early 1970s.[23] In the mid-1970s, national sentiment changed to a "get tough with criminals" approach; the publication of crime statistics and the media coverage of street crime convinced the public that crime was out of hand.

According to Clemens Bartollas and John P. Conrad, the "permissive" approach that "kept offenders in the community became less and less acceptable. Supporters of the punishment model were quick to urge incarceration as a more fitting way of dealing with crime."[24] In spite of financial pressures and declining government and social support for community-based corrections in the 1970s, crowding in correctional institutions significantly increased the use of community-based corrections during the 1980s: "Federal court orders in thirty-six states to relieve crowded prison conditions meant that the states had to do something. Although prison construction remained a possible long-term solution, more immediate relief was clearly needed. Community-based corrections, particularly probation and parole, suddenly gained favor of judges and politicians, and the number of those on probation soon skyrocketed and of those on parole significantly increased."[25]

Far fewer criminal offenders are confined in prisons than are involved in community-based corrections. Probation is a way to keep offenders in the community while they comply with court-imposed conditions. Under the supervision of a probation officer, **probation** is the correctional service that allows an offender to remain in the community while complying with certain rules and conditions imposed by the court. Probation involves the *suspension* of a sentence *conditional on good behavior* with community supervision imposed for a certain period of time. In other words, probation allows a convicted person to remain at liberty while subject to certain conditions and restrictions.[26]

Probation is the correctional service that allows an offender to remain in the community while complying with court-imposed conditions.

Major Objectives of Probation

During the past fifteen years the objectives of probation have changed. The following are considered to be the five major objectives of probation in the United States currently:

1. To protect the community
2. To execute the sanctions imposed by the court
3. To assist offenders to change
4. To support victims of crime
5. To effectively utilize and coordinate community resources for substance abuse treatment, vocational evaluation, and job training for probationers

Sources: B. R. McCarthy and B. J. McCarthy Jr., *Community-Based Corrections*, 3rd ed., Belmont, CA: Wadsworth, 1997, p. 97; H. Boon, B. Fulton, et al., *Results-Driven Management Implementing Performance-Based Measures in Community Corrections*, Lexington, KY: American Probation and Parole Association, 1995, p. 39.

In the United States, four times as many criminals are placed on probation as are sent to correctional facilities. According to the Bureau of Justice Statistics (BJS), more than 4 million adults are under federal-, state-, or local-jurisdiction probation.

- Among offenders on probation, slightly more than half (53 percent) have been convicted for committing a felony, 45 percent for a misdemeanor, and 1 percent for other infractions.
- Women constitute about 22 percent of the nation's probationers.
- Approximately 55 percent of the adults on probation are white, 31 percent are black, and 12 percent are Hispanic.[27]

Probation has its roots in English common law, which allowed clergymen accused of crime to be released from criminal courts and dealt with by the church. In the United States, probation dates back to 1841, when Boston shoemaker John Augustus was successful in obtaining court releases for offenders to whom he provided rehabilitative assistance. His efforts on behalf of offenders also led to the development of the bail system. As a formal correctional system in the United States, however, probation did not develop until the twentieth century.

The Model Penal Code and Probation Outcomes

Standards for sentencing to probation are specified in the Model Penal Code.

The *Model Penal Code* was established in 1962 to improve consistency and reasonableness in the application of penal sanctions in the United States. The code lists criteria for probation. Judges do not always follow the criteria, however; they may sentence offenders to probation who should be incarcerated or incarcerate offenders who should be put on probation. Several states prohibit judges from granting probation to convicted felons, but in most states convicted felons may be granted probation.

The Model Penal Code on Probation

According to the Model Penal Code, the following criteria determine eligibility for probation:

1. The offender's crime did not cause or threaten serious harm.
2. The offender did not intend to cause or threaten serious harm but acted under strong provocation.
3. There were substantial mitigating circumstances that tend to excuse or justify what the offender did.
4. The victim induced or aided in the commission of the crime.
5. The offender has compensated, or will compensate, the victim for damages the offender has caused; has no prior criminal record or has led a law-abiding life for a considerable period of time and is likely to benefit from probation.
6. The offender's criminal conduct took place in circumstances unlikely to recur; character and attitude indicate unlikely future criminal conduct.
7. Imprisonment would cause undue hardship to the offender and the offender's family.

Source: American Law Institute, *Model Penal Code: Official Draft and Explanatory Notes*, Philadelphia: American Law Institute, 1985, sec. 7.01.

Under the federal criminal code and in many states, serving a jail term may be a condition of probation. This is termed *split sentencing.* Between 15 and 20 percent of convicted federal offenders receive some type of split sentence that includes jail or prison time as a condition of probation. As more stringent sentencing laws take effect, this percentage is expected to increase in the future.[28]

Conditions of probation vary from one community to another, but common requirements include restitution to victims, payment of fines, random drug testing, and community-service assignments. Many of these conditions of probation meet the desire to consider victims' needs first and then to teach offenders responsible behavior.[29]

If the probationer violates the rules of probation in what is termed a **technical violation,** his or her probation may be revoked by the court. The individual begins serving the original sentence or, if never sentenced, is then sentenced by the court. Of course, the offender will have his or her probation revoked if another offense is committed.

The success of probation is questionable. In a major study by the Rand Corporation, Joan Petersilia and her associates followed almost 1,700 men who were granted probation in California for felony offenses. The results of a forty-month follow-up study indicated that 65 percent (almost 1,100 men) were rearrested; 51 percent (over 850) were convicted; and over 34 percent (568) were incarcerated. Significantly, 75 percent of the new charges reported were for such serious crimes as robbery, burglary, and larceny. Eighteen percent of the men were convicted of serious violent crimes.[30]

Probationers nevertheless did better in the community than offenders released from prison after serving their sentences. In another study comparing more than 500 released offenders with more than 500 probationers

A probationer who violates the rules of probation is said to have committed a **technical violation,** in which case probation may be revoked.

matched for gender, crime, and the like, Petersilia and associates reported a higher rate of recidivism among released prisoners than probationers. For example, 63 percent of the probationers were rearrested compared with 72 percent of the released prisoners. In addition, 38 percent of the probationers had new charges filed against them, compared with 53 percent of the ex-prisoners. Only about one-third (31 percent) of the probationers were reincarcerated, compared with almost half (47 percent) of the ex-prisoners. The report also stated that, in spite of the fact that there were more new offenses committed by ex-prisoners, they were no more serious than those committed by probationers.[31]

Cassia Spohn and David Holleran recently studied the effect of imprisonment on recidivism rates of felony offenders in Missouri. The purpose of their study was to evaluate the deterrent effect of imprisonment. They compared **recidivism** rates—rates of repeat offending—for offenders placed on probation with those for offenders sentenced to prison. Their findings include the following:

> **Recidivism** is the term for repeat offending. A recidivist is someone who repeatedly commits crimes.

- There is no evidence that imprisonment reduces the likelihood of recidivism.
- Offenders sentenced to prison have higher rates of recidivism.
- Offenders sentenced to prison recidivate more quickly than offenders who are placed on probation.
- Imprisonment appears to have a clearer "criminogenic" effect on drug offenders than on non–drug offenders.[32]

Shock Probation and Intensive Probation Supervision

Shock probation gives offenders a prison experience to deter them from further offending, whereas intensive probation supervision involves proactive monitoring in the community.

A variation on probation as an alternative to prison is **shock probation**, which is granted by the court following a brief period of incarceration. Shock probation is based on the idea that, if an offender had a sample of what prison is "all about," he or she would be more likely to follow the guidelines of his or her period of probation and less likely to commit another crime. Shock probation, also sometimes called shock incarceration, also enables judges to grant offenders community alternatives after having the experience of prison life.

> **Shock probation** is an alternative to prison that is granted by the court following a brief period of incarceration.

Basically, under shock probation, the offender is resentenced after he or she is incarcerated for a few months:

- The offender is first given a long maximum sentence by the court.
- He or she is then eligible for supervised community release at the judge's discretion.
- The offender does not know when he or she will be released on probation.
- After serving some time, the offender may petition the court for probation.
- Judges may permit the offender to serve the remainder of his or her sentence on probation only if he or she qualifies according to the guidelines set by the court.

In studies on the effectiveness of shock probation compared to regular probation, some researchers report that shock probationers had a 17 percent rate of reincarceration versus an 11 percent rate for regular probationers. Other studies have reported that shock probation is 80 to 90 percent effective.[33]

Intensive probation supervision (IPS) or Intensive supervised probation (ISP) is a type of probation in which small caseloads of clients are monitored intensively in the community by probation officers.

Another variation of probation that has been implemented in the great majority of states is termed **intensive probation supervision (IPS)** or **intensive supervised probation (ISP)**. In this type of probation, small caseloads of fifteen to forty clients are monitored intensively in the community by probation officers. The goals of IPS are

1. to divert offenders who would have normally been sent to overcrowded prisons;
2. to have better control over high-risk offenders in the community through more rigorous security procedures than in traditional probation programs;
3. to reorient offenders toward a more productive life;
4. to reintegrate offenders into society by maintaining community ties and avoiding the problems of imprisonment.[34]

Although some research has reported success with such programs, it remains to be seen whether IPS can significantly reduce offenses in the community.[35]

After reading this section, you should be able to

1. describe the main categories of community-based corrections;
2. define *probation* and list its five major objectives;
3. identify criteria for determining eligibility for probation according to the Model Penal Code;
4. explain how shock probation and intensive probation supervision (IPS) work.

14.5 OTHER INTERMEDIATE SANCTIONS AND ALTERNATIVES

Intermediate sanctions are punishments that are less severe than incarceration but more involved than probation.

Intermediate sanctions is the term given to punishments that fall short of incarceration but involve more than standard probation. Steps beyond intensive probation supervision, for example, include home confinement, or house arrest, and high-tech monitoring. Other intermediate sanctions are restitution, forfeiture, and fines.

Home Confinement and Electronic Monitoring

House arrest and electronic monitoring have become popular measures in community-based corrections today.

Home confinement is the sentencing of offenders to confinement in their own residence or in an alternative shelter or group home for the duration of their sentence.

Home confinement, or house arrest, is increasingly used throughout the United States as a low-cost alternative to imprisonment. Given the high cost of maintaining prisoners, many state courts are sentencing offenders to confinement in their own residence or in an alternative shelter or group home for the duration of their sentence. The convict spends extended periods of time in his or her house or apartment instead of in a jail or prison cell. If permitted by the court, the convict may leave the house for work, health care, or a religious function. At times, house convicts are required to pay probation-supervision fees or victim restitution by performing community service.

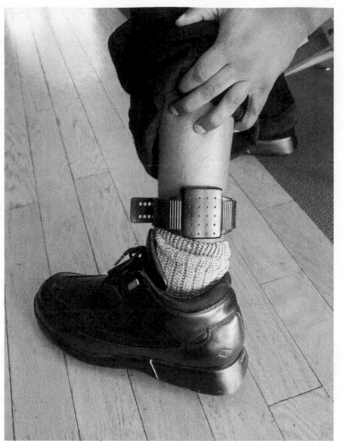

This criminal offender is wearing an electronic monitoring device on his ankle. Which type of high-tech monitoring device, active or passive, is this offender probably wearing?

Annually, there are approximately 10,000 people placed under house arrest in the United States. About 50,000 people across the nation already sentenced to house arrest are also electronically monitored. The number of criminal offenders who are electronically monitored has grown from less than one hundred in 1986 to the tens of thousands in the 1990s and may soon grow into the hundreds of thousands.[36]

Electronic monitoring involves having criminal offenders wear—on the neck, ankle, or wrist—an electronic device that sends signals to a control office. Some devices track the offender's location and movements. Some systems (active) send a continuous signal to the control office. If the offender leaves his or her house without authorization, the signal is broken, and the authorities are alerted and able to respond accordingly. Other electronic-monitoring systems (passive) will, through computer generation, phone the convict, who then has to respond by voice or monitoring device within a designated time frame.

House arrest combined with electronic monitoring is viewed by some as a revolutionary development in American correctional policy because of its effectiveness and low costs combined with its attractiveness as an alternative to overcrowded prisons. Criminologists and corrections researchers are currently studying a wide variety of issues related to electronically monitored house arrest, including the legal, constitutional, and ethical aspects involved—from the potential for excessive government intrusion into citizens' lives to the operational aspects of the systems.[37]

Electronic monitoring involves having criminal offenders wear—on the neck, ankle, or wrist—an electronic device that sends signals to a control office.

Restitution, Forfeiture, and Fines

Other intermediate sanctions are victim-focused and require offenders to make up for their offenses against the community.

Restitution is an intermediate sanction that requires an offender to pay damages to the victim (*monetary restitution*) or to perform community service (*community-service restitution*) as punishment for his or her criminal acts. It is cost-beneficial and enables less serious offenders the opportunity to engage in a constructive activity. Today, many thousands of misdemeanants serve their time by performing a wide variety of community, health, and welfare services in places ranging from schools to nursing homes and hospitals. In addition to benefiting the community, the criminal justice system, the offender, and the victim, restitution programs have saved communities thousands of dollars that would have been spent to maintain offenders in detention centers and correctional facilities.

People are supportive of restitution programs because they achieve the utilitarian goal of punishment and the goal of ensuring just deserts.[38] According to researchers, restitution works well in the United States in that 75 to 90 percent of offenders fulfilled their restitution orders. A similar percentage of offenders had no subsequent contact with the criminal justice systems.[39]

Even though in some states forfeiture is a civil matter, **forfeiture** is primarily a criminal sanction that involves the seizing of an offender's real and personal property. As mentioned in Chapter 11, forfeiture reappeared in the U.S. criminal justice system with the passage of the Racketeer Influenced and Corrupt Organizations Act (RICO) and the Continuing Criminal Enterprises Act (CCE). These measures legally enable various law enforcement agencies to seize any and all property derived from illegal conspiracies and enterprises. Forfeiture has been used extensively by the government to seize the enormous illegal profits of drug dealers and pornography rings and has also been used against white-collar criminals.

Fines are intermediate sanctions that require the convicted defendant to make a monetary payment as punishment for his or her criminal act. Fines are more common in misdemeanors and may be used as the only sanction. Fines may also be levied in addition to imprisonment or probation.

> **Forfeiture** is a criminal sanction that involves the seizing of an offender's real and personal property.

After reading this section, you should be able to

1. define intermediate sanctions;
2. explain home confinement and electronic monitoring as intermediate sanctions;
3. describe the use of restitution, forfeiture, and fines in addition to suspended sentences with probation.

14.6 PAROLE

Parole is the conditional release of a prisoner before a full sentence has been served. It refers to the release of an offender from a correctional institution after part of the sentence has been served, on the condition that the offender remain under the custody and supervision of the institution (or other state-approved agency) until a final discharge is granted. Parole was initially

> **Parole** is the conditional release of a prisoner before a full sentence has been served.

adopted as a formal release system in 1876 with the creation of the Elmira Reformatory in New York State. The **Elmira system** employed indeterminate sentences and early supervised release for good behavior. The system of combining parole with indeterminate sentencing spread rather quickly. By 1922, forty-five states had enacted parole laws; by 1944, all states had adopted such legislation.

The **Elmira system** employed indeterminate sentences and early supervised release for good behavior.

Methods of Parole Release and Parolee Characteristics

Almost 80 percent of all state prisoners will be released to parole supervision through discretionary or mandatory parole.

Record-high numbers of people are on parole at the state level. Currently there are about 660,000 adults under state parole supervision (up from 502,000 in 1990).[40] There are two methods of parole release:

(1) *Discretionary parole* exists when a parole board has authority to conditionally release prisoners based on a statutory or administrative determination of eligibility. Discretionary releases to parole have dropped from 39 percent of releases in 1990 to the 20 to 25 percent range today. Currently about sixteen states have abolished discretionary parole for all offenders.

(2) *Mandatory parole* generally occurs in jurisdictions using determinate-sentencing statutes in which inmates are conditionally released from prison after serving a specified portion of their original sentence minus any good time earned. Mandatory releases to parole have steadily increased from 117,000 in 1990 to about 250,000 today (from about 29 percent to about 45 percent).[41]

A prisoner becomes eligible for parole only after serving a specific part of the sentence. The decision to grant parole is made by an authority such as a *parole board,* which has the power to grant or revoke parole (or to discharge a parolee altogether). A parole board typically has exclusive responsibility for determining when an offender may be released. It also specifies the conditions of parole. When making a decision on a release, most members of parole boards are primarily concerned with evaluating whether the offender is likely to commit a serious crime while on parole, whether the person would benefit from a continued period of confinement, and whether the offender would become a worse risk if confinement continued. Granting parole is an "administrative decision," whereas probation is exclusively a function of the criminal courts.

The parolee is under the supervision of a community parole officer for the balance of his or her unexpired sentence. As with probation, this supervision is governed by specific conditions of release, and the parolee may be returned to prison for violations of such conditions.[42]

Persons entering state parole are now older than those who entered parole in 1990 (from thirty-one to thirty-four years). The racial and ethnic composition is as follows: 41 percent blacks, 39 percent whites, and 19 percent Hispanics. About 12 percent of entries to state parole are female. The background characteristics of state prisoners expected to be released to the community during a one-year period recently studied by the BJS were as follows:

- Fifty-six percent had one or more prior incarcerations, and 25 percent had three or more prior incarcerations.
- Eighty-four percent reported being involved in drugs or alcohol at the time of the offense that led to their incarceration.
- Nearly 25 percent were assessed as being alcohol-dependent.

Parole

- At least 95 percent of all state prisoners will be released from prison at some point. Almost 80 percent will be released to parole supervision.
- From 1990 to 2001, the state parole population grew at a slower rate than the state prison population.
- As reported earlier, the rate of growth in the prison population has slowed since 1999. This slowdown is partially due to the rise in the number of releases from prison (from 400,000 in 1990 to over 600,000 annual releases today).
- Relative to the prison population, the growth in the state parole population was much more modest (increasing from 500,000 in 1990 to 650,000 by 2001).

- On average, from 1990 to 2001 the prison population increased 5.3 percent per year. The state parole population rose 2.4 percent per year. However, since 1999, the rate of growth in state prisons has nearly stabilized.
- The low rate of growth in parole supervision relative to the growth in the prison population reflects changes in sentencing and parole release policies. These changes have resulted in increasing lengths of stay in prison and declining prison release rates.

Source: U.S. Department of Justice, Office of Justice Programs, Bureau of Justice Statistics, "Reentry Trends in the United States," October 25, 2002, **http://www.ojp.usdoj.gov/bjs/reentry/characteristics.htm**.

- Twenty-one percent had committed the offense to obtain money for drugs.
- Fourteen percent were assessed as mentally ill.
- Twelve percent reported being homeless at the time of the arrest.[43]

Parole Outcomes

Research suggests that the success of parole as a deterrent to crime is debatable.

Does parole reduce recidivism? Does it help the parolee adjust to life in the community? In the 1970s, Irvin Waller compared arrest rates of male discharges and parolees at six, twelve, and twenty-four months following prison release. Arrest rates were lower for parolees at six months, but no differences existed at twelve and twenty-four months. Waller reported, "The effectiveness of parole in terms of reducing recidivism within twelve months and twenty-four months, or in the long run, is an illusion."[44]

Howard Sacks and Charles Logan studied parolees who were already in the community and prisoners who were released directly from prison, and found that parolees were significantly less likely to fail than released prisoners when measured by such factors as time of the first conviction, seriousness of the offense, and time in the community as opposed to time incarcerated.[45] Nevertheless, a 1989 federal study of 16,000 parolees in eleven states reported that, within three years, 63 percent had been rearrested for a serious misdemeanor or felony, and 47 percent had been convicted of a new crime (41 percent were sent back to prison).[46]

What are the more recent success rates for state parolees? Before examining the data, three terms must be defined:

1. *Discharges* refers to individuals exiting parole supervision.
2. *Successful discharges* include persons who have completed the term of conditional supervision.

3. *Unsuccessful discharges* include revocations of parole, returns to prison or jail, and absconders. Parolees who are transferred to other jurisdictions and those who die while under supervision are not included in the calculation of success/failure rates.[47]

Among state parole discharges in a recent year studied by the Bureau of Justice Statistics,

- forty-three percent were returned to prison or jail;
- forty-two percent successfully completed their term of supervision (relatively unchanged since 1990);
- ten percent absconded.

Additional findings include the following:

- In every year during the 1990s, first releases were more likely to have been successful on parole than re-releases. (*Re-releases* are persons leaving prison after having served time either for a violation of parole or other conditional release or for a new offense committed while under parole supervision.)
- In every year between 1990 and 1999, state prisoners released by a parole board had higher success rates than those released through mandatory parole.
- Among parole discharges in 1999, 54 percent of discretionary parolees were successful compared to 33 percent of those who received mandatory parole.[48]

During the past two decades, parole has been under attack. In his analysis of parole, Joel Samaha reports that the following factors have contributed to this attack: "the decline in rehabilitation as a correctional policy, the growth of determinate and mandatory sentencing, the efforts to control discretion in criminal justice, and the resurgence of retribution and incapacitation as penal policies."[49] Determinate and mandatory sentencing have been replacing the indeterminate sentences that prevailed in the past. The indeterminate sentence is at the core of parole. In many states it is being replaced by mandatory, flat, or presumptive sentencing (a statutorily determined prison sentence that offenders who have been convicted will presumably receive if committed by the court to prison) that seriously limits eligibility for parole.

Both conservatives and liberals oppose parole. Conservatives oppose it because they see it as based on invalid rehabilitation policies that coddle criminals by releasing them well before their sentenced time. Liberals argue that parole boards have too much discretionary power and are irrational and discriminatory.[50] Andrew von Hirsch and Kathleen J. Hanrahan, in an analysis of abolishing parole, report the following criticisms: "[P]rocedures that govern the decision to grant parole are vague and have not been controlled by due process considerations. . . . [S]ome inmates may be subject to the unfair denial of parole, while some who are undeserving may benefit. . . . [P]arole authorities [are unable] to either predict who will make a successful adjustment on parole or to accurately monitor parolees' behavior in the community. It is unjust to decide whether to release an individual from prison based on what we expect that person to do in the future. After all, we have no way of determining that accurately."[51]

Parole boards have been abolished in the federal government and in sixteen states. In an analysis of corrections, Bartollas and Conrad report that, although the movement to abolish parole may have peaked in the United States, limitations have been placed "on the discretion of paroling authorities in many states, particularly concerning the release and supervision of offenders."[52] That is,

The Truth about Polly Klaas

Richard Allen Davis was a dangerous violent felon. He was sentenced to life in prison in 1976 for kidnapping and other violent crimes. His criminal record was littered with instance after instance of predatory behavior. The paroling authority in the State of California knew this. His disregard for human life and safety, even while in prison, was a profound reminder of the need to keep this individual isolated from the community as long as possible. While in prison, the parole board reviewed his case six times, and six times the parole board rejected any possibility of release.

But the forces of change were at work in California. Politicians pledged to be "tough on crime." The obvious answer—"Abolish parole." And they got their wish. The requirement of earning the approval of the parole board before even a dangerous offender could be released was abolished. New standard sentences mandated automatic release after service of a set portion of the sentence. Offenders already incarcerated came under the provisions of the new law. Release dates were churned out by the prison system's computers for thousands of prisoners then in custody. When the computers had done their job, there was no turning back. Richard Allen Davis had already served the amount of prison time that the new law and its mandatory release provisions demanded. He had a mandatory sentence alright—including a mandatory release. On the night of June 27, 1993, Richard Allen Davis walked out of prison, a free man. Less than four months later, in the safe darkness of a girlhood slumber party, Richard Allen Davis is alleged to have kidnapped and brutally murdered a little girl. Her name was Polly Klaas.

No one can say with certainty all that would have happened to Richard Allen Davis if parole had not been abolished in California. But there is overwhelming evidence that if the parole board had still been in control of release, Richard Allen Davis would have been in prison the night that Polly Klaas was murdered.[1]

[1]Information from California Board of Prison Terms.

Source: Abolishing Parole: Why the Emperor Has No Clothes, American Probation and Parole Association, 1995. Used by permission.

guidelines have been developed for deciding whether inmates are eligible for parole. The degree of professionalism of the parole board and the consistency of supervision practices have been debated by penologists. To some researchers, parole has been called upon to "be responsive to the competing concerns of the public, victims, and offenders."[53]

After reading this section, you should be able to

1. define parole and contrast parole with probation;
2. discuss the methods of parole release and issues surrounding those methods;
3. explain the main criteria parole boards use in granting parole;
4. summarize data on parolee characteristics and rates of parole violation;
5. explain why many people oppose parole and why the federal government and some states no longer use parole boards.

RELEASE AND REENTRY PROGRAMS

Reentry programs help offenders make the transition from a correctional institution to the community. Participation in a reentry program often is a condition of parole. The United States has the following types of reentry programs: prerelease, work release, educational release, home furlough, and halfway houses.

Prerelease programs enable inmates to attend a three- to four-week training program to prepare them for release into the community. The training includes information on such things as how to find and keep a job, getting a driver's license, and family responsibilities. In some states, prerelease training programs are mandatory, although their helpfulness and effectiveness are questionable.[54]

Over the past several decades, work-release programs have been used by many prison systems. Under **work-release programs**, the prisoner is allowed to leave the prison (or community treatment center or halfway house) for a certain number of hours each day to work or train in the community. Many states, such as New York, California, and Texas, with their large corrections departments, have only 1 to 2 percent of their prison populations in work-release programs. Because of our nation's high unemployment rates and pressure from citizens not to have work-release centers in their communities (released prisoners compete with regular citizens for jobs), the popularity of these programs has diminished in many states.[55]

Educational and occupational- and vocational-training programs have also been available for many prisoners. A number of U.S. trade schools, colleges, and universities provide courses in prisons for inmates who are qualified and express interest. In **educational-release programs**, inmates attend community colleges and universities in the surrounding area. Inmates from Trenton State Prison in Rahway, New Jersey, have attended Mercer Community College, for

A **work-release program** is a reentry program in which a prisoner is allowed to leave the prison (or community treatment center or halfway house) for a certain number of hours each day to work or train in the community.

Educational-release programs pay for prison inmates to attend colleges and universities.

Inmates can be assigned to a halfway house as an alternative to prison, which the community may or may not support. What are the goals of their participation in a halfway house program? What other reentry programs might be available to these probationers or parolees? According to the restorative justice model, what behaviors should be part of their reentry into the community?

example. Inmates in the California prison system have attended classes on the campuses of the University of California and returned at night to housing provided by the state.[56] Recently, however, many states have reduced or eliminated college prison programs due to budgetary restraints and political pressure to provide more college funding for the noncriminal population.

Furloughs and Halfway Houses

In addition to release programs, minimum-security reentry alternatives include home furlough and assignment to a halfway house.

Home-furlough programs enable inmates with minimum-security status, especially those living in work-release centers or halfway houses, to take a temporary leave from the institution. Furloughs, also called home visits, are usually on weekends and are from forty-eight to seventy-two hours in length. Although some states allow minimum-security inmates to have a furlough after serving only six months of time, most states restrict furloughs to inmates who are reaching the end of their prison term. Many states that regularly granted furloughs in the past have been much more restrictive recently due to the "get tough on criminals" attitude that has gained momentum over the past decade and the publicity given to criminals on leave who have committed serious crimes.[57]

The *halfway house* is a community-based corrections facility to which inmates are assigned either prior to or following a period of incarceration. Both probationers and parolees are placed in halfway houses. They serve the offender who is beginning his or her sentence ("halfway in") as an alternative to prison and those who are completing their sentences ("halfway out") to help in their community reintegration. Many provide group and individual counseling in areas such as substance abuse, employment, and family relationships. Researchers have reported that halfway houses are as effective as other alternatives in reducing rates of recidivism. They also help offenders find employment and probably cost less than imprisonment.[58]

Restorative Justice

The concept of restorative justice is a focus of community-based corrections today.

Throughout the 1960s and 1970s, the development of community-based corrections became one of the most significant changes in American corrections. Community-based programs are less costly than imprisonment and provide the potential for rehabilitating offenders and reintegrating them into the larger community. However, the effectiveness of rehabilitation efforts, whether in an institutional or community setting, has been called into serious question over the past decade or so. During the late 1980s and 1990s, there was a significant decrease in the emphasis placed on rehabilitative goals and a significant increase in a correctional policy based on incarceration, retribution, and deterrence, particularly for serious criminal offenders.

Recently, however, many Americans have called for the application of restorative justice to traditional approaches in the criminal justice system. As Anne Seymour and Trudy Gregorie report, "The principles of restorative justice evoke a significant shift from America's traditionally retributive approach to justice."[59]

Restorative justice has been viewed as a philosophy for justice and fairness. During the past several years, this philosophy has taken on important

Restorative justice is a judicial approach "based upon a shared set of values that determines how conflicts can be resolved and how damaged relationships can be repaired or improved."

TABLE 14.1   CHARACTERISTICS OF THE RETRIBUTIVE AND RESTORATIVE MODELS OF JUSTICE

Retributive Justice	Restorative Justice
Crimes are acts against the state.	Crimes are acts against another individual or the community.
Crime is controlled by the criminal justice system.	Crime control comes from the community.
Punishment holds offenders accountable.	Assuming responsibility and taking action to remedy harm result in accountability.
Victims are part of the community protected by the criminal justice system.	Victims are harmed by crime and are central in determining accountability.
Justice is pursued through the adversarial system.	Justice is pursued using dialogue and reconciliation, negotiation, and reparation.
The focus is on punishing the crime that occurred in the past.	The focus is on the consequences of the crime and on how to make the victim and community whole again.
Punishment changes behavior through retribution and deterrence.	Punishment alone is not effective, because it disrupts possibilities for harmony within the community.

Source: J. S. Albanese, *Criminal Justice,* brief ed., p. 400. Published by Allyn & Bacon, Boston, MA. Copyright © 2001 by Pearson Education. Reprinted by permission of the publisher.

practical applications as it supplants the retributive model. Researchers state that restorative justice is "based upon a shared set of values that determines how conflicts can be resolved and how damaged relationships can be repaired or improved."[60] Katherine Van Wormer believes that restorative justice does not condemn the *actor* but condemns the criminal *act*. She states that restorative justice "holds offenders accountable, involves all participants, and encourages repentant offenders to earn their way back into good standing in society."[61]

As a value-based approach to criminal justice, the idea of restorative justice causes confusion and controversy among justice professionals who are traditionally based in agency structure and the retributive model.[62] Table 14.1 compares and contrasts retributive and restorative justice.

READING ABSTRACT

Restorative Justice for Young Offenders and Their Victims

BY ANNE SEYMOUR AND TRUDY GREGORIE

In this reading the authors examine the application of restorative justice to the traditional approaches in U.S. criminal justice—especially juvenile justice. The authors present seven core values of restorative justice developed at a conference sponsored by the National Institute of Corrections. The article then reviews restorative justice legislation and policy and victim's issues, followed by an analysis of the effectiveness of restorative justice. The reading concludes with a review of promising practices and victim awareness.

See reading on page 440.

After reading this section, you should be able to

1. describe several different types of reentry and release programs and their goals;
2. evaluate the effectiveness of reentry programs in helping offenders and protecting communities;
3. contrast the concepts and goals of restorative justice and retributive justice;
4. describe community corrections based on the concept of restorative justice;
5. based on Reading 14.2, evaluate the use of restorative justice in juvenile corrections.

CHAPTER SUMMARY

Corrections involve the treatment, incapacitation, and punishment of criminal offenders who have been convicted in a court of law. In the United States, there are about ten thousand correctional agencies—residential facilities, juvenile and adult probation and parole agencies, and so on—established to correct, treat, and administer postadjudicatory care to convicted criminal offenders.

Over the centuries, retribution has been a major social response to crime. Retribution is the notion that a wrongdoer should be punished in order to compensate for his or her criminal acts. Beccaria and Bentham argued that the proper objective of punishment should be to protect society and its laws. They believed that punishment should not be inflicted for vengeance; rather, the primary purpose of punishment should be the reduction or deterrence of crime.

The Quakers believed that imprisonment should have a deterrent function, but, more importantly, it should serve the purpose of reforming and rehabilitating the inmate as well. From the 1940s to the 1960s, rehabilitation of offenders, at least in theory, was a dominant goal of imprisonment and other forms of correction.

During the 1970s and into the 1980s, there was a return to retributivism, or the "justice model," which stresses that offenders are responsible people and, therefore, deserve to be punished if they violate the law (pp. 411–414).

Jails are basically local detention facilities. Prisons are federal or state correctional facilities for the incarceration of felony offenders for terms of longer than one year. There are over five hundred state and federal prisons in the United States.

In spite of many positive goals, programs, and services in the majority of our nation's correctional facilities, the reality of the prison experience is quite different for many prisoners. Researchers report that many prison atmospheres are oppressive and punitive, and many prisoners are subject to harsh discipline and repressive regulations (pp. 414–420).

Community-based corrections consist of pretrial release, diversion, probation, residential and reentry programs, and parole. Community-based corrections are rooted in the nineteenth century but blossomed in the 1960s and early 1970s.

Probation allows a convicted person to remain at liberty while subject to certain conditions and restrictions. If the probationer makes a technical violation, his or her probation may be revoked by the court. The success of probation is questionable. There are many variations on probation, such as shock probation and intensive probation supervision (IPS) (pp. 420–424).

Home confinement, or house arrest, is increasingly used throughout the United States as a low-cost alternative to imprisonment. The electronic monitoring of criminal offenders has also grown significantly during the past ten years. Restitution, forfeiture, and fines are additional intermediate sanctions used in the United States (pp. 424–426).

Parole is the conditional release of a prisoner before a full sentence has been served. During the past two decades, parole has come under attack by both conservatives and liberals. Parole boards have been dismantled in the federal government and in sixteen states (pp. 426–430).

Reentry programs, such as prerelease, work release, educational release, home furlough, and halfway houses, help offenders make the transition from a correctional institution to the community. Recently, many Americans have called for the application of restorative justice to traditional approaches in the criminal justice system (pp. 431–434).

Study Guide

Chapter Objectives

- Define corrections.
- Explain what is meant by the concept of retribution.
- Explain Beccaria and Bentham's views on punishment and deterrence.
- Describe the solitary system of imprisonment.
- Briefly discuss the silent system of imprisonment.
- Explain what is meant by rehabilitation of offenders.
- Briefly describe retributivism (the justice model).
- Define the utilitarian punishment model.
- Define jails and prisons.
- Describe prison populations, rates, characteristics, and trends.
- Briefly describe prison conditions in the United States.
- Examine U.S. prison release, rearrest, and reentry levels.

- Describe the main categories of community-based corrections.
- List the five major objectives of probation.
- List four of the many criteria that determine eligibility for probation according to the Model Penal Code.
- Explain shock probation *and* intensive probation supervision (IPS).
- Describe home confinement and electronic monitoring.
- Describe restitution, forfeiture, and fines.
- Define parole, and discuss issues regarding parole in the United States.
- Describe three reentry programs.
- Describe restorative justice.
- Examine the issues of restorative justice for juveniles.

Key Terms

Auburn system (413)
Boot camps (416)
Corrections (411)
Deterrence (412)
Educational-release programs (431)
Electronic monitoring (425)
Elmira system (427)
Forfeiture (426)
Home confinement (424)
Intensive probation supervision (IPS) (424)
Intensive supervised probation (ISP) (424)

Intermediate sanctions (424)
Jail (414)
Justice model (414)
Lex talionis (411)
Maximum-security prisons (416)
Medium-security prisons (416)
Minimum-security prisons (416)
Parole (426)
Pennsylvania system (413)
Prison (415)
Probation (420)
Recidivism (423)
Rehabilitation (413)

Restorative justice (432)
Retribution (411)
Retributivism (414)
Shock probation (423)
Silent system (413)
Solitary system (412)
Technical violation (422)
Utilitarian punishment model (414)
Work-release programs (431)

Self-Test
Multiple Choice

1. The famous Code of Hammurabi stressed the doctrine of
   a. *mens rea*
   b. *caveat emptor*
   c. *lex talionis*
   d. *rex borribulus*

2. The Quakers believed that imprisonment should have a
   a. deterrent function
   b. reforming function
   c. rehabilitative function
   d. all of the above

3. Proponents of the utilitarian punishment model
   a. believe in free will
   b. believe that punishment is an effective deterrent against crime
   c. resent the lower quality of American life caused by the crime problem
   d. all of the above

4. About how many prisoners are being held in U.S. prisons and jails today?
   a. 1 million
   b. 2 million
   c. 5 million
   d. 10 million

5. Probation
   a. allows a convicted person to remain at liberty
   b. has its root in French common law
   c. dates back to the late 1700s
   d. requires an offender to comply with court-imposed conditions

6. Shock probation
   a. involves a limited amount of low-level electroshock treatment
   b. is a form of probation granted by the court following a brief period of incarceration
   c. is granted by the prison parole board following a brief period of incarceration
   d. is granted by the intensive-probation-supervision board following a brief period of incarceration

7. Intensive supervised probation (ISP)
   a. has been abolished in most states
   b. offers little, if any, hope of relieving prison over-crowding
   c. is intended to help offenders avoid the problems of imprisonment
   d. is organized in caseloads of 100 to 150 clients

8. Parole
   a. is the conditional release of a prisoner before a full sentence has been served
   b. is opposed by conservatives but not by liberals
   c. is opposed by liberals but not by conservatives
   d. has been abolished in all but eleven states

9. Which of the following is not a reentry program?
   a. prerelease
   b. postrelease
   c. work release
   d. halfway houses

10. Home-furlough programs
    a. are no longer available in the state prison systems
    b. enable maximum-security inmates to go home on weekends
    c. have been much more restrictive recently
    d. are basically the same as halfway houses

True–False

T F   1. Under the silent system, each prisoner was required to live and work in solitary confinement throughout his or her entire sentence.

T F   2. Rehabilitation of offenders has never been a dominant goal of imprisonment in the United States.

T F   3. Lifetime chances of a person going to prison are higher for men than for women.

T F   4. Over one-half of the increase in state prison population since 1990 is due to an increase in the prisoners convicted of violent offenses.

T F   5. The incarceration rate in the United States continues to rise between four and five percent per year.

T F   6. At least 95 percent of all state prisoners will be released from prison at some point in time.

T F   7. Probation is the release of an offender—under custody of the state—after the offender has served a portion of his or her sentence.

T F   8. Parole boards have been abolished in the federal government and in over half of the states.

T F   9. State parole success has been basically unchanged since 1990.

T F   10. Restorative justice is considered by most criminologists to be an outdated philosophy for justice.

Fill-In

1. _____ and _____ believed that punishment should not be inflicted for vengeance; rather, the primary purpose of punishment should be the reduction or deterrence of crime.
2. Proponents of the _____ believe that criminals are deterred from crime only through the awareness that unlawful behavior will result in a period of isolation from society.
3. _____ is the release of an individual from a pre-trial detention center or jail pending case adjudication.
4. _____ is the correctional service that allows an offender, under supervision, to remain in the community while complying with court-imposed conditions.
5. _____ is a form of probation granted by the court following a brief period of incarceration.
6. If a probationer violates the rules of probation, he or she has committed a _____ and his or her probation may be revoked by the court.
7. _____ is a type of probation wherein small caseloads of clients are monitored intensively in the community by probation officers.
8. _____ is the conditional release of a prisoner before a full sentence has been served.
9. _____ programs enable inmates—usually those with minimum-security status who live in work-release centers or halfway houses—to take a temporary leave from the institution.

Matching

1. *Lex talionis*
2. Probation
3. Boot camps
4. Retribution
5. Justice model
6. Halfway house
7. Quakers
8. Electronic monitoring
9. ISP
10. Utilitarian punishment model

A. Retributivism
B. Small caseloads monitored intensively
C. Program tracking prisoners' location and movements
D. Suspension of a sentence conditional on good behavior
E. Modeled after U.S. military basic training
F. Payback for criminal acts
G. Reentry program
H. Solitary system
I. Proponents believe in free will
J. Reciprocal revenge for crime

Essay Questions

1. Reread the section of the text on the goals of punishment. What do you believe the goals of punishment should be? Just for a moment, assume that you or a very close, loved member of your family has become a victim of a serious crime. How should the perpetrator of this crime be punished? Why?
2. After reading the text materials on prison conditions, try to meet with a friend, neighbor, or student who has been in a jail or prison. Have him or her describe the experience to you. How does it compare with your ideas about prison life and what you have read in the text?
3. Assume that you have been appointed director of a state prison system. How will you organize your prison system? What will it look like? How do you think the inmates will respond to the changes you institute? Do you think other states will follow your system?
4. After reading about probation and parole as cost-beneficial alternatives to imprisonment and examining the trend toward violent and drug-related crimes in our society, do you believe that probation and parole are suitable solutions to prison overcrowding? Are intermediate sanctions such as intensive supervision programs and home confinement viable alternatives?

The Goals of Punishment: The Return to Retributivism and the Utilitarian Model

Source: C. Bartollas and J. P. Conrad, Introduction to Corrections, *2nd ed., New York: Harper-Collins College, 1992, pp. 123–126, 128, 129. Reprinted by permission of Pearson Education.*

BY CLEMENS BARTOLLAS AND JOHN P. CONRAD

THE RETURN TO RETRIBUTIVISM

Until the 1970s there was little overt dissension on the utilitarian goals of punishment. The Benthamite triad—deterrence, incapacitation, and rehabilitation—was assumed by both theoreticians and practitioners to contain the governing justifications for the administration of the various sanctions against the criminal embodied in our criminal laws. The 1970 Declaration of Principles of the American Prison Association was explicit in its support of the indeterminate sentence as the criterion for sentencing required by the "rehabilitative ideal." It continued to be the firm policy of correctional practitioners, in spite of increasing skepticism about the feasibility of rehabilitation.

Two American academics reopened the debate. In an aggressively forthright tract, *We Are the Living Proof,* David Fogel, a correctional administrator who transferred to academia as a professor of criminal justice, challenged the very foundations of the "rehabilitative ideal." He attacked the administration of the indeterminate sentence, arguing that the rehabilitation of offenders or their failure to achieve it should be irrelevant to the sentencing decision. The wide disparity of sentences for the same crimes depended more on the personal values of judges than on any consideration of fairness. Therefore, Fogel proposed that criminal codes should be revised to provide for uniformity in sentencing, making some allowances for mitigating or aggravating factors involved in the offense. In place of the "medical model" of sentencing, so long enshrined in correctional ideology, Fogel urged that his proposed reforms should be known as the justice model.

The concept of just deserts is the pivotal philosophical basis of the justice model. Fogel contends that offenders are volitional and responsible human beings and, therefore, deserve to be punished if they violate the law. This punishment shows offenders that they are responsible for their behavior. Decisions concerning offenders, then, should be based not on their needs, but on the penalties they deserve for their acts. This nonutilitarian position is not intended to achieve social benefits or advantages, such as deterrence or rehabilitation, but instead is designed to punish offenders because they deserve it; it is their "just deserts" for the social harm they have inflicted upon society.

The punishment given offenders must be proportionate to the social harm they have done. Fogel believes that the just deserts approach offers a more rational ground for the construction of correctional policies and offers a "set of principles for the rehabilitation of the system itself":

> The retributive position, in contrast (to rehabilitation), is essentially nonutilitarian, holding that punitive sanctions should be imposed on the offender simply for the sake of justice. Punishment is deserved; the form and severity of the punishment must, however, be proportionate to the criminal act. The right of the state to impose treatment of one sort or another on the offender holds no place in this approach.

In 1976, Andrew von Hirsch, as executive director of the Committee for the Study of Incarceration, drafted the report of the committee's study, which was published under the title *Doing Justice: The Choice of Punishments.* The committee's orientation calls for sentences administered on the basis of just deserts, very much like Fogel's justice model. The fundamental principle is that the *severity of punishment should be commensurate with the seriousness of the wrong.* Neither deterrence, nor incapacitation, nor rehabilitation should enter into the sentencing decision. The principle was clearly stated and explained but, unlike Fogel's justice model, the proposed sentence structure was not related to past sentencing practice.

The commensurate deserts proposal found in *Doing Justice* was later developed by Andrew von Hirsch and Kathleen Hanrahan into a modified desert model. This new retributionist rationale for punishment attempted to put into practice the moral bases of retributionism. Some of the salient recommendations in these proposals were the following:

- weighting the punishments for a crime to fit the degree of seriousness of the offense;
- the time spent in prison should be reduced for all crimes in keeping with the relative weights of seriousness . . . ;
- determinate or fixed-time sentences should be imposed upon conviction . . . ;
- parole should be abolished or at least radically modified to reduce discretion;
- prison conditions should be modified to produce a fair and just environment in which to serve flat-time sentences . . . ;
- incarceration should not be used to achieve other goals: crime prevention, rehabilitation, or general deterrence.

The flat terms that result from the movement toward retributivism have been fairly inflexible compared to the policies of indeterminate sentencing. The public perception of crime and drugs on the streets has put pressure on legislators and judges to increase the length of sentences with serious consequences for the country's overcrowded prisons. Both liberals and hardline conservatives welcomed an end to the inequitable indeterminate sentence. As the crime wave continued without abatement, the conservative preference for longer terms gained sway. An unprecedented increase of prison populations has been the predictable result.

In the 1990s, and today, the justice model continues to have its supporters and its critics. The critics charge that the concept of just deserts or "just punishment" is a fatal weakness, because making retribution the ultimate aim of the correctional process breeds a policy of despair rather than one of hope. In this regard, it is argued that while the idea of just deserts has been around for centuries, it has never totally dominated the penal policy of any advanced society. Critics also state that while the justice model may have broad support in theory, there is little evidence that it is producing a more humane system. They point out that determinate sentencing has even been used by state legislatures to create more punitive and prolonged sentences. Furthermore, the criticism is made that prisons are worse today than in 1975, when Fogel began to gain the ear of politicians and correctional administrators. Fogel agrees that the justice model has fallen short of its intended objectives: "I am encouraged by the rhetoric of the nationwide acceptance of the justice model, but there are precious few places that have accepted it as a mission."

UTILITARIAN PUNISHMENT MODEL

In the mid-1970s, the United States returned to the philosophy of utilitarian punishment to deal with serious juvenile as well as adult crime. The utilitarian punishment philosophy is grounded on the assumption that punishment is necessary to deter offenders and to protect society from crime. Thus, punishment is justified because of its presumed social advantages. Proponents of this approach, the correctional right, make the argument that if we are unable to improve offenders through rehabilitative programs, we can at least assure that they are confined and that potential lawbreakers are deterred by the consequences incurred by those who do break the law.

James Q. Wilson and Ernest van den Haag, leading spokespersons for utilitarian punishment philosophy, have described the main points of this hardline approach. First, proponents of utilitarian punishment philosophy resent losses in the quality of American life caused by the problem of crime. They feel that a paramount duty of government is to provide the necessary social controls so that citizens are secure in their lives, liberties, and pursuit of happiness. Because the duty of the government is to protect the rights and liberties of its citizens, punishment should be used against those who violate the law of the state.

Second, punishment is an effective deterrent against crime. Van den Haag is particularly convinced of the deterrent effects of sanctions, believing that the "first line of social defense is the cost imposed for criminal activity." The higher the cost, the more likely that it will deter crime.

> If a given offender's offenses are rational in the situation in which he lives—if what he can gain exceeds the likely cost to him by more than the gain from legitimate activities he does—there is little that can be "corrected" in the offender. Reform will fail. It often fails for this reason. What has to be changed is not the personality of the offender, but the cost-benefit ratio, which makes his offense rational. That ratio can be changed by improving and multiplying his opportunities for legitimate activity and the benefits they yield, or by decreasing his opportunity for illegitimate activities, or by increasing their cost to him, including punishment.

Third, proponents of utilitarian punishment philosophy believe in free will—that is, that offenders can reason and have freely chosen to violate the law. Such offenders are not controlled by any past or present forces, and, therefore, they deserve punishment for the social harm they have inflicted on society.

Fourth, criminals are deterred from crime only through the awareness that unlawful behavior will result in a period of isolation from society. Hardliners dismiss the community-based movement, because they claim that offenders do not take the justice process seriously until they "do some prison time."

In sum, hardliners today are informing policymakers that a panacea is available: That is, the simple solution to the crime problem is to increase the cost, especially for street offenders. Wilson and van den Haag, chief high priests of this "get tough" approach, promise that such a strategy will protect the community and deter would-be offenders.

The basic problem with implementing a crime-control policy based on the principles of utilitarian punishment philosophy is that the celerity and certainty of punishment cannot at present be attained by the criminal justice system. No one involved seems to know how the time lag between the commission of the crime and the punishment for the crime can be significantly shortened. Nor does anyone appear to know how the certainty of arrest and conviction can be raised to an acceptable level. But because the celerity and the certainty of punishment cannot be attained, policymakers are being urged by some to become more severe in punishing criminals.

Critics also claim that a crime-control policy based on utilitarian punishment philosophy focuses almost entirely on street crime and is blind to the more serious violations of trust inherent in economic or white-collar crime. Furthermore, advocates of this crime-control model are accused of neglecting the social and structural conditions—such as poverty, unemployment, and social injustice—that may lead to crime. Marxist criminologists add that this crime-control position solidifies the power of the middle class, thereby preventing the structural transformation of an exploitative economic system. . . .

The critique of retributivism draws on incidents of callous brutality, and on the indifference of a retribution-oriented correctional system to the maintenance of standards of decency. Federal courts have been consistent in their requirement that although prison officials cannot be obliged to rehabilitate the offenders committed to them, they may not administer their institutions in such a way that inmates have no opportunities to improve themselves. Modern criminal justice looks back on what the offender has done and mandates a punishment that fits the crime, not the criminal. It also looks forward and demands that punishment must make it possible for the criminal to become, in Plato's formulation, "a better man, or, failing this, at least less of a wretch."

CRITICAL THINKING

1. According to this article, why has there been a return to the retributive model of criminal justice?
2. What is wrong with the retributive model?
3. How is the utilitarian model of punishment different?

READING 14.2

Restorative Justice for Young Offenders and Their Victims

Source: Corrections Today *64, no. 1, February 2002, pp. 90–93. Reprinted with permission of the American Correctional Association, Lanham, MD.*

"Treatment and punishment standing alone are not capable of meeting the intertwined needs of the community, victim, offender and family."

—Mission statement of the Pinal County Department of Juvenile Court Services in Florence, Arizona

BY ANNE SEYMOUR AND TRUDY GREGORIE

As the juvenile justice system and juvenile corrections professionals seek new approaches that focus on prevention, early intervention and a greater emphasis on victims' needs, a new framework has emerged. This framework seeks to balance the rights and interests of young offenders, their victims and the community, and engage all three groups as clients of juvenile justice services and as resources in a more effective response to youth crime. Restorative justice, the guiding philosophical foundation for this new, more balanced vision, promotes juvenile justice interventions that focus on basic community needs and expectations. Communities expect justice systems to improve public safety, sanction juvenile crime, and habilitate and reintegrate offenders. True balance is achieved when juvenile justice professionals consider all three of these needs and goals in each case and when a juvenile justice system allocates its resources equally to meet each need.

The principles of restorative justice evoke a substantial shift from America's traditionally retributive approach to justice. Initially offered as a philosophy for justice and fairness, restorative justice has taken on many important practical applications during the past decade. Unlike America's framework for juvenile justice, restorative justice is not a system or a network of agencies. Rather, restorative justice is based upon a shared set of values that determines how conflicts can be resolved and how damaged relationships can be repaired or improved. This value-based approach to justice can cause confusion in justice professions that have traditionally been based on structures and agencies. However, the ultimate goal of restorative justice is to infuse its shared values and practical applications into America's traditional approaches to juvenile justice.

RESTORATIVE JUSTICE VALUES

At a 1996 national restorative justice teleconference sponsored by the National Institute of Corrections, a panel of experts identified seven core values of restorative justice:

- Crime is an offense against human relationships;
- Victims and the community are central to justice processes;
- The first priority of justice processes is to assist victims;
- The second priority of justice processes is to restore the community, to the degree possible;
- The offender has a personal responsibility to victims and to the community for crimes committed;
- The offender will develop improved competency and understanding as a result of the restorative justice experience; and
- Stakeholders share responsibilities for restorative justice through partnerships for action.

In developing programs based on restorative justice, these underlying principles should form the foundation for planning, implementation and evaluation.

LEGISLATION AND PUBLIC POLICY

In a nationwide survey to determine states' juvenile justice laws, policies and programs based on the values and principles of restorative justice and the Balanced and Restorative Justice (BARJ) models, the BARJ project at Florida Atlantic University found that:

- Nineteen states have adopted restorative justice statutes;
- Twenty states articulate restorative justice in agency policies;
- Thirty-two states articulate restorative justice in agency mission statements;
- Thirty-six states incorporate restorative justice into program plans;
- Thirteen states have developed evaluation/outcome measures for restorative justice programs and activities; and
- Thirty-three states articulate restorative justice principles in multiple documents.

The 19 states that have restorative juvenile justice statutes are: Alabama, Alaska, Arizona, California, Colorado, Connecticut, Idaho, Illinois, Louisiana, Maine, Maryland, Missouri, Montana, Oregon, Pennsylvania, South Carolina, Utah, Virginia and Washington.[1] (For more information about BARJ, visit web site: http://www.favedu/divdept/caupa/cji, or call (954) 762–5668.)

Additionally, the National Survey of Victim Services in Adult and Juvenile Correctional Agencies[2] was conducted in 1996 by the National Center for Victims of Crime. The survey offered insight into the types of restorative justice initiatives that have been implemented by juvenile correctional agencies. It found that: 13 percent of juvenile agencies used confrontation, 24 percent mediation, 24 percent conciliation, 29 percent impact of crime on victims programs, and 37 percent victims impact panels or classes.

CRIME VICTIMS

While restorative justice holds great promise for victims, many victims and service providers remain suspect of both the concept and its applications. Some of their fears and concerns are based on actual experiences such as judges ordering victim/offender mediation without the victim's knowledge and/or consent. Others are based on victims' perceptions, such as reading older publications about restorative justice that are offender-focused with little attention paid to victims' needs or concerns. If victims and service providers are truly to be stakeholders in restorative justice, their fears and concerns must be addressed in a meaningful way.

Restorative justice provides victims with a viable alternative to an adversarial justice process that traditionally has ignored their interests and needs. While victims are increasingly being afforded considerable constitutional and statutory rights, they are seldom considered "partners in justice." Restorative justice offers victims the opportunity to join as equal partners with community representatives, professionals who assist offenders, justice practitioners and victim service providers in planning, implementing, evaluating and improving restorative justice programs and practices. Victim satisfaction often is directly related to the levels of participation and respect they are afforded by the juvenile justice system—levels that are substantially increased through restorative justice approaches. When victims are excluded or diluted in restorative justice partnerships, the end result is likely to be continued growth in adversarial opposition.

EFFECTIVENESS OF RESTORATIVE JUSTICE

As more states and jurisdictions move toward performance-based evaluative measures, so must restorative justice consider effective approaches to measuring success and to identifying components that need improvement. The victims committees of the American Correctional Association and the American Probation and Parole Association have developed recommendations for evaluating restorative justice programs and initiatives.[3] The following are measures included in the committees' recommendations:

- Does the agency's and/or program's mission statement incorporate language that addresses victims as clients and victims' needs?
- Are there staff and/or volunteers designated to provide victims with assistance, information and referral either in a full-time capacity or as a percentage of the job requirements? Do job descriptions and/or duty statements clarify specific responsibilities to victims and to restorative justice initiatives?
- Does the agency or initiative use victims and service providers in an advisory capacity to guide the development of restorative justice policies, procedures and programs? What is the structure of the Victim Advisory Council or Community Advisory Council? Have its recommendations and efforts had a measurable impact on program implementation?
- Does the agency or program provide orientation, continuing education and training to its staff and volunteers about victims' needs and rights, victim trauma and supportive services available to victims? If so, how often are training programs held? How many professionals and volunteers are trained? Are participants' retention and application of what they learned measured at follow-on intervals?
- What is the effect of restorative justice on victims' awareness of their rights and available services? What are the scope and specific activities/products used to inform and involve victims? Are these services and products available in multiple languages, teletypewriter and Braille and in measures commensurate with victims' ages and cognitive development? Are they available in jurisdictions large and small, urban and rural?
- Can an increase in the number of victims who are accessing their core rights be determined? Such increases include the number of victims who request (and receive): notification of the case or offender status; restitution and/or other financial/legal obligations; protective orders or other measures to increase victim safety and security; the right to submit a victim impact statement—written, oral, through audio/videotape, and/or by teleconference—to the hearing site; and information about and referrals to supportive services offered either in the community or by the juvenile justice system.
- Does the agency or initiative measure victim satisfaction with its programs and services, either through surveys, focus groups or direct interviews? What are the cumulative results of victim satisfaction assessments?
- Can any reduction in victims' short- and/or long-term trauma be directly attributed to their participation in restorative justice processes and programs?
- How many restorative community service hours were requested, ordered and/or completed with victims:

requesting direct service from offenders, having direct input into the community service placement from a list provided by the community corrections agency, or requesting that offenders provide community service to the victim assistance or community-based agency of the victim's choice?

- How many victims voluntarily participate in victim/offender programming, which includes community reparative boards, family group conferencing, healing or sentencing circles, victim impact programs and panels, and victim/offender mediation or dialogue?
- How many of these programs are sponsored? What were the outcomes of such programs? What was the level of victim satisfaction in participating in such programs?
- How many community volunteers are involved in restorative justice initiatives, particularly those who provide victims with assistance and support? How many community volunteer hours are performed?

In addition, the job performance measures of juvenile justice professionals must be changed to reflect the delivery of victim assistance and services. In the traditional justice system, great emphasis is placed on the number of cases processed, their outcomes in terms of findings and services/programs provided to adjudicated juvenile offenders. With a restorative justice approach, the evaluation measures for victim assistance and services described above should be incorporated into job descriptions and duty statements. Only when professional advancement is based on victim assistance will the victim component of restorative justice be fully realized and implemented.

PROMISING PRACTICES

Community service that is viable and visible can be very restorative for victims, offenders and the community. In addition, restorative community service can directly benefit the victim (only at the victim's request and with his or her consent) or directly benefit victim service or community service organizations such as constructing a domestic violence shelter, providing volunteers for victim-related fund-raising events, or cutting ribbons for the annual public awareness campaign sponsored by Mothers Against Drunk Driving.

In Deschutes County, Ore., merchant accountability boards involve panels of local shopkeepers and merchants who have experienced low-level offenses such as shoplifting and graffiti. Juvenile offenders appear before the boards to learn how chronic offenses against merchants detrimentally affect their businesses and the community in the form of higher prices and increased security expenditures. Often, the offenders perform their community service in the stores owned by members of the merchant accountability boards, which provides both meaningful work experience and mentoring from positive adult figures.

The Lincoln Action Program in Nebraska sponsors a youth violence alternatives project that includes an innovative program called Victims First. The goal of Victims First is "to help victims of property damage crime, while giving youths a firsthand look at the impact of crime on family, friends, neighbors and the community." At-risk youths and nonviolent offenders are supervised by adult mentors—both staff and volunteers—while cleaning up and enhancing security for property crime victims. Following victim-specific community service, the youths have the opportunity to hear from victims about the physical, emotional and financial effects of the crime. Victims First also sponsors fund-raisers that benefit crime victims organizations.

VICTIM AWARENESS

How can restorative justice proponents increase victim awareness about, and involvement in, their efforts? Here are 10 steps they can take to reach this goal:

- Learn about different types of victimization;
- Become educated about victim trauma;
- Recognize that each victim is unique;
- Learn who provides victim services in the community—both system-based and community-based;
- Participate in victim coalitions that promote rights and services for victims;
- Establish policies and procedures to guide the implementation of all victim-related programs within the context of a restorative justice framework;
- Establish a victim advisory council within all agencies that promote restorative justice approaches;
- Provide internal training for staff and volunteers on victim issues;
- Provide cross-training about all program activities to victim service providers and allied professionals; and
- Know, understand and implement core victims' rights, which include notification, restitution, input/involvement and protection.

By identifying and seeking to meet the needs of crime victims, juvenile justice practitioners can validate victims' pain and trauma and include them as true "clients" of the juvenile justice process. Victims can provide valuable input into how juvenile offenders can be held accountable, and can participate in programming that meets their own needs, as well as those of offenders. The end result is a juvenile justice process that is truly just for all stakeholders.

ENDNOTES

1. O'Brien, S., G. Bazemore and M. Umbreit. 2000. Restorative juvenile justice policy development and implementation assessment: A national survey of states. Ft. Lauderdale, Fla.: Balanced and Restorative Justice Project and Office of Juvenile Justice and Delinquency Prevention.
2. Seymour, A. 1997. National survey of victim services in adult and juvenile correctional agencies. Arlington, Va.: National Center for Victims of Crime and Office for Victims of Crime, U.S. Department of Justice.
3. Seymour, A. 1999. Restorative justice victim-related performance measures. Lanham, Md.: American Correctional Association; Lexington, Ky.: American Probation and Parole Association.

Note: Anne Seymour is a national public safety consultant and serves as co-chair of the American Correctional Association's (ACA) Restorative Justice Committee. Trudy Gregorie is director of training at the National Center for Victims of Crime and is co-chair of ACA's Victims Committee. Both have many years of experience in victims' rights and services, juvenile justice, and restorative justice. They serve as project staff for the national Promising Practices and Strategies for Victim Services in Corrections project.

CRITICAL THINKING

1. What is meant by victim awareness?
2. In what ways does restorative justice focus on victims and their communities?
3. Why are the goals of the restorative justice model especially suited to juvenile justice?

End Notes

CHAPTER 1

1. E. Sutherland and D. Cressey, *Criminology*, 8th ed., Philadelphia: Lippincott, 1960, pp. 8–9.
2. D. E. Hebding and L. Glick, *Introduction to Sociology*, 4th ed., New York: McGraw-Hill, 1992, pp. 10–11.
3. M. R. Haskell and L. Yablonsky, *Crime and Delinquency*, 3rd ed., Chicago: Rand McNally College Publishing, 1978, p. 4.
4. P. W. Tappan, *Crime, Justice, and Correction*, New York: McGraw-Hill, 1960, pp. 3–22.
5. Haskell and Yablonsky, *Crime and Delinquency*, p. 5.
6. H. C. Black, *Black's Law Dictionary*, St. Paul, MN: West, 1979, p. 334.
7. L. Yablonsky, *Criminology: Crime and Criminality*, 4th ed., New York: Harper and Row, 1990, pp. 6–8.
8. Ibid., p. 6.
9. Black, *Law Dictionary*, p. 335.
10. Ibid., pp. 334–35.
11. Yablonsky, *Criminology*, p. 9.

CHAPTER 2

1. W. F. Whyte, *Street Corner Society*, 2nd ed., Chicago: University of Chicago Press, 1955.
2. S. L. Hills and R. Santiago, *Tragic Magic: The Life and Crimes of a Heroin Addict,* Wadsworth Publishing, 1992, p. 1.
3. Federal Bureau of Investigation, Uniform Crime Reports, *Crime in the United States, 2001*, Washington, DC: Government Printing Office, October 28, 2002, pp. 1–17, **http://www.fbi.gov/ucr/ucr.htm** (accessed May 25, 2003); hereafter cited as FBI, Uniform Crime Reports.
4. Ibid.
5. U.S. Department of Justice, Office of Justice Programs, Bureau of Justice Statistics, *Criminal Victimization in the United States, 1991: A National Crime Victimization Survey Report*, National Crime Victimization Survey, NCJ-139563, December 1992, pp. 141–47; U.S. Department of Justice, Office of Justice Programs, Bureau of Justice Statistics, *Criminal Victimization in the United States, 2001: A National Crime Victimization Survey*, National Crime Victimization Survey, NCJ-197064, pp. 1–143; hereafter cited as BJS, National Crime Victimization Survey. Both reports were accessed on May 25, 2003, through **http://www.ojp.usdoj.gov/bjs/.**
6. L. Savitz, "Official Statistics," in *Contemporary Criminology*, L. Savitz and N. Johnston, eds., New York: Wiley, 1982, pp. 3–15.
7. L. W. Sherman, *The Quality of Police Arrest Statistics*, Washington, DC: Police Foundation, 1984.

8. L. Sherman and B. Glick, "The Quality of Arrest Statistics," *Police Foundation Reports* 2, 1984, pp. 1–8.
9. BJS, National Crime Victimization Survey.
10. A. Blumstein and J. Wallman, *The Crime Drop in America*, Cambridge, England: Cambridge University Press, 2000; G. Lafree, review of *The Crime Drop in America*, M. Quimet, "Explaining the American and Canadian Crime 'Drop' in the 1990's," *Canadian Journal of Criminology*, 44, no. 1, January 2002.
11. J. Levine, "The Potential for Crime Over-reporting in Criminal Victimization Surveys," *Criminology* 14, 1976, pp. 307–30.
12. U.S. Department of Justice, Office of Justice Programs, Bureau of Justice Statistics, National Incident-Based Reporting System, **http://www.fbi.gov/ucr/nibrs. htm** (accessed May 24, 2004).
13. J. F. Short and F. I. Nye, "Reported Behavior as a Criterion of Deviant Behavior," *Social Problems* 5, 1957–1958, pp. 207–13.
14. See F. W. Dunford and D. S. Elliot, "Identifying Career Offenders Using Self-Reported Data," *Journal of Research in Crime and Delinquency* 21, pp. 57–86.
15. L. Johnston, P. O'Malley, and J. Bachman, *Monitoring the Future, 1990*, Ann Arbor, MI: Institute for Social Research, 1991.
16. J. S. Wallerstein and C. J. Wyle, "Our Law-Abiding Law Breakers," *Probation* 25, March–April 1947, pp. 107–12.
17. M. A. Peterson and H. B. Braiker, *Who Commits Crimes: A Survey of Prison Inmates*, Cambridge, MA: Oelgeschlager, Gunn and Hain, 1981, pp. xix–xxi.
18. FBI, Uniform Crime Reports.
19. BJS, National Crime Victimization Survey.
20. U.S. Department of Justice, Office of Justice Programs, Bureau of Justice Statistics, *Reporting Crime to the Police, 1992–2000*, by T. Hart and C. Rennison, March 2003, NCJ-195710.
21. M. Hindelang, "Causes of Delinquency: A Partial Replication and Extension," *Social Problems* 20, 1973, pp. 471–87. See also J. Short and I. Nye, "Extent of Undetected Delinquency, Tentative Conclusions," *Journal of Criminal Law, Criminology, and Police Science* 49, 1958, pp. 296–302.
22. FBI, Uniform Crime Reports.
23. Ibid.
24. BJS, National Crime Victimization Survey.
25. FBI, Uniform Crime Reports; U.S. Department of Justice, Office of Justice Programs, Bureau of Justice Statistics, *Bureau of Justice Statistics, 2002: At a Glance*, by D. B. Adams and L. E. Reynolds, August 2002, NCJ-194449, p. 7.
26. FBI, Uniform Crime Report, *Crime in the United States, 2005,* Washington, DC: Government Printing Office
27. U.S. Department of Justice, Office of Justice Programs, Bureau of Justice Statistics, *Report to the Nation on Crime and Justice*, 2nd ed., March 1988, NCJ-105506, p. 11.
28. Cited in ibid.
29. J. Laub, D. Clark, L. Siegel, and J. Garofolo, *Trends in Juvenile Crime in the United States, 1973–1983*, Albany, NY: Hindelang Research Center, 1987.
30. M. Gottfredson and T. Hirschi, "The True Value of Lambda Would Appear to Be Zero: An Essay on Career Criminals, Selective Incapacitation, Cohort Studies, and Related Topics," *Criminology* 24, 1986, pp. 213–34.
31. L. Cohen and K. Land, "Age Structure and Crime: Symmetry versus Asymmetry and the Projection of Crime Rates through the 1990s," *American Sociological Review* 52, 1987, pp. 170–83; T. Hirschi and M. Gottfredson, "Age and the Explanation of Crime," *American Journal of Sociology* 89, 1983, pp. 552–84; M. Gottfredson and T. Hirschi, "The Methodological Adequacy of Longitudinal Research on Crime," *Criminology* 25, 1987, pp. 581–614. See also D. J. Steffensmeier, E. A. Allan, M. D. Hater, and C. Streifel, "Age and the Distribution of Crime," *American Journal of Sociology* 94, 1989, pp. 803–31.
32. J. Q. Wilson and R. Herrnstein, *Crime and Human Nature*, New York: Simon and Schuster, 1985, pp. 126–47.
33. K. Kercher, "Explaining the Relationship between Age and Crime: The Biological vs. Sociological Model," paper presented at the annual American Society of

Criminology meeting, Montreal, Canada, November 1987; A. Blumstein, J. Cohen, and D. Farrington, "Criminal Career Research: Its Value for Criminology," *Criminology* 26, 1988, pp. 1–35; D. Farrington, L. E. Ohlin, and J. Q. Wilson, *Understanding and Controlling Crime: Toward a New Research Strategy*, New York: Springer-Verlag, 1986.

34. A. Barnett, A. Blumstein, and D. Farrington, "Probabilistic Models of Youthful Criminal Careers," *Criminology* 25, 1987, pp. 83–107. See also D. Steffensmeier, E. A. Allen, M. Harer, and C. Streifel, "Age and the Distribution of Crime: Variant or Invariant?" paper presented at the annual American Society of Criminology Meeting, Montreal, Canada, November 1987.

35. FBI, Uniform Crime Reports.

36. BJS, National Crime Victimization Survey.

37. FBI, Uniform Crime Reports.

38. U.S. Department of Justice, Office of Justice Programs, Bureau of Justice Statistics, *Women Offenders*, October 3, 2000, NCJ-175688; FBI, Uniform Crime Reports; BJS, National Crime Victimization Survey.

39. Ibid.

40. Ibid.

41. D. S. Eitzen and M. B. Zinn, *Social Problems*, New York: Simon and Schuster, 1992, p. 488.

42. BJS, *Report to the Nation on Crime and Justice*, p. 48.

43. Eitzen and Zinn, *Social Problems*, pp. 487–88.

44. D. Elliot, S. Ageton, and D. Huizinga, "Reconciling Race and Class Differences in Self-Reported and Official Estimates of Delinquency," *American Sociological Review* 45, 1980, pp. 95–110. See also D. Elliot and D. Huizinga, "Social Class and Delinquent Behavior in a National Youth Panel, 1976–1980," *Criminology* 21, 1983, pp. 149–77.

45. Short and Nye, "Extent of Undetected Delinquency."

46. C. Tittle, W. Villemez, and D. Smith, "The Myth of Social Class and Criminality: An Empirical Assessment of the Empirical Evidence," *American Sociological Review* 43, 1978, pp. 643–56.

47. C. Tittle and R. Meier, "Specifying the SES/Delinquency Relationship," *Criminology* 28, 1990, pp. 271–301.

CHAPTER 3

1. D. R. Cressey, "Crime," in *Contemporary Social Problems*, 2nd ed., New York: Harcourt, Brace and World, 1966, pp. 136–92.

2. L. Glick and D. E. Hebding, *Introduction to Social Problems*, Reading, MA: Addison-Wesley, 1980, pp. 223–25.

3. E. Monachesi, "Cesare Beccaria," in *Pioneers in Criminology*, H. Mannheim, ed., 2nd ed., Montclair, NJ: Patterson Smith, 1972, pp. 36–50.

4. Ibid.

5. Ibid.

6. E. H. Johnson, *Crime, Correction, and Society*, 3rd ed., Homewood, IL: Dorsey Press, 1974, p. 170.

7. C. Beccaria, *On Crimes and Punishments*, H. Paolucci, trans., Indianapolis: Bobbs-Merrill, 1963, pp. 8–13, 30–33, 45–58, 62–64, 99; also C. Beccaria, *An Essay On Crimes and Punishments*, E. D. Ingraham, trans., 2nd Amer. ed., Philadelphia: Nicklin, 1819, pp. 15, 20–23, 28–34, 47, 60, 74–80, 93–99, 148–57.

8. Ibid.

9. Ibid.

10. Ibid.

11. Ibid.

12. C. Beccaria, *Essay on Crimes and Punishments*, 5th ed., London: Symonds, 1804, p. 205.

13. J. Bentham, *An Introduction to the Principles of Morals and Legislation*, L. J. Lafleur, ed., New York: Hafney, 1948, p. 2.

14. G. Geis, "Jeremy Bentham," in Mannheim, *Pioneers in Criminology*, pp. 54–55.
15. Ibid., p. 58.
16. Ibid., p. 60.
17. Monachesi, "Cesare Beccaria," p. 49.
18. R. Korn and L. McCorkle, *Criminology and Penology*, New York: Holt, Rinehart and Winston, 1966, pp. 403–5; and C. Beccaria, *An Essay on Crimes and Punishments*, London: Almon, 1767.
19. Glick and Hebding, *Introduction to Social Problems*, pp. 214–15; W. C. Reckless, *The Crime Problem*, 3rd ed., New York: Appleton-Century-Crofts, 1961, p. 233.
20. D. E. Hebding and L. Glick, *Introduction to Sociology*, 4th ed., New York: McGraw-Hill, 1992, pp. 5, 7–8. The discussions of positivism and Comte are based largely on a discussion of these topics in Hebding and Glick.
21. G. B. Vold and T. J. Bernard, *Theoretical Criminology*, New York: Oxford University Press, 1986, p. 35.
22. M. E. Wolfgang, "Cesare Lombroso," in Mannheim, *Pioneers in Criminology*, pp. 232–91.
23. Glick and Hebding, *Introduction to Social Problems*, p. 215; C. Lombroso, *Crime, Its Causes and Remedies*, H. P. Horton, trans., Boston: Little, Brown, 1911; E. H. Sutherland and D. R. Cressey, *Criminology*, 9th ed., Philadelphia: Lippincott, 1974, p. 53.
24. Wolfgang, "Cesare Lombroso," p. 246.
25. Ibid.
26. Ibid., p. 270.
27. Ibid., pp. 271–72.
28. Ibid., p. 271.
29. T. Sellin, "Enrico Ferri," in Mannheim, *Pioneers in Criminology*, pp. 361–84.
30. Ibid., p. 368.
31. Ibid.
32. E. Ferri, *L'omicida nella psicologia e nella psicopatologia criminale*, 2nd ed.; *L'omicidio-Suicido: Responsabilita giuridica*, 5th ed., Torino, Italy: UTET, 1925, pp. 54–55.
33. Sellin, "Enrico Ferri," p. 369.
34. Vold and Bernard, *Theoretical Criminology*, p. 41.
35. Sellin, "Enrico Ferri," pp. 378–79.
36. R. Garofalo, *Criminology*, R. W. Millar, trans., Boston: Little, Brown, 1914; and F. A. Allen, "Raffaele Garofalo," in Mannheim, *Pioneers in Criminology*.
37. Garofalo, *Criminology*, p. 33. See also Vold and Bernard, *Theoretical Criminology*, p. 43.
38. Allen, "Raffaele Garofalo," p. 321.
39. Garofalo, *Criminology*, pp. 23, 31.
40. Allen, "Raffaele Garofalo," pp. 324–26.
41. Ibid.
42. Garofalo, *Criminology*, pp. 95–96.
43. Ibid., p. 92; Allen, "Raffaele Garofalo," p. 326.
44. Allen, "Raffaele Garofalo," pp. 327–28.
45. Garofalo, *Criminology*, p. 97.
46. Allen, "Raffaele Garofalo," pp. 327–28.
47. Ibid., pp. 328–30.
48. Ibid.
49. Ibid.
50. Ibid.
51. Vold and Bernard, *Theoretical Criminology*, p. 41.
52. Ibid.
53. Ibid.
54. D. B. Cornish, and R. V. Clarke, "Situational Prevention, Displacement of Crime, and Rational Choice Theory," in *Situational Crime Prevention: From Theory into Practice*, K. Heal and G. Laycock, eds., London, H.M.S.O., 1986; D. B. Cornish and R. V. Clarke, *The Reasoning Criminal: Rational Choice Perspectives on Offending*, New York: Springer-Verlag, 1986; D. B. Cornish and R. V. Clarke, "Understanding Crime Displacement: An Application of Rational Choice Theory," *Criminology* 25, 1984, pp. 933–47.

55. D. J. Shoemaker, *Theories of Delinquency: An Examination of Explanations of Delinquent Behavior*, 3rd ed., New York: Oxford University Press, 1996; F. Schmalleger, *Criminology Today*, 2nd ed., Upper Saddle River, NJ: Prentice Hall, 1999; R. L. Akers, 2000 *Criminological Theories: Introduction and Evaluation*, 3rd ed., Los Angeles: Roxbury, 2000.

56. R. V. Clarke, ed., *Situational Crime Prevention: Successful Case Studies*, 2nd ed., Guilderland, NY: Harrow and Heston, 1997.

57. T. Marvell and C. Moody, "Specification Problems, Police Levels, and Crime Rates," *Criminology* 34, 1996, pp. 609–47.

58. G. Kelling, T. Pate, D. Dieckman, and C. Brown, *The Kansas City Preventive Patrol Experiment: A Summary Report*, Washington, DC: Police Foundation, 1974.

59. L. Sherman, "Police Crackdowns," *National Institute of Justice Reports*, March–April 1990, pp. 2–6.

60. National Center for Policy Analysis, *Crime and Punishment in America, 1997*, Dallas, 1997; T. Marvell and C. Moody, "The Impact of Enhanced Prison Terms for Felonies Committed with Guns," *Criminology* 33, 1995, pp. 247–81; E. Stevens and B. Payne, "Applying Deterrence Theory in the Context of Corporate Wrongdoing: Limitations on Punitive Damages," *Journal of Criminal Justice* 27, 1999, pp. 195–209.

61. National Center for Policy Analysis, *Crime and Punishment*.

62. L. E. Cohen and M. Felson, "Social Change and Crime Rate Trends: A Routine Activity Approach," *American Sociological Review* 44, 1979, pp. 588–608.

63. Ibid.; and D. Glaser, *Social Deviance*, Chicago: Markham, 1971.

64. Cohen and Felson, "Social Change and Crime Rate Trends."

CHAPTER 4

1. G. B. Vold and T. J. Bernard, *Theoretical Criminology*, 3rd ed., New York: Oxford University Press, 1986, pp. 84–85.

2. C. Lombroso, *Crime, Its Causes and Remedies*, H. P. Horton, trans., Boston: Little, Brown, 1912.

3. G. Lombroso Ferrero, *Criminal Man according to the Classification of Cesare Lombroso*, New York: Putnam, 1911.

4. A. E. Fink, *The Causes of Crime: Biological Theories in the United States, 1800–1915*, Philadelphia: University of Pennsylvania Press, 1938.

5. C. Goring, *The English Convict: A Statistical Study*, London: His Majesty's Stationery Office, 1913, p. 173; quoted in Vold and Bernard, *Theoretical Criminology*, pp. 6–9.

6. E. A. Hooton, *The American Criminal: An Anthropological Study*, Cambridge, MA: Harvard University Press, 1939.

7. Vold and Bernard, *Theoretical Criminology*, pp. 56–57.

8. W. H. Sheldon, *Varieties of Delinquent Youth: An Introduction to Constitutional Psychiatry*, New York: Harper and Bros., 1949; see also E. Kretchmer, *Physique and Character*, W. H. J. Sprott, trans., New York: Harcourt Brace, 1925.

9. S. Glueck and E. Glueck, *Physique and Delinquency*, New York: Harper, 1956; see also S. Glueck and E. Glueck, *Unraveling Juvenile Delinquency*, Cambridge, MA: Harvard University Press, 1950.

10. J. B. Cortés, *Delinquency and Crime: A Biopsychosocial Approach; Empirical, Theoretical, and Practical Aspects of Criminal Behavior*, New York: Seminar Press, 1972.

11. Vold and Bernard, *Theoretical Criminology*, p. 65.

12. J. Lange, *Verbrechen als Schicksal: Studien an kriminellen Zwillingen*, Leipzig, Germany: George Thieme, 1929; translation by C. Haldane, *Crime and Destiny*, New York: Boni, 1930.

13. D. Rowe and J. Rodgers, "The Ohio Twin Project and ADSEX Studies: Behavior Genetic Approaches to Understanding Antisocial Behavior," paper presented at the American Society of Criminology meeting, Montreal, Canada, November 1987; G. Carey, "Twin Imitation for Antisocial Behavior: Implications for

Genetic and Family Environment Research," *Journal of Abnormal Psychology* 101, 1992, pp. 18–25.

14. Vold and Bernard, *Theoretical Criminology*, p. 89.

15. B. Hutchings and S. A. Mednick, "Criminality in Adoptees and Their Adoptive and Biological Parents: A Pilot Study," in *Biosocial Bases in Criminal Behavior*, S. A. Mednick and K. O. Christiansen, eds., New York: Gardner, 1977; R. R. Crowe, "The Adoptive Offspring of Women Criminal Offenders," *Archives of General Psychiatry* 27, no. 5, November 1972, pp. 600–3; F. Schulsinger, "Psychopathy: Heredity and Environment," *International Journal of Mental Health* 1, 1972, pp. 190–206.

16. S. A. Mednick, W. Gabrielli, and B. Hutchings, "Genetic Influences in Criminal Behavior: Evidence from an Adoption Cohort," in *Prospective Studies of Crime and Delinquency*, K. Teilmann et al., eds., Boston: Kluver-Nijhoff, 1983; S. A. Mednick, T. Moffitt, W. Gabrielli, and B. Hutchings, "Genetic Factors in Criminal Behavior: A Review," in *Development of Antisocial and Prosocial Behavior: Research, Theories, and Issues*, D. Olweus, J. Block, and M. Radke-Yarrow, eds., Orlando: Academic Press, 1986.

17. Vold and Bernard, *Theoretical Criminology*, p. 91.

18. P. A. Jacobs, M. Brunton, and M. M. Melville, "Aggressive Behavior, Mental Subnormality, and the XYY Male," *Nature* 208, December 1965, pp. 1351–52.

19. T. R. Sarbin and J. E. Miller, "Demonism Revisited: The XYY Chromosomal Anomaly," *Issues in Criminology* 5, no. 2, Summer 1970, p. 199.

20. H. A. Witkin et al., "Criminality Aggression and Intelligence among XYY and XXY Men," in *Biosocial Bases of Criminal Behavior*, S. A. Mednick and K. O. Christiansen, eds., New York: Gardner, 1977.

21. D. J. Rapp, *Allergies and the Hyperactive Child*, New York: Simon and Schuster, 1981; M. Krassner, "Diet and Brain Function," *Nutrition Reviews* 44, 1986; D. H. Fishbein and S. Pease, "The Effects of Diet on Behavior: Implications for Criminology and Corrections," *Research on Corrections* 1, 1988, pp. 1–45.

22. N. Ward, "Assessment of Chemical Factors in Relation to Child Hyperactivity," *Journal of Nutritional and Environmental Medicine* 7, 1997, pp. 333–42.

23. S. Schoenthaler and W. Doraz, "Types of Offenses Which Can Be Reduced in an Institutionalized Setting Using Nutritional Intervention," *International Journal of Biosocial Research* 4, 1983, pp. 74–84; S. Schoenthaler, "Diet and Crime: An Empirical Examination of the Value of Nutrition in the Control and Treatment of Incarcerated Juvenile Offenders," *International Journal of Biosocial Research* 4, 1982, pp. 25–39.

24. E. Podolsky, "The Chemistry of Murder," *Pakistan Medical Journal* 15, 1964, pp. 9–14; D. Hill and W. Sargent, "A Case of Matricide," *Lancet* 244, 1943, pp. 526–27.

25. M. Virkkunen, "Insulin Secretion during the Glucose Tolerance Test among Habitually Violent and Impulsive Offenders," *Aggressive Behavior* 12, 1986, pp. 303–10; M. Virkkunen, "Reactive Hypoglycemic Tendency among Habitually Violent Offenders," *Nutrition Reviews Supplement* 44, 1986, pp. 94–103; J. A. Yaryura-Tobias and E. Neziroglu, "Violent Behavior, Brain Dysrhythmia, and Glucose Dysfunction: A New Syndrome," *Journal of Orthopsychiatry* 4, 1975, pp. 182–88.

26. Vold and Bernard, Theoretical Criminology, p. 99.

27. G. Heath et al., "Behavior Changes in Nonpsychotic Volunteers following the Administration of Taraxein, the Substance Extracted from Serum of Schizophrenic Patients," *American Journal of Psychiatry* 114, 1958, pp. 917–20; see also T. Millon, *Modern Psychopathology: A Biosocial Approach to Maladaptive Learning and Functioning*, Philadelphia: Saunders, 1969, p. 154.

28. E. F. Coccaro, R. J. Kavoussi, R. L. Hauger, T. B. Cooper, and C. F. Ferris, "Cerebrospinal Fluid Vasopressin Levels: Correlates with Aggression and Serotonin Function in Personality Disordered Subjects," *Archives of General Psychiatry* 55, August 1998; A. S. Unis, E. H. Cook, J. G. Vincent, D. K. Gjerde, B. D. Perry, C. Mason, and J. Mitchell, "Platelet Serotonin in Adolescents with Conduct Disorder," *Biological Psychiatry* 42, no. 7, Oct. 1, 1997, pp. 553–59; A. S. New, R. L. Trestmen, V. Mitropoulou, D. S. Benishay, E. Coccaro, J. Silverman, and L. J.

Siever, "Serotonergic Function and Self-Injurious Behavior in Personality Disorder Patients," *Psychiatry Research* 69, 1997, pp. 17–26; A. J. Cleare and A. J. Bond, "Does Central Serotonergic Function Correlate Inversely with Aggression? A Study Using D-fenfluramine in healthy subjects," *Psychiatric Research* 69, 1997, pp. 89–95.

29. T. E. Moffitt, G. L. Brammer, A. Caspi, J. P. Fawcett. M. Raleigh, A. Yuwiler, and P. Silva, "Whole Blood Serotonin Relates to Violence in an Epidemiological Study," *Biological Psychiatry* 43, no. 6, March 15, 1998, pp. 446–57.

30. L. Glick and D. E. Hebding, "Environment," in *Introduction to Social Problems*, Reading, MA: Addison-Wesley, 1980, pp. 427–72; A. Schauss, *Diet, Crime, and Delinquency*, Berkeley, CA: Parker House, 1980.

31. A. R. Mawson and K. W. Jacobs, "Corn Consumption, Tryptophan, and Cross-National Homicide Rates," *Journal Orthomolecular Psychiatry* 7, 1978, pp. 227–30; "A Clean America: Will People Pay the Price?" *U.S. News & World Report*, February 7, 1977; R. Wunderlich, "Neuroallergy as a Contributing Factor to Social Misfits: Diagnosis and Treatment," in *Ecologic-Biochemical Approaches to Treatment of Delinquents and Criminals*, L. Hippchen, ed., New York: Von Nostrand Reinhold, 1978, pp. 229–53.

32. E. E. Maccoby and C. N. Jacklin, "Sex Differences in Aggression," *Child Development* 51, 1980, pp. 964–80.

33. J. M. Dabbs Jr. "Testosterone, Crime, and Misbehavior among 692 Male Prison Inmates," *Personality and Individual Differences* 18, no. 5, 1995.

34. J. M. Dabbs Jr. and M. F. Hargrove, "Age, Testosterone, and Behavior among Female Prison Inmates," *Psychosomatic Medicine* 59, 1997, pp. 477–80.

35. L. E. Kreuz and R. M. Rose, "Assessment of Aggressive Behavior and Plasma Testosterone in a Young Criminal Population," *Psychosomatic Medicine* 34, 1972, pp. 321–32.

36. W. Gove, "The Effect of Age and Gender on Deviant Behavior: A Biopsychosocial Perspective," in *Gender and the Life Course*, A. S. Rossi, ed., New York: Aldine, 1985, pp. 11–144.

37. Dabbs and Hargrove, "Age, Testosterone, and Behavior."

38. L. Ellis and P. Coontz, "Androgens, Brain Functioning, and Criminality: The Neurohormonal Foundations of Antisociality," in *Crime in Biological, Social, and Moral Contexts*, L. Ellis and H. Hoffman, eds., New York: Praeger, 1990, pp. 162–93.

39. P. O. Alm, B. af Klinteberg, K. Humble, J. Leppert, S. Sorensen, R. Tegelman, L. H. Thorell, and L. Lidberg, "Criminality and Psychopathy as Related to Thyroid Activity in Former Juvenile Delinquents," *Acta Psychiatrica Scandinavica* 94, no. 2, August 1, 1996, pp. 112–17.

40. E. G. Stalenheim, L. von Knorring, and L. Wide, "Serum Levels of Thyroid Hormones as Biological Markers in a Swedish Forensic Psychiatric Population," *Biological Psychiatry* 43, no. 10, May 15, 1998, pp. 755–61.

41. *Diagnostic and Statistical Manual of Mental Disorders: DSM-III*, 3rd. ed., Washington, DC: American Psychiatric Association, 1980, pp. 101–79: See also *Diagnostic and Statistical Manual of Mental Disorders: DSM-III-R*, 3rd ed., rev., Washington, DC: American Psychiatric Press, 1987; and *Diagnostic and Statistical Manual of Mental Disorders: DSM-IV*, 4th ed., Washington, DC: American Psychiatric Association, 1994, pp. 175–278.

42. A. J. Sallett, "Mini-course on Alcohol," *Drug Notes* 1, Utica: SUNY Institute of Technology at Utica/Rome, 1990, pp. 2–4.

43. *DSM-III-R*, pp. 150–51; also *DSM-IV*, pp. 175–278.

44. U.S. Department of Justice, Office of Justice Programs, Bureau of Justice Statistics, *Violent Crime in the United States*, Washington, DC: Government Printing Office, March 1991, p. 17.

45. Vold and Bernard, *Theoretical Criminology*, p. 98.

46. L. Yeudall, O. Fedora, and D. Fromm, "A Neuropsychosocial Theory of Persistent Criminality: Implications for Assessment and Treatment," in *Advances in Forensic Psychology and Psychiatry*, R. Rieber, ed., Norwood, NJ: Ablex 1987, pp. 119–91.

47. *DSM-III-R*, pp. 118–20.

48. H. K. Kletchka, "Violent Behavior Associated with Brain Tumor," *Minnesota Medicine* 49, 1966, pp. 1853–55.

49. Studies reporting these findings can be found in S. A. Mednick et al., "Biology and Violence," in *Criminal Violence*, M. E. Wolfgang and N. A. Weiner, eds., Beverly Hills, CA: Sage, 1982, pp. 46–52.

50. Z. A. Zayed, S. A. Lewis, and R. P. Britain, "An Encephalographic and Psychiatric Study of 32 Insane Murderers," *British Journal of Psychiatry* 115, 1969, pp. 1115–24.

51. D. Williams, "Neural Factors Related to Habitual Aggression—Consideration of Differences between Habitual Aggressives and Others Who Have Committed Crimes of Violence," *Brain* 92, 1969, pp. 503–20.

52. D. R. Bars, F. La Marr Heyrend, C. D. Simpson, and J. C. Munger, "Use of Visual Evoked-Potential Studies and EEG Data to Classify Aggressive Explosive Behavior of Youths," *Psychiatric Services* 52, January 2001, pp. 81–86.

53. *DSM-IV.*

54. *DSM-III-R*, pp. 41–45; see also ibid., pp. 78–85; T. Moffitt and P. Silva, "Self-Reported Delinquency, Neropsychological Deficit, and History of Attention Deficit Disorder," *Journal of Abnormal Child Psychology* 16, 1988, pp. 553–69.

CHAPTER 5

1. S. Halleck, *Psychiatry and the Dilemmas of Crime*, Berkeley and Los Angeles: University of California Press, 1971; D. Abrahamsen, *Crime and the Human Mind*, New York: Columbia University Press, 1944.

2. S. Freud, *An Outline of Psychoanalysis*, New York: Norton, 1963; D. E. Hebding and L. Glick, *Introduction to Sociology*, 4th ed., New York: McGraw-Hill, 1992, pp. 93–95.

3. Ibid.

4. Ibid.; S. Freud, *The Ego and the Id*, London: Hogarth, 1927.

5. A. Aichorn, *Wayward Youth*, New York: Viking, 1963; Vold and T. J. Bernard, *Theoretical Criminology*, 3rd ed., New York: Oxford University Press, 1986, p. 116.

6. C. R. Bartol, *Criminal Behavior: A Psychosocial Approach*, Englewood Cliffs, NJ: Prentice-Hall, 1980; Vold and Bernard, *Theoretical Criminology*, p. 116.

7. S. L. Brodsky, *Psychologists in the Criminal Justice System*, Urbana: University of Illinois Press, 1973; S. L. Brodsky, "Criminal and Dangerous Behavior," in *Abnormal Psychology*, D. Rimm and J. Somervill, eds., New York: Academic Press, 1977; F. A. Henn, M. Herjanic, and R. H. Vanderpearl, "Forensic Psychiatry: Profiles of Two Types of Sex Offenders," *American Journal of Psychiatry* 133, 1976, pp. 694–96; J. Monahan, *Predicting Violent Behavior: An Assessment of Clinical Techniques*, Beverly Hills, CA: Sage, 1981; J. G. Rabkin, "Criminal Behavior of Discharged Mental Patients: A Critical Appraisal of the Research," *Psychological Bulletin* 86, 1979, pp. 1–27.

8. D. Klassen, and W. O'Connor, "Crime Inpatient Admissions, and Violence among Male Patients," *International Journal of Law and Psychiatry* 11, 1988, pp. 305–12; D. Klassen, and W. O'Conner, "Assessing the Risk of Violence in Released Mental Patients: A Cross-Validation Study," *Psychological Assessment: A Journal of Consulting and Clinical Psychology* 1, 1990, pp. 75–81; J. Monahan, "Mental Disorder and Violent Behavior: Perceptions and Evidence," *American Psychologist* 47, 1992, pp. 511–21.

9. H. Belfrage, "A Ten-Year Follow-Up of Criminals in Stockholm Mental Patients: New Evidence for a Relationship between Mental Disorder and Crime," *British Journal of Criminology* 38, no. 1, Winter 1998, pp. 145–55.

10. J. Monahan, "Mental Disorder and Violent Behavior: Perceptions and Evidence," *American Psychologist* 47, 1992, pp. 511–21; J. Swanson, and C. Holzer, "Violence and the ECA Data," *Hospital and Community Psychiatry* 42, 1991, pp. 79–80; J. Swanson, C. Holzer, V. Ganju, and R. Jono, "Violence and Psychiatric Disorder in the Community: Evidence from the Epidemiologic Catchment Area Surveys," *Hospital and Community Psychiatry* 41, 1990, pp. 761–70.

11. L. N. Robbins, and D. A. Regier, *Psychiatric Disorders in America: The Epidemiologic Catchment Area Study*, New York: Free Press, 1991; H. J. Steadman, S. Fabisiak, J. Dovoskin, and E. Holobean, "A Survey of Mental Disability among State Prison Inmates," *Hospital and Community Psychiatry* 38, 1987, pp. 1086–90; L. Teplin, "The Prevalence of Severe Mental Disorder among Male Urban Jail Detainees: Comparisons with the Epidemiologic Catchment Area Program," *American Journal of Public Health* 80, 1990, pp. 663–69.

12. U.S. Department of Justice, Bureau of Justice Statistics, *Mental Health and Treatment of Inmates and Prisoners*, Washington, DC: Government Printing Office, July 1999.

13. C. R. Bartol, Criminal Behavior: *A Psychosocial Approach*, Englewood Cliffs, NJ: Prentice-Hall, 1980; J. Monahan and H. Steadman, "Crime and Mental Disorder: An Epidemiological Approach," in *Crime and Justice*, vol. 4, M. Tonry and N. Morris, eds., Chicago: University of Chicago Press, 2002.

14. E. H. Sutherland and D. R. Cressey, *Criminology*, 9th ed., Philadelphia: Lippincott, 1974.

15. J. Bonta, M. Law, and K. Hanson, "The Prediction of Criminal and Violent Recidivism among Mentally Disordered Offenders: A Meta-Analysis," *Psychological Bulletin* 123, 1998, pp. 123–42.

16. Ibid.

17. P. A. Bandura and A. H. Walters, *Social Learning and Personality Development*, New York: Holt, Rinehart and Winston, 1963; A. Bandura, *A Social Learning Analysis*, Englewood Cliffs, NJ: Prentice-Hall, 1977; A. Bandura, *Social Learning Theory*, Englewood Cliffs, NJ: Prentice-Hall, 1977.

18. Ibid.

19. L. Glick and D. E. Hebding, *Introduction to Social Problems*, Reading, MA: Addison-Wesley, 1980; C. R. Huesmann and N. Malamuth, "Media Violence and Antisocial Behavior," *Journal of Social Issues* 42, 1986, pp. 1–7; S. Messner, "Television Violence and Violent Crime: An Aggregate Analysis," *Social Problems* 33, 1986, pp. 218–35; C. Kruttschnitt, L. Heath, and D. Ward, "Family Violence, Television Viewing Habits, and Other Adolescent Experiences Related to Violent Criminal Behavior," *Criminology* 243, 1986, pp. 235–67.

20. C. Burt, "The Inheritance of Mental Ability," *American Psychologist* 13, 1958, pp. 1–15; W. Healy and A. Bronner, *Delinquency and Criminals: Their Making and Unmaking*, New York: Macmillan, 1926; H. Goddard, *Efficiency and Levels of Intelligence*, Princeton, NJ: Princeton University Press, 1920; E. Sutherland, "Mental Deficiency and Crime," in *Social Attitudes*, K. Young, ed., New York: Holt, 1931; T. Hirschi and M. Hindelang, "Intelligence and Delinquency: A Revisionist Review," *American Sociological Review* 42, 1977, pp. 471–586; D. Denno, "Victim, Offender, and Situational Characteristics of Violent Crime," *Journal of Criminal Law and Criminology* 77, 1986, pp. 1142–58; T. Moffitt, W. Gabrielli, S. Mednick, and E. Schulsinger, "Socioeconomic Status, IQ, and Delinquency," *Journal of Abnormal Psychology* 90, 1981, pp. 152–86.

21. P. R. Giancola, and A. Zeichner, "Intellectual Ability and Aggressive Behavior in Nonclinical-Nonforensic Males," *Journal of Psychopathology and Behavioral Assessment* 16, no. 2, 1994, pp. 121–30.

22. R. Goodman, "The Relationship between Normal Variation in IQ and Common Childhood Psychopathology: A Clinical Study," *European Child and Adolescent Psychiatry* 4, no. 3, July 1995, pp. 187–96.

23. J. Slawson, *The Delinquent Boys*, Boston: Budget, 1926; D. W. Denno, "Sociological and Human Developmental Explanations of Crime: Conflict or Consensus?" *Criminology* 23, 1985, pp. 711–40; D. W. Denno, "Victim, Offender, and Situational Characteristics of Violent Crime," *Journal of Criminal Law and Criminology* 77, 1986, pp. 1142–58; S. Menard and B. Morse, "A Structuralist Critique of the IQ-Delinquency Hypothesis: Theory and Evidence," *American Journal of Sociology* 89, 1984, pp. 1347–78.

24. L. J. Siegel, *Criminology*, St. Paul, MN: West, 1992, p. 178.

25. L. Kohlberg, *The Philosophy of Moral Development*, vol. 1, San Francisco: Harper and Row, 1981; L. Kohlberg, "Stage and Sequence; The Cognitive-Developmental Approach to Socialization," in *Handbook of Socialization Theory and Research*, D. A. Goslin, ed., Chicago: Rand McNally, 1969.

26. J. J. Conger and A. C. Petersen, *Adolescence and Youth*, New York: Harper and Row, 1984; R. M. Lerner and J. A. Shea, "Social Behavior in Adolescence," in *Handbook of Developmental Psychology*, B. B. Wolman, ed., Englewood Cliffs, NJ: Prentice-Hall, 1982, pp. 503–25.

27. C. Gilligan, *In a Different Voice: Psychological Theory and Women's Development*, Cambridge, MA: Harvard University Press, 1982; D. Baumrind, "A Dialectical Materialist's Perspective on Knowing Social Reality," *New Directions for Child Development* 2, 1978.

28. *Diagnostic and Statistical Manual of Mental Disorders*, 3rd ed. *(DSM-III)*, Washington DC: American Psychiatric association, 1980; *Diagnostic and Statistical Manual of Mental Disorders*, 4th ed. *(DSM-IV)*, Washington, DC: American Psychiatric Association, 1994, pp. 645–50.

29. Ibid.

30. Ibid.

31. Ibid.

32. Ibid.

33. Hare, R. D., *Harvard Mental Health Letter*, September 1995, "Linking Brain Dysfunction to Disordered/Criminal/Psychopathic Behavior," in *Crime Times* 2, no. 1, 1996, p. 3.

34. *DSM-III, DSM-IV*, pp. 645–50.

CHAPTER 6

1. W. I. Thomas and F. Znaniecki, *The Polish Peasant in Europe and America*, New York: Knopf, 1927.

2. Ibid.

3. C. R. Shaw and H. D. McKay, *Juvenile Delinquency and Urban Areas: A Study of Rates of Delinquents in Relation to Differential Characteristics of Local Communities in American Cities*, Chicago: University of Chicago Press, 1942.

4. E. W. Burgess, "The Growth of the City," in *The City*, R. E. Park, E. W. Burgess, and R. D. McKenzie, eds., Chicago: University of Chicago Press, 1928.

5. Shaw and McKay, *Juvenile Delinquency and Urban Areas*.

6. G. B. Vold and T. J. Bernard, *Theoretical Criminology*, 3rd ed., New York: Oxford University Press, 1986, pp. 173–80.

7. Ibid.

8. R. Bursik, "Social Disorganization and Theories of Crime and Delinquency: Problems and Prospects," *Criminology* 26, 1988, pp. 521–39; R. Sampson and W. B. Groves, "Community Structure and Crime: Testing Social Disorganization Theory," *American Journal of Sociology* 94, 1989, pp. 774–802; P. O. Wikstrom and L. Colman, "Crime and Crime Trends in Different Urban Environments," *Journal of Quantitative Criminology* 6, 1990, pp. 7–28; S. Messner and K. Tardiff, "Economic Inequality and Level of Homicide: An Analysis of Urban Neighborhoods," *Criminology* 24, 1986, pp. 297–317.

9. Vold and Bernard, *Theoretical Criminology*, p. 185.

10. É. Durkheim, *Suicide: A Study in Sociology*, bk. 2, J. A. Spaulding and G. Simpson, trans., Glencoe, IL: Free Press, 1951.

11. R. K. Merton, *Social Theory and Social Structure*, New York: Free Press, 1965, pp. 132–57.

12. Ibid.

13. Ibid.

14. R. Agnew, "Foundation for a General Strain Theory of Crime and Delinquency," *Criminology* 30, 1992, pp. 47–87.

15. R. Agnew, T. Brezina, J. P. Wright, and F. T. Cullen, "Strain, Personality Traits, and Delinquency: Extending General Strain Theory," *Criminology* 40, 2002, pp. 43–72.

16. J. P. Hoffman and F. G. Cerbone, "Stressful Life Events and Delinquency Escalation in Early Adolescence," *Criminology* 14, 1999, pp. 83–111; J. P. Hoffman and A. Miller, "A Latent Variable Analysis of General Strain Theory," *Journal of*

Quantitative Criminology 14, 1998, pp. 83–111; R. Paternoster and P. Mazerolle, "General Strain Theory and Delinquency: A Replication and Extension," *Journal of Research in Crime and Delinquency* 31, 1994, pp. 235–26; P. Mazerolle and A. Piquero, "Violent Responses to Strain: An Examination of Conditioning Influences," *Violence and Victims* 12, 1997, pp. 3–24.

17. Mazerolle and Piquero, "Violent Responses to Strain."
18. P. Mazerolle and J. Maahs, "General Strain and Delinquency: An Alternative Examination of Conditioning Influences," paper presented at the annual meeting of the American Society of Criminology, Washington, DC, November 1998.
19. Agnew, Brezina, Wright, and Cullen, "Strain, Personality Traits, and Delinquency."
20. Vold and Bernard, *Theoretical Criminology*, p. 194.
21. L. Glick and D. E. Hebding, *Introduction to Social Problems*, Reading, MA: Addison-Wesley, 1980, pp. 221–22.
22. Ibid.
23. A. K. Cohen, *Delinquent Boys: The Culture of the Gang*, New York: Free Press, 1955. See also ibid.
24. G. Sykes and D. Matza, "Techniques of Neutralization: A Theory of Delinquency," *American Sociological Review* 22, December 1957, pp. 664–70.
25. R. A. Cloward and L. E. Ohlin, *Delinquency and Opportunity: A Theory of Delinquent Gangs*, Glencoe, IL: Free Press, 1960.
26. Vold and Bernard, *Theoretical Criminology*, p. 214.
27. Ibid. See also W. B. Miller, "Lower-Class as a Generating Milieu of Gang Delinquency," *Journal of Social Issues* 14, 1958, pp. 5–19.
28. Ibid.
29. Ibid.
30. O. Lewis, "The Culture of Poverty," in *Explosive Forces in Latin America*, J. J. TePaske and S. N. Fisher, eds., Columbus: Ohio State University Press, 1964. See also L. R. Della Fave, "The Culture of Poverty Revisited: A Strategy for Research," *Social Problems* 21, no. 5, June 1974, pp. 609–21.
31. Della Fave, "Culture of Poverty Revisited."
32. Lewis, "Culture of Poverty."
33. A. Etzioni, *Social Problems*, Englewood Cliffs, NJ: Prentice Hall, 1976, pp. 9, 14–15, 28–29, 31–32.
34. Glick and Hebding, *Introduction to Social Problems*.
35. M. Wolfgang and F. Ferracuti, *The Subculture of Violence: Towards an Integrated Theory in Criminology*, London: Tavistock, 1967.
36. Ibid.
37. Ibid.
38. L. Cao, A. Adams, and V. J. Jensen, "A Test of the Black Subculture of Violence Thesis: A Research Note," *Criminology* 35, 1997, pp. 367–79.

CHAPTER 7

1. E. H. Sutherland, *Principles of Criminology*, 4th ed., Philadelphia: Lippincott, 1947, pp. 5–9; see also E. H. Sutherland and D. R. Cressey, *Criminology*, 9th ed., Philadelphia: Lippincott, 1974.
2. G. B. Vold and T. J. Bernard, *Theoretical Criminology*, 3rd ed., New York: Oxford University Press, 1988, p. 225.
3. Sutherland and Cressey, *Principles of Criminology*, pp. 75–77.
4. Ibid.
5. D. R. Cressey, "Application and Verification of the Differential Association Theory," *Journal of Criminal Law, Criminology, and Police Science* 43, no. 1, 1952, pp. 43–52.
6. T. Hirschi, *Causes of Delinquency*, Berkeley and Los Angeles: University of California Press, 1969, pp. 132–57.
7. M. L. DeFleur and R. Quinney, "A Reformulation of Sutherland's Association Theory and a Strategy for Empirical Verification," *Journal of Research in Crime and Delinquency* 3, January 1966, pp. 1–22.

8. R. Akers, *Deviant Behavior: A Social Learning Approach*, Belmont, CA: Wadsworth, 1973, pp. 45–61, 177–81; R. L. Burgess and R. L. Akers, "A Differential Association-Reinforcement Theory of Criminal Behavior," *Social Problems* 14, Fall 1968, pp. 128–47.

9. Vold and Bernard, *Theoretical Criminology*, p. 224.

10. D. Glaser, "Differential Identification," in *Social Deviance: Readings in Theory and Research*, H. N. Pontel, ed., Upper Saddle River, NJ: Prentice Hall, 1999, p. 146.

11. D. Glaser, "Criminality Theory and Behavioral Images," *American Journal of Sociology*, 61, 1956, pp. 433–44; D. Glaser, "Role Models and Differential Association," in *Deviance: The Interactionist Perspective*, E. Rubington and M. S. Weinberg, eds., New York: Macmillan, 1973, pp. 369–73.

12. D. Glaser, *Crime in Our Changing Society*, New York: Holt, Rinehart and Winston, 1978.

13. Vold and Bernard, *Theoretical Criminology*, p. 232.

14. T. Hirschi, *Causes of Delinquency*, Berkeley and Los Angeles: University of California Press, 1969, p. 34.

15. Ibid.; see also Vold and Bernard, *Theoretical Criminology*, p. 232.

16. Hirschi, *Causes of Delinquency*, p. 34.

17. In support of Hirschi: M. Hindelang, "Causes of Delinquency: A Partial Replication and Extension," *Social Problems* 2, 1973, pp. 471–87; R. Agnew and D. Peterson, "Leisure and Delinquency," *Social Problems* 36, 1989, pp. 332–48; P. Van Voorhis, E. Cullen, R. Mathers, and C. Chenoweth Garner, "The Impact of Family Structure and Quality on Delinquency: A Comparative Assessment of Structural and Functional Factors," *Criminology* 26, 1988, pp. 235–61. Critical of Hirschi: R. Agnew, "Social Control Theory and Delinquency: A Longitudinal Test," *Criminology* 23, 1985, pp. 47–61; M. Krohn and J. Massey, "Social Control and Delinquent Behavior: An Examination of the Elements of the Social Bond," *Sociological Quarterly* 21, 1980, pp. 529–43; R. La Grange and H. Raskin White, "Age Differences in Delinquency: A Test of Theory," *Criminology* 23, 1985, pp. 19–45.

18. Vold and Bernard, *Theoretical Criminology*, p. 248.

19. M. R. Gottfredson and T. Hirschi, *A General Theory of Crime*, Stanford, CA: Stanford University Press, 1990.

20. Ibid.

21. Ibid., pp. 88–105.

22. Ibid.

23. J. Gibbs, D. Giever, and J. Martin, "Parental Management and Self Control: An Emperical Test of Gottfredson and Hirschi's General Theory," *Journal of Research in Crime and Delinquency* 35, 1998, pp. 40–70; C. Herbert, "The Implications of Self-Control Theory for Workplace Offending," paper presented at the American Society of Criminology meeting, San Diego, CA, 1997; D. Giever, D. Lynskey, and D. Monnet, "Gottfredson and Hirschi's General Theory of Crime and Youth Gangs: An Emperical Test on a Sample of Middle School Youth," paper presented at the American Society of Criminology meeting, San Diego, CA, 1997.

24. G. Geis, "On the Absence of Self-Control as the Basis for a General Theory of Crime: A Critique," *Theoretical Criminology* 4, 2000, pp. 35–54; K. Calavita and H. N. Pontell, "Savings and Loan Fraud as Organized Crime: Toward a Conceptual Typology of Corporate Illegality," *Criminology* 31, 1993, pp. 519–48; K. Polk, "Review of a General Theory of Crime," *Crime and Delinquency* 37, 1991, pp. 575–81; G. E. Reed and P. C. Yeager, "Organizational Offending and Neoclassical Criminology: Challenging the Reach of a General Theory of Crime," *Criminology* 34, 1996, pp. 357–82.

25. D. S. Eitzen, *Social Structures and Social Problems in America*, Boston: Allyn and Bacon, 1974, p. 11.

26. D. E. Hebding and L. Glick, *Introduction to Sociology*, 4th ed., New York: McGraw-Hill, 1992, p. 199.

27. E. Goode, *Deviant Behavior*, 2nd ed., Englewood Cliffs, NJ: Prentice-Hall, 1984.

28. Hebding and Glick, *Introduction to Sociology*, p. 218.

29. R. Quinney, *Critique of the Legal Order*, Boston: Little, Brown, 1974; R. Quinney, "Crime Control in a Capitalist Society," in *Critical Criminology*, I. Taylor, P. Walton, and J. Young, eds., London: Routledge and Kegan Paul, 1975.
30. R. Quinney, *The Social Reality of Crime*, Boston: Little, Brown, 1970, pp. 15–23.
31. Ibid., pp. 15–24; see also Vold and Bernard, *Theoretical Criminology*, pp. 277–80.
32. G. B. Vold, *Theoretical Criminology*, 1st ed., New York: Oxford University Press, 1958, pp. 208–9.
33. Ibid.
34. Vold and Bernard, *Theoretical Criminology*, p. 279.
35. Ibid.; see also P. L. Berger and T. Luckman, *The Social Construction of Reality*, Garden City, NY: Doubleday, 1966.
36. Ibid.
37. Quinney, *Social Reality of Crime*.
38. Goode, *Deviant Behavior*.
39. Ibid.
40. Hebding and Glick, *Introduction to Sociology*, p. 200.
41. D. J. Curran and C. M. Renzetti, *Theories of Crime*, 2nd ed., Boston: Allyn and Bacon, 2001, p. 211.
42. L. Glick and D. E. Hebding, *Introduction to Social Problems*, Reading, MA: Addison-Wesley, 1980.
43. Ibid.
44. Curran and Renzetti, *Theories of Crime*, p. 224.
45. J. Messerschmidt, *Capitalism, Patriarchy, and Crime*, Totowa, NJ: Rowman and Littlefield. See also ibid.
46. Curran and Renzetti, *Theories of Crime*.
47. Ibid, p. 225.
48. Ibid.
49. Glick and Hebding, *Introduction to Social Problems*, pp. 84–7.
50. Ibid.
51. Curran and Renzetti, *Theories of Crime*, p. 212.
52. Glick and Hebding, *Introduction to Social Problems*, pp. 116–17.
53. Curran and Renzetti, *Theories of Crime*, p. 212.
54. Ibid.
55. J. Flavin, "Feminism for the Mainstream Criminologist: An Invitation," *Journal of Criminal Justice* 29, 2001, pp. 271–85.
56. H. S. Becker, *Outsiders: Studies in the Sociology of Deviance*, New York: Free Press, 1963, pp. 9, 34, 37–39.
57. Ibid.; see also Glick and Hebding, *Introduction to Social Problems*.
58. Hebding and Glick, *Introduction to Sociology*, pp. 198–99.
59. Ibid., p. 218.

CHAPTER 8

1. U.S. Department of Justice, Office of Justice Programs, Bureau of Justice Statistics, National Crime Victimization Survey, *Criminal Victimization*, Washington, DC: Government Printing Office, January 29, 2003, p. 1.
2. U.S. Department of Justice, Office of Justice Programs, Bureau of Justice Statistics, *Reporting Crime to the Police, 1992–2000*, Washington, DC: Government Printing Office, March 9, 2003, NCJ-195710, p. 2.
3. Federal Bureau of Investigation, Uniform Crime Reports, *Crime in the United States, 2001*, "Section II—Crime Index Offenses Reported," Washington, DC: Government Printing Office, March 26, 2003, pp. 37–39.
4. U.S. Department of Justice, Office of Justice Programs, Bureau of Justice Statistics, National Crime Victimization Survey, *Personal Crimes, 2002*, "Victim Characteristics," Table 26, "Number of incidents and ratio of victimizations to incidents, by type of crime," Washington, DC: Government Printing Office, March 9, 2003.

5. Bureau of Justice Statistics, *Reporting Crime to the Police, 1992–2000*, p. 3.

6. U.S. Department of Justice, Office of Justice Programs, Bureau of Justice Statistics, "Assault Rates," *Bureau of Justice Statistics Assault Trends*, Washington, DC: Government Printing Office, September 9, 2002, p. 1.

7. E. Brod, "A New Form of Warfare: Employees 'Get Even' in the Age of Layoffs," *USA Today Magazine*, November 1994, pp. 58–60.

8. M. Purdey, "Workplace Homicides Provoke Suits and Better Security," *New York Times*, February 14, 1994; M. Braverman and S. R. Braverman, "Seeking Solutions to Violence on the Job," *USA Today Magazine,* May 1994, pp. 29–31.

9. Ibid.

10. D. T. Duhart, *Violence in the Workplace, 1993–99*, special report of the National Crime Victimization Survey, U.S. Department of Justice, Office of Justice Programs, Bureau of Justice Statistics, Washington, DC: Government Printing Office, December 2001, NCJ-190076.

11. Braverman and Braverman, "Seeking Solutions."

12. J. E. O'Brien, "Violence in Divorce-Prone Families," *Journal of Marriage and the Family* 33, November 1971, pp. 692–98.

13. Ibid; and L. A. Coser, "Some Social Functions of Violence," in *Patterns of Violence*, M. E. Wolfgang, ed., Annals of the American Academy of Political and Social Science 364, Philadelphia: American Academy of Political and Social Science, 1966; L. A. Coser, "The Functions of Conflict," in *Sociological Theory: A Book of Readings*, L. A. Coser and B. Rosenberg, eds., New York: Macmillan, 1957, pp. 218–19.

14. O'Brien, "Violence in Divorce-Prone Families."

15. S. Steinmetz, "Violence in Families," in *Research and Theory in Family Science*, R. D. Day, K. R. Gilbert, and W. R. Burr, eds., Pacific Grove, CA: Brooks/Cole, 1995, pp. 255–69.

16. S. Steinmetz and M. A. Straus, eds., *Violence in the Family*, New York: Dodd, Mead, 1974: D. J. Sonkin, *Learning to Live without Violence: A Handbook for Men*, 2nd ed., San Francisco: Volcano, 1985; W. H. Meredith, D. A. Abbott, and S. L. Adams, "Family Violence: Its Relation to Marital and Parental Satisfaction and Family Strengths," *Journal of Family Violence* 1, 1986, pp. 299–305.

17. R. I. Parnas, "The Police Response to the Domestic Disturbance," *Wisconsin Law Review* 914, Fall, pp. 914–60.

18. E. Giradet, "City's Poor Women Abused, Study Says," *Chicago Tribune*, March 26, 1995.

19. C. M. Rennison, *Intimate Partner Violence, 1993–2001,* crime data brief of the U.S. Department of Justice, Office of Justice Programs, Bureau of Justice Statistics, Washington, DC: Government Printing Office, February 2003, NCJ-197838, pp. 1–2.

20. Ibid.

21. S. X. Radbill, "A History of Child Abuse and Infanticide," in Steinmetz and Straus, *Violence in the Family*, pp. 173–79.

22. R. J. Gelles, "Child Abuse Psychopathology: A Sociological Critique and Reformulation," in Steinmetz and Straus, *Violence in the Family*, pp. 190–204; American Association for Protecting Children, *Highlights of Official Child Neglect and Abuse Reporting, 1984*, Denver: American Humane Society, 1986.

23. Steinmetz and Straus, *Violence in the Family*.

24. M. A. Straus and R. J. Gelles, "Societal Change and Change in Family Violence from 1975 to 1985 as Revealed by Two National Surveys," *Journal of Marriage and the Family* 48, August 1986, pp. 465–79; M. A. Straus and R. J. Gelles, *Physical Violence in American Families*, New Brunswick, NJ: Transaction, 1990; R. Gelles, and D. Loseke, eds., *Current Controversies on Family Violence*, Newbury Park, CA: Sage, 1993; U.S. Department of Health and Human Services, National Center on Child Abuse and Neglect, National Child Abuse and Neglect Data System, "No. 336 Child Abuse and Neglect Cases Substantiated and Indicated—Victim Characteristics," Working Paper 2, 1991 Summary Data Component, May 1993; Working Paper 2, 1992 Summary Data Component, May 1994.

25. Steinmetz, "Violence in Families."

26. R. J. Gelles and M. A. Straus, *Intimate Violence*, New York: Simon and Schuster, 1988, pp. 77–97; also R. J. Gelles and M. A. Straus, "Profiling Violent Families," in *Diversity and Change in Families: Patterns, Prospects, and Policies*, eds., M. R. Rank and E. L. Kain, Englewood Cliffs, NJ: Prentice Hall, 1995, pp. 370–87.

27. Ibid.

28. W. J. Goode, "Force and Violence in the Family," *Journal of Marriage and the Family* 33, November 1971, pp. 624–36.

29. D. Gil, *Violence against Children: Physical Child Abuse in the United States*, Cambridge, MA: Harvard University Press, 1970; R. J. Gelles, "Child Abuse as Psychopathology: A Sociological Critique and Reformulation," *American Journal of Orthopsychiatry* 43, 1973, pp. 611–62; R. J. Gelles, "Poverty and Violence Toward Children," *American Behavioral Scientist* 35, 1992, pp. 258–74; J. D. McLeod and M. J. Shanahan, "Poverty, Parenting, and Children's Mental Health," *American Sociological Review* 58, 1993, pp. 351–66; M. F. Maden and D. F. Wrench, "Significant Findings in Child Abuse Research," *Victimology* 2, 1977, pp. 196–224; J. Garbarino, "The Incidence and Prevalence of Child Maltreatment," in *Family Violence*, L. Ohlin and M. Tonry, eds., Chicago: University of Chicago Press, 1989, pp. 219–61; Gelles and Straus, *Intimate Violence*; M. A. Straus, R. J. Gelles, and S. K. Steinmetz, *Behind Closed Doors: Violence in the American Family*, Garden City, NY: Anchor, 1980; C. Kruttschnitt, J. D. McLeod, and M. Dornfeld, "The Economic Environment of Child Abuse," *Social Problems* 41, no. 2, May 1994, pp. 299–314.

30. Steinmetz, "Violence in Families."

31. M. Sewell, "Some Causes of Jealousy in Young Children," in Steinmetz and Straus, *Violence in the Family*, p. 6.

32. P. G. Ney, "Transgenerational Abuse," in *Intimate Violence: Interdisciplinary Perspectives*, E. C. Viano, ed., Washington, DC: Hemisphere 1992.

33. R. J. Gelles and C. P. Cornell, *Intimate Violence in Families*, 2nd. ed., Newbury Park, CA: Sage, 1987.

34. Goode, "Force and Violence in the Family."

35. Gelles, "Child Abuse as Psychopathology."

36. Straus and Gelles, *Physical Violence in American Families*.

37. M. A. Straus, *Beating the Devil out of Them: Corporal Punishment in American Families*, New York: Lexington Books, 1994.

38. Ibid.; M. Woodall, "A Passionate Plea Calling Spanking Harmful and Futile," *Philadelphia Inquirer*, January 8, 1995.

39. Ibid.

40. Ibid.

41. B. Egeland, "A History of Abuse Is a Major Risk Factor for Abusing the Next Generation," in Gelles and Loseke, *Current Controversies on Family Violence*.

42. Ibid.

43. Ibid.

44. C. S. Widom, *The Cycle of Violence*, a Research in Brief of the National Institute of Justice, Washington, DC: U.S. Department of Justice, October 1992, pp. 1–6.

45. H. C. Raffali, "The Battered Child: An Overview of a Medical, Legal, and Social Problem," in *Deviance, Action, Reaction, Interaction: Studies in Positive and Negative Deviance*, F. R. Scarpitti and P. T. McFarlane, eds., Reading, MA: Addison-Wesley, 1975.

46. Gelles and Straus, *Intimate Violence*, pp. 77–97; also Gelles and Straus, "Profiling Violent Families."

47. Ibid.

48. Ibid.

49. Ibid.

50. R. J. Gelles, "Through a Sociological Lens: Social Structure and Family Violence," in Gelles and Loseke, *Current Controversies on Family Violence*; Gelles and Cornell, *Intimate Violence in Families*.

51. B. Strong and C. DeVault, *The Marriage and Family Experience*, Minneapolis: West, 1995.

52. Ibid.; Gelles and Cornell, *Intimate Violence in Families*; F. I. Nye, "Fifty Years of Family Research," *Journal of Marriage and the Family* 50, May 1988, pp. 305–16.

53. H. S. Erlanger, "Social Class Differences in Parents' Use of Physical Punishment," in Steinmetz and Straus, *Violence in the Family*.

54. T. Bernard, "Angry Aggression among the 'Truly Disadvantaged,'" *Criminology* 28, 1990, pp. 73–96.

55. D. B. Sugerman, "An Analysis of Risk Markers in Husband to Wife Violence: The Current State of Knowledge," *Violence and Victims* 1, 1986, pp. 101–24; A. Brown, *When Battered Women Kill*, New York: Free Press, 1987; and L. E. Walker, *The Battered Woman Syndrome*, New York: Springer, 1984.

56. Gil, *Violence against Children*; also see Straus, *Beating the Devil out of Them*.

57. C. Swift, "Preventing Family Violence: Family-Focused Programs," in *Violence in the Home: Interdisciplinary Perspectives*, M. Lystad, ed., New York: Brunner/Mazel, 1986.

58. Steinmetz, "Violence in Families."

59. H. C. Black, *Black's Law Dictionary*, St. Paul, MN: West, 1979, p. 1134.

60. Uniform Crime Reports, *Crime in the United States*, 2001, p. 29.

61. M. A. Wolfgang, R. M. Figlio, P. E. Tracy, and S. I. Singer, *The National Survey of Crime Severity*, Washington, DC: Government Printing Office, 1985.

62. S. Brownmiller, *Against Our Will: Men, Women, and Rape*, New York: Simon and Schuster, 1975.

63. Uniform Crime Reports, *Crime in the United States, 2001*, p. 29.

64. Bureau of Justice Statistics, *Personal Crimes, 2002*, "Victim Characteristics," Table 26.

65. H. Eigenberg, "The National Crime Survey and Rape: The Case of the Missing Question," *Justice Quarterly* 7, 1990, pp. 655–73.

66. U.S. Department of Justice, Office of Justice Programs, Bureau of Justice Statistics, "Crime Facts at a Glance," Washington, DC: Government Printing Office, September 1, 2002, p. 1; Uniform Crime Reports, *Crime in the United States*, 2001, pp. 37–39.

67. U.S. Department of Justice, Office of Justice Programs, Bureau of Justice Statistics, "Criminal Victimization in the United States—Statistical Tables Index—Definitions," Washington, DC: Government Printing Office, pp. 4–5.

68. D. Symons, *The Evolution of Human Sexuality*, New York: Oxford University Press, 1979.

69. P. R. Sanday, "Rape in Its Cultural Context," *Journal of Social Issues* 37, no. 4, 1981.

70. D. Russell, *The Politics of Rape*, New York: Stein and Day, 1975.

71. P. H. Gebhard et al., *Sex Offenders: An Analysis of Types*, New York: Harper and Row, 1965, pp. 197–206.

72. R. Rada, ed., *Clinical Aspects of the Rapist*, New York: Grune and Stratton, 1978, pp. 122–30.

73. A. N. Groth and J. Birnbaum, *Men Who Rape*, New York: Plenum, 1979.

74. Ibid.

CHAPTER 9

1. U.S. Department of Justice, Federal Bureau of Investigation, Bureau of Justice Statistics, Uniform Crime Reports, Washington, DC. **http://www.ojp.usdoj.gov/bjs/**, April 12, 2003.

2. D. Williamson, "Robbery," in *Atlas of Crime: Mapping the Criminal Landscape*, L. S. Turnbull, E. H. Hendrix, and B. D. Dent, eds., Phoenix: Oryx, 2000, pp. 43–50.

3. Bureau of Justice Statistics, *Robbery Victims*, by C. W. Harlow, Washington, DC: U.S. Government Printing Office, 1989, pp. 1–5; Uniform Crime Reports, April 12, 2003.

4. Federal Bureau of Investigation, Uniform Crime Reports, *Crime in the United States*, 2001; "Section II—Crime Index Offenses Reported," Washington, DC: U.S. Government Printing Office, March 26, 2003, pp. 32–35.

5. Ibid.

6. J. Conklin, *Robbery and the Criminal Justice System*, Philadelphia: Lippincott, 1972.

7. Uniform Crime Reports, April 12, 2003; U.S. Department of Justice, Office of Justice Programs, Bureau of Justice Statistics, National Crime Victimization Report, *Criminal Victimization, 2002*, Washington, DC: Government Printing Office, January 29, 2003.

8. Ibid.

9. F. H. McClintock and E. Gibson, *Robbery in London*, London: Macmillan, 1961.

10. I. Sommers and D. R. Baskin, "The Situational Context of Violent Female Offending," *Journal of Research in Crime and Delinquency* 30, no. 2, May 1993, pp. 136–62.

11. R. Lejeune, "The Management of a Mugging," *Urban Life* 6, 1977, pp. 123–48.

12. P. Cook, "A Strategic Choice Analysis of Robbery," in *Sample Surveys of the Victims of Crime*, W. G. Skogan, ed., Cambridge, MA: Ballinger, 1976; see also Sommers and Baskin, "Situational Context."

13. D. Walsh, *Heavy Business: Commercial Burglary and Robbery*, London: Routledge and Kegan Paul, 1986.

14. F. Fenney, "Robbers as Decision-Makers," in *The Reasoning Criminal: Rational Choice Perspectives on Offending*, D. Cornish and R. Clark, eds., New York: Springer-Verlag, 1986, pp. 53–71; see also Sommers and Baskin, "Situational Context."

15. Ibid.; see also P. Cook, "Robbery in the United States: An Analysis of Recent Trends and Patterns," in *Violence: Patterns, Causes, Public Policy*, N. Weiner, M. Zahn, and R. Sagi, eds., New York: Harcourt Brace Jovanovich, 1990, pp. 85–97.

16. Sommers and Baskin, "Situational Context."

17. J. Katz, "The Motivation of the Persistent Robber," in *Crime and Justice: An Annual Review of Research* 14, M. Tonry, ed., Chicago: University of Chicago Press, 1991, pp. 277–89, 298–300.

18. H. C. Black, *Black's Law Dictionary*, 5th ed., St. Paul, MN: West, 1979, pp. 661, 869, 918–19, 933.

19. Ibid., p. 869.

20. Ibid.

21. Ibid., p. 919.

22. Ibid., p. 819.

23. U.S. Department of Justice, Office of Justice Programs, Bureau of Justice Statistics, *Homicide Trends in the United States: 2000 Update*, crime data brief, by J. A. Fox and M. W. Zawitz, January 2003, NCJ-197471, Washington, DC; and Uniform Crime Reports, *Crime in the United States*, 2001, pp. 19–20.

24. Uniform Crime Reports, *Crime in the United States*, 2001, pp. 19–20.

25. Ibid; *Homicide Trends in the United States*; and U.S. Department of Justice, Office of Justice Programs, Bureau of Justice Statistics, *Age Patterns in Violent Victimizations, 1976–2000*, by P. Klaus and C. M. Rennison, Washington, DC, February 2002, NCJ-190104.

26. Uniform Crime Reports, *Crime in the United States, 2001*, p. 27.

27. Ibid., pp. 22, 27.

28. M. Riedel, "Stranger Violence: Perspectives, Issues, and Problems," *Journal of Criminal Law and Criminology* 78, 1987, pp. 223–58.

29. A. Toufexis, "When Kids Kill Abusive Parents," *Time*, November 23, 1992, pp. 60–61.

30. Bureau of Justice Statistics, Crime Data Brief, *Homicide Trends in the U.S.* by J. A. Fox and M. W. Zawitz, BJS, January, 2003, NJS-197471, Washington, DC.

31. Uniform Crime Reports, *Crime in the United States*, 2001, p. 27.

32. M. Wolfgang, "Victim-Precipitated Criminal Homicide," *Journal of Criminal Law, Criminology, and Police Science* 48, no. 1, May–June 1957, pp. 1–4, 6–11.

33. Ibid.

34. Ibid.

35. Ibid.

36. W. R. Holcomb and A. E. Daniel, "Homicide without Apparent Motive," *Behavioral Sciences and the Law* 6, 1988, pp. 429–39.

37. *Homicide Trends in the United States.*
38. R. M. Holmes and S. T. Holmes, "Understanding Mass Murder: A Starting Point," *Federal Probation* 56, no. 1, March 1992, pp. 53–61.
39. Ewing, *When Children Kill.*
40. J. Levin and J. A. Fox, *Mass Murder: America's Growing Menace*, 2nd ed., New York: Plenum, 1991.
41. C. R. Shaw and H. D. McKay, *Juvenile Delinquency and Urban Areas*, Chicago: University of Chicago Press, 1942.
42. M. E. Wolfgang and F. Ferracuti, *The Subculture of Violence: Towards an Integrated Theory in Criminology*, London: Tavistock, 1967.
43. K. R. Williams and R. L. Flewelling, "The Social Production of Criminal Homicide: A Comparative Study of Disaggregated Rates in American Cities," *American Sociological Review* 53, June 1988, pp. 421–31.
44. Several of the theoretical perspectives presented here are based on a more extensive analysis by Williams and Flewelling in ibid. See also, with respect to this particular point, S. Hackney, "Southern Violence," in *Violence in America*, D. Graham and T. R. Gurr, eds., New York: Bantam, 1969, pp. 505–27; and R. D. Gastil, "Homicide and a Regional Culture of Violence," *American Sociological Review* 36, 1971, pp. 412–27.
45. S. E. Messner, "Regional and Racial Effects on the Urban Homicide Rate: The Subculture of Violence Revisited," *American Journal of Sociology* 88, 1983, pp. 997–1007; S. E. Messner, "Regional Differences in the Economic Correlates of Urban Homicide Rates," *Criminology* 21, 1983, pp. 477–88; W. G. Doerner, "Why Does Johnny Reb Die When Shot? The Impact of Medical Resources upon Whodunnit," *Sociological Inquiry* 53, 1983, pp. 1–15; L. Huff-Corzine, J. Corzine, and D. C. Moore, "Southern Exposure: Deciphering the South's Influence on Homicide Rates," *Social Forces* 64, 1986, pp. 906–24; R. J. Sampson, "Race and Criminal Violence: A Demographically Disaggregated Analysis of Urban Homicide," *Crime and Delinquency* 31, 1985, pp. 47–82; and, for a contending argument, D. F. Hawkins, *Homicide among Black Americans*, Lanham, MD: University Press of America, 1986.
46. Williams and Flewelling, "Social Production."
47. Ibid. See also D. Humphries and D. Wallace, "Capitalist Accumulation and Urban Crime, 1950–1971," *Social Problems* 28, 1980, pp. 179–93; J. R. Blau and P. M. Blau, "Metropolitan Structure and Violent Crime," *American Sociological Review* 47, 1982, pp. 114–28; K. R. Williams, "Economic Sources of Homicide: Reestimating the Effects of Poverty and Inequality," *American Sociological Review* 49, 1984, pp. 283–89; R. D. Crutchfield, M. R. Geerken, and W. R. Gove, "Crime Rate and Social Integration: The Impact of Metropolitan Mobility," *Criminology* 20, 1982, pp. 467–78.
48. Shaw and McKay, *Juvenile Delinquency*; Williams and Flewelling, "Social Production"; R. J. Bursik Jr., "Urban Dynamics and Ecological Studies of Delinquency," *Social Forces* 63, 1984, pp. 393–413.
49. Crutchfield, Geerken, and Gove, "Crime Rate."
50. Williams and Flewelling, "Social Production."
51. A. Bandura and R. H. Walters, *Social Learning and Personality Development*, New York: Holt, Rinehart and Winston, 1963; L. R. Huesmann and L. D. Eton, "Cognitive Processes and the Persistence of Aggressive Behavior," *Aggressive Behavior* 10, 1984, pp. 243–51.
52. D. Lewis et al., "Neuropsychiatric, Psychoeducational, and Family Characteristics of 14 Juveniles Condemned to Death in the United States," *American Journal of Psychiatry* 145, 1988, pp. 584–88.
53. Toufexis, "When Kids Kill"; Ewing, *When Children Kill*; K. M. Heide, "A Typology of Adolescent Parricide Offenders," paper presented at the annual meeting of the American Society of Criminology, Baltimore, November 1990.
54. R. Johnson, *Aggression in Man and Animals*, Philadelphia: Saunders, 1972.
55. J. E. Boothe, L. H. Bradley, T. M. Flick, K. E. Keough, and S. P. Kirk, "America's Schools Confront Violence," *USA Today Magazine*, January 1994, pp. 33–35.
56. "Facing Tough Issues Head On: Ridding the Schools of Drugs and Violence," in *Safety Initiatives in Urban Public Schools*, Washington, DC: Council of the Great

City Schools, December 1993; H. W. Hughes, "From Fistfights to Gunfights: Preparing Teachers and Administrators to Cope with Violence in School," paper presented at the annual meeting of the American Association of Colleges for Teacher Education, Chicago, February 16–19, 1994; U.S. Department of Education, *Safe, Disciplined, Drug-Free Schools: A Background Paper for the Goals 2000: Educate America Satellite Town Meeting*, July 20, 1993, Washington, DC.

57. R. Riley, "Goals 2000 in Brief," July 27, 1994, pkickbush, America Online, November 22, 2002.

58. "Goals 2000 and School Safety: The Safe Schools Act of 1994," July 27, 1994, pkickbush, America Online, November 22, 2002.

59. Ibid.

60. R. Weitzer, ed., *Current Controversies in Criminology*, Upper Saddle River, NJ: Prentice Hall, 2003, p. 69.

61. U.S. Department of Justice, Community Relations Service, *Hate Crime: The Violence of Intolerance*, December 2001, http://www.usdoj.gov/crs/pubs/ crs_pub_hate_crime_bulletin_1201.htm.

62. National Criminal Justice Reference Service, "Hate Crime Resources—Facts and Figures," August 2, 2003, http://www.ncjrs.org/hate_crimes/facts.html.

63. "Hate Crime: The Violence of Intolerance."

64. Ibid.

65. Ibid.

66. Ibid.

67. "Hate and Bias Crime," chap. 22, sec. 1 of 2001 National Victim Assistance Academy, http://www.ojp.usdoj.gov/ovc/assist/nvaa2001/chapter22_1.html.

68. Ibid.

69. National Criminal Justice Reference Service, "Hate Crime Resources—Legislation," August 2, 2003, http://www.ncjrs.org/hate_crimes/legislation.html.

70. "Hate and Bias Crimes."

71. Ibid.

72. Ibid.

73. Ibid

74. *Hate Crime: The Violence of Intolerance.*

75. Interpol, "The Fight against Terrorism," http://www.interpol.com/Public/Icpo/FactSheets/FS200102.asp, August 8, 2003.

76. Federal Bureau of Investigation, *Terrorism in the United States, 1995*, Washington, DC: Government Printing Office, 1997, http://www.fbi.gov/terrorinfo/counterrorism/waronterrorhome.htm, August 1, 2003.

77. CNN. com, "Terror in the Philippines," http://www.cnn.com/SPECIALS/2001/; August 8, 2003; BBC News, "Who Are the Abu Sayyaf?" December 30, 2000, http://news.bbc.co.uk/l/hi/world/asia-pacific/719623.stm.

78. BBC News, "Who Is Osama Bin Laden?" September 18, 2001, http://news.bbc.co.uk/l/hi/world/south-asia/115236.stm.

79. M. A. Lee, "The Swastika and the Crescent," *Intelligence Report*, no. 105, Spring 2002, pp. 18–26.

80. "Hate and Bias Crimes."

81. D. J. Daniels, "The Challenge of Domestic Terrorism to American Criminal Justice," *Corrections Today* 64, no. 7, December 2002, pp. 66–69.

82. S. Misra, "High-Tech Terror," *American City and County* 118, no. 6, June 2003.

83. Ibid.

84. C. E. Simonsen and J. R. Spindlove, "Defining Terrorism," in *Terrorism Today: The Past, the Players, the Future*. Upper Saddle River, NJ: Prentice Hall, 2000, pp. 3–30.

85. Federal Bureau of Investigation, War on Terrorism, Counterterrorism, web page, http://www.fbi.gov/terrorinfo/counterrorism/waronterrorhome.htm.

86. Daniels, "The Challenge of Domestic Terrorism."

87. House Committee on Government Reform, *Homeland Security: Information Sharing Responsibilities, Challenges, and Key Management Issues*, 108th Congress, 1st session, May 8, 2003, http://www.gao.gov/cgi-bin/getrpt?GAO-03-715T.

88. Ibid.

89. Ibid.

90. Charles Doyle, Senior specialist American Law Division, "The USAPATRIOT Act: A Sketch," Congressional Research Service, Order Code RS21203, April 18, 2002 from *The USA PATRIOT Act: A Legal Analysis*, CRS Report RL31377. pages CRS-1 thru CRS-5.

91. Charles Lewis, and Adam Mayle, "Justice Dept. Drafts Sweeping Expansion of Anti-Terrorism Act," The Center For Public Integrity, Feb. 7, 2003.

CHAPTER 10

1. U.S. Department of Justice, Federal Bureau of Investigation, Uniform Crime Reports, *Crime in the United States, 2001,* "Section II—Crime Index Offenses Reported," Washington, DC: Government Printing Office, October 28, 2002, pp. 1–52; U.S. Department of Justice, Office of Justice Programs, Bureau of Justice Statistics, "Crime Characteristics," March 20, 2003; U.S. Department of Justice, Office of Justice Programs, Bureau of Justice Statistics, National Crime Victimization Survey, *Criminal Victimization 2000: Changes 1999–2002 with Trends 1993–2000,* by C. M. Rennison, Washington, DC, June 2001, NCJ-187007; U.S. Department of Justice, Office of Justice Programs, Bureau of Justice Statistics, *Sourcebook of Criminal Justice Statistics, 2001,* April 2003.

2. Uniform Crime Reports, *Crime in the United States, 2001,* pp. 1–52.

3. Bureau of Justice Statistics, *Sourcebook.*

4. Uniform Crime Reports, *Crime in the United States, 2001,* pp. 1–52; U.S. Department of Justice, Office of Justice Programs, Bureau of Justice Statistics, "Theft Rates," table in "Crime Facts at a Glance," **http://www.ojp.usdoj.gov/bjs/gance/theft.htm**, accessed September 9, 2002; U.S. Department of Justice, Federal Bureau of Investigation, Preliminary Semiannual Uniform Crime Report, January–June 2002, Washington, DC, December 16, 2002, pp. 1–2.

5. Uniform Crime Reports, *Crime in the United States, 2001,* pp. 51–52.

6. Ibid.

7. Bureau of Justice Statistics, *Sourcebook.*

8. Ibid.

9. J. Hepburn, "Occasional Criminals," in *Major Forms of Crime,* R. Meier, ed., Beverly Hills, CA: Sage, 1984, pp. 73–94.

10. E. H. Sutherland, *The Professional Thief, by a Professional Thief,* Chicago: University of Chicago Press, 1937.

11. Ibid.

12. S. L. Messinger, "Some Reflections on 'Professional Crime' in West City," President's Commission on Law Enforcement, as cited in G. M. Sykes, *Criminology,* New York: Harcourt Brace Jovanovich, 1978, pp. 113–14; see also J. A. Inciardi, *Careers in Crime,* Chicago: Rand McNally, 1975.

13. Sykes, *Criminology.*

14. C. Klockars, *The Professional Fence,* New York: Free Press, 1976; J. Rosecrance, "The Stooper: A Professional Thief in the Sutherland Manner," *Criminology* 24, no. 1, 1986, pp. 29–40; D. Steffensmeir, *The Fence: In the Shadow of Two Worlds,* Totowa, NJ: Rowman and Littlefield, 1986.

15. Uniform Crime Reports, *Crime in the United States, 2001,* pp. 53–55; U.S. Department of Justice, Office of Justice Programs, Bureau of Justice Statistics, "Motor Vehicle Theft Rates," table in "Crime Facts at a Glance," **http://www.ojp.usdoj.gov/bjs/glance/mvt.htm**, accessed September 9, 2002.

16. C. McCaghy, P. Giordano, and T. Knicely Henson, "Auto Theft," *Criminology* 15, 1977, pp. 367–81.

17. Ibid.

18. N. G. La Vigne, J. K. Fleury, and J. Szakas, "Auto Theft and Detecting Chop Shop Locations," in *Atlas of Crime: Mapping the Criminal Landscape,* L. S. Turnbull, E. H. Hendrix, and B. D. Dent, Phoenix: Oryx, 2000, pp. 60–67.

19. Ibid.

20. "Carjackings Become Deadly: Crime Trend Linked to Anti-theft Devices," *Oklahoman,* September 20, 1992.

21. Ibid.
22. Ibid; S. Shane, "More Teenagers Today Are Going Places—in Your Car," *Baltimore Sun,* May 31, 1992.
23. J. Ray, "Every Twelfth Shopper: Who Shoplifts and Why?" *Social Casework* 68, 1987, pp. 234–39; A. Buckle and D. P. Farrington, "An Observational Study of Shoplifting," *British Journal of Criminology* 24, 1984, pp. 63–72.
24. Uniform Crime Reports, *Crime in the United States, 2001,* p. 47; T. L. Baumer and D. P. Rosenbaum, *Combating Retail Theft: Programs and Strategies,* Boston: Butterworth, 1984.
25. M. Owen Cameron, *The Booster and the Snitch,* New York: Free Press, 1964.
26. Ibid.
27. Ibid.; see also T. N. Gibbens, C. Palmer, and J. Prince, "Mental Health Aspects of Shoplifting," *British Medical Journal* 3, 1971, pp. 612–15; and R. Moore, "Shoplifting in Middle America: Patterns and Motivational Correlates," *International Journal of Offender Therapy and Comparative Criminology* 28, 1984, pp. 53–64.
28. E. Blankenburg, "The Selectivity of Legal Sanctions: An Empirical Investigation of Shoplifting," *Law and Society Review* 11, 1976, pp. 109–29; L. Klemke, "Does Apprehension for Shoplifting Amplify or Terminate Shoplifting Activity?" *Law and Society Review* 12, 1978, pp. 390–403; L. Cohen and R. Stark, "Discrimination Labeling and the Five-Finger Discount: An Empirical Analysis of Differential Shoplifting Dispositions," *Journal of Research on Crime and Delinquency* 11, 1974, pp. 25–35.
29. H. C. Black, Black's *Law Dictionary,* 5th ed., St. Paul, MN: West, 1979, pp. 594–95.
30. Uniform Crime Reports, *Crime in the United States,* 2001, pp. 1–52.
31. Bureau of Justice Statistics, *Sourcebook.*
32. Ibid.
33. Uniform Crime Reports, *Crime in the United States, 2001,* pp. 44–47.
34. Ibid.; U.S. Department of Justice, Office of Justice Programs, Bureau of Justice Statistics, "Burglary Rates," table in "Crime Facts at a Glance," http://www.ojp.usdoj.gov/bjs/glance/burg.htm.
35. Bureau of Justice Statistics, *Sourcebook.*
36. N. Shover, "Burglary," in *Crime and Justice: An Annual Review of Research,* vol. 14, M. Tonry and J. Q. Wilson, eds., Chicago: University of Chicago Press, 1991.
37. N. Shover, "Structures and Careers in Burglary," *Journal of Criminal Law, Criminology, and Police Science* 63, 1972, pp. 540–49.
38. P. Cromwell, J. Olson, and D. Wester Avary, *Breaking and Entering: An Ethnographic Analysis of Burglary,* Newbury Park, CA: Sage, 1991.
39. Ibid.; P. Letkemann, *Crime as Work,* Englewood Cliffs, NJ: Prentice-Hall, 1973.
40. G. Rengert and J. Wasilchick, *Suburban Burglary: A Time and Place for Everything,* Springfield, IL: Thomas, 1985.
41. Ibid.
42. S. M. Walcott, "Burglary," in Turnbull, Hendrix, and Dent, *Atlas of Crime,* pp. 53–59.
43. L. Yablonsky, *Criminology,* New York: Harper and Row, 1990, p. 77.
44. L. W. Sherman, P. R. Garten, and M. E. Buerger, "Hot Spots of Predatory Crime: Routine Activities and the Criminology of Place," *Criminology* 27, 1989, pp. 27–55.
45. J. Samaha, *Criminal Justice,* St. Paul, MN: West, 1991; J. H. Skolnick and D. H. Bayley, *The New Blue Line: Police Innovation in Six American Cities,* New York: Free Press, 1986.
46. Inciardi, *Careers in Crime,* pp. 33–35.
47. Klockars, *Professional Fence,* pp. 171–72.
48. Steffensmeir, *Fence.*
49. Uniform Crime Reports, *Crime in the United States,* 2001, pp. 56–58.
50. W. W. Bennett and K. M. Hess, *Investigating Arson,* St. Paul, MN: West, 1981, pp. 387–410.
51. Uniform Crime Reports, *Crime in the United States,* 2001, pp. 56–58.
52. Ibid.; M. J. Kartes Jr., "A Look at Fire Loss during 1986," *Fire Journal,* September–October 1987; J. Hall Jr., *U.S. Arson Trends and Patterns,* Quincy,

MA: National Fire Protection Association, March 2001, updated April 2002, pp. 1–2.

53. Law Enforcement Assistance Administration, *Arson and Arson Investigation,* Washington, DC: U.S. Government Printing Office, October 1987. See also Bennett and Hess, *Investigating Arson.*

54. *Diagnostic and Statistical Manual of Mental Disorders: DSM-III,* 3rd ed. Washington, DC: American Psychiatric Association, 1980, pp. 294–95.

55. Federal Emergency Management Agency, United States Fire Administration, *Interviewing and Counseling Juvenile Firesetters,* Washington, DC: U.S. Government Printing Office, 1989.

56. L. E. Somers, *Economic Crimes,* New York: Clark Boardman, 1984.

57. Bennett and Hess, *Investigating Arson.*

58. Ibid.

CHAPTER 11

1. E. H. Sutherland, *White-Collar Crime,* New York: Dryden, 1949.

2. Ibid.; see also E. H. Sutherland and D. R. Cressey, *Criminology,* 9th ed., Philadelphia: Lippincott, 1974.

3. U.S. Department of Justice, Office of Justice Programs, Bureau of Justice Statistics, *Report to the Nation on Crime and Justice,* 2nd ed., M. W. Zawitz, ed., Washington, DC, 1988, NCJ-105506, March, p. 9.

4. D. R. Simon and D. S. Eitzen, *Elite Deviance,* 4th ed., Boston: Allyn and Bacon, 1993; and the National White Collar Crime Center (NW3C), **http://www.nw3c.org/.**

5. Simon and Eitzen, *Elite Deviance,* p. 115.

6. Ibid.

7. R. Mokhiber and R. Weissman, "The 100 Top Corporate Criminals," AlterNet.org, April 26, 2000, **http://www.alternet.org/story.html?ID=1075;** *Corporate Crime Reporter* 10, no. 6, February 12, 1996.

8. Mokhiber and Weissman, "100 Top Corporate Criminals"; NW3C, *Embezzlement/Employee Theft,* September 2002, **http://www.nw3c.org/.**

9. Mokhiber and Weissman, "100 Top Corporate Criminals"; *Corporate Crime Reporter* 13, no. 7, February 15, 1999.

10. "WorldCom to Pay Record Fine," *Houston Chronicle,* May 20, 2003.

11. Simon and Eitzen, *Elite Deviance,* p. 115.

12. "WorldCom to Pay Record Fine."

13. A. Bequai, *White-Collar Crime: A 20th-Century Crisis,* Lexington, MA: Lexington Books, 1978.

14. Bureau of Justice Statistics, *Report to the Nation,* p. 9.

15. Ibid.

16. H. C. Black, *Black's Law Dictionary,* 5th ed., St Paul, MN: West, 1979, p. 468.

17. NW3C, *Embezzlement/Employee Theft.*

18. R. Willis, "White-Collar Crime: The Threat from Within," *Management Review,* 75, no. 6, June 1986, pp. 22–27, 30; J. Clark and R. Hollinger, *Theft by Employees in Work Organizations: Executive Summary,* Washington, DC: National Institute of Justice, 1983.

19. P. Cole, "Are ATMs Easy Targets for Crooks?" *Business Week,* March 6, 1989, p. 30.

20. Ibid.

21. *Time,* February 16, 1981.

22. Willis, "White-Collar Crime."

23. Ibid.

24. NW3C, *Embezzlement/Employee Theft,* September, 2002. **http://www.nw3c.org/.**

25. Ibid., and A. Resnik, "Man apologizes after stealing from society," *Cincinnati Enquirer,* April 13, 2001.

26. Willis, "White-Collar Crime."

27. D. R. Cressey, *Other People's Money: A Study in the Social Psychology of Embezzlement,* New York: Free Press, 1953.

28. Ibid.

29. D. Zeitz, *Women Who Embezzle or Defraud: A Study of Convicted Felons*, New York: Praeger, 1981; G. Nettler, "Embezzlement without Problems," *British Journal of Criminology* 14, 1974, pp. 70–77.

30. Willis, "White-Collar Crime."

31. Ibid.; Clark and Hollinger, *Theft by Employees*.

32. Willis, "White-Collar Crime."

33. Ibid.

34. Clark and Hollinger, *Theft by Employees*.

35. NW3C, *Embezzlement/Employee Theft*.

36. AARP, *Telemarketing Fraud*, 2002, cited in NW3C, *Telemarketing Fraud*, February 2003, http://www.nw3c.org/.

37. Simon and Eitzen, *Elite Deviance*, p. 114; see also D. McClintick, "The Biggest Ponzi Scheme: A Reporter's Journal," in *Swindled! Classic Business Frauds of the Seventies*, D. Moffitt, ed., Princeton, NJ: Dow Jones Books, 1976, pp. 90–126.

38. Cited in R. Lewis, "Stock Schemes a New Peril," *American Association of Retired People Bulletin* 34, no. 7, July–August 1993, pp. 1, 6–7.

39. Cited in ibid.

40. Ibid.

41. *Black's Law Dictionary*, p. 595.

42. P. Duke, "The IRS Excels at Tracking the Average Earner but Not the Wealthy," *Wall Street Journal*, April 15, 1991; see also A. Murray, "IRS Is Losing Battle against Tax Evaders Despite New Gear," *Wall Street Journal*, April 10, 1984.

43. P. E. Tracy and J. A. Fox, "A Field Experiment on Insurance Fraud in Auto Body Repair," *Criminology* 27, 1989, pp. 589–603.

44. NW3C, *Computer Crime: Computer as the Instrument of Crime*, September 2002, http://www.nw3c.org/.

45. Ibid.

46. Willis, "White-Collar Crime."

47. Ibid.

48. Ibid.

49. Ibid.

50. Ibid.

51. N. L. Winter and U. J. Dymon, "Environmental Crime," in *Atlas of Crime: Mapping the Criminal Landscape*, L. S. Turnbull, E. H. Hendrix, and B. D. Dent, eds., Phoenix, AZ: Oryx, 2000, pp. 68–81.

52. NW3C, *Environmental Crime*, September 2002, http://www.nw3c.org/.

53. Ibid.

54. "The U.S.: No Water to Waste," *Time*, August 20, 1990, p. 61.

55. G. T. Miller Jr., *Living in the Environment: An Introduction to Environmental Science*, 6th ed., Belmont, CA: Wadsworth, 1990.

56. U.S. Bureau of the Census, *Statistical Abstract of the United States, 1992*, 112th ed., Washington, DC: Government Printing Office, 1992.

57. W. H. Corson, ed., *The Global Ecology Handbook: What You Can Do about the Environmental Crisis*, Boston: Beacon, 1990.

58. Mokhiber and Weissman, "100 Top Corporate Criminals."

59. U.S. Environmental Protection Agency, *Pollution and Your Health*, Washington, DC: Office of Public Affairs, May 6, 1976.

60. Corson, *Global Ecology Handbook*.

61. Ibid.

62. Cited in P. R. Ehrlich and A. H. Ehrlich, *Population, Resources, Environment: Issues in Human Ecology*, 2nd ed., San Francisco: Freeman, 1972, pp. 146–56.

63. Miller, *Living in the Environment*.

64. J. F. DiMento and G. Forti, "'Green Managers Don't Cry': Criminal Environmental Law and Corporate Strategy" in *Contemporary Issues in Crime and Criminal Justice: Essays in Honor of Gilbert Geis*, H. N. Pontell and D. Shichor, eds., Upper Saddle River, NJ: Prentice Hall, 2001, pp. 253–64.

65. Sutherland and Cressey, *Criminology*, pp. 75–77.

66. J. Braithwaite, "Toward a Theory of Organizational Crime," paper presented at the Annual Meeting of the American Society of Criminology, Montreal, Canada, November 1987.

67. T. Hirschi and M. Gottfredson, "Causes of White-Collar Crime," *Criminology* 25, 1987, pp. 949–74; see also M. Gottfredson and T. Hirschi, *A General Theory of Crime,* Stanford, CA: Stanford University Press, 1990.

68. H. Edelhertz and C. Rogovin, eds., *A National Strategy for Containing White-Collar Crime,* Lexington, MA: Lexington Books, 1980, pp. 122–24.

69. K. Carlson and J. Chaiken, *White-Collar Crime,* Washington, DC: Bureau of Justice Statistics, 1987; D. Manson, *Tracking Offenders: White Collar Crime,* Washington, DC: Bureau of Justice Statistics, 1986.

70. G. D. Robin, "The Corporate and Judicial Disposition of Employee Thieves," *Wisconsin Law Review,* Summer 1967, pp. 635–702.

71. M. L. Benson and E. Walker, "Sentencing the White-Collar Offender," *American Sociological Review* 53, 1988, pp. 583–607; S. P. Shapiro, "Collaring the Crime, Not the Criminal: 'Liberating' the Concept of White-Collar Crime," paper presented at the Sutherland Conference, Indiana University, Bloomington, Indiana, May 12–15, 1990.

72. M. Clinard and P. Yeager, *Corporate Crime,* New York: Free Press, 1980; P. Yeager, "Structural Bias in Regulatory Law Enforcement: The Case of the U.S. Environmental Protection Agency," *Social Problems* 34, 1987, pp. 330–44.

73. American Management Association, as reported in *Nation's Business,* November 1978.

74. L. J. Siegel, *Criminology,* St. Paul, MN: West, 1993, p. 377.

75. G. Geis, "White Collar and Corporate Crime," in *Major Forms of Crime,* R. Meier, ed., Beverly Hills, CA: Sage, 1984, pp. 145–54.

76. S. Klepper and D. Nagin, "The Deterrent Effect of Perceived Certainty and Severity of Punishment Revisited," *Criminology* 27, 1989, pp. 721–46.

77. Siegel, *Criminology.*

78. Ibid.

79. Ibid.; see also J. Braithwaite and G. Geis, "On Theory and Action for Corporate Crime Control," *Crime and Delinquency* 28, 1982, pp. 292–314.

80. Siegel, *Criminology.*

81. M. Weidenbaum, "Protecting the Environment," *Society* 27, no. 1, November–December 1989, pp. 49–56.

82. Ibid.

83. Willis, "White-Collar Crime."

84. Ibid.

85. N. Jaspan, *Mind Your Own Business,* Englewood Cliffs, NJ: Prentice Hall, 1974.

86. Ibid.; see also Willis, "White-Collar Crime."

87. Willis, "White-Collar Crime."

88. R. L. Worsnop, "Mafia Crackdown (A Melting Pot of Organized Crime)," *Congressional Quarterly Researcher* 2, no. 12, 1992, pp. 267+.

89. Bureau of Justice Statistics, *Report to the Nation,* p. 8.

90. President's Commission on Organized Crime, *The Impact: Organized Crime Today; Report to the President and the Attorney General,* Washington, DC, April 1986.

91. F. A. J. Ianni and E. Reuss-Ianni, eds., *The Crime Society: Organized Crime and Corruption in America,* New York: New American Library, 1976, p. xvi.

92. U.S. Task Force on Organized Crime, *Organized Crime,* Washington, DC: Government Printing Office, 1976.

93. D. R. Cressey, *Theft of a Nation: The Structure and Operations of Organized Crime in America,* New York: Harper and Row, 1969.

94. F. A. J. Ianni and E. Reuss-Ianni, *A Family Business: Kinship and Control in Organized Crime,* New York: Russell Sage, 1973.

95. P. Reuter, *Disorganized Crime: Illegal Markets and the Mafia,* Cambridge, MA: MIT Press, 1983.

96. D. Bell, "Crime as an American Way of Life: A Queer Ladder of Social Mobility," in *The End of Ideology,* D. Bell, ed., New York: Free Press, 1965; A. A. Block, *The Business of Crime: A Documentary Study of Organized Crime in the American Economy,* Boulder, CO: Westview, 1991; J. E. Conklin, ed., *The Crime*

Establishment: Organized Crime and American Society, Englewood Cliffs, NJ: Prentice Hall, 1973; M. H. Halley, *Life under Bruno: The Economics of an Organized Crime Family,* Philadelphia: Philadelphia Crime Commission, 1991.
97. Bureau of Justice Statistics, *Report to the Nation.*
98. Ibid.

CHAPTER 12

1. U.S. Department of Health and Human Services, National Institutes of Health, National Institute on Drug Abuse (NIDA), *National Household Survey on Drug Abuse: Population Estimates, 1988,* Washington, DC: Government Printing Office, 1989, DHHS Publication no. (ADM) 89–1636; U.S. Department of Health and Human Services, Substance Abuse and Mental Health Services Administration, Office of Applied Studies, 2001 National Survey on Drug Use and Health (NSDUH), updated April 4, 2003, Washington, DC, http://www.samhsa.gov/oas/nhsda/2klnhsda/vol1/chapter2.htm.

2. Ibid.

3. D. Giacopassi and M. Vandiver, "University Students' Perceptions of Tobacco, Cocaine, and Homicide Fatalities," *American Journal of Drug and Alcohol Abuse,* 25, no. 1, 1999, pp. 163–72; M. McGinnis and W. Foege, "Actual Causes of Death in the United States," *Journal of the American Medical Association* 270, no. 18, 1993, pp. 2207–12.

4. L. Glick and D. Hebding, "Drugs and Alcohol," in *Introduction to Social Problems,* Reading, MA: Addison-Wesley, 1980, pp. 237–75.

5. U.S. Commission on Marihuana and Drug Abuse, *Drug Use in America: Problem in Perspective; Second Report,* Washington, DC: Government Printing Office, 1973; see also U.S. Department of Justice, Bureau of Justice Statistics, "Public Opinion about Drugs," in *Drugs and Crime Facts, 1992,* Washington, DC, March 1993, NCJ-139561; U.S. Department of Health and Human Services, Substance Abuse and Mental Health Services Administration, Office of Applied Studies, *NSDUH Report,* February 7, 2003.

6. Ibid.

7. E. Goode, *Drugs in American Society,* New York: Knopf, 1972; see also Glick and Hebding, *Introduction to Social Problems;* D. Hebding and L. Glick, "Majority Varieties of Deviant Behavior, Drug Abuse, and Alcoholism," in *Introduction to Sociology,* 4th ed., New York: McGraw-Hill, 1992, pp. 184–93.

8. NIDA, *Cocaine/Crack: The Big Lie,* 1989, DHHS Publication no. (ADM) 89–1427.

9. Goode, *Drugs in American Society;* S. Cohen, *The Substance Abuse Problems,* New York: Haworth, 1981; NIDA, *Cocaine/Crack.*

10. J. Fort and C. Cory, *American Drugstore,* Boston: Educational Associates, 1975; Goode, *Drugs in American Society;* Glick and Hebding, *Introduction to Social Problems.*

11. Fort and Cory, *American Drugstore;* and Glick and Hebding, *Introduction to Social Problems.*

12. G. W. Lawson and C. A. Cooperrider, *Clinical Psychopharmacology,* Rockville, MD: Aspen, 1988; Fort and Cory, *American Drugstore.*

13. Drugs and Crime Data Center and Clearinghouse, *Drugs, Crime, and the Justice System: A National Report from the Bureau of Justice Statistics (DCJS),* M. W. Zawitz, ed., Washington, DC: U.S. Department of Justice, Bureau of Justice Statistics NCJ-133652, December 1992.

14. *NSDUH Report,* February 7, 2003.

15. Ibid.

16. U.S. Department of Justice, Office of Justice Programs, Bureau of Justice Statistics, *Drugs and Crime Facts,* May 9, 2002, p. 2. For a detailed current analysis of drug use and crime in the United States go to http://www.ojp.usdoj.gov/bjs/dcf/duc.htm, or use "Bureau of Justice Statistics" as your Internet search keyword and go to "Drug Use and Crime."

17. Ibid.; and U.S. Department of Justice, Office of Justice Programs, Bureau of Justice Statistics, *Violence in the Workplace, 1993–99,* Washington, DC, December 2001, NCJ-190076.

18. U.S. Department of Justice, Office of Justice Programs, Bureau of Justice Statistics, *Substance Abuse and Treatment of Adults on Probation, 1995,* Washington, DC, March 1998, NCJ-166611; U.S. Department of Justice, Office of Justice Programs, Bureau of Justice Statistics, *Mental Health and Treatment of Inmates and Probationers,* Washington, DC, July 1999, NCJ-174463; *Drugs and Crime Facts,* May 9, 2002.

19. U.S. Department of Justice, Office of Justice Programs, Bureau of Justice Statistics, *Mental Health and Treatment of Inmates and Probationers,* Washington, DC, July 1999, NCJ-174463; and *Drugs and Crime Facts,* May 9, 2002.

20. National Council on Alcoholism (NCA), 1987, *Facts on Alcoholism and Alcohol-Related Problems;* National Council on Alcoholism and Drug Dependence, "Facts and Information: Alcoholism and Drug Dependence Are America's Number One Health Problem," June 2002, **http://www.ncadd.org/facts/numberoneprob.html.**

21. *DCJS,* p. 25.

22. Cohen, *Substance Abuse Problems,* p. 7; see also *DCJS,* pp. 20, 27.

23. Drugs and Crime Data Center and Clearinghouse, *Street Terms: Cocaine, Heroin, and Marijuana,* 1991.

24. Cohen, *Substance Abuse Problems,* pp. 287–93.

25. *NSDUH Report,* February 7, 2003.

26. Fort and Cory, *American Drugstore;* and M. B. Clinard, *Sociology of Deviant Behavior,* 4th ed., New York: Holt, Rinehart and Winston, 1974.

27. *DCJS; NSDUH Report,* February 7, 2003.

28. NIDA, *National Household Survey on Drug Abuse: Population Estimates, 1991,* Washington, DC: Government Printing Office, December 1992, p. 26. *NSDUH Report,* February 7, 2003.

29. *DCJS,* p. 41.

30. *NSDUH Report,* February 7, 2003.

31. *DCJS,* pp. 41, 151.

32. Ibid, p. 24.

33. NIDA, *National Household Survey,* 1991, pp. 11, 26; *NSDUH Report,* February 7, 2003.

34. *DCJS,* p. 24.

35. Goode, *Drugs in American Society.*

36. Glick and Hebding, *Introduction to Social Problems,* p. 246.

37. *Street Terms,* p. 24.

38. Bureau for International Narcotics and Law Enforcement Affairs, *International Narcotics Control Strategy Report, 2002,* March 2003, pp. 1–2, **http://www.state.gov/g/inl/rls/nrcrpt/2002/html/17942.htm.**

39. Ibid.

40. Cohen, *Substance Abuse Problems,* pp. 76–77.

41. E. Goode, *Deviant Behavior,* 3rd ed., Englewood Cliffs, NJ: Prentice Hall, 1990.

42. Cohen, *Substance Abuse Problems,* pp. 76–77.

43. NIDA, *National Household Survey, 1991; NSDUH Report,* February 7, 2003.

44. *Street Terms.*

45. Ibid., p. 24.

46. D. W. Goodwin, "Alcoholism and Genetics," *Archives of General Psychiatry* 42, 1985, pp. 171–74.

47. R. J. Williams, *Alcoholism: The Nutritional Approach,* Austin: University of Texas Press, 1959; Glick and Hebding, *Introduction to Social Problems,* pp. 237–75; see also Cohen, *Substance Abuse Problems.*

48. S. Rathus and J. Nevid, *Abnormal Psychology,* Englewood Cliffs, NJ: Prentice-Hall, 1991, pp. 344–54.

49. U.S. Department of Health, Education and Welfare, National Institute on Alcohol Abuse and Alcoholism (NIAAA), *Alcohol Abuse and Alcoholism,* Washington, DC: U.S. Government Printing Office, 1972; NCA, *Facts on Alcoholism.*

50. Goode, *Drugs in American Society*, p. 3.
51. Cohen, *Substance Abuse Problems*.
52. Glick and Hebding, *Introduction to Social Problems*.
53. P. Laurie, *Drugs: Medical, Psychological, and Social Facts*, Baltimore: Penguin, 1970, p. 13.
54. Goode, *Drugs in American Society*.
55. C. Winick, "Physician Narcotic Addicts," *Social Problem*, 9, pp. 174–86.
56. A. Lindesmith, *Addiction and Opiates*, Chicago: Aldine, 1968; see also R. Akers, *Deviant Behavior: A Social Learning Approach*, Belmont, CA: Wadsworth, 1973.
57. NIAAA, *Alcohol Abuse and Alcoholism*.
58. Laurie, *Drugs*.
59. N. Kessel and H. Walton, *Alcoholism*, Baltimore: Penguin, 1976, pp. 56–68.
60. J. Platt and C. Labate, *Heroin Addiction: Theory, Research, and Treatment*, New York: Wiley, 1976.
61. NIAAA, *Alcohol Abuse and Alcoholism*.
62. A. Bass, "Mental Ills, Drug Abuse Linked," *Boston Globe*, November 21, 1990.
63. Glick and Hebding, *Introduction to Social Problems*.
64. E. H. Sutherland and D. R. Cressey, *Criminology*, 9th ed., Philadelphia: Lippincott, 1974.
65. Akers, *Deviant Behavior*, pp. 49–57, 84–85, 123, 133.
66. H. S. Becker, "Becoming a Marijuana User," in *Readings in General Sociology*, 4th ed., R. O'Brien, C. Schrag, and W. Martin, eds., New York: Houghton Mifflin, 1969, pp. 280–85.
67. Goode, *Drugs in American Society*, pp. 81, 112, 135, 167–79.
68. R. Quinney, *Criminology*, Boston: Little, Brown, 1975, p. 128.
69. Ibid.; see also Akers, *Deviant Behavior*.
70. U.S. Department of Justice, Office of Justice Programs, Bureau of Justice Statistics, "Drug Control Budget," in *Drugs and Crime Facts*, Washington, DC, May 16, 2003.
71. U.S. Department of Justice, Office of Justice Programs, Bureau of Justice Statistics, "Drug Law Violations: Enforcement," in *Drugs and Crime Facts*, October 28, 2002, updated May 16, 2003.
72. Ibid.
73. R. Straus, "Alcoholism and Problem Drinking," in *Contemporary Social Problems*, R. Merton and R. Nisbet, eds., p. 212; Glick and Hebding, *Introduction to Social Problems*.
74. Glick and Hebding, *Introduction to Social Problems*, pp. 264–65.
75. Goode, *Drugs in American Society*.
76. *DCJS*, pp. 91–125; Executive Office of the President, Office of National Drug Control Policy, *The President's National Drug Control Strategy, 2004*, Washington, DC, March 2004, **http://www.whitehousedrugpolicy.gov/publications/policy/ndcs04/2004ndcs.pdf**.
77. Ibid.; C. E. Reasons, "The Addict as Criminal," *Crime and Delinquency* 21, no. 1, January 1975, pp. 19–27; and *Drugs and Crime Facts*, May 9, 2002.
78. Goode, *Drugs in American Society*.
79. U.S. Department of Justice, Office of Justice Programs, Bureau of Justice Statistics, *Substance Abuse and Treatment, State and Federal Prisons, 1997*, Washington, DC, January 1999, NCJ-172871.
80. A. B. Smith and H. Pollack, "Crimes without Victims," *Saturday Review*, December 4, 1971; Hebding and Glick, *Introduction to Sociology*.
81. J. Feinberg, *Social Philosophy*, Englewood Cliffs, NJ: Prentice-Hall, 1973, chaps. 1–3.
82. H. C. Black, *Black's Law Dictionary*, 5th ed., St. Paul, MN: West, 1979, p. 100.
83. J. Boyles, "Prostitution," in *Atlas of Crime: Mapping the Criminal Landscape*, L. S. Turnbull, E. H. Hendrix, and B. D. Dent, eds., Phoenix: Oryx, 2000, pp. 140–48.
84. C. Esselzstyn, "Prostitution in the United States," *Annals* 376, 1968, pp. 126–43; S. Rathus, *Human Sexuality*, New York: Holt, Rinehart and Winston, 1983.
85. J. Mall, "A Study of S.F.'s Unhappy Hookers," *Los Angeles Times*, February 19, 1982; M-D. Janus, B. Scanlon, and V. Price, "Youth Prostitution," in *Child*

Pornography and Sex Rings, A. Wolbert Burgess, ed., Lexington, MA: Lexington Books, 1989, pp. 127–46.

86. C. Winick and P. Kinsie, *The Lively Commerce,* Chicago: Quadrangle, 1971.
87. K. Daly, "The Social Control of Sexuality: A Case Study of the Criminalization of Prostitution in the Progressive Era," *Research in Law, Deviance, and Social Control* 9, 1988, pp. 171–206.
88. H. Greenwald, *The Call Girl,* New York: Ballantine, 1958.
89. Ibid.; see also G. Hotaling and D. Finkelhor, *The Sexual Exploitation of Missing Children,* Washington, DC: U.S. Department of Justice, 1988; P. Gebhard, "Misconceptions about Female Prostitutes," *Medical Aspects of Human Sexuality* 3, July 1969, pp. 28–30; Winick and Kinsie, *Lively Commerce;* and J. James, "Prostitutes and Prostitution," in *Deviants: Voluntary Action in a Hostile World,* E. Sagarin and E. Montanino, eds., New York: Scott, Foresman, 1977.
90. Boyles, "Prostitution."
91. *Webster's New World Dictionary of the American Language,* 2nd college ed., Cleveland, OH: Prentice-Hall, 1986, p. 1109.
92. *Black's Law Dictionary,* p. 1045.
93. Ibid.; *Miller v. California,* 413 U.S. 15, 24–25; 93 S.Ct. 2607, 2615; 37 L.Ed.2d 419 (1973).
94. *Pope* v. *Illinois,* 107 S.Ct.1918 (1987).
95. U.S. Commission on Obscenity and Pornography, *The Report of the Commission on Obscenity and Pornography,* Washington, DC: Government Printing Office, 1970.
96. J. Court, "Sex and Violence: A Ripple Effect," in *Pornography and Aggression,* N. Malamuth and E. Donnerstein, eds., Orlando: Academic Press, 1984.
97. E. Donnerstein, D. Linz, and S. Penrod, *The Question of Pornography: Research Findings and Policy Implications,* New York: Free Press, 1987.
98. U.S. Attorney General's Commission on Pornography, *Attorney General's Commission on Pornography: Final Report,* Washington, DC: U.S. Department of Justice, 1986.
99. U.S. Attorney General's Commission on Pornography, *Final Report of the Attorney General's Commission on Pornography,* Nashville: Rutledge Hill Press, 1986; ibid.
100. *Attorney General's Commission on Pornography: Final Report.*
101. A. Belanger et al., "Typology of Sex Rings Exploiting Children," in Burgess, *Child Pornography and Sex Rings,* pp. 51–81; J. Hurst, "Children—A Big Profit Item for the Smut Peddlers," *Los Angeles Times,* May 26, 1977, cited in L. Lederer, ed., *Take Back the Night,* New York: Morrow, 1980.
102. *New York* v. *Ferber,* 50 L.W. 5077 (1982).
103. "The Communications Decency Act Defined," CNN Interactive, 1997, http://www.cnn.com/us/9703/cda.scotus/what.is.cda/; "Decency Act Blocked," *Time,* June 14, 1996, http://www.time.com/time/nation/article/0,8599,6790,00.html; "Filtering Law Sparks Fight," ABC News.com, December 20, 2000, http://more.abcnews.go.com/sections/scitech/DailyNews/library_filters001220.html.
104. Ibid.
105. Arkansas Shared Technical Architecture, "Summary of the Children's Internet Protection Act," 2002, http://www.techarch.state.ar.us/domains/network/resources/CIPA.htm; ADLAW by Request, "Congress Defends Children's Internet Protection Act," April 16, 2001, http://www.adlawbyrequest.com/legislation/CIPA41601.shtml; Wisconsin Department of Public Instruction, "Children's Internet Protection Act Questions and Answers," and "FAQ on E-Rate Compliance with the Neighborhood Children's Internet Protection Act," September 27, 2002, http://www.dpi.state.wi.us/dpi/dlcl/pld/cipafaq.html.

CHAPTER 13

1. U.S. Department of Justice, Bureau of Justice Statistics, "The Response to Crime: An Overview of the Criminal Justice System," in *Report to the Nation on Crime and Justice*, 2nd ed., Washington, DC, March 1988, NCJ-105506, pp. 56–61.

2. U.S. Department of Justice, Bureau of Justice Statistics, "The Justice System," August 6, 2001, http://www.ojp.usdoj.gov/bjs/justsys.htm.

3. "The Response to Crime."

4. "The Justice System."

5. Ibid.

6. Ibid.

7. N. Kop, M. Euwema, and W. Schaufeli, "Burnout, Job Stress, and Violent Behaviour among Dutch Police Officers," *Work and Stress* 13, no. 4, 1999, pp. 326–40; D. A. Alexander, L. G. Walker, G. Innes, and B. L. Irving, *Police Stress at Work*, London: Police Foundation, 1993; F. H. Biggam, K. G. Power, R. R. MacDonald, W. B. Carcary, and E. Moodie, "Self-Perceived Occupational Stress and Distress in a Scottish Police Force," *Work and Stress* 11, no. 2, 1997, pp. 118–33; J. M. Brown and E. A. Campbell, "Sources of Occupational Stress in the Police," *Work and Stress* 4, no. 4, 1990, pp. 305–18; J. M. Brown and E. A. Campbell, *Stress and Policing: Sources and Strategies*, Chichester, England, Wiley, 1994.

8. J. Samaha, *Criminal Justice*, 2nd ed., St. Paul: West, 1991, p. 122; E. B. Weston and K. M. Wells, *Law Enforcement and Criminal Justice*, Pacific Palisades, CA: Goodyear, 1972; R. Lane, *Policing the City: Boston, 1822–1885*, Cambridge, MA: Harvard University Press, 1967; R. Lane, "Urban Crime and Police in Nineteenth-Century America," in *Crime and Justice: An Annual Review of Research*, vol. 2, N. Morris and M. Tonry, eds., Chicago: University of Chicago Press, 1980, pp. 1–45; M. H. Moore and G. L. Kelling, "Learning from Police History," *Public Interest*, Spring 1983, p. 51; E. Parks, "From Constabulary to Police Society," in *Criminal Law in Action*, 2nd ed., W. Chambliss, ed., New York: Macmillan, 1984, pp. 209–22.

9. Ibid.; and W. R. Miller, "Cops and Bobbies, 1830–1870," in *Thinking about Police: Contemporary Readings*, 2nd ed., C. B. Klockars and S. D. Mastrofski, eds., New York: McGraw Hill, 1991, pp. 73–88.

10. Ibid.

11. Ibid.

12. M. H. Haller, "Chicago Cops, 1890–1925," in Klockars and Mastrofski, *Thinking about Police*, pp. 88–100.

13. C. D. Uchida, "The Development of the American Police," in *Critical Issues in Policing*, R. Dunham and G. P. Alpert, eds., Prospect Heights, IL: Waveland, 1989, p. 24; Samaha, *Criminal Justice*, p. 124.

14. N. Douthit and A. Vollmer, in Klockars and Mastrofski, *Thinking about Police*, pp. 101–14.

15. Ibid.

16. Ibid.

17. Samaha, *Criminal Justice*, pp. 125–27.

18. R. A. Staufenberger, "The Role of the Police," in *Progress in Policing: Essays on Change*, Cambridge, MA: Ballinger, 1980, pp. 13–18; President's Commission on Law Enforcement and the Administration of Justice, *Task Force Report: Crime and Its Impact*, Washington, DC: U.S. Government Printing Office, 1969.

19. M. M. Freeley and A. D. Sarat, *The Policy Dilemma: Federal Crime Policy and Enforcement, 1968–1978*, Minneapolis: University of Minnesota Press, 1980; Samaha, *Criminal Justice*, pp. 125–27.

20. Samaha, *Criminal Justice*, p. 231.

21. U.S. Department of Justice, Bureau of Justice Statistics, *Census of State and Local Law Enforcement Agencies, 2000*, October 2002, Washington, DC, NCJ-194066, p. 1.

22. T. Adams, *Law Enforcement*, Englewood Cliffs, NJ: Prentice Hall, 1968.

23. D. A. Torres, *Handbook of Federal Police and Investigative Agencies*, Westport, CT: Greenwood, 1985.

24. CNN.com, "Ex-FBI Spy Hannssen sentenced to Life, Apologizes," May 14, 2002, http://www.cnn.com/2002/LAW/05/10/hanssen.sentenced; B. Bender, "FBI Responds to Re-address the Terrorist Threat," Jane's Information Group, June 3, 2002, http://www.janes.com/; Anti-Defamation League, "ADL Commends FBI Restructuring Effort," November 18, 1999, press release, http://www.adl.org/PresRele/Mise_00/3526_00.asp; ABCNEWS.com, "Restructuring

for Terrorism," May 29, 2002, http://www.ABCNEWS.com/; Guardian Unlimited, "FBI Rebuked over 'Illegal' Spying," August 23, 2002, http://www.guardian.co.uk/usa/story/0,12271,779746,00.html; ABCNEWS.com, "FBI Chief Tells Warning Ignored Before Sept. 11," September 5, 2002, http://www.ABCNEWS.com/; Time.com, "The Bombshell Memo: Coleen Rowley's Memo to FBI Director Robert Mueller," May 21, 2002, http://www.time.com/time/covers/1101020603/memo.html; S. Walker, *Popular Justice*, New York: Oxford University Press, 1980; *Philadelphia Inquirer*, September 30, 1993.

25. BJS, *Report to the Nation*; BJS, *Census, 2000*, p. 4.

26. President's Commission on Law Enforcement, *Task Force Report*; see also Klockars and Mastrofski, *Thinking about Police*.

27. President's Commission on Law Enforcement, *Task Force Report*.

28. BJS, *Report to the Nation*, p. 62.

29. J. Q. Wilson and G. Kelling, "Broken Windows: The Police and Neighborhood Safety," *Atlantic Monthly*, March 1982, pp. 29–38; See also H. Goldstein, "Toward Community Oriented Policing: Potential Basic Requirements, and Threshold Questions," *Crime and Delinquency* 33, no. 1, 1987, pp. 6–30; C. B. Klockars, "The Rhetoric of Community Policing," in *Community Policing: Rhetoric and Reality*, J. R. Green and S. Mastrofski, eds., New York: Praeger, 1988, pp. 239–58.

30. J. Webster, "Police Task and Time Study," *Journal of Criminal Law, Criminology, and Police Science* 61, 1970, pp. 94–100; E. Birtner, *The Function of the Police in Modern Society*, Chevy Chase, MD: National Institute of Mental Health, 1970; J. R. Lilly, "What Are the Police Now Doing?" *Journal of Police Science and Administration* 6, 1978, pp. 51–60; S. Mastrofski, "The Police and Non-crime Services," in *Evaluating Performance of Criminal Justice Agencies*, G. Whitaker and C. Philips, eds., Beverly Hills, CA: Sage, 1983.

31. J. R. Greene and C. B. Klockars, "What Police Do," in Klockars and Mastrofski, *Thinking about Police*, pp. 273–84.

32. BJS, "The Justice System."

33. Lawrence W. Sherman, "Policing for Crime Prevention," in *Preventing Crime: What Works, What Doesn't, What's Promising*, report to the United States Congress prepared for the National Institute of Justice by L. W. Sherman, D. Gottfredson, D. MacKenzie, J. Eck, P. Reuter, and S. Bushway, n.d., http://www.ncjrs.org/works/chapter8.htm and http://www.ncjrs.org/works.org/works.

34. Ibid.

35. Ibid.

36. N. G. Holton and L. L. Lamar, *The Criminal Courts: Structures, Personnel, and Processes*, New York: McGraw-Hill, 1991, pp. 50, 56, 100; BJS, "the Sentencing of Criminals and Changing Correctional Practices and Alternatives," in *Report to the Nation*, pp. 90–93, 96–97, 100–101.

37. Holten and Lamar, *Criminal Courts*, p. 59.

38. Ibid.

39. U.S. Department of Justice, Bureau of Justice Statistics, *The Prosecution of Felony Arrests*, Washington, DC, 1989, and *Sourcebook of Criminal Justice Statistics, 1992*, 20th anniversary ed., Washington, DC, 1993, p. 442.

40. Samaha, *Criminal Justice*, p. 320.

41. Ibid.

42. Holten and Lamar, *Criminal Courts*, p. 59.

43. Ibid., p. 93.

44. Ibid.

45. BJS, "Response to Crime," p. 90.

46. Ibid.

47. "17 Years of Executions," *Philadelphia Inquirer*, May 9, 1993; L. A. Greenfield, *Capital Punishment*, 1991, Bulletin of the Bureau of Justice Statistics, Washington, DC, 1992.

48. U.S. Department of Justice, Bureau of Justice Statistics, "Capital Punishment Statistics," June 13, 2003, http://www.ojp.usdoj.gov/bjs/cp.htm.

49. M. Wolfgang and M. Riedel, "Race, Judicial Discretion, and the Death Penalty," *Annals of the American Academy of Political and Social Sciences*, 407, 1973,

pp. 119–33; Greenfield, *Capital Punishment, 1991*; L. A. Greenfield, *Capital Punishment, 1989*, Bulletin of the Bureau of Justice Statistics, Washington, DC, 1990; J. E. Jacoby and R. Paternoster, "Sentencing Disparity and Jury Packing: Further Challenges to the Death Penalty," *Journal of Criminal Law and Criminology* 73, 1982, pp. 379–87; G. Vito and T. Keil, "Capital Sentencing in Kentucky: An Analysis of Factors Influencing Decision Making in the Post-Gregg Period," *Journal of Criminal Law and Criminology* 79, 1988, pp. 483–503; J. E. Jacoby, "The Deterrence and Brutalizing Effects of the Death Penalty," in *The Death Penalty in South Carolina*, B. L. Pearson, ed., Columbia, SC: Acluse, 1981; T. Keil and G. Vito, "Race, Homicide Severity, and Application of the Death Penalty: A Consideration of the Barnett Scale," *Criminology* 27, 1989, pp. 511–32; and BJS, "Capital Punishment Statistics."

50. Ibid.
51. D. Baldus, C. Pulaski, and G. Woodworth, "Comparative Review of Death Sentences: An Empirical Study of the Georgia Experience," *Journal of Criminal Law and Criminology* 74, 1983, pp. 661–90.
52. Death Penalty Information Center, "Facts about the Death Penalty," http://www.deathpenaltyinfo.org/FactSheet.pdf.
53. A. M. Platt, *The Child Savers*, Chicago: University of Chicago Press, 1969, pp. 73–80; A. L. Mauss, *Social Problems as Social Movements*, Philadelphia: Lippincott, 1975, pp. 128–38.
54. BJS, "Response to Crime," pp. 71–82.
55. Ibid.

CHAPTER 14

1. R. Korn and L. McCorkle, *Criminology and Penology*, New York: Holt, Rinehart and Winston, 1966, pp. 374–98, 403–5; L. Glick and D. Hebding, *Introduction to Social Problems*, Reading, MA: Addison Wesley, 1980.
2. Ibid.; see also C. Beccaria, *An Essay on Crimes and Punishments*, London: Almon, 1767.
3. Korn and McCorkle, *Criminology and Penology*, pp. 410–14; Glick and Hebding, *Introduction to Social Problems*.
4. Ibid.
5. Ibid.
6. U.S. National Advisory Commission on Criminal Justice Standards and Goals, Corrections, Washington, DC, 1973, p. 43.
7. U.S. Department of Justice, Office of Justice Programs, Bureau of Justice Statistics, "Jail Statistics," April 6, 2003, http://www.ojp.usdoj.gov/bjs/jails.htm.
8. H. Mattick, "The Contemporary Jail in the United States," in *Handbook of Criminology*, D. Glaser, ed., Chicago: Rand McNally, 1974; S. Kline, *Jail Inmates*, 1989, bulletin of the Bureau of Justice Statistics, Washington, DC, 1990.
9. C. Bartollas and J. P. Conrad, *Introduction to Corrections*, 2nd ed., New York: HarperCollins, 1992, p. 332.
10. D. L. MacKenzie, "'Boot Camp' Programs Grow in Number and Scope," *National Institute of Justice Research in Action* 222, November–December 1990, pp. 1–8; D. L. MacKenzie et al., "Shock Incarceration: Rehabilitation or Retribution?" *Journal of Rehabilitation* 14, 1989, pp. 25–40; D. L. MacKenzie, "Boot Camp Prisons: Components, Evaluations, and Empirical Issues," *Federal Probation*, September 1990, pp. 44–52; Bartollas and Conrad, *Introduction to Corrections*, p. 336.
11. D. Parent, "Shock Incarceration Programs," paper presented at the American Correctional Association Winter Conference, Phoenix, Arizona, 1988.
12. U.S. Department of Justice, Office of Justice Programs, Bureau of Justice Statistics, "Key Crime and Justice Facts at a Glance," June 18, 2003, http://www.ojp.usdoj.gov/bjs/glance/corrtyp.htm and http://www.ojp.usdoj.gov/bjs/glance/incrt.htm.

13. R. Hawkins and G. P. Allpert, *American Prison Systems: Punishment and Justice*, Englewood Cliffs, NJ: Prentice Hall, 1989.
14. Bartollas and Conrad, *Introduction to Corrections*, pp. 338–48.
15. Ibid.; and Hawkins and Allpert, *American Prison Systems*.
16. Ibid.; B. S. Alper, *Prisons Inside Out*, Cambridge, MA: Ballinger, 1974; T. R. Clear and G. E Cole, *American Corrections*, Monterey, CA:, Brooks/Cole, 1986.
17. Ibid.
18. P. Macci, H. Teitelbaum, and J. Prather, "Population Density and Inmate Misconduct Rates in the Federal Prison System," *Federal Probation* 41, 1977, pp. 26–31; E. Megargee, "The Association of Population Density, Reduced Space, and Uncomfortable Temperatures with Misconduct in a Prison Community," *American Journal of Community Psychology* 5, 1977, pp. 289–98; G. McCain, V. Cox, and E. Paulus, *The Effect of Prison Crowding on Inmate Behavior*, Washington, DC: Government Printing Office, 1981.
19. P. G. Zimbardo, "Pathology of Imprisonment," *Society* 9, April 1972.
20. U.S. Department of Justice, Office of Justice Programs, Bureau of Justice Statistics, "Reentry Trends in the United States," June 13, 2003, **http://www.ojp.usdoj.gov/bjs/reentry/releases.htm**.
21. Ibid.
22. Ibid., **http://www.ojp.usdoj.gov/bjs/reentry/recidivism.htm**.
23. Bartollas and Conrad, *Introduction to Corrections*, pp. 192–93.
24. Ibid.
25. Ibid., p. 194.
26. U.S. Department of Justice, Bureau of Justice Statistics, *Report to the Nation on Crime and Justice*, 2nd ed., Washington, DC, March 1988, WCJ-105506, p. 58, and "Probation and Parole Statistics," June 13, 2003, **http://www.ojp.usdoj.gov/bjs/pandp.htm**.
27. BJS, "Probation and Parole Statistics."
28. M. Block and W. Rhodes, *The Impact of Federal Sentencing Guidelines*, Washington, DC: National Institute of Justice, 1987.
29. Bartollas and Conrad, *Introduction to Corrections*, p. 222.
30. J. Petersilia et al., *Granting Felons Probation: Public Risks and Alternatives*, Santa Monica, CA: Rand Corporation, 1985.
31. J. Petersilia et al., *Prison versus Probation in California*, Santa Monica, CA: Rand Corporation, 1986, pp. i–vii.
32. C. Spohn and D. Holleran, "The Effects of Imprisonment on Recidivism Rates of Felony Offenders: A Focus on Drug Offenders," *Criminology*, 40, no. 2, May 2002, pp. 329–58.
33. E. J. Latessa and G. E. Vito, "The Effects of Intensive Supervision on Shock Probationers," *Journal of Criminal Justice* 16, 1988, pp. 319–30; D. L. MacKenzie and J. W. Shaw, "Inmate Adjustment and Change during Shock Incarceration: The Impact of Correctional Boot Camp Programs," *Justice Quarterly* 7, 1990, pp. 125–50; H. Allen et al., *Probation and Parole in America*, New York: Free Press, 1985.
34. S. Gettinger, "Intensive Supervision: Can It Rehabilitate Probation?" *Corrections Magazine* 9, April 1983, pp. 7–18.
35. B. Erwin and L. Bennett, *New Dimensions in Probation: Georgia's Experience with Intensive Probation Supervision (IPS)*, Washington, DC: National Institute of Justice, 1987; F. S. Pearson and A. G. Harper, "Contingent Intermediate Sentences," *Crime and Delinquency* 36, 1990, pp. 75–86.
36. J. Petersilia, *Exploring the Option of House Arrest*, Santa Monica, CA: Rand Corporation, 1986; J. Petersilia, *Expanding Options for Criminal Sentencing*, Santa Monica, CA: Rand Corporation, 1987; M. Renzema and D. Skelton, "Use of Electronic Monitoring in the United States: 1989 Update," *NIJ Reports*, November–December 1990, pp. 9–13; G. Graham, "High Tech Monitoring: Are We Losing the Human Element?" *Corrections Today*, December 1988, pp. 92–93; K. Peck, "High-Tech: House Arrest," *Progressive*, July 1988, pp. 26–28; J. Walker, "Sharing the Credit, Sharing the Blame: Managing Political Risks in Electronically Monitored House Arrest," *Federal Probation, U.S. Courts*, June 1990, pp. 16–19.

37. Walker, "Sharing the Credit"; A. Esteves, "Electronic Incarceration in Massachusetts: A Critical Analysis," *Social Justice* 17, 1991, pp. 76–90; K. Morane and C. Linder, "Probation and High-Technology Revolution: Is Reconceptualization of the Traditional Probation Officer Role Model Inevitable?" *Criminal Justice Review* 3, 1987, pp. 25–32.

38. B. Galaway, "Restitution as Innovation or Unfulfilled Promise?" *Federal Probation* 52, no. 3, 1988, pp. 3–14.

39. P. Schneider, A. Schneider, and W. Griffith, *Two Year Report on the National Evaluation of the Juvenile Restitution Evaluation Project V*, Eugene, OR: Institute of Policy Analysis, 1982; J. Hudson and B. Galaway, "Financial Restitution: Toward an Invaluable Program Model," *Canadian Journal of Criminology* 31, 1989, pp. 1–18.

40. BJS, "Reentry Trends," http://www.ojp.usdoj.gov/bjs/reentry/growth.htm.

41. Ibid., http://www.ojp.usdoj.gov/bjs/reentry/releases.htm.

42. BJS, *Report to the Nation*, p. 58.

43. BJS, "Reentry Trends," http://www.ojp.usdoj.gov/bjs/reentry/characteristics.htm.

44. I. Waller, *Men Released from Prison*, Toronto, Canada: University of Toronto Press, 1974, p. 190.

45. H. Sacks and C. Logan, *Parole—Crime Prevention? Or Crime Postponement?* Storrs: University of Connecticut School of Law Press, 1980, pp. 1–13.

46. A. Beck and B. Shipley, *Recidivism of Prisoners Released in 1983*, Washington, DC: Bureau of Justice Statistics, 1989.

47. BJS, "Reentry Trends," http://www.ojp.usdoj.gov/bjs/reentry/success.htm.

48. Ibid.

49. J. Samaha, *Criminal Justice*, 2nd ed., St. Paul, MN: West, 1991, p. 548.

50. Ibid.

51. A. von Hirsch and K. J. Hanrahan, *Abolish Parole? Summary of Report Submitted to the National Institute of Law Enforcement and Criminal Justice, Law Enforcement Assistance Administration, U.S. Department of Justice*, Washington, DC: National Institute of Law Enforcement, 1978.

52. Bartollas and Conrad, *Introduction to Corrections*, p. 256.

53. Ibid.

54. Ibid., pp. 269–76.

55. Ibid.

56. Ibid.

57. Ibid.

58. K. F. Schoen, "The Community Corrections Act," *Crime and Delinquency* 24, October 1978, pp. 459–64; C. Eskridge, R. Seiter, and E. Carlson, "Community Based Corrections: From the Community to the Community," in *Critical Issues in Corrections*, V. Webb and R. Roberg, eds., St. Paul, MN: West, 1981, pp. 171–203.

59. A. Seymour and T. Gregorie, "Restorative Justice for Young Offenders and Their Victims," *Corrections Today* 64, no. 1, February 2002, pp. 90–93.

60. Ibid.

61. K. Van Wormer, "Restoring Justice," *USA Today Magazine*, November 2001, pp. 32–34.

62. Seymour and Gregorie, "Restorative Justice."

The **addict robber** is dependent on drugs and steals to support his or her habit.

Addiction is the condition in which a person becomes physically dependent on a drug and so will go through withdrawal if drug use ceases.

ADHD, or **attention deficit/hyperactivity disorder,** has been linked to delinquency and crime.

Adjudication is the decision making that occurs in formal court proceedings.

Aggravated assault is an attack or attempted attack with a weapon, regardless of whether an injury occurred, or an attack without a weapon when serious injury resulted.

August Aichorn believed that criminality is the result of an underdeveloped superego and an unregulated id.

Air contamination results from the release of industrial and other wastes into the air.

Alcohol is a central nervous system depressant.

Alcohol abuse is a pattern of frequent and excessive alcohol consumption that leads to many devastating long-term consequences, both physical and mental.

The **alcoholic robber** steals for reasons related to excessive alcohol use.

Amateur burglars tend to be relatively unskilled and commit only occasional burglaries along with a variety of other crimes.

Amateur shoplifters, also called **snitches,** shoplift out of greediness or because they need the merchandise.

The **amateur thief** is an occasional criminal uncommitted to a criminal value system.

Amphetamines are synthetic stimulants, including substances such as Methedrine, Dexedrine, and Benzedrine.

In **anger rape,** the rapist expresses his hostility toward women in general by selecting a victim and raping her.

Animal assault is assault committed against an animal.

Antisocial personality disorder (APD)—at times called the **sociopathic personality**—involves a history of continuous and chronic antisocial behavior that violates others' rights and may also be criminal.

Arson is any willful or malicious burning or attempt to burn, with or without intent to defraud, a dwelling house, public building, motor vehicle or aircraft or personal property of another.

The **Auburn system** or **silent system** was a system of imprisonment within which prisoners were permitted to work side by side, but at no time were they allowed to speak or even glance at one another.

Barbiturates are depressant drugs, including commonly used substances such as Phenobarbital, Nembutal, and Amtal.

Battery is an attack that results in striking or touching the victim.

Howard S. Becker believed that deviance results from social judgments relative to group norms that are applied as labels to certain forms of behavior.

Behavioral theories assume that all human behavior, including criminal behavior, is learned.

Jeremy Bentham was an early classical theorist who based his ideas on utilitarianism, *felicitious calculus*, and "the greatest happiness."

Biocriminologists are scientists and researchers who study the biological factors affecting delinquent and criminal behavior and who develop biological theories to explain it.

Biosocial theories claim that certain biological factors increase the probability that a person will act criminally but that these factors do not necessarily determine behavior.

Boot camps are forms of imprisonment that are styled after the U.S. military basic-training model.

The **U.S. Customs and Border** is a federal agency in charge of examining all cargo entering the country and investigating smuggling, cargo and criminal frauds, and currency violations.

Robert Burgess and **Ronald Akers** developed **differential-association reinforcement theory,** which links differential association with concepts and principles of behavioral psychology.

According to the UCR, **burglary** is the unlawful entry of a structure to commit a felony or theft.

Capital punishment refers to the death penalty.

Carjacking is a serious crime in which the perpetrator forces a driver from his or her vehicle and steals it.

Case study is a scientific method of data collection used in the study of crime; it involves the comprehensive study of a single person, group, community, or institution.

The **chemicalistic fallacy** is the view that drug *A* causes behavior *X,* and that what we see as behavior and effects associated with a given drug are solely a function of the biochemical properties of that drug.

Child abuse includes physical abuse and neglect, sexual abuse, emotional abuse, abandonment or inadequate supervision, and exploitation.

The **child-saving movement** (late 1800s) was a social movement committed to the idea of saving "wayward youth" from the effects of a "bad environment" in the home and in the community.

A **chop shop** is a garage where stolen cars are broken down into their component parts for resale.

Civil, or tort law deals with noncriminal offenses that are handled by civil rather than criminal courts.

According to the **classical school of criminology,** human behavior is rational, people have the ability to choose right from wrong, and people rationally choose to commit criminal acts.

Clearance rate refers to the number of cases solved or closed compared to the number that remain open.

Richard Cloward and **Lloyd Ohlin** believed that three distinct types of delinquent subcultures exist: the **criminal, conflict,** and **retreatist** subcultures.

Cocaine (coke) is a stimulant that is processed from the leaves of coca plants.

Cognitive theories focus on people's mental processes, including how they perceive the environment and resolve problems.

Albert Cohen believed that a delinquent subculture exists because it offers a solution to the status problems and frustrations that working-class boys experience in their efforts to achieve middle-class success.

Community-based corrections are correctional measures that are applied in the community rather than in jails and prisons.

Computer crime is the use of computer hardware or software in property crimes against others and includes vandalism, information theft, unauthorized personal use, burglary by modem, and financial fraud.

Auguste Comte, the founder of sociology and positivism, believed that both external and internal forces are important for understanding human behavior.

Using a **concentric zone model,** they scientifically studied the relationship between crime rates and various community zones.

Various **conditioning factors** affect strain through internal or external constraints on behavior.

Conduct disorders are characterized by a repetitive and persistent pattern of aggressive conduct that violates the rights of others.

Conflict is a product of social interaction and an effort to resolve a decision-making impasse.

According to **conflict theory,** the sources of crime are found in conflicts that arise as a result of the laws, customs, and distribution of wealth and power in the society.

Conflict perspective is based on the premise that wealth and power may vary across groups. Inequality generates conflicting social values, the basis of much crime.

Conformity refers to behavior that complies with the norms of a community or society.

Consumer fraud occurs when a consumer of goods and services surrenders his or her money through a misrepresentation of a material fact or through deceit. In **business-opportunity fraud,** the consumer is persuaded by the perpetrator to invest money in a business that is worth much less than is indicated or stated.

Controlled experiment is a scientific method for collecting information in which measurements of behaviour in an experimental group and in a control group are compared.

At the **conventional level,** the child's world expands to include such factors as liking or disliking, approval or disapproval.

Corrections involve the treatment, incapacitation, and punishment of criminal offenders who have been convicted in a court of law.

Crack cocaine is a stimulant derived from cocaine.

Crimes of violence include the offenses of criminal homicide, rape, robbery, and aggravated assault.

Crimes against property include the offenses of burglary, larceny-theft, auto theft, and arson.

Criminal behavior is any behavior that is in violation of the criminal law.

Criminal cases arise when agents of government bring lawsuits against persons alleged to have committed crimes or a variety of other offenses as defined in the statutes or codes.

The **criminal justice system** consists of the police, the courts, and the correctional system.

The **criminalization of domestic violence** is the process of dealing with assaultive behavior in families through the passage and enforcement of civil and criminal laws.

Criminologists identify crime problems, collect and analyze data, and communicate research findings to inform criminal justice and related public policy.

Criminology is the scientific study of crime, criminals, and criminal behavior.

Cult murder occurs when members of a cult kill strangers or other cult members.

Culture of poverty claims that the shared experience of poverty leads to the development of a unique way of life that actively opposes middle class beliefs and values.

Cyberterrorism is the premeditated misuse or threatened misuse of computers, the Internet, and information technology to gain a political or social objective.

Dark figure of crime is the range of crimes that are committed in society but are undiscovered, unreported, or unrecorded.

The **defense counsel** or attorney represents the accused in the criminal process.

A **delinquent response** occurs when youths reject middle-class standards and turn to the delinquent subculture of the gang.

Delinquent subculture refers to a subculture within which young people, through participation and gradual absorption into group life, become socialized to a variety of norms, beliefs, and skills necessary for committing delinquent acts.

The **Department of Homeland Security (DHS)** is a federal agency with law enforcement functions related to the war on terrorism. It was formed by the U.S. government to consolidate federal counterterrorism initiatives. The **Homeland Security Act of 2002** established a single contact point for local and state government officials to address equipment, emergency planning, training, and other needs for emergency response.

Depressants are psychoactive substances that decrease or depress the functioning of the central nervous system.

Detached observation is a method of observation wherein the observer remains outside of the group under study.

Deterrence is the act of preventing a criminal act before it occurs, through the threat of punishment and sanctions.

Beccaria and Bentham argued that the proper objective of punishment should be to protect society and its laws and that punishment should be inflicted for its deterrent effect, not for vengeance. **Deterrence** refers to demonstrating the certainty and severity of punishment to discourage further crime by the offender (specific deterrence) and by others (general deterrence).

Deterrence theory stresses the idea that an individual's choice is influenced by the fear of punishment.

Deviant behavior is behavior that does not conform to the social norms of society.

Dietary factors and conditions strongly affected by them, such as **hypoglycemia,** may be related to various types of behavioral disorders and violent behaviors.

Differential anticipation theory says that a person is likely to behave in ways that will yield the greatest rewards with the least punishment.

Differential association theory of addiction says that people learn drug use and addiction through interaction with others who exhibit such behavior.

Differential-association reinforcement theory applies the principles of operant conditioning to the theory of differential association.

Edwin H. Sutherland believed that criminal behavior is learned. **Differential association theory** stresses the importance of one's associates (or peers) in that learning.

Disaster fraud is fraud committed against a person, a group of individuals, or the government after a human-made or natural disaster or catastrophe.

Fraternal or **dizygotic** (DZ) **twins** have only half of their genes in common and develop from separate eggs fertilized at the same time.

Domestic terrorism is terrorism that originates and is carried out within one country.

Scientifically, a **drug** is any substance other than food which by its chemical nature affects the structure or function of a living organism. Socially, a **drug** is any substance that has been arbitrarily defined as a drug by certain segments of society.

Drug abuse is the excessive or compulsive use of a drug to the degree that it is harmful to the user's health or social functioning, or to the extent that it can result in harmful consequences to others.

Drug abuse violations are local and/or state offenses relating to the unlawful possession, sale, use, growing, manufacturing, and making of narcotic drugs including opium or cocaine and their derivatives, marijuana, synthetic narcotics, and dangerous non-narcotic drugs such as barbiturates.

Sociologist **Émile Durkheim** introduced the concept of **anomie,** meaning "normlessness," as a source of strain.

The **economic model of crime** stresses that criminal behavior follows a calculation whereby the criminal explores the perceived costs, rewards, and risks of alternative actions.

Ecstasy is an amphetamine analog and is the common name for 3-4 methylene-dioxymethamphetamine, or **MDMA.**

Educational-release programs pay for prison inmates to attend colleges and universities.

EEG abnormalities have been linked to criminality.

The **ego** is that part of the personality which is conscious and rational.

Eldercide refers to the murder of persons age 65 and over.

Electronic monitoring involves having prisoners wear—on the neck, ankle, or wrist—an electronic device that sends signals to a control office.

The **Elmira system** employed indeterminate sentences and early supervised release for good behavior.

Embezzlement is the taking or converting to one's own use money or property with which one has been entrusted.

Employee theft is theft by an employee from his or her employer.

Environmental crimes are acts or omissions that violate federal, state, or local environmental standards by endangering human health and the environment.

Environmental factors are products in the environment that have been linked to behavioral disorders.

Exchange theory stresses that in our social interactions with others, we continually weigh the perceived benefits or rewards against the perceived risks or costs.

The **Federal Bureau of Investigation (FBI)** is the most important federal law enforcement agency.

Federal courts administer federal laws.

Felicitous calculus is a **moral calculus** developed by Jeremy Bentham for estimating the probability that a person will engage in a particular kind of behavior.

Felonies are the more serious of the two basic types of crimes usually resulting in a penalty of one year or more in prison.

Feminism is a perspective that emphasizes the way gender has been used as a basis for unequal treatment and the importance of collectively ending sexism in America.

Feminist theory focuses on women's experiences and issues that they face in society.

Feminists focus on the various inequalities between women and men.

A **fence** is a receiver of stolen goods who operates in conjunction with thieves and burglars to dispose of those goods.

Enrico Ferri was a positivist who developed a scientific classification of criminals and focused on the causes of crime, criminal sociology, social reform, and effective criminal justice.

Fines are intermediate sanctions that require the convicted defendant to make a monetary payment as punishment for his or her criminal act.

First-degree murder is all murder perpetrated by means of a person, or by lying in wait, or by any other kind of willful, deliberate, and premeditated killing, or committed in the perpetration of, or attempt to perpetrate, any arson, rape, robbery, or burglary.

Flunitrazepam is a central nervous system depressant.

Miller proposed six **focal concerns** that characterize lower-class culture: trouble, toughness, smartness, excitement, fate, and autonomy.

The UCR defines **forcible rape** similarly but also includes assaults or attempts to commit rape by force or threat of force.

Forfeiture is a criminal sanction that involves the seizing of an offender's real and personal property.

Fraud, or false pretenses, involves the acquiring of another person's property through deception or cheating.

Functionalism is a theoretical perspective which contends that social order is realized because people reach a normative consensus, that is, agreement over right and wrong.

The **funneling effect** moves some people along for further criminal processing while it releases others from the system.

Gang murder involves teenage gang members who, as part of their group organization and activities, murder others.

Raffaele Garofalo was a positivist who rejected the doctrine of free will.

GBL is an analog of GHB.

GHB is a central nervous system depressant.

Daniel Glaser developed **differential identification theory,** which says that an individual pursues criminal behavior to the extent that he or she identifies with real or imaginary persons who accept his or her criminal behavior.

Michael Gottfredson and **Travis Hirschi** developed a **general theory of crime (GTC),** which explains crime as the outcome of an individual's low self-control in combination with situational conditions conducive to criminal behavior.

The **halfway house** is a community-based corrections facility to which inmates are assigned either prior to or following a period of incarceration.

Hallucinogens are psychoactive substances that cause mild to intense distortions of visual and auditory functions.

The **Harrison Narcotics Tax Act of 1914** limited possession of opiates to particular registered parties and assigned enforcement responsibility to the Narcotics Division of the Treasury Department.

Hate crime is the violence of intolerance and bigotry, intended to hurt and intimidate someone because of his or her race, ethnicity, national origin, religion, sexual orientation, or disability.

Heterogeneity means mixed, or consisting of different elements or parts.

Travis Hirschi's control theory states that a person who is tightly bonded to groups such as the family, peers, or school is less likely to commit delinquent or criminal acts than a person who is not bonded to such groups.

Home confinement is the sentencing of offenders to confinement in their own residence or in an alternative shelter or group home for the duration of their sentence.

Home-furlough programs enable inmates to take a temporary leave from the institution.

In **home-improvement fraud,** consumers are persuaded to pay inflated prices for home improvements. In **real estate and land fraud,** consumers are persuaded to pay inflated prices for property or land of much less value.

Homicide is the killing of one human being by the act, procurement, or omission of the other. [It is] the act of a human being . . . taking away the life of another human being.

Aggression and violence in men and women are linked to **hormonal levels.**

The **id** is a person's basic biological drives and impulses.

Identity theft is the theft of a person's identity for the purpose of stealing property.

Illicit drug use is the use of prescription-type psychotherapeutic drugs for nonmedical purposes or the use of illegal drugs.

Infanticide refers to the murder of infants and children under age 5.

An **integrated theory** is a theory in which two or more of the major criminological theories are used together in a new theoretical perspective.

Intensive probation supervision (IPS) or **Intensive supervised probation (ISP)** is a type of probation in which small caseloads of clients are monitored intensively in the community by probation officers.

Interactionist perspective focuses on social behavior from the standpoint of the individuals involved in day-to-day interaction and defines criminal behavior as a product of social learning.

Intermediate sanctions are punishments that are less severe than incarceration but more involved than probation.

The **Internal Revenue Service (IRS)** is the federal agency in charge of investigating violations of federal taxes, such as income, stamp, and excise taxes.

Interpol is one of the world's preeminent international police organizations.

Intimate homicide refers to the murder of a spouse or domestic or sexual partner.

Intimate partner violence refers to violent victimizations committed by current or former spouses or sexual partners.

A **jail** is a secured local detention facility used to retain arrested individuals who are awaiting arraignment, trial, conviction, or sentencing.

The **judge** is the senior officer in a court of criminal law.

The **judicatory process** involves prosecution, defense, and sentencing or other outcome of a criminal trial.

Just deserts is a justice perspective according to which those who violate others' rights deserve to be punished.

The **justice model** stresses the idea that offenders are responsible people and therefore deserve to be punished if they violate the law.

The **Juvenile Court Act of 1899** paved the way for the establishment of the first juvenile court, in Illinois.

Juvenile delinquency refers to illegal acts committed by young people, usually sixteen to eighteen years of age or younger.

Lawrence Kohlberg focused on the importance of moral and ethical reasoning. Kohlberg's **theory of moral development** proposes a series of stages linked to child development in which moral judgments become part of a more complex system of personal ethics.

Labeling theory stresses that what is deviant is always dependent on, and in a sense created by, group norms and social reactions to human acts.

Larceny–theft is the unlawful taking, carrying, leading, or riding away of property from the possession or constructive possession of another.

The **Law Enforcement Assistance Administration (LEAA)** was created in the 1960s to achieve a high level of criminal justice reform in the United States.

Laws are formal norms that have been codified as punishable offenses against society or its citizens.

Learning violence theory stresses the idea that violent behavior is learned from the family and society.

Lex talionis ("an eye for an eye") was an ancient penal practice that was based on the motive of reciprocal revenge for crime.

Lower-class focal concerns theory focuses on gang delinquency and argues that the lower class has a separate, identifiable culture distinct from the culture of the middle class.

LSD and **PCP** are manufactured hallucinogens.

Mala prohibita acts that are viewed as criminal because the law says so.

Mala in se acts that are viewed as criminal because they are wrong, immoral, or evil in themselves.

The **male socialization** perspective on rape holds that rape is a function of the way males are socialized to be dominant in our culture.

Manslaughter is the unlawful killing of another without malice, either expressed or implied.

Marijuana, after alcohol, is the most widely used mind-altering drug.

Karl Marx was an early conflict theorist who believed that our social reality must be understood in terms of the class struggle for the underlying mode of production.

Mass murder involves the killing of several victims in one event.

Maximum-security prisons have been carefully designed to house the most dangerous and most violent inmates.

Merton's **means/ends theory** says that anomie results from a lack of integration of culturally prescribed goals and the availability of legitimate or institutionalized means for goal attainment.

Medium-security prisons are designed to house prisoners who are considered more dangerous and more prone to escape.

Mens rea means "guilty mind" *Meas rea* defines criminal intent.

Methamphetamine is a stimulant that is synthesized from phenyl-2-propanone (P2P), an immediate precursor chemical.

Walter B. Miller believed that crime and delinquency stem from this lower-class culture, which has its own values system that evolved in response to living in urban slums.

Minimum-security prisons house inmates who are considered to be low security risks.

Misdemeanors are the lesser of the two basic types of crime, usually punishable by no more than one year in prison.

The **Model Penal Code** lists criteria for probation.

Moderate or liberal feminism stresses that all people are created equal and that all people should have equal opportunity.

Identical or **monozygotic (MZ) twins** are genetically identical; that is, they develop from a single fertilized egg that divides into two embryos.

Motor vehicle theft (MVT) is the theft or attempted theft of a motor vehicle, including automobiles, trucks, buses, motorcycles, motor scooters, and snowmobiles.

Multiple-drug use involves a drug user taking additional drugs to either dampen or heighten the effects of another drug.

Murder is the unlawful killing of a human being by another with malice aforethought, either expressed or implied.

Narcotics are depressants that include opiates such as opium, morphine, heroin, and codeine, and synthetic drugs such as methadone and Demerol.

Natural crime, for Garofalo, consisted of conduct that offends the basic moral sentiments of pity and probity.

National Crime Victimization Survey (NCVS) annually presents information on crime victimization in the United States. The Census Bureau has administered the NCVS for the **Bureau of Justice Statistics (BTS)** since the program began in 1973.

Negligent homicide is a criminal offense committed by one whose negligence is the direct and proximate cause of another's death.

Neurophysiology is the study of the physiology of the central nervous system. Brain dysfunction and brain damage have been linked to criminality.

A **neurotic** person is a person who is less seriously mentally ill.

The British **New Police,** or "bobbies," were the first paid uniformed police force.

The **National Crime Information Center (NCIC)** provides information on criminals to law enforcement agencies in all fifty states.

National Incident-Based Reporting System (NIBRS) is an incident-based reporting system through which crime data are collected on each single crime occurrence.

The **National White Collar Crime Center (NW3C)** is a federally funded nonprofit organization that aids law enforcement in the investigation of white-collar crime. See http://www.nw3c.org.

Objectivity refers to the ability and willingness to study the subject matter of a given field without prejudice or bias.

Occupational crime is crime committed by any persons in the context of their employment.

Opium is a narcotic/depressant drug of which **morphine** is a derivative.

An **opportunistic robber** does little planning and has no long-term commitment to robbery.

Organized crime is a continuing, structured collectivity of persons who utilize criminality, violence, and a willingness to corrupt in order to gain and maintain power and profit.

The English **parish constable watch system** provided civic protection through unpaid night watchmen.

Parole is the conditional release of a prisoner before a full sentence has been served.

The **parole board** typically has exclusive responsibility for determining when an offender may be released.

Parricide is the murder of parents by their children.

Participant observation is a method of observation wherein the observer actually joins and participates in the group or community being studied.

Part I crimes or index crimes, include murder, nonnegligent manslaughter, forcible rape, robbery, aggravated assault, burglary, larceny-theft, motor vehicle theft, and arson.

Part II crimes are all other crimes except traffic violations, including fraud, embezzlement, vandalism, and gambling.

Personality is the organization of attitudes, beliefs, habits, and behavior, in addition to other characteristics, that develop in an individual through social interaction with others.

Personality theories stress the importance of various personal traits in an attempt to explain why some people become addicted to drugs and alcohol.

Personality theories, in general, stress that the possession of certain characteristics predisposes individuals to criminal behavior. When combined, these characteristics make up what some psychologists term the **criminal personality.**

Personality traits are enduring patterns of perceiving, relating to, and thinking about oneself and others, exhibited in a wide range of social and personal contexts.

Lombroso believed that **physical stigmata,** such as a long lower jaw, flattened nose, and long, apelike arms, identify a criminal. These biological characteristics were seen as **atavism,** or a throwback to earlier states in human evolution.

Plea bargaining is negotiating an agreement between the prosecution and the defense in which a criminal case is decided outside of the courtroom, which thus has a funneling effect.

The **police** are an organized civil force that has the important functions of law enforcement and the control of crime.

A **Ponzi scam** is a classic fraudulent pyramid scheme in which early investors are paid off with proceeds from sales to later participants. It is called a **pyramid scheme** because in the business structure, which resembles a pyramid, a small number of people at the top receive payments from a broad base of investors who never see returns on their investment.

Population is a large category of people from which a sample is selected.

Pornography—derived from the Greek word *pornographos* (*porne,* a prostitute, and *graphein,* to write)—is any medium intended primarily to arouse sexual desire.

Positivism emphasizes the techniques of observation, the comparative method, and experimentation in the development of knowledge concerning human behavior and the nature of society.

At the **postconventional,** or **principled, level,** the person judges the rightness or wrongness of actions not according to their consequences but according to ethical principles.

Power is the ability to realize one's own will even against the resistance of others.

In **power rape,** the rapist is usually insecure about his masculinity.

Precision involves maintaining a high degree of accuracy in the collection and analysis of data.

Predatory crimes are instrumental offenses committed for material gain.

Predatory violations are illegal acts in which someone definitely and intentionally takes or damages the person or property of another.

Types of community-based corrections include **pretrial release, diversion, probation, reentry programs,** and **parole.**

A **prison** is a state or federal correctional institution for the incarceration of felony offenders for terms of longer than one year.

Probation is the correctional service that allows an offender to remain in the community while complying with court-imposed conditions.

Problem-oriented policing is policing for crime prevention through a focus on risk factors in the community.

Professional burglars have a technical and professional competence in their field.

A **professional robber** has a long-term commitment to robbery as a source of livelihood.

Professional shoplifters steal for profit.

The **professional thief** devotes his or her entire working time and energy to larceny, in which every act is carefully planned.

Property crimes include larceny-theft, burglary, motor vehicle theft, fencing, fraud, and arson.

Prosecution is criminal proceedings against a defendant.

The **prosecutor** is a government attorney who represents the state and the people against persons who have been accused of committing criminal acts.

Prostitution is performing an act of sexual intercourse for hire, or offering or agreeing to perform an act of sexual intercourse or any unlawful sexual act for hire.

Psychoactive drugs are chemical substances that affect the user's central nervous system and thus influence mood, perceptions, emotions, and behavior.

The **psychological perspective** on rape reports that rapists are mentally ill or have a serious personality disorder.

Psychological theories of addiction stress the importance of investigating the people who use drugs rather than the drugs themselves.

Psychopathological explanations for assaultive and violent behavior involve the idea of mental illness.

A **psychotic** person is a person who is more seriously mentally ill.

People who have the impulse disorder termed **pyromania** recurrently fail to control or resist impulses to set fires.

Richard Quinney developed the **social-reality-of-crime theory,** which integrates ideas about power and authority in the form of **six propositions** about the social construction of criminality.

Radical feminism emphasizes the family's role in the personal oppression of women.

Rape is unlawful sexual intercourse with a female without her consent and the unlawful carnal knowledge of a woman by a man forcibly and against her will.

Rational choice theory focuses on the situational aspects of criminal behavior and stresses that a criminal rationally chooses both the crime to commit and the target of the crime.

Reaction formation occurs when youths reject middle-class standards and turn to the delinquent subculture of the gang.

The **reasonableness doctrine** (from the 1987 *Pope* v. *Illinois* decision) states that a work is considered obscene if a reasonable individual applying objective, nationally developed standards would consider the material in question lacking in any social value.

Recidivism is the term for repeat offending. A recidivist is someone who repeatedly commits crimes.

A **reference group** is a group that a person takes into account when evaluating his or her own behavior or self-concept.

Rehabilitation is a goal of imprisonment; its aim is to help offenders become useful and productive members of society by instilling the appropriate standards, attitudes, and skills necessary for an acceptable life after release.

Reinforcement theory is based on the idea that people tend to continue in activities they find pleasurable.

The **release rate** is the number of releases per 100 sentenced prisoners at the beginning of each year, plus the number admitted to prison during the year.

Research design precisely defines the types of data to be collected, the sources and the methods to be used in gathering data, and the time period for the study.

Restitution is an intermediate sanction that requires an offender to pay damages to the victim (**monetary restitution**) or to perform community service (**community-service restitution**) as punishment for his or her criminal acts.

Restorative justice is a judicial approach based upon a shared set of values that determines how conflicts can be resolved and how damaged relationships can be repaired or improved.

According to Merton, **retreatism, rebellion, innovation,** and **ritualism** are four methods of adaptation, constituting deviant, criminal, or anomic behavior, that occur when legitimate means to goal attainment are blocked.

Retribution is the notion that a wrongdoer should be forced to "pay back" or compensate for his or her criminal acts.

Retribution, incapacitation, deterrence, rehabilitation, and **restitution** are the conflicting social goals of sentencing.

Retributivism ("justice model") is a goal of punishment that stresses the idea that offenders are responsible people and, therefore, deserve to be punished if they violate the law.

RICO, or **The Racketeer Influenced and Corrupt Organizations Act,** is the government's principal weapon against organized crime.

Robbery is the taking or attempt to take anything of value from the care, custody, or control of a person or persons by force or the threat of force or violence and/or by putting the victim in fear.

Robert Agnew proposes a **general strain theory (GST)** to explain criminal and delinquent behavior, defining three major types of strain caused by negative interpersonal relationships.

Robert Merton modified and adapted Durkheim's concept of anomie to explain deviant behavior such as crime and delinquency.

Routine activities theory (RAT) stresses the idea that criminals are not impulsive or unpredictable, because they balance the costs as well as benefits of committing crimes.

In **sadistic rape,** anger and power over the victim become eroticized.

The **Safe Schools Act** (of Goals 2000) authorizes the U.S. education secretary to award grants to school districts to help reduce violence in schools.

Sample is a set of subjects selected from a population.

School violence refers to acts of violence committed in American schools.

Second-degree murder is all types of murder other than first-degree murder.

The **Secret Service, ATF,** and **IRS** are all important law enforcement agencies that operate under the U.S. Treasury Department.

In **a self-fulfilling prophecy,** one's belief that a condition is true (when it is not) actually creates the condition.

A **sentence** is a criminal sanction issued against a convicted defendant.

Serial murder involves the killing of several victims over a period of time.

Sexism is a system of social, economic, political, and psychological activities and pressures that supress or discriminate against people because they are female.

Clifford Shaw and **Henry McKay,** of the Chicago school of criminology, popularized the social disorganization approach to crime and delinquency through the study of urban social ecology.

Shock probation is an alternative to prison that is granted by the court following a brief period of incarceration.

Shoplifting is the stealing or theft of goods from retail stores and merchants.

Sibling assault is assault by one sibling against another. **Elder assault** is assaultive behavior against grandparents and the elderly. **Parent assault** is assault committed against a parent or parents by children.

Sigmund Freud, the founder of psychoanalysis, believed that crime is the result of an overdeveloped superego.

Simple assault is an attack without a weapon resulting in no injury, minor injury, or undetermined injury requiring less than two days of hospitalization.

A **situational inducement** is a short-run influence on a person's behavior that increases risk taking, such as peer influence (social factors) or financial problems (psychological factors).

Social change refers to change in the structure and organization of social relationships of a society.

Social control theory asserts that social controls—such as arrest, imprisonment, loss of status, or loss of income—increase the costs of violent behavior.

Social control theory stresses the idea that people in society commit delinquent and criminal acts because of the weakness of forces restraining them from doing so, not because of the strength of forces driving them to do so.

Social disintegration theories explain violent crime as a product of the deterioration of community integration.

Social disorganization theory stresses that crime increases when traditional social guidelines no longer work or when there is a decline in group unity due to ineffective behavior patterns.

Socialization is the process by which individuals internalize many of the socially approved values, attitudes, beliefs, and behavioral patterns of their society.

According to **social learning theory,** people learn vicariously by observing the consequences that behaviors have for others.

In criminology, **social learning theory** focuses on the idea that people learn aggressive behavior in the same way they learn other social behavior—through socialization.

Social norms are standards and rules of accepted behavior; **laws** are the codified rules or norms of a society.

Social organization is the actual patterning and regulation of people's interactions in society, including social norms.

Social structure refers to the roles, statuses, and institutions through which society is organized.

Socialist feminism emphasizes women's economic oppression and believes in the necessity of a socialist revolution as a prerequisite for women's complete liberation.

The **sociobiological view** stresses that rape may be an instinctive male drive developed over thousands of years that encourages men to have sexual relations with many women as a way of favoring their genes while perpetuating the human species.

Sociocultural factors important in explaining assault include child-rearing practices and childhood socialization.

The **sociocultural view** stresses that rape is embedded in a cultural configuration that includes male dominance and interpersonal violence.

Sociological theories of addiction stress the importance of group factors and the influence of a person's social environment. Sociological explanations view drug use and addiction as products of **social learning.**

Quakers of Pennsylvania spearheaded the movement to have imprisonment take the place of other forms of punishment. They started the **solitary system** (or **Pennsylvania system**), a system of imprisonment in which each prisoner was required to live and work in solitary confinement throughout the entire sentence.

In **split sentencing,** offenders serve a jail or prison sentence as a condition of probation.

Spouse assault is assault against one's own spouse—husband or wife.

In Kohlberg's **stage theory,** at the **preconventional level,** a child will base his or her moral judgments on the desire to avoid punishment.

State courts administer the laws of the states within which they operate.

Status offenses are criminal offenses that apply specifically to youths.

Steroids are manufactured drugs used in bodybuilding and to enhance athletic performance.

Stimulants are psychoactive substances that increase the functioning of the central nervous system.

Strain theory views crime and delinquency as a result of the anger and frustration people feel because of their inability to achieve the "American dream."

Structural adaptation theories view violence as an adaptive response to the social-structural conditions under which people live.

Subcultural theories focus on the nature and origins of delinquent subcultures.

Subcultural theories of substance abuse view drug use and addiction as the product of a drug subculture.

The type of **subculture** that forms depends on members' differential opportunities for deviance and support for that deviance.

Subculture of violence theories focus on the approval of violence, and the use of violence to resolve interpersonal conflicts, in a subculture's value system and social norms.

The **subculture of violence,** a theory developed by **Marvin Wolfgang** and **France Ferracuti,** hypothesizes a subculture that condones violent behavior.

Subcultures are diverse subgroups that share the general culture but maintain some unique norms that distinguish them from the wider culture.

The **superego** is a morality or "social conscience" learned during childhood.

Survey research, involving the use of **questionnaires,** and **interviews,** is the most common method of data collection for criminologists.

Gresham Sykes and **David Matza** argued that the delinquent subculture does not totally reject middle-class standards and attempts to "neutralize" delinquent acts.

In **tax fraud,** a taxpayer underreports or does not report taxable income; purposely attempts to evade or defeat a payment of owed taxes; and is willful, i.e., voluntarily and intentionally violates a known legal duty.

A probationer who violates the rules of probation is said to have committed a **technical violation,** in which case probation may be revoked.

Telescoping occurs in crime victimization surveys when respondents report on criminal events that occurred prior to the study's time frame.

Terrorism is the use or threatened use of violence to gain a political objective.

Theory is a means of explaining natural occurrences through statements about the relationships between observable phenomena.

William I. Thomas and **Florian Znaniecki,** theorists of the Chicago school, examined how social disorganization can create personal disorganization and criminal behavior.

Transnational terrorism is terrorism that originates in one country and takes place in another.

Uniform Crime Reports (UCR) the FBI publishes a report containing the most extensive set of U.S. crime statistics available.

Uniform Crime Reporting Program (UCRP) is the country's major sources of crime data and information produced by city, country, and state law enforcement agencies.

The **U.S. Marshal Service, INS, DEA,** and **OCRU** are all important law enforcement agencies of the U.S. Justice Department.

The **U.S. Supreme Court** interprets and applies the U.S. Constitution and decides conflicts between state and federal laws.

The **utilitarian punishment model** is a philosophy of punishment based on the assumption that punishment is necessary to protect society from crime and also to deter offenders.

Utilitarian punishment philosophy is based on the assumption that punishment is necessary to protect society from crime and also to deter offenders.

Utilitarianism is the doctrine that the purpose of all actions should be to bring about the greatest happiness for the greatest number of people.

Values are conceptions of worth or desireability, and they make up our judgments of moral and immoral, good and bad, right and wrong, and so forth.

Victimization surveys seek information from victims of crime whereas **self-report surveys** ask respondents to describe current and past criminal activities.

Victim-precipitated murder is applied to criminal homicides in which the victim contributes directly to precipitating the crime.

Sex-related and other crimes based solely on moral laws are often referred to as **victimless crimes.**

Violence is any behavior that threatens or causes physical damage to a person or object.

August Vollmer was the father of police reform and professionalism in the United States.

Water contamination results from the introduction of industrial and other wastes to water, such as toxic chemicals and substances, nitrates, and oils.

White-collar crime, according to the DOJ, refers to a group of nonviolent crimes that generally involve deception or abuse of power.

Sutherland defined **white-collar crime** as crime committed by a person of respectability and high social status in the course of his or her occupation.

Workplace violence refers to violence between workers or between managers and employees that occurs in or around the workplace.

A **work-release program** is a reentry program in which a prisoner is allowed to leave the prison (or community treatment center or halfway house) for a certain number of hours each day to work or train in the community.

XYY males have an extra Y chromosome that may predispose them to engage in criminal behavior.

Answers

CHAPTER 1

Multiple Choice	True-False	Fill-In	Matching
1. d	1. T	1. Criminology	1. J
2. d	2. T	2. Evaluator	2. F
3. c	3. F	3. Scientific	3. E
4. a	4. F	4. Objectivity	4. D
5. b	5. T	5. Interactionist	5. G
6. b	6. T	6. Deviant	6. H
7. b	7. F	7. Conformity	7. I
8. b	8. F	8. Laws	8. C
9. d	9. T	9. Relative	9. B
10. d	10. T	10. Civil or tort	10. A

CHAPTER 2

Multiple Choice	True-False	Fill-In	Matching
1. d	1. F	1. Control	1. G
2. a	2. F	2. Thief	2. D
3. b	3. T	3. UCR	3. C
4. d	4. F	4. Dark figure	4. H
5. b	5. F	5. NCVS	5. B
6. b	6. T	6. Self-report	6. J
7. b	7. T	7. Greater	7. I
8. b	8. F	8. NIBRS	8. A
9. a	9. T	9. Juvenile	9. F
10. c	10. T	10. Day; night	10. E
	11. F	11. Aging-out	
	12. F	12. Economic	

CHAPTER 3

Multiple Choice	True-False	Fill-In	Matching
1. d	1. F	1. Classical	1. G
2. a	2. F	2. Beccaria, Bentham	2. D
3. d	3. F	3. Laws	3. F
4. d	4. T	4. Pain	4. I
5. b	5. T	5. Calculus	5. C
6. d	6. T	6. Comte	6. J
7. b	7. F	7. Lombroso	7. B
8. d	8. T	8. Of criminology	8. A
9. c	9. F	9. Ferri	9. E
10. d	10. F	10. Death, Partial elimination, Enforced reparation	10. H
11. b	11. F	11. Deterrence theory	11. L
12. a		12. Routine activities theory	12. K
13. d			
14. a			
15. d			

CHAPTER 4

Multiple Choice	True-False	Fill-In	Matching
1. a	1. F	1. Mesomorph	1. G
2. d	2. T	2. XYY	2. C
3. b	3. F	3. Testosterone	3. H
4. d	4. T	4. Hypoglycemia	4. D
5. c	5. T	5. Neurophysiological	5. E
6. d	6. F	6. Biological	6. I
7. d	7. F	7. Alcohol; drugs	7. B
8. c	8. F	8. ADHD	8. J
9. d	9. T	9. Biocriminologists	9. A
10. b	10. T	10. Biological	10. F

CHAPTER 5

Multiple Choice	True-False	Fill-In	Matching
1. d	1. T	1. Personality	1. E
2. a	2. T	2. Guilt	2. C
3. a	3. F	3. Schizophrenia	3. J
4. d	4. F	4. Social Learning	4. I
5. d	5. F	5. direct effects	5. H
6. b	6. T	6. Cognitive	6. B
7. c	7. T	7. Preconventional	7. G
8. c	8. T	8. Criminal Behavior	8. D
9. d	9. F	9. APD—Antisocial Personality Disorder	9. A
10. d			10. F
		10. Sociopaths or conduct disordered	

CHAPTER 6

Multiple Choice	True-False	Fill-In	Matching
1. d	1. T	1. Social disorganization	1. C
2. c	2. T	2. Organization	2. F
3. a	3. F	3. Durkheim	3. I
4. a	4. T	4. Anomie	4. G
5. b	5. F	5. Innovation	5. J
6. d	6. T	6. GST	6. A
7. c	7. F	7. Strain	7. H
8. c	8. F	8. Subcultural	8. B
9. d	9. F	9. Status	9. D
10. b	10. T	10. Neutralization	10. E
11. b	11. F	11. Criminal	11. K
12. a	12. T	12. Retreatist	12. L
13. b	13. F		13. N
14. a	14. T		14. M
15. d	15. T		15. O

CHAPTER 7

Multiple Choice	True-False	Fill-In	Matching
1. a	1. T	1. Differential association	1. F
2. b	2. F	2. Learning	2. B
3. c	3. F	3. Identification	3. E
4. b	4. T	4. Control	4. C
5. a	5. T	5. Attachment	5. D
6. d	6. T	6. Social	6. A
7. d	7. T	7. Conflict	7. G
8. d	8. F	8. Marx	8. I
9. d	9. T	9. Socialist	9. H
10. c	10. T	10. Feminism	
11. d	11. T	11. Deviance	
		12. Labeling	

CHAPTER 8

Multiple Choice	True-False	Fill-In	Matching
1. c	1. T	1. Aggravated	1. H
2. b	2. F	2. Conflict	2. E
3. c	3. T	3. authority	3. G
4. d	4. T	4. husband	4. F
5. a	5. T	5. three	5. J
6. d	6. F	6. observing	6. B
7. d	7. F	7. Violence	7. I
8. b	8. F	8. Rape	8. A
9. a	9. T	9. Sadistic	9. D
10. a	10. T	10. Anger	10. C
11. c	11. T		
12. c	12. F		

CHAPTER 9

Multiple Choice	True-False	Fill-In	Matching
1. d	1. T	1. Robbery	1. I
2. a	2. F	2. Professional	2. C
3. d	3. F	3. Opportunistic	3. A
4. c	4. F	4. Instrumental	4. H
5. d	5. T	5. Murder	5. J
6. b	6. T	6. Victim-precipitated murder	6. E
7. d	7. F	7. Motives	7. G
8. a	8. T	8. Mass murder	8. D
9. d	9. F	9. Random	9. F
10. b	10. F	10. Learning violence	10. B
11. d	11. T	11. "Equalizers"	11. L
12. d	12. T	12. Epidemic	12. K
13. d	13. F	13. Reactive	
14. d	14. T	14. Transnational	
15. d	15. T	15. Terrorist	
	16. T		
	17. T		
	18. T		
	19. F		

CHAPTER 10

Multiple Choice	True-False	Fill-In	Matching
1. d	1. T	1. Larceny-theft	1. G
2. d	2. T	2. Professional	2. F
3. d	3. F	3. Geographic Information Systems	3. D
4. a	4. F	4. Carjacking	4. C
5. a	5. F	5. Snitches	5. A
6. d	6. T	6. Fraud	6. B
7. b	7. F	7. Burglar (or car thief)	7. H
8. b	8. F	8. Community watch or neighborhood watch	8. E
9. d	9. T	9. Pyromania	9. I
10. c			

CHAPTER 11

Multiple Choice	True-False	Fill-In	Matching
1. c	1. T	1. White-collar	1. H
2. d	2. F	2. Embezzlement	2. E
3. a	3. T	3. Consumer	3. F
4. d	4. T	4. Ponzi	4. B
5. d	5. F	5. Logic	5. J
6. b	6. T	6. Separation	6. D
7. b	7. F	7. Organized crime	7. C
8. d	8. T	8. Violence	8. A
9. c	9. F	9. *La Cosa Nostra:* Mafia	9. G
10. a	10. F	10. RICO	10. I

CHAPTER 12

Multiple Choice	True-False	Fill-In	Matching
1. d	1. F	1. Depressants	1. D
2. b	2. T	2. Withdrawal	2. C
3. c	3. T	3. Harrison	3. B
4. b	4. T	4. Social learning	4. A
5. c	5. T	5. Becker	5. I
6. d	6. T	6. Subcultural	6. H
7. a	7. T	7. Predatory	7. E
8. d	8. F	8. Madam	8. F
9. d	9. T	9. Reasonableness doctrine	9. J
10. a	10. F		10. G

CHAPTER 13

Multiple Choice	True-False	Fill-In	Matching
1. d	1. T	1. Discretion	1. G
2. b	2. F	2. Arrest	2. J
3. b	3. T	3. Prosecution	3. I
4. d	4. F	4. Adjudication	4. F
5. d	5. T	5. FBI	5. H
6. c	6. T	6. Retribution	6. C
7. a	7. F	7. Restitution	7. E
8. a	8. F	8. Defense counsel (or) attorney	8. D
9. a	9. T	9. Sentence	9. A
		10. DNA	10. B

CHAPTER 14

Multiple Choice	True-False	Fill-In	Matching
1. c	1. F	1. Beccaria and Bentham	1. J
2. d	2. F	2. Utilitarian punishment philosophy	2. D
3. d	3. T	3. pretrial release	3. E
4. b	4. T	4. Probation	4. F
5. d	5. F	5. Shock probation	5. A
6. b	6. T	6. Technical violation	6. G
7. c	7. F	7. Intensive probation supervision	7. H
8. a	8. F	8. Parole	8. C
9. b	9. T	9. Home furlough	9. B
10. c	10. F		10. I

Louisiana Pacific Corporation, 315
Lower-class cultural theory, 157
Lower-class focal concerns, 156–158
LPC. *See* Louisiana Pacific Corporation
LSD, 349–350
Lyons, Michael, 105

M

Maahs, Jeff, 153
Mafia, 323
Magnetic resonance imaging, 115
Mala in se, 17, 315
Mala prohibita, 17, 315
Male socialization, rape and, 221
Mandatory parole, 427–428
Manslaughter, 245
  nonnegligent, 35
MAOA. *See* Monoamine oxidase-A
Marijuana, 342
  trafficking, 343
Marx, Karl, 179, 182
Mass murder, 251–252
Mass Murder, 252, 270–273
Matza, David, 155
Maximum security, 416
Mazerolle, Paul, 153
McCarthy, Julie M., 105
McGuffin, Peter, 105
McKay, Henry, 146–147
MDMA trafficking, 344
Mean world syndrome, 141
Measurement of crime, 28–61
  aggravated assault, 35–36
  arson, 35–36
  assault
    aggravated, 35
    simple, 36
  breaking, or entering, 36
  Bureau of Justice Statistics, 40
  burglary, 35–36
  buying stolen property, 36
  carrying weapons, 36
  commercialized vice, 36
  counterfeiting, 36
  crime patterns, 46–52
    age, crime and, 47–49
    aging-out phenomenon, 48
    ecological factors in crime patterns, 46–47
    gender, crime and, 49–50
    poverty, 50–51
    profiles, 47
    race, crime and, 50–51
    racial minorities, 50
    racism, 50
    undereducated persons, 51
    unemployment, 50–51
  criminal homicide, 35
  curfew, 36
  "Dark figure of crime," 38
  data collection, 29–34
  disorderly conduct, 36
  driving under influence, 36
  drug abuse violations, 36
  drunkenness, 36
  embezzlement, 35–36
  entering, 36
  family, offenses against, 36
  Federal Bureau of Investigation, 35
  forcible rape, 35
  forgery, 36
  fraud, 35–36
  gambling, 35–36
  index crimes, 35
  larceny, 35–36
  liquor laws, 36
  loitering laws, 36
  manslaughter, nonnegligent, 35
  motor vehicle theft, 35–36
  murder, 35
  National Crime Victimization Survey, 40–41
    limitations of, 41–43
    Uniform Crime Reports, compared, 42

National Incident-Based Reporting System, 43–44
  nonnegligent manslaughter, 35
  offenses against, 36
  place, in crime profile, 47
  possessing stolen property, 36
  possessing weapons, 36
  property, crimes against, 35
  prostitution, 36
  questionnaires, 29–30
    problems with, 30
  rape, forcible, 35
  receiving stolen property, 36
  robbery, 35–36
  runaways, 36
  sex offenses, 36
  simple assault, 36
  social class, crime and, 50–51
  stolen property, 36
  suspicion of crime, 36
  telescoping, 42
  theft, 35–36
    motor vehicle, 35
  time factors, 46–47
  time of day, in crime profile, 47
  undiscovered crime, 38
  Uniform Crime Report, limitations of, 38–40
  Uniform Crime Reporting, offenses in, 35–36
  Uniform Crime Reporting Program, 35
  Uniform Crime Reports, 35–40
    aggravated assault, 36
    arson, 36
    assault, simple, 36
    burglary, 36
    criminal homicide, 35
    curfew, 36
    disorderly conduct, 36
    driving under influence, 36
    drug abuse violations, 36
    drunkenness, 36
    embezzlement, 36
    family, offenses against, 36
    forcible rape, 35
    forgery, 36
    fraud, 35–36
    gambling, 36
    index crimes, 35
    larceny, 36
    limitations of, 38–40
    liquor laws, 36
    motor vehicle theft, 36
    murder, 35
    National Crime Victimization Survey, compared, 42–43
    property, crimes against, 35
    prostitution, 36
    robbery, 36
    runaways, 36
    sex offenses, 36
    stolen property, 36
    suspicion of crime, 36
    Uniform Crime Reporting, offenses in, 35–36
    vagrancy, 36
    vandalism, 36
    violent crime, 35
    weapons, 36
  unrecorded crime, 38
  unreported crime, 38
  vagrancy, 36
  vandalism, 35–36
  vice, commercialized, 36
  victims, characteristics of, 46–52
  violent crime, 35
  weapons, 36
Mechanisms of control, 13
Media, violence in, 129
Media Violence and Youth, 129, 139–141
Medium-security, 416
Mednick, Sarnoff A., 105
Mens rea, 16
Menstruation, effect on behavior, 113
Mental retardation, 117
Mercury, effect on behavior, 111

Merton, Robert, 148, 150
  anomie/strain theory, 148–149
Mesomorphs, 103
Messerschmidt, James, 182
Methamphetamine, 343
Methylated idoleamines, effect on behavior, 111
Milk, effect on behavior, 109
Miller
  J. Mitchell, 26–27, 57–61
  Walter B., 157–158
Minimal brain damage, 116
Minimal brain dysfunction, 116
Minimal cerebral dysfunction, 117
Minimum-security, 416
Misdemeanors, 14
Mission offenders, 258
Mission-oriented serial killers, 252
Model Penal Code, 421–423
Modeling theory. *See* Social learning theory
Moderate feminism, 184
Moffitt, Terrie, 108, 111
Monetary restitution, 426
Monoamine oxidase-A, 108
Monosodium glutamate, effect on behavior, 109
Monozygotic (MZ) twins, 104
Moral calculus, 70
Morality crimes, 332–377
Morphine, 346
Motor vehicle theft, 35–36, 280–282
MRI. *See* Magnetic resonance imaging
MSG. *See* Monosodium glutamate
Multiple-drug use, 340–342
Murder, 35, 244–255
  characteristics of murderers, 246–249
  circumstances leading to, 250–251
  intimate homicide, 247
  mass murder, 251–252
  school violence, 254–255
  serial murder, 251–252
  weapons used in, 246
Murray, John P., 129, 139–141
Mutilation, 234
MVT. *See* Motor vehicle theft
Myers, David L., 90–98

N

Nagin, Daniel, 320
Narcotics, 346
National Crime Information Center, 384–385
National Crime Victimization Survey, 40–41, 275
  limitations of, 41–43
  Uniform Crime Reports, compared, 42
National Incident-Based Reporting System, 43–44
Natural crime, 77
Natural explanations for crime, 64–65
Nature of criminal behavior, 12–15
Nature of deviant behavior, 12
NCIC. *See* National Crime Information Center
NCVS. *See* National Crime Victimization Survey
Neglect, 210
Negligent homicide, 245
Nelson, Toni, 222, 234–239
Neurophysiological factors, 114–117
  attention deficit/hyperactivity disorder, 116–117
  brain-wave abnormalities, 115–116
Neurophysiology, 114
Neurotic, 123–124
New Police, 381
Newman, Horatio H., 105
NIBRS. *See* National Incident-Based Reporting System
Nonnegligent manslaughter, 35
Normal learned behavior, criminal behavior as, 170
Normality of crime, Durkheim on, 18–20
Norms, 11, 13
  becoming laws, 14–15
  conformity to, 13
  formal, 14
  social, 11
Nurturing, 108

Photo Credits

p. 2: Adam Eastland/Alamy Images;

p. 4: Kathy McLaughlin/The Image Works;

p. 5: Shelly Gazin/Bettmann/Corbis;

p. 8: Joel Gordon Photography/Design Conceptions;

p. 11: Chuck Savage/CORBIS;

p. 14: David Buton/Corbis Saba;

p. 16: Bob Daemmrich/The Image Works;

p. 19: Bettmann/Corbis;

p. 28: AP Images/Brian Kersey;

p. 33: Nadav Neuhaus/CORBIS;

p. 37: Joel Gordon Photography/Design Conceptions;

p. 39: Spencer Grant/PhotoEdit, Inc.;

p. 50: Joel Gordon Photography/Design Conceptions;

p. 62: Shannon Stapleton/REUTERS/Landov LLC;

p. 64: Bettmann/Corbis;

p. 70: Andrew Butterton/Alamy Images;

p. 76: Bettmann/Corbis;

p. 80: Patrick Giardino/Bettmann/Corbis;

p. 100: Phototake Inc./Alamy Images;

p. 104: Ryan McVay/PhotoDisc/Getty Images Royalty Free;

p. 107: Skjold Photographs;

p. 109: Michael Newman/PhotoEdit, Inc.;

p. 114: Design Pics Inc./Alamy Images;

p. 116: AP Images/Jim McKnight;

p. 122: Don Farrall/Getty Images;

p. 125: Keystone/The Image Works;

p. 126: Stephen Fery/Getty Images;

p. 127: Radius Images/Alamy Images;

p. 129: Joel Gordon Photography/Design Conceptions;

p. 132: Emely/Corbis Zefa Collection;

p. 142: Jeff Greenberg/The Image Works;

p. 144: Ralf-Finn Hestoft/CORBIS;

p. 148: Jean-Michel Turpin/CORBIS;

p. 151: Joel Gordon Photography/Design Conceptions;

p. 155: Lucas Jackson/Landov LLC;

p. 157: Joel Gordon Photography/Design Conceptions;

p. 159: Bill Bachman/PhotoEdit, Inc.;

p. 168: AP Images/Rick Bowmer;

p. 171: Janine Wiedel Photolibrary/Alamy Images;

p. 175: Bill Aron/PhotoEdit, Inc.;

p. 178: Chris Pizzello/Landov LLC;

p. 180: Image Source/CORBIS;

p. 186: Joel Gordon Photography/Design Conceptions;

p. 200: Dwayne Newton/PhotoEdit, Inc.;

p. 202: Dwayne Newton/PhotoEdit, Inc.;

p. 204: KEVIN LAMARQUE/Reuters America LLC/Corbis;

p. 206: Photofusion Picture Library/Alamy Images;

p. 217: AP Images;

p. 240: Paul Conklin/PhotoEdit, Inc.;

p. 242: AP Images/Nashville Police Department;

p. 255: Bob Daemmrich/The Image Works;

p. 257: Kateland Photo;

p. 262: Spencer Platt/Getty Images;

p. 274: Vince Streano/Stone/Getty Images;

p. 282: Michael Newman/PhotoEdit, Inc.;

p. 284: Annie Griffiths Belt/CORBIS;

p. 290: AP Images/Michael Heinz/Journal and Courier;

p. 293: James Shaffer/PhotoEdit, Inc.;

p. 302: David Young-Wolff/PhotoEdit, Inc.;

p. 307: Lisa Berkshire/Illustration Works/CORBIS;

p. 310: Steven Peters/Stone/Getty Images;

p. 311: Angela Jimenez/Getty Images;

p. 317: Kapoor Baldev/Sygma/Corbis;

p. 332: Janine Wiedel Photolibrary/Alamy Images;

p. 334: Carl Court/Bloomberg News/Landov LLC;

p. 339: Mikael Karlsson/Arresting Images;

p. 341: Sean Murphy/Stone/Getty Images;

p. 378: Bob Daemmrich/The Image Works;

p. 381: Shaun Best/ Reuters America LLC/Corbis;

p. 385: U.S. Customs/Getty Images;

p. 396: AP Images;

p. 399: Joel Gordon Photography/Design Conceptions;

p. 410: Corbis/Bettmann;

p. 413: Robert Holmes/Bettmann/Corbis;

p. 425: Dwayne Newton/PhotoEdit, Inc.;

p. 431: Joel Gordon Photography/Design Conceptions.